Methods for Achieving Your Purpose in Writing

The Brief Bedford Reader centers on common ways of thinking and writing about all kinds of subjects, from everyday experiences to public policies to scientific theories. Whatever your purpose in writing, one or more of these ways of thinking—or methods of development—can help you discover and shape your ideas in individual paragraphs or entire papers.

The following list connects various purposes you may have for writing and the methods for achieving those purposes. The blue boxes along the right edge of the page correspond to tabs on later pages where each method is explained.

PURPOSE	METHOD	
To tell a story about your subject, possibly to enlighten readers or to explain something to them	Narration	
To help readers understand your subject through the evidence of their senses—sight, hearing, touch, smell, taste	Description	
To explain your subject with instances that show readers its nature or character	Example	
To explain or evaluate your subject by helping readers see the similarities and differences between it and another subject	Comparison and Contrast	
To inform readers how to do something or how something works—how a sequence of actions leads to a particular result	Process Analysis	
To explain a conclusion about your subject by showing readers the subject's parts or elements	Division or Analysis	
To help readers see order in your subject by understanding the kinds or groups it can be sorted into	Classification	
To tell readers the reasons for or consequences of your subject, explaining why or what if	Cause and Effect	
To show readers the meaning of your subject—its boundaries and its distinctions from other subjects	Definition	
To have readers consider your opinion about your subject or your proposal for it	Argument and Persuasion	

THE BRIEF BEDFORD READER

Thirteenth Edition

X. J. Kennedy

Dorothy M. Kennedy

Jane E. Aaron

Ellen Kuhl Repetto

bedford/st.martin's
Macmillan Learning
Boston | New York

For Bedford/St. Martin's

Vice President, Editorial, Macmillan Learning Humanities: Edwin Hill
Editorial Director, English: Karen S. Henry
Senior Publisher for Composition, Business and Technical Writing, Developmental Writing:
   Leasa Burton
Executive Editor: John E. Sullivan III
Developmental Editor: Sherry Mooney
Production Editor: Louis C. Bruno Jr.
Media Producer: Rand Thomas
Publishing Services Manager: Andrea Cava
Senior Production Supervisor: Jennifer Wetzel
Executive Marketing Manager: Joy Fisher Williams
Assistant Editor: Jennifer Prince
Project Management: Jouve
Senior Photo Editor: Martha Friedman
Photo Researcher: Julie Tesser
Permissions Editor: Kalina Ingham
Senior Art Director: Anna Palchik
Text Design: Anna Palchik, Dorothy Bungert/EriBen Graphics, and Jean Hammond
Cover Design: William Boardman
Cover Image: Dariush M / Shutterstock
Composition: Jouve
Printing and Binding: LSC Communications

Manufactured in the United States of America.

1   0   9   8   7   6

f   e   d   c   b   a

For information, write: Bedford/St. Martin's, 75 Arlington Street, Boston, MA 02116
   (617-399-4000)

ISBN 978-1-319-03118-3 (Student Edition)
ISBN 978-1-319-07424-1 (Instructor's Edition)

ACKNOWLEDGMENTS
Text acknowledgments and copyrights appear at the back of the book on pages 559–61, which constitute an extension of the copyright page. Art acknowledgments and copyrights appear on the same pages as the art selections they cover.

PREFACE FOR INSTRUCTORS

"A writer" says Saul Bellow, "is a reader moved to emulate." In a nutshell, the aim of *The Brief Bedford Reader* is to move students to be writers, through reading and emulating the good writing of others.

Like its popular predecessors, this thirteenth edition pursues that aim both rhetorically and thematically. We present the rhetorical methods realistically, as we ourselves use them — as instinctive forms that assist invention and fruition and as flexible forms that mix easily for any purpose a writer may have. Further, we make numerous thematic connections among selections, both to spark students' interest in reading and to show how different writers tackle similar subjects with unique results.

Filling in this outline is a wealth of features, new and enduring.

NEW FEATURES

ENGAGING NEW READINGS BY REMARKABLE WRITERS As always, we have been enthralled with freshening the book's selections. In searching for essays academic yet lively, we discovered exceptional rhetorical models that will, we trust, also capture students' interest. The twenty-eight new selections include classic pieces by writers such as N. Scott Momaday and Joan Didion; recent works by established favorites such as Diane Ackerman, Bruce Catton, and Annie Lamott, and contemporary voices such as Issa Rae, Brian Doyle, and Colson Whitehead.

FOCUS ON STUDENT WORK *The Brief Bedford Reader* now features more student writing than any other textbook of its kind. Twenty-four models of

exemplary college work (ten of them new to this edition) include samples of
a student's critical reading and response; ten annotated examples of student
writing in academic genres such as lab reports, field observations, and policy
proposals; eleven essays given the same treatment as the professional writing;
and two new annotatated research papers.

**A GREATER EMPHASIS ON THE CONNECTION BETWEEN READING AND
WRITING**   More than ever, *The Brief Bedford Reader* demonstrates that critical reading and academic writing are related processes that naturally inform
and build off each other. At the request of instructors who use the book, we
have thoroughly revised and reorganized the material on academic reading
and writing in Part One, with increased attention throughout the text to writing in response to sources, whether one or many.

- **A stronger focus on reading to write.** Offering more guidance on active
  and critical reading than any other rhetorical reader, we stress the inter-
  connectedness of reading and writing in Chapter 1, with a clearer overview of annotating texts and a new discussion of writing in response as a
  component of critical thinking.

- **Expanded coverage of key writing topics.** Chapter 2 now examines the
  writing situation in more detail, clarifying the distinctions between writing to reflect, entertain, explain, or persuade, and explaining how an
  awareness of purpose and audience influences a writer's choices. Placing
  fresh emphasis on supporting a thesis with ideas gleaned from reading,
  the chapter also features a newly integrated discussion of synthesizing
  evidence, with multiple examples of acceptable and unacceptable summaries, paraphrases, and quotations.

- **Examples of writing that responds to reading.** In addition to the essay-
  in-progress that concludes Chapter 2, *The Brief Bedford Reader* for the
  first time features multiple student and professional essays that respond,
  directly or indirectly, to other works in the book. Student writer Rachel
  O'Connor, for instance, shares her critical reading of Shirley Jackson's
  "The Lottery," and composition instructor Barbara B. Parsons offers a rhe-
  torical analysis of Brent Staples's "Black Men and Public Space." Janelle
  Asselin makes a point-by-point rebuttal of an argument presented by
  Chuck Dixon and Paul Rivoche, while Jon Overton counters Brianne
  Richson's call for trigger warnings on syllabi. And Luis Alberto Urrea, in
  "Barrio Walden," reveals how he was influenced by the writings of Henry
  David Thoreau, "What I Lived For" in particular.

- **A new Appendix, "Finding and Documenting Sources,"** gathers the
  details on research and source citation where students are most likely to

look for guidance. Freshened guidelines emphasize asking questions, finding and evaluating sources, creating annotated bibliographies, and avoiding plagiarism; and updated help with documenting sources reflects the most recent versions of both MLA style and APA style, offering dozens of current models and new annotated student essays for each. Ten additional examples of documented writing are spread throughout the book.

A FRESH TAKE ON THE WRITERS' COMMENTS ON WRITING   After their essays, more than half of the book's writers offer comments on everything from reading to grammar to how they developed the particular piece we reprint. Besides providing rock-solid advice, these comments — eighteen of them new — prove that for the pros, too, writing is usually a challenge. New notes following the comments highlight the writers' key points, telling students where in the book they can find additional resources and suggesting how they might apply the insights to their own work.

For easy access, the "Writers on Writing" commentaries are listed in a new Directory under the topics they address. Look up *Revision*, for instance, and find that Junot Díaz, Shirley Jackson, Anne Lamott, and Colson Whitehead, among others, have something to say about this crucial stage of the writing process.

TRADEMARK FEATURES

EXCELLENT SELECTIONS BY WELL-KNOWN AUTHORS   All of them models of exceptional writing, the essays in *The Brief Bedford Reader* vary in authorship, topic, even length and format. We offer clear and interesting applications of the methods of development by noted writers such as Anna Quindlen, Brent Staples, Amy Tan, and David Sedaris. Half the selections are by women, and a third touch on cultural diversity. They range in subject from family to science, from language to psychology, from food to politics.

EXTENSIVE THEMATIC CONNECTIONS   *The Brief Bedford Reader* provides substantial opportunities for topical class discussion and writing. A pair of essays in each chapter addresses the same subject, from the ordinary (embarrassment) to the controversial (privilege). Eight of those pairings are new, and the thoroughly refreshed chapter on argument now includes one new essay pair and a new casebook. At least one "Connections" writing topic after every selection suggests links to other selections in the book. And an alternate table of contents arranges the book's selections under more than three dozen topics and academic disciplines (nine new).

REALISTIC TREATMENT OF THE RHETORICAL METHODS   *The Brief Bedford Reader* treats the methods of development not as empty forms but as tools for inventing, for shaping, and, ultimately, for accomplishing a purpose.

- **A practical guide.** The chapters on reading and writing in Part One and the introductions to the rhetorical methods in Part Two are simple and clear, with many explanations and suggestions distilled into bulleted lists and boxed guidelines so that students can easily follow and use the book's advice on their own. Each chapter introduction links the method to the range of purposes it can serve and gives step-by-step guidance for writing and revising. (For quick reference, the purpose/method links also appear inside the front cover, where they are keyed to the marginal page tabs that appear in each chapter introduction.)

- **A "Focus" box in every rhetorical chapter** highlights an element of writing that is especially relevant to that method — for example, verbs in narration, concrete words in description, parallelism in comparison and contrast, and tone in argument and persuasion. To show these elements in context, most selections include a question about them.

- **Annotated examples** of a textbook passage and a college writing assignment end each chapter introduction to demonstrate academic applications of the methods across the disciplines.

- **An emphasis on mixing the methods** takes the realistic approach even further. We show how writers freely combine methods to achieve their purposes: Each rhetorical introduction discusses how that method might work with others, and at least one "Other Methods" question after every selection helps students analyze how methods work together. Most significantly, Part Three provides an anthology of works by celebrated writers that specifically illustrate mixed methods. The headnotes for these selections point to where each method comes into play.

ABUNDANT EDITORIAL APPARATUS   As always, we've surrounded the selections with a wealth of material designed to get students reading, thinking, and writing. To help structure students' critical approach to the selections, each one is preceded by a headnote on the author and one on the selection itself, which outlines the selection's cultural and historical contexts. Each selection is followed by sets of questions on meaning, writing strategy, and language and at least five writing suggestions. One writing suggestion encourages students to explore their responses in their journals; another suggests how to develop the journal writing into an essay; and others emphasize critical writing, research, and connections among selections.

Besides the aids provided with every selection, the book also includes additional writing topics at the end of every rhetorical chapter (with several new suggestions in each), a Glossary of Useful Terms that defines key terms used in the book (all those printed in SMALL CAPITAL LETTERS), and a comprehensive index that alphabetizes not only authors and titles but also all important topics (including the elements of composition).

ATTENTION TO GENRE   *The Brief Bedford Reader* is still the only rhetorical reader to show students how they can apply the methods of development to various genres of writing. Integrated discussions throughout Part One introduce students to the concept of genre and help them understand how purpose, audience, and convention affect a writer's choices. And in each rhetorical chapter in Part Two, an annotated sample of a student-written document demonstrates a specific application of method to genre, with brief guidelines for writing different kinds of projects. Three of these documents—a criminal justice report, a critical reading of literature, and a policy proposal—are new to this edition.

ENGAGING VISUAL DIMENSION   *The Brief Bedford Reader* emphasizes the visual as well as the verbal. Chapter 1, on reading, provides a short course in thinking critically about images, with a photograph serving as a case study. Each rhetorical chapter then opens with a striking image—an ad, a photograph, a drawing—(a third of them new) with accompanying text and questions to invite students' own critical reading and show how the rhetorical methods work visually. Finally, several of the book's selections either take images as their starting points or use illustrations to explain or highlight key ideas.

EXTENSIVE INSTRUCTOR'S MANUAL   Available as a separate manual, online on the book page at *macmillanlearning.com*, or bound into the instructor's edition, *Notes and Resources for Teaching The Brief Bedford Reader* suggests ways to integrate journaling and collaboration into writing classes; discusses uses for the book's chapters on critical reading, academic writing, and research and documentation; and provides tips on using visuals and multimedia selections in a writing course. In addition, *Notes and Resources* discusses every method, every selection (with new multimedia resource suggestions and with possible answers provided for all questions), and every "Writers on Writing" feature.

TWO VERSIONS   *The Brief Bedford Reader* has a sibling. A longer edition, *The Bedford Reader*, features sixty-eight essays instead of fifty, including eight selections (rather than four) in Part Three.

ADDITIONAL RESOURCES

Bedford/St. Martin's offers multiple resources that can help you and your students get even more out of *The Brief Bedford Reader* and your course. To learn more about or to order any of the following products at a significant discount, contact your Bedford/St. Martin's sales representative or visit *macmillanlearning.com*.

E-BOOK OPTION   *The Brief Bedford Reader* is also available as an e-book. For details, visit *macmillanlearning.com/ebooks*.

LAUNCHPAD SOLO FOR READERS AND WRITERS   Offering instruction tailored to individual students' unique needs, *LaunchPad Solo for Readers and Writers* features several innovative digital tools.

- **Reading comprehension quizzes** for every selection in *The Brief Bedford Reader*.
- **Pre-built units that support a learning arc.** Each unit includes a pre-test, multimedia instruction and assessment, help for multilingual writers, and a post-test that assesses what students have learned about critical reading, the writing process, using sources, grammar, style, and mechanics.
- **Video introductions** offer overviews of many unit topics and illustrate the concepts at hand.
- **Adaptive quizzing for targeted learning.** Most units include Learning-Curve, game-like quizzing that focuses on the areas in which each student needs the most help.
- **The ability to monitor student progress.** Instructors can use the Gradebook to see which students are on track and which need additional help.

Order ISBN 978-1-319-09777-6 to package *LaunchPad Solo for Readers and Writers* with *The Brief Bedford Reader*, or visit *macmillanlearning.com /catalog/readwrite* for more information.

WRITER'S HELP 2.0   Built on research with more than 1,600 student writers, this online writing resource helps students find answers whether they are searching for advice on their own or as part of an assignment. The smart search feature leads to trusted content from best-selling handbooks, even when students use novice terms such as *flow* and *getting unstuck*. And Writer's Help 2.0 includes LearningCurve, game-like quizzing that adapts to what students already know and helps them focus on what they need to learn, as well as reading comprehension quizzes for every essay in *The Brief Bedford Reader*.

Order ISBN 978-1-319-09776-9 to package *Writer's Help 2.0, Hacker Version*, or ISBN 978-1-319-09778-3 for *Writer's Help 2.0, Lunsford Version*, with *The Brief Bedford Reader*; students who rent or buy a used book can purchase access at *macmillanlearning.com/writershelp2*. Instructor access is free. For technical support, visit *macmillanlearning.com/getsupport*.

PORTFOLIOS   The third edition of *Portfolio Keeping*, by Nedra Reynolds and Elizabeth Davis, provides all the information students need to use the portfolio method successfully in a writing course. *Portfolio Teaching*, a companion guide for instructors, provides practical support for you and your writing-program administrator. Contact your sales representative for a package ISBN.

JOIN OUR COMMUNITY!   *The Macmillan English Community* is now the home for all Bedford/St. Martin's professional resources, featuring Bedford *Bits*, a popular blog site offering new ideas for the composition classroom and composition teachers. Connect and converse with a growing team of Bedford authors and top scholars who blog on *Bits*: Andrea Lunsford, Nancy Sommers, Steve Bernhardt, Traci Gardner, Barclay Barrios, Jack Solomon, Susan Bernstein, Elizabeth Wardle, Doug Downs, Liz Losh, Jonathan Alexander, and Donna Winchell. In addition, you'll find an expanding collection of additional resources that support your teaching. Download titles from the publisher's professional resource series to support your teaching, review projects in the pipeline, sign up for professional development webinars, start a discussion, ask a question, and follow your favorite members. Visit *community .macmillan.com* to join the conversation.

ACKNOWLEDGMENTS

Hundreds of teachers and students over the years have helped us shape *The Brief Bedford Reader*. For this edition, the following teachers offered insights from their experiences that encouraged worthy changes: Mary Jane Atkins, Pierce Collegel; Richard Birk, North Central State College; Mary Bradley, Eastern Florida State College; Jessica Dennis, Tiffin University; Christina Devlin, Montgomery College; Kathryn Erickson, Eastern Florida State College; Cynthia Fillmore, Grossmont College; Donna French, Valencia College; Krystal Hering, Des Moines Area Community College; Debra Lee, Nash Community College; Crystal Manboard, Northwest Vista College; Ami Massengill, Nashville State Community College-Cookeville Campus; Todd McCann, Bay de Noc Community College; Mary Nolan-Coffman, Santa Moncia College; Lauren Rice, Des Moines Area Community College; Michael Rudd, Springfield Technical Community College; Madelyn Troxclair, Seattle Central College.

We are as ever deeply in debt to the creative people at and around Bedford/ St. Martin's. Leasa Burton, Steve Scipione, John Sullivan, Maura Shea, and Karen Henry contributed insight and support. Sherry Mooney, developing the book, was an invaluable collaborator: She helped to plan and implement the revisions and new features, hunted for readings, researched and drafted some of the apparatus, and calmly steered the ship through unexpected storms. Jennifer Prince ably assisted, especially in reaching out to student writers and coordinating the inclusion of their essays. William Boardman created the refreshing new cover. Louis Bruno planned and oversaw the production of the book. And Kevin Bradley, with remarkable patience and flexibility, transformed the raw manuscript into the book you hold.

CONTENTS

A writer with multiple sclerosis thinks she knows why the media carry so few images of people like herself with disabilities: Viewers might conclude, correctly, that "there is something ordinary about disability itself."

2   THE WRITING PROCESS   29

Inspired by reading Nancy Mairs's "Disability" (Chap. 1), a student writer argues that
television should "portray psychological disability as a part of everyday life, not a
crime."

12 ARGUMENT AND PERSUASION: Stating Opinions and Proposals   404

CONTENTS BY THEME AND DISCIPLINE

CHILDHOOD

CLASS

COMMUNICATION AND LANGUAGE

COMMUNITY

COMPUTER TECHNOLOGY

CRIME

DEATH

DIVERSITY

EDUCATION

ETHICS

FAMILY

FOOD

GENDER AND SEXUALITY

HEALTH AND DISABILITY

HISTORY

HUMOR AND SATIRE

INTERNATIONAL STUDIES

JOURNALISM

LAW

LITERATURE

MARRIAGE

MYTH AND LEGEND

THE NATURAL ENVIRONMENT

SCIENCE

SELF-DISCOVERY

SOCIAL CUSTOMS

SPORTS AND LEISURE

HOW (AND WHY) TO USE THIS BOOK

Many prophets have predicted the doom of words on paper, and they may yet be proved correct. Already, many of us are reading books and magazines mainly on mobile devices and communicating mostly by text messages. But even if we do discard paper and pens, the basic aims and methods of writing will not fundamentally change. Whether in print or on screen, we will need to explain our thoughts to others plainly and forcefully.

Our aim with *The Brief Bedford Reader* is to provide you with ample and varied resources that will help you develop your skills as a reader and writer. In this academic toolbox, you'll find not only interesting models of good writing but also useful advice, reference guides, ideas for writing, and practical strategies that you can apply to your own work.

THE SELECTIONS

Essays

In this book, we trust, you'll find many selections you will enjoy and want to discuss. *The Brief Bedford Reader* features work by some of the finest nonfiction writers and even a few famous literary figures.

The selections deal with more than just writing; they cut broadly across a college curriculum. You'll find professional essays and textbook paragraphs on science, history, business, culture, technology, sports, and politics. Some writers recall their childhoods, their problems and challenges. Some explore academic concerns such as the goals of education and the physics of mass movement. Some touch on matters likely to spark debate: free speech, class privilege, race relations, child labor. Some writers are serious; others, funny. In all, these selections mirror the kinds of reading you will meet in your other courses. Such reading is the intellectual storehouse of well-informed people with lively minds — who, to be sure, aren't found only on college campuses.

We have chosen the essays with one main purpose in mind: to show you how good writers write. Don't be discouraged if at first you find an immense gap in quality between Joan Didion's writing and yours. Of course there's a gap: Didion is an immortal with a unique style that she perfected over half a century. You don't have to judge your efforts by comparison. The idea is to gain whatever writing techniques you can. If you're going to learn from other writers, why not go to the best of them?

Student Examples

You can glean many skills by reading the work of seasoned writers, but you can also learn from your peers. Students, too, produce writing worth studying, as proved by Scott Beltran, Andrea Roman, Koji Frahm, and many others. In every chapter in Part Two, you'll find student pieces among the professional selections, at least one of them annotated to show you how the writers' strategies work. These examples vary in subject, approach, and GENRE, but every one of them shows how much student writers can achieve with a little inspiration and effort.

Visuals

The selections in *The Brief Bedford Reader* go beyond the written word. Much of what we "read" in the world is visual information, as in paintings and drawings, or visual-with-verbal information, as in advertisements and cartoons. In all, we include sixteen visual works. Some of them are subjects of writing, as when a writer analyzes a news photo or a bar graph. Other visual works stand free, offering themselves to be understood, interpreted, and perhaps enjoyed, just as prose and fiction do. To help you get the most from these images, we offer advice on reading visuals, with a sample analysis of a photograph, in Chapter 1.

We combine visual material with written texts to further a key aim of *The Brief Bedford Reader*: to encourage you to think critically about what you see, hear, and read. Like everyone else, you face a daily barrage of words and pictures. Mulling over the views of the writers, artists, and others represented in this book — figuring out their motives and strategies, agreeing or disagreeing with their ideas — will help you learn to manage, digest, and use in your own writing whatever media you encounter.

THE METHODS OF DEVELOPMENT

The selections in *The Brief Bedford Reader* fall into distinct sections. In Part Two, the heart of the book, each of ten chapters explains a familiar method of developing ideas, such as NARRATION, DESCRIPTION, EXAMPLE, CAUSE AND EFFECT, or DEFINITION. These methods are extraordinarily useful tools for achieving your PURPOSE in writing, whatever that purpose may be. They can help you discover what you know, what you need to know, how to think critically about your subject, and how to shape your ideas.

An introduction to each chapter outlines the method, explains its uses, and shows how you can apply it to your own writing. The reading selections that follow illustrate the method at work. Examining these selections, you'll discover two important facts about the methods of development. First, they are flexible: Two people can use the same method for quite different ends, and just about any method can point a way into just about any subject in any medium.

The second fact about the methods of development is this: A writer never sticks to just one method all the way through a piece of writing. Even when one method predominates, you'll see the writer pick up another method, let it shape a paragraph or more, and then move on to yet another method — all to achieve some overriding aim. Part Three offers an anthology of classic and contemporary selections that illustrate how, in most writing, the methods work together.

THE PRACTICAL GUIDANCE

Overviews of Reading, Writing, and Research

The selections in *The Brief Bedford Reader* are meant to be enjoyed, but also to give you ideas for your own writing. We include two chapters in Part One to help you build your critical reading and writing skills as you work with the readings. You might want to read these chapters straight through as a general guide or turn back to them as necessary for reference, or both.

Chapter 1 explains the connection between reading and writing, outlines the goals of CRITICAL READING, and provides concrete advice for approaching written and visual works with an open, questioning mind. To demonstrate what academic reading entails, we include a sample essay and accompany it with one student's notes and with our own interpretations of the writer's meanings and strategies.

In Chapter 2 we walk you through the stages of the writing process, following the same student as she works from rough idea to final draft. Like the first chapter, this one features bulleted points and boxed checklists to help you find the information you need. It addresses in particular the challenges of ACADEMIC WRITING, whether in responding to individual selections or developing an idea with reference to multiple works. It also includes a brief overview of common editing challenges and shows you how to solve them.

The Appendix goes over the basics of finding and using sources in academic writing. It offers dozens of citation models for both MLA and APA styles and includes two annotated student research papers.

Reading Questions and Writing Prompts

Following every essay in *The Brief Bedford Reader*, you'll find a battery of questions that can help you analyze the selection and respond to it. First, a suggestion for responding in your JOURNAL to what you've just read encourages you to think about the writer's themes and your reactions to them. Next, you'll find critical reading questions that can help you read beneath the surface of the work, teasing out the elements that contribute to the writer's success and even those that don't. (You can see a sample of how these questions work when we analyze Nancy Mairs's essay "Disability," starting on p. 12.)

After these questions are at least four suggestions for writing, including one that proposes turning your journal entry into an essay, one that links the selection with one or two others in the book, and one that asks you to read the selection and write about it with your critical faculties alert. Additional suggestions for writing appear at the end of each chapter. We intend these prompts not as rigid taskmasters but as helpful guides. Certainly you can respond to them exactly as written, but if they spark other insights for you, by all means pursue your inspiration. Writing is always best when it comes from a real interest in the subject and a desire to write about it.

Glossary and Index

In this introduction and throughout the following chapters, certain words appear in CAPITAL LETTERS. These are key terms helpful in discussing both the selections in this book and the reading and writing you do. If you'd like to see such a term defined and illustrated, you can find it in the Glossary of Useful Terms on pages 536–50. The Glossary offers more than just brief definitions. It is there to provide you with further explanation, examples, and support.

You can also find the help you need by consulting the Index, located at the back of the book. Say you're revising a draft and your instructor has commented that your essay needs a clearer thesis, but you're not sure what that means or what to do. Look up THESIS, and you'll discover exactly where in *The Brief Bedford Reader* you can find advice for clarifying and expressing your main idea.

THE WRITERS ON WRITING

A final word. The writers represented in this book did not produce their readable and informative texts on the first try, as if by magic, leaving the rest of us to cope with writer's block, awkward sentences, and all the other difficulties of writing. As proof, we visit their workshops. Following more than half the selections are comments by their writers, revealing how they write (or wrote), offering their tricks, setting forth things they admire about good writing. Accompanying the comments are tips on how you can apply the writers' insights to your own work, and a directory at the back of the book points you toward their advice on such practical matters as drafting, finding your point, and revising. No doubt you'll notice some contradictions in these comments: The writers disagree about when and how to think about readers, about whether outlines have any value, about whether style follows subject or vice versa. The reason for the differences of opinion is, simply, that no two writers follow the same path to finished work. Even the same writer may take a left instead of the customary right turn if the writing situation demands a change. A key aim of providing the writers' statements is to suggest the sheer variety of routes open to you, the many approaches to writing and strategies for succeeding at it.

Let's get started then.

PART ONE

ACADEMIC READING AND WRITING

1

CRITICAL READING

Reading and writing are interconnected. Deepen your mastery of one, and you deepen your mastery of the other. The experience of carefully reading an excellent writer, noticing not only what the writer has to say but also the quality of its saying, rubs off (if you are patient and perceptive) on your own writing. For any writer, then, reading is indispensable. It turns up fresh ideas; it stocks the mind with information, understanding, and examples; it instills critical awareness of one's own surroundings.

Whatever career you enter, reading will be an integral part of your work. You may be trying to understand a new company policy, seeking the truth in a campaign ad, researching a scientific development, or looking for pointers to sharpen your skills. Such reading, like writing itself, demands effort. Unlike the casual reading you might do to pass the time or entertain yourself, CRITICAL READING involves looking beneath the surface of a text, seeking to understand the creator's intentions, the strategies for achieving them, and their effects. This book offers dozens of selections that reward critical reading and can teach you how to become a better writer. To learn from a selection, plan to spend an hour or two in its company. Seek out some quiet place — a library, a study cubicle, your room. Switch off the music and the phone. The fewer the distractions, the easier your task will be and the more you'll enjoy it.

How do you read critically? Exactly how, that is, do you engage with a work, master its complexities, learn from it, and respond? To find out, we'll model critical-thinking processes that you can apply to the written and visual selections in this book, taking a close look at an essay and a photograph for examples.

READING ACTIVELY

Previewing

Critical reading starts before you read the first word of a piece of writing. You take stock of what's before you, locating clues to the work's content and the writer's biases. Whenever you approach a written work, make a point of assessing these features beforehand:

- **The title.** Effective titles do more than lure readers in; they also hint at what to expect from a work. Often the title will tell you the writer's subject, as with Anna Quindlen's "Homeless." Sometimes the title immediately states the main point the writer will make: "I Want a Wife." Some titles spell out the method a writer proposes to follow: "Grant and Lee: A Study in Contrasts." And the title may reveal the writer's attitude toward the material, as "Live Free and Starve" does.

- **The author.** Whatever you know or can learn about a writer — upbringing, special training, previous publications, outlook, ideology — can often help you predict something about a work. Is the writer a political conservative or a liberal? a feminist? an athlete? an internationally renowned philosopher? a popular comedian? By knowing something about the background or beliefs of a writer, you may guess beforehand a little of what he or she will say.

- **The genre.** Identifying the type, or GENRE, of a work can tell you much about the writer's intentions and likely strategies. Genres vary widely; they include critical analyses, business reports, works of literature, humor pieces, and newspaper columns — among many others. The conventions of a given genre necessarily direct a writer's choices. For instance, you can assume that a scholarly article will take an academic tone, lay out arguments and evidence carefully, and cite other published works. The same approach in a personal narrative, however, would confuse most readers.

- **Where the work was published.** Clearly, it matters to a writer's credibility whether an article called "Creatures of the Dark Oceans" appears in a science magazine or in a supermarket tabloid. But no less important, knowing where a work first appeared can tell you for whom the writer was writing. Good writers, as you will see, develop an awareness of their AUDIENCE and shape their messages to appeal to particular readers' interests and needs.

- **When the work was published.** Knowing the year a work appeared may give you another key to understanding it. A 2017 article on ocean creatures will contain statements of fact more advanced and reliable than an essay printed in 1917 — although the older work might offer valuable information and insights, too.

To help provide such prereading knowledge, this book supplies biographical information about the writers and tells you something about the sources and original contexts of the selections, in notes just before each essay. It can be tempting to skip over such introductory materials, but we encourage you to look at them. Doing so will help you become a more efficient reader in the end.

Annotating

To learn from other writers how to write well, you'll want to read the essays in this book multiple times. On the first reading, focus on what the author has to say, without getting hung up on every particular. If you encounter any words or concepts that you don't know, take them in stride; you can always circle them and look them up later. Begin by getting a feel for the gist of the essay; later, you will examine the details and strategies that make it work.

In giving an essay a second or third going-over, critical readers find a pencil (or stylus) indispensable. A pencil in hand concentrates the attention wonderfully, and, as often happens with writing, it can lead to unexpected connections. (Some readers favor highlighting key words or lines, but you can't use color alone to note *why* a word or an idea is important.)

You can annotate your own material in several ways, developing a personal system that works best for you:

- **Underline essential ideas,** and double-underline repeated points or concepts.
- **Mark key passages** with checks or vertical lines.
- **Write questions** in the margins.
- **Note associations** with other works you've read, seen, or heard.
- **Vent your feelings** ("Bull!" "Yes!" "Says who?").

If you can't annotate what you're reading — because it's borrowed or your device doesn't have that functionality — make your notes on a separate sheet of paper or in an electronic bookmark or file.

Writing while reading helps you uncover the hidden workings of an essay, so that you, as much as any expert, can judge its effectiveness. You'll develop an opinion about what you read, and you'll want to express it. While reading this way, you're being a writer. Your pencil marks or keystrokes will jog your memory, too, when you review for a test, take part in class discussion, or write about what you've read.

To show what a reader's annotations on an essay might look like, we give you Nancy Mairs's "Disability" with a student's marginal notes, written over the course of several readings. The same student, Rosie Anaya, wrote an essay spurred by the ideas she found in reading Mairs's work; it appears at the end of the next chapter.

NANCY MAIRS

A self-described "radical feminist, pacifist, and cripple," Nancy Mairs aims to "speak the 'unspeakable.'" Her poetry, memoirs, and essays deal with many sensitive subjects, including her struggles with multiple sclerosis. Born in Long Beach, California, in 1943, Mairs grew up in New Hampshire and Massachusetts. She received a BA from Wheaton College and an MFA in creative writing and a PhD in English literature from the University of Arizona. While working on her advanced degrees, Mairs taught high-school and college writing courses. Her second book of poetry, *In All the Rooms of the Yellow House* (1984), received a Western States Arts Foundation book award. Mairs's essays are collected in several volumes, including *Carnal Acts* (1990), *Waist High in the World* (1996), *A Troubled Guest* (2001), and *A Dynamic God* (2007). In 2008 she received the Arizona Literary Treasure Award. In addition to working as a writer, Mairs is a public speaker and a research associate with the Southwest Institute for Research on Women.

Disability

As a writer afflicted with multiple sclerosis, Mairs is in a unique position to examine how the culture responds to people with disabilities. In this essay from *Carnal Acts*, she examines media depictions of disability and argues with her usual unsentimental candor that the media must treat disability as normal. The essay was first published in 1987 in the *New York Times*. To what extent is Mairs's critique still valid today?

For months now I've been consciously searching for repre- 1
sentations of myself in the media, especially television. I know
I'd recognize this self because of certain distinctive, though not
unique, features: I am a forty-three-year-old woman crippled with
multiple sclerosis; although I can still totter short distances with
the aid of a brace and a cane, more and more of the time I ride in
a wheelchair. Because of these appliances and my peculiar gait,
I'm easy to spot even in a crowd. So when I tell you I haven't
noticed any women like me on television, you can believe me.

"myself" = a person
with a disability
living a full life

!

Actually, last summer I did see a woman with multiple scle- 2
rosis portrayed on one of those medical dramas that offer an
illness-of-the-week like the daily special at your local diner. In
fact, that was the whole point of the show: that this poor young
woman had MS. She was terribly upset (understandably, I assure
you) by the diagnosis, and her response was to plan a trip to
Kenya while she was still physically capable of making it, against
the advice of the young, fit, handsome doctor who had fallen in
love with her. And she almost did it. At least, she got as far as
a taxi to the airport, hotly pursued by the doctor. But at the last
she succumbed to his blandishments and fled the taxi into his
manly protective embrace. No escape to Kenya for this cripple.

Wait, I've seen
characters with
wheelchairs. Plenty.

A movie shows
disability defining a
woman's life.

emotions

again!

Capitulation into the arms of a man who uses his medi- 3
cal powers to strip one of even the urge toward independence
is hardly the sort of representation I had in mind. But even if
the situation had been sensitively handled, according to the
woman her right to her own adventures, it wouldn't have been
what I'm looking for. Such a television show, as well as films
like *Duet for One* and *Children of a Lesser God*, in taking disability
as its major premise, excludes the complexities that round out
a character and make her whole. It's not about a woman who
happens to be physically disabled; it's about physical disability as
the determining factor of a woman's existence.

Also The Soloist, and
A Beautiful Mind

The complaint: these
shows miss the point

Take it from me, physical disability looms pretty large in 4
one's life. But it doesn't devour one wholly. I'm not, for instance,
Ms. MS, a walking, talking embodiment of a chronic incur-
able degenerative disease. In most ways I'm just like every other
woman of my age, nationality, and socioeconomic background.
I menstruate, so I have to buy tampons. I worry about smoker's
breath, so I buy mouthwash. I smear my wrinkling skin with
lotions. I put bleach in the washer so my family's undies won't

Details
have a point
she buys things the
advertisers sell.

be dingy. I drive a car, talk on the telephone, get runs in my pantyhose, eat pizza. In most ways, that is, I'm the advertisers' dream: Ms. Great American Consumer. And yet the advertisers, who determine nowadays who will get represented publicly and who will not, deny the existence of me and my kind absolutely.

Ads don't show disability either — still true?

I once asked a local advertiser why he didn't include dis- 5
abled people in his spots. His response seemed direct enough: "We don't want to give people the idea that our product is just for the handicapped." But tell me truly now: If you saw me pouring out puppy biscuits, would you think these kibbles were only for the puppies of the cripples? If you saw my blind niece ordering a Coke, would you switch to Pepsi lest you be struck sightless? No, I think the advertiser's excuse masked a deeper and more anx-ious rationale: To depict disabled people in the ordinary activi-ties of daily life is to admit that there is something ordinary about disability itself, that it may enter anybody's life. If it is effaced completely, or at least isolated as a separate "problem," so that it remains at a safe distance from other human issues, then the viewer won't feel threatened by her or his own physi-cal vulnerability.

Hah! Snarky.
emotions

✓ *scary thought*

effaced? (means erased, or made to disappear)

This kind of effacement or isolation has painful, even dan- 6
gerous consequences, however. For the disabled person, these include self-degradation and a subtle kind of self-alienation not unlike that experienced by other minorities. Socialized human beings love to conform, to study others and then mold them-selves to the contours of those whose images, for good reasons or bad, they come to love. Imagine a life in which feasible others — others you can hope to be like — don't exist. At the least you might conclude that there is something queer about you, something ugly or foolish or shameful. In the extreme, you might feel as though you don't exist, in any meaningful social sense, at all. Everyone else is "there," sucking breath mints and splashing cologne and swigging wine coolers. You're "not there." And if not there, nowhere.

effects — IMPORTANT

emotions

What about individuality?

emotions

But this denial of disability imperils even you who are able- 7
bodied, and not just by shrinking your insight into the physi-cally and emotionally complex world you live in. Some disabled people call you TAPs, or Temporarily Abled Persons. The fact is that ours is the only minority you can join involuntarily, without warning, at any time. And if you live long enough, as you're

Problem affects people without disabilities too — interesting point.

✓

increasingly likely to do, you may well join it. The transition will probably be difficult from a physical point of view no matter what. But it will be a good bit easier <u>psychologically</u> if you are accustomed to seeing disability as a normal characteristic, one that complicates but does not ruin human existence. Achieving this integration, for disabled and able-bodied people alike, requires that we insert disability daily into our field of vision: quietly, naturally, in the small and common scenes of our ordinary lives.

main idea

DEVELOPING AN UNDERSTANDING

Apart from your specific notes on an essay, you'll also need a place to work out your comprehension using the strategies and detailed analyses discussed below and on the following pages. For such responses, you may find a JOURNAL handy. It can be a repository of your ideas, a comfortable place to record thoughts about what you read. You may be surprised to find that the more you write in an unstructured way, the more you'll have to say when it's time to write a structured essay.

Summarizing

It's good practice, especially with more difficult essays, to SUMMARIZE the content in writing to be sure you understand it or, as often happens, to come to understand it. (We're suggesting here that you write summaries for yourself, but the technique is also useful when you discuss other people's works in your writing, as shown on pp. 43–44.)

In summarizing a work of writing, you digest, *in your own words*, what the author says: You take the essence of the author's meaning, without the supporting evidence and other details that make the whole convincing or interesting. If the work is short, you may want to make this a two-step procedure: First write a summary sentence for every paragraph or related group of paragraphs; then summarize those sentences in two or three others that capture the heart of the author's meaning.

Here is a two-step summary of "Disability." (The numbers in parentheses refer to paragraph numbers in the essay.) First, the longer version:

(1) Mairs searches the media in vain for depictions of women like herself with disabilities. (2) One TV movie showed a woman recently diagnosed with multiple sclerosis, but she chose dependence over independence. (3) Such shows oversimplify people with disabilities by making disability

central to their lives. (4) People with disabilities live lives and consume goods like everyone else, but the media ignore them. (5) Showing disability as ordinary would remind nondisabled viewers that they are vulnerable. (6) The media's exclusion of others like themselves deprives people with disabilities of role models and makes them feel undesirable or invisible. (7) Nondisabled viewers lose an understanding that could enrich them and would help them adjust to disability of their own.

Now the short summary:

> Mairs believes that the media, by failing to depict disability as ordinary, both marginalize viewers with disabilities and impair the outlook and coping skills of the "Temporarily Abled."

Thinking Critically

Summarizing will start you toward understanding the author's meaning, but it is just a first step. Once you comprehend the gist of a text, you're ready to examine its deeper meanings and intentions and apply them to your own work and life. (A TEXT may be a written document, but it may also be a photograph, an experiment, a conversation, a work of art, a Web site, or any other form of communication.)

We're talking here about critical thinking — not "negative," the common conception of *critical*, but "thorough, thoughtful, inquisitive, judgment forming." When you approach something critically, you harness your faculties, your fund of knowledge, and your experiences to understand, appreciate, and evaluate the text. Critical thinking is a process involving several overlapping operations: analysis, inference, synthesis, and evaluation.

Analysis

A way of thinking so essential that it has its own chapter in this book (Chap. 8), ANALYSIS separates an item into its parts. Say you're listening to a new song by a band you like: Without thinking much about it, you isolate melodies, lyrics, and instrumentals. Critical readers analyze essays more consciously, by looking at an author's main idea, support for that idea, special writing strategies, and other elements. To show you how the beginnings of such an analysis might look, we examine these elements in "Disability" later in this chapter.

Inference

Next you draw conclusions about a work based on your store of information and experience, your knowledge of the creator's background and biases, and your analysis. Say that after listening to the new song, you conclude

> **CHECKLIST FOR CRITICAL READING**
>
> ✔ **Analyze.** Examine the elements of the work, such as thesis, purpose and audience, genre, evidence, structure, and language.
>
> ✔ **Infer.** Interpret the underlying meanings of the elements and the assumptions and intentions of the author.
>
> ✔ **Synthesize.** Form an idea about how the elements function together to produce a whole and to deliver a message.
>
> ✔ **Evaluate.** Judge the quality, significance, or value of the work.

that it reveals the band's interest in the Caribbean soca scene. Now you are using INFERENCE. When you infer, you add to the work, making explicit what was only implicit.

Inference is especially important in discovering a writer's ASSUMPTIONS: opinions or beliefs, often unstated, that direct the writer's ideas, supporting evidence, writing strategies, and language choices. A writer who favors gun control, for instance, may assume without saying so that an individual's rights may be infringed for the good of the community. A writer who opposes gun control might assume the opposite, that an individual's right is superior to the community's good.

Synthesis

During SYNTHESIS, you use your special aptitudes, interests, and training to reconstitute a text so that it now contains not just the original elements but also your sense of their underpinnings, relationships, and implications. What is the band trying to accomplish with its new song? Has the musical style changed? Answering such questions leads you to link elements into a whole or to link two or more wholes.

Synthesis is the core of much academic writing. Sometimes you'll respond directly to a text, or you'll use it as a springboard to another subject. Sometimes you'll show how two or more texts resemble each other or how they differ. Sometimes you'll draw on many texts to answer a question or support an argument. In all these cases, you'll put your reading to use to develop your own ideas.

Evaluation

When you EVALUATE, you determine the adequacy, significance, or value of a work: Is the band getting better or just standing still? In evaluating an essay you answer a question such as whether you are moved as the author intended, whether the author has proved a case, or whether the effort was even worthwhile. Not all critical thinking involves evaluation, however;

often you (and your teachers) will be satisfied with analyzing, inferring, and synthesizing ideas without judging a text's overall merit.

Using this book, you'll learn to think critically about an essay by considering what the author's purpose and main idea are, how clear they are, and how well supported. You'll isolate which writing techniques the author has used to special advantage, what hits you as particularly fresh, clever, or wise — and what *doesn't* work, too. You'll discover exactly what the writer is saying, how he or she says it, and whether, in the end, it was worth saying. In class discussions and in writing, you'll tell others what you think and why.

ANALYZING ESSAYS

To help you in your critical reading, questions after every selection in this book direct your attention to specific elements of the writer's work. Here we introduce the three categories of questions — on meaning, writing strategy, and language — and show how they might be applied to Nancy Mairs's "Disability" (p. 12).

QUESTIONS FOR ANALYZING AN ESSAY

MEANING

✔ **What is the thesis,** or main point? Where is stated?

✔ **What is the writer's purpose?** What does the essay try to acomplish?

WRITING STRATEGY

✔ **Who is the intended audience?** What assumptions does the writer make about readers' knowledge, perspectives, and interests?

✔ **How are supporting details structured?** What methods does the writer use to organize ideas? How does the writer achieve unity and coherence?

✔ **What evidence does the writer provide** to support the main idea? Is it sufficient and compelling?

LANGUAGE

✔ **What is the overall tone of the essay?** Is it appropriate, given the writer's purpose and audience?

✔ **How effective are the writer's words?** Are their meanings clear? What connotations do they hold?

✔ **Does the writer use any figures of speech,** such as metaphor, simile, hyperbole, personification, or irony? How well do they lend meaning and vibrancy to the writer's thoughts?

Meaning

By *meaning*, we're getting at what the words say literally, of course, but also what they imply and, more generally, what the author's aims are. When reading an essay, look especially for the THESIS and try to determine the author's PURPOSE for writing.

- **Thesis.** Every essay has — or should have — a point, a main idea the writer wants to communicate. Many writers come right out and sum up this idea in a sentence or two, a THESIS STATEMENT. They may provide it in the first or second paragraph, give it somewhere in the middle of the essay, or hold it for the end. Mairs, for instance, develops her thesis over the course of the essay and then states it in paragraph 7:

  Achieving this integration [of seeing disability as normal], for disabled and able-bodied people alike, requires that we insert disability daily into our field of vision: quietly, naturally, in the small and common scenes of our ordinary lives.

  Sometimes a writer will not state his or her thesis outright at all, although it remains in the background controlling the work and can be inferred by a critical reader. If you find yourself confused about a writer's point — "What *is* this about?" — it will be up to you to figure out what the author is trying to say.

- **Purpose.** By *purpose*, we mean the writer's apparent reason for writing: what he or she was trying to achieve. In making a simple statement of a writer's purpose, we might say that a person writes *to reflect* on an experience or observation, *to entertain* readers, *to explain* something to them, or *to persuade* them. To state a purpose more fully, we might say that a writer writes not just to persuade, for instance, but to motivate readers to accept a particular idea or take a specific action. In the case of "Disability," it seems that Mairs's purpose is twofold: to explain her view of the media and to convince readers that lack of representation hurts people without disabilities as much as it does people with disabilities.

Writing Strategy

Almost all writing is a *transaction* between a writer and an audience, maybe one reader, maybe millions. To the extent that writers hold our interest, make us think, and convince us to accept a thesis, it pays to ask, "How do they succeed?" (When writers bore or anger us, we ask why they fail.) Conscious writers make choices intended to get readers on their side so that they can achieve their purpose. These choices are what we mean by STRATEGY in writing.

- **Audience.** We can tell much about a writer's intended audience from the context in which the piece was first published. And when we know something of the audience, we can better analyze the writer's decisions, from the choice of supporting details to the use of a particular tone. Mairs's original audience, for instance, was the readers of the *New York Times*, as the introduction to "Disability" on page 12 informs us. She could assume educated readers with diverse interests who are not themselves disabled or even familiar with disability. So she fills them in, taking pains to describe her disability (par. 1) and her life (4). For her thoughtful but somewhat blinkered audience, Mairs mixes a blend of plain talk, humor, and insistence to give them the facts they need, win them over with common humanity, and convey the gravity of the problem.

- **Method.** A crucial part of a writer's strategy is how he or she develops ideas to achieve a particular purpose or purposes. As Chapters 3–12 of this book illustrate, a writer may draw on one or more familiar methods of development to make those ideas concrete and convincing. Mairs, for instance, uses COMPARISON AND CONTRAST to show similarities and differences between herself and nondisabled people (pars. 1, 4, 5). She offers EXAMPLES: of dramas she dislikes (2–3), of products she buys (4), and of ads in which people with disabilities might appear (5). With DESCRIPTION she shows the flavor of her life (4) and the feelings she has experienced (6). And with CAUSE AND EFFECT she explains why disability is ignored by the media (5) and what that does to people with disabilities (6) and those without (7). Overall, Mairs uses these methods to build an ARGUMENT, asserting and defending an opinion.

- **Evidence.** Typically, each method of development benefits from — and lends itself to — different kinds of support. For this EVIDENCE, the writer may use facts, reasons, examples, expert opinions — whatever best delivers the point. (We have more to say about the uses of evidence in the introductions to Chapters 3–12.) Mairs draws on several types of evidence to develop her claims, including personal experiences and emotions (pars. 1, 4, 5), details to support her generalizations (2, 4, 5), and the opinion of an advertiser (5).

- **Structure.** A writer must mold and arrange ideas to capture, hold, and direct readers' interest. Writing that we find clear and convincing almost always has UNITY (everything relates to the main idea) and COHERENCE (the relations between parts are clear). All the parts fit together logically. In "Disability," Mairs first introduces herself and establishes her complaint (pars. 1–5). Then she explains and argues the negative effects of "effacement" on people with disabilities (6) and the positive effects that normalizing disability would have on people who are not presently disabled (7). As often occurs in arguments, Mairs's organization builds to her main idea, her thesis, which readers might find difficult to accept at the outset.

Language

To examine the element of language is to go even more deeply into an essay and how it was made. A writer's tone, voice, and choice of words in particular not only express meaning but also convey the writer's attitudes and elicit those attitudes from readers.

- **Tone.** The TONE of a piece of writing is the equivalent of tone of voice in speaking. Whether it's angry, sarcastic, or sad, joking or serious, tone carries almost as much information about a writer's purpose as the words themselves do. Mairs's tone mixes lightness with gravity, humor with intensity. Sometimes she uses IRONY, saying one thing but meaning another, as in "If you saw my blind niece ordering a Coke, would you switch to Pepsi lest you be struck sightless?" (par. 5). She's blunt, too, revealing intimate details about her life. Honest and wry, Mairs invites us to see the media's exclusion as ridiculous and then leads us to her uncomfortable conclusion.

- **Word choice.** Tone comes in part from DICTION, a writer's choices regarding words and sentence structures — academic, casual, or otherwise. Mairs is a writer whose diction is rich and varied. Expressions from common speech, such as "what I'm looking for" (par. 3), lend her prose vigor and naturalness. At the same time, Mairs is serious about her argument, so she puts it in serious terms, such as "denial of disability imperils even you who are able-bodied" (7). Pay attention also to the CONNOTATIONS of words — their implied meanings and associations. Such subtle nuances can have a profound effect on both a writer's meaning and readers' understanding of it. In "Disability," the word with the strongest connotations may be "cripple" (2, 5) because it calls up insensitivity: By using this word, Mairs stresses her frankness but also suggests that negative attitudes determine what images the media present.

- **Imagery.** One final use of language is worth noting: those concrete words and phrases that appeal to readers' senses. Such IMAGES might be straightforward, as in Mairs's portrayal of herself as someone who "can still totter short distances with the aid of a brace and a cane" (par. 1). But often writers use FIGURES OF SPEECH, bits of colorful language that capture meaning or attitude better than literal words can. For instance, Mairs says that people "study others and then mold themselves to the contours of those whose images . . . they come to love" (6). That figure of speech is a *metaphor*, stating that one thing (behavioral change) is another (physical change). Elsewhere Mairs uses *simile*, stating that one thing is *like* another ("an illness-of-the-week like the daily special at your local diner," 2), and *understatement* ("physical disability looms pretty large in one's life," 4). More examples of figures of speech appear in the Glossary of Useful Terms, page 543.

Many of the reading questions in this book point to figures of speech, to oddities of tone, to particulars of diction, or to troublesome or unfamiliar words. Writers have few traits more valuable than a fondness for words and a willingness to experiment with them.

EXAMINING VISUAL IMAGES

We often forget that a visual text, just as much as a written work, was created for a reason. No matter what it is — advertisement, infographic, painting, video, photograph, cartoon — an image originated with a person or persons who had a purpose, an intention for how that image should look and how viewers should respond to it.

In their origins, then, visual images are not much different from written texts, and they are no less open to critical thinking that will uncover their meanings and effects. To a great extent, the method for critically "reading" visuals parallels the one for essays outlined earlier in this chapter. In short, as the checklist on the facing page indicates, you start with an overview of the image and then analyze its elements, make inferences, synthesize, and evaluate.

As you do when reading written works, always write while examining a visual image or images. Jotting down responses, questions, and other notes will not only help you remember what you were thinking but also jog further thoughts into being.

To show the critical method in action, we'll look closely at the photograph on page 24. Further examples of visual works appear elsewhere in this book as well: For images that support written works, see pages 202 and 268 (photo-

QUESTIONS FOR EXAMINING AN IMAGE

THE BIG PICTURE

✔ **What is the source of the work?** Who was the intended audience?

✔ **What does the work show overall?** What appears to be happening?

✔ **Why was the work created** — to educate, to sell, to shock, to entertain?

ANALYSIS

✔ **Which elements of the image stand out?** What is distinctive about each?

✔ **What does the composition of the image emphasize?** What is pushed to the background or the sides?

INFERENCE

✔ **What do the elements of the work suggest** about the creator's intentions and assumptions?

✔ **If words accompany the work, what do they say?** How are they sized and placed in relation to the visual elements? How do the written and visual parts interact?

SYNTHESIS

✔ **What general appeal does the work make to viewers?** For instance, does it emphasize logic, emotion, or value?

✔ **What feelings, memories, moods, or ideas does the work summon from viewers' own store of experiences?** Why would its creator try to establish these associations?

EVALUATION

✔ **Does the work fulfill its creator's intentions?** Was it worth creating?

✔ **How does the work affect you?** Are you moved? amused? bored? offended?

graphs), 352–55 (drawings), and 359 (a bar graph). And Chapters 3–12 each open with a visual that gives you a chance to try critical viewing on your own.

Seeing the Big Picture

To examine any visual representation, it helps first to get an overview, a sense of the whole and its context. On such a first glance, consider who created it — for instance, a painter, a teacher, an advertiser — when it was created, and why.

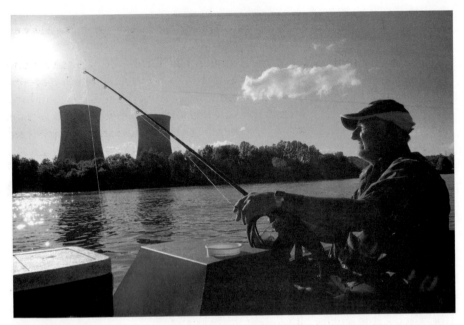

Robin Nelson

The photograph above was taken by photojournalist Robin Nelson near the Watts Bar nuclear power plant in Spring City, Tennessee, for a 2011 photo essay in *Mother Jones*, a magazine known for its progressive outlook. The year before, an earthquake and tsunami had destroyed nuclear reactors in Japan, causing global alarm. Nelson's picture shows a solitary older man fishing from a boat with his hands resting on its steering wheel; the Chicamauga Reservoir and two cooling towers appear in the background. (The tower on the left has operated since 1996; a new reactor for the other tower was under construction at the time of the photograph and was slated to begin operation within a year.)

Taking a Critical Look

After you've gained an overview of an image, you can start making the kinds of deeper inquiry — analysis, inference, synthesis, and evaluation — that serve as the foundation of any critical reading, whatever form the text may take.

Analysis

To analyze a visual work, focus on the elements that contribute to the whole — not just the people, animals, or objects depicted but also artistic elements such as lighting, color, shape, and balance. Notice which elements stand out and what seems to be emphasized. If spoken or written words accompany the work, examine their relation to the visual components as well as what they say.

In Nelson's photograph, the dominant elements are the towers and the man, whose smile suggests contentment. A fishing rod and line occupy the center of the image, visually connecting the man, the towers, and the water. The pole points at the sun in the upper left corner. The sun reflects off the water and puts parts of the man in shadow; the towers are reflected in the water as well. A line of trees runs across the midline of the photo, highlighting the natural environment. The sky is clear, with one cloud floating in the upper right. And in the foreground we see what appear to be a container for bait and a cooler.

Inference

Identifying the elements of a visual leads you to consider what they mean and how the image's creator has selected and arranged them so that viewers will respond in certain ways. You make explicit what may only be implicit in the work — the creator's intentions and assumptions.

We can guess at Robin Nelson's intentions for the photograph. On the one hand, it seems to support nuclear power as harmless: The bright sun, clear sky, sparkling water, and lush trees imply an unspoiled environment, and the man appears unworried about fishing near the plant. On the other hand, Nelson would know that most readers of *Mother Jones* are concerned about the safety of nuclear power and that the cooling towers alone would raise red flags for many; certainly the cloud in the otherwise clear sky and the deep shadow obscuring most of the fisherman hint at danger. The photographer may see these opposites as reflecting the controversy over nuclear power.

Synthesis

Linking the elements and your inferences about them will move you into a new conception of a visual representation: your own conclusions about its overall message and effect.

As we see it, Nelson's photograph represents Americans' mixed feelings about nuclear power. The looming towers, the cloud, and the shadowing seem ominous, suggesting risks facing the area around the plant and the country as a whole. The beauty of the scenery evokes our appreciation of nature; the implied pleasure of fishing evokes our approval as it intensifies our concerns for the man's safety. The juxtaposition of the power plant, the environment, and a single human being seems to represent the intersecting forces of nature and society and the complex implications of nuclear energy for both.

Evaluation

Often in criticizing visual works, you'll take one step beyond synthesis to judge the quality, significance, or value of the work.

Robin Nelson's photograph seems to us masterful in delivering a message. As Nelson seems to have intended, he distills strong, contradictory feelings about nuclear power and environmental protection into a deceptively simple image of a man fishing. Viewers' own biases, positive or negative, will affect their responses to Nelson's image and the meanings they derive from it.

READING TO WRITE

As we said at the start of this chapter, reading and writing are interconnected. Not only will reading the work of other writers help you develop your skills as a communicator, but much of the reading you do will result in writing. You might be prompted to write by an assignment for a class, or you might be moved to respond for your own reasons, perhaps to express your agreement with — or outrage at — an opinion posted online, or simply to work out your thoughts for yourself. Responding to texts in some way — the natural outcome of reading them critically — will occupy much of your academic career.

Building Knowledge

In college you will read and write in many disciplines — history, psychology, chemistry, and so on — each with its own subjects, approaches, and genres for shaping ideas and information. As varied as your readings may be, however, they will all share the goals and requirements of ACADEMIC WRITING: The writers build and exchange knowledge by thinking critically and writing effectively about what they read, see, hear, or do.

For a taste of such academic knowledge building, you can take a look at any of the selections in this book that synthesize information and ideas gleaned from a SOURCE or sources — such as Rachel O'Connor's critical reading of Shirley Jackson's short story "The Lottery" (p. 90), Laila Ayad's examination of a historical photograph (p. 267), Marie Javdani's study of the global effects of the drug trade (p. 345), Margaret Lundberg's environmental argument for vegetarianism (p. 514), or Eric Kim's overview of recent developments in neuroscience (p. 530).

You may notice that regardless of discipline, these essays follow certain conventions of academic writing:

- **Each writer presents a clearly stated thesis** — a debatable idea about a subject — and attempts to gain readers' agreement with it.

- **The writers provide evidence to support the thesis,** drawing on one or more texts, or works that can be examined or interpreted.

- **The writers analyze meaning, infer assumptions, and synthesize texts with their own views.** Academic writers do not merely summarize sources; they grapple with them — in short, they read and write critically.

- **They assume an educated audience** — one that can be counted on to read critically in turn. The writers express their ideas clearly, provide the information readers need to analyze those ideas, and organize points and evidence effectively. Further, they approach their subjects seriously and discuss evidence and opposing views fairly.

- **The essays acknowledge the use of sources,** often using in-text citations and a bibliography in a format appropriate for the discipline.

This book will show you how to achieve your own academic writing by responding directly to what you read (below), integrating evidence ethically and effectively (Chap. 2), and orchestrating — and documenting — multiple sources to develop and support your ideas (Appendix).

Forming a Response

The essay by Rosie Anaya at the end of the next chapter (p. 59) illustrates one genre of academic writing, the critical response: Anaya summarizes Nancy Mairs's essay "Disability" (p. 12), explores its implications, and uses it as a springboard to her own related subject, which she supports with personal observation and experience.

Just as Anaya responds to Mairs's essay, so you can respond to any essay in this book, or for that matter to any text you read, see, or hear. Using evidence from the text, from your own experiences, and sometimes from additional sources, you can take a variety of approaches to writing about what you read:

- **Agree with and extend the author's ideas,** providing additional examples or exploring related ideas.
- **Agree with the author on some points,** but disagree on others.
- **Disagree with the author** on one or more key points.
- **Explain how the author achieves a particular EFFECT,** such as enlisting your sympathy or sparking your anger.
- **Judge the overall effectiveness of the essay** — for instance, how well the writer supports the thesis, whether the argument is convincing, or whether the author succeeds in his or her stated or unstated purpose.

These suggestions assume that you are responding to a single work, but of course you may take on two or even more works at the same time. You might, for instance, use the method of comparison and contrast to show how two stories are alike or different, or find your own way between competing arguments on an issue.

Some works you read will spark an immediate reaction, maybe because you disagree or agree strongly right from the start. Other works may require a more gradual entry into the author's meaning and what you think about it. At the same time, you may have an assignment that narrows the scope of your response — for instance, by asking you to look at tone or some other element of the work or by asking you to agree or disagree with the author's thesis.

Whatever your initial reaction or your assignment, you can use the tools discussed in this chapter to generate and structure your response: summary, analysis, inference, synthesis, and evaluation. As you work out a response, you'll certainly need to make notes of some sort: For instance, Rosie Anaya's annotations on Mairs's essay on pages 12–15 include questions raised while reading, highlights of key quotations, summaries of Mairs's ideas, interpretations of their meanings, and the beginnings of Anaya's ideas in response. Such notes may grow increasingly focused as you refine your response and return to the work to interpret it further and gather additional passages to discuss.

Knowledge builds as you bring your own perspectives to bear on what others have written, making your own contributions to what has come before. By reading carefully and writing thoughtfully in response, you're well on your way to becoming an academic writer yourself.

2

THE WRITING PROCESS

The CRITICAL THINKING discussed in the previous chapter will serve you in just about every role you'll play in life — consumer, voter, friend, parent. As a student and a worker, though, you'll find critical thinking especially important as the foundation for writing. Whether to demonstrate your competence or to contribute to discussions and projects, writing will be the main way you communicate with teachers, supervisors, and peers.

Writing is no snap: As this book's Writers on Writing attest, not even professionals can produce thoughtful, detailed, attention-getting prose in a single draft. Writing well demands, and rewards, a willingness to work recursively — to begin tentatively and then to double back, to welcome change and endure frustration, to recognize progress and move forward.

This recursive writing process is not really a single process at all, not even for an individual writer. Some people work out meticulous plans ahead of time; others prefer to just start writing; still others will work one way for one project and a different way for another. Generally, though, writers do move through distinct stages between initial idea and finished work: discovery, drafting, revising, and editing.

In examining these stages, we'll have the help of a student, Rosie Anaya, who wrote an essay for this book responding to Nancy Mairs's essay "Disability." Along with the finished essay (pp. 59–60), Anaya also shares her notes and multiple drafts.

ASSESSING THE WRITING SITUATION

Any writing you do will occur in a specific situation. What are you writing about? Whom are you writing for? Why are you writing about this subject to these people? What will they expect of you? Subject, audience, and purpose are the main components of the writing situation, discussed in detail in this section. We also touch on another component, genre (or type of writing), which relates to audience and purpose.

Subject

The SUBJECT of a work is what it is about, or the general topic. Your subject may be specified or at least suggested in an assignment. "Discuss one of the works we've read this semester in its historical and social context," reads a literature assignment; "Can you draw up a proposal for holiday staffing?" asks your boss. If you're left to your own devices and nothing occurs to you, try the discovery techniques explained on pages 32–34 to find a topic that interests you.

In this book we provide ideas that will also give you practice in working with assignments. After each reading selection, a variety of writing prompts suggest possible subjects; more writing topics conclude each chapter. You may not wish to take any of our suggestions exactly as worded; they may merely inspire your own thoughts — and thus what you want to say.

Audience

We looked at AUDIENCE in the previous chapter as a way of understanding the decisions other writers make. When *you* are doing the writing, considering audience moves from informative to necessary.

You can conceive of your audience generally — for instance, your classmates, subscribers to a particular newspaper or blog, members of the city council. Usually, though, you'll want to think about the characteristics of readers that will affect how they respond to you:

- **Who will read your work?** What in the makeup of readers will influence their responses? How old are they? Are they educated? Do they share your values? Are they likely to have some misconceptions about your subject?

- **What do readers need to know?** To get them to understand you or agree with you, how much background should you provide? How thoroughly must you support your ideas? What kinds of evidence will be most effective?

Knowing whom you're addressing and why tells you what approach to take, what EVIDENCE to gather, how to arrange ideas, even what words to use. Imagine, for instance, that you are writing two reviews of a new movie, one for students who read the campus newspaper, the other for amateur and professional filmmakers who read the trade journal *Millimeter*. For the first audience, you might write about the actors, the plot, and especially dramatic scenes. You might judge the film and urge your readers to see it — or to avoid it. Writing for *Millimeter*, you might discuss special effects, shooting techniques, problems in editing and in mixing picture and sound. In this review, you might use more specialized and technical terms. An awareness of the interests and knowledge of your readers, in each case, would help you decide how to write.

Purpose

While you are considering readers' backgrounds and inclinations, you'll also be refining your PURPOSE. As we discussed earlier (p. 19), writers generally write with one of four broad goals in mind:

- **To reflect** on an experience, an observation, or an idea. Reflective writing is most common in personal journals or diaries, but writers often mull over their thoughts for others to read, especially in essays that draw on NARRATION or DESCRIPTION.

- **To entertain** others, perhaps by relating a thrilling event or by poking fun at a subject. Fiction is often meant to entertain, of course, but so are Web comics, many popular blogs, celebrity gossip magazines, and several of the selections in this book.

- **To explain** something, typically by sharing information gleaned from experience or investigation. Such is the case with most newspapers and textbooks, for instance, as well as science and business reports, research papers, or biographies.

- **To persuade** members of an audience to accept an idea or take a particular action. Almost all writing offers an ARGUMENT of some sort, whether explicitly or implicitly. Opinion pieces and proposals are the most obvious examples; most academic writing seeks to convince readers of the validity of a THESIS, or debatable assertion, as well.

You may know your basic purpose for writing early on — whether you want to explain something about your subject or argue something about it, for instance. To be most helpful, though, your idea of purpose should include what you want readers to think or do as a result of reading your writing, as in the following examples:

> To explain two therapies for autism in young children so that parents and educators can weigh the options
>
> To defend term limits for state legislators so that voters who are undecided on the issue will support limits
>
> To analyze Shakespeare's *Macbeth* so that theatergoers see the strengths as well as the flaws of the title character
>
> To propose an online system for scheduling work shifts so that company managers decide to implement it

We have more to say about purpose in the introductions to the rhetorical methods (Chaps. 3–12). Each method, such as EXAMPLE and CAUSE AND EFFECT, offers useful tools for achieving your purposes in writing.

Genre

Closely tied to audience and purpose is the type of writing, the GENRE, that you will use to shape your ideas. Your assignment might specify the genre: Have you been asked to write a personal narrative? a critical analysis? an argumentative response? These and other genres have distinctive features — such as organization, kinds of evidence, and even TONE — that readers expect.

You will find many examples of different genres in this book. In a sense each method of development (CLASSIFICATION, DEFINITION, and so on) is itself a genre, and its conventions and strategies are covered in the chapter devoted to it (Chaps. 3–12). Each chapter introduction also shows the method at work in a specific academic genre, such as a field observation or a review. And the book's selections illustrate a range of genres, from personal reflection and memoir to objective reporting and critical evaluation. The best way to learn about genres and readers' expectations is to read widely and attentively.

DISCOVERING IDEAS

During the initial phase of the writing process, you'll feel your way into an assignment. This DISCOVERY period is the time when you critically examine any TEXT that is part of the assignment and begin to generate ideas. When writing about selections in this book, you'll be reading and rereading and writing, coming to understand the work, figuring out what you think of it, figuring out what you have to *say* about it.

From marginal notes to jotted phrases, lists, or half-finished paragraphs of response, the discovery stage should always be a writing stage. You may even produce a rough draft. The important thing is to let yourself go: Do not, above all, concern yourself with making beautiful sentences or correcting errors. Such self-consciousness at this stage will only jam the flow of thoughts. Several techniques can help you open up, among them writing in a journal, freewriting, and exploring the methods of development.

Keeping a Journal

A JOURNAL is a record of your thoughts *for yourself.* You can keep a journal on paper or on a computer or mobile device. When you write in it, you don't have to worry about being understood by a reader or making mistakes: You are free to get your thoughts down however you want.

Kept faithfully — say, for ten or fifteen minutes a day — a journal can limber up your writing muscles, giving you more confidence and flexibility. It can also provide a place to work out personal difficulties, explore half-formed ideas, make connections between courses, or respond to reading. (For examples of one student's journal notes, see p. 53.)

Freewriting

Another technique for limbering up, usually in response to a specific writing assignment rather than as a regular habit, is *freewriting.* When freewriting, you write without stopping for ten or fifteen minutes, not halting to reread, criticize, edit, or admire. You can use partial sentences, abbreviations, question marks for uncertain words. If you can't think of anything to write about, jot "can't think" over and over until new words come. (They will.)

You can use this technique to find a subject for writing or to explore ideas on a subject you already have. When you've finished, you can separate the promising passages from the dead ends, and then use those promising bits as the starting place for more freewriting or perhaps a freely written first draft.

Exploring the Methods of Development

In Part Two of this book each of the ten chapters explains a familiar method of developing ideas. In the discovery stage, approaching your subject with these methods in mind can reveal its potential:

- **Narration.** Tell a story about the subject, possibly to enlighten or entertain readers or to explain something to them. Answer the journalist's questions: who, what, when, where, why, how?
- **Description.** Explain or evoke the subject by focusing on its look, sound, feel, smell, taste — the evidence of the senses.

- **Example.** Point to instances, or illustrations, of the subject that clarify and support your idea about it.
- **Comparison and contrast.** Set the subject beside something else, noting similarities or differences or both, for the purpose of either explaining or evaluating.
- **Process analysis.** Explain step by step how to do something or how something works — in other words, how a sequence of actions leads to a particular result.
- **Division or analysis.** Slice the subject into its parts or elements in order to show how they relate and to explain your conclusions about the subject.
- **Classification.** Show resemblances and differences among many related subjects, or the many forms of a subject, by sorting them into kinds or groups.
- **Cause and effect.** Explain why or what if, showing reasons for or consequences of the subject.
- **Definition.** Trace a boundary around the subject to pin down its meaning.
- **Argument and persuasion.** Formulate an opinion or make a proposal about the subject.

You can use the methods of development singly or together to find direction, ideas, and supporting details. Say you already have a sense of your purpose for writing: Then you can search the methods for one or more that will help you achieve that purpose by revealing and focusing your ideas. Or say you're still in the dark about your purpose: Then you can apply each method of development systematically to throw light on your subject, helping you see it from many possible angles.

DRAFTING

Sooner or later, the discovery stage yields to DRAFTING: writing out sentences and paragraphs, linking thoughts, focusing them. For most writers, drafting is the occasion for exploring ideas, filling in the details to support them, beginning to work out the shape and aim of the whole. A few suggestions for drafting:

- **Give yourself time,** at least a couple of hours.
- **Find a quiet place to work,** somewhere you won't be disturbed.
- **Stay loose** so that you can wander down intriguing avenues or consider changing direction altogether.
- **Keep your eyes on what's ahead,** not on possible errors, "wrong" words, or bumpy sentences. This is an important message that many inexperienced writers miss: It's okay to make mistakes. You can fix them later.

Expect to draft in fits and starts, working in chunks and fleshing out points as you go. And don't feel compelled to follow a straight path from beginning to end. If the opening paragraph is giving you trouble, skip it until later. In fact, most writers find that drafting is easier and more productive if they work on the body of the essay first, leaving the introduction and conclusion until everything else has been worked out.

Focusing on a Thesis

Your essay will need to center on a THESIS, a core idea to which everything else relates. When you write with a clear-cut thesis in mind, you head toward a goal. Without the focus of a thesis, an essay wanders and irritates and falls flat. With a focus, a draft is much more likely to click.

You may start a project with a thesis already in mind, or your idea might take shape as you proceed through the writing process. Sometimes you may have to write one or more drafts to know exactly what your point is. But early on, try to express your main idea in a sentence or two, called a THESIS STATEMENT, like these from essays in this book:

> That first encounter, and those that followed, signified that a vast, unnerving gulf lay between nighttime pedestrians — particularly women — and me.
> — Brent Staples, "Black Men and Public Space"

> Inanimate objects are classified into three major categories — those that don't work, those that break down and those that get lost.
> — Russell Baker, "The Plot against People"

> A bill [to prohibit import of goods produced with children's labor] is of no use unless it goes hand in hand with programs that will offer a new life to these newly released children.
> — Chitra Divakaruni, "Live Free and Starve"

As these diverse examples reveal, a thesis shapes an essay. It gives the writer a clearly defined aim, focusing otherwise scattered thoughts and providing a center around which the details and supporting points can gather.

An effective thesis statement, like the ones above, has a few important qualities:

- **It asserts an opinion, taking a position on the subject.** A good thesis statement moves beyond facts or vague generalities, as in "That first encounter was troubling" or "This bill is a bad idea."
- **It projects a single, focused idea.** A thesis statement may have parts (such as Baker's three categories of objects), but those parts should all relate to a single, central point.

- **It accurately forecasts the scope of the essay,** neither taking on too much nor leaving out essential parts.
- **It hints at the writer's purpose.** From their thesis statements, we can tell that Staples and Baker mean to explain, whereas Divakaruni intends mainly to persuade.

Every single essay in this book has a thesis because a central, controlling idea is a requirement of good writing. As you will see, writers have great flexibility in presenting a thesis statement — how long it might be, where it appears, even whether it appears. For your own writing, we advise stating your thesis explicitly and putting it near the beginning of your essay — at least until you've gained experience as a writer. The stated thesis will help you check that you have the necessary focus, and the early placement will tell your readers what to expect from your writing. We offer additional suggestions for focusing your thesis and crafting your thesis statement, with examples, later in this chapter (p. 40–41) and in each of the introductions to the methods of development (Chaps. 3–12).

Supporting the Thesis

The BODY of an essay consists of the subpoints and supporting evidence that develop the main idea. In some way, each sentence and paragraph should serve to support your thesis by making it clear and explicit to readers. You will likely need to experiment and explore your thoughts before they fully take shape, tackling your essay in multiple drafts and filling in (or taking out) details as you go, adjusting your thesis to fit your ideas. Most writers do.

Developing Ideas

You may have gotten a start at expressing your thoughts in the discovery stage, in which case you can build on what you've already written in your journal or during freewriting sessions. Or you may find yourself staring at a blank screen. In either case, it's usually best to focus first on the parts you're most comfortable with, keeping your thesis, your purpose, and your audience in mind.

Earlier we saw that the methods of development can help you discover ideas about a subject (see pp. 33–34). They can also help you find, present, and structure evidence as you draft. Suppose, for example, that you set out to explain what makes a certain singer unique. You want to discuss her voice, her music, her lyrics, her style. While putting your ideas down, it strikes you that you can best illustrate the singer's distinctions by showing the differences between her and another singer. To achieve your purpose, then, you draw on the method of COMPARISON AND CONTRAST; and as you proceed, the method prompts you to notice differences you had missed.

Each method typically benefits from — and lends itself to — a particular kind of support. Narration and description might draw on personal experience, for instance, while a CAUSE-AND-EFFECT or PROCESS ANALYSIS may require objective information such as verifiable facts. Give the methods a try. See how flexible they are, coming into play as you need them to develop parts of your essay.

Organizing the Evidence

How you ORGANIZE your evidence depends on your purpose and your audience: What is your aim? What do you want readers to think or feel? What's the best way to achieve that? For instance, anyone writing a proposal to solve a problem wants to cover all the reasonable solutions and make a case for one or more. But one writer might bring readers gradually to her favored solution by first discussing and rejecting the alternatives, while another might grab readers' attention by focusing right away on his own solution, dispensing with alternatives only near the end. In either case, the choices aren't random but depend on the writer's understanding of readers — their assumptions, their biases, and their purposes for reading.

Some methods of development lend themselves to familiar patterns of organization, which we discuss in the introductions to Chapters 3–12. In a narrative essay or a process analysis, for instance, you would probably put events in CHRONOLOGICAL ORDER. Other methods require that you put more thought into how you arrange your points. In an essay developed by example, you might use a CLIMACTIC ORDER, starting with the weakest point and ending with the most compelling one (or vice versa). And a descriptive essay might take a SPATIAL ORDER, following details the way an eye might scan a scene: left to right, near to far, and so forth.

Some writers like to plan the order of their points in advance, perhaps with a rough outline or simply a list of points to cover. If concerns about the organization leave you feeling stuck or frustrated, however, focus instead on getting your ideas into sentences and paragraphs; you can rearrange things in revision.

Shaping the Introduction and Conclusion

The opening and closing paragraphs of an essay serve as bookends for the thoughts and information presented in the body. The INTRODUCTION identifies and narrows the subject for readers, capturing their interest and giving them a reason to continue reading. The CONCLUSION creates a sense of completion, bringing readers back to the main idea and satisfying them that you have accomplished what you set out to do as a writer.

Because of the importance of these paragraphs, and because it is difficult to set up and close out material that has not yet been drafted, most writers find that it works best to turn to the introduction and conclusion *after* the rest of the essay has begun to take shape.

The Introduction

The opening paragraph or paragraphs of an essay invite readers in. At a minimum, your introduction will state the subject and lead to your main idea, often presented in a thesis statement. But an effective introduction also grabs readers' attention and inspires them to read on.

Introductions vary in length, depending on their purpose. A research paper may need several paragraphs to set forth its central idea and its plan of organization; a brief, informal essay may need only a sentence or two for an introduction. Whether long or short, a good introduction tells readers no more than they need to know when they begin reading.

Here are a few possible ways to open an essay effectively:

- **Present startling facts** about your subject.
- **Tell an** ANECDOTE, a brief story that illustrates your subject.
- **Give background information** so that readers will understand your subject or see why it is important.
- **Begin with an arresting quotation** that sets up your subject or previews your main idea.
- **Ask a challenging question.** (In your essay, you'll go on to answer it.)

Whatever technique you try, strive to make a good first impression and establish a positive, engaging tone, taking care to match the voice in the body of your essay. Avoid beginning with a hedge such as *It seems important to understand why* . . . ; and stay away from mechanical phrasing such as *In this essay, I will explain* . . . or *The purpose of this paper is to show.* . . . Such openings bore readers and give them little incentive to read on.

The Conclusion

A conclusion is purposefully crafted to give a sense of unity to the whole essay. The best conclusions evolve naturally out of what has gone before and convince readers that the essay is indeed at an end, not that the writer has run out of steam.

Conclusions vary in type and length depending on the nature and scope of the essay. A long research paper may require several paragraphs of summary to review and emphasize the main points. A short essay, however, may benefit from a few brief closing sentences.

Although there are no set formulas for closing, consider these options:

- **Restate the thesis of your essay,** and possibly summarize your main points.
- **Mention the broader implications** or significance of your topic.
- **Give a final example,** pulling all the parts of your discussion together.
- **Offer a prediction** for the future.
- **End with the most important point,** or the culmination of your essay's development.
- **Suggest how readers can apply the information you have provided** in their own lives or work.
- **End with a bit of drama or flourish.** Tell an anecdote, offer an appropriate quotation, ask a question, make a final insightful remark, circle back to the introduction. Keep in mind, however, that an ending shouldn't sound false and gimmicky. It truly has to conclude.

In concluding an essay, beware of diminishing the impact of your writing by finishing on a weak note. Resist the urge to apologize for what you have or have not written, or to cram in a final detail that would have been better placed elsewhere.

REVISING

If it helps to get you writing, you may want to view a draft as a kind of dialog with readers, fulfilling their expectations, answering the questions you imagine they would ask. But some writers save this kind of thinking for the next stage, REVISION. Literally "re-seeing," revision involves stepping outside the intense circle of you-and-the-material to see the work as a reader will, with whatever qualities you imagine that reader to have.

The first task of revising is to step back and view your draft as a whole, looking at the big picture and ignoring details like grammar and spelling. Let a draft sit for a while before you come back to revise it: at least a few hours, ideally a day or more. When you return with fresh eyes and a refreshed mind, you'll be in a better position to see what works, what doesn't, and what needs your attention. The checklist on the next page and the ensuing discussion can guide you to the big-picture view. Specific revision guidelines for each method of development appear in the introductions to Chapters 3–12.

QUESTIONS FOR REVISION

✔ **Will my purpose be clear to readers?** Have I achieved it?

✔ **What are readers' expectations for this kind of writing?** Have I met them?

✔ **What is my thesis?** Have I supported it for readers? Is my thesis statement clear and to the point?

✔ **Is the essay unified?** Can readers see how all parts relate to the thesis?

✔ **Have I developed my points well?** Have I supplied enough details, examples, and other specifics so that readers can understand me and follow my reasoning?

✔ **Is the essay coherent?** Can readers see how the parts relate?

✔ **Is the organization clear?** Can readers follow it?

Purpose and Genre

Earlier we looked at purpose and genre as important considerations in planning an essay. They are even more important in revision. Like many writers, in the discovery and experimentation of drafting you may lose track of your original direction. Did you set out to write a critical analysis of a reading but end up with a summary? Did you rely on personal experience when you were supposed to integrate evidence from sources? Did you set out to persuade readers but not get beyond explanation? That's okay. You've jumped the first hurdle simply by putting your thoughts into words. Now you can add, delete, and reorganize until your purpose will be clear to readers and you meet their expectations for how it should be fulfilled.

Thesis

As you've developed your ideas and your draft, you've also been developing your thesis, the main idea that you want to get across to readers. The thesis may be stated up front or hover in the background, but it should be clear to readers and the rest of the essay should support it. Almost always, you will need to revise your thesis as your ideas take form and your purpose for writing becomes clear to you. You may find that you need to adjust your thesis to reflect what you ended up writing in your draft, or you may need to rework your supporting ideas so that they adequately develop your thesis.

Pay attention, too, to your thesis statement itself. Few writers craft a perfect statement on the first try. In each of the following pairs, for example, the draft statement is too vague to work as a hook: It conveys the writer's general opinion but not its basis. Each revised statement clarifies the point.

DRAFT   The sculpture is a beautiful piece of work.

REVISED   Although it may not be obvious at first, this smooth bronze sculpture unites urban and natural elements to represent the city dweller's relationship with nature.

DRAFT   The sculpture is a waste of money.

REVISED   The huge bronze sculpture in the middle of McBean Park demonstrates that so-called public art may actually undermine the public interest.

When you revise, make a point of checking your thesis and your thesis statement against the guidelines listed earlier in this chapter (p. 35) and discussed in the introduction to every method chapter in Part Two. You want to ensure that your thesis takes an arguable position on your subject, that it focuses on a single idea, that it reflects the actual content of your essay, and that it gives a sense of your purpose for writing.

Unity

Drafting freely, as you should, can easily take you into some of the byways of your topic. A goal of revision, then, is to deal with digressions so that your essay has UNITY, with every paragraph relating to the thesis and every sentence in a paragraph relating to a single idea, often expressed in a TOPIC SENTENCE. You may choose to cut a digression altogether or to rework it so that it connects to the main idea. Sometimes you may find that a digression is really what you want to write about and then opt to recast your thesis instead. For more help, see "Focus on Paragraph and Essay Unity" on page 372.

Development

While some points in your draft may have to be sacrificed for the sake of unity, others will probably want more attention. Be sure that any general statements you make are backed up with evidence: details, examples, analysis, information from sources, whatever it takes to show readers that your point is valid. The introductions to the methods in Chapters 3–12 offer suggestions for developing specific kinds of essays; take a look, too, at "Focus on Paragraph Development" on pages 295–96.

Coherence

Drafting ideas into sentences can be halting work, and a first draft can seem jumbled as a result. In revision, you want to help readers follow your thoughts by improving COHERENCE: the clear flow and relation of parts.

You can achieve coherence through your use of paragraphs, transitions, and organization.

PARAGRAPHS help readers grasp related information in an essay by developing one supporting point at a time: All of the sentences hang together, defining, explaining, illustrating, or supporting one central idea. Check all your paragraphs to be sure that each sentence connects with the one preceding and that readers will see the connection without having to stop and reread. One way to clarify such connections is with TRANSITIONS: linking words and phrases such as *in addition, moreover,* and *at the same time.* (We have more to say about transitions in "Focus on Paragraph Coherence" on p. 257–58.)

Be sure, too, that each paragraph follows logically from those before it and leads clearly to those that follow, and that any material from your reading and other sources is integrated logically and smoothly (see the next section). Constructing an outline of what you've written can help you see how well your thoughts hold together. Expect to experiment, moving paragraphs around, deleting some and adding others, before everything clicks into place.

INTEGRATING READING

Writing about what you have read will occupy you for much of your college career, as you rely on books, periodical articles, interviews, Web sites, and other materials to establish and extend your own contributions to academic conversations. The selections in this book, for instance, can serve as sources for your writing: You might analyze them, respond to them, or use them to support your own ideas. Such SYNTHESIS, as we note in Chapter 1, is the core of academic writing. Much of your synthesis of others' work will come as you present evidence from your reading and integrate that evidence into your own text. An important goal of revision, then, is to ensure that you have used such materials honestly and effectively.

Exercising Caution

When you write with sources, your readers expect you to distinguish your own contributions from those of others, honestly acknowledging material that originated elsewhere. To do otherwise — to deliberately or accidentally copy another's idea, data, or wording without acknowledgment — is considered stealing. Called PLAGIARISM, this theft is a serious offense.

Plagiarism is often a result of careless note taking or drafting. The simplest way to avoid problems is always to acknowledge your sources, clearly marking the boundaries between your ideas and those picked up from other writers. Integrate source materials carefully, following the suggestions provided on the following pages. And cite your sources in an appropriate documentation style, such as MLA for English or APA for the social sciences. (See the Appendix for detailed guidelines and documentation models.)

Summarizing, Paraphrasing, and Quoting

As you revise, make sure you have used the ideas and information in sources to support your own ideas, not to direct or overwhelm them. Depending on the importance and complexity of source material, you might summarize it, paraphrase it, or quote it directly. *All summaries, paraphrases, and quotations must be acknowledged in source citations.*

Summary

In a SUMMARY you use your own words to condense a paragraph, an entire article, or even a book into a few lines that convey the source's essential meaning. We discussed summarizing as a reading technique on pages 15–16, and the advice and examples there apply here as well. When responding to a text, you might use a brief summary to catch readers up on the gist of the author's argument or a significant point in the argument. Here, for example, is a summary of Anna Quindlen's "Homeless," which appears on pages 164–66:

> SUMMARY   Quindlen argues that reducing homeless people to the abstract issue of homelessness can obscure the fundamental problem of the homeless individual: He or she needs a home (164–66).

Notice that a summary identifies the source's author and page numbers and uses words that are *not* the author's. A summary that picks up any of the author's distinctive language or neglects to acknowledge that the idea is borrowed from a source counts as plagiarism and must be rewritten. In an early draft of "Mental Illness on Television" (p. 58), for instance, Rosie Anaya inadvertently plagiarized this passage from Nancy Mairs's "Disability":

> ORIGINAL QUOTATION   "But this [media] denial of disability imperils even you who are able-bodied, and not just by shrinking your insight into the physically and emotionally complex world you live in. Some disabled people call you TAPs, or Temporarily Abled Persons. The fact is that ours is the only minority you can join involuntarily, without warning, at any time. . . . The transition will probably be difficult from a physical point of view no matter what. But it will be a good bit easier psychologically if you are accustomed to seeing disability as a normal characteristic, one that complicates but does not ruin human existence."

> PLAGIARISM   Media misrepresentation of disability hurts not only viewers with disabilities but also Temporarily Abled Persons.

In forgetting to name Mairs as the source and in using the phrase "Temporarily Abled Persons" without quotation marks, Anaya stole Mairs's idea. Here is her revision:

> ACCEPTABLE SUMMARY   Mairs argues that media misrepresentation of disability hurts not only viewers with disabilities but also "Temporarily Abled Persons," or those without disabilities (13–15).

Paraphrase

When you PARAPHRASE, you restate a specific passage in your own words. Paraphrase adheres more closely than summary to the source author's line of thought, so it's useful for presenting an author's ideas or data in detail. Generally, use paraphrase rather than quotation for this purpose, since paraphrase shows that you're in command of your evidence and lets your own voice come through. Here is a quotation from Quindlen's essay and a paraphrase of it:

> ORIGINAL QUOTATION   "Homes have stopped being homes. Now they are real estate."
>
> PARAPHRASE   Quindlen points out that people's dwellings seem to have lost their emotional hold and to have become just investments (165).

As with a summary, note that a paraphrase cites the original author and page number. And like a summary, a paraphrase must express the original idea in an entirely new way, both in word choice and in sentence structure. The following attempt to paraphrase a line from an essay by David Cole slips into plagiarism through sloppiness:

> ORIGINAL QUOTATION   "We stand to be collectively judged by our treatment of immigrants, who may appear to be 'other' now but in a generation will be 'us.'"
>
> PLAGIARISM   Cole argues that we will be judged as a group by how we treat immigrants, who seem to be different now but eventually will be the same as us (110).

Even though the writer identifies Cole as the source and provides a page number, much of the language and the sentence structure are also Cole's. It's not enough to change a few words — such as "collectively" to "as a group," "they may appear to be 'other'" to "they may seem different," and "in a generation" to "eventually." In contrast, this acceptable paraphrase restates Cole's point in completely new language *and* a new sentence structure:

> ACCEPTABLE PARAPHRASE   Cole argues that the way the United States deals with immigrants now will come back to haunt it when those immigrants eventually become part of mainstream society (110).

Quotation

Quotations from sources can both support and enliven your own ideas — *if* you choose them well. When analyzing a source such as an essay in this book, you may need to quote some passages in order to give the flavor of the author's words and evidence for your analysis. Too many quotations, however, will clutter your essay and detract from your voice. Select quotations that are relevant to the point you are making, that are concise and pithy, and that use lively, bold, or original language. Sentences that lack distinction — for example, a statement providing statistics on immigration rates — should be paraphrased.

Always enclose quotations in quotation marks and cite the source author and page number. For a blatant example of plagiarism, look at the following use of a quotation from Anna Quindlen's "Homeless":

ORIGINAL QUOTATION   "It has been customary to take people's pain and lessen our own participation in it by turning it into an issue, not a collection of human beings."

PLAGIARISM   As a society we tend to lessen our participation in other people's pain by turning it into an issue.

By not acknowledging Quindlen at all, the writer takes claim for her idea and for much of her wording. A source citation would help — at least the idea would be credited — but still the expression of the idea would be stolen because there's no indication that the language is Quindlen's. Here is a revision with citation and quotation marks:

ACCEPTABLE QUOTATION   Quindlen suggests that our tendency "to take people's pain and lessen our own participation in it by turning it into an issue" dehumanizes homeless people (166).

You may adapt quotations to fit your sentences, provided you make clear how you've changed them. If you omit something from a quoted passage, signal the omission with the three spaced periods of an ellipsis mark as shown:

In Quindlen's view, "the thing that seems most wrong with the world . . . right now is that there are so many people with no homes" (165).

If you need to insert words or phrases into a quotation to clarify the author's meaning or make the quotation flow with your own language, show that the insertion is yours by enclosing it in brackets:

Quindlen points out that "we work around [the problem], just as we walk around" the homeless people we encounter (166).

Synthesizing Ideas

When you write about a text, your perspective on it will be your thesis — the main point you have in response to the text or as a result of examining it. As you develop and revise your essay, keep your ideas front and center, pulling in material from the text as needed for support. In each paragraph, your idea should come first and, usually, last: State the idea, use evidence from the reading to support it, and then interpret the evidence.

You can see a paragraph structured like this in Rosie Anaya's essay "Mental Illness on Television" at the end of this chapter:

SYNTHESIS

However, in depicting one type of disability, the media are, if anything, worse than they were three decades ago. Mairs doesn't address mental illness, but it falls squarely into the misrepresentation she criticizes. It has never been shown, in Mairs's words, "as a normal characteristic, one that complicates but does not ruin human existence" (15). Thus people who cope with a psychological disability such as depression, bipolar disorder, or obsessive-compulsive disorder as part of their lives do not see themselves in the media. And those who don't have a psychological disability now but may someday do not see that mental illness is usually a condition one can live with.

> Anaya's idea
>
> Evidence from Mairs's text
>
> Anaya's interpretation of Mairs's idea

Understand that synthesis is more than summary, which just distills what the text says or shows. Summary has its uses, especially in understanding a writer's ideas (p. 15) and in presenting evidence from source material (p. 43), but it should not substitute for your own ideas. Contrast the preceding paragraph from Anaya's essay with the following early draft passage in which Anaya uses summary to present evidence:

SUMMARY

Mairs argues that media misrepresentation of disability hurts not only viewers with disabilities but also those without disabilities (14). The media either ignore disability altogether or present it as the defining characteristic of a person's life (13–15). In doing so, they deny "Temporarily Abled Persons" the opportunity to see disability as something common that may be difficult to adjust to but does not destroy one's life (14–15).

> Mairs's idea
>
> Mairs's idea
>
> Mairs's idea

With synthesis, you're always making it clear to readers what *your* idea is and how the evidence from your reading supports that idea. To achieve this clarity, you want to fit evidence from other texts into your sentences and show what you make of it. In this passage, the writer drops a quotation awkwardly into her paragraph and doesn't clarify how it relates to her idea:

NOT INTEGRATED   Homelessness affects real people. "[W]e work around it, just as we walk around it when it is lying on the sidewalk or sitting in the bus terminal — the problem, that is" (Quindlen 166).

In the revision below, the writer uses "but" and the SIGNAL PHRASE "as Quindlen points out" to link the quotation to the writer's idea and to identify the source author:

INTEGRATED   Homelessness affects real people, but, as Quindlen points out, "we work around it, just as we walk around it when it is lying on the sidewalk or sitting in the bus terminal — the problem, that is" (166).

A final note: Whether you are synthesizing information and ideas from one text or several, remember that all source material must be acknowledged with in-text citations and a list of works cited or references at the end of your paper. The Appendix at the back of this book (pp. 491–535) provides detailed guidelines and ample models for both the MLA and APA styles of documenting sources.

EDITING

You will find that you produce better work when you approach revision as at least a two-step process. First revise, focusing on fundamental, whole-essay matters such as purpose, organization, and synthesis. Only then turn to EDITING, focusing on surface issues such as grammar and word choice to improve the flow of your writing and to fix the mistakes that tend to get in the way of readers' understanding.

The checklist below covers the most common opportunities and problems, which are explained on the pages following. Because some challenges tend to pop up more often when writing with a particular method, you'll find additional help in the introductions to Chapters 3–12, in boxes labeled "Focus on . . ." that highlight specific issues and provide tips for solving them.

QUESTIONS FOR EDITING

✔ **Are my language and tone appropriate** for my purpose, audience, and genre?

✔ **Do my words say what I mean,** and are they as vivid as I can make them?

✔ **Are my sentences smooth and concise?** Do they use emphasis, parallelism, variety, and other techniques to clarify meaning and hold readers' interest?

✔ **Are my sentences grammatically sound?** In particular, have I avoided sentence fragments, run-on sentences, comma splices, mismatched subjects and verbs, unclear pronouns, unclear modifiers, and inconsistencies?

✔ **Are any words misspelled?**

Effective Language

Many of us, when we draft, fall back on the familiar language we use when chatting with friends: We might rely on COLLOQUIAL EXPRESSIONS such as *get into* and *freak out* or slip into texting shortcuts such as *u* for "you" and *idk* for "I don't know." This strategy can help us to put ideas together without getting sidetracked by details. But patterns of casual communication are usually too imprecise for college writing, where word choices can dramatically affect how readers understand your ideas.

As a critical reader, you take note of writers' language and consider how their choices affect the meaning and impact of their work (see pp. 21–22). As a writer, you should devote similar attention to your own choices, adapting your general language and your specific words to reflect your purpose, your meaning, and your audience.

A few guidelines:

- **Adopt a relatively formal voice.** Replace overly casual or emotional language with standard English DICTION and a neutral TONE. (Refer to pp. 540–41 and 549–50 of the Glossary and to "Focus on Tone" on p. 416.)

- **Choose an appropriate point of view.** In most academic writing, you should prefer the more objective third PERSON (*he, she, it, they*) over the first person (*I*) or the second person (*you*). There are exceptions, of course: A personal narrative written without *I* would ring strange to most ears, and a how-to process analysis often addresses readers as *you*.

- **Check that words have the meanings you intend.** The DENOTATION of a word is its dictionary meaning — for example, *affection* means "caring regard." A CONNOTATION, in contrast, is an emotional association that a word produces in readers, as *passion* evokes intensity or *obsession* evokes compulsion. Using a word with the wrong denotation muddies meaning, while using words with strong connotations can shape readers' responses to your ideas — for good or for ill.

- **Use concrete and specific words.** Effective writing balances ABSTRACT and GENERAL words, which provide outlines of ideas and things, with CONCRETE and SPECIFIC words, which limit and sharpen. You need abstract and general words such as *old* and *transportation* for broad statements that convey concepts or refer to entire groups. But you also need concrete and specific words such as *crumbling* and *streetcar line* to make meaning precise and vivid. See "Focus on Specific and Concrete Language" on page 108.

- **Be creative.** You can make your writing more lively and forceful with FIGURES OF SPEECH, expressions that imply meanings beyond or different from their literal meanings, such as *curled tight like a rosebud* or *feelings trampled to dirt*. Be careful not to resort to CLICHÉS, worn phrases that have lost their power (*hour of need, thin as a rail*), or to combine figures of speech into confusing or absurd images, such as *The players flooded the soccer field like bulls ready for a fight*.

Clear and Engaging Sentences

Effective sentences are the product of careful attention to meaning and read-ability. Editing for emphasis, parallelism, and variety will ensure that readers can follow your ideas without difficulty and stay interested in what you have to say.

Emphasis

While drafting, simply getting ideas down in sentence form can be chal-lenge enough. But once the ideas are down, it becomes apparent that some are more important than others. Editing for emphasis offers an opportunity to clar-ify those relationships for readers. As you do so, focus on the following changes:

- **Put verbs in the active voice.** A verb in the ACTIVE VOICE expresses action by the subject (*He recorded a new song*), whereas a verb in the PASSIVE VOICE expresses action done *to* the subject (*A new song was recorded*, or, adding who did the action, *A new song was recorded by him*). The active voice is usually more emphatic and therefore easier to follow. See "Focus on Verbs" on page 69.

- **Simplify wordy sentences.** Unnecessary padding deflates readers' inter-est. Weed out any empty phrases or meaningless repetition:

  WORDY The nature of social-networking sites is such that they reconnect lost and distant friends but can also for all intents and purposes dredge up old relationships, relationships that were better left forgotten.

  CONCISE Social-networking sites reconnect lost and distant friends but can also dredge up old relationships that were better left forgotten.

  See also "Focus on Clarity and Conciseness" on pages 336–37.

- **Combine sentences.** You can often clarify meaning by merging sentences. Use *coordination* to combine and balance equally important ideas, joining them with *and, but, or, nor, for, so,* or *yet*:

  UNEMPHATIC Many restaurant meals are high in fat. Their sodium content is also high. To diners they seem harmless.

  EMPHATIC Many restaurant meals are high in fat and sodium, but to diners they seem harmless.

Use *subordination* to de-emphasize less important ideas, placing minor information in modifying words or word groups:

UNEMPHATIC Restaurant menus sometimes label certain options. They use the label "healthy." These options are lower in fat and sodium.

EMPHATIC Restaurant menus sometimes label as "healthy" the options that are lower in fat and sodium.

Parallelism

Another way to clarify meaning is to give parallel structure to related words, phrases, and sentences. PARALLELISM is the use of similar grammatical forms for elements of similar importance, either within or among sentences.

PARALLELISM WITHIN A SENTENCE Binge drinking can worsen heart disease and cause liver failure.

PARALLELISM AMONG SENTENCES Binge drinking has less well-known effects, too. It can cause brain damage. It can raise blood sugar to diabetic levels. And it can reduce the body's ability to fight off infections.

Readers tend to stumble over elements that seem equally important but are not in parallel form. As you edit, look for groups of related ideas and make a point of expressing them consistently:

NONPARALLEL Even occasional binges can cause serious problems, from the experience of blackouts to getting arrested to injury.

PARALLEL Even occasional binges can cause serious problems, from blackouts to arrests to injuries.

For more on parallel structure, see "Focus on Parallelism" on pages 176–77.

Sentence Variety

Sentence after sentence with the same length and structure can be stiff and dull. By varying sentences, you can hold readers' interest while also achieving the emphasis you want. The techniques to achieve variety include adjusting the lengths of sentences and varying their beginnings. For examples and specifics, see "Focus on Sentence Variety" on pages 144–45.

Common Errors

Writers sometimes think of grammar as a set of rules that exist solely to give nitpickers a chance to point out mistakes. But basic errors can undermine an otherwise excellent piece of writing by distracting readers or creating confusion. The guidelines here can help you catch some of the most common problems.

Sentence Fragments

A *sentence fragment* is a word group that is punctuated like a sentence but is not a complete sentence. Experienced writers sometimes use fragments for effect, but readers usually stumble over incomplete sentences. For the sake of clarity, make sure every sentence has a subject and a verb and expresses a complete thought:

FRAGMENT Snowboarding a relatively young sport.

COMPLETE Snowboarding is a relatively young sport.

FRAGMENT Many ski resorts banned snowboards at first. Believing they were dangerous and destructive.

COMPLETE Many ski resorts banned snowboards at first, believing they were dangerous and destructive.

Run-on Sentences and Comma Splices

When two or more sentences run together with no punctuation between them, they create a *run-on sentence*. When they run together with only a comma between them, they create a *comma splice*. Writers usually correct these errors by separating the sentences with a period, with a semicolon, or with a comma along with *and, but, or, nor, for, so,* or *yet*:

RUN-ON Snowboarding has become a mainstream sport riders are now as common as skiers on the slopes.

COMMA SPLICE Snowboarding has become a mainstream sport, riders are now as common as skiers on the slopes.

EDITED Snowboarding has become a mainstream sport. Riders are now as common as skiers on the slopes.

EDITED Snowboarding has become a mainstream sport; riders are now as common as skiers on the slopes.

EDITED Snowboarding has become a mainstream sport, and riders are now as common as skiers on the slopes.

Subject-Verb Agreement

Most writers know to use singular verbs with singular subjects and plural verbs with plural subjects, but matching subjects and verbs can sometimes be tricky. Watch especially for these situations:

- **Don't mistake a noun that follows the subject for the actual subject.** In the examples below, the subject is *appearance*, not *snowboarders* or *Olympics*:

MISMATCHED The appearance of snowboarders in the Olympics prove their status as true athletes.

MATCHED The appearance of snowboarders in the Olympics proves their status as true athletes.

- **With subjects joined by** and **, use a plural verb.** Compound word groups are treated as plural even if the word closest to the verb is singular:

    MISMATCHED The cross course and the half-pipe shows the sport's versatility.

    MATCHED The cross course and the half-pipe show the sport's versatility.

Pronouns

We tend to use pronouns without thinking much about them. Problems occur when usage that feels natural in speech causes confusion in writing:

- **Check that each pronoun refers clearly to an appropriate noun.** Rewrite sentences in which the reference is vague or only implied:

    VAGUE Students asked the administration to add more parking spaces, but it had no effect.

    CLEAR Students asked the administration to add more parking spaces, but their pleas had no effect.

    IMPLIED Although commuter parking is hard to find, they keep driving to campus.

    CLEAR Although commuters know that parking is hard to find, they keep driving to campus.

- **Take care with indefinite pronouns.** Although people often use pronouns such as *anybody, anyone, everyone,* and *somebody* to mean "many" or "all," these indefinite pronouns are technically singular, not plural:

    MISMATCHED Everyone should change their passwords frequently.

    MATCHED Everyone should change his or her passwords frequently.

    MATCHED All computer users should change their passwords frequently.

Misplaced and Dangling Modifiers

A *modifier* describes another word or group of words in a sentence. Make sure that modifiers clearly describe the intended words. Misplaced and dangling modifiers can be awkward or even unintentionally amusing:

    MISPLACED I swam away as the jellyfish approached in fear of being stung.

    CLEAR In fear of being stung, I swam away as the jellyfish approached.

    DANGLING Floating in the ocean, the clouds drifted by.

    CLEAR Floating in the ocean, I watched as the clouds drifted by.

Shifts

Be consistent in your use of verb tense (past, present, and so on), person (*I, you, he/she/it, they*), and voice (active or passive). Unnecessary shifts can confuse readers. For details, see "Focus on Verbs" on page 69 and "Focus on Consistency" on page 216.

AN ESSAY-IN-PROGRESS

In the following pages, you have a chance to follow Rosie Anaya as she develops an essay through journal writing and several drafts. She began the writing process early, while reading and annotating Nancy Mairs's "Disability" (p. 12). Inspired by Mairs's argument, Anaya writes about another group that has been "effaced" by the media.

Discovering Ideas and Drafting

Journal Notes on Reading

Haven't the media gotten better about showing people with disabilities since Mairs wrote this essay? Lots of TV shows have characters who just happen to use wheelchairs. But I see why she has a problem: I would be bothered, too, if I didn't see people like me represented. I would feel left out, probably hurt, maybe angry.

Mairs is doing more: Invisibility is a problem for healthy people too — anybody could become disabled and wouldn't know that people with disabilities live full, normal lives.

Interesting that she mentions emotions so many times: The references to feelings and psychology raise a question about people with mental disabilities, like depression or schizophrenia. How are *they* represented by the media? Definitely *not* as regular people: Stories in the news about emotionally disturbed people who go over the edge and hurt or even kill people. And *Criminal Minds* etc. always using some kind of psychological disorder to explain a crime.

Except the problem with mental illness isn't just invisibility — it's negative stereotyping. What if you're represented as a danger to yourself and others? That's got to be worse.

First Draft

Nancy Mairs is upset with television and movies that don't show physical disability as a feature of normal life. She says the media shows disability consuming a character's life or it doesn't show disability at all, and she wants to see "representations of myself in the media, especially television" (p. no.).

Mairs makes a convincing argument that the media should portray physical disability as part of everyday life because "effacement" leaves the rest of us unprepared to cope in the case that we should eventually become disabled ourselves. As she explains it, anybody could become disabled, but because we rarely see people with disabilities living full, normal lives on tv, we assume that becoming disabled means life is pretty much over (p. no.). It's been three decades since Mairs wrote her essay, and she seems to have gotten her wish. Plenty of characters on television today who have a disability are not defined by it. But psychological disabilities are disabilities too, and they have never been shown "as a normal characteristic, one that complicates but does not ruin human existence" (p. no.).

Television routinely portrays people with mental illness as threats to themselves and to others. Think about all those stories on the evening news about a man suffering from schizophrenia who went on a shooting spree before turning his gun on himself, or a mother who drowned her own children in the throes of depression, or a bipolar teenager who commits suicide. Such events are tragic, no doubt, but although the vast majority of people with these illnesses hurt nobody, the news implies that they're all potential killers.

Fictional shows, too, are always using some kind of psychological disorder to explain why someone committed a crime. On *Criminal Minds* a woman with "intermittent explosive disorder" impulsively kills multiple people after she is released from a psychiatric hospital and stops taking her medication. On *Rizzoli and Isles* a serial abductor's actions are blamed on "a long history of mental illness" that started with depression after he saw his father kill his mother and developed a perverse need to recreate their relationship with victims of his own. And the entire premise of *Dexter* is that the trauma of witnessing his mother's brutal murder turned the title character into a serial killer. Dexter is an obsessive-compulsive killer who justifies his impulses by killing only other killers. Early in the series, viewers learned that his nemesis, the "Ice Truck Killer," who at one point was engaged to Dexter's adopted sister and then tried to kill her, was actually his long-lost brother. Every season featured a different enemy, and each one of them had some kind of stated or implied mental illness: The "Doomsday Killer" of season six, for example, was a psychotic divinity student who went off his meds and suffered from delusions.

It is my belief that the presentation of psychological disability may do worse than the "effacement" of disability that bothered Mairs. People with mental illness are discouraged from seeking help and are sent deeper into isolation and despair. This negative stereotype hurts us all.

Revising

Anaya's first draft was a good start. She found an idea worth pursuing and explored her thoughts. But as with any first draft, her essay needed work. To improve it, Anaya revised extensively, cutting digressions in some places and adding support in others. Her revised draft, you'll see, responds to "Disability" more directly, spells out Mairs's points and Anaya's own ideas in more detail, and builds more thoroughly on what Mairs had to say.

Revised Draft

Mental Illness on Television

In her essay "Disability" Nancy Mairs ~~is upset with~~ argues that **television and movies** ~~that don't~~ fail to **show physical disability as a feature of normal life.** ~~She~~ **Instead, Mairs says, the media shows disability consuming a character's life or it doesn't show disability at all**~~, and she wants to see "representations of myself in the media, especially television"~~ (~~p. no.~~ 13). But Mairs wrote her essay in 1987. Since then the situation has actually improved for physical disability. At the same time, another group — those with mental illness — have come to suffer even worse representation.

~~Mairs makes a convincing argument~~ **Mairs's purpose in** writing her essay was to persuade her readers **that the media should portray physical disability as part of everyday life because** ~~"effacement"~~ otherwise it denies or misrepresents disability, and it **leaves** ~~the rest of us~~ "Temporarily Abled Persons" (those without disability, for now) **unprepared to cope in the case that** ~~we~~ **they** should eventually become disabled ~~ourselves~~ **themselves** (14-15). ~~As she explains it, anybody could become disabled, but because we rarely see people with disabilities living full, normal lives on tv, we assume that becoming disabled means life is pretty much over (p. no.). It's been three decades since Mairs wrote her essay, and~~ **Three decades later, Mairs** ~~she~~ **seems to have gotten her wish. Plenty of characters on television today who have a disability are not defined by it.** Lawyer and superhero Matt Murdoch on *Daredevil* is blind. Daphne Vasquez on *Switched at Birth* (as well as many of her friends and their

Uses a less abrupt, more formal tone.

Deletes a quotation to remove a side issue and tighten the introduction.

Adds a thesis statement.

Explains Mairs's idea more clearly.

Provides page numbers in Mairs's essay.

Adds examples to support the assertion about TV today.

parents) is deaf. Security analyst Patton Plame of *NCIS: New Orleans* uses a wheelchair equipped with a computer to help his team solve crimes, Joe Swanson of *Family Guy* is also paraplegic. A current ad campaign for TJ Maxx features a wheelchair dance team, and Amy Purdy, an athlete with two prosthetic feet, is featured on a TV spot for Toyota. The media still has a long way to go in representing physical disability, but it has made progress.

However, the media depiction of one type of disability is, if anything, worse than it was three decades ago. Although Mairs doesn't address mental illness in "Disability," mental illness falls squarely into the misrepresentation she criticizes. ~~But p~~Psychological disabilities are disabilities too, ~~and~~ but they have never been shown "as a normal characteristic, one that complicates but does not ruin human existence" (~~p. no.~~ 15). People who cope with a disability such as depression, bipolar disorder, or obsessive-compulsive disorder as parts of their lives do not see themselves in the media; those who don't have a psychological disability now but may someday do not see that mental illness is usually a condition they can live with.

The depictions of mental illness actually go beyond Mairs's concerns, as the media actually exploits it. Television routinely portrays people with mental illness as threats to themselves and to others. Think about all those stories on the evening news about a man suffering from schizophrenia who went on a shooting spree before turning his gun on himself, or a mother who drowned her own children in the throes of depression, or a bipolar teenager who commits suicide. ~~Such events are tragic, no doubt, but although the vast majority of people with these illnesses hurt nobody, the news implies that they're all potential killers.~~ Fictional shows, too, are always using some kind of psychological disorder to explain why someone committed a crime. On *Criminal Minds* a woman with "intermittent explosive disorder" impulsively kills multiple people after she is released from a psychiatric hospital and stops taking her medication~~,~~. ~~and~~ ~~O~~on *Rizzoli and Isles* a serial abductor's actions are blamed on "a long history of mental illness" beginning ~~that started~~ with depression. ~~after he saw his father kill his mother and developed a perverse need~~

Adds a transition to tighten the connection with Mairs's essay.

More fully develops the idea about mental illness as a "normal characteristic."

Adds a transition to link back to Mairs and the thesis.

Combines related paragraphs ("Fictional shows" used to start a new paragraph).

~~to recreate their relationship with victims of his own. And the entire premise of Dexter is that the trauma of witnessing his mother's brutal murder turned the title character into a serial killer. Dexter is an obsessive-compulsive killer who justifies his impulses by killing only other killers. Early in the series, viewers learned that his nemesis, the "Ice Truck Killer," who at one point was engaged to Dexter's adopted sister and then tried to kill her, is actually his long-lost brother. Every season has featured a different enemy, and each one of them has had some kind of stated or implied mental illness: The "Doomsday Killer" of season six, for example, was a psychotic divinity student who went off his meds and suffered from delusions.~~

Removes digressions and simplifies examples to improve unity.

These programs highlight mental illness to get viewers' attention. But the media is also telling us that the proper response to people with mental illness is to be afraid of them. Mairs argues that invisibility in the media can cause people with disabilities to feel unattractive or inappropriate (14). **It is my belief that the presentation of psychological disability may do worse.** ~~than the "effacement" of disability that bothered Mairs.~~ **People with mental illness are discouraged from seeking help and are sent deeper into isolation and despair.** Those feelings are often cited as the fuel for violent outbursts, but ironically the media portrays such violence as inevitable with mental illness. ~~This negative stereotype hurts us all.~~

Expands paragraph to link to Mairs's essay and lend authority to Anaya's point.

More complex and varied depictions of all kinds of impairments, both physical and mental, will weaken the negative stereotypes that are harmful to all of us. With mental illness especially, we would all be better served if psychological disability was portrayed by the media as a part of everyday life. It's not a crime.

Provides a new conclusion that explains why the topic is important and ends with a flourish.

Works Cited

Adds a list of works cited. (See pp. 491–535.)

"Breath Play." *Criminal Minds*, season 10, episode 17, CBS, 11 Mar. 2015. *Netflix*, www.netflix.com/search/criminalminds. Accessed 19 July 2015.

"Deadly Harvest." *Rizzoli and Isles*, season 6, episode 3, TNT, 23 July 2015.

Mairs, Nancy. "Disability." *The Bedford Reader*, edited by X. J. Kennedy et al., 13th ed., Bedford/St. Martin's, 2017, pp. 13-15.

TJ Maxx. Advertisement. Fox, 21 July 2015.

Toyota. Advertisement. TNT, 23 July 2015.

Editing

With her thesis clarified, the connections between her argument and Mairs's tightened, and her ideas more fully developed, Anaya was satisfied that her essay was much improved and just about finished. She still had some work to do, though. In editing, she corrected errors, cleaned up awkward sentences, and added explanations. Here we show you her changes to one paragraph.

Edited Paragraph

Mairs's purpose in ~~writing her essay~~ "Disability" ~~was~~ is to persuade ~~her~~ readers that the media should portray physical disability as part of everyday life because otherwise ~~it denies~~ they deny or misrepresent~~s~~ disability~~,~~ and ~~it~~ leave~~s~~ "Temporarily Abled Persons" (those without disability, for now) unprepared to cope ~~in the case that they should eventually~~ if they become disabled ~~themselves~~ (14-15). Three decades later, Mairs seems to have gotten her wish. ~~Plenty of~~ for characters ~~on television today~~ who have a disability but are not defined by it. Lawyer and superhero Matt Murdoch on *Daredevil* is blind. ~~Daphne Vasquez~~ Several characters on *Switched at Birth* ~~(as well as many of her friends and their parents) is~~ are deaf. Security analyst Patton Plame of *NCIS: New Orleans* uses a wheelchair equipped with a computer to help his team solve crimes~~,~~. Police officer Joe Swanson of *Family Guy* is also paraplegic. A current ad campaign for TJ Maxx features a wheelchair dance team, and ~~Amy Purdy, an athlete with two prosthetic feet, is featured on~~ a TV spot for Toyota highlights Amy Purdy, an athlete with two prosthetic feet. The media still ~~has~~ have a long way to go in representing physical disability, but ~~it has~~ they have made progress.

Reduces wordiness; corrects tense shift.

Corrects pronoun-antecedent and subject-verb agreement (*media* is plural).

Reduces wordiness.

Adds coordination for emphasis.

Reduces wordiness.

Fixes comma splice.

Eliminates passive voice and creates parallelism.

Corrects subject-verb and pronoun-antecedent agreement.

Final Draft

Mental Illness on Television

In her essay "Disability," Nancy Mairs argues that the media, such as television and movies, fail to show physical disability as a feature of normal life. Instead, Mairs says, they show disability consuming a character's life or they don't show disability at all. Mairs wrote her essay in 1987, and since then the situation has actually improved for depiction of physical disability. At the same time, another group — those with mental illness — has come to suffer even worse representation.

Mairs's purpose in "Disability" is to persuade readers that the media should portray physical disability as part of everyday life because otherwise they deny or misrepresent disability and leave "Temporarily Abled Persons" (those without disability, for now) unprepared to cope if they become disabled (14-15). Three decades later, Mairs seems to have gotten her wish for characters who have a disability but are not defined by it. Lawyer and superhero Matt Murdoch on *Daredevil* is blind. Several characters on *Switched at Birth* are deaf. Security analyst Patton Plame of *NCIS: New Orleans* uses a wheelchair equipped with a computer to help his team solve crimes. Police officer Joe Swanson of *Family Guy* is also paraplegic. A current ad campaign for TJ Maxx features a wheelchair dance team, and a TV spot for Toyota highlights Amy Purdy, an athlete with two prosthetic feet. The media still have a long way to go in representing physical disability, but they have made progress.

However, in depicting one type of disability, the media are, if anything, worse than they were three decades ago. Mairs doesn't address mental illness, but it falls squarely into the misrepresentation she criticizes. It has never been shown, in Mairs's words, "as a normal characteristic, one that complicates but does not ruin human existence" (15). Thus people who cope with a psychological disability such as depression, bipolar disorder, or obsessive-compulsive disorder as part of their lives do not see themselves in the media. And those who don't have a psychological disability now but may someday do not see that mental illness is usually a condition one can live with.

Unfortunately, the depictions of mental illness also go beyond Mairs's concerns, because the media actually exploit it. Television routinely portrays people with mental illness as

Introduction summarizes Mairs's essay and sets up Anaya's thesis.

Thesis statement establishes Anaya's main idea.

Page numbers in parentheses refer to "Works Cited" at end of paper.

Examples provide support for Anaya's analysis.

Comparison and contrast extend Mairs's idea to Anaya's new subject.

Follow-up comments explain what the quotation contributes to Anaya's thesis.

Topic sentence introduces new idea.

threats to themselves and to others. TV news often features
stories about a man suffering from schizophrenia who goes on
a shooting spree before turning his gun on himself, a mother
with depression who drowns her own children, or a teenager
with bipolar disorder who commits suicide. Fictional programs,
especially crime dramas, regularly use mental illness to develop
their plots. On *Criminal Minds* a woman with "intermittent
explosive disorder" impulsively kills multiple people after she
is released from a psychiatric hospital and stops taking her
medication, and on *Rizzoli and Isles* a serial abductor's actions
are blamed on "a long history of mental illness" beginning with
depression. These programs and many others like them highlight
mental illness to get viewers' attention, and they strongly
imply that the proper response is fear. Mairs argues that the
invisibility of physical disability in the media can cause people
with disabilities to feel unattractive or inappropriate (14), but
the presentation of psychological disability may do worse. It can
prevent people with mental illness from seeking help and send
them deeper into isolation and despair. Those feelings are often
cited as the fuel for violent outbursts, but ironically the media
portray such violence as inevitable with mental illness.

   Seeing more complex and varied depictions of people living
with all kinds of impairments, physical and mental, can weaken
the negative stereotypes that are harmful to all of us. With
mental illness especially, we would all be better served if the
media would make an effort to portray psychological disability as
a part of everyday life, not a crime.

Examples provide evidence for Anaya's point.

Paraphrase explains one of Mairs's points in Anaya's own words.

Cause-and-effect analysis applies Mairs's idea to Anaya's thesis.

Conclusion reasserts the thesis and explains the broader implications of the subject.

Works Cited

"Breath Play." *Criminal Minds*, season 10, episode 17, CBS, 11
      Mar. 2015. *Netflix*, www.netflix.com/search/criminalminds.
      Accessed 19 July 2015.
"Deadly Harvest." *Rizzoli and Isles*, season 6, episode 3, TNT, 23
      July 2015.
Mairs, Nancy. "Disability." *The Bedford Reader*, edited by X. J. Kennedy
      et al., 13th ed., Bedford/St. Martin's, 2017, pp. 13-15.
TJ Maxx. Advertisement. Fox, 21 July 2015.
Toyota. Advertisement. TNT, 23 July 2015.

List of "Works Cited" at the end of the paper gives complete publication information for Anaya's sources. (See pp. 491–535.)

PART TWO

THE METHODS

3

NARRATION

Telling a Story

◀ **Narration in a drawing**

Demetri Martin is a popular stand-up comedian known for intelligent wit and for the clever graphs and drawings he incorporates into his act. He has published two books of such artwork: *This Is a Book by Demetri Martin* (2011), which also includes comic essays, and *Point Your Face at This* (2013). "Reality is a concept that depends on where you point your face," he says in the epigraph to the second book — an idea illustrated with this drawing. In Martin's trademark simple style, the sketch focuses on just the lower legs of two people to tell a brief narrative, or story. What experience is depicted here? What do the details in each part of the sequence tell us about the characters, and what do they contribute to the narrative? What effect does Martin achieve by not showing the couple more fully? How does the unusual perspective shape your understanding of what has happened?

THE METHOD

"What happened?" you ask a friend who sports a swollen black eye. Unless he merely grunts, "A golf ball," he may answer you with a narrative — a story, true or fictional.

"Okay," he sighs, "you know The Tenth Round? That gym down by the docks that smells like formaldehyde? Last night I heard they were giving away $500 to anybody who could stand up for three minutes against this karate expert, the Masked Samurai. And so . . ."

You lean forward. At least, you lean forward *if* you love a story. Most of us do, particularly if the story tells us of people in action or in conflict, and if it is told briskly, vividly, or with insight into the human condition. NARRATION, or storytelling, is therefore a powerful method by which to engage and hold the attention of listeners — readers as well. A little of its tremendous power flows to the blogger who encapsulates events in a critical social moment, and to the lawyer who pulls together the threads of a compelling case.

The term *narrative* takes in abundant territory. A narrative may be short or long, factual or imagined, as artless as a tale told in a locker room or as artful as a novel by Toni Morrison. A narrative may instruct and inform, or simply entertain. It may set forth some point or message, or it may be no more significant than a horror tale that aims to curdle your blood. Because narration can both put across ideas and hold attention, the ability to tell a story — on paper, as well as in conversation — may be one of the most useful skills you can acquire.

THE PROCESS

Purpose and Shape

At least a hundred times a year, you probably turn to narration, not always to tell an entertaining story, but often to report information or to illustrate an idea. Every good story has a purpose, because a narrative without a point is bound to irritate readers.

In academic writing, you will use mainly brief narratives, or ANECDOTES, that recount single incidents as a way of supporting an explanation or argument with the flesh and blood of real life. That is, although a narrative can run from the beginning of an essay to the end, as those later in this chapter do, more often in your writing a narrative will be only a part of what you have to say. It will serve a larger purpose. For instance, say you're writing about therapies for autism and you want readers to see how one particular method works. In a paragraph or so, you can narrate a session you observed between a child and his teacher. Your purpose will determine which of the session's events you relate — not every action and exchange but the ones that, in your eyes, convey the essence of the therapy and make it interesting for readers.

The Thesis

In writing a news story, a reporter often begins by placing the main event in the opening paragraph (called the *lead*) so that readers get the essentials up front. Similarly, in using an anecdote to explain something or to argue a point, you'll want to tell readers directly what the story demonstrates. But in most other kinds of narration, whether fiction or nonfiction, whether to entertain or to make an idea clear, the storyteller refrains from revealing the gist of the story, its point, right at the beginning.

In fact, many narratives do not contain a THESIS STATEMENT, an assertion of the idea behind the story, because such a statement can rob the reader of the very pleasure of narration, the excitement of seeing a story build. That doesn't mean the story lacks a thesis, however — far from it. The writer has every obligation to construct the narrative as if a thesis statement shows the way at the start, even when it doesn't.

By the end of the story, that thesis should become obvious, as the writer builds toward a memorable CONCLUSION. Most storytellers end with a bang if they can, often by surprising the reader with a final moment of IRONY, or an unexpected twist to the tale. In the drawing that opens this chapter, for instance, Demetri Martin shows a marriage proposal that ends in a breakup. For another example, take specific notice in this chapter of Shirley Jackson's ending for "The Lottery" (*after* you've read the whole story, that is). The final impact need not be as dramatic as Martin's or Jackson's, either. As Junot Díaz demonstrates in his narrative in this chapter, you can achieve a lot just by working up to your point, and stating your thesis at the very end. You can sometimes make your point just by saving the best incident — the most dramatic or the funniest — for last.

The Narrator in the Story

Every story has a NARRATOR, the person telling the tale. The narrator's role in relation to the story determines the POINT OF VIEW, or angle of seeing, that shapes the telling. Generally, writers use different points of view to tell different kinds of stories.

- **Narratives that report personal experience:** Whether you are telling of a real or a fictional event, your narrator will be the one who was there. The telling will probably be SUBJECTIVE: You will use the first PERSON ("I did this; we did that") and choose details and language to express the feelings of the narrator — your own feelings when you are recounting your actual experience or the imagined feelings of a character you have invented. Of course, any experience told in the first person can use some artful telling and structuring, as the personal narratives in this chapter — by Amy Tan and Naomi Shihab Nye — both demonstrate.

- **Narratives that report others' experiences:** When a story isn't your own but someone else's, you proceed differently as narrator. You use the third person, *he, she, it,* or *they*: "The experimenter did this; she did that." Your approach may be subjective, building in the real or imagined feelings of the person experiencing the events — as Junot Díaz does in this chapter, reporting his mother's story. Or your approach may be OBJECTIVE, sticking to the facts as observed by you or by others. In objective narration — typical of writing such as news stories, history books, lab reports, and some fiction — you show what transpired as accurately and dispassionately as possible. In this chapter you can see objective narration in the police log by Scott Beltran and in the short story by Shirley Jackson.

A final element of the narrator's place in the story is verb tense, whether present (*I stare, she stares*) or past (*I stared, she stared*). The present tense is often tempting because it gives events a sense of immediacy. Told as though everything were happening right now, the story of the Masked Samurai might begin: "I duck between the ropes and step into the ring. My heart is thudding fast." But the present tense can seem artificial because we're used to reading stories in the past tense, and it can be difficult to sustain throughout an entire narrative. (See p. 216 on consistency in tenses.) The past tense may be more removed, but it is still powerful.

What to Emphasize

Discovery of Details

Whether you tell of your own experience or of someone else's, even if it is brief, you need a whole story to tell. If the story is complex, do some searching and discovering in writing. One trusty method to test your memory (or to make sure you have all the necessary elements of a story) is that of a news reporter. Ask yourself:

- **What happened?**
- **Who took part?**
- **When?**

- **Where?**
- **Why did it happen?**
- **How did it happen?**

Journalists call this handy list of questions "the five *W*'s and the *H*." The *H* — *how* — isn't merely another way of asking what happened. It means: In exactly what way or under what circumstances? If the event was a break-in, how was it done — with an ax or with a bulldozer?

Scene versus Summary

If you have prepared well — searching your memory or doing some research — you'll have far more information on hand than you can use in your narrative. You'll need to choose carefully, to pick out just those events and details that will accomplish your purpose with your readers.

A key decision is to choose between the two main strategies of narration:

- **Tell a story by SCENE, visualizing each event as vividly and precisely as if you were there.** Think of the scene as if it were in a film, with your reader sitting before the screen. This is the strategy Shirley Jackson uses in her account of a tense crowd's behavior as, gathered in a small town square, they anticipate who will be at the center of an annual tradition (in "The Lottery," p. 90). Instead of just mentioning people, you portray them. You recall dialog as best you can, or you invent some that could have been spoken. You include DESCRIPTION (a mode of writing to be dealt with fully in the next chapter). You might prolong one scene for an entire essay, or you could draw a scene in only two or three sentences (as Scott Beltran does in his police log on pp. 71–73).

- **Tell a story by SUMMARY, relating events concisely.** Instead of depicting people and their surroundings in great detail, you set down just the essentials of what happened. Such is the strategy Junot Díaz uses in "The Dreamer" (p. 84) to tell of his mother's childhood determination to get an education. Most of us employ this method in the everyday stories we tell, for it takes less time and fewer words. When chosen well, the economy of a story told in summary may be as effective as the lavish detail of a story told in scenes.

As always, your choice of a strategy depends on your answers to the questions you ask yourself: What is my purpose? Who is my audience? Whether to flesh out a scene fully, how much detail to include — these choices depend on what you seek to do and on how much your audience needs to know to follow you. You may find that you want to use both strategies in telling a single story, passing briskly from one scene to the next, distilling events of lesser importance. Were you to write, let's say, the story of your grandfather's emigration from Cuba, you might just summarize his decision to leave Cuba and his settlement in Florida. These summaries could frame and emphasize a detailed telling of the events that you consider essential and most interesting — his nighttime escape, his harrowing voyage in a small boat, his surprising welcome by immigration authorities.

Dialog

In this book we are primarily concerned with the kind of writing you do every day in college: nonfiction writing in which you explain ideas, organize information you have learned, analyze other people's ideas, or argue a case. In fiction, though, we find an enormously popular and appealing use of narration and certain devices of storytelling from which all writers can learn. For these reasons, this chapter includes one celebrated short story by a master storyteller, Shirley Jackson. But fiction and fact barely separate Jackson's tale and the equally compelling true stories in this chapter. All of the authors strive to make people and events come alive for us. Many of them also use a tool that academic writers generally do not: DIALOG. Reported speech, in quotation marks, is invaluable for revealing characters' feelings, as Amy Tan and Naomi Shihab Nye demonstrate with their tales from real life.

Organization

In any kind of narration, the simplest approach is to set down events in CHRONOLOGICAL ORDER, following the sequence in which they occurred. To do so is to have your story already organized for you.

Chronological order is an excellent pattern to follow unless you can see some special advantage in violating it. Ask: What am I trying to do? If you are trying to capture your readers' attention right away, you might begin *in medias res* (Latin, "in the middle of things") and open with a colorful, dramatic event, even though it took place late in the chronology. If trying for dramatic effect, you might save the most exciting or impressive event for last, even though it actually happened early. By this means, you can keep your readers in suspense for as long as possible. (You can return to earlier events in a FLASHBACK, an earlier scene recalled.) Let your purpose be your guide.

No matter what order you choose, either following chronology or departing from it, make sure your audience can follow it. The sequence of events has to be clear. This calls for TRANSITIONS that mark time, whether they are brief phrases that point out exactly when each event happened ("seven years later," "a moment earlier") or whole sentences that announce an event and clearly locate it in time ("Passing by the gym on Friday evening, I noticed the sign: 'Go Three Minutes with the Masked Samurai and Win $500.' "). See *Transitions* in the Glossary for a list of possibilities.

FOCUS ON VERBS

Narration depends heavily on verbs to clarify and enliven events. Strong verbs sharpen meaning and encourage you to add other informative details:

> WEAK   The wind <u>made</u> an awful noise.

> STRONG   The wind <u>roared</u> around the house and <u>rattled</u> the trees.

Forms of *make* (as in the example above) and forms of *be* (as in the next example) can sap the life from narration:

> WEAK   The noises <u>were</u> alarming to us.

> STRONG   The noises <u>alarmed</u> us.

Verbs in the ACTIVE VOICE (the subject does the action) usually pack more power into fewer words than verbs in the PASSIVE VOICE (the subject is acted upon):

> WEAK PASSIVE   We <u>were besieged</u> in the basement by the wind, as the water at our feet <u>was swelled</u> by the rain.

> STRONG ACTIVE   The wind <u>besieged</u> us in the basement, as the rain <u>swelled</u> the water at our feet.

While strengthening verbs, also ensure that they're consistent in tense. The tense you choose for relating events, present or past, should not shift unnecessarily.

> INCONSISTENT TENSES   We <u>held</u> a frantic conference to consider our options. It <u>takes</u> only a minute to decide to stay put.

> CONSISTENT TENSE   We <u>held</u> a frantic conference to consider our options. It <u>took</u> only a minute to decide to stay put.

See page 49 for further discussion of passive versus active verbs and page 216 for advice on avoiding shifts in tense.

CHECKLIST FOR REVISING A NARRATIVE

✔ **Thesis.** What is the point of your narrative? Will it be clear to readers by the end? Even if you don't provide a thesis statement, your story should focus on a central idea. If you can't risk readers' misunderstanding — if, for instance, you're using narration to support an argument or explain a concept — then have you stated your thesis outright?

✔ **Point of view.** Is your narrator's position in the story appropriate for your purpose and consistent throughout? Check for awkward or confusing shifts in point of view (subjective or objective; first or third person) and in the tenses of verbs (present to past or vice versa).

✔ **Selection of events.** Have you selected and emphasized events to suit your audience and fulfill your purpose? Tell the important parts of the story in the greatest detail. Summarize the less important, connective events.

✔ **Organization.** If your organization is not strictly chronological (first event to last), do you have a compelling reason for altering it? If you start somewhere other than the beginning of the story or use flashbacks at any point, will your readers benefit from your creativity?

✔ **Transitions.** Have you used transitions to help clarify the order of events and their duration?

✔ **Dialog.** If you have used dialog, quoting participants in the story, is it appropriate for your purpose? Is it concise, telling only the important, revealing lines? Does the language sound like spoken English?

✔ **Verbs.** Do strong, active verbs move your narrative from event to event? Are verb tenses consistent?

NARRATION IN ACADEMIC WRITING

A Geology Textbook

In this paragraph from *The Earth: An Introduction to Physical Geology*, the authors Edward J. Tarbuck and Frederick K. Lutgens use narration to illustrate a powerful geological occurrence. Following a paragraph that explains landslides more generally, this narrative places the reader at a historic event.

The news media periodically relate the terrifying and often grim details of landslides. On <u>May 31, 1970</u>, one such event occurred when a gigantic rock avalanche buried more than 20,000 people in Yungay and Ranrahirca, Peru. There was little warning of the impending disaster; it began and ended in just <u>a matter of a few minutes</u>. The avalanche started 14 kilometers from Yungay, near the summit of 6,700-meter-high Nevados Huascaran, the loftiest

Generalization illustrated by narrative

Anecdote helps explain landslides:

• Sudden beginning

peak in the Peruvian Andes. Triggered by the ground motion from a strong offshore earthquake, a huge mass of rock and ice broke free from the precipitous north face of the mountain. <u>After plunging nearly one kilometer</u>, the material pulverized on impact and immediately began rushing down the mountainside, made fluid by trapped air and melted ice. The initial mass ripped loose additional millions of tons of debris <u>as it roared downhill</u>. The shock waves produced by the event created thunderlike noise and stripped nearby hillsides of vegetation. Although the material followed a previously eroded gorge, a portion of the debris jumped a 200–300-meter-high bedrock ridge that had protected Yungay from past rock avalanches and buried the entire city. <u>After inundating another town in its path</u>, Ranrahirca, the mass of debris <u>finally</u> reached the bottom of the valley where its momentum carried it across the Rio Santa and tens of meters up the opposite bank.

• Fast movement

• Irresistible force

Transitions (underlined) clarify sequence and pace of events

A Police Log

What is it like to work in law enforcement? What takes place on a typical shift? What procedures are the police expected to follow, and why? To learn the answers to such questions, criminal justice students — and sometimes civilians — are often given the opportunity to ride along on patrol with seasoned officers and observe their activities.

Whatever else the risks and rewards of the job, policing involves a good deal of paperwork. Every incident must be recorded in writing — sometimes in formal reports, but more often in simple activity logs. Kept by all police departments and often published in local newspapers, such logs provide straightforward public records of calls for help, motor vehicle stops, interactions with suspected criminals, and similar events. Always in chronological order, these narratives are generally presented as briefly and objectively as possible, written in the past tense and third-person point of view, and limited to the facts of each case: what happened, who was involved, where and when the events took place. Even so, as novelist Brian Doyle observes (p. 160), police logs offer some of the most engaging writing produced for general readers.

For an introductory criminal justice class at Lone Star College–Montgomery in Texas, student Scott Beltran went on a Saturday-night ride-along with the Crime Reduction Unit (CRU) of the Houston Police Department. Like the officers themselves, he kept an activity log through the shift. He also ANALYZED each event to better understand the experience. The final report he wrote and turned in to his instructor is excerpted on the following pages.

2000: CRU Roll Call. Two Sergeants take muster to make sure all officers are present and accounted for. After muster they discuss any intelligence on open cases they're actively investigating, and then they formulate a strategy to decide what part of town to focus their efforts. . . .

2030–2130: Officer Smith and I teamed up with one other unit and began conducting sweeps of previously identified drug trafficking locations. . . . During these sweeps, the officers were on alert for any type of suspicious activity, such as loitering, and they approached everyone in the area for at least some sort of brief questioning, but almost no one was detained or arrested. Officer Smith explained that these sweeps were done not only to make arrests, but also to establish HPD's presence in high-crime areas and to get the word out that Houston Police are proactively working to stop crime.

2200: We responded to an "officer needs assistance" call in the 800 block of N. Shepherd Drive. When we arrived there was one other unit on the scene; they already had two males and a female in custody. One male and the female were being detained for possession of crack cocaine, and the other male was being held for a parole violation warrant. After some investigation . . . it was determined that there were possibly more drugs in the suspect's apartment. The officers asked for, and were granted, consent to search the apartment. The officers asked the suspect to sign a "Consent to Search" form, which she did voluntarily. This was witnessed and signed by two other officers. After a quick search of the residence, the officers located a small amount of marijuana, a chemical mixing beaker, and a hot plate that appeared to have been used to cook, or make drugs. These items were seized and the suspects were charged with possession of a controlled substance. . . . All three suspects were transported to the central police station in downtown Houston. . . .

0030: Officer Smith initiated a stop of a black Dodge Charger for the windows being tinted too dark. While running the driver's license through the system he determined that the driver was wanted out of Louisiana for a felony warrant, but the warrant stipulated arrest-in-state only. Officer Smith attempted to contact the agency that issued the warrant to determine if they wanted him to make the arrest. While he was waiting for the Louisiana agency to return his phone call, Officer Smith made contact with the passenger, the owner of the vehicle, and got consent to search the car. A search was completed and nothing illegal was found. Because he still hadn't gotten in touch with a supervisor in Louisiana, he took down all of the suspect's information and released him. . . .

0400: While traveling northbound we came upon a vehicle stopped at a red light in the 6500 block of the Gulf Freeway. With our windows rolled up we could still easily hear the vehicle's stereo system playing at a high volume. Officer Smith initiated a stop of the vehicle for violation of a city noise ordinance. After the vehicle pulled off the road we observed the driver making obvious furtive gestures while reaching toward the passenger seat. Officer Smith made contact with the driver and noticed that he was acting very nervous and appeared to be under the influence of some type of stimulant. Officer Smith removed the driver from the vehicle to investigate further. The driver admitted that he had been using cocaine and that he had a small amount still in the car. . . . Officer Smith placed a call to the District Attorney's office to make sure they would accept charges. The DA did accept the charges and the suspect was charged with Felony Possession of a Controlled Substance and booked into the central police station.

Narration by scene

0530: All of the Officers in the CRU met back at the station for an end of shift muster and de-briefing.

Narration concludes with the end of shift

AMY TAN

Amy Tan is a gifted storyteller whose first novel, *The Joy Luck Club* (1989), met with critical acclaim and huge success. The relationships it details between immigrant Chinese mothers and their Chinese American daughters came from Tan's firsthand experience. She was born in 1952 in Oakland, California, the daughter of immigrants who had fled China's civil war in the late 1940s. She majored in English and linguistics at San José State University, where she received a BA in 1973 and an MA in 1974. After two more years of graduate work, Tan became a consultant in language development for disabled children and then a freelancer writing reports and speeches for business corporations. Bored with such work, Tan began writing fiction to explore her ethnic ambivalence and to find her voice. Since *The Joy Luck Club*, she has published several more novels — most recently *The Valley of Amazement* (2013) — as well as children's books and *The Opposite of Fate* (2003), a collection of autobiographical essays. She is also a founding member of the Rock Bottom Remainders, a "literary garage band" made up of popular writers.

Fish Cheeks

In Tan's novel *The Bonesetter's Daughter* (2001), one of the characters says, "Good manners are not enough. . . . They are not the same as a good heart." Much of Tan's writing explores those tensions between keeping up appearances and having true intentions. In the brief narrative that follows, the author deftly portrays the contradictory feelings of a girl with feet in different cultures. The essay first appeared in *Seventeen*, a magazine for teenage girls and young women, in 1987.

For another entertaining story about a cultural misunderstanding, read the next essay, Naomi Shihab Nye's "Museum."

I fell in love with the minister's son the winter I turned fourteen. He was not Chinese, but as white as Mary in the manger. For Christmas I prayed for this blond-haired boy, Robert, and a slim new American nose.

When I found out that my parents had invited the minister's family over for Christmas Eve dinner, I cried. What would Robert think of our shabby Chinese Christmas? What would he think of our noisy Chinese relatives who lacked proper American manners? What terrible disappointment would he feel upon seeing not a roasted turkey and sweet potatoes but Chinese food?

On Christmas Eve I saw that my mother had outdone herself in creating   3
a strange menu. She was pulling black veins out of the backs of fleshy prawns.
The kitchen was littered with appalling mounds of raw food: A slimy rock cod
with bulging eyes that pleaded not to be thrown into a pan of hot oil. Tofu,
which looked like stacked wedges of rubbery white sponges. A bowl soaking
dried fungus back to life. A plate of squid, their backs crisscrossed with knife
markings so they resembled bicycle tires.

And then they arrived — the minister's family and all my relatives in a   4
clamor of doorbells and rumpled Christmas packages. Robert grunted hello,
and I pretended he was not worthy of existence.

Dinner threw me deeper into despair. My relatives licked the ends of their   5
chopsticks and reached across the table, dipping them into the dozen or so
plates of food. Robert and his family waited patiently for platters to be passed
to them. My relatives murmured with pleasure when my mother brought out
the whole steamed fish. Robert grimaced. Then my father poked his chopsticks
just below the fish eye and plucked out the soft meat. "Amy, your favorite," he
said, offering me the tender fish cheek. I wanted to disappear.

At the end of the meal my father leaned back and belched loudly, thank-   6
ing my mother for her fine cooking. "It's a polite Chinese custom to show you
are satisfied," explained my father to our astonished guests. Robert was looking down at his plate with a reddened face. The minister managed to muster
up a quiet burp. I was stunned into silence for the rest of the night.

After everyone had gone, my mother said to me, "You want to be the   7
same as American girls on the outside." She handed me an early gift. It was a
miniskirt in beige tweed. "But inside you must always be Chinese. You must be
proud you are different. Your only shame is to have shame."

And even though I didn't agree with her then, I knew that she understood   8
how much I had suffered during the evening's dinner. It wasn't until many
years later — long after I had gotten over my crush on Robert — that I was
able to fully appreciate her lesson and the true purpose behind our particular
menu. For Christmas Eve that year, she had chosen all my favorite foods.

Journal Writing

Do you sympathize with the shame Tan feels because of her family's differences from
their non-Chinese guests? Or do you think she should have been more proud to share
her family's customs? Think of an occasion when, for whatever reason, you were
acutely aware of being different. How did you react? Did you try to hide your difference in order to fit in, or did you reveal or celebrate your uniqueness?

Questions on Meaning

1. Why does Tan cry when she finds out that the boy she is in love with is coming to dinner?

2. Why does Tan's mother go out of her way to prepare a disturbingly traditional Chinese dinner for her daughter and guests? What one sentence best sums up the lesson Tan was not able to understand until years later?

3. How does the fourteen-year-old Tan feel about her Chinese background? about her mother?

4. What is Tan's PURPOSE in writing this essay? Does she just want to entertain readers, or might she have a weightier goal?

Questions on Writing Strategy

1. How does Tan draw the reader into her story right from the beginning?

2. How does Tan use TRANSITIONS both to drive and to clarify her narrative?

3. What is the IRONY of the last sentence of the essay?

4. **OTHER METHODS** Paragraph 3 is a passage of pure DESCRIPTION. Why does Tan linger over the food? What is the EFFECT of this paragraph?

Questions on Language

1. The simile about Mary in the second sentence of the essay is surprising. Why? Why is it amusing? (See FIGURES OF SPEECH in the Glossary for a definition of *simile*.)

2. How does the narrator's age affect the TONE of this essay? Give EXAMPLES of language particularly appropriate to a fourteen-year-old.

3. In which paragraph does Tan use strong verbs most effectively?

4. Make sure you know the meanings of the following words: prawns, tofu (par. 3); clamor (4); grimaced (5); muster (6).

Suggestions for Writing

1. **FROM JOURNAL TO ESSAY** Using Tan's essay as a model, write a brief narrative based on your journal sketch (p. 75) about a time when you felt different from others. Try to imitate the way Tan integrates the external events of the dinner with her own feelings about what is going on. Your story may be humorous, like Tan's, or more serious.

2. Take a perspective like that of the minister's son, Robert: Write a narrative essay about a time when you had to adjust to participating in a culture different from your own. It could be a meal, a wedding or other rite of passage, a religious ceremony, a trip to another country. What did you learn from your experience, about yourself and others?

3. **CRITICAL WRITING** From this essay one can INFER two very different sets of ASSUMPTIONS about the extent to which immigrants should seek to integrate themselves into the culture of their adopted country. Take either of these positions, in favor of or against assimilation (cultural integration), and make an ARGUMENT for your case.

4. **CONNECTIONS** Both Amy Tan and Naomi Shihab Nye, in "Museum" (next page), write about embarrassment, but their POINTS OF VIEW are not the same: Tan's is a teenager's lament about not fitting in; Nye's is an adult's celebration of a past mistake. In an essay, ANALYZE the two authors' uses of narration to convey their perspectives. What details do they focus on? What internal thoughts do they report? Is one essay more effective than the other? Why, or why not?

NAOMI SHIHAB NYE

Naomi Shihab Nye is an accomplished writer of poetry, fiction, and prose for young readers and adults alike. Born in 1952 in St. Louis, Missouri, she earned a BA in English and world religions from Trinity University in 1974 and teaches as a visiting writer at schools and colleges across the country. Growing up, Nye was enchanted by the lyricism of her father's Palestinian folktales and her mother's American lullabies; she published her first poem in a children's magazine when she was seven years old. Since then, Nye's entranced and entrancing writing has appeared regularly in *The Horn Book, The Texas Observer, World Literature Today,* and other magazines and in her wide-ranging books, including *Habibi* (1997), a young-adult novel based on Nye's own time living in Jerusalem as a teenager; *Sitti's Secrets* (1994) and *Benito's Dream Bottle* (1995), picture books for children; and *Honeybee* (2008), poems and essays for adults. She has also compiled or translated several anthologies of world and student poetry, among them *This Same Sky* (1992) and *Salting the Ocean* (2000). In 2010 Nye was elected a chancellor of the Academy of American Poets. She lives in San Antonio, Texas, and enjoys singing.

Museum

Themes of human connection and cultural exchange run throughout Nye's work. In this story from *Honeybee,* she leads us fleeing giddily from an honest mistake. Like all of her writing, this romp shows Nye's unparalleled exuberance for everyday life and her skill at expressing it.

The preceding essay, Amy Tan's "Fish Cheeks," also tells a tale of embarrassment.

I was 17, and my family had just moved to San Antonio. A local magazine 1
featured an alluring article about a museum called the McNay, an old mansion once the home of an eccentric many-times-married watercolorist named Marian Koogler McNay. She had deeded it to the community to become a museum upon her death. I asked my friend Sally, who drove a cute little convertible and had moved to Texas a year before we did, if she wanted to go there. Sally said, "Sure." She was a good friend that way. We had made up a few words in our own language and could dissolve into laughter just by saying them. Our mothers thought we were a bit odd. On a sunny Saturday afternoon, we drove over to Broadway. Sally asked, "Do you have the address of this place?"

"No," I said, "just drive very slowly and I'll recognize it, there was a picture in the magazine." I peered in both directions and pointed, saying, "There, there it is, pull in!" The parking lot under some palm trees was pretty empty. We entered, excited. The museum was free. Right away, the spirit of the arched doorways, carved window frames, and elegant artwork overtook us. Sally went left; I went right. A group of people seated in some chairs in the lobby stopped talking and stared at us.

"May I help you?" a man said. "No," I said. "We're fine." I didn't like to 2 talk to people in museums. Tours and docents got on my nerves. What if they talked a long time about a painting you weren't that interested in? I took a deep breath, and moved on to another painting — fireworks over a patio in Mexico, maybe? There weren't very good tags in this museum. In fact, there weren't any. I stood back and gazed. Sally had gone upstairs. The people in the lobby had stopped chatting. They seemed very nosy, keeping their eyes on me with irritating curiosity. What was their problem? I turned down a hallway. Bougainvilleas and azaleas pressed up right against the windows. Maybe we should have brought a picnic. Where was the Moorish courtyard? I saw some nice sculptures in another room, and a small couch. This would be a great place for reading. Above the couch hung a radiant print by Paul Klee,[1] my favorite artist, blues and pinks merging softly in his own wonderful way. I stepped closer. Suddenly I became aware of a man from the lobby standing behind me in the doorway.

"Where do you think you are?" he asked. I turned sharply. "The McNay 3 Art Museum!" He smiled then, and shook his head. "Sorry to tell you. The McNay is three blocks over, on New Braunfels Street. Take a right when you go out of our driveway, then another right." "What is this place?" I asked, still confused. He said, "Well, we thought it was our home." My heart jolted. I raced past him to the bottom of the staircase and called out, "Sally! Come down immediately! Urgent!" I remember being tempted to shout something in our private language, but we didn't have a word for this. Sally came to the top of the stairs smiling happily and said, "You have to come up here, there's some really good stuff! And there are old beds too!" "No, Sally, no," I said, as if she were a dog, or a baby. "Get down here. Speed it up. This is an emergency." She stepped elegantly down the stairs as if in a museum trance, looking puzzled. I just couldn't tell her out loud in front of those people what we had done. I actually pushed her toward the front door, waving my hand at the family in

---

[1] Paul Klee (1879–1940) was a Swiss artist in the German Expressionist school, known for his childish yet sophisticated imagery. — Eds.

the chairs, saying, "Sorry, ohmygod, please forgive us, you have a really nice place." Sally stared at me in the parking lot. When I told her, she covered her mouth and doubled over with laughter, shaking. We were still in their yard. I imagined them inside looking out the windows at us. She couldn't believe how long they let us look around without saying anything, either. "That was really friendly of them!" "Get in the car," I said sternly. "This is mortifying."

The real McNay was fabulous, splendid, but we felt a little nervous the whole time we were there. Van Gogh, Picasso, Tamayo.[2] This time, there were tags. This time, we stayed together, in case anything else weird happened.   4

We never told anyone.   5

Thirty years later, a nice-looking woman approached me in a public place. "Excuse me," she said. "I need to ask a strange question. Did you ever, by any chance, enter a residence, long ago, thinking it was the McNay Museum?"   6

Thirty years later, my cheeks still burned. "Yes. But how do you know? I never told anyone."   7

"That was my home. I was a teenager sitting with my family talking in the living room. Before you came over, I never realized what a beautiful place I lived in. I never felt lucky before. You thought it was a museum. My feelings changed about my parents after that too. They had good taste. I have always wanted to thank you."   8

Journal Writing

Why do you suppose Nye remembers in such vivid detail a minor event that happened more than thirty years ago? What small embarrassments or misadventures from your youth seem momentous even now? List these incidents, along with some notes about their importance.

Questions on Meaning

1. What is Nye's PURPOSE in this essay? Obviously, she wants to entertain readers, but does she have another purpose as well?

2. How does Nye explain why she and her friend walked into the home of strangers and wandered around? What do you imagine the family thought was going on?

---

[2] All groundbreaking modern artists. Cubist Pablo Picasso (1881–1973) was Spanish; Post-Impressionist Vincent van Gogh (1853–90) was Dutch; Surrealist Rufino Tamayo (1899–1991) was Mexican. — EDS.

3. What does the incident represent for Nye? What does it represent for the daughter of the household? How did the teenager's feelings about herself and her parents change after the other teenagers left the house, and why?

4. In your own words, try to express Nye's THESIS, or the moral of her story.

Questions on Writing Strategy

1. Does Nye narrate primarily by summary or by scene? How effective do you find her choice?

2. Discuss the author's POINT OF VIEW. Is her perspective that of a seventeen-year-old or that of an adult writer reflecting on her experience?

3. Nye writes poetry and books both for children and for adult readers. Who seems to be the intended AUDIENCE for this story? Why do you think so?

4. **OTHER METHODS** "Museum" implicitly COMPARES AND CONTRASTS Nye's and the family's appreciation for luxury and fine art. What are some of the differences (and similarities) that Nye implies?

Questions on Language

1. Look up any of the following words that you don't already know: eccentric (par. 1); docents, bougainvilleas, azaleas, Moorish (2); mortifying (3).

2. Nye uses short and simple sentences through most of this essay. Why do you suppose that is? What does "Museum" gain (or lose) from lack of sentence variety? (If necessary, see pp. 49–53 and 144 on sentence structure.)

3. How does Nye use DIALOG to make the story easy to follow?

4. "Our mothers thought we were a bit odd," Nye writes in the first paragraph. Pick out a few other instances of understatement in the essay. What is their effect? (For an explanation of *understatement*, look under FIGURES OF SPEECH in the Glossary.)

Suggestions for Writing

1. **FROM JOURNAL TO ESSAY** Choose one embarrassing incident from the list of experiences you wrote for your journal, and narrate the incident as vividly as you can. Include the details: Where did the event take place? What did people say? How were they dressed? What was the weather like? Follow Nye's model in putting CONCRETE IMAGES to work for an idea, in this case an idea about the significance of the incident to you then and now.

2. Nye and her friend were clearly amused when they discovered their mistake, but entering a private home uninvited — even unintentionally — can have serious consequences. Many states, including Texas, authorize homeowners to use deadly force against intruders regardless of immediate threat to their own safety. Write a serious argumentative essay that addresses the issue of gun rights and self-defense. To what extent should homeowners be allowed to shoot first and ask questions

later in the case of home invasion? What about someone on the street who simply feels threatened? Under what circumstances, if any, should personal freedoms be limited in the name of public safety? (You might want to do some research on what's known as the "castle doctrine" and on "stand your ground" laws to learn more about the issue.) Be sure to include evidence to support your opinion and to ARGUE your position calmly and rationally. You could, if you wish, include ANECDOTES — whether based on Nye's story or other incidents you know of — to help develop your argument.

3. **CRITICAL WRITING** Using your answer to the second Question on Meaning (p. 80) as a starting point, tell Nye's story from the father's or the daughter's point of view. What do you imagine they were talking about when Naomi and Sally walked in? What did they think was happening? Were they amused, or do you suppose they felt annoyed, even frightened? What lessons did they take from the incident? You could take a humorous approach, as Nye does, or you could choose to be more serious.

4. **CONNECTIONS** Write an essay about the humor gained from IRONY, relying on Nye's essay and Amy Tan's "Fish Cheeks" (p. 74). Why is irony often funny? What qualities does self-effacing humor have? Quote and PARAPHRASE from Nye's and Tan's essays for your support.

––––––––––––

Naomi Shihab Nye on Writing

In an interview with Nye for *Pif Magazine*, Rachel Barenblatt asked, "What is your advice to writers, especially young writers who are just starting out?" This was her response:

Number one: Read, Read, and then Read some more. Always Read. Find the voices that speak most to *you*. This is your pleasure and blessing, as well as responsibility!

It is crucial to make one's own writing circle — friends, either close or far, with whom you trade work and discuss it — as a kind of support system, place-of-conversation, and energy. Find those people, even a few, with whom you can share and discuss your works — then do it. Keep the papers flowing among you. Work does not get into the world by itself. We must help it. . . . Let that circle be sustenance.

There is so much goodness happening in the world of writing today. And there is plenty of *room* and appetite for new writers. I think there always was. Don't let anybody tell you otherwise. Attend all the readings you can, and get involved in giving some, if you like to do that. Be part of your own writing community. Often the first step in doing this is simply to let yourself become identified as One Who Cares About Writing!

My motto early on was "Rest and be kind, you don't have to prove anything" — Jack Kerouac's advice about writing — I still think it's true. But working always felt like resting to me.

The Brief Bedford Reader on Writing

Naomi Shihab Nye's advice to beginning writers echoes our own. For more on how reading can make you a better writer, see Chapter 1 on Critical Reading, especially "Reading to Write" on pages 26–28. You can learn about the roles of AUDIENCE and PURPOSE in writing on pages 19–20 and 30–32. And for additional tips on writing freely without trying "to prove anything," see "Drafting," on pages 34–39.

JUNOT DÍAZ

Junot Díaz is a writer well loved for his unique voice and unflinching fiction, which typically involves young Dominicans struggling with obstacles. Born in 1968 in Santo Domingo, Dominican Republic, he immigrated to New Jersey with his family in 1975. As a poor child who had trouble speaking English and who felt like an outsider, Díaz immersed himself in comic books and science fiction and discovered that writing helped him cope with his difficulties. He earned degrees in literature and history from Rutgers University in 1992 and an MFA in creative writing from Cornell University in 1995. Díaz's critically acclaimed work includes the collections of short stories *Drown* (1996) and *This Is How You Lose Her* (2012) and the novel *The Brief Wondrous Life of Oscar Wao* (2007), which centers on the brutalities of Dominican history and an awkward boy's struggles to adapt. Díaz won a National Book Critics Circle Award and a Pulitzer Prize for that novel; he has also been recognized with a PEN/Malamud Award, a Dayton Literary Peace Prize, an O. Henry Prize, and a Guggenheim Fellowship. He received a MacArthur "genius" grant in 2012. A frequent contributor to *The New Yorker* and the fiction editor at the *Boston Review*, Díaz teaches writing at the Massachusetts Institute of Technology.

The Dreamer

In this essay Díaz relates a remarkable episode of his mother's life in the Dominican Republic. In expressing his admiration for her determination to learn, Díaz hints at the myriad ways a young girl's daring has influenced his own life and work. "The Dreamer" first appeared in *More*, a women's magazine, in 2011.

I think of my mother, of course. She's one of those ironwill rarely speak figures that haunt. See her in New Jersey, in the house with the squirrels in the back that she feeds sparingly (they shouldn't get fat) and that she chides when she thinks they're acting up. You wouldn't know it looking at her in that kitchen, but she grew up one of those poor Third World–country girls. The brutalized backbone of our world. The kind of Dominican girl who was destined never to get off the mountain or out of the *campo*.[1] Her own mother a straight-haired terror. Expected her to work on the family farm until she died or was married off, but my mother in those small spaces between the work cultivated dreams, that unbreakable habit of the young. When the field hands were hurt or fell ill, she was the one who cared for them. Opened in her a horizon. A dream of being a nurse in the capital, where she heard that every

1

---

[1] Spanish, "countryside." — Eds.

block had electricity. But to be a nurse, you needed education, and while there were some girls who attended the one-room school at the base of the hill, my mother was not one of them. Her mother, my grandmother, demanded that she stay on the farm, that she stay a mule. No one more threatened by the thought of an educated girl than my grandmother. Any time my mother was caught near the schoolhouse, my grandmother gave her a beating. And not the beatings of the First World but the beatings of the Third — which you do not so easily shake off.

So the months passed and the horizon started to dim, and that's the way it should have stayed, but then the world, so far away, intervened. For his own complicated reasons the dictator of that time, Trujillo,[2] passed a mandatory-education act stipulating that all Dominican children under the age of fifteen had to be in school and not stuck out in the fields. All children. Any parent keeping a child from school would be imprisoned! Nothing short of the threat of a year inside a Trujillo prison could snap the resistance that rural Dominicans had to the idea of educating their young.   2

My mother heard about the law, of course. And she brooded on it. The house, like all other houses in the Dominican Republic, had a portrait of Trujillo hanging in it. I guess my mother figured if anyone was going to protect her from my grandmother's wrath, it was going to be him.   3

She'd only learn later how little our dictator protected her or anyone else.   4

The news of the school came at a crucial time. My mother's family was preparing for its seasonal move up higher into the hills, in the mist-soaked highlands where the coffee was waiting, but my mother had other plans. Two days before the move, she got down on her knees beside a stagnant puddle of water, put her mouth in it and drank deeply.   5

She was so sick that the family decided to head into the hills without her. The coffee could not wait. My mother was left with a cousin, and as soon as my grandmother was out of sight, my mother, bent over double from the stomach pains, hobbled down to the schoolhouse and reported my grandmother.   6

I want to go to school, was what she told the teacher.   7

What should have happened was that the teacher should have laughed and sent her poor ass back to the hills to pick coffee. But as it turned out, the teacher was an idealistic young woman from the capital — God bless all idealistic educators — and she took my mother's claim seriously. Went to the police, who *always* took Trujillo's laws seriously, and so when my grandmother came back to fetch her daughter, she found my mother attending school.   8

[2] General Rafael Trujillo took over rule of the Dominican Republic in a 1930 military coup. His regime was characterized by violent oppression and lasted until he was assassinated in 1961. — Eds.

And when she tried to drag my mother up to the hills, the police put her   9
in handcuffs, and that was that.

"Your grandmother beat me almost every day," my mother explained, "but   10
I got my education."

She never did become a nurse, my mother. Immigration got in the way   11
of that horizon — once in the United States, my mother never could master
English, no matter how hard she tried, and my God, did she try. But strange
how things work — her son became a reader and a writer, practices she
encouraged as much as possible. I write professionally now, and life is long and
complicated, and who knows how things might have turned out under different circumstances, but I do believe that who I am as an artist, everything that
I've ever written, was possible because a seven-year-old girl up in the hills of
Azua knelt before a puddle, found courage in herself and drank. Every time
I'm in trouble in my art, I try to think of that girl. I think of that thirst, of that
courage. I think of her.

Journal Writing

Díaz writes that his mother was severely beaten by her own mother, and distinguishes
"the beatings of the First World [from] the beatings of the Third — which you do not
so easily shake off" (par. 1). How do you react to this distinction? Why would beatings
in developing countries be especially brutal? Do degrees of abuse matter? Why would
any parent beat a child? And why wouldn't families, neighbors, or authority figures
(such as teachers) step in to stop the abuse? Explore your thoughts on any of these
questions in your journal.

Questions on Meaning

1. Why does Díaz admire his mother as he does? What does her experience represent to him?

2. Does Díaz have a THESIS? In which sentence or sentences does he state the point
   of his story most directly?

3. What would you say is Díaz's PURPOSE in this essay? Is it simply to inform readers
   about his mother's quest for an education, or does he seem to have another purpose in mind?

4. "She'd only learn later how little our dictator protected her or anyone else," Díaz
   writes in paragraph 4. What does he mean? Based on this statement and other
   references to Rafael Trujillo in the essay, what can you INFER about life in the
   Dominican Republic under his dictatorship?

Questions on Writing Strategy

1. Take note of the first and last sentences in "The Dreamer." How are they related, and what is their effect?

2. In telling his mother's story, does Díaz take mostly an objective or a subjective POINT OF VIEW? How effective do you find his choice?

3. This essay originally appeared in a women's magazine. What evidence in the text reveals that Díaz was writing for an AUDIENCE of female readers?

4. **OTHER METHODS** Explain the CAUSE-AND-EFFECT relationships Díaz outlines in his narrative. What actions — and whose — made it possible for his mother to attend school? What impact did her education have on her life? on his?

Questions on Language

1. Be sure you know how to define the following words: ironwill, chides, cultivated (par. 1); intervened, stipulating (2); brooded (3); stagnant (5).

2. In what sense does Díaz use the word *horizon* (pars. 1, 2, and 11)? What makes this IMAGE particularly appropriate to the story's meaning?

3. The first paragraph of this essay is loaded with sentence fragments, such as "The brutalized backbone of our world." Where else do you find incomplete sentences? What do they contribute to (or take away from) Díaz's VOICE and the effectiveness of his narrative?

4. Díaz quotes his mother twice. Why do you suppose he uses quotation marks around her words in paragraph 10 but not in paragraph 7?

Suggestions for Writing

1. **FROM JOURNAL TO ESSAY** Building on your journal entry, compose an essay that examines one of the causes or effects of child abuse, in the United States or elsewhere. If you have had some experience with abuse (as a counselor, a bystander, a victim, or an abuser) and you care to write about it, you might develop your thesis based on your experience and observation; otherwise, draw on information you have gleaned from the media and your reading, being sure to acknowledge any sources you use.

2. Using Díaz's essay as a model, compose an essay in which you contemplate and explain your sense of identity. How do you define yourself? Has any one person had a significant effect on who you are? How so?

3. **CRITICAL WRITING** Write an essay in which you ANALYZE Díaz's use of language in this essay or a portion of it. How would you characterize his DICTION? What are some especially creative uses of language? What overall EFFECT does Díaz create with the language he uses?

4. **CONNECTIONS** In "Live Free and Starve" (p. 340), Chitra Divakaruni also writes about children in desperate circumstances. Write an essay that COMPARES AND

CONTRASTS Díaz's and Divakaruni's attitudes toward child labor. Taken together, what do these two authors seem to believe is the best recourse for a family struggling in poverty? What do they suggest are a parent's responsibilities to children? a community's? a government's? What is each writer saying about the role of education in particular? How do you respond to their ideas?

Junot Díaz on Writing

In a 2009 essay for Oprah Winfrey's O magazine, Díaz tells the story of how, in his mind, he became a writer. It begins with failure. He had drafted seventy-five pages of his second book, then got stuck. "It wasn't that I couldn't write," he explains. "I wrote every day. I actually worked really hard at writing. At my desk by seven a.m., would work a full eight and more. Scribbled at the dinner table, in bed, on the toilet, on the No. 6 train, at Shea Stadium. I did everything I could. But none of it worked. . . . I wrote and I wrote and I wrote, but nothing I produced was worth a damn."

Díaz goes on to say that he kept trying all the same. "Want to talk about stubborn? I kept at it for five straight years. Five damn years. Every day failing for five years? I'm a pretty stubborn, pretty hard-hearted character, but those five years of fail did a number on my psyche. On me. Five years, sixty months? It just about wiped me out." Frustrated and despondent, he considered pursuing another line of work: "I knew I couldn't go on much more the way I was going. I just couldn't. . . . So I put the manuscript away. All the hundreds of failed pages, boxed and hidden in a closet. I think I cried as I did it."

"I slipped into my new morose half-life," Díaz recalls. "Started preparing for my next stage, back to school in September." And then, on a sleepless night, "sickened that I was giving up, but even more frightened by the thought of having to return to the writing," Díaz pulled the pages out of storage. "I figured if I could find one good thing in the pages I would go back to it," he explains. "Spent the whole night reading everything I had written, and guess what? It was still terrible. In fact with the new distance the lameness was even worse than I'd thought. . . . I didn't have the heart to go on. But I guess I did. . . . I separated the seventy-five pages that were worthy from the mountain of loss, sat at my desk, and despite every part of me shrieking no no no no, I jumped back down the rabbit hole again." And after five more years of struggle and regular bouts "of being utterly, dismayingly lost," he finally completed The Brief Wondrous Life of Oscar Wao.

"That," concludes Díaz, is his "tale in a nutshell. Not the tale of how I came to write my novel but rather of how I became a writer. Because, in truth, I didn't become a writer the first time I put pen to paper or when I finished my first book (easy) or my second one (hard). You see, in my view a writer is a writer not because she writes well and easily, because she has amazing talent, because everything she does is golden. In my view a writer is a writer because even when there is no hope, even when nothing you do shows any sign of promise, you keep writing anyway. Wasn't until that night when I was faced with all those lousy pages that I realized, really realized, what it was exactly that I am."

The Brief Bedford Reader on Writing

Díaz seems to have inherited a good streak of his mother's determination and willingness to make personal sacrifices — as indeed he suggests in "The Dreamer." Although you probably can't imagine discarding hundreds of pages of manuscript during REVISION, you can surely empathize with the frustrations of failed writing and the agony of starting over. Have you ever, like Díaz, tossed out most of a DRAFT? How might "one good thing" justify, or even require, starting over? See our suggestions in "Revising," pages 39–42.

SHIRLEY JACKSON

Shirley Jackson was a fiction writer best known for horror stories that probe the dark side of human nature and social behavior. But she also wrote humorously about domestic life, a subject she knew well as a wife and the mother of four children. Born in 1916 in California, Jackson moved as a teenager to upstate New York, and graduated from Syracuse University in 1940. She started writing as a young girl and was highly disciplined and productive all her life. She began publishing stories in 1941, and eventually her fiction appeared in *The New Yorker*, *Harper's*, *Good Housekeeping*, and many other magazines. Her tales of family life appeared in two books, *Life among the Savages* (1953) and *Raising Demons* (1957). Her suspense novels, which were more significant to her, included *The Haunting of Hill House* (1959) and *We Have Always Lived in the Castle* (1962). After Jackson died in 1965, her husband, the literary critic Stanley Edgar Hyman, published two volumes of her stories, novels, and lectures: *The Magic of Shirley Jackson* (1966) and *Come Along with Me* (1968).

The Lottery

By far Jackson's best-known work and indeed one of the best-known short stories ever written, "The Lottery" first appeared in *The New Yorker* in 1948 to loud applause and louder cries of outrage. The time was just after World War II, when Nazi concentration camps and the dropping of atomic bombs had revealed the horrors of organized human cruelty. Jackson's husband, denying that her work purveyed "neurotic fantasies," argued instead that it was fitting "for our distressing world." Is the story still relevant today?

The morning of June 27th was clear and sunny, with the fresh warmth of a full-summer day; the flowers were blossoming profusely and the grass was richly green. The people of the village began to gather in the square, between the post office and the bank, around ten o'clock; in some towns there were so many people that the lottery took two days and had to be started on June 26th, but in this village, where there were only about three hundred people, the whole lottery took less than two hours, so it could begin at ten o'clock in the morning and still be through in time to allow the villagers to get home for noon dinner.

The children assembled first, of course. School was recently over for the summer, and the feeling of liberty sat uneasily on most of them; they tended to gather together quietly for a while before they broke into boisterous play, and their talk was still of the classroom and the teacher, of books and reprimands. Bobby Martin had already stuffed his pockets full of stones, and the other boys soon followed his example, selecting the smoothest and roundest stones; Bobby and Harry Jones and Dickie Delacroix — the villagers pronounced this name "Dellacroy" — eventually made a great pile of stones in one corner of the square and guarded it against the raids of the other boys. The girls stood aside, talking among themselves, looking over their shoulders at the boys, and the very small children rolled in the dust or clung to the hands of their older brothers or sisters.

Soon the men began to gather, surveying their own children, speaking of planting and rain, tractors and taxes. They stood together, away from the pile of stones in the corner, and their jokes were quiet and they smiled rather than laughed. The women, wearing faded house dresses and sweaters, came shortly after their menfolk. They greeted one another and exchanged bits of gossip as they went to join their husbands. Soon the women, standing by their husbands, began to call to their children, and the children came reluctantly, having to be called four or five times. Bobby Martin ducked under his mother's grasping hand and ran, laughing, back to the pile of stones. His father spoke up sharply, and Bobby came quickly and took his place between his father and his oldest brother. 3

The lottery was conducted — as were the square dances, the teenage club, the Halloween program — by Mr. Summers, who had time and energy to devote to civic activities. He was a round-faced, jovial man and he ran the coal business, and people were sorry for him, because he had no children and his wife was a scold. When he arrived in the square, carrying the black wooden box, there was a murmur of conversation among the villagers, and he waved and called, "Little late today, folks." The postmaster, Mr. Graves, followed him, carrying a three-legged stool, and the stool was put in the center of the square and Mr. Summers set the black box down on it. The villagers kept their distance, leaving a space between themselves and the stool, and when Mr. Summers said, "Some of you fellows want to give me a hand?" there was a hesitation before two men, Mr. Martin and his oldest son, Baxter, came forward to hold the box steady on the stool while Mr. Summers stirred up the papers inside it. 4

The original paraphernalia for the lottery had been lost long ago, and the black box now resting on the stool had been put into use even before Old Man Warner, the oldest man in town, was born. Mr. Summers spoke frequently to the villagers about making a new box, but no one liked to upset even as much tradition as was represented by the black box. There was a story that the present box had been made with some pieces of the box that had preceded it, the one that had been constructed when the first people settled down to make a village here. Every year, after the lottery, Mr. Summers began talking again about a new box, but every year the subject was allowed to fade off without 5 anything's being done. The black box grew shabbier each year; by now it was no longer completely black but splintered badly along one side to show the original wood color, and in some places faded or stained.

Mr. Martin and his oldest son, Baxter, held the black box securely on the stool until Mr. Summers had stirred the papers thoroughly with his hand. Because so much of the ritual had been forgotten or discarded, Mr. Summers had been successful in having slips of paper substituted for the chips of wood that had been used for generations. Chips of wood, Mr. Summers had argued, had been all very well when the village was tiny, but now that the population was more than three hundred and likely to keep on growing, it was necessary to use something that would fit more easily into the black box. The night before the lottery, Mr. Summers and Mr. Graves made up the slips of paper and put them in the box, and it was then taken to the safe of Mr. Summers's coal company and locked up until Mr. Summers was ready to take it to the square next morning. The rest of the year, the box was put away, sometimes one place, sometimes another; it had spent one year in Mr. Graves's barn and another year underfoot in the post office, and sometimes it was set on a shelf in the Martin grocery and left there.

There was a great deal of fussing to be done before Mr. Summers declared the lottery open. There were the lists to make up — of heads of families, heads of households in each family, members of each household in each family. There was the proper swearing-in of Mr. Summers by the postmaster, as the official of the lottery; at one time, some people remembered, there had been a recital of some sort, performed by the official of the lottery, a perfunctory, tuneless chant that had been rattled off duly each year; some people believed that the official of the lottery used to stand just so when he said or sang it, others believed that he was supposed to walk among the people, but years and years ago this part of the ritual had been allowed to lapse. There had been, also, a ritual salute, which the official of the lottery had had to use in addressing each person who came up to draw from the box, but this also had changed with time, until now it was felt necessary only for the official to speak to each person approaching. Mr. Summers was very good at all this; in his clean white shirt and blue jeans, with one hand resting carelessly on the black box, he seemed very proper and important as he talked interminably to Mr. Graves and the Martins.

Just as Mr. Summers finally left off talking and turned to the assembled villagers, Mrs. Hutchinson came hurriedly along the path to the square, her sweater thrown over her shoulders, and slid into place in the back of the crowd. "Clean forgot what day it was," she said to Mrs. Delacroix, who stood next to her, and they both laughed softly. "Thought my old man was out back stacking wood," Mrs. Hutchinson went on, "and then I looked out the window and the kids was gone, and then I remembered it was the twenty-seventh and came a-running." She dried her hands on her apron, and Mrs. Delacroix said, "You're in time, though. They're still talking away up there."

Mrs. Hutchinson craned her neck to see through the crowd and found her   9
husband and children standing near the front. She tapped Mrs. Delacroix on the arm as a farewell and began to make her way through the crowd. The people separated good-humoredly to let her through; two or three people said, in voices just loud enough to be heard across the crowd, "Here comes your Missus, Hutchinson," and "Bill, she made it after all." Mrs. Hutchinson reached her husband, and Mr. Summers, who had been waiting, said cheerfully, "Thought we were going to have to get on without you, Tessie." Mrs. Hutchinson said, grinning, "Wouldn't have me leave m'dishes in the sink, now, would you, Joe?" and soft laughter ran through the crowd as the people stirred back into position after Mrs. Hutchinson's arrival.

"Well now," Mr. Summers said soberly, "guess we better get started, get   10
this over with, so's we can go back to work. Anybody ain't here?"

"Dunbar," several people said. "Dunbar, Dunbar."   11

Mr. Summers consulted his list. "Clyde Dunbar," he said. "That's right.   12
He's broke his leg, hasn't he? Who's drawing for him?"

"Me, I guess," a woman said, and Mr. Summers turned to look at her.   13
"Wife draws for her husband," Mr. Summers said. "Don't you have a grown boy to do it for you, Janey?" Although Mr. Summers and everyone else in the village knew the answer perfectly well, it was the business of the official of the lottery to ask such questions formally. Mr. Summers waited with an expression of polite interest while Mrs. Dunbar answered.

"Horace's not but sixteen yet," Mrs. Dunbar said regretfully. "Guess I gotta 14
fill in for the old man this year."

"Right," Mr. Summers said. He made a note on the list he was holding.   15
Then he asked, "Watson boy drawing this year?"

A tall boy in the crowd raised his hand. "Here," he said. "I'm drawing   16
for m'mother and me." He blinked his eyes nervously and ducked his head as several voices in the crowd said things like "Good fellow, Jack," and "Glad to see your mother's got a man to do it."

"Well," Mr. Summers said, "guess that's everyone. Old Man Warner make it?"   17

"Here," a voice said, and Mr. Summers nodded.   18

A sudden hush fell on the crowd as Mr. Summers cleared his throat and   19
looked at the list. "All ready?" he called. "Now, I'll read the names — heads of families first — and the men come up and take a paper out of the box. Keep the paper folded in your hand without looking at it until everyone has had a turn. Everything clear?"

The people had done it so many times that they only half listened to the   20
directions, most of them were quiet, wetting their lips, not looking around.
Then Mr. Summers raised one hand high and said, "Adams." A man disen-
gaged himself from the crowd and came forward. "Hi, Steve," Mr. Summers
said, and Mr. Adams said, "Hi, Joe." They grinned at one another humorlessly
and nervously. Then Mr. Adams reached into the black box and took out a
folded paper. He held it firmly by one corner as he turned and went hastily
back to his place in the crowd, where he stood a little apart from his family,
not looking down at his hand.

"Allen," Mr. Summers said, "Anderson. . . . Bentham."   21

"Seems like there's no time at all between lotteries anymore," Mrs. Delacroix   22
said to Mrs. Graves in the back row. "Seems like we got through with the last one
only last week."

"Time sure goes fast," Mrs. Graves said.   23

"Clark. . . . Delacroix."   24

"There goes my old man," Mrs. Delacroix said. She held her breath while   25
her husband went forward.

"Dunbar," Mr. Summers said, and Mrs. Dunbar went steadily to the box   26
while one of the women said, "Go on, Janey," and another said, "There she goes."

"We're next," Mrs. Graves said. She watched while Mr. Graves came   27
around from the side of the box, greeted Mr. Summers gravely, and selected
a slip of paper from the box. By now, all through the crowd there were men
holding the small folded papers in their large hands, turning them over and
over nervously. Mrs. Dunbar and her two sons stood together, Mrs. Dunbar
holding the slip of paper.

"Harburt. . . . Hutchinson."   28

"Get up there, Bill," Mrs. Hutchinson said, and the people near her   29
laughed.

"Jones."   30

"They do say," Mr. Adams said to Old Man Warner, who stood next to   31
him, "that over in the north village they're talking of giving up the lottery."

Old Man Warner snorted. "Pack of crazy fools," he said. "Listening to the   32
young folks, nothing's good enough for *them*. Next thing you know, they'll be
wanting to go back to living in caves, nobody work anymore, live *that* way
for a while. Used to be a saying about 'Lottery in June, corn be heavy soon.'
First thing you know, we'd all be eating stewed chickweed and acorns. There's
always been a lottery," he added petulantly. "Bad enough to see young Joe
Summers up there joking with everybody."

"Some places have already quit lotteries," Mrs. Adams said.   33

"Nothing but trouble in *that*," Old Man Warner said stoutly. "Pack of   34
young fools."

"Martin." And Bobby Martin watched his father go forward. "Overdyke. . . .   35
Percy."

"I wish they'd hurry," Mrs. Dunbar said to her older son. "I wish they'd hurry."   36

"They're almost through," her son said.   37

"You get ready to run tell Dad," Mrs. Dunbar said.   38

Mr. Summers called his own name and then stepped forward precisely and   39
selected a slip from the box. Then he called, "Warner."

"Seventy-seventh year I been in the lottery," Old Man Warner said as he   40
went through the crowd. "Seventy-seventh time."

"Watson." The tall boy came awkwardly through the crowd. Someone   41
said, "Don't be nervous, Jack," and Mr. Summers said, "Take your time, son."

"Zanini."   42

After that, there was a long pause, a breathless pause, until Mr. Summers,   43
holding his slip of paper in the air, said, "All right, fellows." For a minute,
no one moved, and then all the slips of paper were opened. Suddenly, all the
women began to speak at once, saying, "Who is it?" "Who's got it?" "Is it the
Dunbars?" "Is it the Watsons?" Then the voices began to say, "It's Hutchinson.
It's Bill," "Bill Hutchinson's got it."

"Go tell your father," Mrs. Dunbar said to her older son.   44

People began to look around to see the Hutchinsons. Bill Hutchinson   45
was standing quiet, staring down at the paper in his hand. Suddenly, Tessie
Hutchinson shouted to Mr. Summers, "You didn't give him time enough to
take any paper he wanted. I saw you. It wasn't fair!"

"Be a good sport, Tessie," Mrs. Delacroix called, and Mrs. Graves said,   46
"All of us took the same chance."

"Shut up, Tessie," Bill Hutchinson said.   47

"Well, everyone," Mr. Summers said, "that was done pretty fast, and now   48
we've got to be hurrying a little more to get done in time." He consulted his
next list. "Bill," he said, "you draw for the Hutchinson family. You got any
other households in the Hutchinsons?"

"There's Don and Eva," Mrs. Hutchinson yelled. "Make *them* take their   49
chance!"

"Daughters draw with their husbands' families, Tessie," Mr. Summers said   50
gently. "You know that as well as anyone else."

"It wasn't *fair*," Tessie said.   51

"I guess not, Joe," Bill Hutchinson said regretfully. "My daughter draws with   52
her husband's family, that's only fair. And I've got no other family except the kids."

"Then, as far as drawing for families is concerned, it's you," Mr. Summers   53
said in explanation, "and as far as drawing for households is concerned, that's
you, too. Right?"

"Right," Bill Hutchinson said.   54

"How many kids, Bill?" Mr. Summers asked formally.   55

"Three," Bill Hutchinson said. "There's Bill, Jr., and Nancy, and little   56
Dave. And Tessie and me."

"All right, then," Mr. Summers said. "Harry, you got their tickets back?" 57

Mr. Graves nodded and held up the slips of paper. "Put them in the box,   58
then," Mr. Summers directed. "Take Bill's and put it in."

"I think we ought to start over," Mrs. Hutchinson said, as quietly as she 59
could. "I tell you it wasn't *fair*. You didn't give him time enough to choose.
Everybody saw that."

Mr. Graves had selected the five slips and put them in the box, and he   60
dropped all the papers but those onto the ground, where the breeze caught
them and lifted them off.

"Listen, everybody," Mrs. Hutchinson was saying to the people around   61
her.

"Ready, Bill?" Mr. Summers asked, and Bill Hutchinson, with one quick   62
glance around at his wife and children, nodded.

"Remember," Mr. Summers said, "take the slips and keep them folded   63
until each person has taken one. Harry, you help little Dave." Mr. Graves took
the hand of the little boy, who came willingly with him up to the box. "Take
a paper out of the box, Davy," Mr. Summers said. Davy put his hand into the
box and laughed. "Take just *one* paper," Mr. Summers said. "Harry, you hold
it for him." Mr. Graves took the child's hand and removed the folded paper
from the tight fist and held it while little Dave stood next to him and looked
up at him wonderingly.

"Nancy next," Mr. Summers said. Nancy was twelve, and her school   64
friends breathed heavily as she went forward, switching her skirt, and took
a slip daintily from the box. "Bill, Jr.," Mr. Summers said, and Billy, his face
red and his feet overlarge, nearly knocked the box over as he got a paper out.
"Tessie," Mr. Summers said. She hesitated for a minute, looking around defi-
antly, and then set her lips and went up to the box. She snatched a paper out
and held it behind her.

"Bill," Mr. Summers said, and Bill Hutchinson reached into the box and   65
felt around, bringing his hand out at last with the slip of paper in it.

The crowd was quiet. A girl whispered, "I hope it's not Nancy," and the   66
sound of the whisper reached the edges of the crowd.

"It's not the way it used to be," Old Man Warner said clearly. "People ain't 67
the way they used to be."

"All right," Mr. Summers said. "Open the papers. Harry, you open little   68
Dave's."

Mr. Graves opened the slip of paper and there was a general sigh through   69
the crowd as he held it up and everyone could see that it was blank. Nancy
and Bill, Jr., opened theirs at the same time, and both beamed and laughed,
turning around to the crowd and holding their slips of paper above their heads.

"Tessie," Mr. Summers said. There was a pause, and then Mr. Summers   70
looked at Bill Hutchinson, and Bill unfolded his paper and showed it. It was
blank.

"It's Tessie," Mr. Summers said, and his voice was hushed. "Show us her   71
paper, Bill."

Bill Hutchinson went over to his wife and forced the slip of paper out of   72
her hand. It had a black spot on it, the black spot Mr. Summers had made the
night before with the heavy pencil in the coal-company office. Bill Hutchinson held it up and there was a stir in the crowd.

"All right, folks," Mr. Summers said. "Let's finish quickly."   73

Although the villagers had forgotten the ritual and lost the original black   74
box, they still remembered to use stones. The pile of stones the boys had made
earlier was ready; there were stones on the ground with the blowing scraps of
paper that had come out of the box. Mrs. Delacroix selected a stone so large
she had to pick it up with both hands and turned to Mrs. Dunbar. "Come on,"
she said. "Hurry up."

Mrs. Dunbar had small stones in both hands, and she said, gasping for   75
breath, "I can't run at all. You'll have to go ahead and I'll catch up with you."

The children had stones already, and someone gave little Davy Hutchin-   76
son a few pebbles.

Tessie Hutchinson was in the center of a cleared space by now, and she   77
held her hands out desperately as the villagers moved in on her. "It isn't fair,"
she said. A stone hit her on the side of the head.

Old Man Warner was saying, "Come on, come on, everyone." Steve   78
Adams was in front of the crowd of villagers, with Mrs. Graves beside him.

"It isn't fair, it isn't right," Mrs. Hutchinson screamed and then they were   79
upon her.

Journal Writing

Think about rituals in which you participate, such as those involving holidays, meals,
religious observances, family vacations, sporting events — anything that is repeated
and traditional. List some of these in your journal and write about their significance
to you.

Questions on Meaning

1. The PURPOSE of all fiction might be taken as entertainment or self-expression. Does Jackson have any other purpose in "The Lottery"?
2. When does the reader know what is actually going to occur?
3. Describe this story's community on the basis of what Jackson says of it.
4. What do the villagers' attitudes toward the black box indicate about their feelings toward the lottery?

Questions on Writing Strategy

1. Jackson uses the third PERSON (*he, she, it, they*) to narrate the story, and she does not enter the minds of her characters. Why do you think she keeps this distant POINT OF VIEW?
2. On your first reading of the story, what did you make of the references to rocks in paragraphs 2–3? Do you think they effectively forecast the ending?
3. Jackson has a character introduce a controversial notion in paragraph 31. Why does she do this?
4. **OTHER METHODS** Jackson is exploring — or inviting us to explore — CAUSES AND EFFECTS. Why do the villagers participate in the lottery every year? What does paragraph 32 hint might have been the original reason for it?

Questions on Language

1. Dialog provides much information not stated elsewhere in the story. Give three examples of such information about the community and its interactions.
2. Check a dictionary for definitions of the following words: profusely (par. 1); boisterous, reprimands (2); jovial, scold (4); paraphernalia (5); perfunctory, duly, interminably (7); petulantly (32).
3. In paragraph 64 we read that Mrs. Hutchinson "snatched" the paper out of the box. What does this verb suggest about her attitude?
4. Jackson admits to setting the story in her Vermont village in the present time (that is, 1948). Judging from the names of the villagers, where did these people's ancestors originally come from? What do you make of the names Delacroix and Zanini? What is their significance?
5. Unlike much fiction, "The Lottery" contains few FIGURES OF SPEECH. Why do you think this is?

Suggestions for Writing

1. **FROM JOURNAL TO ESSAY** Choose one of the rituals you wrote about in your journal (p. 97), and compose a narrative about the last time you participated in this ritual. Use DESCRIPTION and dialog to convey the significance of the ritual and your own and other participants' attitudes toward it.

2. In his 1974 book *Obedience to Authority*, the psychologist Stanley Milgram reported and analyzed the results of a study he had conducted that caused a furor among psychologists and the general public. Under orders from white-coated "experimenters," many subjects administered what they believed to be life-threatening electric shocks to other people whom they could hear but not see. In fact, the "victims" were actors and received no shocks, but the subjects thought otherwise and many continued to administer stronger and stronger "shocks" when ordered to do so. Find *Obedience to Authority* in the library and COMPARE AND CONTRAST the circumstances of Milgram's experiment with those of Jackson's lottery. For instance, who or what is the order-giving authority in the lottery? What is the significance of seeing or not seeing one's victim?

3. **CRITICAL WRITING** Jackson has said that a common response she received to "The Lottery" was "What does this story mean?" (She never answered the question.) In an essay, interpret the meaning of the story as *you* understand it. (What does it say, for instance, about conformity, guilt, or good and evil?) You will have to INFER meaning from such features as Jackson's TONE as narrator, the villagers' dialog, and, of course, the events of the story. Your essay should be supported with specific EVIDENCE from the story. (For a sample of another student's interpretation of "The Lottery," see Rachel O'Connor's critical analysis on p. 260.)

4. **CONNECTIONS** Although very different from Jackson's story, Firoozeh Dumas's essay "Sweet, Sour, and Resentful" (p. 233) also focuses on observing a tradition. Taken together, what do these two pieces seem to say about the benefits and the dangers of adhering to tradition? Write an essay in which you explore the pros and cons of maintaining rituals, giving examples from these selections and from your own experience.

ADDITIONAL WRITING TOPICS

Narration

1. Write a narrative with one of the following as your subject. It may be (as your instructor may advise) either a first-PERSON memoir or a story written in the third person, observing the experience of someone else. Decide before you begin what your PURPOSE is and whether you are writing (1) an anecdote, (2) an essay consisting mainly of a single narrative, or (3) an essay that includes more than one story.

   A lesson you learned the hard way
   A trip into unfamiliar territory
   An embarrassing moment that taught you something
   A monumental misunderstanding
   An accident
   An adventure or misadventure
   A friendship
   An unexpected encounter
   A loss that lingers
   A moment of triumph
   A story about a famous person
   A legend from family history
   A conflict or contest
   A fierce storm
   A historical event of significance

2. Tell a true story of your early or recent school days, either humorous or serious, relating a struggle you experienced (or still experience) in school.

3. Write a fictional narrative, set in the past, present, or future, of a ritual that demonstrates something about the people who participate in it. The ritual can be, but need not be, as sinister as Shirley Jackson's lottery; yours could concern bathing, eating, dating, going to school, driving, growing older.

Note: Writing topics combining narration and description appear on page 139.

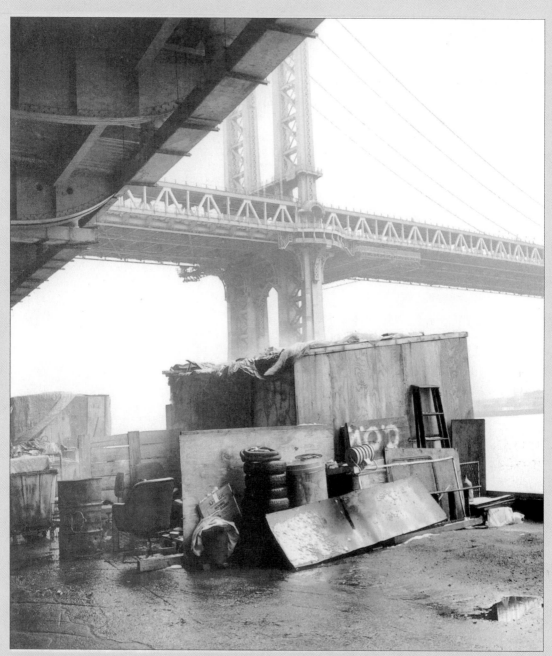

Photograph: Margaret Morton © OmbraLuce LLC

4

DESCRIPTION

Writing with Your Senses

◀ **Description in a photograph**

Margaret Morton photographs homeless communities in New York City. This photograph, titled *Doug and Mizan's House, East River,* depicts a makeshift dwelling on a Manhattan riverbank. Consider Morton's photograph as a work of description — revealing a thing through the perceptions of the senses. What do you see through her eyes? What is the house made of? What do the overhanging structure on the upper left and the bridge behind the house add to the impression of the house? If you were standing in the picture, in front of the house, what might you hear or smell? If you touched the house, what textures might you feel? What main idea do you think Morton wants this photograph to convey?

THE METHOD

Like narration, DESCRIPTION is a familiar method of expression, already a working part of your life. In any chat, you probably do your share of describing. You depict in words someone you've met by describing her clothes, the look on her face, the way she walks. You describe somewhere you've been, something you admire, something you just can't stand. In a message to a friend back home, you describe your college (concrete buildings, crowded walks, pigeons scuttling); or perhaps you describe your brand-new secondhand car, from the glitter of its hubcaps to the odd antiques wedged in its seat cushions. You can hardly go a day without describing (or hearing described) some person, place, or thing. Small wonder, then, that in written discourse description is almost as indispensable as words.

Description reports the testimony of your senses. It invites your readers to imagine that they, too, not only see but perhaps also hear, taste, smell, and touch the subject you describe. Usually, you write a description for either of two PURPOSES:

- **Convey information without bias,** using description that is OBJECTIVE (or *impartial, public,* or *functional*). You describe your subject so clearly and exactly that your reader will understand it or recognize it, and you leave your emotions out. The description in academic writing is usually objective: A biology report on a particular species of frog, for instance, might detail the animal's appearance (four-inch-wide body, bright-orange skin with light-brown spots), its sounds (hoarse clucks), and its feel (smooth, slippery). In writing an objective description your purpose is not to share your feelings. You are trying to make the frog or the subject easily recognized.

- **Convey perceptions with feeling,** using description that is SUBJECTIVE (or *emotional, personal,* or *impressionistic*). This is the kind included in a magazine advertisement for a new car. It's what you write in your message to a friend setting forth what your college is like — whether you are pleased or displeased with it. In this kind of description, you may use biases and personal feelings — in fact, they are essential.

For a splendid example of subjective description, read the following passenger's-eye view of a storm at sea by Charles Dickens. Notice how the writer's words convey the terror of the event:

> Imagine the ship herself, with every pulse and artery of her huge body swollen and bursting . . . sworn to go on or die. Imagine the wind howling, the sea roaring, the rain beating; all in furious array against her. Picture the sky both dark and wild, and the clouds in fearful sympathy with the waves,

making another ocean in the air. Add to all this the clattering on deck and
down below; the tread of hurried feet; the loud hoarse shouts of seamen; the
gurgling in and out of water through the scuppers; with every now and then
the striking of a heavy sea upon the planks above, with the deep, dead, heavy
sound of thunder heard within a vault; and there is the head wind of that
January morning.

Think of what a starkly different description of the very same storm the captain might set down — objectively — in the ship's log: "At 0600 hours, watch
reported a wind from due north of 70 knots. Whitecaps were noticed, in height
two ells above the bow. Below deck water was reported to have entered the
bilge. . . ." But Dickens, not content simply to record information, strives to
ensure that his emotions are clear.

Description is usually found in the company of other methods of writing.
Often, for instance, it will enliven NARRATION and make the people in the
story and the setting unmistakably clear. Writing a PROCESS ANALYSIS in her
essay "Sweet, Sour, and Resentful" (p. 233), Firoozeh Dumas begins with a
description of her family's hometown in Iran. Description will help a writer in
examining the EFFECTS of a storm or in COMPARING AND CONTRASTING two paintings. Keep description in mind when you try expository and argumentative
writing. The method is key to clarity and to readers' interest.

THE PROCESS

Purpose and Audience

Understand, first of all, why you are writing about your subject and thus
what kind of description is called for. Is it appropriate to perceive and report
without emotion or bias — and thus write an objective description? Or is it
appropriate to express your personal feelings as well as your perceptions — and
thus write a subjective description?

Give some thought also to your AUDIENCE. What do your readers need to
be told, if they are to share the perceptions you would have them share? If,
let's say, you are describing a downtown street on a Saturday night for an audience of fellow students who live in the same city, then you need not dwell on
the street's familiar geography. What must you tell? Only those details that
make the place different on a Saturday night. But if you are remembering your
home city, and writing for readers who don't know it, you'll need to establish
a few central landmarks to sketch (in their minds) an unfamiliar street on a
Saturday night.

Before you begin to write a description, go look at your subject. If that is
not possible, your next best course is to spend a few minutes imagining the

subject until, in your mind's eye, you can see every speck of it. Then, having fixed your subject in mind, ask yourself which of its features you'll need to report to your particular audience, for your particular purpose. Ask yourself, "What am I out to accomplish?"

Dominant Impression and Thesis

When you consider your aim in describing, you'll begin to see what impression you intend your subject to make on readers. Let your description, as a whole, convey this one DOMINANT IMPRESSION. If you are writing a subjective description of an old house, laying weight on its spooky atmosphere to make readers shiver, then you might mention its squeaking bats and its shadowy halls. If, however, you are describing the house in a classified ad, for an audience of possible buyers, you might focus instead on its eat-in kitchen, working fireplace, and proximity to public transportation. Details have to be carefully selected. Feel no obligation to include every perceptible detail. To do so would only invite chaos — or perhaps, for the reader, tedium. Pick out the features that matter most.

Your dominant impression is like the THESIS of your description — the main idea about your subject that you want readers to take away with them. When you use description to explain or to argue, it's usually a good strategy to state that dominant impression outright, tying it to your essay's thesis or a part of it. In the biology report on a species of frog, for instance, you might preface your description with a statement like this one:

> A number of unique features distinguish this frog from others in the order Anura.

Or in an argument in favor of cleaning a local toxic-waste site, you might begin with a description of the site and then state your point about it:

> This landscape is as poisonous as it looks, for underneath its barren crust are enough toxic chemicals to sicken an entire village.

When you use subjective description more for its own sake — to show the reader a place or a person, to evoke feelings — you needn't always state your dominant impression as a THESIS STATEMENT, as long as the impression is there dictating the details.

Organization

To help them arrange the details of a description, many writers rely on their POINT OF VIEW — the physical angle from which they're perceiving and describing. As an observer who stays put and observes steadily, you can make a carefully planned inspection tour of your subject, using SPATIAL ORDER (from left to right, from near to far, from top to bottom, from center to periphery), or perhaps moving from prominent objects to tiny ones, from dull to bright, from commonplace to extraordinary — or vice versa.

The plan for you is the one that best fulfills your purpose, arranging details so that the reader receives the exact impression you mean to convey. If you were to describe, for instance, a chapel in the middle of a desert, you might begin with the details of the lonely terrain. Then, as if approaching the chapel with the aid of a zoom lens, you might detail its exterior before going on inside. That might be a workable method *if* you wanted to create the dominant impression of the chapel as an island of beauty in the midst of desolation. Say, however, that you had a different impression in mind: to emphasize the spirituality of the chapel's interior. You might then begin your description inside the structure, perhaps with its most prominent feature, the stained glass windows. You might mention the surrounding desert later in your description, but only incidentally.

Whatever pattern you follow, stick with it all the way through so that your arrangement causes no difficulty for the reader. In describing the chapel, you wouldn't necessarily proceed in the way you explored the structure in person, first noting its isolation, then entering and studying its windows, then going outside again to see what the walls were made of, then moving back inside to look at the artwork. Instead, you would lead the reader around and through (or through and around) the structure in an organized manner. Even if a scene is chaotic, the prose should be orderly.

Details

Luckily, to write a memorable description, you don't need a ferocious storm or any other awe-inspiring subject. As Brad Manning and N. Scott Momaday demonstrate later in this chapter, you can write about your family as effectively as you write about a hurricane. The secret is in the vividness, the evocativeness of the details. Momaday, for instance, uses many IMAGES to call up concrete sensory experiences, including FIGURES OF SPEECH (expressions that do not mean literally what they say). Using *metaphor*, he writes that "the walls have closed in upon my grandmother's house" to express his change in perception when he returns to the house as an adult. And using *simile*, Momaday describes grasshoppers "popping up like corn" to bring a sense of stinging suddenness to life for his readers.

FOCUS ON SPECIFIC AND CONCRETE LANGUAGE

When you write effective description, you'll convey your subject as exactly as possible. You may use figures of speech, as discussed above, and you'll definitely rely on language that is *specific* (tied to actual things) and *concrete* (tied to the senses of sight, hearing, touch, smell, and taste). Such language enables readers to behold with the mind's eye — and to feel with the mind's fingertips.

The first sentence below shows a writer's first-draft attempt to describe something she saw. After editing, the second sentence is much more vivid.

VAGUE   Beautiful, scented wildflowers were in the field.

CONCRETE AND SPECIFIC   Backlighted by the sun and smelling faintly sweet, an acre of tiny lavender flowers spread away from me.

When editing your description, keep a sharp eye out for vague words such as *delicious*, *handsome*, *loud*, and *short* that force readers to create their own impressions or, worse, leave them with no impression at all. Using details that call on readers' sensory experiences, tell why delicious or why handsome, how loud or how short. When stuck for a word, conjure up your subject and see it, hear it, touch it, smell it, taste it.

Note that *concrete* and *specific* do not mean "fancy": Good description does not demand five-dollar words when nickel equivalents are just as informative. The writer who uses *rubiginous* instead of *rusty red* actually says less because fewer readers will understand the less common word and all readers will sense a writer showing off.

CHECKLIST FOR REVISING A DESCRIPTION

✔ **Subjective or objective.** Is the description appropriately subjective (emphasizing feelings) or objective (unemotional) for your purpose?

✔ **Dominant impression.** What is your dominant impression of the subject? If you haven't stated it, will your readers be able to pinpoint it accurately?

✔ **Point of view and organization.** Do your point of view and organization work together to make the subject clear for readers? Are they consistent?

✔ **Details.** Have you provided all of the details — and just those details — needed to convey your dominant impression? What needs expanding? What needs condensing or cutting?

✔ **Specific and concrete language.** Have you used words that express your meaning exactly and appeal to the senses of sight, hearing, touch, taste, and smell?

DESCRIPTION IN ACADEMIC WRITING

An Art History Textbook

Description interprets a familiar painting in the following paragraphs from *Janson's History of Art* by H. W. Janson et al. The details "translate" the painting, creating a bridge between the reader and the text's reproduction of the work.

While working on *The Battle of Anghiari*, Leonardo painted his most famous portrait, the *Mona Lisa*. The delicate *sfumato* already noted in the *Madonna of the Rocks* is here so perfected that it seemed miraculous to the artist's contemporaries. The forms are built from layers of glazes so gossamer-thin that the entire panel seems to glow with a gentle light from within. But the fame of the *Mona Lisa* comes not from this pictorial subtlety alone; even more intriguing is the psychological fascination of the sitter's personality. Why, among all the smiling faces ever painted, has this particular one been singled out as "mysterious"? Perhaps the reason is that, as a portrait, the picture does not fit our expectations. The features are too individual for Leonardo to have simply depicted an ideal type, yet the element of idealization is so strong that it blurs the sitter's character. Once again the artist has brought two opposites into harmonious balance. The smile, too, may be read in two ways: as the echo of a momentary mood, and as a timeless, symbolic expression (somewhat like the "Archaic smile" of the Greeks . . .). Clearly, the *Mona Lisa* embodies a quality of maternal tenderness which was to Leonardo the essence of womanhood. Even the landscape in the background, composed mainly of rocks and water, suggests elemental generative forces.

(Sfumato: soft gradations of light and dark)

Main idea (topic sentence) of the paragraph, supported by description of "pictorial subtlety" (above) and "psychological fascination" (below)

Details (underlined) contribute to dominant impression

A Field Observation

In many of your classes, particularly those in the social sciences, you will be asked to observe people or phenomena in particular settings and to describe what your senses perceive. A systematic observation may produce evidence for an ARGUMENT, as when a writer describes the listlessness of kittens in an animal shelter to encourage support for a spay-and-neuter program. Just as often, however, an observation results in an objective report providing information from which readers draw their own conclusions. Like any description, such a field report emphasizes details and uses concrete language to convey the writer's perceptions. Because the writer's purpose is to inform, the report takes a neutral, third-PERSON (*he, she, they*) point of view, uses unemotional language, and refrains from interpretation or opinion — or withholds such analysis for a separate section near the end.

For an education class in child development, Nick Fiorelli spent a morning in a private preschool, observing the teachers' techniques and the children's behaviors and taking note of how they interacted. The paragraphs below, excerpted from his finished report, "Teaching Methodologies at Child's Play Preschool," describe both the classroom itself and some of the activities Fiorelli witnessed. The full report goes on to outline the educational philosophies and developmental theories that inform the school's approach, with additional examples and descriptions from Fiorelli's visit.

The preschool's Web site explains that it draws on elements of Waldorf, Montessori, Reggio Emillia, and other educational models. This background was evident in the large and colorful classroom, which included separate interest areas for different activities. The room was also open and well lit, with long windows that looked out on a playground and an expansive lawn. The walls of the room were decorated with students' paintings and drawings. Colored rugs, floor tiles, or rubber mats indicated the boundaries of each activity area.

> Background information sets the stage

> Organization moves from the periphery to the center, then around the room's distinct areas

> Dominant impression: structured creativity

At first, the general atmosphere appeared noisy and unstructured, but a sense of order emerged within a few minutes of observation. At a sturdy wooden art table, two students used safety scissors to cut shapes from sheets of red construction paper. Behind them, a child in a red smock stood at a small wooden easel and painted with a foam brush. Another strung multicolored beads on a string. Next to the art table, two children at a sensory station poured wet sand and rocks through an oversize funnel into a miniature sandbox, while a third filled a clear plastic tank with water from a blue enameled pail. A teacher moved between the two tables, encouraging the students and asking questions about their play. In the back of the room, at a literacy area with a thick blue rug and low yellow bookshelves, six students lolled on beanbag chairs, pillows, and a low brown couch, listening to a teacher read a story from an illustrated children's book. She paused on each page to help the children connect the pictures with the story.

> Concrete details contribute to the dominant impression

BRAD MANNING

Brad Manning was born in Little Rock, Arkansas, in 1967 and grew up near Charlottesville, Virginia. While a student at Harvard University he played intramural sports and wrote articles and reviews for the *Harvard Independent*. He graduated in 1990 with a BA in history and religion. Now living in Charlottesville, Manning is a psychiatrist specializing in the treatment of children and adolescents.

Arm Wrestling with My Father

In this essay written for his freshman composition course, Manning explores his physical contact with his father over the years, perceiving gradual changes that are, he realizes, inevitable. For Manning, description provides a way to express his feelings about his father and to comment on relations between sons and fathers. In the essay after Manning's, N. Scott Momaday uses description for similar ends, but his subject is the death of his grandmother.

"Now you say when" is what he always said before an arm-wrestling match. He liked to put the responsibility on me, knowing that he would always control the outcome. "When!" I'd shout, and it would start. And I would tense up, concentrating and straining and trying to push his wrist down to the carpet with all my weight and strength. But Dad would always win; I always had to lose. "Want to try it again?" he would ask, grinning. He would see my downcast eyes, my reddened, sweating face, and sense my intensity. And with squinting eyes he would laugh at me, a high laugh, through his perfect white teeth. Too bitter to smile, I would not answer or look at him, but I would just roll over on my back and frown at the ceiling. I never thought it was funny at all.

That was the way I felt for a number of years during my teens, after I had lost my enjoyment of arm wrestling and before I had given up that same intense desire to beat my father. Ours had always been a physical relationship, I suppose, one determined by athleticism and strength. We never communicated as well in speech or in writing as in a strong hug, battling to make the other gasp for breath. I could never find him at one of my orchestra concerts. But at my lacrosse games, he would be there in the stands, with an angry look, ready to coach me after the game on how I could do better. He never helped me write a paper or a poem. Instead, he would take me outside and show me a new move for my game, in the hope that I would score a couple of goals and gain confidence in my ability. Dad knew almost nothing about lacrosse and his movements were all wrong and sad to watch. But at those times I could just feel how hard he was trying to communicate, to help me, to show the love he had for me, the love I could only assume was there.

His words were physical. The truth is, I have never read a card or a letter written in his hand because he never wrote to me. Never. Mom wrote me all the cards and letters when I was away from home. The closest my father ever came, that I recall, was in a newspaper clipping Mom had sent with a letter. He had gone through and underlined all the important words about the dangers of not wearing a bicycle helmet. Our communication was physical, and that is why we did things like arm wrestle. To get down on the floor and grapple, arm against arm, was like having a conversation. 3

This ritual of father-son competition in fact had started early in my life, back when Dad started the matches with his arm almost horizontal, his wrist an inch from defeat, and still won. I remember in those battles how my tiny shoulders would press over our locked hands, my whole upper body pushing down in hope of winning that single inch from his calm, unmoving forearm. "Say when," he'd repeat, killing my concentration and causing me to squeal, "I did, I did!" And so he'd grin with his eyes fixed on me, not seeming to notice his own arm, which would begin to rise slowly from its starting position. My greatest efforts could not slow it down. As soon as my hopes had disappeared I'd start to cheat and use both hands. But the arm would continue to move steadily along its arc toward the carpet. My brother, if he was watching, would sometimes join in against the arm. He once even wrapped his little legs around our embattled wrists and pulled back with everything he had. But he did not have much and, regardless of the opposition, the man would win. My arm would lie at rest, pressed into the carpet beneath a solid, immovable arm. In that pinned position, I could only giggle, happy to have such a strong father. 4

My feelings have changed, though. I don't giggle anymore, at least not around my father. And I don't feel pressured to compete with him the way I thought necessary for years. Now my father is not really so strong as he used to be and I am getting stronger. This change in strength comes at a time when I am growing faster mentally than at any time before. I am becoming less my father and more myself. And as a result, there is less of a need to be set apart from him and his command. I am no longer a rebel in the household, wanting to stand up against the master with clenched fists and tensing jaws, trying to impress him with my education or my views on religion. I am no longer a challenger, quick to correct his verbal mistakes, determined to beat him whenever possible in physical competition. 5

I am not sure when it was that I began to feel less competitive with my 6
father, but it all became clearer to me one day this past January. I was home
in Virginia for a week between exams, and Dad had stayed home from work
because the house was snowed in deep. It was then that I learned something I
never could have guessed.

I don't recall who suggested arm wrestling that day. We hadn't done it for 7
a long time, for months. But there we were, lying flat on the carpet, face to
face, extending our right arms. Our arms were different. His still resembled
a fat tree branch, one which had leveled my wrist to the ground countless
times before. It was hairy and white with some pink moles scattered about.
It looked strong, to be sure, though not so strong as it had in past years. I
expect that back in his youth it had looked even stronger. In high school he
had played halfback and had been voted "best-built body" of the senior class.
Between college semesters he had worked on road crews and on Louisiana
dredges. I admired him for that. I had begun to row crew in college and that
accounted for some small buildup along the muscle lines, but it did not seem
to be enough. The arm I extended was lanky and featureless. Even so, he
insisted that he would lose the match, that he was certain I'd win. I had to
ignore this, however, because it was something he always said, whether or not
he believed it himself.

Our warm palms came together, much the same way we had shaken 8
hands the day before at the airport. Fingers twisted and wrapped about once
again, testing for a better grip. Elbows slid up and back making their little
indentations on the itchy carpet. My eyes pinched closed in concentration
as I tried to center as much of my thought as possible on the match. Arm
wrestling, I knew, was a competition that depended less on talent and experience than on one's mental control and confidence. I looked up into his eyes
and was ready. He looked back, smiled at me, and said softly (did he sound
nervous?), "You say when."

It was not a long match. I had expected him to be stronger, faster. I was 9
conditioned to lose and would have accepted defeat easily. However, after
some struggle, his arm yielded to my efforts and began to move unsteadily
toward the carpet. I worked against his arm with all the strength I could find.
He was working hard as well, straining, breathing heavily. It seemed that this
time was different, that I was going to win. Then something occurred to me,
something unexpected. I discovered that I was feeling sorry for my father. I
wanted to win but I did not want to see him lose.

It was like the thrill I had once experienced as a young boy at my grand- 10
father's lake house in Louisiana when I hooked my first big fish. There was
that sudden tug that made me leap. The red bobber was sucked down beneath
the surface and I pulled back against it, reeling it in excitedly. But when my

cousin caught sight of the fish and shouted out, "It's a keeper," I realized that I would be happier for the fish if it were let go rather than grilled for dinner. Arm wrestling my father was now like this, like hooking "Big Joe," the old fish that Lake Quachita holds but you can never catch, and when you finally think you've got him, you want to let him go, cut the line, keep the legend alive.

Perhaps at that point I could have given up, letting my father win. But it was so fast and absorbing. How could I have learned so quickly how it would feel to have overpowered the arm that had protected and provided for me all of my life? His arms have always protected me and the family. Whenever I am near him I am unafraid, knowing his arms are ready to catch me and keep me safe, the way they caught my mother one time when she fainted halfway across the room, the way he carried me, full grown, up and down the stairs when I had mononucleosis, the way he once held my feet as I stood on his shoulders to put up a new basketball net. My mother may have had the words or the touch that sustained our family, but his were the arms that protected us. And his were the arms now that I had pushed to the carpet, first the right arm, then the left. ¹¹

I might have preferred him to be always the stronger, the one who carries me. But this wish is impossible now; our roles have begun to switch. I do not know if I will ever physically carry my father as he has carried me, though I fear that someday I may have that responsibility. More than once this year I have hesitated before answering the phone late at night, fearing my mother's voice calling me back to help carry his wood coffin. When I am home with him and he mentions a sharp pain in his chest, I imagine him collapsing onto the floor. And in that second vision I see me rushing to him, lifting him onto my shoulders, and running. ¹²

A week after our match, we parted at the airport. The arm-wrestling match was by that time mostly forgotten. My thoughts were on school. I had been awake most of the night studying for my last exam, and by that morning I was already back into my college-student manner of reserve and detachment. To say goodbye, I kissed and hugged my mother and I prepared to shake my father's hand. A handshake had always seemed easier to handle than a hug. His hugs had always been powerful ones, intended I suppose to give me strength. They made me suck in my breath and struggle for control, and the way he would pound his hand on my back made rumbles in my ears. So I offered a handshake; but he offered a hug. I accepted it, bracing myself for the impact. Once our arms were wrapped around each other, however, I sensed a different message. His embrace was softer, longer than before. I remember how it surprised me and how I gave an embarrassed laugh as if to apologize to anyone watching. ¹³

I got on the airplane and my father and mother were gone. But as the plane lifted my throat was hurting with sadness. I realized then that Dad must ¹⁴

have learned something as well, and what he had said to me in that last hug was that he loved me. Love was a rare expression between us, so I had denied it at first. As the plane turned north, I had a sudden wish to go back to Dad and embrace his arms with all the love I felt for him. I wanted to hold him for a long time and to speak with him silently, telling him how happy I was, telling him all my feelings, in that language we shared.

In his hug, Dad had tried to tell me something he himself had discovered.   15
I hope he tries again. Maybe this spring, when he sees his first crew match, he'll advise me on how to improve my stroke. Maybe he has started doing pushups to rebuild his strength and challenge me to another match — if this were true, I know I would feel less challenged than loved. Or maybe, rather than any of this, he'll just send me a card.

Journal Writing

Manning expresses conflicting feelings about his father. How do you respond to his conflict? When have you felt strongly mixed emotions about a person or an event, such as a relative, friend, breakup, ceremony, move? Write a paragraph or two exploring your feelings.

Questions on Meaning

1. In paragraph 3 Manning says that his father's "words were physical." What does this mean?

2. After his most recent trip home, Manning says, "I realized then that Dad must have learned something as well" (par. 14). What is it that father and son have each learned?

3. Manning says in the last paragraph that he "would feel less challenged than loved" if his father challenged him to a rematch. Does this statement suggest that he did not feel loved earlier? Why, or why not?

4. What do you think is Manning's PURPOSE in this essay? Does he want to express love for his father, or is there something more as well?

Questions on Writing Strategy

1. Why does Manning start his essay with a match that leaves him "too bitter to smile" and then move backward to earlier bouts of arm wrestling?

2. In the last paragraph Manning suggests that his father might work harder at competing with him and pushing him to be competitive, or he might just send his

son a card. Why does Manning present both of these options? Are we supposed to know which will happen?

3. Explain the fishing ANALOGY Manning uses in paragraph 10.

4. **OTHER METHODS** Manning's essay is as much a NARRATIVE as a description: The author gives brief stories, like video clips, to show the dynamic of his relationship with his father. Look at the story in paragraph 4. How does Manning mix elements of both methods to convey his powerlessness?

Questions on Language

1. Manning uses the word *competition* throughout this essay. Why is this a more accurate word than *conflict* to describe Manning's relationship with his father?

2. What is the EFFECT of "the arm" in this sentence from paragraph 4: "But the arm would continue to move steadily along its arc toward the carpet"?

3. In paragraph 9 Manning writes, "I wanted to win but I did not want to see him lose." What does this apparent contradiction mean?

4. If any of these words is unfamiliar, look it up in a dictionary: embattled (par. 4); dredges, crew (7); conditioned (9); mononucleosis (11).

Suggestions for Writing

1. **FROM JOURNAL TO ESSAY** Expand your journal entry (p. 115) into a descriptive essay that brings to life your mixed feelings about a person or an event. Focus less on the circumstances and happenings than on emotions, both positive and negative.

2. Write an essay that describes your relationship with a parent or another close adult. You may want to focus on just one aspect of your relationship, or one especially vivid moment, in order to give yourself the space and time to build many sensory details into your description.

3. Arm wrestling is a highly competitive sport with a long history. Research the sport in the library or on the Internet. Then write a brief essay that traces its history and explains its current standing.

4. **CRITICAL WRITING** In paragraph 12 Manning says that "our roles have begun to switch." Does this seem like an inevitable switch, or one that this father and son have been working to achieve? Use EVIDENCE from Manning's essay to support your answer. Also consider whether Manning and his father would respond the same way to this question.

5. **CONNECTIONS** Like "Arm Wrestling with My Father," the next essay, N. Scott Momaday's "The Way to Rainy Mountain," depicts the lasting influence of a family member. In an essay, COMPARE AND CONTRAST the two essays on this point. What conclusions do the authors draw about aging and maturity? How do they resolve their conflicts with older generations?

Brad Manning on Writing

For this book, Brad Manning offered some valuable concrete advice on writing as a student.

You hear this a lot, but writing takes a long time. For me, this is especially true. The only difference between the "Arm Wrestling" essay and all the other essays I wrote in college (and the only reason it's in this book and not thrown away) is that I rewrote it six or seven times over a period of weeks.

If I have something to write, I need to start early. In college, I had a bad habit of putting off papers until 10 p.m. the night before they were due and spending a desperate night typing whatever ideas the coffee inspired. But putting off papers didn't just lower my writing quality; it robbed me of a good time.

I like starting early because I can jot down notes over a stretch of days; then I type them up fast, ignoring typos; I print the notes with narrow margins, cut them up, and divide them into piles that seem to fit together; then it helps to get away for a day and come back all fresh so I can throw away the corny ideas. Finally, I sit on the floor and make an outline with all the cutouts of paper, trying at the same time to work out some clear purpose for the essay.

When the writing starts, I often get hung up most on trying to "sound" like a good writer. If you're like me and came to college from a shy family that never discussed much over dinner, you might think your best shot is to sound like a famous writer like T. S. Eliot and you might try to sneak in words that aren't really your own like *ephemeral* or *the lilacs smelled like springtime*. But the last thing you really want a reader thinking is how good or bad a writer you are.

Also, in the essay on arm wrestling, I got hung up thinking I had to make my conflict with my father somehow "universal." So in an early draft I wrote in a classical allusion — Aeneas lifting his old father up onto his shoulders and carrying him out of the burning city of Troy.[1] I'd read that story in high school and guessed one classical allusion might make the reader think I knew a lot more. But Aeneas didn't help the essay much, and I'm glad my teacher warned me off trying to universalize. He told me to write just what was true for me.

But that was hard, too, and still is — especially in the first draft. I don't know anyone who enjoys the first draft. If you do, I envy you. But in my early drafts, I always get this sensation like I have to impress somebody and

---

[1] In the *Aeneid*, by the Roman poet Virgil (70–19 BC), the mythic hero Aeneas escapes from the city of Troy when it is sacked by the Greeks and goes on to found Rome. — Eds.

I end up overanalyzing the effects of every word I am about to write. This self-consciousness may be unavoidable (I get self-conscious calling L.L. Bean to order a shirt), but, in this respect, writing is great for shy people because you can edit all you want, all day long, until it finally sounds right. I never feel that I am being myself until the third or fourth draft, and it's only then that it gets personal and starts to be fun.

When I said that putting off papers robbed me of a good time, I really meant it. Writing the essay about my father turned out to be a high point in my life. And on top of having a good time with it, I now have a record of what happened. And my ten-month-old son, when he grows up, can read things about his grandfather and father that he'd probably not have learned any other way.

The Brief Bedford Reader on Writing

Brad Manning has some good advice for other college writers, especially about taking the time to plan (pp. 30–32), organize (p. 37), and revise (pp. 39–42) a draft, often many times over. For guidelines on how to edit your writing as he did, especially to establish and maintain your own VOICE, refer to pages 47–53 of Chapter 2.

N. SCOTT MOMADAY

Navarre Scott Momaday was born in 1934 on the Kiowa Indian Reservation in Oklahoma and grew up there and on other reservations in the Southwest. His father was a Kiowa, his mother a descendant of white pioneers, and their fusion of Native and European American cultures permeates Momaday's work. He has always pursued an academic career, earning a BA in 1958 from the University of New Mexico and a PhD in 1963 from Stanford University, teaching at several universities, and writing on poetry. At the same time he has been one of the country's foremost interpreters of American Indian history, myths, and landscapes. His first novel, *House Made of Dawn* (1968), won the Pulitzer Prize, and he has since published more than fifteen books, including *The Names* (memoir, 1976), *In the Presence of the Sun* (stories and poems, 1992), *In the Bear's House* (poems, essays, and artwork, 1999), and *Again the Far Morning* (poems, 2011). In 2007 he was awarded the National Medal of Arts. Momaday is also a playwright and a painter and is active with the Kiowa Gourd Dance Society. He teaches at the University of Arizona.

The Way to Rainy Mountain

Like the previous essay, Brad Manning's "Arm Wrestling with My Father," this one explores a relationship with family. "The Way to Rainy Mountain" is the introduction to a book of that title, published in 1969, in which Momaday tells Kiowa myths and history and his own story of discovering his heritage. Writing on the occasion of his grandmother's death, Momaday begins and ends this essay in the same place, the Oklahoma plain where the Kiowa tribe was brought down by the US government. In between he visits the sites where the Kiowas had formed the powerful, noble society from which his grandmother sprang.

A single knoll rises out of the plain in Oklahoma, north and west of the [1] Wichita Range.[1] For my people, the Kiowas, it is an old landmark, and they gave it the name Rainy Mountain. The hardest weather in the world is there. Winter brings blizzards, hot tornadic winds arise in the spring, and in summer the prairie is an anvil's edge. The grass turns brittle and brown, and it cracks beneath your feet. There are green belts along the rivers and creeks, linear groves of hickory and pecan, willow and witch hazel. At a distance in July or August the steaming foliage seems almost to writhe in fire. Great green and

---

[1] The Wichita Mountains are southwest of Oklahoma City. — EDS.

yellow grasshoppers are everywhere in the tall grass, popping up like corn to sting the flesh, and tortoises crawl about on the red earth, going nowhere in the plenty of time. Loneliness is an aspect of the land. All things in the plain are isolate; there is no confusion of objects in the eye, but one hill or one tree or one man. To look upon that landscape in the early morning, with the sun at your back, is to lose the sense of proportion. Your imagination comes to life, and this, you think, is where Creation was begun.

I returned to Rainy Mountain in July. My grandmother had died in the spring, and I wanted to be at her grave. She had lived to be very old and at last infirm. Her only living daughter was with her when she died, and I was told that in death her face was that of a child. 2

I like to think of her as a child. When she was born, the Kiowas were living that last great moment of their history. For more than a hundred years they had controlled the open range from the Smoky Hill River to the Red, from the headwaters of the Canadian to the fork of the Arkansas and Cimarron.[2] In alliance with the Comanches, they had ruled the whole of the southern Plains. War was their sacred business, and they were among the finest horsemen the world has ever known. But warfare for the Kiowas was preeminently a matter of disposition rather than of survival, and they never understood the grim, unrelenting advance of the US Cavalry. When at last, divided and ill-provisioned, they were driven onto the Staked Plains in the cold rains of autumn, they fell into panic. In Palo Duro Canyon they abandoned their crucial stores to pillage and had nothing then but their lives. In order to save themselves, they surrendered to the soldiers at Fort Sill and were imprisoned in the old stone corral that now stands as a military museum.[3] My grandmother was spared the humiliation of those high gray walls by eight or ten years, but she must have known from birth the affliction of defeat, the dark brooding of old warriors. 3

Her name was Aho, and she belonged to the last culture to evolve in North America. Her forebears came down from the high country in western Montana nearly three centuries ago. They were a mountain people, a mysterious tribe of hunters whose language has never been positively classified in any major group. In the late seventeenth century they began a long migration to the south and east. It was a journey toward the dawn, and it led to a golden age. Along the way the Kiowas were befriended by the Crows, who gave them the culture and religion of the Plains. They acquired horses, and their ancient nomadic spirit was suddenly free of the ground. They acquired Tai-me, the sacred Sun 4

[2] Momaday describes an area covering much of present-day Kansas and Oklahoma as well as the Texas Panhandle and parts of Colorado and New Mexico. — Eds.

[3] The Palo Duro Canyon is south of Amarillo, Texas, and Fort Sill is southwest of Oklahoma City, near the Wichita Mountains. — Eds.

Dance doll, from that moment the object and symbol of their worship, and so shared in the divinity of the sun. Not least, they acquired the sense of destiny, therefore courage and pride. When they entered upon the southern Plains they had been transformed. No longer were they slaves to the simple necessity of survival; they were a lordly and dangerous society of fighters and thieves, hunters and priests of the sun. According to their origin myth, they entered the world through a hollow log. From one point of view, their migration was the fruit of an old prophecy, for indeed they emerged from a sunless world.

Although my grandmother lived out her long life in the shadow of Rainy   5
Mountain, the immense landscape of the continental interior lay like memory in her blood. She could tell of the Crows, whom she had never seen, and of the Black Hills,[4] where she had never been. I wanted to see in reality what she had seen more perfectly in the mind's eye, and traveled fifteen hundred miles to begin my pilgrimage.

Yellowstone, it seemed to me, was the top of the world, a region of deep   6
lakes and dark timber, canyons and waterfalls. But, beautiful as it is, one might have the sense of confinement there. The skyline in all directions is close at hand, the high wall of the woods and deep cleavages of shade. There is a perfect freedom in the mountains, but it belongs to the eagle and the elk, the badger and the bear. The Kiowas reckoned their stature by the distance they could see, and they were bent and blind in the wilderness.

Descending eastward, the highland meadows are a stairway to the   7
plain. In July the inland slope of the Rockies is luxuriant with flax and buckwheat, stonecrop and larkspur. The earth unfolds and the limit of the land recedes. Clusters of trees, and animals grazing far in the distance, cause the vision to reach away and wonder to build upon the mind. The sun follows a longer course in the day, and the sky is immense beyond all comparison. The great billowing clouds that sail upon it are shadows that move upon the grain like water, dividing light. Farther down, in the land of the Crows and Blackfeet, the plain is yellow. Sweet clover takes hold of the hills and bends upon itself to cover and seal the soil. There the Kiowas paused on their way; they had come to the place where they must change their lives. The sun is at home on the plains. Precisely there does it have the certain character of a god. When the Kiowas came to the land of the Crows, they could see the dark lees of the hills at dawn across the Bighorn River, the profusion of light on the grain shelves, the oldest deity ranging after the solstices. Not yet would they veer southward to the caldron of the land that lay below; they must wean

[4] The Black Hills are in western South Dakota. Yellowstone (next paragraph) is in northwestern Wyoming. In paragraphs 7–8, Momaday describes movement eastward across the top of Wyoming. — Eds.

their blood from the northern winter and hold the mountains a while longer in their view. They bore Tai-me in procession to the east.

A dark mist lay over the Black Hills, and the land was like iron. At the 8 top of a ridge I caught sight of Devil's Tower[5] upthrust against the gray sky as if in the birth of time the core of the earth had broken through its crust and the motion of the world was begun. There are things in nature that engender an awful quiet in the heart of man; Devil's Tower is one of them. Two centuries ago, because they could not do otherwise, the Kiowas made a legend at the base of the rock. My grandmother said:

> Eight children were there at play, seven sisters and their brother. Suddenly the boy was struck dumb; he trembled and began to run upon his hands and feet. His fingers became claws, and his body was covered with fur. Directly there was a bear where the boy had been. The sisters were terrified; they ran, and the bear after them. They came to the stump of a great tree, and the tree spoke to them. It bade them climb upon it, and as they did so it began to rise into the air. The bear came to kill them, but they were just beyond its reach. It reared against the tree and scored the bark all around with its claws. The seven sisters were borne into the sky, and they became the stars of the Big Dipper.

From that moment, and so long as the legend lives, the Kiowas have kinsmen in the night sky. Whatever they were in the mountains, they could be no more. However tenuous their well-being, however much they had suffered and would suffer again, they had found a way out of the wilderness.

My grandmother had a reverence for the sun, a holy regard that now is 9 all but gone out of mankind. There was a wariness in her, and an ancient awe. She was a Christian in her later years, but she had come a long way about, and she never forgot her birthright. As a child she had been to the Sun Dances; she had taken part in those annual rites, and by them she had learned the restoration of her people in the presence of Tai-me. She was about seven when the last Kiowa Sun Dance was held in 1887 on the Washita River above Rainy Mountain Creek.[6] The buffalo were gone. In order to consummate the ancient sacrifice — to impale the head of a buffalo bull upon the medicine tree — a delegation of old men journeyed into Texas, there to beg and barter for an animal from the Goodnight herd. She was ten when the Kiowas came together for the last time as a living Sun Dance culture. They could find no buffalo; they had to hang an old hide from the sacred tree. Before the dance could begin, a company of soldiers rode out from Fort Sill under orders to

---

[5] Devil's Tower is an 865-foot stone outcropping in northeastern Wyoming, now a national monument. — Eds.

[6] The Washita runs halfway between Oklahoma City and the Wichita Mountains. — Eds.

disperse the tribe. Forbidden without cause the essential act of their faith, having seen the wild herds slaughtered and left to rot upon the ground, the Kiowas backed away forever from the medicine tree. That was July 20, 1890, at the great bend of the Washita. My grandmother was there. Without bitterness, and for as long as she lived, she bore a vision of deicide.[7]

Now that I can have her only in memory, I see my grandmother in the   10 several postures that were peculiar to her: standing at the wood stove on a winter morning and turning meat in a great iron skillet; sitting at the south window, bent above her beadwork, and afterwards, when her vision failed, looking down for a long time into the fold of her hands; going out upon a cane, very slowly as she did when the weight of age came upon her; praying. I remember her most often at prayer. She made long, rambling prayers out of suffering and hope, having seen many things. I was never sure that I had the right to hear, so exclusive were they of all mere custom and company. The last time I saw her she prayed standing by the side of her bed at night, naked to the waist, the light of a kerosene lamp moving upon her dark skin. Her long, black hair, always drawn and braided in the day, lay upon her shoulders and against her breasts like a shawl. I do not speak Kiowa, and I never understood her prayers, but there was something inherently sad in the sound, some merest hesitation upon the syllables of sorrow. She began in a high and descending pitch, exhausting her breath to silence; then again and again — and always the same intensity of effort, of something that is, and is not, like urgency in the human voice. Transported so in the dancing light among the shadows of her room, she seemed beyond the reach of time. But that was illusion; I think I knew then that I should not see her again.

Houses are like sentinels in the plain, old keepers of the weather watch.   11 There, in a very little while, wood takes on the appearance of great age. All colors wear soon away in the wind and rain, and then the wood is burned gray and the grain appears and the nails turn red with rust. The windowpanes are black and opaque; you imagine there is nothing within, and indeed there are many ghosts, bones given up to the land. They stand here and there against the sky, and you approach them for a longer time than you expect. They belong in the distance; it is their domain.

Once there was a lot of sound in my grandmother's house, a lot of com-   12 ing and going, feasting and talk. The summers there were full of excitement and reunion. The Kiowas are a summer people; they abide the cold and keep to themselves, but when the season turns and the land becomes warm and vital they cannot hold still; an old love of going returns upon them. The aged visitors who came to my grandmother's house when I was a child were made

[7] The killing of a divine being or beings (from Latin words meaning "god" and "kill"). — Eds.

of lean and leather, and they bore themselves upright. They wore great black hats and bright ample shirts that shook in the wind. They rubbed fat upon their hair and wound their braids with strips of colored cloth. Some of them painted their faces and carried the scars of old and cherished enmities. They were an old council of warlords, come to remind and be reminded of who they were. Their wives and daughters served them well. The women might indulge themselves; gossip was at once the mark and compensation of their servitude. They made loud and elaborate talk among themselves, full of jest and gesture, fright and false alarm. They went abroad in fringed and flowered shawls, bright beadwork and German silver. They were at home in the kitchen, and they prepared meals that were banquets.

There were frequent prayer meetings, and great nocturnal feasts. When I 13 was a child I played with my cousins outside, where the lamp-light fell upon the ground and the singing of the old people rose up around us and carried away into the darkness. There were a lot of good things to eat, a lot of laughter and surprise. And afterwards, when the quiet returned, I lay down with my grandmother and could hear the frogs away by the river and feel the motion of the air.

Now there is a funeral silence in the rooms, the endless wake of some 14 final word. The walls have closed in upon my grandmother's house. When I returned to it in mourning, I saw for the first time in my life how small it was. It was late at night, and there was a white moon, nearly full. I sat for a long time on the stone steps by the kitchen door. From there I could see out across the land; I could see the long row of trees by the creek, the low light upon the rolling plains, and the stars of the Big Dipper. Once I looked at the moon and caught sight of a strange thing. A cricket had perched upon the handrail, only a few inches away from me. My line of vision was such that the creature filled the moon like a fossil. It had gone there, I thought, to live and die, for there, of all places, was its small definition made whole and eternal. A warm wind rose up and purled like the longing within me.

The next morning I awoke at dawn and went out on the dirt road to 15 Rainy Mountain. It was already hot, and the grasshoppers began to fill the air. Still, it was early in the morning, and the birds sang out of the shadows. The long yellow grass on the mountain shone in the bright light, and a scissortail hied above the land. There, where it ought to be, at the end of a long and legendary way, was my grandmother's grave. Here and there on the dark stones were ancestral names. Looking back once, I saw the mountain and came away.

Journal Writing

"The Way to Rainy Mountain" is about Momaday's associations between his grandmother and Rainy Mountain. Think of somebody special to you and a specific place that you associate with this person. Jot down as many details about the person and place as you can.

Questions on Meaning

1. What is the significance of Momaday's statement that the Kiowas "reckoned their stature by the distance they could see" (par. 6)? How does this statement relate to the ultimate fate of the Kiowas?

2. Remembering his grandmother, Momaday writes, "She made long, rambling prayers out of suffering and hope, having seen many things" (par. 10). What is the key point here, and how does the concept of prayer connect with the essay as a whole?

3. What do you think Momaday's main idea is? What thread links all the essay's parts?

4. What seems to be Momaday's PURPOSE in writing this essay? Can we read this as more than a personal story about a visit to his grandmother's grave?

Questions on Writing Strategy

1. Who is Momaday's AUDIENCE? Do you think he is writing for other Kiowa descendants? for non-Indians? for others who have lost an older relative?

2. "Loneliness is an aspect of the land," Momaday writes (par. 1). To what extent do you think this sentence captures the DOMINANT IMPRESSION of the essay? If you perceive a different impression, what is it?

3. How does Momaday organize his essay? (It may help to plot the structure by preparing a rough outline.) How effective do you find this organization, and why?

4. Would you characterize Momaday's description as SUBJECTIVE or OBJECTIVE? What about his use of language suggests one over the other?

5. **OTHER METHODS** Besides description, Momaday relies on mixing other methods, such as NARRATION, EXAMPLE, COMPARISON AND CONTRAST, and CAUSE AND EFFECT. What is the purpose of the comparison in paragraphs 12–14?

Questions on Language

1. If you do not know the meanings of the following words, look them up in a dictionary: anvil (par. 1); infirm (2); preeminently, pillage, affliction (3); nomadic (4); cleavages (6); lees, profusion, deity, caldron (7); engender, tenuous (8); reverence, consummate (9); inherently (10); purled (14); hied (15).

2. Momaday uses many vivid FIGURES OF SPEECH. Locate at least one use each of metaphor, simile, and hyperbole (review these terms in the Glossary if necessary). What does each of these figures convey?

3. Momaday's first and last paragraphs present contrasting IMAGES of Rainy Mountain and the surrounding plain: At first, "the prairie is an anvil's edge" and the "grass turns brittle and brown"; in the end, "the birds sang out of the shadows" and the "long yellow grass on the mountain shone in the bright light." How does this contrast serve Momaday's purpose?

4. Notice Momaday's use of PARALLELISM in describing the visitors to his grandmother's house (par. 12) — for instance, "They wore.... They rubbed.... They made...." What does the parallelism convey about the people being described?

Suggestions for Writing

1. **FROM JOURNAL TO ESSAY** Develop your journal entry (p. 125) into an essay that describes both the person and the place, using concrete and specific details to make the connection between them clear to your readers.

2. Momaday writes about his ancestors and a way of life very different from that of the present. For this assignment you may need to investigate your family's history. Write an essay that describes your ancestors' way of life. (Your ancestors may be as recent as your grandparents or as distant as your research allows.) Who were these people? How did they live? How does that way of life differ from the way you and your family live now? Be specific in your description and comparison, providing concrete details and examples for clarity.

3. One of Momaday's underlying themes in this essay is the difficulties American Indians often face on reservations. Do some research about the conditions of reservation life. Then write an essay in which you report your findings.

4. **CRITICAL WRITING** In an essay, ANALYZE Momaday's attitudes toward the Kiowas as revealed in the language he uses to describe them. Support your THESIS (your central idea about Momaday's attitudes) with specific quotations from the essay.

5. **CONNECTIONS** Both Momaday and Manning write about traditions and the evolution of relationships in their families. Write an essay that contrasts the sense of continuity in Manning's essay with the sense of loss and change in Momaday's. Are there also similarities in the feelings and influences they describe?

DIANE ACKERMAN

Diane Ackerman is a poet and essayist who writes extensively on the natural world. She was born in Waukegan, Illinois, in 1948 and grew up mostly in gritty Allentown, Pennsylvania. She studied English at Penn State (BA, 1970) and, after completing an MFA (1973) and PhD (1978) at Cornell University, took up travel, college teaching, and constant writing. A former staff writer for *The New Yorker*, Ackerman is consistently praised for her detailed scientific observations, expressed with a poet's knack for sensuous language and a child's sense of wonder. She has published several books of poetry, including *The Planets: A Cosmic Pastoral* (1976) and *I Praise My Destroyer* (1998), and more than a dozen works of exuberant nonfiction ranging from memoir to philosophy to anthropology, most notably *A Natural History of the Senses* (1991) and *The Zookeeper's Wife* (2008). Ackerman is also a regular contributor to *Smithsonian*, *National Geographic*, *Parnassus*, and many other magazines and literary journals. She lives in Ithaca, New York, where she is an avid gardener and cyclist.

Black Marble

Ackerman's latest book, *The Human Age: The World Shaped by Us* (2014), offers a refreshingly optimistic take on the causes and implications of our changing environment. Suggesting that the world has entered a new geological era and calling it the *Anthropocene*, or "Human Age," Ackerman insists that "our relationship with nature has changed . . . radically, irreversibly, but by no means all for the bad." In this chapter from the book, she imagines what travelers from outer space might encounter as they approach the Earth — and what we might make of their observations.

As our spaceship enters the roulette wheel of a new solar system, hope starts building its fragile crystals once again. Disappointment has dogged our travels, but we are nomads with restless minds, and this sun resembles our own middle-aged star. Like ours, it rules a tidy jumble of planets looping in atypical orbits, some unfurling a pageant of seasons, others hard-hearted, monotone, and remote. They're a strange assortment for siblings, with many small straggling hangers-on, but we've encountered odder night-fellows, and variety is their lure. One fizzy giant trails dozens of sycophantic moons; another floats inside a white cocoon. We weave between rocky, hard-boiled worlds, swing by a blimp tugging a retinue of jagged moons, dodge the diffuse rubble of asteroids, skirt a hothouse of acid clouds and phantom light. 1

Slowing to a hyperglide, we admire all the dappled colors, mammoth canyons of razor-backed rust, ice-spewing volcanoes, fountains fifty miles high, 2

hydrocarbon lakes, scarlet welts and scourges, drooling oceans of frozen methane, light daggers, magma flows, sulfur rain, and many other intrigues of climate
and geology. Yet there's no sign of living, breathing life forms anywhere. We
are such a lonely species. Maybe this solar system will be the harbor where
we find others like ourselves, curious, questing beings of unknown ardor or
bloom. Life will have whittled them to fit their world, it doesn't matter how.

One more planet to survey, and then it's on to the next port of call.   3

On a small water planet flocked over by clouds, sequins sparkle every-   4
where. Racing toward it with abandon, we give in to its pull, and orbit in step
with nightfall shadowing the world, transfixed by the embroidery of gold and
white lights — from clusters and ribbons to willful circles and grids. *Crafted*
lights, not natural auroras or lightning, but *designed*, and too many, too regular,
too rare to ignore.

In 2003, aboard the Space Station, Don Pettit[1] felt his heart pin-wheel   5
whenever he viewed Earth's cities at night. *If only everyone could see Earth like
this*, he thought, *they'd marvel at how far we've come, and they'd understand what
we share.* A born tinkerer, he used spare parts he found in the Space Station
to photograph the spinning planet with pristine clarity, as if it were sitting
still. When he returned home he stitched the photographs together into a
video montage, an orbital tour of Earth's cities at night, which he posted on
YouTube. His voice-over identifies each glowing spiderweb as we sail toward it
with him, as if we too were peering out of a Space Station window: "Zurich,
Switzerland; Milan, Italy; Madrid, Spain.

"Cities at night are caught in a triangle," he says with awe tugging at his   6
voice, "between culture, geography, and technology. . . . Cities in Europe display a characteristic network of roads that radiate outwards. . . . London, with
a tour down the English coast to Bristol. Cairo, Egypt, with the Nile River
seen as a dark shape running south to north, the Pyramids of Giza are well lit
at night . . . Tel Aviv on the left, Jerusalem on the right . . ."

Glowing gold, green, and yellow, the Middle Eastern cities seem especially   7
lustrous. He points out India's hallmark — village lights dotted over the countryside, softly glowing as through a veil. Then we fly above Manila, where geo-
metrical lights define the waterfront. The dragon-shaped lights of Hong Kong
flutter under us, and the southeast tip of South Korea. In the welling darkness
of the Korea Strait, a band of dazzling white grains is a fleet of fishing boats
shining high-intensity xenon lamps as lures.

---

[1] Don Pettit (born 1955) is an American astronaut, chemical engineer, and NASA
photographer. He worked aboard the International Space Station from November 2002 to
May 2003. — Eds.

"There's Tokyo, Brisbane, the San Francisco Bay, Houston," Pettit notes.   8

We don't intend our cities to be so beautiful from space. They're human-   9
ity's electric fingerprints on the planet, the chrome-yellow energy that flows
through city veins. Dwarfed by the infinite dome of space with its majestic
coliseum of stars, we've created our own constellations on the ground and
named them after our triumphs, enterprises, myths, and leaders. Copenhagen
("Merchants Harbor"), Amsterdam ("A Dam on the Amstel River"), Ottawa
("Traders"), Bogotá ("Planted Fields"), Cotonou ("Mouth of the River of
Death"), Canberra ("Meeting Place"), Fleissenberg ("Castle of Diligence"),
Ouagadougou ("Where People Get Honor and Respect"), Athens (City of
Athena, Greek goddess of wisdom). We play out our lives amid a festival of
lights. The story the lights tell would be unmistakable to any space traveler:
some bold life form has criss-crossed the planet with an exuberance of cities,
favoring settlements along the coast and beside flowing water, and connecting
them all with a labyrinth of brilliantly lit roads, so that even without a map
the outlines of the continents loom and you can spot the meandering rivers.

The silent message of this spectacle is timely, strange, and wonderful.   10
We've tattooed the planet with our doings. Our handiwork is visible everywhere, which NASA has captured with graphic poignancy in *Black Marble*,
its December 7, 2012, portrait of Earth ablaze at night. A companion to the
famous *Blue Marble* photograph of Earth that appeared forty years ago, this
radical new self-portrait promises to awaken and inspire us just as mightily.

On December 7, 1972, the crew of *Apollo 17*, the last manned lunar mis-   11
sion, shot the *Blue Marble* photograph of the whole Earth floating against the
black velvet of space. Africa and Europe were eye-catching under swirling
white clouds, but the predominant color was blue. This was the one picture
from the Apollo missions that dramatically expanded our way of thinking. It
showed us how small the planet is in the vast sprawl of space, how entwined
and spontaneous its habitats are. Despite all the wars and hostilities, when
viewed from space Earth had no national borders, no military zones, no visible
fences. One could see how storm systems swirling above the Amazon might
affect the grain yield half a planet away in China. An Indian Ocean hurricane,
swirling at the top of the photo, had pummeled India with whirlwinds and
floods only two days before. Because it was nearly winter solstice, the white
lantern of Antarctica glowed. The entire atmosphere of the planet — all the
air we breathe, the sky we fly through, even the ozone layer — was visible as
the thinnest rind.

Released during a time of growing environmental concern, it became an   12
emblem of global consciousness, the most widely distributed photo in human
history. It gave us an image to float in the lagoon of the mind's eye. It helped
us embrace something too immense to focus on as a single intricately known

and intricately unknown organism. Now we could see Earth in one eye-gulp, the way we gaze on a loved one. We could paste the image into our *Homo sapiens* family album. Here was a view of every friend, every loved one and acquaintance, every path ever traveled, all together in one place. No wonder it adorned so many college dorm rooms. As the ultimate group portrait, it helped us understand our global kinship and cosmic address. It proclaimed our shared destiny.

NASA's new image of city lights, a panorama of the continents emblazoned with pulsating beacons, startles and transforms our gaze once again. Ours is the only planet in our solar system that glitters at night. Earth is 4.5 billion years old, and for eons the nighttime planet was dark. In a little over two hundred years we've wired up the world and turned on the lights, as if we signed the planet in luminous ink. In another forty years our scrawl won't look the same. There are so many of us who find urban life magnetic that our cities no longer simply sprawl — they've begun to grow exponentially. Millions of us pack up, leave jobs and neighbors behind, and migrate to the city every year, joining nearly two-thirds of all the people on Earth. In the future, more and more clusters will appear, with even wider lattices and curtains of lights connecting them. Many display our curious tastes and habits. A harlequin thread drawn from Moscow to Vladivostok and dipping into China is the Trans-Siberian Railway. A golden streak through a profound darkness, the Nile River pours between the Aswan Dam and the Mediterranean Sea. A trellis connecting bright dots is the US interstate highway system. The whole continent of Antarctica is still invisible at night. The vast deserts of Mongolia, Africa, Arabia, Australia, and the United States look almost as dark. So, too, teeming jungles in Africa and South America, the colossal arc of the Himalayas, and the rich northern forests of Canada and Russia. But shopping centers and seaports sizzle with light, as if they're frying electrons. The single brightest spot on the entire planet isn't Jerusalem or the Pyramids of Giza, though those do sparkle, but a more secular temple of neon, the Las Vegas Strip.

Newer settlements in the American West tend to be boxy, with streets that bolt north-south and east-west, before trickling into darkness at the fringes of town. In big cities like Tokyo, the crooked, meandering lines of the oldest neighborhoods glow mantis-green from mercury vapor streetlights, while the newer streets wrapped around them shine orange from modern sodium vapor lamps.

Our shimmering cities tell all (including us) that Earth's inhabitants are thinkers, builders and rearrangers who like to bunch together in hivelike settlements, and for some reason — bad night vision, primal fear, sheer vanity, to scare predators, or as a form of group adornment — we bedeck them all with garlands of light.

Journal Writing

Imagine you're an alien visiting Earth for the first time, and that the spaceship has touched down in the neighborhood you currently occupy (or, if you prefer, in a region you have lived in or visited in the past). Look around and describe what you find, absorbing as much as you can and taking nothing for granted. Consider, for instance, the area's physical attributes, any movements you perceive, subtle or overpowering scents, the weather, and any human alterations to the natural surroundings such as roads, buildings, and power lines. Jot down your impressions in your journal.

Questions on Meaning

1. What DOMINANT IMPRESSION does Ackerman create of the Earth as viewed from space at night?

2. What would you say is Ackerman's PURPOSE in this essay? Does she express her purpose in a THESIS STATEMENT, or is it implied?

3. What does Ackerman mean when she says in paragraph 2, "Life will have whittled them to fit their world, it doesn't matter how"? Where in the essay does she return to this notion, and why?

4. In what ways does light serve as a SYMBOL for Ackerman?

Questions on Writing Strategy

1. Reread the first four paragraphs of the essay closely. What sense do you make of Ackerman's introduction? What is the EFFECT of opening the way she does?

2. How does Ackerman organize her description?

3. What does Ackerman seem to ASSUME about the interests and knowledge of her AUDIENCE? To what extent do you fit her assumptions?

4. Ackerman's description is based on viewing online SOURCES. What are they? What strategies does she use to SYNTHESIZE information and ideas from her sources without losing her own voice? How well does she succeed?

5. **OTHER METHODS** Where in the essay does Ackerman use COMPARISON AND CONTRAST to explain her meaning to readers? What does the method contribute to her essay?

Questions on Language

1. Ackerman uses an abundance of FIGURES OF SPEECH in this essay, most notably metaphor, but also simile and personification. Find at least two or three examples of each and comment on their effectiveness.

2. How would you characterize Ackerman's DICTION and TONE? Is her language appropriate given her subject? Why, or why not?

3. Ackerman uses a number of words that may not be familiar to you. Consult a dictionary if you need help defining the following: nomads, atypical, sycophantic, retinue, diffuse (par. 1); hyperglide, hydrocarbon, scourges, magma, ardor (2); transfixed, auroras (4); pristine, orbital (5); lustrous, xenon (7); coliseum, enterprises, exuberance, labyrinth (9); poignancy (10); lunar, entwined, solstice, ozone (11); lagoon, *Homo sapiens* (12); luminous, exponentially, lattices, harlequin, colossal, secular (13); mantis (14); primal (15). From what field(s) of academic study does much of her vocabulary derive?

Suggestions for Writing

1. **FROM JOURNAL TO ESSAY** Working from your journal entry (p. 131), write an essay that describes a particular aspect of your corner of the planet Earth from the perspective of someone experiencing it for the first time. Draw on as many of the five senses as you like, but make your description as lively as possible, letting your feelings influence your selection of details, what you say about them, and the dominant impression you create.

2. Go online and find the *Blue Marble* and *Black Marble* photographs that Ackerman describes so subjectively. Pick one (or both) of the photographs, and in a paragraph or essay of your own, describe it as *objectively* as possible, leaving emotions out of your description and focusing on the observable details.

3. **CRITICAL WRITING** Using your response to the first Question on Language (p. 131) as a starting point, analyze Ackerman's use of sensory IMAGES in "Black Marble." How does the abundant imagery and figurative language help convey her ideas about a changing environment? What else do the images contribute to the essay?

4. **CONNECTIONS** Like Ackerman, *National Geographic*, in "Wild Weather" (p. 330), Randall Munroe, in "Everybody Jump" (p. 352), and Margaret Lundberg, in "Eating Green" (p. 514) address the issue of human impacts on the planet. While Ackerman suggests such impacts might be beneficial, Munroe believes they are negligible, Lundberg asserts that they are damaging, and *National Geographic* implies they are catastrophic. What do you think? Write a brief essay about your view of one aspect of the environment. Do you regard energy consumption, carbon emissions, climate change, overpopulation, or dwindling natural resources as critical problems? Do you believe that governments are taking adequate steps to protect the environment? Do you believe that the actions of individuals can make a difference? Your essay may but need not be an ARGUMENT: That is, you could explain your answer to any of these questions or argue a specific point. Either way, choose a narrow focus and use examples and details to support your ideas, drawing on evidence from any of these selections as appropriate.

SVEN BIRKERTS

Born in Pontiac, Michigan, in 1951 to immigrants from Latvia, Sven Birkerts grew up near Detroit "wrestling," as he once put it, "with the ghosts of another culture." For much of his childhood he heard only Latvian at home and was regularly regaled with stories of a happier life in northern Europe before World War II. Birkerts was a voracious reader in his youth and studied literature at the University of Michigan, earning a bachelor's degree in 1973. He stumbled on his career as a literary critic in the early 1980s while working as a bookstore clerk. On a whim he wrote a review of a novel for his own enjoyment and submitted it to a journal; to his surprise the amateur effort led to regular assignments. Birkerts's essays have been collected in several volumes, starting with *An Artificial Wilderness: Essays on Twentieth-Century Literature* (1987) and including *The Gutenberg Elegies: The Fate of Reading in an Electronic Age* (1994), *The Art of Time in Memoir: Then, Again* (2008), *The Other Walk* (2011), and *Changing the Subject: Art and Attention in the Internet Age* (2015). He has also taught college writing and is a co-author of two literature textbooks. Often praised for his lack of pretention, Birkerts is known for his skill at distilling complex thoughts into simple prose. He lives in Arlington, Massachusetts, a suburb of Boston.

Ladder

Birkerts's book *The Other Walk* (2011) mixes critical analysis and personal reflection and was praised by *Publisher's Weekly* for "the humor and insights conveyed in [its] enchanting and well-crafted essays," such as the one we include here. In "Ladder," Birkerts describes with precision and embarrassment what it felt like to discover a crippling phobia at a most inopportune time.

It was already there when I came around the side of the house. I saw it in 1 that sidelong way you register one thing while looking for another. I was trying to find the man I'd spoken to on the phone, who had hired me for the day, and there he was, cross-legged on the grass, wearing a bright white T-shirt, with a full head of silvery hair, camera hair, though he didn't really look like the kind of older man who would go to all the trouble. But maybe he was, because when he heard me coming and turned full-face I saw he was handsome, lady-killer handsome the way some older men are, and these men are always vain. He was cleaning paintbrushes — they were neatly lined up on a sheet of newspaper — and he didn't get up. He had strong-looking arms, maybe even an old-style tattoo. I was looking, staring, at his face, but not so distracted that I didn't take in the other thing. Off to my right, propped up against the side of the house, going up and up in sections, was the tallest ladder I'd ever seen. I felt a bump in my stomach. I hadn't even really turned yet, or followed the ladder up into the light to see where the ends were propped against the highest gable. I was still making my way across the grass, and the man, I don't remember his name anymore, was squinting up and saluting me, or maybe lifting his arm to block the sun, saying, "Here to do some work?" I nodded and said I was. That was the deal. I'd been living on the edge all winter in our little seaside Maine town, buying dented canned goods at discount and even signing on one day with my girlfriend, Sally, to deliver phone books in nearby Biddeford, the mill town in which every other person was named Pelletier or Thibodeaux — and we were required to check off the right recipient and address. Thibodeaux, Thibodeaux, Thibodeaux . . . We quit after a day. Next I'd put up a sign in our little cracker-box post office offering my odd-job services for a laughably low hourly rate. My logic: who could resist?

And now it was one of the first real spring days and this man had called 2 with a job, and my attention was evenly split between the shock of his sea-soned movie-star looks and my growing awareness of that ladder. Did I already know how it was with me and heights? How could I not? I was in my early twenties and had done enough playing in trees and high places as a kid to have an idea. I'd always been a reluctant climber, though maybe I'd later chalked it off as a fear outgrown — as if a decade of not testing the edge would have made it go away. I don't know. I only know that the man — my boss — walked me over to where the ladder stood flat on its grips and showed me my bucket and brushes and handed me a rag that I tucked into my belt. But just before he did that — this comes back with close-up clarity — he reached his thumb and forefinger into the two corners of his mouth and took out his teeth. Out. The whole apparatus. He pulled it from his mouth and held it up like one of those party jokes that you wind with a key. I looked away — I felt embarrassed — and when I glanced back I must have done a double take. Impossible. His face had completely fallen in on itself — the strong jaw was gone, the mouth was crimped like the top of a string bag. I watched as he bent down and set the teeth on another sheet of newspaper in the grass.

When he straightened up, I was face-to-face with an old man with a thick, 3 groomed head of silver hair. I don't know if he had any idea of the effect he had just achieved. He was standing with me by the ladder, telling me to make sure I got enough paint onto the wood, and I was nodding, agreeing, and already registering — I'm sure of it — that first nervous heaviness in my legs, and that tightness in the chest that starts you drawing deep breaths as if a good deep rush of air will make everything better. And then I was on the ladder, starting, a few rungs up, hauling the bucket with my left hand, the shore in sight, the ground still an easy jump. I had that instinct, or instruction, picked up somewhere, to keep my gaze straight ahead, taking in the lapping shingles row by row, the voice that said, "Don't look, just climb." Which I did, so carefully, every bit of my focus on my legs and hands, and on keeping the line of the vertical steady — no twists or turns, just plant the foot on the rung and pull with my one free arm, the right arm, the other gripping the bucket, which I was to hang on a hook next to where I painted — and I was already telling myself the facts of the matter, that people did this all the time, everywhere; that the ladder was strong, well planted at the base; and that little wobbles would naturally be magnified as sensations, that there was no real danger, and that even if I were to fall — *I would not fall* — it would be nothing more than a bad bump and some embarrassment at this point. So I stepped and pulled and steadied and watched myself in slow blurry sections pass by the frame of the first big window, which I knew was about halfway up.

But here the ordinary sequence stops. This upward progress was not happening in units anymore, never mind the rungs lined up ahead of me. Somewhere between one step and another the time stream balked, then stopped and started backing up. Every movement was suddenly breaking into its parts, the one arm aware of itself lifting, wrapping its fingers around the metal of the next rung, the other hand feeling in its joints the cut of the handle, the weight of the bucket, the weathered shingles mere inches away now gathering into the clearest detail: nail heads, streaks and smears and hardened little droplets of ancient paint, the ribbing of the wood grain visible under the color. "Don't look down, just climb." And I could feel it then, on my skin, up the armholes, the April wind, sweetly cool even in the spots of full sun, which I knew without looking was moving in and out behind the clouds. The moment of the shift. It comes now. I hear myself breathing and realize that I've stopped. I don't remember stopping, but all at once I know that I've been staring and staring at the same few warps and scratches. How long? I don't know. The window below me rattles in the breeze, I hear it. Suddenly I can't help myself: I turn my head just slightly to the left and I look down. Mainly to see if the man, my boss, is still there somewhere, but also because I need to know where I am. I feel a kind of thud as the scene clicks in. Ground, grass. He's not anywhere on the left side. Nor — I've moved my head so carefully, as if that little action could make a difference — on the other. The lawn falls away in either direction, empty. I am halfway up the side of the tallest house I've ever seen, and I'm alone. And that little twist of the neck was like breaking the seal. The calm, the focus, whatever story I was telling myself up here, is gone. I take in the great wide lawn, and over there, tiny as a kit for dolls, the newspaper with its row of tiny brushes lined up, and one corner flipping up in the breeze. That repeating movement makes me feel sick, that and the ground all at once so far away, the wind now pulling at the back of my shirt, and I feel the fingers of my right hand tighten their grasp and my chest and stomach push in harder against the rungs. What have I done? I can't unsee the distance down, or lose

4

the sense of the ladder shrinking away to nothing below me and above me. My hand hurts where I hold the metal, and now my knees go soft, just like that. I have the weight of the bucket in my other hand. For the first time I think, *Let it go, just drop it* — drop it and reach up with that hand, as if maybe with both hands gripping I can make it down. But somehow I can't make myself loosen my hold on the bucket, or do anything. Except close my eyes. Close my eyes and start to count, slowly: *One thousand one, one thousand two* . . . I don't know how high I get, but after enough numbers I feel something in me settle, I say to myself, *OK now*, and as I say that I get my fingers to go loose, and then without ever taking them away from the ladder I slide them, along the rung to the right-hand side, and then down the metal slowly, clutching between thumb and forefinger, until I reach the nearer rung, which I grab, and as I do that I let my left leg loose to find the lower support, and this I find, and lower the other leg, foot, shuddering my torso inch by inch down along the rungs, and again repeating the whole sequence, gaining just the first slight ease as the ground lifts slightly toward me, again, again, until I reach the first rung and take the backward step to earth, almost crazy with reaching it, bending to set the bucket down, letting go my other grip and straightening slowly up . . . and only then becoming aware of the man standing right in back of me. He's arrived from somewhere, and I know he's seen the whole of it, and at the same time I can feel that the fingers of my left hand, free from the clutch and the weight, are shaking. But I have no doubt, no question. Standing there, I notice where the shadows — mine, his — break from the grass against the side of the house, and I say to him without turning around, "I can't go up that high. I didn't know it before." I wait for a moment. When I finally turn and meet his eye, he shrugs, saying basically, *What can you do?* He's wearing a painter's cap now, flecked with white paint, and I see that he has put the teeth back in — and he looks good, not quite Paul Newman,[1] but very handsome. Obviously a lady-killer.

Journal Writing

Using Birkerts's essay as a springboard, consider any irrational fears that you may have. Are you afraid of heights, for instance, or snakes or spiders or tight spaces? Does any one instance involving your phobia stand out in your memory? Write about the experience in your journal.

[1] Paul Newman (1925–2008) was a movie actor famous for striking good looks that seemed to improve as he aged. — Eds.

Questions on Meaning

1. How would you describe the writer's PURPOSE in this essay? What DOMINANT IMPRESSION does Birkerts create?

2. In describing turning his head while high up during his climb, Birkert says, "that little twist of the neck was like breaking the seal" (par. 4)? What do you think he means? What phenomenon does "breaking the seal" ALLUDE to?

3. Why did the author seek out odd jobs like a day of house painting? How do those circumstances hint at the deeper implications of his fear?

4. Why is Birkerts terrified by the ladder? What does it represent to him?

Questions on Writing Strategy

1. What strategy does Birkerts use to connect with his readers? How well does he succeed, in your estimation?

2. What point of view does Birkerts take, and how does he arrange the details of his description?

3. What is the intended effect of the unusually long final paragraph?

4. **OTHER METHODS** Where does Birkerts use COMPARISON AND CONTRAST? What do these passages contribute to the essay?

Questions on Language

1. Consult a dictionary if you are unsure of the meaning of any of the following: sidelong, vain, gable (par. 1); lapping (3); balked (4).

2. In paragraph 1 Birkerts describes his boss as "lady-killer handsome." What does that mean? Where in his essay does Birkerts come back to this idea, and what is the EFFECT of the repetition?

3. Point to a few instances in the essay that make particularly effective use of CONCRETE details and sensory IMAGES to convey Birkerts's feelings.

Suggestions for Writing

1. **FROM JOURNAL TO ESSAY** Write an essay on the experience you explored in your journal, using SUBJECTIVE description to convey the effect a phobia had on you.

2. Have you ever initiated a course of action but then, as events unfolded, lost control of the situation? What happened, and how did you respond? Write a NARRATIVE essay in which you relate your experience.

3. Think of some job you have held, whether something temporary like a day of house painting or more structured work for a regular employer. What was the job? Did you do it because you wanted to, because you needed the income, or for some other reason? How do you feel about working? Write about your work experience,

using PROCESS ANALYSIS to explain the mechanics of the job to a new or future employee. Or, if you wish, use description and narration to convey the effect the experience had on you.

4. **CRITICAL WRITING** In an essay, ANALYZE the image that Birkerts presents of himself. Consider specific examples of his language and TONE, along with what he says about himself and his implied attitude toward traditional measures of masculinity.

5. **CONNECTIONS** Both Sven Birkerts's "Ladder" and the pair of students essays on trigger warnings in Chapter 12 (pp. 426–435) examine how anxiety can interfere with completing an important task. Write an essay that considers the extent to which attitude affects a person's ability to cope with fears and worries, using these three essays and your own experience for examples and EVIDENCE.

ADDITIONAL WRITING TOPICS

Description

1. Try this in-class writing experiment. Describe another person in the room so clearly and unmistakably that when you read your description aloud, your subject will be recognized. (Be OBJECTIVE. No insulting descriptions, please!)

2. Write a paragraph describing one subject from each of the following categories. It will be up to you to make the general subject refer to a particular person, place, or thing. Write at least one paragraph as an objective description and at least one as a SUBJECTIVE description.

PERSON

A friend or roommate
A rap, pop, or country musician
A parent or grandparent
A child you know
A prominent politician
A historical figure

THING

A city or rural bus
A favorite toy or gadget
A painting or photograph
A foggy day
A season of the year
A musical instrument

PLACE

An office
A classroom
A college campus
A peaceful spot
A waiting room
A lake or pond

3. In a brief essay, describe your ideal place — perhaps an apartment or dorm room, a home office, a restaurant, a gym, a store, a garden, a dance club, a theater. With concrete details, try to make the ideal seem actual.

Narration and Description

4. Use a combination of NARRATION and description to develop any one of the following topics, or a topic they suggest for you:

Your first day on the job or at college
A vacation
Returning to an old neighborhood
Getting lost
An encounter with a wild animal
Delivering bad (or good) news

LOW-ENERGY DRINKS

LeLIEVRE

5

EXAMPLE

Pointing to Instances

◀ **Examples in a cartoon**

This cartoon by Glen Le Lievre, first published in *The New Yorker*, uses the method of example in a complex way. Most simply, the drawings propose instances of the general category stated in the title — imaginary "low-energy drinks." At the same time, the humor of the examples comes from their contrast with real caffeine-laced high-energy drinks such as Red Bull, Monster Energy, Xtreme Shock Fruit Punch, and Zippfizz Liquid Shot. Whom are these drinks marketed to? (Consider visiting a grocery store or a gas station minimart to see some samples up close.) Whom does their marketing ignore? How would you express the general idea of Le Lievre's cartoon?

THE METHOD

"There have been many women runners of distinction," a writer begins, and quickly goes on, "among them Joan Benoit Samuelson, Florence Griffith Joyner, Grete Waitz, Uta Pippig, and Marla Runyan."

You have just seen examples at work. An EXAMPLE (from the Latin *exemplum*: "one thing selected from among many") is an instance that reveals a whole type. By selecting an example, a writer shows the nature or character of the group from which it is taken. In a written essay, examples will often serve to illustrate a general statement, or GENERALIZATION. Here, for instance, the writer Linda Wolfe makes a point about the food fetishes of Roman emperors (Domitian and Claudius ruled in the first century AD).

> The emperors used their gastronomical concerns to indicate their contempt of the country and the whole task of governing it. Domitian humiliated his cabinet by forcing them to attend him at his villa to help solve a serious problem. When they arrived he kept them waiting for hours. The problem, it finally appeared, was that the emperor had just purchased a giant fish, too large for any dish he owned, and he needed the learned brains of his ministers to decide whether the fish should be minced or whether a larger pot should be sought. The emperor Claudius one day rode hurriedly to the Senate and demanded they deliberate the importance of a life without pork. Another time he sat in his tribunal ostensibly administering justice but actually allowing the litigants to argue and orate while he grew dreamy, interrupting the discussions only to announce, "Meat pies are wonderful. We shall have them for dinner."

Wolfe might have allowed the opening sentence of her paragraph — the TOPIC SENTENCE — to remain a vague generalization. Instead, she supports it with three examples, each a brief story of an emperor's contemptuous behavior. With these examples, Wolfe not only explains and supports her generalization but also animates it.

The method of giving examples — of illustrating what you're saying with a "for instance" — is not merely helpful to all kinds of writing; it is essential. Writers who bore us, or lose us completely, often have an ample supply of ideas; their trouble is that they never pull their ideas down from the clouds. A dull writer, for instance, might declare, "The emperors used food to humiliate their governments," and then, instead of giving examples, go on, "They also manipulated their families," or something — adding still another large, unillustrated idea. Specific examples are *needed* elements in effective prose. Not only do they make ideas understandable, but they also keep readers from falling asleep.

Example   **143**

THE PROCESS

The Generalization and the Thesis

Examples illustrate a generalization, such as Linda Wolfe's opening statement about the Roman emperors. Any example essay is bound to have such a generalization as its THESIS, expressed in a THESIS STATEMENT. Here are examples from the essays in this chapter:

> That first encounter, and those that followed, signified that a vast, unnerving gulf lay between nighttime pedestrians — particularly women — and me.
> — Brent Staples, "Black Men and Public Space"

> The truth is, I slip in and out of my black consciousness, as if I'm in a racial coma. Sometimes, I'm so deep in my anger, my irritation, my need to stir change, that I can't see anything outside of the lens of race. At other times I feel guilty about my apathy.
> — Issa Rae, "The Struggle"

> I think we love animals as images because we miss them in the flesh, and I think we love them as images because they matter to us spiritually in ways we cannot hope to articulate.
> — Brian Doyle, "A Note on Mascots"

> Sometimes I think we would be better off [in dealing with social problems such as homelessness] if we forgot about the broad strokes and concentrated on the details.
> — Anna Quindlen, "Homeless"

The thesis statement establishes the backbone, the central idea, of an essay developed by example. Then the specifics flesh the idea out for readers, bringing it to life.

The Examples

An essay developed by example will often start with a random observation. That is, you'll see something — a man pilfering a dollar from a child's lemonade stand, a friend copying another friend's homework, a roommate downloading pirated movies — and your observation will suggest a generalization (perhaps a statement about the problem of stealing). But a mere example or two probably won't demonstrate your generalization for readers and thus won't achieve your PURPOSE in writing. For that you'll need a range of instances.

Where do you find more? In anything you know — or care to learn. Start close to home. Seek examples in your own immediate knowledge and experience. Explore your conversations with others, your studies, and the storehouse of information you have gathered from books, newspapers, radio, TV, and the Internet as well as from popular hearsay: proverbs and sayings, popular songs, bits of wisdom you've heard voiced in your family.

Now and again, you may feel an irresistible temptation to make up an example out of thin air. Suppose you have to write about the benefits — any benefits — that rocket science has conferred on society. You might imagine one such benefit: the prospect of one day being able to vacation in outer space and drift about like a soap bubble. That imagined benefit would be all right, but it is obviously a conjecture that you dreamed up. An example from fact or experience is likely to carry more weight. Do a little digging on the Internet or in recent books and magazines. Your reader will feel better informed to be told that science — specifically, the NASA space program — has produced useful inventions. You add:

> Among these are the smoke detector, originally developed as Skylab equipment; the inflatable air bag to protect drivers and pilots, designed to cushion astronauts in splashdowns; a walking chair that enables paraplegics to mount stairs and travel over uneven ground, derived from the moonwalkers' surface buggy; and the technique of cryosurgery, the removal of cancerous tissue by fast freezing.

By using specific examples like these, you render the idea of "benefits to society" more concrete and more definite. Such examples are not mere decoration for your essay; they are necessary if you are to hold your readers' attention and convince them that you are worth listening to.

When giving examples, you'll find other methods useful. Sometimes, as in the paragraph by Linda Wolfe, an example takes the form of a NARRATIVE (Chap. 3): an ANECDOTE or a case history. Sometimes an example embodies a vivid DESCRIPTION of a person, place, or thing (Chap. 4).

Lazy writers think, "Oh well, I can't come up with any example here — I'll just leave it to the reader to find one." The flaw in this ASSUMPTION is that the reader may be as lazy as the writer. As a result, a perfectly good idea may be left suspended in the stratosphere.

FOCUS ON SENTENCE VARIETY

While accumulating and detailing examples during drafting — both essential tasks for a successful essay — you may find yourself writing strings of similar sentences:

Example **145**

Example

UNVARIED   One example of a movie that deals with chronic illness is *Rockingham Place*. Another example is *The Beating Heart*. Another is *Tree of Life*. These three movies treat misunderstood or little-known diseases in a way that increases the viewer's sympathy and understanding. *Rockingham Place* deals with a little boy who suffers from cystic fibrosis. *The Beating Heart* deals with a mother of four who is weakening from multiple sclerosis. *Tree of Life* deals with brothers who are both struggling with muscular dystrophy. All three movies show complex, struggling human beings caught blamelessly in desperate circumstances.

The writer of this paragraph was clearly pushing to add examples and to expand them, but the resulting passage needs editing so that the writer's labor isn't so obvious. In the more readable and interesting revision, the sentences vary in structure, group similar details, and distinguish the specifics from the generalizations:

VARIED   Three movies dealing with disease are *Rockingham Place*, *The Beating Heart*, and *Tree of Life*. In these movies people with little-known or misunderstood diseases become subjects for the viewer's sympathy and understanding. A little boy suffering from cystic fibrosis, a mother weakening from multiple sclerosis, a pair of brothers coping with muscular dystrophy — these complex, struggling human beings are caught blamelessly in desperate circumstances.

As you review your draft, be alert to repetitive sentence structures and look for opportunities to change them: Try coordinating and subordinating ideas, varying the beginnings and endings of sentences, shortening some and lengthening others (see pp. 49–50).

CHECKLIST FOR REVISING AN EXAMPLE ESSAY

✔ **Generalization.** What general statement do your examples illustrate? Will it be clear to readers what ties the examples together?

✔ **Support.** Do you have enough examples to establish your generalization, or will readers be left needing more?

✔ **Specifics.** Are your examples detailed? Does each one capture some aspect of the generalization?

✔ **Relevance.** Do all your examples relate to your generalization? Should any be cut because they go off track?

✔ **Sentence variety.** Have you varied sentence structures for clarity and interest?

EXAMPLES IN ACADEMIC WRITING

An Economics Textbook

The following paragraph from *Microeconomics*, by Lewis C. Solmon, appears amid the author's explanation of how markets work. To dispel what might seem like clouds of theory, the author here brings an abstract principle down to earth with a concrete and detailed example.

> The primary function of the market is to bring together suppliers and demanders so that they can trade with one another. Buyers and sellers do not necessarily have to be in face-to-face contact; they can signal their desires and intentions through various intermediaries. For example, the demand for green beans in California is not expressed directly by the green bean consumers to the green bean growers. People who want green beans buy them at a grocery store; the store orders them from a vegetable wholesaler; the wholesaler buys them from a bean cooperative, whose manager tells local farmers of the size of the current demand for green beans. The demanders of green beans are able to signal their demand schedule to the original suppliers, the farmers who raise the beans, without any personal communication between the two parties.

Generalization to be illustrated

Single extended example

A Job-Application Letter

To obtain the kinds of jobs a college education prepares you for, you'll submit a résumé that presents your previous work experience, your education, and your qualifications for a specific career field. To capture the prospective employer's interest, you'll introduce yourself and your résumé with a cover letter.

Rather than merely repeat or summarize the contents of a résumé, a job-application letter highlights the connections between your background and the employer's need for someone with particular training and skills. Typically brief and tightly focused on the job in question, an application letter aims to persuade the reader to look at the accompanying résumé and then to follow up with an interview.

When college junior Kharron Reid was applying for a summer internship implementing computer networks for businesses, he put together a résumé tailored for a specific opportunity posted at his school's placement office. (See the résumé on p. 298.) His cover letter, opposite, pulls out examples from the résumé to support the statement (in the second-to-last paragraph) that "my education and my hands-on experience with network development have prepared me for the opening you have."

Example   147

137 Chester St., Apt. E
Allston, MA 02134
February 21, 2017

Dolores Jackson
Human Resources Director
E-line Systems
75 Arondale Avenue
Boston, MA 02114

Dear Ms. Jackson:

I am applying for the network development internship in your
information technology department, advertised in the career
services office of Boston University.

| Introduction states purpose of letter |

I have considerable experience in network development from
summer internships at NBS Systems and at Pioneer Networking.
At NBS I planned and laid the physical platforms and configured
the software for seven WANs on Windows Server 2016. At Pioneer, I laid the physical platforms and configured the software
to connect eight workstations into a LAN. Both internships
gave me experience in every stage of network development.

| Generalization about experience |
| Two examples of experience |

In my three years in Boston University's School of Management,
I have concentrated on developing skills in business administration and information systems. I have completed courses in
organizational behavior, computer science (including programming), and networking and data communications. At the same
time, I have become proficient in Unix, Windows 10/8, Windows
Server 2016/2012, and Red Hat Enterprise Linux.

| Generalization about education and skills |
| Two sets of examples about education and skills |

As the enclosed résumé indicates, my education and my hands-
on experience with network development have prepared me for
the opening you have.

| Concluding paragraphs summarize qualifica- tions, refer reader to résumé, and invite a response |

I am available for an interview at your convenience. Please call
me at (617) 555–4009 or e-mail me at kreid@bu.edu.

Sincerely,

Kharron Reid

Kharron Reid

BRENT STAPLES

Brent Staples is a member of the editorial board of the *New York Times*, where he writes on culture, politics, and special education, advocating for children with learning disabilities. Born in 1951 in Chester, Pennsylvania, Staples has a BA in behavioral science from Widener University in Chester and a PhD in psychology from the University of Chicago. Before joining the *New York Times* in 1985, he worked for the *Chicago Sun-Times*, the *Chicago Reader*, *Chicago* magazine, and *Down Beat* magazine. He has also taught psychology and contributed to the *New York Times Magazine*, *New York Woman*, *Ms.*, *Harper's*, and other periodicals.

Black Men and Public Space

"Black Men and Public Space" first appeared in the December 1986 issue of *Harper's* magazine and was then published, in a slightly different version, in Staples's memoir, *Parallel Time: Growing Up in Black and White* (1994). To explain a recurring experience of African American men, Staples relates incidents when he has been "an avid night walker" in the urban landscape. Sometimes his only defense against others' stereotypes is to whistle.

In the essay following this one, "The Struggle," Issa Rae offers a contemporary woman's counterpoint to Staples's perspective.

My first victim was a woman — white, well dressed, probably in her late twenties. I came upon her late one evening on a deserted street in Hyde Park, a relatively affluent neighborhood in an otherwise mean, impoverished section of Chicago. As I swung onto the avenue behind her, there seemed to be a discreet, uninflammatory distance between us. Not so. She cast back a worried glance. To her, the youngish black man — a broad six feet two inches with a beard and billowing hair, both hands shoved into the pockets of a bulky military jacket — seemed menacingly close. After a few more quick glimpses, she picked up her pace and was soon running in earnest. Within seconds she disappeared into a cross street.

That was more than a decade ago. I was twenty-two years old, a graduate student newly arrived at the University of Chicago. It was in the echo of that terrified woman's footfalls that I first began to know the unwieldy inheritance I'd come into — the ability to alter public space in ugly ways. It was clear that she thought herself the quarry of a mugger, a rapist, or worse. Suffering a bout of insomnia, however, I was stalking sleep, not defenseless wayfarers. As a softy who is scarcely able to take a knife to a raw chicken — let alone hold one to a person's throat — I was surprised, embarrassed, and dismayed all at once. Her flight made me feel like an accomplice in tyranny. It also made it clear that I was indistinguishable from the muggers who occasionally seeped into the area from the surrounding ghetto. That first encounter, and those that followed, signified that a vast, unnerving gulf lay between nighttime pedestrians — particularly women — and me. And I soon gathered that being perceived as dangerous is a hazard in itself. I only needed to turn a corner into a dicey situation, or crowd some frightened, armed person in a foyer somewhere, or make an errant move after being pulled over by a policeman. Where fear and weapons meet — and they often do in urban America — there is always the possibility of death.

In that first year, my first away from my hometown, I was to become thor-   3
oughly familiar with the language of fear. At dark, shadowy intersections, I could cross in front of a car stopped at a traffic light and elicit the *thunk, thunk, thunk, thunk* of the driver — black, white, male, or female — hammering down the door locks. On less traveled streets after dark, I grew accustomed to but never comfortable with people crossing to the other side of the street rather than pass me. Then there were the standard unpleasantries with policemen, doormen, bouncers, cabdrivers, and others whose business it is to screen out troublesome individuals *before* there is any nastiness.

I moved to New York nearly two years ago and I have remained an avid   4
night walker. In central Manhattan, the near-constant crowd cover minimizes tense one-on-one street encounters. Elsewhere — in SoHo, for example, where sidewalks are narrow and tightly spaced buildings shut out the sky — things can get very taut indeed.

After dark, on the warrenlike streets of Brooklyn where I live, I often   5
see women who fear the worst from me. They seem to have set their faces on neutral, and with their purse straps strung across their chests bandolier-style, they forge ahead as though bracing themselves against being tackled. I understand, of course, that the danger they perceive is not a hallucination. Women are particularly vulnerable to street violence, and young black males are drastically overrepresented among the perpetrators of that violence. Yet these truths are no solace against the kind of alienation that comes of being ever the suspect, a fearsome entity with whom pedestrians avoid making eye contact.

It is not altogether clear to me how I reached the ripe old age of twenty-   6
two without being conscious of the lethality nighttime pedestrians attributed to me. Perhaps it was because in Chester, Pennsylvania, the small, angry industrial town where I came of age in the 1960s, I was scarcely noticeable

against a backdrop of gang warfare, street knifings, and murders. I grew up one of the good boys, had perhaps a half-dozen fistfights. In retrospect, my shyness of combat has clear sources.

As a boy, I saw countless tough guys locked away; I have since buried several, too. They were babies, really — a teenage cousin, a brother of twenty-two, a childhood friend in his mid-twenties — all gone down in episodes of bravado played out in the streets. I came to doubt the virtues of intimidation early on. I chose, perhaps unconsciously, to remain a shadow — timid, but a survivor. 7

The fearsomeness mistakenly attributed to me in public places often has a perilous flavor. The most frightening of these confusions occurred in the late 1970s and early 1980s, when I worked as a journalist in Chicago. One day, rushing into the office of a magazine I was writing for with a deadline story in hand, I was mistaken for a burglar. The office manager called security and, with an ad hoc posse, pursued me through the labyrinthine halls, nearly to my editor's door. I had no way of proving who I was. I could only move briskly toward the company of someone who knew me. 8

Another time I was on assignment for a local paper and killing time before an interview. I entered a jewelry store on the city's affluent Near North Side. The proprietor excused herself and returned with an enormous red Doberman pinscher straining at the end of a leash. She stood, the dog extended toward me, silent to my questions, her eyes bulging nearly out of her head. I took a cursory look around, nodded, and bade her good night. 9

Relatively speaking, however, I never fared as badly as another black male journalist. He went to nearby Waukegan, Illinois, a couple of summers ago to work on a story about a murderer who was born there. Mistaking the reporter for the killer, police officers hauled him from his car at gunpoint and but for his press credentials would probably have tried to book him. Such episodes are not uncommon. Black men trade tales like this all the time. 10

Over the years, I learned to smother the rage I felt at so often being taken for a criminal. Not to do so would surely have led to madness. I now take precautions to make myself less threatening. I move about with care, particularly late in the evening. I give a wide berth to nervous people on subway platforms during the wee hours, particularly when I have exchanged business clothes for jeans. If I happen to be entering a building behind some people who appear skittish, I may walk by, letting them clear the lobby before I return, so as not to seem to be following them. I have been calm and extremely congenial on those rare occasions when I've been pulled over by the police. 11

And on late-evening constitutionals I employ what has proved to be an excellent tension-reducing measure: I whistle melodies from Beethoven and 12

Vivaldi and the more popular classical composers. Even steely New Yorkers hunching toward nighttime destinations seem to relax, and occasionally they even join in the tune. Virtually everybody seems to sense that a mugger wouldn't be warbling bright, sunny selections from Vivaldi's *Four Seasons*. It is my equivalent of the cowbell that hikers wear when they know they are in bear country.

Journal Writing

Staples explains how he perceives himself altering public space. Write in your journal about a time when you felt as if *you* altered public space — in other words, you changed people's attitudes or behavior just by being in a place or entering a situation. If you haven't had this experience, write about a time when you saw someone else alter public space in this way.

Questions on Meaning

1. What is the PURPOSE of this essay? Do you think Staples believes that he (or other African American men) will cease "to alter public space in ugly ways" (par. 2) in the near future? Does he suggest any long-term solution for "the kind of alienation that comes of being ever the suspect" (5)?

2. In paragraph 5 Staples says he understands that the danger women fear when they see him "is not a hallucination." Do you take this to mean that Staples perceives himself to be dangerous? Explain.

3. Staples says, "I chose, perhaps unconsciously, to remain a shadow — timid, but a survivor" (par. 7). What are the usual CONNOTATIONS of the word *survivor*? Is "timid" one of them? How can you explain this apparent discrepancy?

Questions on Writing Strategy

1. The concept of altering public space is relatively abstract. How does Staples convince you that this phenomenon really takes place?

2. Staples employs a large number of examples in a fairly short essay. How does he avoid having the piece sound like a list? How does he establish COHERENCE among all these examples? (Look, for example, at details and TRANSITIONS.)

3. **OTHER METHODS** Many of Staples's examples are actually ANECDOTES — brief NARRATIVES. The opening paragraph is especially notable. Why is it so effective?

Questions on Language

1. What does the author accomplish by using the word *victim* in the essay's opening line? Is the word used literally? What TONE does it set for the essay?

2. Be sure you know how to define the following words, as used in this essay: affluent, uninflammatory (par. 1); unwieldy, tyranny, pedestrians (2); intimidation (7); congenial (11); constitutionals (12).

3. The word *dicey* (par. 2) comes from British slang. Without looking it up in your dictionary, can you figure out its meaning from the context in which it appears?

Suggestions for Writing

1. **FROM JOURNAL TO ESSAY** Write an essay narrating your experience of either altering public space yourself or being a witness when someone else did so. What changes did you observe in people's behavior? Was your behavior similarly affected? In retrospect, do you think your reactions were justified?

2. Write an essay using examples to show how a trait of your own or of someone you know well always seems to affect people, whether positively or negatively.

3. The ironic term "driving while black" expresses the common perception that African American drivers are more likely than white drivers to be pulled over by police for minor infractions — or no infraction at all. Research and write an essay about the accuracy of this perception in one state or municipality: Is there truth to it? If African Americans have been discriminated against, what, if anything, has been done to address the problem?

4. **CRITICAL WRITING** Consider, more broadly than Staples does, what it means to alter public space. Staples would rather not have the power to do so, but it *is* a power, and it could perhaps be positive in some circumstances (wielded by a street performer, for instance, or the architect of a beautiful new building on campus). Write an essay that expands on Staples's idea and examines the pros and cons of altering public space. Use specific examples as your EVIDENCE.

5. **CONNECTIONS** Like Brent Staples, Issa Rae, in "The Struggle" (p. 155), considers misplaced expectations of African Americans. In an essay, examine the POINTS OF VIEW of these two authors. How does point of view affect each author's selection of details and tone?

Brent Staples on Writing

In comments written especially for this book, Brent Staples talks about the writing of "Black Men and Public Space": "I was only partly aware of how I felt when I began this essay. I knew only that I had this collection of experiences (facts) and that I felt uneasy with them. I sketched out the experiences one by one and strung them together. The bridge to the essay — what I wanted to say, but did not know when I started — sprang into life quite unexpectedly as I sat looking over these experiences. The crucial sentence comes right after the opening anecdote, in which my first 'victim' runs away from me: 'It was in the echo of that terrified woman's footfalls that I first began to know the unwieldy inheritance I'd come into — the ability to alter public space in ugly ways.' 'Aha!' I said. 'This is why I feel bothered and hurt and frustrated when this happens. I don't want people to think I'm stalking them. I want some fresh air. I want to stretch my legs. I want to be as anonymous as any other person out for a walk in the night.'"

A news reporter and editor by training and trade, Staples sees much similarity between the writing of a personal essay like "Black Men and Public Space" and the writing of, say, a murder story for a daily newspaper. "The newspaper murder," he says, "begins with standard newspaper information: the fact that the man was found dead in an alley in such-and-such a section of the city; his name, occupation, and where he lived; that he died of gunshot wounds to such-and-such a part of his body; that arrests were or were not made; that such-and-such a weapon was found at the scene; that the police have established no motive; etc.

"Personal essays take a different tack, but they, too, begin as assemblies of facts. In 'Black Men and Public Space,' I start out with an anecdote that crystallizes the issue I want to discuss — what it is like to be viewed as a criminal all the time. I devise a sentence that serves this purpose and also catches the reader's attention: 'My first victim was a woman — white, well dressed, probably in her late twenties.' The piece gives examples that are meant to illustrate the same point and discusses what those examples mean.

"The newspaper story stacks its details in a specified way, with each piece taking a prescribed place in a prescribed order. The personal essay begins often with a flourish, an anecdote, or the recounting of a crucial experience, then goes off to consider related experiences and their meanings. But both pieces rely on reporting. Both are built of facts. Reporting is the act of finding and analyzing facts.

"A fact can be a state of the world — a date, the color of someone's eyes, the arc of a body that flies through the air after having been struck by a car. A fact can also be a feeling — sorrow, grief, confusion, the sense of being pleased, offended, or frustrated. 'Black Men and Public Space' explores the relationship between two sets of facts: (1) the way people cast worried glances at me and sometimes run away from me on the streets after dark, and (2) the frustration and anger I feel at being made an object of fear as I try to go about my business in the city."

Personal essays and news stories share one other quality as well, Staples thinks: They affect the writer even when the writing is finished. "The discoveries I made in 'Black Men and Public Space' continued long after the essay was published. Writing about the experiences gave me access to a whole range of internal concerns and ideas, much the way a well-reported news story opens the door onto a given neighborhood, situation, or set of issues."

The Brief Bedford Reader on Writing

Staples provides an enlightening illustration of how writing generates ideas, rather than merely recording them. As often happens, he discovered his THESIS by writing about his subject, that is, by working out his examples and finding the connecting threads in the process. And as Staples observes, although personal essays and newspaper stories are different GENRES, both types of writing rely on gathering EVIDENCE first, before starting to draft. For tips on "finding and analyzing facts" for your own writing, see "Developing Ideas" in Chapter 2, pages 36–37.

ISSA RAE

Jo-Issa Rae Diop was born in 1985 and raised in Potomac, Maryland, and Los Angeles, California, with extended stays with family in Senegal (a country in West Africa). Frustrated by the lack of positive roles for black women in television and film, she started producing and acting in her own online programming while a student at Stanford University, adopted the screen name Issa Rae in 2008, and created the award-winning Web series *The Misadventures of Awkward Black Girl* shortly out of college with funding from a Kickstarter campaign. The popular comedy follows a self-deprecating introvert, "J," as she navigates the pitfalls of social interaction; it has captured more than twenty million views and the attention of traditional media outlets including *Elle*, *Forbes*, *Essence*, MSNBC, and HBO. Rae's first book of memoir and essays, also titled *The Misadventures of Awkward Black Girl*, was published in 2015. She lives in Los Angeles.

The Struggle

In this selection from her book, Rae tackles the fraught subject of race with characteristically acerbic wit. While Brent Staples in the previous essay expresses embarrassment at strangers' reactions to his skin color, Rae has a different problem with stereotypes: Her peers don't think she's "black enough."

I don't remember the exact day I demilitarized from my blackness. It's all 1
a blur and since I'm fairly certain that militants never forget, and I forget stuff *all* the time, I guess I wasn't meant to be one.

I love being black; that's not a problem. The problem is that I don't 2
want to always *talk* about it because honestly, talking about being "black" is extremely tiring. I don't know how Al Sharpton and Jesse Jackson do it. I know why Cornel West and Tavis Smiley do it.[1] They *love* the attention and the groupies. But the rest of these people who talk, think, and breathe race every single day — how? Just how? Aren't they exhausted?

The pressure to contribute to these conversations now that we have a 3
black president is even more infuriating.

"What do you think about what's going on in the world? And how our 4
black president is handling it?" asks a race baiter.

"It's all good, I guess," I want to answer, apathetically, with a Kanye shrug. 5
"I'm over it." But am I really? Could I be even if I wanted to?

---

[1] The Reverend Jesse Jackson (1941–) and Baptist minister Al Sharpton (1954–) are prominent civil rights activists; Dr. Cornel West (1953–) is a public intellectual and college professor; Tavis Smiley (1964–) is a talk show host. — Eds.

Even now, I feel obligated to write about race. It's as though it's expected 6
of me to acknowledge what we all already know. The truth is, I slip in and out
of my black consciousness, as if I'm in a racial coma. Sometimes, I'm so deep
in my anger, my irritation, my need to stir change, that I can't see anything
outside of the lens of race.

At other times I feel guilty about my apathy. But then I think, *isn't this* 7
what those who came before me fought for? The right *not* to have to deal with
race? If faced with a choice between fighting until the death for freedom and
civil rights and living life without any acknowledgment of race, they'd choose
the latter.

Growing up as a young black girl in Potomac, Maryland, was easy. I never 8
really had to put much thought into my race, and neither did anybody else.
I had a Rainbow Coalition of friends of all ethnicities, and we would carelessly skip around our elementary school like the powerless version of Captain
Planet's Planeteers. I knew I was black. I knew there was a history that accompanied my skin color and my parents taught me to be proud of it. End of story.

All that changed when my family moved to Los Angeles and placed me 9
in a middle school where my blackness was constantly questioned — and
not even necessarily in the traditional sense, i.e., "You talk white, Oreo girl"
or "You can't dance, white girl." Those claims were arguable, for the most
part. My biggest frustration in the challenge to prove my "blackness" usually
stemmed from two very annoying, very repetitive situations.

SITUATION #1: "I'm not even black, and I'm blacker than you." It's one 10
thing when other African Americans try to call me out on my race card, but
when people outside my ethnicity have the audacity to question how "down" I
am because of the bleak, stereotypical picture pop culture has painted of black
women, it's a whole other thing. Unacceptable. I can recall a time when I was
having a heated discussion with a white, male classmate of mine. Our eighth-
grade class was on a museum field trip as the bus driver blasted Puff Daddy's
"Been around the World" to drown us out.

It began as a passive competition of lyrics, as we each silently listened for 11
who would mess up first. By the second verse, our lazy rap-whispers escalated
to an aggressive volume, accompanied by rigorous side-eyes by the time we
got to, "Playa please, I'm the macaroni with the cheese," and I felt threatened.
Was this fool seriously trying to outrap me? And why did I care? After the
song ended, he offered his opinion: "Puff Daddy is wack, yo." How dare he?
Not only was I angry, but I felt as if he had insulted my own father (who did I
think I was? Puff Daughter?).

"Puff Daddy is tight," I retorted. He rolled his eyes and said, "Have you 12
heard of [insert Underground rapper]? Now, *he's* dope." I hadn't heard of him,
but I couldn't let this white boy defeat me in rap music knowledge, especially

as others started to listen. "Yeah, I know him. He's not dope," I lied, for the sake of saving face. Perhaps because he saw through me or because he actually felt strongly about this particular artist, he asked me to name which songs I thought were "not dope." Panic set in as I found myself exposed, then — "You don't even know him, huh? Have you even heard of [insert Random Underground rapper]?"

As he continued to rattle off the names of make-believe-sounding MCs, 	13
delighted that he had one-upped me, he managed to make me feel as though my credibility as a black person relied on my knowledge of hip-hop culture. My identity had been reduced to the Bad Boy label clique as this boy seemingly claimed my black card as his own.

Of course, as I grew older and Ma$e found his calling as a reverend, I real- 	14
ized there was more to being black than a knowledge of rap music, and that I didn't have to live up to this pop cultural archetype. I began to take pride in the fact that I couldn't be reduced to a stereotype and that I didn't have to be. This leads me to my next situation.

SITUATION #2: "Black people don't do that." Or so I'm told by a black 	15
person. These, too, are derived from (mostly negative) stereotypes shaped by popular culture. The difference is that in these situations, we black people are the ones buying into these stereotypes.

When I was a teenager, for example, others questioned my blackness 	16
because some of the life choices I made weren't considered to be "black" choices: joining the swim team when it is a known fact that "black people don't swim," or choosing to become a vegetarian when blacks clearly love chicken. These choices and the various positive and negative responses to them helped to broaden my own perspective on blackness and, eventually, caused me to spurn these self-imposed limitations. But not before embarrassing the hell out of myself in a poor attempt to prove I was "down." I'll never forget submitting a school project in "Ebonics" for my seventh-grade English class, just to prove that I could talk *and* write "black." I was trying to prove it to myself just as much as I was to everyone around me.

Even in my early adulthood, post-college, I'd overtip to demonstrate I was 	17
one of the good ones. Only recently have I come to ask, *What am I trying to prove and to whom am I proving it?* Today, I haven't completely rid myself of the feeling that I'm still working through Du Bois's double consciousness.[2]

For the majority of my life I cared too much about how my blackness 	18
was perceived, but *now?* At this very moment? I couldn't care less. Call it

---

[2] In *The Souls of Black Folk* (1903), the sociologist and historian W. E. B. Du Bois famously proposed that African Americans struggle to reconcile the conflict of belonging simultaneously to two cultures in opposition to each other, a mental state he called *double consciousness.* — Eds.

maturation or denial or self-hatred — I give no f%^&s. And it feels great. I've decided to focus only on the positivity of being black, and especially of being a black woman. Am I supposed to feel oppressed? Because I don't. Is racism supposed to hurt me? That's so 1950s. Should I feel marginalized? I prefer to think of myself as belonging to an "exclusive" club.

While experiencing both types of situations — being made to feel not   19 black enough by "down" white people on one hand and not black enough by the blacks in the so-called know on the other — has played a role in shaping a more comfortably black me, in the end, I have to ask: Who is to say what we do and don't do? What we can and can't do? The very definition of "blackness" is as broad as that of "whiteness," yet the media seemingly always tries to find a specific, limited definition. As CNN produces news specials about us, and white and Latino rappers feel culturally dignified in using the N-word, our collective grasp of "blackness" is becoming more and elusive. And that may not be a bad thing.

Journal Writing

Rae shares examples of times when her perception of her "blackness" did not match the expectations of those around her. Think of a defining characteristic you hold for yourself — your race, perhaps, or your gender, your sexual orientation, your nationality, your sports affiliations, your career aspirations, and so forth. Has your sense of who and what you are ever been challenged by others? How, and why? List some such instances in your journal.

Questions on Meaning

1. Rae opens her essay by saying she is tired of discussing race. What, then, would you say was her PURPOSE in writing? Does she have a THESIS?

2. To whom does Rae feel she needs to prove her "blackness"? How do you know?

3. How does Rae characterize society's expectations for black people, especially black women? What does she blame as the source of these stereotypes?

Questions on Writing Strategy

1. "The Struggle" contains one extended example and several brief examples. How does Rae organize them? What is the effect of grouping these "situations" as she does?

2. What ASSUMPTIONS about her readers are evident in Rae's choice of ALLUSIONS, particularly in paragraphs 10–14? Do you need to be familiar with the musicians she mentions to understand her point?

3. **OTHER METHODS**   Rae's essay is in some ways an attempt at DEFINITION. What do her examples of being "not black enough" (par. 19) contribute to that attempt?

Questions on Language

1. Consider Rae's DICTION, especially her use of slang and references to racial slurs such as "Oreo" (par. 9) and "N-word" (19). What is the EFFECT of such language? Where in the essay, if at all, does Rae explain her decision to use it?

2. The words "black" and "blackness" often appear in quotation marks in this essay. Why? What does Rae intend by employing this device?

3. Be sure you know how to define the following words: demilitarized (par. 1); apathetically (5); coalition (8); rigorous (11); archetype (14); Ebonics (16); maturation (18).

Suggestions for Writing

1. **FROM JOURNAL TO ESSAY**   Building on the episodes you recorded in your journal, write about a time or times when others made you think deeply about who you are and how you present yourself to the world. Use Rae's work as a model: Incorporate concrete examples into your essay and try to address the larger social implications of your reflection.

2. Consider an incident from your childhood that has stuck with you. You might choose an embarrassing or frustrating moment, as Rae did in writing about her school-bus rap battle, or a proud or defining event, such as a sports victory or a sudden understanding of a truth. Write a personal reflection, that, like Rae's essay, explains how your understanding of the incident has changed now that you are older.

3. **CRITICAL WRITING**   In an essay, examine Rae's TONE. Is it consistent throughout? Are there passages where she seems self-pitying? mocking? determined? resigned? triumphant? What is the overall tone of the essay? Is it effective? Why?

4. **CONNECTIONS**   COMPARE AND CONTRAST Issa Rae's and Brent Staples's (p. 148) perceptions of "blackness" and of the stereotypes that have been assigned to them. Use specific passages from each essay to support your comparison.

BRIAN DOYLE

Widely admired for his breathless reflections on spirituality, human connection, and the natural world, Brian Doyle defies boundaries of genre and style. Born in 1956 in New York City, he graduated from the University of Notre Dame in 1978, worked for *US Catholic Magazine* and *Boston College Magazine*, and is now the editor of *Portland*, an award-winning quarterly publication for the University of Portland. A frequent contributor to that magazine and to many others, including *The Atlantic Monthly*, *Orion*, *The Sun*, and *Harper's*, Doyle has published two nonfiction books on family and faith, four novels, and multiple collections of short fiction, poetry, and essays, among them *Leaping: Revelations and Epiphanies* (2003), *Grace Notes* (2011), and *So Very Much the Best of Us: Songs of Praise in Prose* (2015) — all consistently lauded for their high quality and Doyle's unique voice. He describes himself as a "shambling shuffling mumbling grumbling muttering muddled maundering meandering male being" with a "deep and abiding love" for his wife, his three children, and basketball.

A Note on Mascots

Whatever he writes, Doyle has a reputation for crafting prose that is unusually poetic; in fact, he calls many of his own works "proems." In this piece from *Children and Other Wild Animals* (2014), he uses examples to ponder the meaning of animals — some of them imaginary or simply odd — standing in as representatives of college sports teams.

The first sports team I remember loving as a child, in the dim dewy days when I was two or three years old and just waking up to things that were not milk and mama and dirt and dogs, was the Fighting Irish of the University of Notre Dame, who were on television every day, it seemed, in our bustling brick Irish Catholic house; and then, inasmuch as I was hatched and coddled near Manhattan, there were Metropolitans and Knickerbockers and Rangers and Islanders; and then, as I shuffled shyly into high school, there were, for the first time, snarling and roaring mammalian mascots, notably the Cougars of my own alma mater, which was plopped in marshlands where I doubt a cougar had been seen for three hundred years; but right about then I started paying attention to how we fetishize animals as symbols for our athletic adventures, and I have become only more attentive since, for I have spent nearly thirty years now working for colleges and universities, and you could earn a degree in zoology just by reading the college sports news, where roar and fly and sprint and lope and canter and gallop and prowl animals from anteater to wasp — among them, interestingly, armadillos, bees, boll weevils, herons, owls, koalas, turtles, moose, penguins, gulls, sea lions, and squirrels, none of which seem especially intimidating or prepossessing, although I know a man in North Carolina who once lost a fistfight with a heron, and certainly many of us have run away from angry bees and moose, and surely there are some among us who could relate stories of furious boll weevils, but perhaps this is not the time, although anyone who *has* a story like that should see me right after class.

There are vast numbers of canids (coyotes, foxes, huskies, salukis, wolves), felids (lions, tigers, panthers, lynx, bobcats), ruminants (bulls, chargers, broncs, broncos, and bronchoes, though no bronchials), mustelids (badgers, wolverine, otters), and denizens of the deep (dolphins, gators, sharks, sailfish, and "seawolves," or orca). There are two colleges which have an aggrieved camel as their mascot. There are schools represented by snakes and tomcats. There is a school whose symbol is a frog and one whose mascot is a large clam and one whose mascot famously is a slug. There is a school whose mascot is the black fly. There are the Fighting Turtles of the College of Insurance in New York. There are schools represented by lemmings and scorpions and spiders. There are the Fighting Stormy Petrels of Oglethorpe University in Georgia. There is a school represented by an animal that has never yet been seen in the Americas, the bearcat of Asia, although perhaps that is meant to be a wolverine, which did once inhabit southern Ohio, and may still live in Cincinnati, which has tough neighborhoods. The most popular mascot appears to be the eagle, especially if you count the fifteen schools represented by golden eagles, which brings us to a round total of eighty-two schools symbolized by a bird Benjamin Franklin considered "a bird of bad moral character, too lazy to fish for himself . . . like those among men who live by sharping & robbing he is generally poor and often very lousy. Besides he is a rank coward . . ." But the two schools that Franklin helped establish are nicknamed the Quakers and the Diplomats, so we can safely ignore Ben on this matter.

And this is not even to delve into the mysterious world of fantastical fauna — blue bears and blue tigers, crimson hawks, trolls, dragons and firebirds, griffins and griffons and gryphons, delta devils and jersey devils (there are a *lot* of devils, which says something interesting), jayhawks and kohawks and duhawks, green eagles and phoenixes, thunderhawks and thunderwolves, the mind reels, and then there is the whole subset of nicknamery that has to do with botany, as evidenced most memorably by the Fighting Violets of New York University, on which image we had better pull this whole essay to the side of the road and sit silently for a moment.

Beyond all the obvious reasons we choose animals as symbols for our sporting teams — their incredible energy and muscle, grace and strength, intelligence and verve, our ancient conviction of their power and magic, ancient associations as clan signs and tribal totems, even more ancient shivers perhaps of fear at animals who hunted and ate us, not to mention the way their images look cool on letterhead and sweatshirts and pennants and fundraising appeals — there is something else, something so deep and revelatory about human beings that I think we do not admit it because it is too sad. I think we love animals as images because we miss them in the flesh, and I think we love them as images because they matter to us spiritually in ways we cannot hope to articulate. The vast majority of us will never see a cougar or a wolverine, not to mention a boll weevil, but even wearing one on a shirt, or shouting the miracle of its name in a stadium, or grinning to see its rippling beauty on the window of a car, gives us a tiny subtle crucial electric jolt in the heart, connects us somehow to what we used to be with animals, which was thrilled and ter-rified. We've lost the salt of that feeling forever, but even a hint of it matters immensely to us as animals too. Maybe that's what we miss the most — the feeling that they are our cousins, and not clans of creatures who once filled the earth and now are shreds of memory, mere symbols, beings who used to be.

Journal Writing

Doyle provides quite a few examples of the many school mascots he has encountered over the years, as well as a reflection on why, generally, we select animals to represent our sports teams. Choose your favorite of the mascots he names and in your jour-nal brainstorm possible explanations for why that particular mascot might be a good choice for a college or university.

Questions on Meaning

1. What do you take to be Doyle's PURPOSE with "A Note on Mascots"? Is it meant to be a straightforward essay, do you think, or more like a poem? Why do you think so?

2. Why does Doyle cite Benjamin Franklin's thoughts on eagles (par. 2)? What might have been the impact if he had chosen to quote, say, a naturalist or sports enthusiast instead?

3. Doyle observes of mascots that "there are a *lot* of devils, which says something interesting" (par. 3). What does he mean? What exactly does it say?

4. How does Doyle explain the appeal of animal mascots? What is his THESIS? Why does he wait until the final paragraph to state it?

Questions on Writing Strategy

1. Examine Doyle's sentences. How varied are they? Taken as a whole, what is the EFFECT of their structures and length?

2. Doyle concludes the first paragraph by dropping the reader into a classroom setting that should be familiar to you. Why? Where else in the essay does he employ a similar strategy? What do these lines reveal about his imagined AUDIENCE?

3. **OTHER METHODS**   Explain how Doyle uses CLASSIFICATION to organize his examples. What does the method contribute to his purpose?

Questions on Language

1. Be sure you know how to define the following words: zoology, boll weevils, prepossessing (par. 1); canids, ruminants, mustelids, denizens (2); fauna, botany (3); verve, totems (4).

2. Doyle's style in this piece is unusual in that he mixes scientific language with the first person (*I* and *we*). Does this POINT OF VIEW seem appropriate, given the author's subject and purpose? Why, or why not? How does it affect his TONE?

3. Doyle identifies several "Fighting" mascots. List them for yourself. What makes these names funny?

4. In his comments on writing (next page), Doyle stresses the importance of using "energized" verbs. Point to any particularly strong verbs you find in "A Note on Mascots." What makes them effective?

Suggestions for Writing

1. **FROM JOURNAL TO ESSAY**   Expand your journal entry into an ARGUMENT proposing that your school should adopt a new mascot. Remember to select several convincing examples to support your choice.

2. Besides sports, where else do you often see animals represented for some purpose beyond their literal existence? Consider Halloween costumes, toys, and television shows, for instance. Do the representations you have observed seem to be fulfilling a longing, such as the one Doyle describes in "A Note on Mascots"? If so, how? If not, what purpose do they seem to serve? Write a reflective essay that contemplates these questions.

3. **CRITICAL WRITING**   Select one of the plants or animals that Doyle highlights and research its current population and habitat. Is Doyle correct that the mascot you chose is something rare that most people will not casually encounter? Have any conservation efforts been made on behalf of the mascot you selected (plants, as well as animals, can be endangered)? How might being a mascot help preserve awareness of the plant or animal you selected? If you chose a mascot that is common or not threatened, make a case for its continuing value as a SYMBOL.

4. **CONNECTIONS**   As a fan, Doyle expresses a certain amount of reverence for sports and their icons. In "Jock Culture" (p. 276), on the other hand, sportswriter Robert Lipsyte argues that athleticism in general fuels unhealthy competition in the working environment. In an essay, consider how Doyle's admiration of sports mascots supports or contradicts Lipsyte's analysis of the implications of Jock Culture for individuals and society.

ANNA QUINDLEN

Anna Quindlen was born in 1953 and graduated from Barnard College in 1974. She worked as a reporter for the *New York Post* and the *New York Times* before taking over the latter's "About New York" column, eventually serving as the paper's deputy metropolitan editor and creating her own weekly column. Quindlen later wrote a twice-weekly op-ed column for the *Times* on social and political issues, earning a Pulitzer Prize for commentary in 1992. She also wrote a biweekly column for *Newsweek* magazine. Quindlen's essays and columns are collected in *Living Out Loud* (1988), *Thinking Out Loud* (1993), and *Loud and Clear* (2004). Her memoir, *Lots of Candles, Plenty of Cake*, appeared in 2012. Quindlen has also published two books for children, three books of non-fiction with a how-to bent, and seven successful novels, most recently *Still Life with Bread Crumbs* (2014). She lives in New York City.

Homeless

In this essay from *Living Out Loud*, Quindlen mingles a reporter's respect for details with a keen sense of empathy, using examples to explore a persistent social issue. When Quindlen wrote, in 1987, homelessness had become a severe and highly visible problem in New York City and elsewhere in the United States. The problem has not abated since then: Using government data, the National Alliance to End Homelessness estimates that more than half a million Americans are homeless on any given day.

Her name was Ann, and we met in the Port Authority Bus Terminal several Januarys ago. I was doing a story on homeless people. She said I was wasting my time talking to her; she was just passing through, although she'd been passing through for more than two weeks. To prove to me that this was true, she rummaged through a tote bag and a manila envelope and finally unfolded a sheet of typing paper and brought out her photographs.

They were not pictures of family, or friends, or even a dog or cat, its eyes brown-red in the flashbulb's light. They were pictures of a house. It was like a thousand houses in a hundred towns, not suburb, not city, but somewhere in between, with aluminum siding and a chain-link fence, a narrow driveway running up to a one-car garage and a patch of backyard. The house was yellow. I looked on the back for a date or a name, but neither was there. There was no need for discussion. I knew what she was trying to tell me, for it was something I had often felt. She was not adrift, alone, anonymous, although her bags and her raincoat with the grime shadowing its creases had made me believe she was. She had a house, or at least once upon a time had had one.

Inside were curtains, a couch, a stove, potholders. You are where you live. She was somebody.

I've never been very good at looking at the big picture, taking the global 3
view, and I've always been a person with an overactive sense of place, the legacy of an Irish grandfather. So it is natural that the thing that seems most wrong with the world to me right now is that there are so many people with no homes. I'm not simply talking about shelter from the elements, or three square meals a day or a mailing address to which the welfare people can send the check — although I know that all these are important for survival. I'm talking about a home, about precisely those kinds of feelings that have wound up in cross-stitch and French knots on samplers over the years.

Home is where the heart is. There's no place like it. I love my home with 4
a ferocity totally out of proportion to its appearance or location. I love dumb things about it: the hot-water heater, the plastic rack you drain dishes in, the roof over my head, which occasionally leaks. And yet it is precisely those dumb things that make it what it is — a place of certainty, stability, predictability, privacy, for me and for my family. It is where I live. What more can you say about a place than that? That is everything.

Yet it is something that we have been edging away from gradually during 5
my lifetime and the lifetimes of my parents and grandparents. There was a time when where you lived often was where you worked and where you grew the food you ate and even where you were buried. When that era passed, where you lived at least was where your parents had lived and where you would live with your children when you became enfeebled. Then, suddenly where you lived was where you lived for three years, until you could move on to something else and something else again.

And so we have come to something else again, to children who do not 6
understand what it means to go to their rooms because they have never had a room, to men and women whose fantasy is a wall they can paint a color of their own choosing, to old people reduced to sitting on molded plastic chairs, their skin blue-white in the lights of a bus station, who pull pictures of houses out of their bags. Homes have stopped being homes. Now they are real estate.

People find it curious that those without homes would rather sleep sitting up 7
on benches or huddled in doorways than go to shelters. Certainly some prefer to do so because they are emotionally ill, because they have been locked in before and they are damned if they will be locked in again. Others are afraid of the violence and trouble they may find there. But some seem to want something that is not available in shelters, and they will not compromise, not for a cot, or oatmeal, or a shower with special soap that kills the bugs. "One room," a woman with a baby who was sleeping on her sister's floor, once told me, "painted blue." That was the crux of it; not size or location, but pride of ownership. Painted blue.

This is a difficult problem, and some wise and compassionate people are   8
working hard at it. But in the main I think we work around it, just as we walk
around it when it is lying on the sidewalk or sitting in the bus terminal —
the problem, that is. It has been customary to take people's pain and lessen
our own participation in it by turning it into an issue, not a collection of
human beings. We turn an adjective into a noun: the poor, not poor people;
the homeless, not Ann or the man who lives in the box or the woman who
sleeps on the subway grate.

Sometimes I think we would be better off if we forgot about the broad   9
strokes and concentrated on the details. Here is a woman without a bureau.
There is a man with no mirror, no wall to hang it on. They are not the homeless. They are people who have no homes. No drawer that holds the spoons.
No window to look out upon the world. My God. That is everything.

Journal Writing

What does the word *home* mean to you? Does it involve material things, privacy,
family, a sense of permanence? In your journal, explore your ideas about this word.

Questions on Meaning

1. What is Quindlen's THESIS?

2. What distinction is Quindlen making in her CONCLUSION with the sentences
   "They are not the homeless. They are people who have no homes"?

3. Why does Quindlen believe that having a home is essential?

Questions on Writing Strategy

1. Why do you think Quindlen begins with the story of Ann? How else might
   Quindlen have begun her essay?

2. What is the EFFECT of Quindlen's examples about her own home?

3. What key ASSUMPTIONS does the author make about her AUDIENCE? Are the
   assumptions reasonable? Where does she specifically address an assumption that
   might undermine her view?

4. How does Quindlen vary the sentences in paragraph 7 that give examples of why
   homeless people avoid shelters?

5. **OTHER METHODS** Quindlen uses examples to support an ARGUMENT. What
   position does she want readers to recognize and accept?

Questions on Language

1. What is the effect of "My God" in the last paragraph?

2. How might Quindlen be said to give new meaning to the old CLICHÉ "Home is where the heart is" (par. 4)?

3. What is meant by "crux" (par. 7)? Where does the word come from?

Suggestions for Writing

1. **FROM JOURNAL TO ESSAY** Write an essay that gives a detailed DEFINITION of *home* by using your own home, hometown, or experiences with homes as supporting examples. (See Chap. 11 if you need help with definition.)

2. Have you ever moved from one place to another? What sort of experience was it? Write an essay about leaving an old home and moving to a new one. Was there an activity or a piece of furniture that helped ease the transition?

3. Write an essay on the problem of homelessness in your town or city. Use examples to support your view of the problem and a possible solution.

4. **CRITICAL WRITING** Write a brief essay in which you agree or disagree with Quindlen's assertion that a home is "everything." Can one, for instance, be a fulfilled person without a home? In your answer, take account of the values that might underlie an attachment to home; Quindlen mentions "certainty, stability, predictability, privacy" (par. 4), but there are others, including some (such as fear of change) that are less positive.

5. **CONNECTIONS** Quindlen makes an emphatic distinction between "the homeless" and "people who have no homes" (par. 9). Read William Lutz's "The World of Doublespeak" (p. 309), which examines how language can be used to distort our perceptions of unpleasant truths. Drawing on what he and Quindlen have to say, write an essay that explores how the way we label a problem like homelessness influences what solutions we may (or may not) be able to find.

Anna Quindlen on Writing

Anna Quindlen started her writing career as a newspaper reporter. "I had wanted to be a writer for most of my life," she recalls in the introduction to her book *Living Out Loud*, "and in the service of the writing I became a reporter. For many years I was able to observe, even to feel, life vividly, but at secondhand. I was able to stand over the chalk outline of a body on a sidewalk dappled with black blood; to stand behind the glass and look down into an operating theater where one man was placing a heart in the yawning chest of another; to sit in the park on the first day of summer and find myself professionally obligated to record all the glories of it. Every day I found answers: who, what, when, where, and why."

Quindlen was a good reporter, but the business of finding answers did not satisfy her personally. "In my own life," she continues, "I had only questions." Then she switched from reporter to columnist at the *New York Times*. It was "exhilarating," she says, that "my work became a reflection of my life. After years of being a professional observer of other people's lives, I was given the opportunity to be a professional observer of my own. I was permitted — and permitted myself — to write a column, not about my answers, but about my questions. Never did I make so much sense of my life as I did then, for it was inevitable that as a writer I would find out most clearly what I thought, and what I only thought I thought, when I saw it written down. . . . After years of feeling secondhand, of feeling the pain of the widow, the joy of the winner, I was able to allow myself to feel those emotions for myself."

The Brief Bedford Reader on Writing

While Brent Staples (p. 148) and Brian Doyle (p. 160) in this chapter both stress the strategies and techniques essay writers can learn from newspaper reporters, Quindlen seems to stress the opposite. For her, GENRE and PURPOSE (see pp. 31–32) impose restrictions as much as they open up possibilities. What did she feel she could accomplish in a column that she could not accomplish in a news article? What evidence of this difference do you see in her essay "Homeless"?

ADDITIONAL WRITING TOPICS

Example

1. Select one of the following general statements, or set forth a general statement of your own that one of these inspires. Making it your central idea (or THESIS), support it in an essay full of examples. Draw your examples from your reading, your studies, your conversations, or your own experience.

   Text messaging has many advantages (or many disadvantages) over making a phone call.

   Individual consumers can (or cannot) help slow down global climate change.

   Friendships don't always start off easily.

   Spending (or saving) is necessary to the nation's economy.

   Each family has its own distinctive culture.

   Certain games, closely inspected, promote violence.

   Graphic novels have become a serious form of literary art.

   Most people can triumph over crushing difficulties.

   Churchgoers aren't perfect.

   Online articles use misleading titles to get readers to click on the stories.

   Local foods, in season, are best for everyone (or not).

   Ordinary lives sometimes give rise to legends.

   Some people are born winners (or losers).

   Music can change lives.

   Certain machines *do* have personalities.

   Some road signs lead drivers astray.

2. In a brief essay, make a GENERALIZATION about the fears, joys, or contradictions that members of minority groups seem to share. To illustrate your generalization, draw examples from personal experience, from outside reading, or from two or three of the essays in this book by the following authors: Nancy Mairs (p. 12), Amy Tan (p. 74), Junot Díaz (p. 84), N. Scott Momaday (p. 119), Brent Staples (p. 148), Issa Rae (p. 155), Andrea Roman (p. 187), Firoozeh Dumas (p. 233), Tal Fortgang (p. 376), Roxane Gay (p. 383), and Linda Chavez (p. 421).

I WAS SPARTAN TO MY FATHER'S ATHENIAN. MODERN TO HIS VICTORIAN.

BUTCH TO HIS NELLY.

UTILITARIAN TO HIS AESTHETE.

6

COMPARISON AND CONTRAST

Setting Things Side by Side

◀ **Comparison and contrast in a graphic memoir**

In the highly praised and influential *Fun Home* (2006), comic artist Alison Bechdel explores the complications of growing up the lesbian daughter of a closeted gay man while living in a nineteenth-century house that held the family's funeral business. In this panel, from the first chapter of the book, she compares herself with her father on four points: politics (ancient Sparta, in Greece, was a warrior society; neighboring Athens focused on education and the arts), cultural sensibilities, gender stereotypes, and values. What striking and not-so-striking differences do you notice? What is the most obvious similarity? What are some more subtle similarities? How would you summarize the conflict Bechdel portrays?

THE METHOD

Which team do you place your money on, the Giants or the Patriots? To go to school full-time or part-time: What are the rewards and drawbacks of each way of life? How do the Republican and the Democratic platforms stack up against each other? In what ways are the psychological theories of Carl Jung like or unlike those of Sigmund Freud? Should we pass laws to regulate medical marijuana or just let recreational use run wild? These are questions that may be addressed by the dual method of COMPARISON AND CONTRAST. In comparing, you point to similar features of the subjects; in contrasting, to different features. (The features themselves you identify by the method of DIVISION or ANALYSIS; see Chap. 8.)

In practice, comparison and contrast are usually inseparable because two subjects are generally neither entirely alike nor entirely unlike. When Bruce Catton sets out to portray the Civil War generals Ulysses S. Grant and Robert E. Lee (p. 193), he considers both their similarities and their differences. Often, as in this case, the similarities make the subjects comparable at all and the differences make comparison worthwhile.

Uses of Comparison and Contrast

Comparison and contrast are especially helpful in academic writing. You can use the method in expository writing to illuminate two or more subjects and demonstrate that you understand your material thoroughly. And in an argument in which you support one of two possible choices, a careful and detailed comparison and contrast may be extremely convincing as you show why you prefer one thing to another, one course of action to another, one idea to another.

Because comparison and contrast reveal knowledge about the subjects under investigation, you will also often be asked to use the method in exams that call for essay answers. Sometimes the examiner will come right out and say, "Compare and contrast nineteenth-century methods of treating drug addiction with those of the present day." Sometimes, however, comparison and contrast won't even be mentioned by name; instead, the examiner may ask, "What resemblances do you find between John Updike's short story 'A & P' and the Grimm fairy tale 'Godfather Death'?" Or, "Explain the relative desirability of holding a franchise against going into business as an independent proprietor." But those — as you realize when you begin to plan your reply — are just other ways of asking you to compare and contrast.

Purposes

A good essay in comparing and contrasting serves a PURPOSE. Most of the time, the writer of such an essay has one of two purposes in mind:

- **To explain the similarities and differences between two things,** the writer shows each of the subjects distinctly by considering both, side by side. With such a purpose, the writer doesn't necessarily find one of the subjects better than the other. In his essay on Grant and Lee, Bruce Catton does not favor either general but concludes that each reflected strong currents of American history.

- **To choose between two things, or EVALUATE them,** the writer shows how one of the subjects is better than the other on the basis of some standard: Which of two films more convincingly captures the experience of being a teenager? Which of two chemical processes works better to clean waste water? To answer either question, the writer has to consider the features of both subjects — both the positive and the negative — and then choose the subject whose positive features more clearly predominate.

THE PROCESS

Subjects for Comparison

Comparison usually works best with two of a kind: two means of reading for the visually impaired, two films on the same theme, two processes for cleaning waste water, two mystery writers, two schools of political thought. When you find yourself considering two subjects side by side or preferring one subject over another, you have already embarked on comparison and contrast. Just be sure that your two subjects display a clear basis for comparison. In other words, they should have something significant in common.

It can sometimes be effective, however, to find similarities between evidently unlike subjects — a city and a country town, say — and a special form of comparison, ANALOGY, equates two very unlike things, explaining one in terms of the other. In an analogy you might explain how the human eye works by comparing it to a simple camera, or you might explain the forces in a thunderstorm by comparing them to armies in battle. In "Tragedy" (p. 199), the pop philosopher Alain de Botton explains the civilizing functions of tabloid news stories by equating them with ancient Greek dramas.

In any comparison, you must have a valid reason for bringing the two things together — that is, the similarities and differences must be significant enough to warrant examination. In a comparison of a city and a country town, for instance, the features must extend beyond the obvious — that people live in them, that both have streets and shops — and venture into likenesses that are more meaningful — perhaps that both places create a sense of community that residents depend on, for instance.

Basis for Comparison and Thesis

Beginning to identify the shared and dissimilar features of your subjects will get you started, but the comparison won't be manageable for you or interesting to your readers unless you also limit it. You would be overly ambitious to try to compare and contrast the Russian way of life with the American way of life in five hundred words; you couldn't include all the important similarities and differences. In a brief paper, you would be wise to select a single basis for comparison: to show, for instance, how representative day-care centers in Russia and the United States are both like and unlike each other.

This basis for comparison will eventually underpin the THESIS of your essay — the claim you have to make about the similarities and dissimilarities of two things or about one thing's superiority over another. Here, from essays in this chapter, are THESIS STATEMENTS that clearly lay out what's being compared and why:

> One would think that language would create the biggest barriers for immigrants but in my mother's case, the biggest obstacles were the small cultural differences.
>
> — Andrea Roman, "We're Not . . ."

> They were two strong men, these oddly different generals, and they represented the strengths of two conflicting currents that, through them, had come into collision.
>
> — Bruce Catton, "Grant and Lee: A Study in Contrasts"

Notice that each author not only identifies his or her subjects (cultural differences, two generals) but also previews the purpose of the comparison.

Organization

Even with a limited basis for comparison, the method of comparison and contrast can be tricky without some planning. We suggest that you make an outline (formal or informal), using one of two organizations described below: subject by subject or point by point.

Say you're writing an essay on two guitarists, Jed and Jake. Your purpose is to explain the distinctive identities of the two players, and your thesis statement might be the following:

Jed and Jake are both excellent guitarists whose differences in style reflect their training.

Here are the two ways you might arrange the BODY of your comparison:

- **Subject by subject.** Set forth all your facts about Jed; then do the same for Jake. Next, sum up their similarities and differences. In your conclusion, state what you think you have shown.

  1. *Jed*
     Training
     Choice of instrument
     Technical dexterity
     Playing style

  2. *Jake*
     Training
     Choice of instrument
     Technical dexterity
     Playing style

  This procedure works well for a paper of a few paragraphs, but for a longer one, it has a built-in disadvantage: Readers need to remember all the facts about subject 1 while they read about subject 2. If the essay is long and lists many facts, a subject-by-subject arrangement may be difficult to hold in mind.

- **Point by point.** Usually more workable in writing a long paper than the first method, the second scheme is to compare and contrast as you go. You consider one point at a time, taking up your two subjects alternately. In this way, you continually bring the subjects together, perhaps in every paragraph. Notice the differences in the outline:

  1. *Training*
     Jed: self-taught
     Jake: classically trained

  2. *Choice of instrument*
     Jed: electric
     Jake: acoustic

  3. *Technical dexterity*
     Jed: highly skilled
     Jake: highly skilled

  4. *Playing style*
     Jed: rapid-fire
     Jake: impressionistic

For either organizing scheme, your conclusion might be as follows: "Although similar in skills, the two differ greatly in aims and in personalities. Jed is better suited to a local club and Jake to a concert hall."

By the way, a subject-by-subject organization works most efficiently for a *pair* of subjects. If you want to write about *three* guitarists, you might first consider Jed and Jake, then Jake and Josh, then Josh and Jed — but it would probably be easier to compare and contrast all three point by point.

Balance and Flexibility

An outline will help you see the shape of your paper and keep your points in mind as you draft. A trick of comparison and contrast will be to balance the treatment of both subjects while allowing them to breathe. You do have to give the subjects equivalence: You can't discuss Jed's on-stage manner without discussing Jake's, too. If you have nothing to say about Jake's on-stage manner, then you might as well omit the point. A surefire loser is the paper that proposes to compare and contrast two subjects but then proceeds to discuss quite different elements in each: Jed's playing style and Jake's choice of material, Jed's fondness for Italian food and Jake's hobby of antique-car collecting. The writer of such a paper doesn't compare and contrast the two musicians at all, but engages in two entirely separate discussions.

Balance your subjects' features, but don't let your outline constrain you too tightly. The reader of a mechanically written comparison-and-contrast essay comes to feel like a weary tennis spectator whose head has to swivel from side to side: now Jed, now Jake; now Jed again, now back to Jake. You need to mention the same features of both subjects, it is true, but no law says *how* you must mention them. You need not follow your outline in lockstep order, or cover similarities and differences at precisely the same length (none of the authors later in this chapter do), or spend a hundred words on Jed's fingering skill just because you spend a hundred words on Jake's. As you write, keep casting your thoughts upon a living, particular world — not twisting and squeezing that world into a rigid scheme.

FOCUS ON PARALLELISM

With several points of comparison and alternating subjects, a comparison will be easier for your readers to follow if you emphasize likenesses and differences in your wording. Take advantage of the technique of parallelism discussed in Chapter 2 (p. 50). PARALLELISM — the use of similar grammatical structures for elements of similar importance — balances a comparison and clarifies the relations between elements. At the same time, lack of parallelism can distract or confuse readers.

To make the elements of a comparison parallel, repeat the forms of related words, phrases, and sentences:

NONPARALLEL Harris expects dieters who follow his plan to limit bread, dairy, and meat, while Marconi's diet forbids few foods.

PARALLEL Harris's diet limits bread, dairy, and meat, while Marconi's diet forbids few foods.

NONPARALLEL Harris emphasizes self-denial, but when following Marconi's plan you can eat whatever you want in moderation.

PARALLEL Harris emphasizes self-denial, but Marconi stresses moderation.

NONPARALLEL If you want to lose weight quickly, choose Harris's diet. You'll have more success keeping the weight off if you follow Marconi's plan.

PARALLEL If you want to lose weight quickly, choose Harris's diet. If you want to keep the weight off, follow Marconi's plan.

CHECKLIST FOR REVISING A COMPARISON-AND-CONTRAST ESSAY

✔ **Purpose.** What is the aim of your comparison: to explain two (or more) subjects or to evaluate them? Will the purpose be clear to readers from the start?

✔ **Subjects.** Are the subjects enough alike, sharing enough features, to make comparison worthwhile?

✔ **Thesis.** Does your thesis establish a limited basis for comparison so that you have room and time to cover all the relevant similarities and differences?

✔ **Organization.** Does your arrangement of material, whether subject by subject or point by point, do justice to your subjects and help readers follow the comparison?

✔ **Balance and flexibility.** Have you covered the same features of both subjects? At the same time, have you avoided a rigid back-and-forth movement that could bore or exhaust a reader?

✔ **Parallelism.** Have you used parallel structure to clarify the subjects and points you are discussing?

COMPARISON AND CONTRAST IN ACADEMIC WRITING

A Communications Textbook

Taken from Steven McCornack's *Reflect and Relate*, the following point-by-point comparison explains a key difference between men and women. The in-text citations, in APA style (see pp. 519–29 of the Appendix), refer readers to a list of sources provided at the end of McCornack's textbook.

<u>Immediately after birth, we begin a lifelong process of gender socialization, learning from others what it means personally, inter-personally, and culturally to be "male" or "female."</u> Girls are typically taught feminine behaviors, such as sensitivity to one's own and others' emotions, nurturance, and compassion (Lippa, 2002). Boys are usually taught masculine behaviors, learning about assertiveness, competitiveness, and independence from others. As a result of gender socialization, men and women often end up forming comparatively different self-concepts (Cross & Madson, 1997). For example, women are more likely than men to perceive themselves as connected to others and to assess themselves based on the quality of these interpersonal connections. Men are more likely than women to think of themselves as a composite of their individual achievements, abilities, and beliefs — viewing themselves as separate from other people. At the same time, the existence of these differences doesn't mean that all men and all women think of themselves in identical ways. Many men and women appreciate and embrace both feminine and masculine characteristics in their self-concepts.

> Point-by-point comparison supporting this topic sentence
>
> 1. First point: Learned behaviors
>   - Girls
>   - Boys
>
> 2. Second point: Self-concepts
>   - Women
>   - Men

A Review

If you browse the Web or flip through any newspaper or magazine, you're bound to spot a review: a writer's assessment of anything from a restaurant to a scholarly book. Commonly assigned in college, too, reviews rely mainly on ANALYSIS to identify and interpret the elements of a subject. But because a review evaluates quality, writers naturally turn to comparison and contrast as well, weighing two or more products, works, or ideas to determine their relative worth. Such a comparison takes its evidence from the subjects themselves, as in descriptions of paintings in an exhibit or quotations from written works.

For a course in popular culture, Charlotte Pak wrote a review of singer Beyoncé Knowles's solo career. Pak chose her subject because "Single Ladies (Put a Ring on It)" bolstered Beyoncé's reputation as a champion of women. Although Pak enjoyed the song, she was bothered by some of the implications in its lyrics, and she decided to investigate the singer's work for similar themes. In the paragraphs below, excerpted from her full review, Pak compares "Single Ladies" with a popular song from the 1960s, with unexpected results.

Critics and fans often view Beyoncé as one of the leaders in
the "strong woman" style that encourages female independence,
equality, and self-worth. These listeners offer her 2009 hit
"Single Ladies (Put a Ring on It)" as a symbol of how far women
have come since the 1950s and 1960s. But this and other songs
by Beyoncé just seem strong when in fact they present women
who are no more independent than the ones portrayed half a
century ago.

A classic example of the older style is the Dixie Cups' 1964
hit "Chapel of Love." The refrain of the song is familiar even
today: "Goin' to the chapel and we're / Gonna get married / . . .
Goin' to the chapel of love." The song itself seems sentimental
and even naive on the surface. In a sweet, dreamy voice, the
female singer imagines marital bliss, as "Birds all sing as if they
knew / Today's the day we'll say 'I do.' " She sings of marriage
as the fulfillment of her life, implying her dependence on a
man. Yet despite the tone and the sentimentality, the song also
suggests equality between the singer and her husband-to-be
within the bounds of traditional marriage: "I'll be his and he'll
be mine." The possession is mutual. Two independent individuals
will say "I do."

In contrast, the singer in Beyoncé's "Single Ladies" seems
pleased to be free from an ex-boyfriend. She dances with another
man in a club while her ex jealously watches: "Don't pay him
any attention / 'Cause you had your turn and now you're gonna
learn / What it really feels like to miss me." Her tone is feisty
and no-nonsense, the voice of a sophisticated and independent
woman. Yet she remains preoccupied with her ex-boyfriend and
still sees herself through his eyes. In the song's chorus — "If
you like it then you shoulda put a ring on it" — the "it" suggests that she has a sense of herself as an object to be possessed rather than an independent being. That suggestion is
explicit in the lines "Pull me into your arms, / Say I'm the one
you own." The wimpy "Chapel of Love" at least offers an image
of equality. "Single Ladies" misleads by casting dependency as
strength.

Marginal annotations:

Basis for comparison:
portrayals of women's
strength

Subject-by-subject
organization supporting
this claim

1. Representative older
   song: "Chapel of Love"
   by the Dixie Cups

   • Quotations from
     song

   • Interpretation

2. Representative
   Beyoncé song:
   "Single Ladies
   (Put a Ring on It)"

   • Quotations from
     song

   • Interpretation

Concluding sentences
express judgment

Comparison and Contrast

DAVID SEDARIS

Winner of the Thurber Prize for American Humor, David Sedaris was born in 1957 and grew up in North Carolina. After graduating from the School of the Art Institute of Chicago in 1987, Sedaris taught writing there part-time and then moved to New York City, where he took various odd jobs. One of these jobs — a stint as a department-store Christmas elf — provided Sedaris with material for "The Santaland Diaries," the essay that launched his career as a humorist after he read it on National Public Radio's *Morning Edition* in 1993. Since then, Sedaris has contributed numerous commentaries to public radio's *Morning Edition* and *This American Life*, and his work appears frequently in *The New Yorker*, *Esquire*, and other magazines. He has published eight collections of essays and fiction, including *Naked* (1997), *Dress Your Family in Corduroy and Denim* (2004), *When You Are Engulfed in Flames* (2008), and *Let's Explore Diabetes with Owls* (2013). Sedaris frequently tours and gives readings of his essays and works in progress; in 2013 he adapted his story "C.O.G.," about an apple-picking job in Oregon, into the script for a feature film. He lives in rural England.

Remembering My Childhood on the Continent of Africa

Many of Sedaris's essays locate comedy in exaggerated depictions of his basically normal North Carolina childhood. In this essay from *Me Talk Pretty One Day* (2000), Sedaris highlights that normality by contrasting it with the distinctly unusual childhood of his partner. For another approach to a similar subject, see the next essay, by student writer Andrea Roman.

When Hugh was in the fifth grade, his class took a field trip to an Ethiopian slaughterhouse. He was living in Addis Ababa at the time, and the slaughterhouse was chosen because, he says, "it was convenient."   1

This was a school system in which the matter of proximity outweighed such petty concerns as what may or may not be appropriate for a busload of eleven-year-olds. "What?" I asked. "Were there no autopsies scheduled at the local morgue? Was the federal prison just a bit too far out of the way?"   2

Hugh defends his former school, saying, "Well, isn't that the whole point of a field trip? To see something new?"   3

"Technically yes, but . . ."   4

"All right then," he says. "So we saw some new things."   5

One of his field trips was literally a trip to a field where the class watched   6
a wrinkled man fill his mouth with rotten goat meat and feed it to a pack of
waiting hyenas. On another occasion they were taken to examine the blood-
ied bedroom curtains hanging in the palace of the former dictator. There were
tamer trips, to textile factories and sugar refineries, but my favorite is always
the slaughterhouse. It wasn't a big company, just a small rural enterprise run
by a couple of brothers operating out of a low-ceilinged concrete building.
Following a brief lecture on the importance of proper sanitation, a small white
piglet was herded into the room, its dainty hooves clicking against the concrete floor. The class gathered in a circle to get a better look at the animal,
who seemed delighted with the attention he was getting. He turned from face
to face and was looking up at Hugh when one of the brothers drew a pistol
from his back pocket, held it against the animal's temple, and shot the piglet,
execution-style. Blood spattered, frightened children wept, and the man with
the gun offered the teacher and bus driver some meat from a freshly slaughtered goat.

When I'm told such stories, it's all I can do to hold back my feelings of   7
jealousy. An Ethiopian slaughterhouse. Some people have all the luck. When
I was in elementary school, the best we ever got was a trip to Old Salem
or Colonial Williamsburg, one of those preserved brick villages where time
supposedly stands still and someone earns his living as a town crier. There
was always a blacksmith, a group of wandering patriots, and a collection of
bonneted women hawking corn bread or gingersnaps made "the ol'-fashioned
way." Every now and then you might come across a doer of bad deeds serving
time in the stocks, but that was generally as exciting as it got.

Certain events are parallel, but compared with Hugh's, my childhood was   8
unspeakably dull. When I was seven years old, my family moved to North
Carolina. When he was seven years old, Hugh's family moved to the Congo.
We had a collie and a house cat. They had a monkey and two horses named
Charlie Brown and Satan. I threw stones at stop signs. Hugh threw stones
at crocodiles. The verbs are the same, but he definitely wins the prize when
it comes to nouns and objects. An eventful day for my mother might have
involved a trip to the dry cleaner or a conversation with the potato-chip
deliveryman. Asked one ordinary Congo afternoon what she'd done with her
day, Hugh's mother answered that she and a fellow member of the Ladies'
Club had visited a leper colony on the outskirts of Kinshasa. No reason was
given for the expedition, though chances are she was staking it out for a future
field trip.

Due to his upbringing, Hugh sits through inane movies never realizing   9
that they're often based on inane television shows. There were no poker-faced
sitcom martians in his part of Africa, no oil-rich hillbillies or aproned brides

trying to wean themselves from the practice of witchcraft. From time to time a movie would arrive packed in a dented canister, the film scratched and faded from its slow trip around the world. The theater consisted of a few dozen folding chairs arranged before a bedsheet or the blank wall of a vacant hangar out near the airstrip. Occasionally a man would sell warm soft drinks out of a cardboard box, but that was it in terms of concessions.

When I was young, I went to the theater at the nearby shopping center 10 and watched a movie about a talking Volkswagen. I believe the little car had a taste for mischief but I can't be certain, as both the movie and the afternoon proved unremarkable and have faded from my memory. Hugh saw the same movie a few years after it was released. His family had left the Congo by this time and were living in Ethiopia. Like me, Hugh saw the movie by himself on a weekend afternoon. Unlike me, he left the theater two hours later, to find a dead man hanging from a telephone pole at the far end of the unpaved parking lot. None of the people who'd seen the movie seemed to care about the dead man. They stared at him for a moment or two and then headed home, saying they'd never seen anything as crazy as that talking Volkswagen. His father was late picking him up, so Hugh just stood there for an hour, watching the dead man dangle and turn in the breeze. The death was not reported in the newspaper, and when Hugh related the story to his friends, they said, "You saw the movie about the talking car?"

I could have done without the flies and the primitive theaters, but 11 I wouldn't have minded growing up with a houseful of servants. In North Carolina it wasn't unusual to have a once-a-week maid, but Hugh's family had houseboys, a word that never fails to charge my imagination. They had cooks and drivers, and guards who occupied a gatehouse, armed with machetes. Seeing as I had regularly petitioned my parents for an electric fence, the business with the guards strikes me as the last word in quiet sophistication. Having protection suggests that you are important. Having that protection paid for by the government is even better, as it suggests your safety is of interest to someone other than yourself.

Hugh's father was a career officer with the US State Department, and 12 every morning a black sedan carried him off to the embassy. I'm told it's not as glamorous as it sounds, but in terms of fun for the entire family, I'm fairly confident that it beats the sack race at the annual IBM picnic. By the age of three, Hugh was already carrying a diplomatic passport. The rules that applied to others did not apply to him. No tickets, no arrests, no luggage search: He was officially licensed to act like a brat. Being an American, it was expected of him, and who was he to deny the world an occasional tantrum?

They weren't rich, but what Hugh's family lacked financially they more 13 than made up for with the sort of exoticism that works wonders at cocktail parties, leading always to the remark "That sounds fascinating." It's a compliment one rarely receives when describing an adolescence spent drinking Icees at the North Hills Mall. No fifteen-foot python ever wandered onto my school's basketball court. I begged, I prayed nightly, but it just never happened. Neither did I get to witness a military coup in which forces sympathetic to the colonel arrived late at night to assassinate my next-door neighbor. Hugh had been at the Addis Ababa teen club when the electricity was cut off and soldiers arrived to evacuate the building. He and his friends had to hide in the back of a jeep and cover themselves with blankets during the ride home. It's something that sticks in his mind for one reason or another.

Among my personal highlights is the memory of having my picture taken   14 with Uncle Paul, the legally blind host of a Raleigh children's television show. Among Hugh's is the memory of having his picture taken with Buzz Aldrin on the last leg of the astronaut's world tour. The man who had walked on the moon placed his hand on Hugh's shoulder and offered to sign his autograph book. The man who led Wake County schoolchildren in afternoon song turned at the sound of my voice and asked, "So what's your name, princess?"

When I was fourteen years old, I was sent to spend ten days with my   15 maternal grandmother in western New York State. She was a small and private woman named Billie, and though she never came right out and asked, I had the distinct impression she had no idea who I was. It was the way she looked at me, squinting through her glasses while chewing on her lower lip. That, coupled with the fact that she never once called me by name. "Oh," she'd say, "are you still here?" She was just beginning her long struggle with Alzheimer's disease, and each time I entered the room, I felt the need to reintroduce myself and set her at ease. "Hi, it's me. Sharon's boy, David. I was just in the kitchen admiring your collection of ceramic toads." Aside from a few trips to summer camp, this was the longest I'd ever been away from home and I like to think I was toughened by the experience.

About the same time I was frightening my grandmother, Hugh and his   16 family were packing their belongings for a move to Somalia. There were no English-speaking schools in Mogadishu, so, after a few months spent lying around the family compound with his pet monkey, Hugh was sent back to Ethiopia to live with a beer enthusiast his father had met at a cocktail party. Mr. Hoyt installed security systems in foreign embassies. He and his family gave Hugh a room. They invited him to join them at the table, but that was as far as they extended themselves. No one ever asked him when his birthday was, so when the day came, he kept it to himself. There was no telephone service between Ethiopia and Somalia, and letters to his parents were sent to Washington and then forwarded on to Mogadishu, meaning that his news was more than a month old by the time they got it. I suppose it wasn't much different than living as a foreign-exchange student. Young people do it all the time, but to me it sounds awful. The Hoyts had two sons about Hugh's age who were always saying things like "Hey that's *our* sofa you're sitting on" and "Hands off that ornamental stein. It doesn't belong to you."

He'd been living with these people for a year when he overheard Mr. Hoyt   17
tell a friend that he and his family would soon be moving to Munich, Germany, the beer capital of the world.

"And that worried me," Hugh said, "because it meant I'd have to find   18
some other place to live."

Where I come from, finding shelter is a problem the average teenager   19
might confidently leave to his parents. It was just something that came with having a mom and a dad. Worried that he might be sent to live with his grandparents in Kentucky, Hugh turned to the school's guidance counselor, who knew of a family whose son had recently left for college. And so he spent another year living with strangers and not mentioning his birthday. While I wouldn't have wanted to do it myself, I can't help but envy the sense of fortitude he gained from the experience. After graduating from college, he moved to France knowing only the phrase "Do you speak French?" — a question guaranteed to get you nowhere unless you also speak the language.

While living in Africa, Hugh and his family took frequent vacations,   20
often in the company of their monkey. The Nairobi Hilton, some suite of high-ceilinged rooms in Cairo or Khartoum: These are the places his people recall when gathered at a common table. "Was that the summer we spent in Beirut or, no, I'm thinking of the time we sailed from Cyprus and took the *Orient Express* to Istanbul."

Theirs was the life I dreamt about during my vacations in eastern North   21
Carolina. Hugh's family was hobnobbing with chiefs and sultans while I ate hush puppies at the Sanitary Fish Market in Morehead City, a beach towel wrapped like a hijab around my head. Someone unknown to me was very likely standing in a muddy ditch and dreaming of an evening spent sitting in a clean family restaurant, drinking iced tea and working his way through an extra-large seaman's platter, but that did not concern me, as it meant I should have been happy with what I had. Rather than surrender to my bitterness, I have learned to take satisfaction in the life that Hugh has led. His stories have, over time, become my own. I say this with no trace of a kumbaya.[1] There is no spiritual symbiosis; I'm just a petty thief who lifts his memories the same way I'll take a handful of change left on his dresser. When my own experiences fall short of the mark, I just go out and spend some of his. It is

[1] From the gospel-folk song with the line "Kumbaya, my Lord, kumbaya," meaning "Come by here." Probably because of its popularity in folk music, the word now also has negative connotations of passivity or touchy-feely spiritualism. — EDS.

with pleasure that I sometimes recall the dead man's purpled face or the report of the handgun ringing in my ears as I studied the blood pooling beneath the dead white piglet. On the way back from the slaughterhouse, we stopped for Cokes in the village of Mojo, where the gas-station owner had arranged a few tables and chairs beneath a dying canopy of vines. It was late afternoon by the time we returned to school, where a second bus carried me to the foot of Coffeeboard Road. Once there, I walked through a grove of eucalyptus trees and alongside a bald pasture of starving cattle, past the guard napping in his gatehouse, and into the waiting arms of my monkey.

Journal Writing

Hugh's experiences living with strangers gave him a "sense of fortitude" (par. 19), according to Sedaris. Have you ever gone through a difficult experience that left you somehow stronger? Write about the struggle in your journal. Was the trouble caused by family relationships? Educational or employment obstacles? Travel experiences? Something else?

Questions on Meaning

1. What is the subject of Sedaris's comparison and contrast in this essay?

2. What do you think is the THESIS of this essay? Take into account both Sedaris's obvious envy of Hugh's childhood and his awareness that Hugh's life was often lonely and insecure. Is the thesis stated or only implied?

3. There is a certain amount of IRONY in Sedaris's envy of Hugh's childhood. What is this irony? How does Sedaris make this irony explicit in paragraph 21?

Questions on Writing Strategy

1. Does Sedaris develop his comparison and contrast subject by subject or point by point? Briefly outline the essay to explain your answer.

2. Point to some of the TRANSITIONS Sedaris uses in moving between his and Hugh's lives.

3. Sedaris refers to Hugh's monkey in paragraphs 8, 16, 20, and 21. In what sense does he use the monkey as a SYMBOL?

4. The first five paragraphs of the essay include a conversation between Sedaris and Hugh about Hugh's childhood. Why do you think the author opened the essay this way?

5. **OTHER METHODS** How does Sedaris use NARRATION to develop his comparison and contrast?

Questions on Language

1. How does Sedaris use PARALLEL STRUCTURE in paragraph 8 to highlight the contrast between himself and Hugh? How does he then point up this parallelism?

2. Sedaris offers the image of himself as a "petty thief" in paragraph 21. What is the effect of this IMAGE?

3. Sedaris's language in this essay is notably SPECIFIC and CONCRETE. Point to examples of such language just in paragraph 6.

4. Consult a dictionary if necessary to learn the meanings of the following words: proximity, petty (par. 2); hyenas (6); hawking, stocks (7); leper (8); hangar (9); machetes (11); diplomatic (12); exoticism, coup, evacuate (13); ornamental, stein (16); fortitude (19); hobnobbing, symbiosis, report, canopy, eucalyptus (21).

Suggestions for Writing

1. **FROM JOURNAL TO ESSAY** Starting from your journal entry (p. 185), write an essay about a difficult experience that shows how it changed you, whether for better or for worse. How are you different now than before? What did the experience teach you?

2. In your library or on the Internet, locate and read reviews of Sedaris's book *Me Talk Pretty One Day*, the source of "Remembering My Childhood," or of another essay collection by Sedaris. Write an essay in which you SYNTHESIZE the reviewers' responses to Sedaris's work.

3. **CRITICAL WRITING** How seriously does Sedaris want the readers of his essay to take him? Write an essay in which you analyze his TONE, citing specific passages from the text to support your conclusions.

4. **CONNECTIONS** Andrea Roman, in "We're Not . . ." (p. 187), writes about a childhood unlike Sedaris's or Hugh's. In an essay, consider how Sedaris and Roman might view each other's childhoods.

ANDREA ROMAN

The daughter of Bolivian immigrants, Andrea Roman was born in 1992 in Washington, DC, and grew up in Rockville, Maryland. She attended Saint Andrews Episcopal School, where she was captain of the varsity girls' soccer team and a volunteer medical translator. As a political science major at Boston College, she volunteered as a Big Sister and served on the cabinet for the school's Organization of Latin American Affairs. Roman graduated in 2014 and is now pursuing a master's degree in education at the University of Pennsylvania, where she works with Teach for America and remains "extremely devoted" to Caporales, a popular Bolivian folk dance.

"We're Not . . ."

Roman wrote "We're Not . . ." at the end of a first-year writing seminar. She revised it with feedback from her classmates and saw it selected for *Fresh Ink*, Boston College's annual collection of student writing. Assigned to write a personal account of a significant event in her life, she chose to focus on a series of disagreements with her mother. Like David Sedaris in the previous essay, Roman compares two distinct cultures, both of them important to the writer's identity.

"No somos pobres, Andrea. Para qué tienes que prestar ropa?"[1] These were words I heard continually from my mother as I grew up. My parents, being immigrants from Bolivia during the eighties, experienced a complete culture clash when they arrived in America. One would think that language would create the biggest barriers for immigrants but in my mother's case, the biggest obstacles were the small cultural differences. Sooner or later, this became a generic formula for strict rules given by my parents: "We're not _____, Andrea. Why do you have to _____?" Typically, the first blank was filled in by the word "American," while the second invariably changed. My mother could not understand that certain unacceptable actions in our culture were quite acceptable here in the States.

I was eleven years old when I first showed up at my house with an article of clothing that was not mine. I had spilled hot chocolate all over my sweater

1

2

---

[1] Spanish, "We're not poor, Andrea. Why do you have to borrow clothes?" — EDS.

during lunch that day. Luckily, my best friend Emily had an extra zip-up in her locker. As any good friend would do, she offered me her sweater to wear for the rest of the day since it was the middle of December. Logically, I accepted the sweater with gratitude and went on with my day as if nothing strange had happened. Little did I know, when my mother picked me up from school, I would receive the familiar speech about how embarrassing my act had been.

"De quien es esa chompa?!" Those were the very first words that came out   3
of my mother's mouth. Not a breath, not an intake of air, just these words in a ridiculing tone: "Whose sweater is that?!" I remained clueless and answered the question, simply, "Emily's." Immediately after my answer, my mother gave me one of the longest speeches I have ever heard. "We're not poor, Andrea. Why do you have to borrow clothes? I buy you clothes. You have sweaters. You wore one this morning!" I could not grasp the magnitude of my mother's anger or disturbance as I did not see what the big deal was in borrowing a sweater. Kids in my class did it all the time without any problem. They'd borrow a sweater one day and give it back the other. It was as simple as that — but not to my mother. "In Bolivia," my mother said, "we do not borrow clothes from other people. It is seen as an insult to the family in saying that we cannot afford to take care of our family. It's a want of an unnecessary thing seeing as you already have your own." The speech went on and on, usually repeating the same points, until I finally got a word in: "I stained my sweater. I had nothing to wear and was cold. I just don't see why it's such a big deal." Boy, was that a mistake. Talking back to my mother was the worst thing I could have done. The second I got home I got a good deep mouth-washing with dishwasher soap as punishment.

"We're not American, Andrea. Why do you want a sleepover?" Sleepovers   4
were a big no to my family. In fact, they were unheard of. "You want to sleep where?" If my girlfriends were having a slumber party over the weekend, I knew better than to ask for permission. I learned this through multiple attempts and failed experiences: *"Mami, puedo ir a dormir donde la Caroline este viernes, porfa?" "Para qué?"* Great. Every time I asked to sleep over at a friend's house my mother's response was always, "Why?"

So I would then respond, "Because all my friends are sleeping over and it's   5
going to be fun and her parents said we could all spend the night."

"Mmm, then no."   6

"Pero por qué???"   7

"Te dije que no."[2]   8

And just like that my attempt to go to a sleepover would end.   9

---

[2] Spanish, "I told you no." — Eds.

"We're not American, Andrea. We don't do that in Bolivia. Everyone has   10
their own house for a reason. If you want to go over to Caroline's your father
will gladly take you and pick you up later tonight, but don't try to convince
him to stay over because it just won't work."

I suppose my mother letting me go to Caroline's for some time was better than   11
nothing, yet I always longed for that sleepover. Growing up, I quickly learned
that what my mother said was the rule in the household. After several attempts
to attend a sleepover, I gave up — not because I didn't want to sleep over, but
because I began to understand why my mother didn't want me to stay over.

Sunday, 1:00 p.m. My family is just getting out of church and deciding   12
where to go for lunch, when all of a sudden I remember that a six-page paper
is due in class on Monday. I assume I had a stunned look on my face, because
my mother asked what was wrong.

"Oh, nothing. I just remembered that I have an essay due tomorrow, so   13
I'll probably have to start working on that rather soon, if that influences our
lunch decision."

"You mean to say that you left all your homework due Monday to do   14
today?"

"Yeah . . ."   15

"Why would you do that? Don't you know Sunday is family day? A day to   16
worship God and be thankful for family?"

"Yes . . ."   17

"Okay then, so you don't have any work due tomorrow right?"   18

"No, Mami, I just said I have an essay due."   19

"Sundays are not the day to leave homework for. That's why you get Friday   20
and Saturday. You have two days to complete it; there is no reason why you
need Sunday, too."

Geesh. My mother sure did accumulate rules over the years.   21

"Okay, Mami, but I really have to do this essay now."   22

"Well you should have thought of that sooner, no?"   23

Silence overtook the car on our way home and I could feel the disappoint-   24
ment on my mother's face.

When I first arrived at Boston College, I immediately knew that my con-   25
servative cultural position would have to become more open-minded. I knew
that not everyone had grown up with strict Bolivian parents, as I had. I would
not have to lose my cultural identity, however.

As I lay in my new bed for the very first time in an unfamiliar room filled   26
with familiar things, I started to ask myself the same question that my hall
mates confronted me with: "Why do you have such a big American flag?" This

question constantly arose when I met someone. Why *did* I have an American flag next to my Bolivian one? My mother instilled Bolivian values in me; Bolivian culture was the only thing I had ever been exposed to, and I loved it. I had just bought this American flag a week before move-in day for my room decorations.

Through my mother's multiple rules, I had become comfortable enough with my identity and culture that showing pride in another country would not take away from my heritage. I now borrow clothes, have sleepovers, and do a ton of work on Sundays, but I have not left behind that little Bolivian girl who received the mouth-washing with dishwasher soap, no matter what flag hangs on my wall.

27

Journal Writing

Write about a time when you were punished for an act that you didn't think was a "big deal." What did you do, and what was the punishment? Was it fair? How did the situation make you feel about your action? about whoever punished you? about yourself? about others involved, such as anyone who may have gotten you into trouble?

Questions on Meaning

1. What is Roman's THESIS? Where does she state it?

2. What seems to be Roman's PURPOSE in this essay? Does she mean to explain or to evaluate? How can you tell?

3. Why was Roman's mother so upset that her daughter borrowed a sweater from a classmate? What prompted her to wash Roman's mouth with soap?

4. Why does Roman hang two flags on the wall of her dorm room? What do they represent to her?

Questions on Writing Strategy

1. What is the function of the extra spaces between certain paragraphs in Roman's essay? What do they indicate?

2. Roman organizes her essay point by point. What points does she compare? What is her basis of comparison?

3. To whom does Roman seem to be writing? Why do you think so?

4. What is notable about Roman's concluding paragraph?

5. **OTHER METHODS**   Roman uses NARRATION to relate three telling episodes involving her mother. What does the dialog contribute to her essay?

Questions on Language

1. How does Roman ensure that English-speaking readers will understand the Spanish phrases she quotes in her essay? Are any statements left unclear to you?

2. Where in the essay does Roman include variations on her mother's complaint "We're not _____, Andrea. Why do you have to _____?" (par. 1)? What is the EFFECT of this repetition?

3. Consult a dictionary if necessary to learn the meanings of the following words: invariably (par. 1), magnitude (3), accumulate (21), instilled (26), heritage (27).

Suggestions for Writing

1. **FROM JOURNAL TO ESSAY**   Based on your journal entry, write an essay in which you narrate your experience (or, perhaps, experiences) with being punished while growing up. As you plan and draft your essay, try to draw a larger point about the results of the punishment(s) on your sense of fairness. What did you learn about yourself and the world around you?

2. Roman writes of differences with her mother that frustrated her but that also helped form her sense of identity. In a narrative and descriptive essay, relate some aspect of a relationship with a parent or other figure of authority that you found troubling or even maddening at the time but that now seems to have shaped you in positive ways. Did a parent (or someone else) push you to study when you wanted to play sports or hang out with your friends? make you attend religious services when they seemed unimportant to you? refuse to let you participate in certain activities? try to direct you onto a path that you didn't care to take?

3. **CRITICAL WRITING**   Roman attributes many of her mother's attitudes to her Bolivian heritage. As an extension of the previous assignment, consider whether Roman's experiences are particular to Bolivian American families or are common in all families, whatever their ethnicity. Are conflicts between children and their parents inevitable, do you think? Why, or why not?

4. **CONNECTIONS**   Much as David Sedaris, in the previous essay, expresses envy for his partner's more exotic childhood in Africa, Roman reveals a certain amount of envy for her classmates' less restrictive American upbringings. Write an essay in which you compare and contrast your own experiences with those of someone you've envied. What in that person's life was attractive to you? Have your feelings, like Sedaris's and Roman's, changed over time? Why, or why not?

Andrea Roman on Writing

Asked how she chose the SUBJECT for "We're Not . . . ," Andrea Roman answered, "I had a lot of difficulty in deciding what to write about because truthfully, I didn't think I was all that interesting." Away from her family, she was painfully homesick and seriously contemplated moving back. Being assigned to write about an event in her life prompted Roman to think about why she was having such a hard time adjusting to college. "After a lot of self-reflection," she says, she pinpointed the source of her discomfort: While at home her "school-life was separate from home-life," at college "school *was* home." For the first time, she felt her "two cultures were colliding." The effort to "integrate" her "American and Bolivian lives," she decided, was a struggle worth exploring in writing.

Roman wrote two drafts and then, with "amazing help" from her teacher and her classmates, was able to "refine and refocus the most important aspects" of her experience. "They informed me of the parts they found most interesting," she explains, "so that I could expand on those specific ideas and events." By the time she was finished, she was gratified to discover that writing had "guided" her "in understanding and embracing the difficult time" she was having. Roman encourages other writers to always ask for feedback as well, particularly when writing about their own lives. "You lived through the story," she points out, "but no one else did. An outsider's perspective can highlight ambiguity and confusion" and help you "be as clear as possible."

The best advice Roman ever received? "Don't hold back, be true, and let yourself go." She explains why this mantra has proven so useful: "Our personal experiences and inspirations can never be taken away from us, and we should not shy away from telling our stories. If we do not share our obstacles and adversities, they will be lost and unheard. When you try to write what you think the audience wants, a feeling of forcedness is apparent. Inversely, when you write truthfully, genuineness becomes evident."

The Brief Bedford Reader on Writing

Roman's experience bears out a lesson that many beginning writers have trouble grasping: DRAFTING provides an opportunity to explore a subject for yourself, to "let yourself go" and discover what you think. REVISION is the time to rework an essay with a particular AUDIENCE in mind. For help identifying the most interesting parts of your drafts and developing those ideas with specifics, you can always turn to your peers — and to pages 39–42 of this book.

BRUCE CATTON

Bruce Catton (1899–1978) was one of America's best-known historians of the American Civil War. As a boy in Benzonia, Michigan, Catton acted out historical battles on local playing fields. In his memoir *Waiting for the Morning Train* (1972), he recalls how he would listen by the hour to the memories of Union army veterans. His studies at Oberlin College were interrupted by service in World War I, and he never finished his bachelor's degree. Instead, he worked as a reporter, columnist, and editorial writer for the *Cleveland Plain Dealer* and other newspapers, then became a speechwriter and information director for government agencies. Of Catton's eighteen books, seventeen were written after he turned fifty. *A Stillness at Appomattox* (1953) won him both a Pulitzer Prize for history and a National Book Award; other notable works include *This Hallowed Ground* (1956) and *Gettysburg: The Final Fury* (1974). From 1954 until his death, Catton edited *American Heritage*, a magazine of history. President Gerald Ford awarded him a Medal of Freedom for his life's accomplishment.

Grant and Lee: A Study in Contrasts

"Grant and Lee: A Study in Contrasts" first appeared in *The American Story*, a book of essays written by eminent historians for interested general readers. Ulysses S. Grant and Robert E. Lee were opposing generals of the Civil War, Grant commanding forces of the North and Lee commanding forces of the South (called the Confederacy). The war lasted from 1861 to 1865, ending with Lee's surrender to Grant during the meeting Catton describes. Contrasting the two great generals allows Catton to portray not only two very different men but also the conflicting traditions they represented. Catton's essay builds toward the conclusion that, in one outstanding way, the two leaders were more than a little alike.

When Ulysses S. Grant and Robert E. Lee met in the parlor of a modest house at Appomattox Court House, Virginia, on April 9, 1865, to work out the terms for the surrender of Lee's Army of Northern Virginia, a great chapter in American life came to a close, and a great new chapter began. 1

These men were bringing the Civil War to its virtual finish. To be sure, other armies had yet to surrender, and for a few days the fugitive Confederate government would struggle desperately and vainly, trying to find some way to go on living now that its chief support was gone. But in effect it was all over when Grant and Lee signed the papers. And the little room where they wrote out the terms was the scene of one of the poignant, dramatic contrasts in American history. 2

193

They were two strong men, these oddly different generals, and they   3
represented the strengths of two conflicting currents that, through them, had
come into final collision.

Back of Robert E. Lee was the notion that the old aristocratic concept   4
might somehow survive and be dominant in American life.

Lee was tidewater Virginia, and in his background were family, culture,   5
and tradition . . . the age of chivalry transplanted to a New World which was
making its own legends and its own myths. He embodied a way of life that had
come down through the age of knighthood and the English country squire.
America was a land that was beginning all over again, dedicated to nothing
much more complicated than the rather hazy belief that all men had equal
rights, and should have an equal chance in the world. In such a land Lee stood
for the feeling that it was somehow of advantage to human society to have a
pronounced inequality in the social structure. There should be a leisure class,
backed by ownership of land; in turn, society itself should be keyed to the land
as the chief source of wealth and influence. It would bring forth (according to
this ideal) a class of men with a strong sense of obligation to the community;
men who lived not to gain advantage for themselves, but to meet the solemn
obligations which had been laid on them by the very fact that they were privileged. From them the country would get its leadership; to them it could look
for the higher values — of thought, of conduct, of personal deportment — to
give it strength and virtue.

Lee embodied the noblest elements of this aristocratic ideal. Through   6
him, the landed nobility justified itself. For four years, the Southern states had
fought a desperate war to uphold the ideals for which Lee stood. In the end,
it almost seemed as if the Confederacy fought for Lee; as if he himself was the
Confederacy . . . the best thing that the way of life for which the Confederacy
stood could ever have to offer. He had passed into legend before Appomattox.
Thousands of tired, underfed, poorly clothed Confederate soldiers, long since
past the simple enthusiasm of the early days of the struggle, somehow considered Lee the symbol of everything for which they had been willing to die. But
they could not quite put this feeling into words. If the Lost Cause, sanctified
by so much heroism and so many deaths, had a living justification, its justification was General Lee.

Grant, the son of a tanner on the Western frontier, was everything Lee   7
was not. He had come up the hard way, and embodied nothing in particular
except the eternal toughness and sinewy fiber of the men who grew up beyond
the mountains. He was one of a body of men who owed reverence and obeisance to no one, who were self-reliant to a fault, who cared hardly anything
for the past but who had a sharp eye for the future.

These frontier men were the precise opposites of the tidewater aristocrats.   8
Back of them, in the great surge that had taken people over the Alleghenies
and into the opening Western country, there was a deep, implicit dissatisfaction with a past that had settled into grooves. They stood for democracy, not
from any reasoned conclusion about the proper ordering of human society, but
simply because they had grown up in the middle of democracy and knew how
it worked. Their society might have privileges, but they would be privileges
each man had won for himself. Forms and patterns meant nothing. No man
was born to anything, except perhaps to a chance to show how far he could
rise. Life was competition.

Yet along with this feeling had come a deep sense of belonging to a   9
national community. The Westerner who developed a farm, opened a shop, or
set up in business as a trader could hope to prosper only as his own community
prospered — and his community ran from the Atlantic to the Pacific and from
Canada down to Mexico. If the land was settled, with towns and highways
and accessible markets, he could better himself. He saw his fate in terms of the
nation's own destiny. As its horizons expanded, so did his. He had, in other
words, an acute dollars-and-cents stake in the continued growth and development of his country.

And that, perhaps, is where the contrast between Grant and Lee becomes   10
most striking. The Virginia aristocrat, inevitably, saw himself in relation to his
own region. He lived in a static society which could endure almost anything
except change. Instinctively, his first loyalty would go to the locality in which
that society existed. He would fight to the limit of endurance to defend it,
because in defending it he was defending everything that gave his own life its
deepest meaning.

The Westerner, on the other hand, would fight with an equal tenacity   11
for the broader concept of society. He fought so because everything he lived
by was tied to growth, expansion, and a constantly widening horizon. What
he lived by would survive or fall with the nation itself. He could not possibly
stand by unmoved in the face of an attempt to destroy the Union. He would
combat it with everything he had, because he could only see it as an effort to
cut the ground out from under his feet.

So Grant and Lee were in complete contrast, representing two diametri-   12
cally opposed elements in American life. Grant was the modern man emerging; beyond him, ready to come on the stage, was the great age of steel and
machinery, of crowded cities and a restless, burgeoning vitality. Lee might
have ridden down from the old age of chivalry, lance in hand, silken banner
fluttering over his head. Each man was the perfect champion of his cause,
drawing both his strengths and his weaknesses from the people he led.

Yet it was not all contrast, after all. Different as they were — in   13
background, in personality, in underlying aspiration — these two great soldiers had much in common. Under everything else, they were marvelous
fighters. Furthermore, their fighting qualities were really very much alike.

Each man had, to begin with, the great virtue of utter tenacity and fidel-   14
ity. Grant fought his way down the Mississippi Valley in spite of acute personal discouragement and profound military handicaps. Lee hung on in the
trenches at Petersburg after hope itself had died. In each man there was an
indomitable quality . . . the born fighter's refusal to give up as long as he can
still remain on his feet and lift his two fists.

Daring and resourcefulness they had, too; the ability to think faster   15
and move faster than the enemy. These were the qualities which gave Lee
the dazzling campaigns of Second Manassas and Chancellorsville and won
Vicksburg for Grant.

Lastly, and perhaps greatest of all, there was the ability, at the end, to turn   16
quickly from war to peace once the fighting was over. Out of the way these
two men behaved at Appomattox came the possibility of a peace of reconcili-
ation. It was a possibility not wholly realized, in the years to come, but which
did, in the end, help the two sections to become one nation again . . . after
a war whose bitterness might have seemed to make such a reunion wholly
impossible. No part of either man's life became him more than the part he
played in their brief meeting in the McLean house at Appomattox. Their
behavior there put all succeeding generations of Americans in their debt. Two
great Americans, Grant and Lee — very different, yet under everything very
much alike. Their encounter at Appomattox was one of the great moments of
American history.

Journal Writing

How do you respond to the opposing political beliefs represented by Grant and Lee?
During the American Civil War, nearly every citizen had an opinion and chose sides.
Do you think Americans today commit themselves as strongly to political and social
causes? In your journal, explain why, or why not.

Questions on Meaning

1. What is Catton's PURPOSE in writing: to describe the meeting of two generals at a
   famous moment in history, to explain how the two men stood for opposing social
   forces in America, or to show how the two differed in personality?

2. SUMMARIZE the background and the way of life that produced Robert E. Lee; then do the same for Ulysses S. Grant. According to Catton, what ideals did each man represent?

3. In the historian's view, what essential traits did the two men have in common? Which trait does Catton think most important of all? For what reason?

4. How does this essay help you understand why Grant and Lee were such determined fighters?

Questions on Writing Strategy

1. From the content of this essay, and from knowing where it first appeared, what can you INFER about Catton's original AUDIENCE? At what places in "Grant and Lee: A Study in Contrasts" does the writer expect of his readers a familiarity with US history?

2. What EFFECT does the writer achieve by setting both his INTRODUCTION and his CONCLUSION in Appomattox?

3. For what reasons does Catton contrast the two generals *before* he compares them? Suppose he had reversed his outline, and had dealt first with Grant's and Lee's mutual resemblances. Why would his essay have been less effective?

4. Closely read the first sentence of every paragraph and underline each word or phrase in it that serves as a TRANSITION. Then review your underlinings. How much COHERENCE has Catton given his essay?

5. What is the TONE of this essay — that is, what is the writer's attitude toward his two subjects? Is Catton poking fun at Lee by imagining the Confederate general as a knight of the Middle Ages, "lance in hand, silken banner fluttering over his head" (par. 12)?

6. **OTHER METHODS** In identifying "two conflicting currents," Catton uses CLASSIFICATION to sort Civil War–era Americans into two groups represented by Lee and Grant. Catton then uses ANALYSIS to tease out the characteristics of each current, each type. How do classification and analysis serve Catton's comparison and contrast?

Questions on Language

1. In his opening paragraph, Catton uses a metaphor: American life is a book containing chapters. Find other FIGURES OF SPEECH in his essay (consulting the Glossary if you need help). What do the figures of speech contribute?

2. What information do you glean from "Lee was tidewater Virginia" (par. 5)?

3. Look up *poignant* in the dictionary. Why is it such a fitting word in paragraph 2? Why wouldn't *touching*, *sad*, or *teary* have been as good?

4. Define *aristocratic* (pars. 4 and 6), *obeisance* (7), and *indomitable* (14) as Catton uses them, based solely on their context in the essay.

Suggestions for Writing

1. **FROM JOURNAL TO ESSAY** Using your journal entry (p. 196) as a starting point, write an essay that offers an explanation for public participation in or commitment to political and social causes today. What fires people up or turns them off? To help focus your essay, zero in on a specific issue, such as education, government spending, health insurance, or terrorism.

2. In your thinking and your attitudes, whom do you more closely resemble — Grant or Lee? Compare and contrast your outlook with that of one of these famous Americans or the other. (A serious tone for this topic isn't required.)

3. Catton writes with respect for the Confederacy and its values as they were exemplified in Robert E. Lee's background and beliefs. The flag that Lee fought under is currently the subject of much heated debate, as some argue that it represents hatred and violence against African Americans, while others insist that it represents Southern tradition and heritage. What is your take on the issue? Should any states or institutions, for instance, fly the Confederate flag on public land? Should individuals display it on their private property or on their persons? Why do you feel the way you do? Present your argument in a brief essay, taking care to consider both sides of the debate.

4. **CRITICAL WRITING** Although slavery, along with other issues, helped precipitate the Civil War, Catton in this particular essay does not deal with it. Perhaps he assumes that his readers will supply the missing context themselves. Is this a fair ASSUMPTION? If Catton had recalled the facts of slavery, would he have undermined any of his assertions about Lee? (Though the general of the proslavery Confederacy, Lee was personally opposed to slavery.) In a brief essay, judge whether or not the omission of slavery weakens the essay, and explain why.

5. **CONNECTIONS** Catton contrasts Robert E. Lee's and Ulysses S. Grant's ideas about the privileges and obligations inherent in aristocracy and democracy, respectively. Tal Fortgang, in "Checking My Privilege" (p. 376), and Roxane Gay, in "Peculiar Benefits" (p. 383), also examine the notion that some people enjoy built-in advantages in American society. In a brief essay full of specific examples, discuss whether the "two diametrically opposed elements in American life" (as Catton calls them in par. 12) still exist in the country today. Is there any "advantage to human society to have a pronounced inequality in the social structure," as Lee believed (5)? Or is it true, as Grant exemplified, that nobody "was born to anything, except perhaps to a chance to show how far he could rise" (8)?

ALAIN DE BOTTON

Alain de Botton is a journalist whom the *Houston Chronicle* has credited with creating his "own subgenre of nonfiction, one that examines the preoccupations of everyday life . . . through the lens of philosophy." He was born in 1969 in Zurich, Switzerland, emigrated to England in 1981, and earned degrees in history and philosophy from Caius College, Cambridge (1991) and King's College London (1992). For a time de Botton directed the graduate philosophy program at London University but decided that the academic world was too rigid and stifling for his tastes. As a writer, de Botton debuted as an experimental novelist in the mid-1990s before inventing the distinct blend of criticism and self-help for which he is known. He has published a dozen such books on subjects ranging from art and architecture to love and sex, including *Status Anxiety* (1994), *How Proust Can Change Your Life* (1997), *The Pleasures and Sorrows of Work* (2006), *Religion for Atheists* (2012), and, most recently, *The News: A User's Manual* (2014). As a producer, he has adapted several of his books into documentaries for PBS and the BBC and recorded lectures for *YouTube*. In 2008 de Botton founded (and still helps to run) the School of Life, an international offering of classes, workshops, and therapies "dedicated to a new vision of education" and designed to foster emotional intelligence in its students. He lives in London.

Tragedy

This essay, a self-contained section of *The News: A User's Manual*, illustrates de Botton's knack for distilling heady concepts for general readers. As he does throughout the book, the author takes a critical look at contemporary journalistic practices. In this case, our self-help philosopher examines the tendency of newspapers and broadcasters to fixate on the most gruesome of tragedies, finding in ancient Greek dramas a possible purpose in telling such stories.

A Manhattan doctor plunged 30 stories to his death from his Upper East Side high-rise yesterday in an apparent suicide, police and witnesses said. The body of Dr. Sheldon "Shelly" Steinbach, 68, an anesthesiologist, slammed into a second-floor balcony at the building, at 246 E. 63rd St., at 9:35 a.m. "I heard a large bang, and we looked outside and saw him. His body just exploded," said resident Jonathan Kershner, 25, who lives two floors above where the doctor landed. "Then a doorman came by saying a woman was looking for her husband," Kershner added. Steinbach had a *Twitter* page but had not updated it since October 2011. The personal description on his account reads: "I am an anesthesiologist in New York City and am having a great day. Married. Love aerobic activities and music."

— *New York Post*

Every time we connect with the news, we can be sure that we will be   1
confronted by graphic accounts of some of the most appalling eventualities
that can befall our species: A depressed man leaps out of the window, a mother
poisons her children, a teacher rapes his pupil, a husband beheads his wife,
a teenager shoots his classmates. The news leads us very reliably into the
crucible of human horror.

A decent impulse is to look away and to insist that such deaths and trau-   2
mas are simply too sad and too private to be subjected to a stranger's gaze.
Any curiosity seems, from this perspective, to be a particularly shameful and
modern kind of pathology.

Motivated by fears of intrusion, the more serious news organizations   3
typically adopt a reserved tone in their reports on the sorts of events that
severely test any faith one might still have in the reasonableness and decency
of mankind.

They leave it to their less dignified colleagues, unfettered by scruples, to   4
evoke the truly vivid details of the latest outrages: to give us a close-up view
of the body after it fell from the balcony, the bedroom where the little child
was tied up or the carving knife with the spouse's blood still on its blade. Their
reward for being willing to undertake such investigations is the occasionally
guilty but concerted and lucrative interest of many millions of readers and
viewers.

It isn't hard to characterize the interest of the public in horror stories as   5
tasteless and unproductive. But beneath the surface banality, we should allow
that we are often — in confused and inarticulate ways — attempting to get at
something important. When immersing ourselves in blood-soaked narratives,
we are not always solely in search of entertainment or distraction; we are not
always being merely prurient or callously appropriating intensities of feeling
that our own lives have failed to provide.

We may also be looking to expose ourselves to barbaric tales to help us   6
retain a tighter hold on our more civilized selves — and in particular, to nur-
ture our always ephemeral reserves of patience, self-control, forgiveness and
empathy.

Rather than just inveigh moralistically against our fascination with hei-   7
nous events, the challenge should be to tweak how they are reported — in
order that they better release their important, yet too often latent, emotional
and societal benefits.

Every year, at the end of March, the citizens of ancient Athens would   8
gather under open skies on the southern slopes of the Acropolis in the Theater
of Dionysus and there listen to the latest works by the great tragedians of

their city. The plot lines of these plays were unmitigatingly macabre, easily matching anything our own news could provide: A man kills his father, marries his mother and gouges out his own eyes (*Oedipus Rex*); a man has his daughter murdered as part of a plan to revenge the infidelity of his brother's wife (*Iphigenia*); a mother murders her two children to spoil her unfaithful husband's plans to start a new family with another woman (*Medea*).[1]

Rather than regarding these stories as grotesque spectacles that all right-minded people should avoid, in his *Poetics* of c. 335 BC, the philosopher Aristotle looked generously upon the human fascination with them. He proposed that, when they are well written and artfully staged, such stories can become crucial resources for the emotional and moral education of a whole society. Despite the barbarity they describe, they themselves can function as civilizing forces.

But in order for this to happen, in order for a *horror* (a meaningless narration of revolting events) to turn into what Aristotle called a *tragedy* (an educative tale fashioned from abominations), the philosopher thought it was vital that the plot should be well arranged and the motives and the personalities of the characters properly outlined to us. Extreme dramatic skill would be required in order for the audience to spontaneously reach a point at which it recognized that the apparently unhinged protagonist of the story, who had acted impetuously, arrogantly and blindly, who had perhaps killed others and destroyed his own reputation and life, the person whom one might at first (had one come across the story in the news) dismissed as nothing but a maniac, was, in the final analysis, rather like us in certain key ways. A work of tragedy would rise to its true moral and edifying possibilities when the audience looked upon the hero's ghastly errors and crimes and was left with no option but to reach the terrifying conclusion: "How easily I, too, might have done the same." Tragedy's task was to demonstrate the ease with which an essentially decent and likeable person could end up generating hell.

If we were entirely sane, if madness did not have a serious grip on one side of us, other people's tragedies would hold a great deal less interest for us. While we circle gruesome stories in the media, we may at a highly unconscious level be exploring shocking but important questions: "If things got really out of hand late one night, and I was feeling wound up and tired and insecure, might I be capable of killing my partner?" "If I was divorced and my spouse

9

10

11

[1] All three are classical Greek dramas. *Oedipus Rex*, by Sophocles (c. 496–406 BC), was first performed around 429 BC. *Iphigenia* and *Medea* were penned by Euripides (c. 480–406 BC) and debuted in 405 BC and 431 BC, respectively. — EDS.

Cascade News

A man drives into his family home to punish his wife, Manchester, 2012.

Erich Lessing / Art Resource, NY

Medea kills her son to punish her husband, Greek jar, c. 330 BC.

Our fascination with crimes may be part of an unconscious effort to make sure we never commit them.

was keeping my children from me, would I ever be able to kill them in a form of twisted revenge?" "Could I ever start chatting with a minor on the Internet and, without quite realizing the enormity of what I was doing, end up trying to seduce him or her?"

For civilization to proceed, we naturally need the answers to be a firm *no* in all cases. There is a serious task for the news here: The disasters we are introduced to should be framed in order to give us the maximum encouragement to practice *not* doing the things that the more chaotic parts of us would — under extreme circumstances — be attracted to exploring. We may never actually fling our children off a bridge at the end of our access day or shoot our partner dead during an argument, but we are all, at times, emotionally in the space where these sorts of things can happen. Tragedies remind us how badly we need to keep controlling ourselves by showing us what happens when people don't.

Tragedies shouldn't only help us to be good, they should also prompt us to be kind. How likely we are to be sympathetic to someone who kills their spouse or children depends in large part on how their story happens to be told to us: what information we are given about them, how we are introduced to their motives and with what degree of insight and complexity their psyches are laid before us.

In Greek tragedies, a Chorus regularly interrupts events to direct sentiments and richly contextualize characters' actions. It tends to speak with solemn respect about the protagonists, whatever the sins they have committed. Such sensitivity ensures that few audience members are likely to leave a performance of *Oedipus Rex* dismissing the unfortunate central character as a "loser" or "psycho."

The news is less careful in its narrations; and our judgements are — as a result — far more intemperate and nastier:

> A Teesside doctor who downloaded more than 1,300 child porn images, including scenes of torture, has been jailed. Police found the "sickening" images on the laptop of James Taylor, 31, from Wensleydale Gardens, Thornaby. The doctor, who worked at Pinderfields Hospital in Wakefield, earlier admitted looking at indecent images of children. Taylor was sentenced to a year and a day in prison by a judge at Teesside Crown Court on Friday and was banned from working with children for life.
>
> — BBC

At first glance, the doctor seems to deserve no sympathy whatsoever. But our decision about how we consider him is crucially dependent on how the facts of his case are presented to us. We could sympathize with more or less anyone if their story was told to us in a certain way — *and we wouldn't necessarily be wrong to do so* (as Dostoevsky or Jesus would have reminded us).[2]

In the context of news reporting, this claim seems contentious, even dangerous, because we have to juggle two ideas which sound opposing: that we can sympathize with a criminal and at the same time firmly condemn his or her crime. The news is tacitly convinced that its audience wouldn't be able to pull off this conceptual feat, and that any sympathy it might express would lead the audience to want to open up the prisons and let murderers roam the streets. It hence remains steadfast in its refusal to undertake the narrative and psychological maneuvers required to humanize criminals. Instead it rushes through their stories. A performance of *Oedipus Rex* might last an hour and a half; the news story in which the doctor appears is 304 words long. 16

Inevitably, a feeling of outrage is likely to be at its height when we confront the headline "Doctor had 'sickening' child porn." But, as we read on, our certainty might be challenged. Towards the end of the piece, we learn, "Ordering Taylor to sign the Sex Offenders Register for 10 years, the judge said: 'As a result of this conviction no doubt your career will come to an end.'" We might feel a chill at the thought of how seven long years of medical school had come to this. The article gives a hint of the panic the doctor must have felt: "The court was told Taylor initially denied being responsible, but later admitted, during police interviews, that he had downloaded the images." And the enormous price that he has subsequently had to pay: "Stephen Rich, defending, told Judge George Moorhouse that Taylor's wife and newborn baby had left him and that his life had collapsed." 17

An addendum informs us that while in prison, the man tried to commit suicide. All this is no less sad than the plot line of *Madame Bovary* or *Hamlet* — and, let's argue, the character of the doctor is not fundamentally any worse; Hamlet is, after all, a murderer and Emma Bovary is guilty of extreme child cruelty.[3] We consider them "tragic" figures — that is, entitled to a degree of complex understanding — because we imagine that there must have been something unusually noble and dignified about their nature and circumstances. But really it is only the generosity of spirit of Flaubert and Shakespeare that elevates Bovary and Hamlet above the ordinary criminal and dissuades us from judging them as harshly as we might the imprisoned doctor. 18

When reporting on a tragedy, the news tends to make dreadful conduct seem unique to a particular person. It resists the wider resonance and the more helpful conclusion: that we are all a hair's breadth away from catastrophe. 19

[2] Russian author Fyodor Dostoevsky (1821–81) is known especially for the philosophical novels *The Brothers Karamazov* (1880) and *Crime and Punishment* (1886), both of which examine questions of murder and morality. — EDS.

[3] *Hamlet*, by William Shakespeare (1564–1616), was first published in print form in 1603. *Madame Bovary*, by French novelist Gustave Flaubert (1821–80), appeared in 1856. — EDS.

This knowledge should, if properly absorbed, sink us into a mood of reflective, mature sadness. We are more implicated than we might like to believe in the misdeeds of other members of our species. A lack of a serious criminal record is in large measure a matter of luck and good circumstance, not proof of an incorruptible nature. A clean conscience is the preserve of those without sufficient imagination. Were life, or what the Greeks termed the gods, ever really to test us, we would almost surely be found wanting — an awareness upon which a measure of understanding towards the guilty should be founded.

The tragedians of ancient Greece never forgot this. They liked to tell us   20
how vicious, stupid, sexual, enraged and blind we could be, but they allowed room for complex compassion as well. Through the examples they leave us, we are coaxed into accepting that we are members of a noble but hideously flawed species; capable of performing amazing feats, ably practicing medicine or parenting with love for many years, and then of turning around and blowing up our existence with a single rash move. We should be scared. The ancient Greeks saw tragic plays once a year, at a specific time, within a particular context and with some knowledge of the works' larger purpose.

By contrast, we take in tragic news stories almost every day, but we rarely   21
recognize them as belonging to a coherent narrative cycle with a distinctive moral to impart. The news doesn't help us to place in a single genre all those incidents in which self-control is lost and the monster within is released. It doesn't, as it should, gather all its varied tales of horror under the unified heading of "Tragedy" and then narrate them in such a way that we can more easily recognize our own smoldering tendencies in the demented actions of the bloody protagonists.

Much of the news is in the end an account of people around the globe,   22
in all sorts of positions, getting things very wrong. They fail to master their emotions, contain their obsessions, judge right from wrong and act decently when there is still time. We shouldn't waste their failures. The news, like literature and history, can serve as that most vital of instruments, a "life simulator" — which is to say, a machine that inserts us into a variety of scenarios stretching far beyond anything we might ordinarily have to cope with and that affords us a chance safely, and at our leisure, to hone our best responses.

Yet too often the news doesn't help us to learn from the experiences of our   23
wretched brethren; it doesn't actively try to spare us and our societies the full force of error at every new turn. If a good life demands that we learn from, and imitate, the example of inspiring figures, it also requires us to undertake close study of those whose behavior should profoundly scare, horrify and warn us. These are two sides of the same coin of growth and development, and it lies within the remit of the news, if not yet on its agenda, to help us with both.

Journal Writing

In his conclusion de Botton remarks that a lot "of the news is in the end an account of people around the globe, in all sorts of positions, getting things very wrong" (par. 22). In your journal, reflect on some things you have gotten wrong. When is the last time you remember slipping up? What was the most significant mistake you ever made? Could it have destroyed you or someone else, or were the potential consequences less serious? What actually happened?

Questions on Meaning

1. What is the PURPOSE of de Botton's essay? Does he seek to justify sloppy or sensationalistic journalism? to defend readers who are drawn to gruesome stories? something else? How do you know?

2. How OBJECTIVE is de Botton's portrayal of contemporary news and Greek tragedy? Does he seem to prefer one GENRE over the other?

3. Does de Botton have a THESIS? Explain the central idea of his essay. What is the basis for comparison?

4. Summarize de Botton's comparison and contrast. What do news reports and Greek tragedies have in common? How are they different? What does de Botton see as the major problem with the reporting he describes?

5. The author refers to three ancient plays (*Oedipus Rex*, *Iphigenia*, and *Medea*) and mentions a few other works of philosophy and literature (such as Aristotle's *Poetics*, Shakespeare's *Hamlet*, and Flaubert's *Madame Bovary*). Does he seem to expect that his audience will understand these ALLUSIONS? Do readers need to be familiar with the texts de Botton cites to understand his comparison or appreciate his meaning?

Questions on Writing Strategy

1. De Botton's comparison is organized point by point — similarities in basic plots, then differences in the writers' sensitivity to context and their audiences' capacity for empathy. What is the EFFECT of this organization? Or, from another angle, what would have been the effect of a subject-by-subject organization — just contemporary news, then just Greek tragedies (or vice versa)?

2. How does de Botton indicate when he's changing points of comparison?

3. "Tragedy" includes two visuals. What do the parallels in the pictures of a video frame and a vase contribute to de Botton's comparison?

4. **OTHER METHODS** Take note of de Botton's reliance on Aristotle's ANALYSIS of drama (pars. 9–10) to support his own interpretation of the news. What, according to the ancient philosopher, are the major elements of tragedy? How is it distinct from horror?

Questions on Language

1. Consult a dictionary if you are unable to determine the meanings of the following words from their context in de Botton's essay: crucible (par. 1); pathology (2); unfettered, scruples, lucrative (4); banality, prurient (5); ephemeral, empathy (6); inveigh, latent (7); unmitigatingly, macabre (8); abominations, protagonist, impetuously, edifying (10); psyches (13); tacitly, steadfast (16); brethren (23).

2. This essay opens with some particularly graphic IMAGES from crime reports. What do you take to be de Botton's intended effect of including such disturbing language? How well does he succeed, in your estimation?

3. The author includes several quotations from newspapers but only SUMMARIZES the plays he cites. Why do you think that is?

4. How would you characterize de Botton's DICTION and TONE? What does his language contribute to the overall effectiveness of his comparison?

Suggestions for Writing

1. **FROM JOURNAL TO ESSAY**   Do you agree with de Botton that most people have the capacity to lose control and fall victim to the kinds of mistakes that make headlines? How common are the kinds of stories he relates? What are your attitudes toward them? Do you tend to sympathize with the characters, for instance, or are you more likely to judge them? Drawing on the mistakes you recalled in your journal (p. 206) for inspiration, write an essay in which you consider the average person's likelihood of committing a heinous crime. Who does these things? Why? What should a civilized society do about it?

2. Analyze the similarities and differences between two characters in your favorite play, film, or TV show. Which aspects of their personalities make them work well together, within the context in which they appear? Which characteristics work against each other, and therefore provide the necessary conflict to hold the reader's or viewer's attention?

3. **CRITICAL WRITING**   Find a recent newspaper story of the gruesome sort de Botton discusses and analyze it using his basis of comparison. Does the reporter, for instance, rush through the details, or does the report provide the kind of background and context that humanizes a subject? Are readers given a reason to sympathize with the perpetrator and learn from his or her example, or is the story mere spectacle? How well does the article conform to the careful style of writing de Botton would like to see more of in the news? Quote, paraphrase, and summarize the story as appropriate to support your conclusions.

4. **CONNECTIONS**   Christopher Beam, in "Blood Loss" (p. 358), also criticizes the news media. But where de Botton believes that crime reports, thoughtfully crafted, can make us better people, Beam suggests that they may actually incite violence and mayhem. What do you think? How much power do the media — newspapers, magazines, television, the Internet — hold over individuals' thoughts and behaviors? Are some forms of reporting more influential than others? Do news accounts affect world events, or merely record them? Taking evidence from both essays as well as your own reading, experience, and observation, write an essay that examines the state of journalism today.

Alain de Botton on Writing

As a generalist, Alain de Botton is known for writing on whatever subjects capture his imagination: His books have examined love, fine art, literature, religion, work, airports, journalism, and more. In a 2014 interview for the *Deloitte Review*, Scott Wilson asked him, "Does wielding such an obviously wide, diverse lens through which to observe, think, and write demand some sort of a process to getting stuff done?" The author responded:

Yes. Broadly speaking, my discipline base is the humanities. So I feed off history, psychology, philosophy, sociology. I'm not a scientist; I'm not an economist. I look at a number of areas related to, let's say, emotional satisfaction or well-being, which encompasses lots of different areas. So it can go as widely as architecture because architecture and the spaces we inhabit are part of what contribute to well-being. Overall I think it's about getting to grips with a topic and trying to find out what belongs to that topic. Really what I'm trying to do is to work out what ideas belong where. It's a chance to structure an order to a topic. So, if I'm writing about architecture, I want to try and gather all my thoughts that are around space and aesthetics and the psychology of location. I want to try and get all those ideas in there. And so the working process starts off relatively freeform and fluid and I'm just trying to get to the main idea. The best analogy is again with architecture. You start with a sketch. You then build it up into detailed plans. You then go into the actual construction of the thing. You put down the main bones and supporting pillars, and then at the very end, you're tidying and decorating the little details, the minor things. So it's very similar to putting up a building except you're putting up chapter three rather than a floor.

The Brief Bedford Reader on Writing

In describing his method of exploring a topic, finding the main idea, planning, drafting, revising, and editing, de Botton likens writing to architecture, one of his favorite academic disciplines. What do you make of this ANALOGY? How else is writing similar to constructing a building? For a concrete overview of the foundations of writing and the stages within it, see Chapter 2, especially pages 30–53.

ADDITIONAL WRITING TOPICS

Comparison and Contrast

1. In an essay replete with EXAMPLES, compare and contrast the two subjects in any one of the following pairs:

   Toys marketed to girls and boys
   Vampires and zombies
   A photograph and a painting
   The special skills of two basketball players
   High school and college
   Introverts and extraverts
   Liberals and conservatives: their opposing views of the role of government
   How city dwellers and country dwellers spend their leisure time
   The presentation styles of two popular comedians
   Science and the humanities

2. Approach a comparison-and-contrast essay on one of the following general subjects by explaining why you prefer one thing to the other:

   Vehicles: hybrid and electric engines; sedans and SUVs; American and Asian; Asian and European
   Smartphone platforms: Apple and Android
   Two buildings on campus or in town
   Two baseball teams
   Two horror movie franchises
   Television when you were a child and television today
   High art and low art
   Malls and main streets
   Two sports
   A vegetarian (or vegan) diet and a meat-based diet

3. Write an essay in which you compare a reality (what actually exists) with an ideal (what should exist). Some possible topics:

   The affordable car
   Available living quarters
   Parenthood
   A job
   A personal relationship
   A companion animal
   The college curriculum
   Public transportation
   Financial aid for college students
   Political candidates

7

PROCESS ANALYSIS

Explaining Step by Step

◀ **Process analysis in a photograph**

In a factory in Shenzhen, China, workers create dolls for export to the United States. This single image catches several steps in the doll-making process. At the very back of the assembly line, flat, unstuffed dolls begin the journey past the ranks of workers who stuff the body parts, using material prepared by other workers on the sides. A supervisor, hands behind his or her back, oversees the process. What do you think the photographer, Wally McNamee, wants viewers to understand about this process? What do you imagine the workers themselves think about it?

THE METHOD

A chemist working for a soft-drink firm is asked to improve on a competitor's product, Hydra Sports Water. First, she chemically tests a sample to figure out what's in the drink. This is the method of DIVISION or ANALYSIS, the separation of something into its parts in order to understand it (see the next chapter). Then the chemist writes a report telling her boss how to make a drink like Hydra Sports Water, but better. This recipe is a special kind of analysis, called PROCESS ANALYSIS: explaining step by step how to do something or how something is done.

Like any type of analysis, process analysis divides a subject into its components: It divides a continuous action into stages. Processes much larger and more involved than the making of a sports drink may also be analyzed. When geologists explain how a formation such as the Grand Canyon developed — a process taking several hundred million years — they describe the successive layers of sediment deposited by oceans, floods, and wind; then the great uplift of the entire region by underground forces; and then the erosion, visible to us today, by the Colorado River and its tributaries, by little streams and flash floods, by crumbling and falling rock, and by wind. Exactly what are the geologists doing in this explanation? They are taking a complicated event (or process) and dividing it into parts. They are telling us what happened first, second, and third, and what is still happening today.

Because it is useful in explaining what is complicated, process analysis is a favorite method of scientists such as chemists and geologists. The method, however, may be useful to anybody. Two PURPOSES of process analysis are very familiar to you:

- **A *directive process analysis* explains how to do something or how to make something.** You make use of it when you read a set of instructions for taking an exam or for assembling a new bookcase ("Lay part A on a flat surface and, using two of the lock tabs provided, attach part B on the left . . .").

- **An *informative process analysis* explains how something is done or how it takes place.** You see it in textbook descriptions of how atoms behave when they split, how lions hunt, and how a fertilized egg develops into a child.

In this chapter, you will find examples of both kinds of process analysis — both the "how to" and the "how." For instance, Anne Lamott and Koji Frahm offer their own directives for writing successfully, while Jessica Mitford spellbindingly explains how corpses are embalmed.

Sometimes process analysis is used imaginatively. Foreseeing that eventually the sun will burn out and all life on Earth will perish, an astronomer who cannot possibly behold the end of the world nevertheless can write a process analysis of it. An exercise in learned guesswork, such an essay divides a vast and almost inconceivable event into stages that, taken one at a time, become clearer and more readily imaginable. Whether it is useful or useless (but fun or scary to imagine), an effective process analysis can grip readers and even hold them fascinated. Say you were proposing a change in the procedures for course registration at your school. You could argue your point until you were out of words, but you would get nowhere if you failed to tell your readers exactly how the new process would work: That's what makes your proposal sing.

Readers, it seems, have an unslakable thirst for process analysis. Leaf through any magazine, and you will find that instructions abound. You may see, for instance, articles telling you how to do a magic trick, make a difficult decision, build muscle, overcome anxiety, and score at stock trading. Less practical, but not necessarily less interesting, are the informative articles: how brain surgeons work, how diamonds are formed, how cities fight crime. Every issue of the *New York Times Book Review* features an entire best-seller list devoted to "Advice, How-to, and Miscellaneous," including books on how to make money in real estate, how to lose weight, how to find a good mate, and how to lose a bad one. Evidently, if anything can still make a busy person crack open a book, it is a step-by-step explanation of how he or she can be a success at living.

THE PROCESS

Here are suggestions for writing an effective process analysis of your own. (In fact, what you are about to read is itself a process analysis.)

1. **Understand clearly the process you are about to analyze.** Think it through. This preliminary survey will make the task of writing far easier for you.

2. **Consider your thesis.** What is the point of your process analysis? Why are you bothering to tell readers about it? The THESIS STATEMENT for a process analysis need do no more than say what the subject is and maybe outline its essential stages, as in this example:

   The main stages in writing a process analysis are listing the steps in the process, drafting to explain the steps, and revising to clarify the steps.

But your readers will surely appreciate something livelier and more pointed, something that says "You can use this" or "This may surprise you" or "Listen up." Here are two thesis statements from essays in this chapter:

Almost all good writing begins with terrible first efforts. You need to start somewhere.

— Anne Lamott, "The Crummy First Draft"

[In a mortuary the body] is in short order sprayed, sliced, pierced, pickled, trussed, trimmed, creamed, waxed, painted, rouged, and neatly dressed — transformed from a common corpse into a Beautiful Memory Picture.

— Jessica Mitford, "Behind the Formaldehyde Curtain"

3. **Think about preparatory steps.** If the reader should do something before beginning the process, list these steps. For instance, you might begin, "Assemble the needed equipment: a 20-milliliter beaker, a 5-milliliter burette, safety gloves, and safety goggles."

4. **List the steps or stages in the process.** Try setting them down in CHRONOLOGICAL ORDER, one at a time — if this is possible. Some processes, however, do not happen in an orderly sequence, but occur all at once. If, for instance, you are writing an account of a typical earthquake, what do you mention first? The shifting of underground rock strata? cracks in the earth? falling houses? bursting water mains? toppling trees? mangled cars? casualties? For this subject the method of CLASSIFICATION (Chap. 9) might come to your aid. You might sort out apparently simultaneous events into categories: injury to people; damage to homes, to land, to public property.

5. **Check the completeness and order of the steps.** Make sure your list includes *all* the steps in the right order. Sometimes a stage of a process may contain a number of smaller stages. Make sure none has been left out. If any seems particularly tricky or complicated, underline it on your list to remind yourself when you write your essay to slow down and detail it with extra care.

6. **Define your terms.** Ask yourself, "Do I need any specialized or technical terms?" If so, be sure to define them. You'll sympathize with your reader if you have ever tried to assemble a bicycle according to a directive that begins, "Position sleeve casing on wheel center in fork with shaft in tongue groove, and gently but forcibly tap in pal-nut head."

7. **Use time-markers or** TRANSITIONS. These words or phrases indicate *when* one stage of a process stops and the next begins, and they greatly aid your reader in following you. Consider, for example, the following paragraph, in which plain medical prose makes good use of helpful time-markers (underlined). (The paragraph is adapted from *Pregnancy and Birth: A Book for Expectant Parents*, by Alan Frank Guttmacher.)

> In the human, <u>thirty-six hours after</u> the egg is fertilized, a two-cell egg appears. A twelve-cell development takes place in <u>seventy-two hours</u>. The egg is <u>still</u> round and has increased little in diameter. In this respect it is like a real estate development. <u>At first</u> a road bisects the whole area, <u>then</u> a cross road divides it into quarters, and <u>later</u> other roads divide it into eighths and twelfths. This happens without the taking of any more land, simply by subdivision of the original tract. <u>On the third or fourth day</u>, the egg passes from the Fallopian tube into the uterus. <u>By the fifth day</u> the original single large cell has subdivided into sixty small cells and floats about the slitlike uterine cavity <u>a day or two longer</u>, <u>then</u> adheres to the cavity's inner lining. <u>By the twelfth day</u> the human egg is already firmly implanted. Impregnation is <u>now</u> completed, <u>as yet</u> unbeknown to the woman. <u>At present</u>, she has not even had time to miss her first menstrual period, and other symptoms of pregnancy are <u>still several days distant</u>.

Brief as these time-markers are, they define each stage of the human egg's journey. When using time-markers, vary them so that they won't seem mechanical. If you can, avoid the monotonous repetition of a fixed phrase (*In the fourteenth stage . . . , In the fifteenth stage . . .*). Even boring time-markers, though, are better than none at all. Words and phrases such as *in the beginning, first, second, next, then, after that, three seconds later, at the same time,* and *finally* can help a process move smoothly in the telling and lodge firmly in the reader's mind.

8. **Be specific.** When you write a first draft, explain your process analysis in generous detail, even at the risk of being wordy. When you revise, it will be easier to delete than to amplify.

9. **Revise.** When your essay is finished, reread it carefully against the checklist on page 217. You might also enlist a friend's help. If your process analysis is directive ("How to Eat an Ice-Cream Cone without Dribbling"), see if your friend can follow the instructions without difficulty. If your process analysis is informative ("How a New Word Enters the Dictionary"), ask whether the process unfolds as clearly in his or her mind as it does in yours.

FOCUS ON CONSISTENCY

While drafting a process analysis, you may start off with subjects or verbs in one form and then shift to another form because the original choice feels awkward. In directive analyses, shifts occur most often with the subjects *a person* and *one*:

> INCONSISTENT   To keep the car from rolling while changing the tire, <u>one</u> should first set the car's emergency brake. Then <u>you</u> should block the three other tires with objects like rocks or chunks of wood.

In informative analyses, shifts usually occur from singular to plural as a way to get around *he* when the meaning includes males and females:

> INCONSISTENT   The poll <u>worker</u> first checks each voter against the registration list. Then <u>they</u> ask the voter to sign another list.

To repair inconsistencies, start with a subject that is both comfortable and sustainable:

> CONSISTENT   To keep the car from rolling while changing the tire, <u>you</u> should set the car's emergency brake. Then <u>you</u> should block the three other tires with objects like rocks or chunks of wood.

> CONSISTENT   Poll <u>workers</u> first check each voter against the registration list. Then <u>they</u> ask the voter to sign another list.

Sometimes, writers try to avoid naming or shifting subjects by using PASSIVE verbs that don't require actors:

> INCONSISTENT   To keep the car from rolling while changing the tire, <u>one</u> should first set the car's emergency brake. Then the three other <u>tires</u> <u>should be blocked</u> with objects like rocks or chunks of wood.

> INCONSISTENT   Poll workers first <u>check</u> each voter against the registration list. Then the voter <u>is asked</u> to sign another list.

In directive analyses, avoid passive verbs by using *you*, as shown in the consistent example above, or by using the commanding form of verbs, in which *you* is understood as the subject:

> CONSISTENT   To keep the car from rolling while changing the tire, first <u>set</u> the car's emergency brake. Then <u>block</u> the three other tires with objects like rocks or chunks of wood.

In informative analyses, passive verbs may be necessary if you don't know who the actor is or want to emphasize the action over the actor. But identifying the actor is generally clearer and more concise:

> CONSISTENT   Poll <u>workers</u> first check each voter against the registration list. Then <u>they</u> ask the voter to sign another list.

CHECKLIST FOR REVISING A PROCESS ANALYSIS

✔ **Thesis.** Does your process analysis have a point? Have you made sure readers know what it is?

✔ **Organization.** Have you arranged the steps of your process in a clear chronological order? If steps occur simultaneously, have you grouped them so that readers perceive some order?

✔ **Completeness.** Have you included all the necessary steps and explained each one fully? Is it clear how each one contributes to the result?

✔ **Definitions.** Have you explained the meanings of any terms your readers may not know?

✔ **Transitions.** Do time-markers distinguish the steps of your process and clarify their sequence?

✔ **Consistency.** Have you maintained comfortable, consistent, and clear subjects and verb forms?

Process Analysis

PROCESS ANALYSIS IN ACADEMIC WRITING

A Psychology Textbook

This passage on our descent into sleep comes from a section in *Psychology*, by Carole Wade and Carol Tavris, on "the most perplexing of all our biological rhythms." Before this paragraph the authors review the history of sleep research; after it they continue to analyze the night-long process that follows this initial descent.

When you first climb into bed, close your eyes, and relax, your brain emits bursts of *alpha waves*. On an EEG recording, alpha waves have a regular, slow rhythm and high amplitude (height). Gradually, these waves slow down even further, and you drift into the Land of Nod, passing through four stages, each deeper than the previous one.

> Steps preceding the process

> Process to be explained with informative analysis

Stage 1. Your brain waves become small and irregular, and you feel yourself drifting on the edge of consciousness, in a state of light sleep. If awakened, you may recall fantasies or a few visual images.

> Step 1

Stage 2. Your brain emits occasional short bursts of rapid, high-peaking waves called *sleep spindles*. Minor noises probably won't disturb you.

> Step 2

Stage 3. In addition to the waves that are characteristic of stage 2, your brain occasionally emits *delta waves*, very slow waves with very high peaks. Your breathing and pulse have slowed down, your muscles are relaxed, and you are hard to waken.   Step 3

Stage 4. Delta waves have now largely taken over, and you are in deep sleep. It will take vigorous shaking or a loud noise to awaken you. Oddly, though, if you walk in your sleep, this is when you are likely to do so.   Step 4

A Lab Report

When scientists conduct experiments to test their hypotheses, or theories, they almost always write reports outlining the processes they followed so that other researchers can attempt to duplicate the outcomes. Laboratory reports are straightforward and objective and are generally organized under standardized headings, such as *Purpose*, *Materials*, *Procedure*, and *Results*. They often include tables, figures, and calculations pertaining to the experiment. Most writers of lab reports put the focus on the experiment by keeping themselves in the background: They avoid *I* or *we* and use the PASSIVE VOICE of verbs (*the solution was heated*, as opposed to *we heated the solution*). The passive voice is not universal, however. Most lab assignments you receive in college will include detailed instructions for writing up the experiment and its results, so the best writing strategy is to follow those instructions to the letter.

For a first-year chemistry experiment, Victor Khoury used mostly household materials to extract and isolate deoxyribonucleic acid (DNA) from an onion. Found in all plants and animals, DNA is the molecule that holds the genetic information needed to create and direct living organisms. Khoury's instructor intended the experiment to teach students basic techniques and interactions in chemistry and to help them understand genetics at a molecular level. In the following excerpt from his lab report, Khoury explains the procedure and the main result.

Procedure

A small onion was coarsely chopped and placed in a   Step 1
1000-ml measuring cup along with 100 ml of a solution consisting of 10 ml of liquid dishwashing detergent, 1.5 g of table salt, and distilled water. The solution was intended to dissolve the   Reason for step
proteins and lipids binding the cell membranes of the onion. The   Step 2
onion pieces were next pressed with the back of a spoon for
30 seconds to break the onion structure down into a mash.   Reason for step

The measuring cup was then placed in a pan of preheated
58°C water for 13 minutes to further separate the DNA from the
walls of the onion cells. For the first 7 minutes, the onion was
continuously pressed with a spoon. After 13 minutes of heating,
the cup of mixture was then placed in a pan of ice water and
the mixture was pressed and stirred for 5 minutes to cool it and
to slow enzyme activity that would otherwise break down the
DNA. The onion mixture was then placed in a coffee filter over a
lab beaker and stored for 1 hour in a 4°C refrigerator in order to
filter and further cool the solution.

After refrigeration, the filtered solution was stirred for
30 seconds and 10 ml were poured into a clean vial. A toothpick
dipped in meat tenderizer was placed into the onion solution
so that the enzymes in the tenderizer would further separate
any remaining proteins from the DNA. Then refrigerated ethyl
alcohol was poured into the vial until it formed a 1-cm layer on
top of the onion solution.

Results

After the solution sat for 2 minutes, the DNA precipitated
into the alcohol layer. The DNA was long, white, and stringy,
with a gelatinous texture. This experiment demonstrated that
DNA can be extracted and isolated using a process of homogeni-
zation and deproteinization. . . .

Step 3

Reason for step

Step 4

Reason for step

Step 5
Reason for step

Steps 6, 7, and 8

Reason for steps
Step 9

Discussion of results

ANNE LAMOTT

Born in San Francisco in 1954, Anne Lamott is a novelist and essayist whom *Amazon* once characterized as "your run-of-the-mill recovering alcoholic and drug addict, born-again Christian, left-wing liberal, and single mother who just so happens to have written *New York Times*–best-selling books." Those books, including *Bird by Bird* (1994), *Traveling Mercies* (1999), *Blue Shoe* (2002), *Imperfect Birds* (2010), and *Small Victories* (2014), touch on subjects ranging from fiction to family to faith and have earned Lamott a devoted following. Her biweekly diary for *Salon*, "Word by Word," ran from 1996 to 1999 and was voted "The Best of the Web" by *Time* magazine. Lamott has taught at the University of California, Davis, and at writing workshops across the country. She lives in northern California.

The Crummy First Draft

Lamott's *Bird by Bird* is an inspiring and often very funny guide to writing. In this excerpt from the book, Lamott advises others how to begin writing by silencing their noisy inner critics.

In the next essay, "How to Write an *A* Paper," college student Koji Frahm offers a different take on succeeding as a writer.

For me and most of the other writers I know, writing is not rapturous. In fact, the only way I can get anything written at all is to write really, really crummy first drafts.

The first draft is the child's draft, where you let it all pour out and then let it romp all over the place, knowing that no one is going to see it and that you can shape it later. You just let this childlike part of you channel whatever voices and visions come through and onto the page. If one of the characters wants to say "Well, so what, Mr. Poopy Pants?" you let her. No one is going to see it. If the kid wants to get into really sentimental, weepy, emotional territory, you let him. Just get it all down on paper, because there may be something great in those six crazy pages that you would never have gotten to by more rational, grown-up means. There may be something in the very last line of the very last paragraph on page six that you just love, that is so beautiful or wild that you now know what you're supposed to be writing about, more or less, or in what direction you might go — but there was no way to get to this without first getting through the first five and a half pages.

I used to write food reviews for *California* magazine before it folded. (My   3
writing food reviews had nothing to do with the magazine folding, although
every single review did cause a couple of canceled subscriptions. Some readers
took umbrage at my comparing mounds of vegetable puree with various
ex-presidents' brains.) These reviews always took two days to write. First I'd go
to a restaurant several times with a few opinionated, articulate friends in tow.
I'd sit there writing down everything anyone said that was at all interesting or
funny. Then on the following Monday I'd sit down at my desk with my notes,
and try to write the review. Even after I'd been doing this for years, panic
would set in. I'd try to write a lead, but instead I'd write a couple of dreadful
sentences, xx them out, try again, xx everything out, and then feel despair and
worry settle on my chest like an x-ray apron. It's over, I'd think, calmly. I'm not
going to be able to get the magic to work this time. I'm ruined. I'm through.
I'm toast. Maybe, I'd think, I can get my old job back as a clerk-typist. But
probably not. I'd get up and study my teeth in the mirror for a while. Then I'd
stop, remember to breathe, make a few phone calls, hit the kitchen and chow
down. Eventually I'd go back and sit down at my desk, and sigh for the next
ten minutes. Finally I would pick up my one-inch picture frame, stare into it
as if for the answer, and every time the answer would come: All I had to do
was to write a really crummy first draft of, say, the opening paragraph. And no
one was going to see it.

So I'd start writing without reining myself in. It was almost just typing,   4
just making my fingers move. And the writing would be *terrible*. I'd write a lead
paragraph that was a whole page, even though the entire review could only
be three pages long, and then I'd start writing up descriptions of the food, one
dish at a time, bird by bird, and the critics would be sitting on my shoulders,
commenting like cartoon characters. They'd be pretending to snore, or rolling
their eyes at my overwrought descriptions, no matter how hard I tried to tone
those descriptions down, no matter how conscious I was of what a friend said
to me gently in my early days of restaurant reviewing. "Annie," she said, "it is
just a piece of *chick*en. It is just a bit of *cake*."

But because by then I had been writing for so long, I would eventually let   5
myself trust the process — sort of, more or less. I'd write a first draft that was
maybe twice as long as it should be, with a self-indulgent and boring beginning,
stupefying descriptions of the meal, lots of quotes from my black-humored
friends that made them sound more like the Manson girls[1] than food lovers,
and no ending to speak of. The whole thing would be so long and incoherent
and hideous that for the rest of the day I'd obsess about getting creamed by a

---

[1] The Manson girls were young, troubled members of the cult led by Charles
Manson (born 1934). In 1969 Manson and some of his followers were convicted of murder in
California. — Eds.

car before I could write a decent second draft. I'd worry that people would read what I'd written and believe that the accident had really been a suicide, that I had panicked because my talent was waning and my mind was shot.

The next day, though, I'd sit down, go through it all with a colored pen, take out everything I possibly could, find a new lead somewhere on the second page, figure out a kicky place to end it, and then write a second draft. It always turned out fine, sometimes even funny and weird and helpful. I'd go over it one more time and mail it in.

Then, a month later, when it was time for another review, the whole process would start again, complete with the fears that people would find my first draft before I could rewrite it.

Almost all good writing begins with terrible first efforts. You need to start somewhere. Start by getting something — anything — down on paper. A friend of mine says that the first draft is the down draft — you just get it down. The second draft is the up draft — you fix it up. You try to say what you have to say more accurately. And the third draft is the dental draft, where you check every tooth, to see if it's loose or cramped or decayed, or even, God help us, healthy.

What I've learned to do when I sit down to work on a crummy first draft is to quiet the voices in my head. First there's the vinegar-lipped Reader Lady, who says primly, "Well, *that's* not very interesting, is it?" And there's the emaciated German male who writes these Orwellian[2] memos detailing your thought crimes. And there are your parents, agonizing over your lack of loyalty and discretion; and there's William Burroughs,[3] dozing off or shooting up because he finds you as bold and articulate as a houseplant; and so on. And there are also the dogs: Let's not forget the dogs, the dogs in their pen who will surely hurtle and snarl their way out if you ever *stop* writing, because writing is, for some of us, the latch that keeps the door of the pen closed, keeps those crazy, ravenous dogs contained. . . .

Close your eyes and get quiet for a minute, until the chatter starts up. Then isolate one of the voices and imagine the person speaking as a mouse. Pick it up by the tail and drop it into a mason jar. Then isolate another voice, pick it up by the tail, drop it in the jar. And so on. Drop in any high-maintenance parental units, drop in any contractors, lawyers, colleagues, children, anyone who is whining in your head. Then put the lid on, and watch all these mouse people clawing at the glass, jabbering away, trying to make you feel crummy because you won't do what they want — won't give them more money, won't

6

7

8

9

10

---

[2] In his novel *1984*, the British writer George Orwell (1903–50) depicts a futuristic world in which a totalitarian government controls citizens' behavior and thoughts. — Eds.

[3] The American novelist William Burroughs (1914–97) wrote experimental and often surreal works on drug addiction and other aspects of contemporary life. — Eds.

be more successful, won't see them more often. Then imagine that there is a volume-control button on the bottle. Turn it all the way up for a minute, and listen to the stream of angry, neglected, guilt-mongering voices. Then turn it all the way down and watch the frantic mice lunge at the glass, trying to get to you. Leave it down, and get back to your crummy first draft.

A writer friend of mine suggests opening the jar and shooting them all in   11 the head. But I think he's a little angry, and I'm sure nothing like this would ever occur to you.

Journal Writing

Describe what usually happens when you begin a writing project. Is the blank paper or screen an invitation or an obstacle? Do the words flow freely or haltingly or not at all? Do you feel creative? competent? helpless? tortured?

Questions on Meaning

1. What is Lamott's THESIS? Which sentences best convey her main idea?

2. According to Lamott, what role can other people, real or imaginary, play in the writing process? Are they helpful?

3. Review the comment by Lamott's friend (par. 8) that "the first draft is the down draft. . . . The second draft is the up draft. . . . And the third draft is the dental draft. . . ." What do you think is the difference in the writer's approach and focus at each stage? In what ways, if any, do these stages relate to your own approach to writing?

4. What do you think Lamott means when she says that "writing is, for some of us, the latch that keeps the door of the pen closed, keeps those crazy, ravenous dogs contained" (par. 9)? What might the dogs and control of them stand for in this IMAGE?

5. What is the PURPOSE of Lamott's piece? To advise inexperienced writers? To relate her own difficulties with writing? Both, or something else? How do you know?

Questions on Writing Strategy

1. Lamott's book *Bird by Bird*, the source of this piece, is subtitled *Some Instructions on Writing and Life*. Who do you believe would find Lamott's advice most useful? Will it be useful to you? Why, or why not?

2. In paragraph 4 Lamott says that she wrote food reviews "one dish at a time" and "bird by bird" (a metaphor from earlier in her book, meaning one step at a time). What steps does her process analysis outline for overcoming obstacles?

3. Process analysis can be directive or explanatory (see p. 212), and Lamott's piece has good examples of both types. In which paragraphs does Lamott use each type? Where does she combine them? What does each type contribute? Is the mixture effective? Why, or why not?

4. What transitions does Lamott use to guide the reader through the steps of her process analysis? Is her use of transitions effective?

5. **OTHER METHODS** Paragraphs 3–7 NARRATE Lamott's experience writing food reviews for a magazine. What is the effect of this story?

Questions on Language

1. Although trying to be encouraging, Lamott uses many negative adjectives to describe her own first efforts: for example, "terrible" (par. 4) and "incoherent" (5). Find some other examples of negative adjectives. Why do you think Lamott uses so many of them?

2. What is Lamott's TONE? How seriously does she take the difficulties facing the writer?

3. Lamott uses several original images, such as the "vinegar-lipped Reader Lady" (par. 9). List some images that made a particular impression on you, and explain their effect.

4. Be sure you know how to define the following words: overwrought (par. 4); self-indulgent, stupefying, waning (5); emaciated, hurtle, ravenous (9); guilt-mongering (10).

Suggestions for Writing

1. **FROM JOURNAL TO ESSAY** Write an essay that explains your own writing process (in general or on a specific project) as you progress from idea to final draft. Enliven the process with specific methods and incidents — techniques of procrastination, ripping up draft after draft, listening to and silencing (or not) your own imagined voices, and so on. Try to draw some conclusions about what the writing process means to you.

2. Writing is, of course, only one way to communicate ideas. Other forms of communication can also be difficult: speaking up in class, making a presentation to a group of people, meeting with a teacher, interviewing for a job, making an important telephone call. Write a process analysis in which you first examine an oral encounter that was particularly difficult for you and then offer advice about how best to tackle such a situation.

3. **CRITICAL WRITING** We are usually taught to respect our parents and other authority figures, but Lamott advises writers to ignore them while composing. Is her advice justified in your view? Are there times when we can, even should, disregard authority? Write an essay about a time when you felt you could accomplish something only by disregarding the advice of someone you would normally listen

to — or, in contrast, when you heeded advice even though it held you back or ignored advice and eventually regretted doing so. How difficult was your action? How did the situation turn out? Looking back, do you believe you did the right thing?

4.   **CONNECTIONS**   Lamott stresses the importance of ignoring the perspectives of others in order to hear your own voice, and in the next essay, Koji Frahm (satirically) encourages writers to be hostile toward their readers. Citing examples from your own experience and from Lamott's and Frahm's essays, write an essay that examines writers' obligations to others versus obligations to themselves. When are we justified in following our own paths regardless of what readers think, and when are we not?

KOJI FRAHM

Koji Frahm was born in 1987 and grew up in Palo Alto, California, a suburb of San Francisco. In high school he competed on the swim team and spent much of his time playing video games. After enrolling at the University of California, Davis, as a biomechanical engineering student, he found himself getting up early to write short stories before classes, and so switched his major to creative writing. He graduated in 2009 and currently lives in Brooklyn, New York, where he runs a makerspace for artists and continues to write.

How to Write an *A* Paper

"How to Write an *A* Paper" was written in response to an assignment given in a freshman composition class. Like Anne Lamott in the previous essay, Frahm considers the challenges and frustrations of writing. Focusing on the advice typically offered to college students, his essay is largely a directive process analysis, but it is also a SATIRE: By outwardly showing us one way to approach a writing project, the author implicitly urges us to do the opposite.

Be nebulous. Scratch that, be amphibological. The vaguer, the better. The reader should be thinking, *what the hell does that mean?* right off the bat. The first sentence is key. Make it short, deadly, and impossible to understand. Convoluted is the term to use here. And remember, I'm not talking indiscernible due to stupidity; I'm talking indiscernible due to smarts. You have to sound brilliant. Scratch that, perspicacious. Be as opaque as a dense fog settling in front of a concrete wall — let them see nothing. Make them understand that you're smarter than they are. The sooner you establish this, the better. Hitting them hard and fast on the first sentence is the quickest way to do it. Make them so unsure of their own acumen from the start that they won't question you afterwards. Get them on the ground, and keep them there. Your God-like intelligence should never be questioned by these mere mortals — that's how you should be writing. Look at your first sentence for a moment and consider this: Is it short? Is it vague? Does it tell the reader nothing about what's going on? If so — bingo. You're in the clear. You can't be marked off if they can't understand your higher parlance — and that's exactly what we're going for.

The end of the introduction means it's thesis time. If you really want to pull this off, end the introduction with no clear thesis. That way, they'll assume the thesis is lurking around somewhere later in the paper like a prowling hyena in Serengeti; and before you KNOW it, they'll forget what they were searching for. You never had one anyway. And if they're really keen for it, they'll probably just extrapolate something from the parts they don't understand later in the paper. You're Shakespeare, remember? You know best.

Be choppy. Scratch that, be desultory. Jump around like a rabbit on fire — never let the reader know where you're headed next. The transitions between your paragraphs should be sudden and unexpected; your sentences short and rapid fire. Your teachers always taught you to be smooth and transitional — screw that. Toss your reader around like a paper bag in a tempest; the only thing they should be doing is covering their heads. Confusion is the key term here. If your reader doesn't look flummoxed and bleary-eyed by paragraph three, you aren't trying hard enough. You're smarter, you're faster, and the only thing they can do is try to keep up.

Paragraph four, all right, now we're getting somewhere. This is the part of the essay where you're taught to bring out the big points. The "meat" of the essay is how teachers sometimes refer to it. That's all garbage. You don't need a plethora of in-depth points or solid evidence to fill up your paper — you just need one. One point. That's all you need. Reiteration is the key term here. I can't stress this part enough. All you need to know is this: keep talking. Be the jammed cassette deck on repeat. Write as if you're being paid a dollar a word, and you have only thirty seconds to type. Just keep pushing through the same old stuff with different wording. Dress it up; do its hair; color its nails; I don't care. Repackage the old, make it look new. Novelty sells the car. Write frivolously. Scratch that, farcically. It'll seem like you're getting deeper and deeper into the topic with every word you say, but really you'll JUST be wasting their time. Analysis is overrated — just keep spitting out what you already said. Regurgitation is the key term here. Vomit your words out and eat them back up, then spit them out a minute later. You're the mother eagle, and the reader is your starving chick. To add weight to this empty package, make sure the paragraph you put your half-digested words in is one of the longest. Nothing says "important" like a hefty paragraph. You would know. You're the smartest.

The thesaurus is your friend. Scratch that, your soul-mate. This whole operation is FUELED by perplexing your reader. If you're the matador, the thesaurus is your cape — you're both coaxing the reader to charge through your charade. An essay is just made up of words, and that's the punch-line of this exploitation. Every word can be more sequestered; every syllable can be more ambagious. Make reading your essay more difficult than solving a Rubik's cube in the dark. Don't write *elderly person*, scratch that off. Write *septuagenarian*. That woman isn't pretty; she's *pulchritudinous* for someone possessing your voluminous vocabulary. And don't worry if the definitions aren't totally the same; it's not as if the reader is going to know what's going on anyway. Obfuscate is the key term here.

Metaphors. It's always good to throw a lot of these in — teachers love this 6 stuff. Make sure they're really random and sporadic, popping up anywhere and everywhere like ferns in the Amazon jungle. Whatever pops into your head at the time, make it a metaphor. Whether it's animals from the Nature Channel you were watching two hours ago, or a Rubik's cube that's sitting on your desk, anything is fair GAME. Forget about clarity or adding depth, your metaphors are there for the same reason neon lights exist — distraction. Your essay should be a patchwork quilt of random metaphors, shrouding your essay from lucidity like the moon blocking the sun during a lunar eclipse. Just stick them everywhere.

Make errors. You heard right. Capitalize some random words throughout 7 your paper. Attach a note to the final document explaining that your computer was on the fritz, and even during printing it was behaving idiosyncratically. *Proofreading couldn't prevent it because it occurred during printing*, the note will say, and how can the teacher blame you? Your computer was haywire,; totally nuts. It was jumping off the walls and banging into the ceiling like a rubber ball fired out of a Civil War cannon, spitting and blasting unnecessary semicolons and punctuation errors into your work. You weren't responsible for what it did. And once you get that across, you can also blame the computer for for any typos or repeated words you may have left in my accident. Just type some OCCASIONAL caps-locked words now and then, and suddenly you're exonerated from all grammatical imperfections. Diabolical is the key term here.

By now you should be closing in like a school of piranha onto a drown- 8 ing ox. You've probably written enough, so you might as well wrap things up. Conclusions are easy. All you need is a quote and your choice of any massive, tear-inducing flaw in society. Take your pick: consumerism consuming our culture, superficiality sucking out our souls, mankind's maniacal instincts, the government's dominance of society's free will, et cetera, et cetera. It doesn't matter. It doesn't even have to pertain to your topic. The beauty with conclusions is you can tie just about anything to anything. If you were writing about the mating habits of rhinos, you could probably conclude with an anecdote about world hunger. The point is that there is no point. Be as random as a herd of buffalo showing up to present the Best Picture award at the Oscars. Just pick something you can rant about for a good half-page and you're in business.

Now for the quote. This is the last thing the reader's nonplussed eyes will 9 see — so make it good. This is the one time in the essay you want them to understand what's going on. After all this confusion they'll be ravenous for something transpicuous — and this is the time to dish it out. What's even better, they'll love you for it. Everyone likes being enlightened. And after your quote, your reader should be more sagacious than Buddha on heroin. Choose one THAT sounds inspirational and profound. Aristotle and Socrates are always solid choices. Once again, it doesn't matter if it actually pertains to your topic. As long as it's half decent, the reader will be grateful. Place this at the end in italics and you're home free.

Congratulations, you're done. Don't worry about proofreading for typos — you took care of the errors, remember? That damn computer of yours. All you have to do now is make sure you turn it in on Wednesday. Sit back and relax; and have a triumphant smile and modest remarks ready for the teacher next week when he praises your work in front of the class. What could go wrong, anyway? We've covered all the bases. An "A" is inevitable. Scratch that, ineluctable . . . which reminds me.   10

I received a paper back this morning and I still haven't checked the grade. Excuse me for a moment; I have to confirm my "A." Consider this a testament to my guide to success. Confidence is the key term here.   11

Be a victim. Scratch that, be a scapegoat. Take the paper and crumple it, throw it away or tuck it away somewhere you won't see it. Who cares anyway? This was a stupid assignment to begin with. It was a puerile assignment with an imbecilic teacher to grade it. What the hell does he know? Confusing Introduction. Lack of Content. Bad Transitions. *Excessive Grammatical Errors?!* You told him the computer was going haywire. Didn't he see the note? What an IDIOT. Obviously it was too much. He probably didn't understand what was going on and decided to take it out on you. What a sucker. Scratch that, a simpleton. His lack of comprehension isn't your fault — the ignoramus. He's taking his confusion out on you, satisfying his own denial by giving you a bad grade. He's just like everybody nowadays. No one takes responsibility for their own problems. People mess up their lives beyond all repair and still have excuses for everything. It's the whole world's fault before anyone will admit it's theirs. *He doesn't like me because . . . It's not my fault, she's the one that . . . I'm late because this stupid . . . blah . . . blah . . . blah . . .* How about a simple "sorry, it's my fault"? It's like the entire damn world would rather blame its problems on other things rather than fixing them. No one is willing to own up to their actions and take the consequences anymore. That's what this is all about. I'm just the hapless victim for all those ignorant fools out there. Those vainglorious dunderheads. Those egocentric imbeciles. It's like a wise man once said: 12

> *You must not lose faith in humanity.*
> *Humanity is an ocean;*
> *if a few drops of the ocean are dirty,*
> *the ocean does not become dirty.*
>   — *Mahatma Gandhi*

Journal Writing

Frahm's essay is SATIRE — that is, an indirect attack on human follies or flaws, using IRONY to urge behavior exactly the opposite of what is really desired. In your journal, explore when you have proposed satirical approaches to challenges that seem overwhelming or ridiculous — for example, suggesting breaking all the dishes so that they don't have to be washed again or barring pedestrians from city streets so that they don't interfere with cars. What kinds of situations might lead you to make suggestions like these?

Questions on Meaning

1. How seriously does Frahm take his subject? Is his main PURPOSE to amuse and entertain, to inform students of ways they can become better writers, to warn about bad teachers, or to make fun of readers? Support your answer with EVIDENCE from the essay.

2. Look closely at Frahm's conclusion (par. 12). Does his writing advice actually promise an A for those who follow it? Why, or why not?

3. Does Frahm have a THESIS? Where in the essay does he explain his reason for not stating it outright?

Questions on Writing Strategy

1. How is Frahm's essay organized? Trace his process analysis carefully to determine whether it happens CHRONOLOGICALLY or follows another order. How effective is this method of organization and presentation?

2. At several points Frahm writes, "___ is the key term here." Find these sentences and underline them. How do they give the essay COHERENCE and UNITY?

3. What is the author's apparent attitude toward readers? What role does he suggest an awareness of AUDIENCE plays in effective writing?

4. Some of the words in Frahm's essay are unnecessarily printed in all-capital letters. What other errors can you find? Why are they there?

5. **OTHER METHODS**   As is the case with any process analysis, "How to Write an A Paper" relies on DIVISION or ANALYSIS of its subject. What does Frahm imply are the elements of good writing?

Questions on Language

1. How do sentences such as "The vaguer, the better" and "Make it short, deadly, and impossible to understand" (par. 1) signal the TONE of this essay from the start? Should they be read literally, ironically, or some other way? How does the tone contribute to Frahm's satire?

2. What consistent sentence subject does Frahm use in "How to Write an A Paper"? Who is to perform the process?

3. Frahm's essay includes many difficult words seemingly plucked from a thesaurus (par. 5), including the following: nebulous, amphibological, perspicacious, acumen, parlance (1); extrapolate (2); desultory, flummoxed (3); plethora, farcically, regurgitation (4); sequestered, ambagious, obfuscate (5); sporadic, lucidity (6); idiosyncratically (7); nonplussed, transpicuous, sagacious (9); ineluctable (10); puerile, hapless, vainglorious (12). Do readers need to know the definitions of these words to understand Frahm's meaning?

4. In paragraph 6 Frahm encourages writers to use "a lot" of metaphors. Point to any metaphors or similes in his essay that strike you as especially imaginative. (See FIGURATIVE LANGUAGE in the Glossary if you need a definition of *metaphor* or *simile*.) What does Frahm say is the purpose of such language? Do you agree?

Suggestions for Writing

1. **FROM JOURNAL TO ESSAY** Choose one of the solutions you wrote about in your journal, or propose a solution to a challenge that your journal entry has suggested. Write an essay detailing this satirical solution, paying careful attention to explaining each step of the process and to maintaining your satiric tone throughout.

2. Write a serious (not satirical) essay that teaches readers how to do something you're good at, such as making fresh guacamole from scratch, writing letters of complaint, or unclogging a sink. You might, like Frahm, imagine a specific group of people as your readers, or you might address your instructions to a more general audience.

3. Try to recall a time when you struggled with or failed at an assignment you thought would be simple. Write a short NARRATIVE about your difficulties. What went wrong? How did the struggle affect you? Did you learn anything?

4. **CRITICAL WRITING** In a brief essay, pick apart Frahm's advice and the ways he applies it to his own writing in "How to Write an A Paper." Consider, for instance, how his first paragraph illustrates the function of his first sentence, or why he includes the quotation by Mahatma Gandhi at the end of the essay. Where else in this essay does Frahm commit the very sins of bad writing that he implicitly identifies? How effective are his choices?

5. **CONNECTIONS** What does Frahm gain or lose by using satire and irony to make his point? What would be the comparative strengths and weaknesses of an essay that straightforwardly and sincerely approached the challenges writers face, such as Anne Lamott's "The Crummy First Draft" (p. 220)?

Koji Frahm on Writing

Asked to reflect on the experience of writing "How to Write an A Paper," Koji Frahm offered the following comments.

I'm still not sure if I like this essay. But with that said, I will admit it was a ton of fun to write. This assignment was to write a parody of another essay. And so, using observation from over the years of all the garbage and terrible techniques people cram into their essays (the idea actually came while discussing Poli Sci papers with a friend), I molded the most ridiculous and multilayered piece I've ever attempted — this being the result. I still have qualms with it; it still doesn't measure up to what I had in mind. But for what it's worth, it's made people chuckle, and that, for me, was the greatest reward of writing this piece.

The Brief Bedford Reader on Writing

Although his essay is a lot of fun for readers, too, Frahm admits that his advice to student writers is "ridiculous and multilayered." For simple and straightforward guidelines on how to write an effective paper, see Chapter 2 of this book.

FIROOZEH DUMAS

Born in Abadan, Iran, in 1966, Firoozeh Dumas immigrated with her family to Whittier, California, at the age of seven, moved back to Iran two years later, then finally settled in the United States two years after that. She earned her bachelor's degree from the University of California at Berkeley in 1988. Dumas, who has said that the worst misconception about Iranians is "that we are completely humorless," took up writing partly to correct such assumptions. Her popular first book, *Funny in Farsi: A Memoir of Growing Up Iranian in America* (2003), portrays the humor in her family's experiences as Middle Eastern immigrants to the United States. Her second book, *Laughing without an Accent: Adventures of an Iranian American, at Home and Abroad* (2008), continues the theme with essays about trying to sell a cross-shaped potato on *eBay* and taking a cruise with fifty-one family members, among other topics. Dumas has written a novel for young readers, *It Ain't So Awful, Falafel* (2016) and contributes to several periodicals — including the *New York Times*, the *Wall Street Journal*, the *Los Angeles Times*, and *Lifetime*. She is also an occasional commentator on National Public Radio.

Sweet, Sour, and Resentful

In this 2009 essay from *Gourmet* magazine, Dumas outlines her mother's pains-taking process of preparing a traditional Persian meal for the dozens of distant relatives and friends of friends who descended on the family's California condo every weekend. Through her mother's weekly routine — from hunting down ingredients to chopping herbs to refusing praise — Dumas reveals much about family, culture, and humility.

My mother's main ingredient in cooking was resentment — not that I   1
can blame her. In 1979, my family was living temporarily in Newport Beach, California. Our real home was in Abadan, a city in the southwest of Iran. Despite its desert location and ubiquitous refineries, Abadan was the quintessential small town. Everybody's father (including my own) worked for the National Iranian Oil Company, and almost all the moms stayed home. The employees' kids attended the same schools. No one locked their doors. Whenever I hear John Mellencamp's "Small Town," I think of Abadan, although I'm guessing John Mellencamp was thinking of somewhere else when he wrote that song.

By the time of the Iranian revolution,[1] we had adjusted to life in   2
California. We said "Hello" and "Have a nice day" to perfect strangers, wore
flip-flops, and grilled cheeseburgers next to our kebabs. We never understood
why Americans put ice in tea or bought shampoo that smelled like strawber-
ries, but other than that, America felt like home.

When the revolution happened, thousands left Iran for Southern   3
California. Since we were one of the few Iranian families already there, our
phone did not stop ringing. Relatives, friends, friends of relatives, friends of
friends, and people whose connection we never quite figured out called us with
questions about settling into this new land. Displaying the hospitality that
Iranians so cherish, my father extended a dinner invitation to everyone who
called. As a result, we found ourselves feeding dozens of people every weekend.

The marathon started on Monday, with my mother planning the menu   4
while letting us know that she was already tired. Fortunately, our rice dishes
were made to be shared; our dilemma, however, was space. Our condo was
small. Our guests squeezed onto the sofa, sat on the floor, or overflowed onto
the patio. We eventually had to explain to our American neighbors why there
were so many cars parked in front of our place every weekend. My mother, her
diplomatic skills in full swing, had me deliver plates of Persian food, decorated
with radish roses and mint sprigs, to them. In time, we learned not to share
fesenjan, pomegranate stew with ground walnuts. "Yes, now that you mention
it, it does look like mud, but it's really good," I'd explain, convincing no one.

Because my mother did not drive, my father took her to buy ingredients   5
every Tuesday after work. In Abadan, my mother and I had started most days
in the market, going from vendor to vendor looking for herbs, vegetables,
and fruits. The fish came from the Karun and Arvand (Shatt al Arab) Rivers,
the *lavash* and the *sangak* breads were freshly baked, and the chickens were
still alive. We were locavores by necessity and foodies without knowing it.
In America, I learned that the time my parents spent shopping was in direct
correlation to the degree of my mother's bad mood. An extra-long trip meant
that my mother could not find everything she needed, a point she would make
loud and clear when she got home: "Why don't they let fruit ripen here?"
"Why are the chickens so huge and flavorless?" "I couldn't find fresh herbs."
"My feet hurt." "How am I supposed to get everything done?"

The first step was preparing the herbs. My mother insisted that the pars-   6
ley, cilantro, and chives for *qormeh sabzi*, herb stew, had to be finely chopped
by hand. The food processor, she explained, squished them. As she and my
father sat across the table wielding huge knives, they argued incessantly.

---

[1] In 1979 fundamentalist rebels led by Ayatollah Ruhollah Khomeini overthrew the
Iranian monarchy and established the Islamic Republic of Iran, a theocratic dictatorship. — EDS.

My father did his best to help her. It wasn't enough. As soon as the mountain of herbs was chopped, my mother started frying them. At any given time, my mother was also frying onions. Every few days, while my father was watching the six o'clock news, my mother would hand him a dozen onions, a cutting board, and a knife. No words were exchanged. Much to my father's relief, I once volunteered for this task, but apparently my slices were neither thin enough nor even. It took my father's precision as an engineer to slice correctly.

While all four burners were in use, my mother mixed the ground beef, rice, split peas, scallions, and herbs for stuffed grape leaves. I chopped the stems of the grape leaves. I had tried stuffing them once, but my rolls, deemed not tight enough, were promptly unrolled and then rerolled by my mother.   7

In between cooking, my mother made yogurt — the thick, sour variety that we couldn't find in America. She soaked walnuts and almonds in water to plump them up; fried eggplants for *kashk-e bademjan*, a popular appetizer with garlic, turmeric, mint, and whey; made *torshi-e limo*, a sour lemon condiment; and slivered orange peels. I had been fired from this task also, having left on far too much pith.   8

By the time our guests arrived, my mother was exhausted. But the work was not finished. Rice, the foundation of the Persian meal, the litmus test of the cook's ability, cannot be prepared ahead of time. To wit, one day in Abadan, the phone rang when my mother was about to drain the rice. During the time it took her to answer the phone and tell her sister that she would call her back, the rice overcooked. Almost forty years later, I still remember my mother's disappointment and her explaining to my father that her sister had time to talk because my aunt's maid did all the cooking. My aunt did not even drain her own rice.   9

We certainly did not have a table big enough to set, so we simply stacked dishes and utensils, buffet-style. As the guest list grew, we added paper plates and plastic utensils. It was always my job to announce that dinner was ready. As people entered the dining room, they gasped at the sight of my mother's table. Her *zereshk polow*, barberry rice, made many emotional. There are no fresh barberries in America (my mother had brought dried berries from Iran in her suitcase), and the sight of that dish, with its distinct deep red hue, was a reminder of the life our guests had left behind.   10

Our dinners took days to cook and disappeared in twenty minutes. As our guests heaped their plates and looked for a place to sit, they lavished praise on my mother, who, according to tradition, deflected it all. "It's nothing," she said. "I wish I could've done more." When they told her how lucky she was to have me to help her, my mother politely nodded, while my father added, "Firoozeh's good at math."   11

On Sundays, my mother lay on the sofa, her swollen feet elevated, fielding   12
thank-you phone calls from our guests. She had the same conversation a
dozen times; each one ended with, "Of course you can give our name to your
cousins." As I watched my mother experience the same draining routine week
after week, I decided that tradition is good only if it brings joy to all involved.
This includes the hostess. Sometimes, even our most cherished beliefs must
evolve. Evolution, thy name is potluck.

Journal Writing

Many people have unique rituals, like Dumas's parents' practice of serving elaborate Persian meals to distant acquaintances every weekend. List some rituals that are
unique to your family, to another group you belong to, or to you alone — for instance,
a holiday celebration, a vacation activity, a way of decompressing after a stressful
week.

Questions on Meaning

1. Why were weekend dinners so important to the author's parents and their guests?
   Consider not just the meals themselves but the larger context that prompted
   them.

2. In which sentence or sentences does Dumas state her THESIS most directly?

3. What would you say is Dumas's PURPOSE in this essay? Is it primarily to entertain readers by describing her family's weekly routine, or does she seem to have
   another purpose in mind?

4. What solution to her mother's exhausting role as hostess does Dumas propose
   in paragraph 12? Do you think her mother would have agreed to it? Why, or
   why not?

Questions on Writing Strategy

1. Why does Dumas begin her essay with an overview of life in Abadan and an
   ALLUSION to the Iranian revolution (pars. 1–3)? What purpose does this opening
   serve?

2. How does Dumas seem to imagine her AUDIENCE? To what extent could she
   ASSUME that readers would appreciate her mother's situation?

3. What steps does Dumas identify in the process of hosting Iranian guests every
   weekend? How does she ensure that her analysis has COHERENCE?

4. **OTHER METHODS**   What role does COMPARISON AND CONTRAST play in paragraph 5?

Questions on Language

1. Explain how Dumas's TONE contributes to the humor in her essay.

2. Where in this essay does Dumas use Persian words? What is their EFFECT?

3. In paragraph 9, Dumas says that rice is "the litmus test" for Iranian cooks. What does she mean? What is a litmus test, and how does the phrase connect to the focus (and title) of her essay?

4. Be sure you know the meanings of the following words: ubiquitous, quintessential (par. 1); Persian (4); locavores, correlation (5); pith (8); lavished, deflected (11); potluck (12).

Suggestions for Writing

1. **FROM JOURNAL TO ESSAY**   Write an essay explaining one of the rituals you listed in your journal. Focus on the details and steps of the ritual itself as well as on the significance it holds for you and for any others who participate in it with you.

2. Research the influx of Iranian families into California during the 1970s. What prompted this migration? What quality of life did newcomers face on arrival? What tensions did their arrival create? In an essay, consider these questions and others your research may lead you to. You may prefer to focus on a different migration from the nineteenth or twentieth century — such as that of Irish to the eastern United States, Chinese to the western United States, or African Americans from the southern to the northern United States.

3. **CRITICAL WRITING**   What impression of herself does Dumas create in this essay? What adjectives would you use to describe the writer as she reveals herself on the page? Cite specific language from the essay to support your ANALYSIS.

4. **CONNECTIONS**   Both Firoozeh Dumas and Amy Tan, in "Fish Cheeks" (p. 74), hint at how as children they felt ashamed of their families because of certain foods. Write an essay in which you COMPARE AND CONTRAST the ways the two writers describe food and how each writer uses food to make a larger point about the need to fit in.

Firoozeh Dumas on Writing

In a 2004 interview with Khaled Hosseini (author of *The Kite Runner* and *A Thousand Splendid Suns*), Firoozeh Dumas explained how writing awakens her memory. As a girl growing up in Iran and the United States, Dumas says she "was always that quiet kid in a room full of adults" who carefully "listened and observed." When she started writing as an adult, her collected observations "just flooded back." Unlike those who experience writer's block, Dumas was easily inspired: "Every time I finished a story, another popped up in its place. It was like using a vending machine: The candy falls down and is immediately replaced by another."

In order to keep up with her vending machine of ideas — and to accommodate her busy family life — Dumas writes "in spurts," often waking at four in the morning. "Once a story is in my head, I'm possessed, and the only thing I can do is write like mad," she told Hosseini. "This means the house gets very messy and dinner is something frozen. I do not read or go to the movies when I am writing, because I can't concentrate on anything else. I also keep writing in my head when I'm not actually writing, which means that I become a terrible listener."

The Brief Bedford Reader on Writing

Have you ever found that the act of writing triggers your memory, as it does for Dumas? Try FREEWRITING (p. 33) and see if it works for you. Many writers find that simply sitting down and writing, even for just a few minutes at a time, can yield surprising results.

JESSICA MITFORD

Born in Batsford Mansion, England, in 1917, the daughter of Lord and Lady Redesdale, Jessica Mitford devoted much of her early life to defying her aristocratic upbringing. In her autobiography *Daughters and Rebels* (1960), she tells how she received a genteel schooling at home, then as a young woman moved to Loyalist Spain during the violent Spanish Civil War. Later she immigrated to the United States, where for a time she worked in Miami as a bartender. She obtained US citizenship in 1944 and became one of her adopted country's most noted reporters: *Time* called her "Queen of the Muckrakers." Exposing with her typewriter what she regarded as corruption, abuse, and absurdity, Mitford wrote *The American Way of Death* (1963, revised as *The American Way of Death Revisited* in 1998), *Kind and Unusual Punishment: The Prison Business* (1973), and *The American Way of Birth* (1992). *Poison Penmanship* (1979) collects articles from *The Atlantic Monthly*, *Harper's*, and other magazines. *A Fine Old Conflict* (1977) is the second volume of Mitford's autobiography. Her biography of a Victorian lighthouse keeper's daughter, *Grace Had an English Heart* (1989), examines how the media transform ordinary people into celebrities. Mitford died at her home in Oakland, California, in 1996.

Behind the Formaldehyde Curtain

The most famous (or infamous) thing Jessica Mitford wrote is *The American Way of Death*, a critique of the funeral industry. In this selection from the book, Mitford analyzes the twin processes of embalming and restoring a corpse, the practices she finds most objectionable. You may need a stable stomach to enjoy the selection, but you'll find it a clear, painstaking process analysis, written with masterly style and outrageous wit. (For those who want to know, Mitford herself was cremated after her death.)

The drama begins to unfold with the arrival of the corpse at the mortuary. 1

Alas, poor Yorick! How surprised he would be to see how his counterpart 2 of today is whisked off to a funeral parlor and is in short order sprayed, sliced, pierced, pickled, trussed, trimmed, creamed, waxed, painted, rouged, and neatly dressed — transformed from a common corpse into a Beautiful Memory Picture. This process is known in the trade as embalming and restorative art, and is so universally employed in the United States and Canada that the funeral director does it routinely, without consulting corpse or kin. He regards as eccentric those few who are hardy enough to suggest that it might be dispensed with. Yet no law requires embalming, no religious doctrine commends it, nor is it dictated by considerations of health, sanitation, or even of personal daintiness. In no part of the world but in Northern America is it widely used. The purpose of embalming is to make the corpse presentable for viewing in a suitably costly container; and here too the funeral director routinely, without first consulting the family, prepares the body for public display.

Is all this legal? The processes to which a dead body may be subjected are   3
after all to some extent circumscribed by law. In most states, for instance, the signature of next of kin must be obtained before an autopsy may be performed, before the deceased may be cremated, before the body may be turned over to a medical school for research purposes; or such provision must be made in the decedent's will. In the case of embalming, no such permission is required nor is it ever sought.[1] A textbook, *The Principles and Practices of Embalming*, comments on this: "There is some question regarding the legality of much that is done within the preparation room." The author points out that it would be most unusual for a responsible member of a bereaved family to instruct the mortician, in so many words, to "embalm" the body of a deceased relative. The very term *embalming* is so seldom used that the mortician must rely upon custom in the matter. The author concludes that unless the family specifies otherwise, the act of entrusting the body to the care of a funeral establishment carries with it an implied permission to go ahead and embalm.

Embalming is indeed a most extraordinary procedure, and one must won-   4
der at the docility of Americans who each year pay hundreds of millions of dollars for its perpetuation, blissfully ignorant of what it is all about, what is done, how it is done. Not one in ten thousand has any idea of what actually takes place. Books on the subject are extremely hard to come by. They are not to be found in most libraries or bookshops.

In an era when huge television audiences watch surgical operations in   5
the comfort of their living rooms, when, thanks to the animated cartoon, the geography of the digestive system has become familiar territory even to the nursery school set, in a land where the satisfaction of curiosity about almost all matters is a national pastime, the secrecy surrounding embalming can, surely, hardly be attributed to the inherent gruesomeness of the subject. Custom in this regard has within this century suffered a complete reversal. In the early days of American embalming, when it was performed in the home of the deceased, it was almost mandatory for some relative to stay by the embalmer's

---

[1] Partly because of Mitford's attack, the Federal Trade Commission now requires the funeral industry to provide families with itemized price lists, including the price of embalming, to state that embalming is not required, and to obtain the family's consent to embalming before charging for it. Shortly before her death, however, Mitford observed that the FTC had "watered down" the regulations and "routinely ignored" consumer complaints about the funeral industry. — EDS.

side and witness the procedure. Today, family members who might wish to be in attendance would certainly be dissuaded by the funeral director. All others, except apprentices, are excluded by law from the preparation room.

A close look at what does actually take place may explain in large measure the undertaker's intractable reticence concerning a procedure that has become his major *raison d'être*. Is it possible he fears that public information about embalming might lead patrons to wonder if they really want this service? If the funeral men are loath to discuss the subject outside the trade, the reader may, understandably, be equally loath to go on reading at this point. For those who have the stomach for it, let us part the formaldehyde curtain. . . .

The body is first laid out in the undertaker's morgue — or rather, Mr. Jones is reposing in the preparation room — to be readied to bid the world farewell.

The preparation room in any of the better funeral establishments has the tiled and sterile look of a surgery, and indeed the embalmer–restorative artist who does his chores there is beginning to adopt the term *dermasurgeon* (appropriately corrupted by some mortician-writers as "demi-surgeon") to describe his calling. His equipment, consisting of scalpels, scissors, augers, forceps, clamps, needles, pumps, tubes, bowls, and basins, is crudely imitative of the surgeon's, as is his technique, acquired in a nine- or twelve-month post-high-school course in an embalming school. He is supplied by an advanced chemical industry with a bewildering array of fluids, sprays, pastes, oils, powders, creams, to fix or soften tissue, shrink or distend it as needed, dry it here, restore the moisture there. There are cosmetics, waxes, and paints to fill and cover features, even plaster of Paris to replace entire limbs. There are ingenious aids to prop and stabilize the cadaver: a Vari-Pose Head Rest, the Edwards Arm and Hand Positioner, the Repose Block (to support the shoulders during the embalming), and the Throop Foot Positioner, which resembles an old-fashioned stocks.

Mr. John H. Eckels, president of the Eckels College of Mortuary Science, thus describes the first part of the embalming procedure: "In the hands of a skilled practitioner, this work may be done in a comparatively short time and without mutilating the body other than by slight incision — so slight that it scarcely would cause serious inconvenience if made upon a living person. It is necessary to remove the blood, and doing this not only helps in the disinfecting, but removes the principal cause of disfigurements due to discoloration."

Another textbook discusses the all-important time element: "The earlier this is done, the better, for every hour that elapses between death and embalming will add to the problems and complications encountered. . . ." Just how soon should one get going on the embalming? The author tells us, "On the basis of such scanty information made available to this profession through its rudimentary and haphazard system of technical research, we must conclude that the best results are to be obtained if the subject is embalmed before life is completely extinct — that is, before cellular death has occurred. In the average case, this would mean within an hour after somatic death." For those who feel that there is something a little rudimentary, not to say haphazard, about this advice, a comforting thought is offered by another writer. Speaking of fears entertained in early days of premature burial, he points out, "One of the effects of embalming by chemical injection, however, has been to dispel fears of live burial." How true; once the blood is removed, chances of live burial are indeed remote.

To return to Mr. Jones, the blood is drained out through the veins and   11
replaced by embalming fluid pumped in through the arteries. As noted in *The Principles and Practices of Embalming*, "every operator has a favorite injection and drainage point — a fact which becomes a handicap only if he fails or refuses to forsake his favorites when conditions demand it." Typical favorites are the carotid artery, femoral artery, jugular vein, subclavian vein. There are various choices of embalming fluid. If Flextone is used, it will produce a "mild, flexible rigidity. The skin retains a velvety softness, the tissues are rubbery and pliable. Ideal for women and children." It may be blended with B. and G. Products Company's Lyf-Lyk tint, which is guaranteed to reproduce "nature's own skin texture . . . the velvety appearance of living tissue." Sun-tone comes in three separate tints: Suntan; Special Cosmetic Tint, a pink shade "especially indicated for female subjects"; and Regular Cosmetic Tint, moderately pink.

About three to six gallons of a dyed and perfumed solution of formalde-   12
hyde, glycerin, borax, phenol, alcohol, and water is soon circulating through Mr. Jones, whose mouth has been sewn together with a "needle directed upward between the upper lip and gum and brought out through the left nostril," with the corners raised slightly "for a more pleasant expression." If he should be bucktoothed, his teeth are cleaned with Bon Ami and coated with colorless nail polish. His eyes, meanwhile, are closed with flesh-tinted eye caps and eye cement.

The next step is to have at Mr. Jones with a thing called a trocar. This is a   13
long, hollow needle attached to a tube. It is jabbed into the abdomen, poked around the entrails and chest cavity, the contents of which are pumped out and replaced with "cavity fluid." This done, and the hole in the abdomen sewn up, Mr. Jones's face is heavily creamed (to protect the skin from burns which may be caused by leakage of the chemicals), and he is covered with a sheet and left unmolested for a while. But not for long — there is more, much more, in store for him. He has been embalmed, but not yet restored, and the best time to start the restorative work is eight to ten hours after embalming, when the tissues have become firm and dry.

The object of all this attention to the corpse, it must be remembered, is to make it presentable for viewing in an attitude of healthy repose. "Our customs require the presentation of our dead in the semblance of normality . . . unmarred by the ravages of illness, disease, or mutilation," says Mr. J. Sheridan Mayer in his *Restorative Art*. This is rather a large order since few people die in the full bloom of health, unravaged by illness and unmarked by some disfigurement. The funeral industry is equal to the challenge: "In some cases the gruesome appearance of a mutilated or disease-ridden subject may be quite discouraging. The task of restoration may seem impossible and shake the confidence of the embalmer. This is the time for intestinal fortitude and determination. Once the formative work is begun and affected tissues are cleaned or removed, all doubts of success vanish. It is surprising and gratifying to discover the results which may be obtained."

The embalmer, having allowed an appropriate interval to elapse, returns to the attack, but now he brings into play the skill and equipment of sculptor and cosmetician. Is a hand missing? Casting one in plaster of Paris is a simple matter. "For replacement purposes, only a cast of the back of the hand is necessary; this is within the ability of the average operator and is quite adequate." If a lip or two, a nose, or an ear should be missing, the embalmer has at hand a variety of restorative waxes with which to model replacements. Pores and skin texture are simulated by stippling with a little brush, and over this cosmetics are laid on. Head off? Decapitation cases are rather routinely handled. Ragged edges are trimmed, and head joined to torso with a series of splints, wires, and sutures. It is a good idea to have a little something at the neck — a scarf or a high collar — when time for viewing comes. Swollen mouth? Cut out tissue as needed from inside the lips. If too much is removed, the surface contour can easily be restored by padding with cotton. Swollen necks and cheeks are reduced by removing tissue through vertical incisions made down each side of the neck. "When the deceased is casketed, the pillow will hide the suture incisions . . . as an extra precaution against leakage, the suture may be painted with liquid sealer."

The opposite condition is more likely to present itself — that of emaciation. His hypodermic syringe now loaded with massage cream, the embalmer seeks out and fills the hollowed and sunken areas by injection. In this procedure the backs of the hands and fingers and the under-chin area should not be neglected.

Positioning the lips is a problem that recurrently challenges the ingenuity of the embalmer. Closed too tightly, they tend to give a stern, even disapproving expression. Ideally, embalmers feel, the lips should give the impression of being ever so slightly parted, the upper lip protruding slightly for a more youthful appearance. This takes some engineering, however, as the lips tend to drift apart. Lip drift can sometimes be remedied by pushing one or two straight pins through the inner margin of the lower lip and then inserting them between the two front upper teeth. If Mr. Jones happens to have no teeth, the pins can just as easily be anchored in his Armstrong Face Former and Denture Replacer. Another method to maintain lip closure is to dislocate the lower jaw, which is then held in its new position by a wire run through holes which have been drilled through the upper and lower jaws at the midline. As the French are fond of saying, *il faut souffrir pour être belle.*[2]

If Mr. Jones has died of jaundice, the embalming fluid will very likely turn   18
him green. Does this deter the embalmer? Not if he has intestinal fortitude. Masking pastes and cosmetics are heavily laid on, burial garments and casket interiors are color-correlated with particular care, and Jones is displayed beneath rose-colored lights. Friends will say "How *well* he looks." Death by carbon monoxide, on the other hand, can be rather a good thing from the embalmer's viewpoint: "One advantage is the fact that this type of discoloration is an exaggerated form of a natural pink coloration." This is nice because the healthy glow is already present and needs but little attention.

The patching and filling completed, Mr. Jones is now shaved, washed,   19
and dressed. Cream-based cosmetic, available in pink, flesh, suntan, brunette, and blond, is applied to his hands and face, his hair is shampooed and combed (and, in the case of Mrs. Jones, set), his hands manicured. For the horny-handed son of toil special care must be taken; cream should be applied to remove ingrained grime, and the nails cleaned. "If he were not in the habit of having them manicured in life, trimming and shaping is advised for better appearance — never questioned by kin."

Jones is now ready for casketing (this is the present participle of the verb   20
"to casket"). In this operation his right shoulder should be depressed slightly "to turn the body a bit to the right and soften the appearance of lying flat on the back." Positioning the hands is a matter of importance, and special rubber positioning blocks may be used. The hands should be cupped slightly for a more life-like, relaxed appearance. Proper placement of the body requires a delicate sense of balance. It should lie as high as possible in the casket, yet not so high that the lid, when lowered, will hit the nose. On the other hand, we are cautioned, placing the body too low "creates the impression that the body is in a box."

Jones is next wheeled into the appointed slumber room where a few last   21
touches may be added — his favorite pipe placed in his hand or, if he was a great reader, a book propped into position. (In the case of little Master Jones a Teddy bear may be clutched.) Here he will hold open house for a few days, visiting hours 10 a.m. to 9 p.m.

[2] You have to suffer to be beautiful. — Eds.

All now being in readiness, the funeral director calls a staff conference   22
to make sure that each assistant knows his precise duties. Mr. Wilber Kriege
writes: "This makes your staff feel that they are a part of the team, with a
definite assignment that must be properly carried out if the whole plan is to
succeed. You never heard of a football coach who failed to talk to his entire
team before they go on the field. They have drilled on the plays they are to
execute for hours and days, and yet the successful coach knows the importance of making even the benchwarming third-string substitute feel that he
is important if the game is to be won." The winning of *this* game is predicated
upon glass-smooth handling of the logistics. The funeral director has notified
the pallbearers whose names were furnished by the family, has arranged for the
presence of clergyman, organist, and soloist, has provided transportation for
everybody, has organized and listed the flowers sent by friends. In *Psychology
of Funeral Service* Mr. Edward A. Martin points out, "He may not always do as
much as the family thinks he is doing, but it is his helpful guidance that they
appreciate in knowing they are proceeding as they should. . . . The important
thing is how well his services can be used to make the family believe they are
giving unlimited expression to their own sentiment."

The religious service may be held in a church or in the chapel of the   23
funeral home; the funeral director vastly prefers the latter arrangement, for
not only is it more convenient for him but it affords him the opportunity to
show off his beautiful facilities to the gathered mourners. After the clergyman
has had his say, the mourners queue up to file past the casket for a last look
at the deceased. The family is *never* asked whether they want an open-casket
ceremony; in the absence of their instruction to the contrary, this is taken for
granted. Consequently well over 90% of all American funerals feature the
open casket — a custom unknown in other parts of the world. Foreigners are
astonished by it. An English woman living in San Francisco described her
reaction in a letter to the writer:

> I myself have attended only one funeral here — that of an elderly fellow
> worker of mine. After the service I could not understand why everyone was
> walking towards the coffin (sorry, I mean casket), but thought I had better
> follow the crowd. It shook me rigid to get there and find the casket open and
> poor old Oscar lying there in his brown tweed suit, wearing a sun-tan makeup
> and just the wrong shade of lipstick. If I had not been extremely fond of the
> old boy, I have a horrible feeling that I might have giggled. Then and there
> I decided that I could never face another American funeral — even dead.

The casket (which has been resting throughout the service on a Classic   24
Beauty Ultra Metal Casket Bier) is now transferred by a hydraulically operated device called Porto-Lift to a balloon-tired, Glide Easy casket carriage

which will wheel it to yet another conveyance, the Cadillac Funeral Coach. This may be lavender, cream, light green — anything but black. Interiors, of course, are color-correlated, "for the man who cannot stop short of perfection."

At graveside, the casket is lowered into the earth. This office, once   25
the prerogative of friends of the deceased, is now performed by a patented mechanical lowering device. A "Lifetime Green" artificial grass mat is at the ready to conceal the sere earth, and overhead, to conceal the sky, is a portable Steril Chapel Tent ("resists the intense heat and humidity of summer and the terrific storms of winter . . . available in Silver Gray, Rose, or Evergreen"). Now is the time for the ritual scattering of earth over the coffin, as the solemn words "earth to earth, ashes to ashes, dust to dust" are pronounced by the officiating cleric. This can today be accomplished "with a mere flick of the wrist with the Gordon Leak-Proof Earth Dispenser. No grasping of a handful of dirt, no soiled fingers. Simple, dignified, beautiful, reverent! The modern way!" The Gordon Earth Dispenser (at $5) is of nickel-plated brass construction. It is not only "attractive to the eye and long wearing"; it is also "one of the 'tools' for building better public relations" if presented as "an appropriate noncommercial gift" to the clergyman. It is shaped something like a saltshaker.

Untouched by human hand, the coffin and the earth are now united.   26

It is in the function of directing the participants through this maze of   27
gadgetry that the funeral director has assigned to himself his relatively new role of "grief therapist." He has relieved the family of every detail, he has revamped the corpse to look like a living doll, he has arranged for it to nap for a few days in a slumber room, he has put on a well-oiled performance in which the concept of *death* has played no part whatsoever — unless it was inconsiderately mentioned by the clergyman who conducted the religious service. He has done everything in his power to make the funeral a real pleasure for everybody concerned. He and his team have given their all to score an upset victory over death.

Journal Writing

Presumably, morticians embalm and restore corpses, and survivors support the work, because the practices are thought to ease the shock of death. Now that you know what goes on behind the scenes, how do you feel about a loved one's undergoing these procedures?

Questions on Meaning

1. What was your emotional response to this essay? Can you analyze your feelings?

2. To what does Mitford attribute the secrecy surrounding the embalming process?

3. What, according to Mitford, is the mortician's intent? What common obstacles to fulfilling it must be surmounted?

4. What do you understand from Mitford's remark in paragraph 10, on dispelling fears of live burial: "How true; once the blood is removed, chances of live burial are indeed remote"?

5. Do you find any implied PURPOSE in this essay? Does Mitford seem primarily out to rake muck, or does she offer any positive suggestions to Americans?

Questions on Writing Strategy

1. What is Mitford's TONE? In her opening two paragraphs, exactly what shows her attitude toward her subject?

2. Why do you think Mitford goes into so much grisly detail in analyzing the processes of embalming and restoration? How does the detail serve her purpose?

3. What is the EFFECT of calling the body Mr. Jones?

4. Paragraph by paragraph, what TRANSITIONS does the author employ?

5. To whom does Mitford address her process analysis? How do you know she isn't writing for an AUDIENCE of professional morticians?

6. Choose one of the quotations from the journals and textbooks of professionals and explain how it serves the author's general purpose.

7. Why do you think Mitford often uses the PASSIVE VOICE to describe the actions of embalmers — for instance, "the blood is drained," "If Flextone is used," and "It may be blended" in paragraph 11? Are the verbs in passive voice effective or ineffective? Why?

8. **OTHER METHODS**   In paragraph 8, Mitford uses CLASSIFICATION in listing the embalmer's equipment and supplies. What groups does she identify, and why does she bother sorting the items at all?

Questions on Language

1. Explain the ALLUSION to Yorick in paragraph 2.

2. What IRONY do you find in this statement in paragraph 7: "The body is first laid out in the undertaker's morgue — or rather, Mr. Jones is reposing in the preparation room"? Pick out any other words or phrases in the essay that seem ironic. Comment especially on those you find in the essay's last two sentences.

3. Why is it useful to Mitford's purpose that she cites the brand names of morticians' equipment and supplies (the Edwards Arm and Hand Positioner, Lyf-Lyk tint)? List all the brand names in the essay that are memorable.

4. Define the following words or terms: counterpart (par. 2); circumscribed, decedent, bereaved (3); docility, perpetuation (4); inherent (5); intractable, reticence, *raison d'être*, formaldehyde (6); "derma-" (in *dermasurgeon*), augers, forceps, distend, stocks (8); somatic (10); carotid artery, femoral artery, jugular vein, subclavian vein, pliable (11); glycerin, borax, phenol (12); trocar, entrails (13); stippling, sutures (15); emaciation (16); jaundice (18); predicated (22); queue (23); hydraulically (24); sere, cleric (25).

Suggestions for Writing

1. **FROM JOURNAL TO ESSAY**   Drawing on your personal response to Mitford's essay in your journal (p. 246), write a brief essay that ARGUES either for or against embalming and restoration. Consider the purposes served by these practices, both for the mortician and for the dead person's relatives and friends, as well as their costs and effects.

2. ANALYZE some other process whose operations may not be familiar to everyone. (Have you ever held a job, or helped out in a family business, that has taken you behind the scenes? How is fast food prepared? How are cars serviced? How is a baby sat? How is a house constructed?) Detail it step by step, including transitions to clarify the steps.

3. **CRITICAL WRITING**   In attacking the funeral industry, Mitford also, implicitly, attacks the people who pay for and comply with the industry's attitudes and practices. What ASSUMPTIONS does Mitford seem to make about how we ought to deal with death and the dead? (Consider, for instance, her statements about the "docility of Americans . . . , blissfully ignorant" [par. 4] and the funeral director's making "the funeral a real pleasure for everybody concerned" [27].) Write an essay in which you interpret Mitford's assumptions and agree or disagree with them, based on your own reading and experience. If you like, defend the ritual of the funeral, or the mortician's profession, against Mitford's attack.

4. **CONNECTIONS**   In "Vampires Never Die" (p. 282), Guillermo del Toro and Chuck Hogan also comment on fears of death, noting that "we have no true jurisdiction over our bodies." Taken together, what do Mitford's and del Toro and Hogan's essays say about the importance of the body in Western culture? Write an essay either defending or criticizing the desire for physical immortality, whether real or imagined.

Jessica Mitford on Writing

"Choice of subject is of cardinal importance," declared Jessica Mitford in *Poison Penmanship*. "One does by far one's best work when besotted by and absorbed in the matter at hand." After *The American Way of Death* was published, Mitford received hundreds of letters suggesting alleged rackets that ought to be exposed, and to her surprise, an overwhelming majority of these letters complained about defective and overpriced hearing aids. But Mitford never wrote a book blasting the hearing aid industry. "Somehow, although there may well be need for such an exposé, I could not warm up to hearing aids as a subject for the kind of thorough, intensive, long-range research that would be needed to do an effective job." She once taught a course at Yale on muckraking, with each student choosing a subject to investigate. "Those who tackled hot issues on campus, such as violations of academic freedom or fail-ure to implement affirmative-action hiring policies, turned in some excellent work; but the lad who decided to investigate 'waste in the Yale dining halls' was predictably unable to make much of this trivial topic."

The hardest problem Mitford faced in writing *The American Way of Death*, she recalled, was doing her factual, step-by-step account of the embalming process. She felt "determined to describe it in all its revolting details, but how to make this subject palatable to the reader?" Her solution was to cast the whole process analysis in the official JARGON of the mortuary industry, draw-ing on lists of taboo words and their EUPHEMISMS (or acceptable synonyms), as published in the trade journal *Casket & Sunnyside*: "Mr., Mrs., Miss Blank, not corpse or body; preparation room, not morgue; reposing room, not laying-out room. . . ." The story of Mr. Jones thus took shape, and Mitford's use of jargon, she found, added macabre humor to the proceedings.

The Brief Bedford Reader on Writing

We aren't sure that the topic of "waste in the Yale dining halls" is nec-essarily trivial, but obviously not everyone would burn to write about it. How do you find a topic worth investigating? Something that will engage you and keep you interested "for the kind of thorough, intensive, long-range research that would be needed to do an effective job"? See our tips in Chapter 2 ("Subject," pp. 30) and the Appendix ("Conducting Research," pp. 492–96).

ADDITIONAL WRITING TOPICS

Process Analysis

1. Write a *directive* process analysis (a "how-to" essay) in which, drawing on your own knowledge, you instruct someone in doing or making something. You might choose to take a serious approach or a light TONE. Either way, divide the process into steps, and be sure to detail each step thoroughly. Here are some possible subjects (any of which may be modified or narrowed):

How to protect one's privacy online
How to enlist people's confidence
How to teach a person to ski
How to book a ride through *Uber* or *Lyft*
How to compose a photograph
How to judge a dog show
How to organize your own rock group
How to eat an artichoke
How to shear a sheep
How to build (or fly) a kite
How to start weight training
How to aid a person who is choking
How to kick a habit
How to win at poker
How to make an effective protest or complaint

Or, if you don't like any of those topics, what else do you know that others might care to learn from you?

2. Working in chronological order, write a careful *informative* (explanatory, not "how-to") analysis of any one of the following processes. Make use of DESCRIPTION where necessary, and be sure to include TRANSITIONS. If one of these topics gives you a better idea for a paper, go with your own subject.

How a student is processed during orientation or registration
How the student newspaper gets published
How a particular Web site generates revenue
How employers find and screen job applicants
How a Bluetooth speaker or an MP3 player works
How fracking extracts natural gas from shale
How a professional umpire (or any other professional) does the job
How an air conditioner (or other household appliance) works
How birds teach their young (or some other process in the natural world: how sharks feed, how a snake swallows an egg, how tsunamis form, how the human liver works)
How police control crowds
How people make up their minds when shopping for cars (or clothes)

© Roz Chast The New Yorker Collection/The Cartoon Bank

8

DIVISION OR
ANALYSIS

Slicing into Parts

◀ **Division or analysis in a cartoon**

The cartoonist Roz Chast is well known for witty and perceptive
comments on the everyday, made through words and simple,
almost childlike drawings. Dividing or analyzing, this cartoon
identifies the elements of a boy's sandwich to discover what they
can tell about the values and politics of the parent who made
the sandwich. The title, "Deconstructing Lunch," refers to a type
of analysis that focuses on the multiple meanings of a subject
and especially its internal contradictions. Summarize what the
sandwich reveals about the boy's parent. What contradictions
do you spot in his or her values or politics? What might Chast
be saying more generally about food choices?

THE METHOD

A chemist working for a soft-drink company is asked to improve on a competitor's product, Hydra Sports Water. To do the job, the chemist first has to figure out what's in the drink. She smells the stuff and tastes it. Then she tests a sample chemically to discover the actual ingredients: water, corn syrup, sodium citrate, potassium chloride, coloring. Methodically, the chemist has performed DIVISION or ANALYSIS: She has separated the beverage into its components. Hydra Sports Water stands revealed, understood, and ready to be bettered.

Division or analysis (the terms are interchangeable) is a key skill in learning and in life. It is an instrument allowing you to slice a large and complicated subject into smaller parts that you can grasp and connect to one another. In fact, it is so fundamental that it underlies every other method of development discussed in this book — for instance, it helps you identify features for DESCRIPTION, spot similarities for COMPARISON AND CONTRAST, or sort out the steps for a PROCESS ANALYSIS (as our chemist did in the previous chapter). With analysis you can comprehend — and communicate — the structure of things. And when it works, you find in the parts an idea or conclusion about the subject that makes it clearer, truer, more comprehensive, or more vivid than it was before you started.

Kinds of Division or Analysis

Although division or analysis always works the same way — separating a whole, singular subject into its elements — the method can be more or less difficult depending on how unfamiliar, complex, or abstract the subject is. Obviously, it's going to be easier to analyze a chicken (wings, legs, thighs, . . .) than a speech by John F. Kennedy (this image, that allusion, . . .), and easier to analyze the structure of a small business than that of a multinational conglomerate.

There are always multiple ways to divide or analyze a subject. One historian, for instance, might study an era by looking at its elections, protest movements, wars, and so forth — following its political components — while another might examine the daily experiences of the people who lived in that period — explaining events in their social context. In other words, the outcome of an analysis depends on the rule or *principle* used to conduct it. This fact accounts for some of the differences among academic disciplines: A psychologist may look at the individual person primarily as a bundle of drives and needs, whereas a sociologist may emphasize the individual's roles in society. Even within a discipline, different factions analyze differently, using different principles of division or analysis. Some psychologists are interested mainly in perception, others mainly in behavior; some focus mainly on emotional development, others mainly on brain chemistry.

Analysis and Critical Thinking

Analysis plays a fundamental role in CRITICAL THINKING, READING, AND WRITING, topics discussed in Chapters 1 and 2. In fact, *analysis* and *criticism* are deeply related: The first comes from a Greek word meaning "to undo"; the second from a Greek word meaning "to separate."

Critical thinking, reading, and writing go beneath the surface of the object, word, image, or whatever the subject is. When you work critically, you divide the subject into its elements, INFER the buried meanings and ASSUMPTIONS that define its essence, and SYNTHESIZE the parts into a new whole that is now informed by your perspective. Say a campaign brochure quotes a candidate for election to the city council as being in favor of "reasonable government expenditures on reasonable highway projects." The candidate will support new roads, right? Wrong. As a critical reader of the brochure, you quickly sense something fishy in the use (twice) of *reasonable*. As an informed reader, you might know (or find out) that the candidate has consistently opposed new roads, so the chances of her finding a highway project "reasonable" are slim. At the same time, her stand has been unpopular, so of course she wants to seem "reasonable" on the issue. Read critically, then, a campaign statement that seems to offer mild support for highways is actually a slippery evasion of any such commitment.

Analysis (a convenient term for the overlapping operations of analysis, inference, and synthesis) is very useful for exposing such evasiveness, but that isn't its only function. You've already done quite a bit of analytical thinking as you critically read the selections in this book. The method will also help you understand a sculpture, perceive the importance of a case study in sociology, or form a response to an environmental impact report. And the method can be invaluable for straight thinking about popular culture, from TV to toys.

THE PROCESS

Subject and Purpose

Keep an eye out for writing assignments requiring division or analysis — in college and work, they won't be hard to find. They will probably include

Division or Analysis

the word *analyze* or a word implying analysis, such as *evaluate, examine, explore, interpret, discuss,* or *criticize.* Any time you spot such a term, you know your job is to separate the subject into its elements, to infer their meanings, to explore the relations among them, and to draw a conclusion about the subject.

Almost any coherent entity — object, person, place, concept — is a fit subject for analysis *if* the analysis will add to the subject's meaning or significance. Little is deadlier than the rote analytical exercise that leaves the parts neatly dissected and the subject comatose on the page. As a writer, you have to animate the subject, and that means finding your interest. What about your subject seems curious? What's appealing? or mysterious? or awful? And what will be your PURPOSE in writing about the subject: Do you simply want to explain it, or do you want to argue for or against it?

Such questions can help you find the principle or framework you will use to divide the subject into parts. Say you've got an assignment to write about a sculpture in a nearby park. Why do you like the sculpture, or why don't you? What elements of its creation and physical form make it art? What is the point of such public art? What does this sculpture do for this park, or what does the park do for the sculpture? Any of these questions could suggest a slant on the subject, a framework for analysis, and a purpose for writing, getting your analysis moving.

Principle of Analysis and Thesis

Finding your principle of analysis will lead you to your essay's THESIS as well — the main point you want to make about your subject. Expressed in a THESIS STATEMENT, this idea will help keep you focused and help your readers see your subject as a whole rather than as a bundle of parts. Here are the thesis statements in two of this chapter's selections:

> Boys — and more and more girls — who accept Jock Culture values often go on to flourish in a competitive sports environment that requires submission to authority, winning by any means necessary, and group cohesion.
> — Robert Lipsyte, "Jock Culture"

> Monsters, like angels, are invoked by our individual and collective needs. Today, much as during that gloomy summer in 1816 [when Dracula was conceived], we feel the need to seek their cold embrace.
> — Guillermo del Toro and Chuck Hogan, "Vampires Never Die"

Readers will have an easier time following your analysis — and will more likely appreciate it — if they have a hook on which to hang the details. Your thesis statement can be that hook if you use it to establish your framework, your principle of analysis. A well-focused thesis statement can help you as well, because it gives you a yardstick to judge how complete, consistent, and supportive your analysis is. Don't be discouraged, though, if your thesis statement doesn't come to you until *after* you've written a first draft and had a chance to discover your interest. Writing about your subject may be the best way for you to find its meaning and significance.

Evidence

Making a valid analysis is chiefly a matter of giving your subject thought, but for the result to seem useful and convincing to your readers, it will have to refer to the real world. The method, then, requires open eyes and a willingness to provide EVIDENCE. The nature of the evidence will depend entirely on what you are analyzing — physical details for a sculpture, quotations for a speech, financial data for a business review, statistics for a psychology case study, and so forth. The idea is to supply enough evidence to justify and support your particular slant on the subject.

In developing an essay by analysis, having an outline at your elbow can be a help. You don't want to overlook any parts or elements that should be included in your framework. You needn't mention every feature in your final draft or give them all equal treatment, but any omissions or variations should be conscious. And you want to use your framework consistently, not switching carelessly (and confusingly) from, say, the form of the sculpture to the cost of public art.

A final caution: It's possible to get carried away with one's own analysis, to become so enamored of the details that the subject itself becomes dim or distorted. You can avoid this danger by keeping the subject literally in front of you as you work (or at least imagining it vividly). It often helps to reassemble your subject at the end of the essay, placing it in a larger context, speculating on its influence, or affirming its significance. By the end of the essay, your subject must be a coherent whole truly represented by your analysis, not twisted, inflated, or obliterated. The reader should be intrigued by your subject, yes, but also able to recognize it on the street.

FOCUS ON PARAGRAPH COHERENCE

Because several elements contribute to the whole of a subject, your analysis will be easier for readers to follow if you frequently clarify what element you are discussing and how it fits with your principle of analysis. Two techniques,

(continued)

especially, can help you guide readers through your analysis: transitions and repetition or restatement.

- **Use TRANSITIONS as signposts to tell readers where you, and they, are headed.** Among other uses, transitions may specify the relations between your points and your principle of analysis (*first, second, another feature*) or may clarify the relations among the points themselves (*even more important, similarly*). Consider how transitions keep readers focused in the following paragraph:

  > Many television comedies, even some that boast live audiences, rely on laugh tracks to fill too-quiet moments. To create a laugh track, an editor uses four overlapping elements of a laugh. The first is style, from titter to belly laugh. The second is intensity, the volume, ranging from mild to medium to earsplitting. The third ingredient is duration, the length of the laugh, whether quick, medium, or extended. And finally, there's the number of laughers, from a lone giggler to a roaring throng. When creating a canned laugh, the editor draws from a bank of hundreds of prerecorded laugh files and blends the four ingredients as a maestro weaves a symphony out of brass, woodwinds, percussion, and strings.

- **Use repetition and restatement to link sentences and tie them to your principle of analysis.** In the preceding paragraph, two threads run through the sentences to maintain the focus: *laugh tracks, laugh track, laugh, laughers,* and *canned laugh*; and *editor, editor,* and *maestro*.

CHECKLIST FOR REVISING A DIVISION OR ANALYSIS ESSAY

✔ **Principle of analysis and thesis.** What is your particular slant on your subject, the rule or principle you have used to divide your subject into its elements? Do you specify it in your thesis statement?

✔ **Completeness.** Have you considered all the subject's elements required by your principle of analysis?

✔ **Consistency.** Have you applied your principle of analysis consistently, viewing your subject from a definite slant?

✔ **Evidence.** Is your division or analysis well supported with concrete details, quotations, data, or statistics, as appropriate?

✔ **Significance.** Why should readers care about your analysis? Have you told them something about your subject that wasn't obvious on its surface?

✔ **Truth to subject.** Is your analysis faithful to the subject, not distorted, exaggerated, or deflated?

DIVISION OR ANALYSIS IN ACADEMIC WRITING
A Political Science Textbook

In this paragraph adapted from *Government by the People*, an introductory political science textbook focused on American government, authors David B. Magleby, Paul C. Light, and Christine L. Nemacheck divide the US Constitution into its essential elements. The careful analysis supports their admiration for the document's simplicity and flexibility.

Despite its brevity, the Constitution firmly established the Framers' experiment in free-government-in-the-making that each generation reinterprets and renews. That is why after more than 225 years we have not had another written Constitution — let alone two, three, or more, like other countries around the world. Part of the reason is the public's widespread acceptance of the Constitution. But the Constitution has also endured because it is a brilliant structure for limited government and one that the Framers designed to be adaptable and flexible. Article I establishes a bicameral Congress, with a House of Representatives and a Senate, and empowers it to enact legislation — for example, governing foreign and interstate commerce. Article II vests the executive power in the president, and Article III vests the judicial power in the Supreme Court and other federal courts that Congress may establish. Article IV guarantees the privileges and immunities of citizens and specifies the conditions for admitting new states. Article V provides for the methods of amending the Constitution, and Article VI specifies that the Constitution and all laws made under it are the supreme law of the land. Finally, Article VII provides that the Constitution had to be ratified by nine of the original thirteen states to go into effect. In 1791, the first ten amendments, the Bill of Rights, were added, and another seventeen amendments have been added since.

Principle of analysis: "brilliant" structure of the Constitution

1. Legislative branch

2. Executive branch
3. Judicial branch
4. Protections for citizens

5. Procedures for amendment

6. Authority
7. Ratification

8. Bill of Rights and later amendments

A Critical Reading

The study of literature — poetry, novels, short fiction, even essays — regularly involves analysis in the form of close readings. Interpretations vary, of course, depending on the reader's chosen principle of analysis. One literary critic, for instance, might divide a poem by looking at its rhymes, meter, imagery, and so forth — following its internal components — while another might examine a short story or novel as an artifact of the author's time and place — connecting its components to its context. In either case, such close readings draw on the text itself for evidence: summarizing, paraphrasing, and quoting the work to give readers the flavor of its content and to support the critic's analysis.

For a composition course using *The Brief Bedford Reader* at Seton Hall University in New Jersey, Rachel O'Connor, a dual major in biology and English, wrote an analysis of Shirley Jackson's short story "The Lottery" (p. 90). She chose to focus on Jackson's use of literary techniques, following MLA style to cite evidence from the story. We excerpt her close reading here to avoid spoilers.

Shirley Jackson's "The Lottery" appears simple on a first read, but close analysis reveals a tale packed with dark social commentary. The story takes place on a glorious summer day, in a small and seemingly docile rural town where an annual lottery is about to take place. It is unclear at first what this lottery entails, but since the term typically has positive connotations, the reader does not suspect the morbidity that lies beneath the surface or the horrors unleashed in the last few lines . . . .

Thesis statement

What makes "The Lottery" so brilliant are the subtle clues Jackson embeds in the text and the deeper moral themes to which they point. The narrative flows smoothly and is compelling enough to consume readers and distract them from noticing the tactics strategically set in place. For example, the first sentence describes the setting as "clear and sunny, with the fresh warmth of a full-summer day" (90). This line is ironic: What appears to be a pleasant community gathering on a beautiful day turns out to be something much more sinister. . . .

Principle of analysis: literary technique

1. Irony

Another early clue is the description, in the second paragraph, of boys gathering stones in their pockets. Although it is not clear what these stones might be used for, the reader is not inclined to think anything of it — until he or she becomes aware of the story's ending. At the same time, the fact that some boys "made a great pile of stones . . . and guarded it against the raids of the other boys" (91) exposes the inherent distrust and hostility the townspeople have for one another despite the appearance of being a close-knit community. . . .

2. Foreshadowing

The gravity of the situation is further suggested through the description of the men, whose "jokes were quiet" and who "smiled rather than laughed" (91). The townspeople's conspicuous efforts to make conversation and act normal hint to the reader that something may be awry. The children's attitude

3. Characterization

toward the lottery is especially troubling. They seem to view it as a game although they are aware of the perverse reality, which indicates their desensitization to violence and loss of innocence. . . . Finally, the winner's insistence that the lottery "isn't fair" and "isn't right" (97) underscores the story's latent theme of the evil often lurking in societal norms.

Jackson, through irony, foreshadowing, and characterization, spins a flawless tale that both entertains and makes readers think. She subtly yet powerfully questions a society that complies with abhorrent practices simply because they are traditional. . . . She challenges readers to make their own moral judgments rather than fall victim to the often unjust mentality of the majority in charge, while simultaneously pulling off a surprise ending wild enough to catch the attention of almost anyone.

Reassembly of elements with a comment on significance

Work Cited

Jackson, Shirley. "The Lottery." *The Bedford Reader*, edited by X. J. Kennedy et al., 13th ed., Bedford/St. Martin's, 2017, pp. 90-97.

List of Works Cited with publication information for the text (see pp. 499–513)

JUDITH ORTIZ COFER

A native of Puerto Rico who has lived most of her life in the United States, Judith Ortiz Cofer writes poetry, fiction, and essays about her heritage and the balancing of two cultures. Born in Hormingueros, Puerto Rico, in 1952, she earned a BA from Augusta College in 1974 and an MA from Florida Atlantic University in 1977. Cofer started out as a bilingual teacher in the schools of Palm Beach County, Florida, and taught English and creative writing at the University of Georgia. Her publications include the poetry collections *Peregrina* (1986) and *Terms of Survival* (1987); the novels *The Line of the Sun* (1989), *The Meaning of Consuelo* (2003), and *If I Could Fly* (2011); the essay collections *Silent Dancing* (1990) and *Woman in Front of the Sun* (2000); mixes of nonfiction, fiction, and poetry in *The Latin Deli* (1993) and *The Year of Our Revolution* (1998); and several children's books, most recently *Animal Jamboree: Latino Folktales* and *The Poet Upstairs* (both 2012). As a native Spanish speaker who challenged herself to learn English, she is always experimenting, she says, with "the 'infinite variety' and power of language."

The Cruel Country

Cofer moved to New Jersey from Puerto Rico with her parents and siblings when she was three years old; the family made frequent visits back to the island and (with the exception of Cofer's father) always considered it home. In this excerpt from her memoir *The Cruel Country* (2015), Cofer draws on a theory of French philosopher Roland Barthes (1915–80) to make sense of why a photograph of her mother moves her as it does. The essay first appeared in *Brevity* magazine in 2012.

In the selection following this one, "The Capricious Camera," student writer Laila Ayad also uses division or analysis to tease out the meanings of a photograph, in her case an image of a little girl in World War II Poland.

> *"Mourning: a cruel country where I'm no longer afraid."*
> — Roland Barthes, *Mourning Diary*

I study a photograph of my mother taken on her return to the Island as a   1
widow in her forties. What do I see? A woman in a bright red top and black pants, neither smiling nor frowning, posed in front of a painted canvas. Her

back is very straight and her hands, showing signs of arthritis in the slightly swollen crooked fingers, are spread flat on her lap.

Something draws the eyes to this woman's face. The camera has caught her in between emotions. We do not know whether she is about to smile or cry.

In his book on photography as memorial, *Camera Lucida*, Roland Barthes talks about the two planes in a photograph that interest him. The first he calls the *studium*, and it represents the actual occasion, meaning, or intent of the photograph. But it is the detail that defies analysis, what Barthes calls the *punctum*, that interests him the most.

The punctum is the point of intersection between viewer and image, that detail that draws us into the picture as a shared human event. It is the thing, whether intended by the photographer or not, that touches you or triggers a quickening of the pulse, an irresistible impulse to look closer.

When I was asked for photos to be displayed at the funeral home, I looked through her albums and found dozens of pictures, but I could not find one that had the right tone, the "air," as Barthes calls it.

My brother had visited our mother several months before her final illness and had found a photo that he scanned and sent to me. She had told him that she did not like it, but had not given a reason. She had kept it put away in a box. I looked at it occasionally, drawn to her haunting look of almost-revelation. It had been taken when she first returned to the Island after my father's death. She looked younger in this photo than I remembered her, maybe because she had taken to wearing conservative, matronly clothes and her hair pulled back while she spent her years as a Navy wife-in-waiting in the United States, the time she always called her *exilio*.[1]

But in this photo she has regained her true age. Her hair is shiny with only a hint of gray at the part, her tan arms are bare, and she looks slim and fit. But in spite of her rejuvenation there is a seriousness that belies the outfit, clearly donned for an evening out.

The punctum of this photo for me is the little spray of white flowers adorning her hair. Doesn't a woman have to be thinking of something celebratory or someone special to put flowers in her hair? I had never seen my mother indulge in anything quite as impractical and frivolous. In fact, she was as concerned about bugs on her body as any child who had experienced the parasite scares of her childhood on a tropical island. I looked at the photo for other signs of her transformation, but kept coming back to the two disparate qualities: the hidden grief in her expression, and the flirtatiousness of the little white flowers in her hair.

[1] Spanish, "exile." — EDS.

On the painted canvas behind her there is an idealized seashore scene at   9
dusk: a background of sinuous palm trees, placid ocean, and a black mountain range. Perhaps this is how our beaches looked once, before the litter, the
hotels and condos, and the tourists. It may have been the image my mother
carried in her mind all those years when she yearned for return.

An ordinary woman, she was a muse to me. It was her ineffable air of timid-   10
ity and even fear, precariously balanced by passionate desires and dreams, of living on her own terms, that I had been trying all of my years as a writer to capture.

But I could not create the visual image I had in my mind's eye. I had to   11
show that photo taken by an anonymous photographer of a woman in the
midst of a struggle, a new widow, alone in a place that had grown strange over
the many years of her absence.

Journal Writing

Flip through a family photo album or scroll through a personal collection of pictures
and pick an image that has a special meaning for you, or one that simply grabs your
attention for some reason. DESCRIBE this photograph in your journal. What is the
"actual occasion, meaning, or intent of the photograph," its "studium," as Roland
Barthes calls it (par. 3)? Who or what is depicted? What are the people wearing? What
are the expressions on their faces? Where was the photo taken? On what elements
does the picture focus? What aspects can be seen in the background? What details
puzzle you, and why?

Questions on Meaning

1. What does Cofer suggest was the reason for her parents' move to the US main-
   land? Why did her mother return to Puerto Rico?

2. What about the photograph of her mother intrigues Cofer as it does?

3. Cofer says her mother "was a muse" (par. 10) to her. What does she mean?

4. What do you think is Cofer's PURPOSE in this essay? Does she have something
   specific she wants the reader to understand?

Questions on Writing Strategy

1. Cofer opens her essay with an epigraph, a short quotation that forecasts a theme.
   How do you interpret the line by Roland Barthes? What theme does it forecast?

2. How does Cofer seem to imagine her AUDIENCE? How reasonable are her
   ASSUMPTIONS about her readers' backgrounds and knowledge?

3. What principle of analysis does Cofer use to interpret her mother's photograph? How does she SYNTHESIZE another writer's ideas to find new meaning in her subject?

4. **OTHER METHODS**   How well can you picture the photograph of Cofer's mother, based on her DESCRIPTION of it? What dominant impression does she create?

Questions on Language

1. What is the double meaning of Cofer's title?

2. How would you describe Cofer's overall TONE? Why is this tone appropriate for her purpose?

3. Consult a dictionary if you need help in defining the following: memorial, planes (par. 3); revelation, matronly (6); rejuvenation, belies, donned (7); disparate (8); sinuous, placid (9); ineffable, precariously (10).

Suggestions for Writing

1. **FROM JOURNAL TO ESSAY**   In an essay, describe the photograph you wrote about in your journal, but also do more: Try to analyze the photo in the contexts of the time it was taken and the impact it has on you now. What was the occasion behind the picture? Who took it, and why? What, for you, is the "punctum" (par. 3) of the image? What meanings can you draw from it?

2. Research the current situation of Puerto Ricans in the United States: citizenship, population, incomes, living conditions, education levels, occupations, and so forth. Then write an essay in which you present your findings.

3. **CRITICAL WRITING**   In an essay, analyze the parallels between Cofer's emotional state after her mother's death and her mother's apparent emotional state when she first became widowed. What point, overall, does Cofer seem to make about the experience of grieving?

4. **CONNECTIONS**   In "The Capricious Camera" (the next essay) Laila Ayad describes a photograph of a young girl and attempts to interpret its historical meanings. Using Cofer's and Ayad's essays for examples, write an essay of your own in which you discuss how writers can create meaning through description and analysis of visual images.

Judith Ortiz Cofer on Writing

Cofer told *Contemporary Authors* in the 1980s why she so often chooses her family as her SUBJECT for writing. She was speaking of her poetry, but the same could be said of her stories and essays as well. "My family is one of the main topics of my poetry," Cofer explained, "the ones left behind on the island of Puerto Rico, and the ones who came to the United States. In tracing their lives, I discover more about mine. The place of birth itself becomes a metaphor for the things we all must leave behind; the assimilation of a new culture is the coming into maturity by accepting the terms necessary for survival. My poetry is the study of this process of change, assimilation, and transformation."

The Brief Bedford Reader on Writing

What is Cofer's apparent PURPOSE in writing about her family as often as she does? For advice on using writing to facilitate your own personal reflection, whether in a JOURNAL or in an essay for others to read, see our notes on pages 19 and 32–33.

LAILA AYAD

Born in 1981, Laila Ayad grew up in Columbia, Maryland, a planned community based on ideals of racial, social, and economic diversity and balance. "Being exposed at an early age to such a diverse community and coming from a multiethnic family have given me great insight into different cultures and perspectives," says Ayad. After graduating from New York University in 2003 with a degree in theater and English literature, Ayad embarked on a successful acting career. When not on stage or screen, she paints and draws and continues to write.

The Capricious Camera

Ayad began college as an art major and produced this essay for a writing class in her sophomore year. Like Judith Ortiz Cofer in the previous selection, Ayad explores the elements of a photograph to find its meaning. The analysis takes her to Nazi Germany before and during World War II.

This essay first appeared in 2001 in *Mercer Street*, a journal of writing by New York University students. Notice that it follows MLA style for in-text parenthetical citations and a list of works cited, as discussed on pages 499–513.

In the years between 1933 and 1945, Germany was engulfed by the rise of a powerful new regime and the eventual spoils of war. During this period, Hitler's quest for racial purification turned Germany not only at odds with itself, but with the rest of the world. Photography as an art and as a business became a regulated and potent force in the fight for Aryan domination, Nazi influence, and anti-Semitism. Whether such images were used to promote Nazi ideology, document the Holocaust, or scare Germany's citizens into accepting their own changing country, the effect of this photography provides enormous insight into the true stories and lives of the people most affected by Hitler's racism. In fact, this photography has become so widespread in our understanding and teaching of the Holocaust that often other factors involved in the Nazis' racial policy have been undervalued in our history textbooks — especially the attempt by Nazi Germany to establish the Nordic Aryans as a master race through the *Lebensborn* experiment, a breeding and adoption program designed to eliminate racial imperfections. It is not merely people of

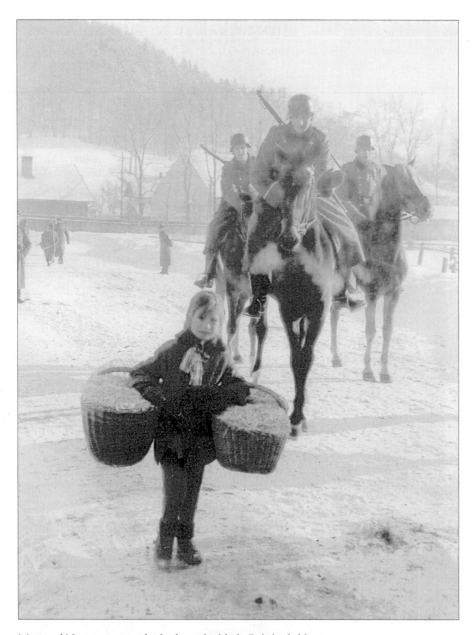

Mounted Nazi troops on the lookout for likely Polish children.

other persecuted races who can become victims in a racial war, but also those we would least expect — the persecuting race itself.

To understand the importance of this often shrouded side of Nazi Germany we might look at the photograph captioned "Mounted Nazi troops on the lookout for likely Polish children." Archived by Catrine Clay and Michael Leapman, this black-and-white photo depicts a young girl in the foreground, carrying two large baskets and treading across a rural and snow-covered countryside, while three mounted and armed Nazi soldiers follow closely behind her. In the distance, we can see farmhouses and a wooden fence, as well as four other uniformed soldiers or guards. Though the photograph accompanies the text without the name of the photographer, year, or information as to where it was found, Clay and Leapman suggest that the photo was taken in Poland between 1943 and 1945.

Who is this young white girl surrounded by armed soldiers? Is she being protected, watched, persecuted? It would be easy enough to assume that she is Jewish, but unlike photos documenting the Holocaust, with *this* image the intent is uncertain. In our general ignorance of the events surrounding this photo, the picture can be deceiving, and yet it is the picture that can also be used to shed light on the story.

Looking just at the photo, and ignoring the descriptive caption, there are some interesting visual and artistic effects that help a viewer better understand the circumstances surrounding the image. One of its most prominent features is the way the photographer decides to focus on only one young child in the foreground, while including seven Nazi soldiers behind her. The effect is overwhelming, and in gazing at the image, one is struck by the magnitude and force of the oppressing men in sharp contrast to the innocence and helplessness of the lone girl. By juxtaposing one child with seven men, the image comes across strongly as both cruel and terribly frightening. In addition, the child in the foreground is a young girl, which only adds to the potency of the image. The photographer makes the soldiers appear far more menacing and unjust, in that there appears to be no physical way in which a young girl could possibly defend herself against these men.

What is additionally interesting about this particular aspect of the photo is that the seven men are not grouped together, or in any way concentrated right next to the child. There are three directly behind the girl, one a little farther behind and to the left, one even slightly farther behind and to the right, and two very far off in the distance, walking in the opposite direction. This placement of the soldiers not only gives the photo an excellent sense of depth, but also conveys to the viewer a sense that the entire surroundings, not just the little girl, are being controlled and surveyed. It allows the viewer to imagine and wonder in what way other children, or perhaps just the other parts of the village, are being similarly restricted. For the young girl, and the viewer, it allows no way out; all angles and directions of the photo are covered by symbols of oppression, producing an eerily suffocating effect.

The child is the only person in the photo looking directly at the pho-   6
tographer. Whether this technique was manipulated on purpose remains to be seen, but it goes without saying that the effect is dramatic. Her gaze is wistful and innocent. In contrast, the men occupying the rest of the photo, and most prominently the three mounted ones in the foreground, are gazing either away or down. While it is uncertain what the soldiers behind the child are staring at, their downward stare causes their heads to hang in almost shameful dis-grace. They do not look at the child, and yet they do not look at the photogra-pher, who is quite obviously standing in front of them. Is this because they do not see that there is a picture being taken, or perhaps the photographer is another soldier, and this picture is simply routine in recording the progress of their work?

If not a Nazi soldier, the photographer could be a Polish citizen; if this   7
were the case, it might change our interpretation of the photo. Suddenly, the girl's facial expression and direct gaze seem pleading, while, for fear of being caught, the photographer snaps the picture quickly, in the exact moment the soldiers are looking away. Perhaps the soldiers did not mind having their pic-ture taken. Many Polish were considered, after all, their racial equals, and maybe they would have respected and appreciated an amateur photographer's interest in their work.

While all of these scenarios are seemingly plausible, the purpose of the   8
photograph is still uncertain. There are also several possibilities. One is that the Nazis commissioned the photograph, as they did others at the time, to properly record the events surrounding the development of their plan. In an article entitled "The Camera as Weapon: Documentary Photography and the Holocaust," Sybil Milton describes the ways in which Nazi photographers worked:

> Nazi professional photographers produced in excess of one-quarter million images. Their work was officially regulated and licensed. . . . All photos were screened by military censors subservient to official directives of the Pro-paganda Ministry. . . . Press photographers of World War II rarely showed atrocities and seldom published prints unfavorable to their own side. (1)

However, while the evidence is compelling, Milton recognizes another possi-bility that significantly changes the motive for the photo: "Portable cameras, and other technical innovations like interchangeable lenses and multiple exposure film, meant that nonprofessionals owned and used cameras with ease. Many soldiers carried small Leica or Ermanox cameras in their rucksacks or pillaged optical equipment from the towns they occupied" (2). While it *is* possible that the photograph was taken by a soldier seeking to document the work in Poland for his own interests, this probability, against the numerous commissioned photographs and the nature of the subject matter being documented, is unlikely. The photo alone, while intriguing in its image, tells only half of the story, and without a definitive context can become akin to a "choose your own adventure" novel. In other words, the possibilities for a photographic purpose are all laid out, but the true meaning or end remains undetermined. Unlike hand-made art, which in its very purpose begs to be viewed through various interpretations, photography, and particularly photojournalism, captures a certain moment in time, featuring specific subject matter, under a genuine set of circumstances. The picture is not invented, it is real life, and in being so demands to be viewed alongside its agenda, for without this context, it may never be fully understood.

When we turn to the caption describing the photograph, "Mounted Nazi   9 troops on the lookout for likely Polish children," the book *Master Race* and its accompanying story can now properly be discussed. Instead of typically dealing with the issues of a racist Nazi Germany as it relates to the Holocaust, and the other forms of racial extermination and discrimination that were subsequently involved, Clay and Leapman's book looks at the other side of the coin. It is important in dealing with and understanding the concept of racism to realize that racists are not simply those who dislike others; they are also those who worship themselves. In *Mein Kampf* Hitler outlined the inspiration for his racial tyranny by saying, "The products of human culture, the achievements in art, science and technology . . . are almost exclusively the creative product of the Aryan" (ch. 3). He was heavily influenced by the work of racially charged popular science writers, such as H. F. K. Gunther, who in his *Ethnology of the German Nation* wrote: "The man of Nordic race is not only the most gifted but also the most beautiful. . . . The man's face is hard and chiseled, the woman's tender, with rose-pink skin and bright triumphant eyes" (qtd. in Clay and Leapman 17). Through the course of the book, the topic of racism in Nazi Germany focuses intently on the concept of racial purification. By following the work of the carefully selected (meaning those of impeccable Aryan ancestry) members of Himmler's elite SS corps, Clay and Leapman introduce the history of Germany's failed *Lebensborn* experiment and the homes that were created by the Third Reich to breed and raise "perfect Aryans" (ix).

In a disturbing segment on Hitler's racial utopia, Clay and Leapman   10 describe the practice of eugenics, improving humankind by eliminating undesirable genetic traits and breeding those that were considered superior. The SS soldiers who are commonly known for forcing the Jews into concentration camps are mentioned, but this time they are discussed as the same men who were ordered to father white babies with volunteer German and Norwegian mothers. However, it is the final fact, the story of the SS soldiers who occupied surrounding countries and then stole children "who looked as if they might further improve the breed," that becomes the focus and ultimate subject matter of the photograph (ix).

Looking at the photograph in this context, the soldier no longer appears 11 to be protecting the Polish children, but hunting them. The word "likely" in the caption denotes this. Children who possessed strong Nordic or Aryan qualities were systematically taken from their native countries, adopted by German parents (who were paid by the Nazi regime), taught to forget their families and former lives, and raised to breed not only many children of their own but, above all, families that would uphold Nazi ideology. For Hitler and Heinrich Himmler, who was appointed Commissar for Consolidating German Nationhood, exterminating the racially impure was merely preparation. It was the process of breeding and stealing children that Himmler considered central and key in the ultimate goal for racial purification:

> Obviously in such a mixture of peoples there will always be some racially good types. Therefore I think that it is our duty to take their children with us, to remove them from their environment, if necessary by robbing or stealing them. . . . My aim has always been the same, to attract all the Nordic blood in the world and take it for ourselves. (qtd. in Clay and Leapman 91)

Additionally, Himmler's objective in targeting children, rather than adults, was a planned and strategic tool. Through teachings at school, children were used to control their parents by being encouraged to report what they did and said. Himmler realized that older people would be less enthusiastic about his ideas, so he made every effort to win the minds of the next generation.

What is perhaps most compelling about the *Lebensborn* experiment 12 and thus most poignant when viewing the photograph is the reminder that for every child that was stolen from nations like Poland, his or her family was being equally betrayed. One Polish girl recounted the events of her kidnapping years later, describing both her and her father's reaction to the incident:

> Three SS men came into the room and put us up against a wall. . . . They immediately picked out the fair children with blue eyes — seven altogether, including me. . . . My father, who tried to stop my being taken away, was threatened by the soldiers. They even said he would be taken to a concentration camp. But I have no idea what happened to him later. (qtd. in Clay and Leapman 95)

The girl who spoke above just as easily could have been the young girl being followed by soldiers in the photograph, only moments after she was taken. Such incidents force us to broaden our sense of whom the Nazis victimized. While there is no mistaking the victimization of the Jewish population and other races in Germany, amidst these better-known hate crimes the Nazis were also perpetrating a horrific exploitation of the so-called "white" race.

The complexities surrounding this photograph remind us that the story of   13 any photograph is liable to contain ambiguity. As an art, photography relies on the imagination of the viewer; not *knowing* provides the viewer with a realm of interesting possibilities. Context matters even with art, and playing with possible contexts gives a photograph diverse meanings. It is in these various viewpoints that we find pleasure, amusement, fear, or wonder. It is perhaps in the shift to photojournalism that determining a particular context becomes even more important. In fact, even if the original photographer saw the image as artistic, subsequent events compel us to try to see the image of the Polish girl with Nazis as journalism. In this endeavor, we must uncover as much as possible about the surrounding context. As much as we can, we need to know this girl's particular story. Without a name, date, place, or relevant data, this girl would fall even further backward into the chapters of unrecorded history.

Works Cited

Clay, Catrine, and Michael Leapman. *Master Race: The* Lebensborn *Experiment in Nazi Germany.* Hodder & Stoughton, 1995.

Hitler, Adolf. *Mein Kampf.* Vol. 2, Eher Verlag, 1926. *Hitler Historical Museum,* 1996–2000, www.hitler.org/writings/Mein_Kampf/. Accessed 1 Dec. 2000.

Milton, Sybil. "The Camera as Weapon: Documentary Photography and the Holocaust." *Annual Scholars' Conference,* Proceedings of the National Conference of Christians and Jews, New York, March 1983. *The Museum of Tolerance,* Simon Wiesenthal Center, 2000, motlc.wiesenthal.com /site/pp.asp?c=gvKVLcMVIuG&b=394975. Accessed 6 Dec. 2000.

"Mounted Nazi Troops on the Lookout for Likely Polish Children." Clay and Leapman, p. 87.

Journal Writing

Ayad uncovers an aspect of Nazi history that is not well known and may seem startling. Think of a time when you learned something that surprised you about history, science, or culture — either in a class or through independent research. In your journal, write about your discovery and how it affected you.

Questions on Meaning

1. Ayad's essay pursues two threads: certain events in German history and certain characteristics of photography, especially photojournalism. Each thread in essence has its own THESIS, stated in paragraphs 1 and 8. What are these theses? Where in the essay does Ayad bring them together?

2. Ayad writes about events in history that she thinks some readers do not know about. What are these events?

3. What do you see as Ayad's PURPOSE in this essay?

Questions on Writing Strategy

1. Why does Ayad devote so much of her essay to discussing the photograph? What is the EFFECT of her speculations about its content and creation?

2. Ayad's AUDIENCE was originally the teacher and students in her writing class. What does she ASSUME readers already know about Nazi Germany? What does she assume they may not know?

3. What is the effect of Ayad's last two sentences? Why does Ayad end this way?

4. **OTHER METHODS**   Where in the essay does Ayad draw on DESCRIPTION? Why is description crucial to her analysis?

Questions on Language

1. What words and phrases does Ayad use in paragraphs 4–6 to communicate her own feelings about the photograph? What are those feelings?

2. Why does Ayad quote Adolf Hitler and H. F. K. Gunther (par. 9), Heinrich Himmler (11), and the Polish woman who was kidnapped as a child (12)? What does Ayad achieve with these quotations?

3. What is the effect of the word *targeting* in paragraph 11?

4. Consult a dictionary if you are unsure of the meanings of any of the following: capricious (title); Aryan, anti-Semitism, ideology, Nordic (par. 1); shrouded (2); juxtaposing (4); suffocating (5); scenarios, plausible, pillaged, definitive (8); extermination, tyranny, impeccable (9); poignant (12); ambiguity, subsequent (13).

Suggestions for Writing

1. **FROM JOURNAL TO ESSAY**   Using your journal writing as a starting point, draft an essay about a surprising discovery you made in a class or on your own. If it will be helpful, do some research to extend your knowledge of the subject. Involve your readers in the essay by distinguishing general knowledge — that is, what they probably know already — from the new information.

2. Locate a photograph that you find especially striking, perhaps in a library book or through an online photo collection such as Instagram or Corbis (*corbisimages.com*).

Write an essay that describes and analyzes the image, using a thesis statement and vivid language to make your interpretation clear.

3. **CRITICAL WRITING**   Some of Ayad's paragraphs are long, especially 1, 8, 9, and 11. How COHERENT are these long paragraphs? Write a brief essay in which you ana-lyze two of them in terms of their organization, the TRANSITIONS or other devices that connect sentences, and any problems with coherence that you see.

4. **CONNECTIONS**   Examine the visual subject of Ayad's essay using the principle of analysis Judith Ortiz Cofer employs in "The Cruel Country" (p. 262). To what extent does Ayad try to establish what Cofer (and Roland Barthes) calls the "studium," or the "actual occasion, meaning, or intent of the photograph"? What for her seems to be the "punctum" of the image, "that detail that draws us into the picture as a shared human event"? What is it for you? Explain your answers in an essay.

ROBERT LIPSYTE

Robert Lipsyte is a sportswriter and broadcast journalist who is equally well known for his young-adult novels. Born in 1938 in the Bronx, he grew up feeling bullied and outcast in the Queens borough of New York City, earned a BA in English from Columbia University at the age of nineteen, and received an MA from the Columbia School of Journalism in 1959. As a reporter and writer for the *New York Times*, Lipsyte published more than five hundred columns; he is also the author of nearly thirty books, including *The Masculine Mystique* (1966), *Free to Be Muhammad Ali* (1978), *An Accidental Sportswriter: A Memoir* (2011), and novels such as *The Contender* (1967) and *The Twin Powers* (2015). Lipsyte was a sports commentator for National Public Radio from 1976 to 1982, an on-air essayist for CBS and NBC from 1982 to 1988, and the host of the public television show *The Eleventh Hour* in the late 1980s, for which he won an Emmy for on-camera achievement in 1990. He continues to write both fiction and nonfiction.

Jock Culture

As Lipsyte tells it, he came into his career by happenstance: Fresh out of college, he needed a job and the *Times* gave him one. That his entry-level position morphed into a career immersed in sports continues to surprise him. Long a sportswriter but never a particular fan, Lipsyte is in a unique position to examine what he sees as a damaging obsession with athleticism and competition in American life. "Jock Culture" first appeared in a special 2011 sports issue of *The Nation*, a newsmagazine usually focused on politics.

In the spring of that hard year, 1968, the Columbia University crew coach, Bill Stowe, explained to me that there were only two kinds of men on campus, perhaps in the world — Jocks and Pukes. He explained that Jocks, such as his rowers, were brave, manly, ambitious, focused, patriotic, and goal-driven, while Pukes were woolly, distractible, girlish, and handicapped by their lack of certainty that nothing mattered as much as winning. Pukes could be found among "the cruddy weirdo slobs" such as hippies, pot smokers, protesters, and, yes, former English majors like me.

I dutifully wrote all this down, although doing so seemed kind of Puke-ish. But Stowe was such an affable *ur*-Jock,[1] twenty-eight years old, funny and articulate, that I found his condescension merely good copy. He'd won an Olympic gold medal, but how could I take him seriously, this former Navy officer who had spent his Vietnam deployment rowing the Saigon River and

---

[1] The German prefix *ur*- means "thorough" or "perfect." — EDS.

running an officers' club? Not surprisingly, he didn't last long at Columbia after helping lead police officers through the underground tunnels to roust the Pukes who had occupied buildings during the antiwar and antiracism demonstrations.

As a thirty-year-old *New York Times* sports columnist then, I was not   3
handicapped by as much lack of certainty about all things as I am now. It was clear to me then that Bill Stowe was a "dumb jock," which does not mean stupid; it means ignorant, narrow, misguided by the values of Jock Culture, an important and often overlooked strand of American life.

These days, I'm not so sure he wasn't right; the world may well be divided   4
into Jocks and Pukes. Understanding the differences and the commonalities between the two might be one of the keys to understanding, first, the myths of masculinity and power that pervade sports, and then why those myths are inescapable in everyday life. Boys — and more and more girls — who accept Jock Culture values often go on to flourish in a competitive sports environment that requires submission to authority, winning by any means necessary, and group cohesion. They tend to grow up to become our political, military, and financial leaders. The Pukes — those "others" typically shouldered aside by Jocks in high school hallways and, I imagine, a large percentage of those who are warily reading this special issue of *The Nation* — were often turned off or away from competitive sports (or settled for cross-country). They were also more likely to go on to question authority and seek ways of individual expression.

This mental conditioning of the Jocks was possible because of the intrin-   5
sic joy of sports. Sports is good. It is the best way to pleasure your body in public. Sports is entertaining, healthful, filled with honest, sustaining sentiment for warm times and the beloved people you shared them with. At its simplest, think of playing catch at the lake with friends.

Jock Culture is a distortion of sports. It can be physically and mentally   6
unhealthy, driving people apart instead of together. It is fueled by greed and desperate competition. At its most grotesque, think killer dodgeball for prize money, the Super Bowl. (The clash between sports and the Jock Culture version is almost ideological, at least metaphorical. Obviously, I am for de-emphasizing early competition and redistributing athletic resources so that everyone, throughout their lives, has access to sports. But then, I am also for world peace.)

Kids are initiated into Jock Culture when youth sports are channeled into   7
the pressurized arenas of elite athletes on travel teams driven by ambitious parents and coaches. A once safe place to learn about bravery, cooperation, and respect becomes a cockpit of bullying, violence, and the commitment to a win-at-all-costs attitude that can kill a soul. Or a brain. It is in Pee Wee football, for example, that kids learn to "put a hat on him" — to make tackles head first rather than the older, gentler way of wrapping your arms around a

ball carrier's legs and dragging him down. Helmet-to-helmet hits start the trauma cycle early. No wonder the current concussion discussion was launched by the discovery of dementia and morbidity among former pro players.

There is no escape from Jock Culture. You may be willing to describe 8
yourself as a Puke, "cut" from the team early to find your true nature as a billionaire geek, Grammy-winning band fag, wonkish pundit, but you've always had to deal with Jock Culture attitudes and codes, and you have probably competed by them. In big business, medicine, the law, people will be labeled winners and losers, and treated like stars or slugs by coachlike authority figures who use shame and intimidation to achieve short-term results. Don't think symphony orchestras, university philosophy departments, and liberal magazines don't often use such tactics.

Jock Culture applies the rules of competitive sports to everything. Boys, 9
in particular, are taught to be tough, stoical and aggressive, to play hurt, to hit hard, to take risks to win in every aspect of their lives. To dominate. After 9/11, I wondered why what seemed like a disproportionate number of athletic women and men were killed. From reading their brief *New York Times* memorials, it seemed as though most were former high school and college players, avid weekend recreationists, or at least passionate sports fans. When I called executives from companies that had offices in the World Trade Center, I discovered it was no coincidence; stock-trading companies in particular recruited athletes because they came to work even if they were sick, worked well in groups, rebounded quickly from a setback, pushed the envelope to reach the goal, and never quit until the job was done. They didn't have to be star jocks, but they did have to have been trained in the codes of Jock Culture — most important, the willingness to subordinate themselves to authority.

The drive to feel that sense of belonging that comes with being part of 10
a winning team — as athlete, coach, parent, cheerleader, booster, fan — is a reflection of Jock Culture's grip on the male psyche and on more and more women. Men have traditionally been taught to pursue their jock dreams no matter the physical, emotional, or financial cost. Those who realized those dreams have been made rich and famous; at the least, they were waved right through many of the tollbooths of ordinary life. Being treated like a celebrity at twelve, freed from normal boundaries, excused from taking out the garbage and from treating siblings, friends, girls responsibly, is no preparation for a fully realized life. No wonder there are so many abusive athletes, emotionally stunted ex-athletes, and resentful onlookers.

At a critical time when masculinity is being redefined, or at least re- 11
examined seriously, this sports system has become more economically, culturally, and emotionally important than ever. More at service to the empire. More dangerous to the common good.

Games have become our main form of mass entertainment (including   12
made-for-TV contests using sports models). Winners of those games become
our examples of permissible behavior, even when that includes cheating, sexual crimes, or dog torturing. And how does that lead us to the cheating, the
lying, the amorality in our lives outside the white lines? It's not hard to connect the moral dots from the field house to the White House.

The recent emergence of girls as competitors of boys has also raised the   13
ante. Boys have traditionally been manipulated by coaches, drill sergeants, and
sales managers by the fear of being labeled a girl ("sissy" and "faggot" have less to
do with homophobia than misogyny). Despite the many ways males can identify themselves as "real men" in our culture — size, sexuality, power, money,
fame — nothing seems as indelible as the mark made in childhood when the
good bodies are separated from the bad bodies, the team from the spectators.
The designated athletes are rewarded with love, attention, and perks. The left-
overs struggle with their resentments and their search for identity.

Of course, the final score is not always a sure thing. There are sensitive   14
linebackers and CEOs, domineering shrinks and violinists. Who won in the
contest between the *Facebook* Puke Mark Zuckerberg and his fiercest competitors, the Olympic rowing Jocks Tyler and Cameron Winklevoss?[2]

"I don't follow that stuff these days," says Bill Stowe, now living in Lake   15
Placid, New York, after retiring as crew coach and fundraiser for the Coast
Guard Academy, a far more comfortable fit than Columbia. "And I have to
tell you, I don't remember separating the world into Jocks and Pukes, although
it sounds good. I liked good brains in my boats, as long as they were willing to
concentrate and pay the price."

Stowe, at seventy-one, is still a conservative Republican. But he doesn't   16
like to talk politics. "It's time to give up the torch," he says. "People are still
living in ignorance, but I'm not running it up the flagpole anymore. Life's too
short to fight." He surprises me when we talk sports. "The big-league thing,
that's a circus. I don't understand how anyone could look up to those guys. But
the real issue is with the kids. Did you read where they're building a $60 mil-
lion football stadium for a high school in Texas? Just for the Jocks. Have you
got any idea how much good you could do, even just in athletics, for all the
other kids with that much money?"

I dutifully write all this down, which doesn't at all seem Puke-ish now.   17
We're on the same page, the coach and I. There's hope.

---

[2] Mark Zuckerberg (born 1984) is the founder and CEO of *Facebook*. Tyler and Cameron
Winkelvoss (born 1981) are twins who accused Zuckerberg, once a fellow Harvard student, of
stealing their idea and computer codes to create his social network. After a protracted legal
battle, the brothers settled for a deal valued at $65 million. — Eds.

Journal Writing

Are you a "Jock" or a "Puke"? Do you play on any athletic teams, or are you content to stay on the sidelines? Did you ever experience or witness any of the aspects of youth sports that Lipsyte describes, whether positive or negative? How did you respond? In your journal, reflect on one such memory.

Questions on Meaning

1. Reread the first three paragraphs of this essay. What do you make of Lipsyte's INTRODUCTION? What event is he reporting, and why is it relevant to his subject?

2. What does Lipsyte mean by "Jock Culture"? How is it distinct from sports in general?

3. What is Lipsyte's THESIS? For whom is Jock Culture harmful, and why?

4. How would you describe the apparent PURPOSE of this essay?

Questions on Writing Strategy

1. What, according to Lipsyte, are the "codes" (par. 8), or elements, of Jock Culture — both positive and negative? What principle of analysis does he apply to his subject?

2. To whom does Lipsyte seem to be writing? Athletes, coaches, students, business leaders, someone else? What ASSUMPTIONS does he make about his readers?

3. Lipsyte brings up the terrorist attacks of September 11, 2001, commenting that "a disproportionate number of athletic women and men were killed" at the World Trade Center (par. 9). Why? What does this detail contribute to his analysis?

4. Why does Lipsyte quote crew coach and former Olympian Bill Stowe in his opening and closing paragraphs? What is the EFFECT of using Stowe's words to frame the essay?

5. **OTHER METHODS**   How does Bill Stowe use CLASSIFICATION to categorize people? How does Lipsyte? What characteristics do "Jocks" have that "Pukes" lack?

Questions on Language

1. What are the CONNOTATIONS of the words *Jock* and *Puke*? Why do you suppose the author chose to repeat these labels coined by Bill Stowe?

2. How would you characterize Lipsyte's TONE? Is it appropriate, given his purpose and AUDIENCE?

3. Point to a few of the metaphors Lipsyte uses to enliven his prose. (See FIGURES OF SPEECH in the Glossary for a definition of *metaphor*.) What do they have in common? What is their effect?

4. Consult a dictionary if any of the following words are unfamiliar: affable, deployment, roust (par. 2); cohesion (4); dementia, morbidity (7); wonkish, pundit (8); stoical (9); psyche (10); amorality (12); ante, misogyny (13).

Suggestions for Writing

1. **FROM JOURNAL TO ESSAY**   Respond to Lipsyte's concerns about the effects of Jock Culture. Do you agree that pressures to compete and a "win-at-all-costs attitude" (par. 7) are destructive forces in society, or do you believe that the values taught by team sports bring positive effects? Why? Start your response with the experience you recounted in your journal, adding additional examples from your observations of others.

2. The concussion crisis that Lipsyte ALLUDES to in paragraph 7 has led some to call for an end to football altogether, or at least for new regulations intended to protect players from brain damage. Research the main arguments for and against such regulations. Then write an essay in which you SUMMARIZE your findings. If your research — or your own experience — leads you to form an opinion favoring one side of the issue, present and support that as well.

3. **CRITICAL WRITING**   Based on this essay, analyze Lipsyte's apparent attitude toward masculinity and the feminist movement. How does he characterize attempts to shift cultural assumptions about men's and women's competitive abilities? Does he believe that gender equity is possible or even desirable? What does he suggest have been (or will be) the effects of feminism? Support your ideas with EVIDENCE from the essay.

4. **CONNECTIONS**   "Jock Culture" is one of several pieces in this book that touch on sports, albeit the only one that's overtly critical. Read as many of the following that interest you: Brad Manning's "Arm Wrestling with My Father" (p. 111), Brian Doyle's "A Note on Mascots" (p. 160), and E. B. White's "Once More to the Lake" (p. 471). How well does Lipsyte's thesis hold up when compared with the feelings others have derived from watching or participating in sporting activities? How do the other writers' experiences support or contradict his analysis of the implications of Jock Culture for individuals and society?

GUILLERMO DEL TORO AND CHUCK HOGAN

Guillermo del Toro and Chuck Hogan are coauthors of *The Strain* (2009), *The Fall* (2010), and *The Night Eternal* (2011) — a trilogy of vampire novels. Although they share an interest in telling a new kind of story about vampires, the authors arrived at their collaboration from very different backgrounds. Born in Guadalajara, Mexico, del Toro began his career as a cinematic makeup artist. He debuted as a director with *Cronos* (1993) and has directed more than a dozen other movies, including both *Hellboy* films (2004, 2008); *Pan's Labyrinth* (2006), which won three Academy Awards; and *Crimson Peak* (2015). Hogan, by contrast, is a Boston-based novelist who was working as a video-store manager when he made his breakthrough with *The Standoff* (1995), a thriller about a tense hostage negotiation. Hogan has since written *The Blood Artists* (1998), *Prince of Thieves* (2004), *The Killing Moon* (2007), *Devils in Exile* (2010), and the screenplay for *13 Hours* (2016). *Prince of Thieves* won the 2005 Hammett Award for literary crime writing and was the basis for the 2010 motion picture *The Town*.

Vampires Never Die

Filmmaker del Toro and novelist Hogan bonded over their fascination with how ancient myths about vampires have been adapted and readapted in popular culture. In this 2009 essay, first published in the *New York Times*, they trace the perpetual craving for vampire stories back to its historical, literary, and scientific roots.

Tonight, you or someone you love will likely be visited by a vampire — on cable television or the big screen, or in the bookstore. Our own novel describes a modern-day epidemic that spreads across New York City. 1

It all started nearly two hundred years ago. It was the "Year without a Summer" of 1816, when ash from volcanic eruptions lowered temperatures around the globe, giving rise to widespread famine. A few friends gathered at the Villa Diodati on Lake Geneva and decided to engage in a small competition to see who could come up with the most terrifying tale — and the two great monsters of the modern age were born. 2

One was created by Mary Godwin, soon to become Mary Shelley, whose Dr. Frankenstein gave life to a desolate creature. The other monster was less created than fused. John William Polidori stitched together folklore, personal 3 resentment and erotic anxieties into "The Vampyre," a story that is the basis for vampires as they are understood today.

With "The Vampyre," Polidori gave birth to the two main branches of vampiric fiction: the vampire as romantic hero, and the vampire as undead monster. This ambivalence may reflect Polidori's own, as it is widely accepted that Lord Ruthven, the titular creature, was based upon Lord Byron — literary superstar of the era and another resident of the lakeside villa that fateful summer. Polidori tended to Byron day and night, both as his doctor and most devoted groupie. But Polidori resented him as well: Byron was dashing and brilliant, while the poor doctor had a rather drab talent and unremarkable physique. 4

But this was just a new twist to a very old idea. The myth, established well before the invention of the word "vampire," seems to cross every culture, language and era. The Indian Baital, the Ch'ing Shih in China, and the Romanian Strigoi are but a few of its names. The creature seems to be as old as Babylonia and Sumer.[1] Or even older. 5

The vampire may originate from a repressed memory we had as primates. Perhaps at some point we were — out of necessity — cannibalistic. As soon as we became sedentary, agricultural tribes with social boundaries, one seminal myth might have featured our ancestors as primitive beasts who slept in the cold loam of the earth and fed off the salty blood of the living. 6

Monsters, like angels, are invoked by our individual and collective needs. Today, much as during that gloomy summer in 1816, we feel the need to seek their cold embrace. 7

Herein lies an important clue: In contrast to timeless creatures like the dragon, the vampire does not seek to obliterate us, but instead offers a peculiar brand of blood alchemy. For as his contagion bestows its nocturnal gift, the vampire transforms our vile, mortal selves into the gold of eternal youth and instills in us something that every social construct seeks to quash: primal lust. If youth is desire married with unending possibility, then vampire lust creates within us a delicious void, one we long to fulfill. 8

In other words, whereas other monsters emphasize what is mortal in us, the vampire emphasizes the eternal in us. Through the panacea of its blood it turns the lead of our toxic flesh into golden matter. 9

In a society that moves as fast as ours, where every week a new "blockbuster" must be enthroned at the box office, or where idols are fabricated by consensus every new television season, the promise of something everlasting, 10

---

[1] Countries of ancient Mesopotamia (in the vicinity of modern-day Iraq), dating back to approximately 4000 BC and 2000 BC, respectively. They are generally considered the origins of Western civilization. — EDS.

something truly eternal, holds a special allure. As a seductive figure, the vampire is as flexible and polyvalent as ever. Witness its slow mutation from the pansexual, decadent Anne Rice[2] creatures to the current permutations — promising anything from chaste eternal love to wild nocturnal escapades — and there you will find the true essence of immortality: adaptability.

Vampires find their niche and mutate at an accelerated rate now — in the past one would see, for decades, the same variety of fiend, repeated in multiple storylines. Now, vampires simultaneously occur in all forms and tap into our every need: soap opera storylines, sexual liberation, noir detective fiction, etc. The myth seems to be twittering promiscuously to serve all avenues of life, from cereal boxes to romantic fiction. The fast pace of technology accelerates its viral dispersion in our culture. 11

But if Polidori remains the roots in the genealogy of our creature, the most widely known vampire was birthed by Bram Stoker in 1897. 12

Part of the reason for the great success of his "Dracula" is generally acknowledged to be its appearance at a time of great technological revolution. The narrative is full of new gadgets (telegraphs, typing machines), various forms of communication (diaries, ship logs), and cutting-edge science (blood transfusions) — a mash-up of ancient myth in conflict with the world of the present. 13

Today as well, we stand at the rich uncertain dawn of a new level of scientific innovation. The wireless technology we carry in our pockets today was the stuff of the science fiction in our youth. Our technological arrogance mirrors more and more the Wellsian[3] dystopia of dissatisfaction, while allowing us to feel safe and connected at all times. We can call, see or hear almost anything and anyone no matter where we are. For most people then, the only remote place remains within. "Know thyself" we do not. 14

Despite our obsessive harnessing of information, we are still ultimately vulnerable to our fates and our nightmares. We enthrone the deadly virus in the very same way that "Dracula" allowed the British public to believe in monsters: through science. Science becomes the modern man's superstition. It allows him to experience fear and awe again, and to believe in the things he cannot see. 15

And through awe, we once again regain spiritual humility. The current vampire pandemic serves to remind us that we have no true jurisdiction over our bodies, our climate or our very souls. Monsters will always provide the 16

---

[2] Anne Rice (born 1941) is an American novelist best known for *Interview with the Vampire* (1976), *The Vampire Lestat* (1985), and *The Queen of the Damned* (1988). — Eds.

[3] H. G. Wells (1866–1946) was an influential English science fiction writer whose works include *The Time Machine* (1895), *The Island of Doctor Moreau* (1896), and *War of the Worlds* (1898). — Eds.

possibility of mystery in our mundane "reality show" lives, hinting at a larger spiritual world; for if there are demons in our midst, there surely must be angels lurking nearby as well. In the vampire we find Eros and Thanatos[4] fused together in archetypal embrace, spiraling through the ages, undying.

Forever.   17

Journal Writing

Do you enjoy vampire stories, whether in books, in movies, or on television? Of the vampire characters in popular culture (past or present), who is your favorite? Why do you think this character appeals to you? In your journal, explore what vampires mean to you. If you don't care for vampire fiction, consider why it leaves you cold.

Questions on Meaning

1. Why do you suppose del Toro and Hogan wrote this essay? Are they merely promoting their novels, or do they have a more serious PURPOSE as well?

2. What is the THESIS of "Vampires Never Die"? Where, if at all, is it stated succinctly?

3. How do del Toro and Hogan explain the appeal of vampires in contemporary culture? In what ways has that appeal changed across time and geography? In what ways has it remained consistent?

4. What is a "social construct" (par. 8)? How is the concept central to the authors' interpretation of vampires?

5. In paragraph 15, del Toro and Hogan say, "Science becomes the modern man's superstition." What do they mean? How do you explain the PARADOX in that statement?

Questions on Writing Strategy

1. "Vampires Never Die" uses advanced academic vocabulary and contains several literary, historical, scientific, and psychological references. How, then, do the authors imagine their AUDIENCE? Are their ASSUMPTIONS reasonable in your case?

2. What principle of analysis do del Toro and Hogan use in examining vampire stories? What enduring elements do they perceive in the characters?

3. Why do del Toro and Hogan speculate in their introduction about the "resentment and erotic anxieties" (par. 3) felt by John William Polidori, the author of

---

[4] Greek gods of love (Eros) and death (Thanatos). — EDS.

the first modern vampire story? What do his personal conflicts have to do with how we think about vampires today?

4. What is the EFFECT of the essay's final paragraph?

5. **OTHER METHODS**   Del Toro and Hogan COMPARE AND CONTRAST new technologies from the late nineteenth and early twenty-first centuries. What similarities do they find?

Questions on Language

1. Make sure you know the meanings of the following words: desolate (par. 3); ambivalence, titular, dashing (4); repressed, sedentary, seminal, loam (6); invoked (7); obliterate, primal (8); panacea (9); consensus, polyvalent, pansexual, permutations, chaste (10); noir, promiscuously, dispersion (11); mash-up (13); dystopia (14); pandemic, mundane, archetypal (16).

2. Explain the double meaning of "twittering" in paragraph 11. Why do you think del Toro and Hogan chose this particular word?

3. What do the authors mean by "a peculiar brand of blood alchemy" (par. 8)? Where else do they use this metaphor? Why is it particularly appropriate for their subject? (For a definition of *metaphor*, see FIGURES OF SPEECH in the Glossary.)

Suggestions for Writing

1. **FROM JOURNAL TO ESSAY**   Expanding on your journal entry, write an essay that analyzes one vampire character from popular culture — such as Bram Stoker's Dracula, Edward from the *Twilight* series, Yvette from Anne Rice's novels, Bill Compton from *True Blood*, or The Master from del Toro and Hogan's trilogy. Break the character down into his (or her) elements, considering backstory as well as personality, and reassemble the parts into a new whole of your understanding.

2. Write an essay that analyzes several examples of another type of writing by examining their shared characteristics and hidden meanings. You may choose any narrowly defined GENRE that's familiar to you: food blog, parenting-advice column, amateur film review, gay romance, alternative-history science fiction, and so on. Be sure to make your principle of analysis clear to your readers.

3. Some cultural analysts have said that the resurgence of vampire stories in the last quarter century can be attributed to the AIDS epidemic that emerged in the 1980s. In your library's database of scholarly journal articles, conduct a key-word search with "vampires and AIDS," and read one or two of the arguments in favor of this theory. (If you prefer, you may search for other academic analyses of vampire lore.) How do you respond to the articles? Do alternate interpretations undermine del Toro and Hogan's analysis, or do they simply complicate it?

4. **CRITICAL WRITING**   Del Toro and Hogan explore CAUSES AND EFFECTS to explain the prevalence of vampires in popular culture. How persuasive is their analysis? Do you agree with them that vampire legends fill psychological and spiritual

voids that have been created by advances in science and technology? Why, or why not?

5. **CONNECTIONS**   In this essay Guillermo del Toro and Chuck Hogan examine how vampires serve as SYMBOLS of human anxieties. Likewise, Brian Doyle, in "A Note on Mascots" (p. 160), observes that animals take on a symbolic function when they're adopted as sports icons. What similarities, if any, do you see between team mascots and long-held myths such as vampires? Is either more culturally significant? Do they represent related fears and needs? Write an essay of your own that examines the deeper implications of such symbols. (You need not choose vampires or sports mascots as your subject: If you've noticed some other symbol that captures your interest, such as zombies or angels, feel free to analyze that instead.) Consider, as well, your own thoughts about interpretations of this sort: Is popular culture worthy of serious inquiry?

Guillermo del Toro and Chuck Hogan on Writing

"Vampires Never Die" was by no means Guillermo del Toro and Chuck Hogan's first experience working together as writers. In 2006 they began collaborating on a trilogy of horror novels about vampires. The project started when Hogan's literary agent sent him a twelve-page outline of del Toro's story idea, originally conceived for the small screen, and told him the director was thinking about trying a novel. "I got a page and a half in before calling [my agent] back and essentially telling him that I would do anything to be involved," Hogan gushed in a 2009 interview with blogger Sarah Weinman. In lieu of a publishing deal or any kind of contract, the authors made a pact on a handshake — "actually more of a bro-hug," according to Hogan — and agreed to join forces. They finished the first installment of the trilogy, *The Strain*, after three years.

Hogan admits to being apprehensive about writing with del Toro, whom he calls "a god of the genre," especially since the storyline was the director's. However, he says that del Toro "completely opened up his story," giving Hogan the freedom to expand and change the NARRATIVE in the drafting stage. In a separate interview with Rick Kleffel on KUSP Central Coast Public Radio, del Toro praised Hogan's contributions to the shape of the story: "The book is full of intimate moments of terror that come from personal experience, and others that Chuck created. . . . Some of the best, most disturbing moments in the book come from his imagination, curiously enough."

Both authors note that, though their drafting processes were loose, revising the book was "rigorous." Exchanging drafts by e-mail, they commented extensively on each other's chapters, a practice that del Toro calls "riffing." As he explains, "I was merciless with his chapters; he was merciless with my chapters." Revisions involved moving or cutting large portions of text. Del Toro often rearranged chapters, and Hogan sometimes scrapped entire sections. Speaking of Hogan's editing style, del Toro jokes that some changes were made "subverticiously" (a word of his own invention): "All of a sudden I would get the manuscript and it was missing one chapter I wrote or half a chapter I wrote." However, it was this kind of harsh revision that in the end made for the "seamless blending" of two writers' talents.

The Brief Bedford Reader on Writing

As collaborators, del Toro and Hogan find distinct advantages in drafting freely, but revising rigorously. Such an approach is not at all unique to team projects, however. For advice on applying the same techniques to your own writing, see pages 34–42 ("Drafting" and "Revising").

ADDITIONAL WRITING TOPICS

Division or Analysis

Using the method of division or analysis, write an essay on one of the following subjects (or choose your own subject). In your essay, make sure your purpose and your principle of division or analysis are clear to your readers. Explain the parts of your subject so that readers know how each relates to the others and contributes to the whole.

The slang or technical terminology of a group such as stand-up comedians or online gamers

An especially *bad* movie, television show, or book

A doll, action figure, or other toy from childhood

A typical sidebar ad for a product such as clothing, deodorant, beer, a luxury car, or an economy car

A machine or an appliance, such as a drone, a motorcycle, a microwave oven, or a camera

An organization or association, such as a social club, a sports league, or a support group

The characteristic appearance of an indie folk singer or a classical violinist

A day in the life of a student

Your favorite poem

A short story, an essay, or another work that made you think

The government of your community

The most popular restaurant (or other place of business) in town

The Bible, Q'uran, or another religious text

An urban legend: hitchhiking ghosts, flickering orbs, gas-station carjackings, haunted cemeteries, buried treasures, and so forth

A painting or a statue

How the Poor, the Middle Class, and the Rich Spend Their Money

Type of Spending	Household Income		
	$15,000–$19,999	$50,000–$69,999	Above $150,000
Food at Home	10.2%	7.7%	5.4%
Food at Restaurants, etc.	4.7%	5.4%	5.4%
Housing	29.2%	26.7%	27.5%
Utilities	11.1%	8.2%	4.8%
Clothes & Shoes	3.6%	3.2%	3.7%
Transportation & Gasoline	20.4%	21.3%	15.5%
Health Care & Health Insurance	8.2%	7.1%	4.5%
Entertainment	4.8%	5.1%	5.7%
Education	1.5%	1.3%	4.4%
Saving for Retirement	2.6%	9.6%	15.9%

Source: Bureau of Labor Statistics. Credit: Lam Thuy Vo / NPR

9

CLASSIFICATION

Sorting into Kinds

◀ **Classification in a table**

How do you spend your money? Does most of it go for rent and
utilities, for instance, or is the bulk of your budget earmarked
for tuition, fees, and books? How do your income and expenses
compare to those of your peers? In this infographic, National
Public Radio's *Planet Money* translates data from the Bureau of
Labor Statistics to show how household budgets in the United
States typically sort out. NPR's table classifies spending patterns
for three economic groups: "the Poor, the Middle Class, and the
Rich." Notice, first, how NPR defines each class. Then examine
the data. The column on the left identifies ten types of spending;
the three other columns compare the percentages of household
income devoted to each category by the groups. What similarities and differences among the categories strike you? Are you
surprised by any of the numbers? Why, or why not?

THE METHOD

To CLASSIFY is to make sense of some aspect of the world by arranging many units — trucks, chemical elements, wasps, students — into more manageable groups. Zoologists classify animals, botanists classify plants — and their classifications help us understand a vast and complex subject: life on earth. To help us find books in a library, librarians classify books into categories: fiction, biography, history, psychology, and so forth. For the convenience of readers, newspapers run classified advertising, grouping many small ads into categories such as "Services" and "Cars for Sale."

Subjects and Reasons for Classification

The subject of a classification essay is always a number of things, such as peaches or political systems. (In contrast, DIVISION or ANALYSIS, the topic of the preceding chapter, usually deals with a solitary subject, a coherent whole, such as *a* peach or *a* political system.) The job of classification is to sort the things into groups or classes based on their similarities and differences. Say, for instance, you're going to write an essay about how people write. After interviewing a lot of writers, you determine that writers' processes differ widely, mainly in the amount of planning and rewriting they entail. (Notice that this determination involves analyzing the PROCESS of writing, separating it into steps. See Chapter 7.) On the basis of your findings, you create groups for planners, one-drafters, and rewriters. Once your groups are defined, and assuming they are valid, your subjects (the writers) almost sort themselves out.

Just as you can analyze a subject in many ways, you can classify a subject according to many principles. One travel guide, for instance, might group places to stay by style of accommodation: resorts, hotels, motels, bed-and-breakfasts, boarding houses, and hostels. A different guidebook might classify options according to price: grand luxury, luxury, moderate, bargain, fleabag, and flophouse.

The principle used in classifying things depends on the writer's PURPOSE. A guidebook classifies accommodations by price to match visitors with hotels that fit their pocketbooks. A linguist might explain the languages of the world by classifying them according to their origins (Romance languages, Germanic languages, Asian languages, Coptic languages . . .), but a student battling with a college language requirement might try to entertain fellow students by classifying languages into three groups: hard to learn, harder to learn, and unlearnable.

Kinds of Classification

Classification schemes vary in complexity, depending on the groups being sorted and the basis for sorting them. In classifying methods of classification, we find two types: binary and complex.

- **Binary classification.** The simplest classification is binary (or two-part), in which you sort things out into (1) those with a certain distinguishing feature and (2) those without it. You might classify a number of persons, let's say, into smokers and nonsmokers, runners and nonrunners, believers and nonbelievers. Binary classification is most useful when your subject is easily divisible into positive and negative categories.

- **Complex classification.** More often, a classification will sort things into multiple categories, sometimes putting members into subcategories. Such is the case with a linguist who categorizes languages by origin. Writing about the varieties of one Germanic language, such as English, the writer could identify the subclasses of British English, North American English, Australian English, and so on.

As readers, we enjoy classifications that strike us as true and familiar. This pleasure may account for the appeal of magazine and Web articles that classify things ("Seven Common Varieties of Moocher," "The Top Ten Most Embarrassing Social Blunders"). Usefulness as well as pleasure may explain the popularity of classifications that EVALUATE things. The magazine *Consumer Reports* sorts products as varied as space heaters and frozen dinners into groups based on quality (excellent, very good, good, fair, and poor), and then, using analysis, discusses each product (of a frozen pot pie: "Bottom crust gummy, meat spongy when chewed, with nondescript old-poultry and stale-flour flavor").

THE PROCESS

Purposes and Theses

Classification will usually come into play when you want to impose order on a complex subject that includes many items. In one essay in this chapter, for instance, Deborah Tannen tackles the seemingly endless opportunities for men and women to miscommunicate with each other. Sometimes you may use classification humorously, as Russell Baker does in another essay in this chapter, to give a charge to familiar experiences.

Whatever use you make of classification, do it for a reason: The files of composition instructors are littered with essays in which nothing was ventured and nothing was gained. Classifications can reveal truth or amuse us, but they can also reveal nothing and bore us. To sort ten North American cities according to their relative freedom from air pollution or their cost of living or the range of services offered to residents might prove highly informative and useful to someone looking for a new place to live. But to sort the cities according to a superficial feature such as the relative size of their cat and dog populations wouldn't interest anyone, probably, except a veterinarian looking for a job.

Your purpose, your THESIS, and your principle of classification will all overlap with your interest in your subject. Say you're curious about how other students write. Is your interest primarily in the materials they use (keyboard, pencil, voice recorder), in where and when they write, or in how much planning and rewriting they do? Any of these could lead to a principle for sorting the students into groups. And that principle should be revealed in your THESIS STATEMENT, letting readers know why you are classifying. Here, from the essays in this chapter, are three examples of classification thesis statements:

> Many of the conversational rituals common among women are designed to take the other person's feelings into account, while many of the conversational rituals common among men are designed to maintain the one-up position, or at least avoid appearing one-down. As a result, when men and women interact — especially at work — it's often women who are at the disadvantage.
>
> — Deborah Tannen, "But What Do You Mean?"

> Inanimate objects are classified into three major categories — those that don't work, those that break down and those that get lost.
>
> — Russell Baker, "The Plot against People"

> [T]hree types [of stars] stand out as the most potentially beneficial to humankind and prolonging its existence: supergiants, yellow dwarfs, and red dwarfs. . . . The red dwarf, however, is or at least will be the most important star because of its incredibly long life span and relative abundance in our immense universe.
>
> — Jean-Pierre De Beer, "Stars of Life"

Categories

For a workable classification, make sure that the categories you choose don't overlap. If you were writing a survey of popular magazines for adults and you were sorting your subject into categories that included women's magazines and sports magazines, you might soon run into trouble. Into which category would you place *Women's Sports?* The trouble is that both categories take in the same item. To avoid this problem, you'd need to reorganize your classification on a different principle. You might sort out the magazines by their audiences: magazines intended for women, magazines intended for men, magazines intended for both women and men. Or you might group them according to subject matter: sports magazines, political magazines, fashion magazines, celebrity magazines, and so on. *Women's Sports* would fit into either of those classification schemes, but into only *one* category in each scheme.

When you draw up a scheme of classification, be sure that you include all essential categories. Omitting an important category can weaken the effect of your essay, no matter how well written it is. It would be a major oversight, for example, if you were to classify the residents of a dormitory according to their religious affiliations and not include a category for the nonaffiliated.

Some form of outline can be helpful to keep the classes and their members straight as you develop and draft ideas. You might experiment with a diagram in which you jot down headings for the groups, with plenty of space around them, letting each heading accumulate members as you think of them. This kind of diagram offers more flexibility than a vertical list or an outline, and is a good aid for keeping categories from overlapping or disappearing.

FOCUS ON PARAGRAPH DEVELOPMENT

A crucial aim of classification is to make sure each group is clear: what's counted in, what's counted out, and why. You'll provide examples and other details to make the groups clear as you develop the paragraph(s) devoted to each.

The following paragraph barely outlines one group in a four-part classification of ex-smokers into zealots, evangelists, the elect, and the serene:

> The second group, evangelists, does not condemn smokers but encourages them to quit. Evangelists think quitting is easy, and they preach this message, often earning the resentment of potential converts.

Contrast this bare-bones adaptation with the actual paragraphs written by Franklin E. Zimring in his essay "Confessions of a Former Smoker":

> By contrast, the antismoking evangelist does not condemn smokers. Unlike the zealot, he regards smoking as an easily curable condition, as a social disease, and not a sin. The evangelist spends an enormous amount of time seeking and preaching to the unconverted. He argues that kicking the habit is not *that* difficult. After all, *he* did it; moreover, as he describes it, the benefits of quitting are beyond measure and the disadvantages are nil.

(continued)

Classification

The hallmark of the evangelist is his insistence that he never misses tobacco. Though he is less hostile to smokers than the zealot, he is resented more. Friends and loved ones who have been the targets of his preachments frequently greet the resumption of smoking by the evangelist as an occasion for unmitigated glee.

In the second sentence of each paragraph, Zimring explicitly contrasts evangelists with zealots, the group he previously defined. And he does more as well: He provides specific examples of the evangelist's message (first paragraph) and of others' reactions to him (second paragraph). These details pin down the group, making it distinct from other groups and clear in itself.

CHECKLIST FOR REVISING A CLASSIFICATION

✔ **Purpose.** Have you classified for a reason? Will readers be able to see why you bothered?

✔ **Principle of classification.** Will readers also see what rule or principle you used for sorting individuals into groups? Is this principle apparent in your thesis sentence?

✔ **Consistency.** Does each representative of your subject fall into one category only, so that categories don't overlap?

✔ **Completeness.** Have you mentioned all the essential categories suggested by your principle of classification?

✔ **Paragraph development.** Have you provided enough information, examples, and other details so that readers can easily distinguish each category from the others?

CLASSIFICATION IN ACADEMIC WRITING

An Anthropology Textbook

This paragraph comes from *Humankind Emerging*, a textbook on human physical and cultural evolution by Bernard Campbell. The author offers a standard classification of hand grips in order to explain one of several important differences between human beings and their nearest relatives, apes and monkeys.

There are two distinct ways of holding and using tools: the *power grip* and the *precision grip*, as John Napier termed them. Human infants and children begin with the power grip and progress to the precision grip. Think of how a child holds a spoon: first in the power grip, in its fist or between its fingers and palm, and later between the tips of the thumb and first two fingers, in the precision grip. Many primates have the power grip also. It is the way they get firm hold of a tree branch. But neither a monkey nor an ape has a thumb long enough or flexible enough to be completely *opposable* through rotation at the wrist, able to reach comfortably to the tips of all the other fingers, as is required for our delicate yet strong precision grip. It is the opposability of our thumb and the independent control of our fingers that make possible nearly all the movements necessary to handle tools, to make clothing, to write with a pencil, to play a flute.

Topic sentence names the principle of classification

Two categories explained side by side

Second category explained in greater detail

A Résumé

Sooner or later, every college student needs a résumé: a one-page overview of skills and experiences that will appeal to a potential employer. Part of the challenge in drafting a résumé is to bring order to what seems a complex and unwieldy subject, a life. The main solution is to classify activities and interests into clearly defined groups: typically work experience, education, and special skills.

The group that poses the biggest challenge is usually work experience: Some résumés list jobs with the most recent first, detailing the specifics of each one; others sort experience into skills (such as computer skills, administrative skills, and communication skills) and then list job specifics under each subcategory. The first arrangement tends to be more straightforward and potentially less confusing to readers. However, college students and recent graduates with few previous jobs often find the second arrangement preferable because it downplays experience and showcases abilities.

The résumé on the following page was prepared by Kharron Reid, who was seeking a paid internship in the field of information systems for the summer between his junior and senior years of college. After experimenting with different organizational strategies, he decided to put the category of work experience first because it related directly to the internships he sought. And he chose to organize his work experience by jobs rather than skills because the companies he had worked for were similar to the companies he was applying to.

For the job-application cover letter Reid wrote to go with the résumé, see page 147 of Chapter 5.

Classification

Kharron Reid
137 Chester Street, Apt. E
Allston, MA 02134
(617) 555-4009
kreid@bu.edu

OBJECTIVE
An internship that offers experience in information systems

EXPERIENCE

NBS Systems Corp., Denniston, MI, June to September 2016

As an intern, helped install seven WANs using Windows Server 2016

- Planned layout for WANs
- Installed physical platform and configured servers

Pioneer Networking, Damani, MI, May to September 2015

As an intern, worked as a LAN specialist using a Unix-based server

- Connected eight workstations onto a LAN by laying physical platform and configuring software
- Assisted network engineer in monitoring operations of LAN

SPECIAL SKILLS
Computer proficiency:

Windows 10/8	Adobe Photoshop	XML
Unix	JIRA	JavaScript
Red Hat Enterprise Linux	HTML	Python

Internet research

EDUCATION

Boston University, School of Management, 2014 to present

Double major: business administration and information systems

Courses: organizational behavior, computer science, advanced programming, networking and data communications

Lahser High School, Bloomfield Hills, MI, 2010 to 2014

Similar to a thesis statement, an objective expresses the applicant's purpose

First major category: work experience

A subcategory for each job includes summaries and specific details

Second major category: special skills

Specific skills

Third major category: education

Specific information relevant to job objective

DEBORAH TANNEN

Deborah Tannen is a linguist who is best known for her popular studies of communication between men and women. Born and raised in New York City, Tannen earned a BA from Harpur College (now part of Binghamton University), MAs from Wayne State University and the University of California at Berkeley, and a PhD in linguistics from Berkeley. She is University Professor at Georgetown University, has published many scholarly articles and books, and lectures on linguistics all over the world. But her renown is more than academic: With television talk-show appearances, speeches to businesspeople and senators, and best-selling books, Tannen has become, in the words of one reviewer, "America's conversational therapist." The books include *You Just Don't Understand* (1990), *The Argument Culture* (1998), *I Only Say This Because I Love You* (2001), and *You Were Always Mom's Favorite!* (2009), the last about communication between sisters. Tannen sits on the board of the PEN/Faulkner Foundation, a nonprofit organization devoted to building audiences for literature.

But What Do You Mean?

Why do men and women so often communicate badly, if at all? This question has motivated much of Tannen's research and writing. Excerpted in *Redbook* magazine from Tannen's book *Talking from 9 to 5* (1994), the essay reprinted here classifies the conversational areas where men and women have the most difficulty communicating in the workplace.

William Lutz's "The World of Doublespeak," the essay following Tannen's, also uses classification to examine communication problems, in the form of misleading verbal substitutions that make "the bad seem good, the negative appear positive."

Conversation is a ritual. We say things that seem obviously the thing to say, without thinking of the literal meaning of our words, any more than we expect the question "How are you?" to call forth a detailed account of aches and pains.

Unfortunately, women and men often have different ideas about what's appropriate, different ways of speaking. Many of the conversational rituals common among women are designed to take the other person's feelings into account, while many of the conversational rituals common among men are

1

2

designed to maintain the one-up position, or at least avoid appearing one-down. As a result, when men and women interact — especially at work — it's often women who are at the disadvantage. Because women are not trying to avoid the one-down position, that is unfortunately where they may end up.

Here, the biggest areas of miscommunication.   3

1. Apologies

Women are often told they apologize too much. The reason they're told   4
to stop doing it is that, to many men, apologizing seems synonymous with putting oneself down. But there are many times when "I'm sorry" isn't self-deprecating, or even an apology; it's an automatic way of keeping both speakers on an equal footing. For example, a well-known columnist once interviewed me and gave me her phone number in case I needed to call her back. I mis-placed the number and had to go through the newspaper's main switchboard. When our conversation was winding down and we'd both made ending-type remarks, I added, "Oh, I almost forgot — I lost your direct number, can I get it again?" "Oh, I'm sorry," she came back instantly, even though she had done nothing wrong and *I* was the one who'd lost the number. But I understood she wasn't really apologizing; she was just automatically reassuring me she had no intention of denying me her number.

Even when "I'm sorry" *is* an apology, women often assume it will be the   5
first step in a two-step ritual: I say "I'm sorry" and take half the blame, then you take the other half. At work, it might go something like this:

A: When you typed this letter, you missed this phrase I inserted.

B: Oh, I'm sorry. I'll fix it.

A: Well, I wrote it so small it was easy to miss.

When both parties share blame, it's a mutual face-saving device. But if one   6
person, usually the woman, utters frequent apologies and the other doesn't, she ends up looking as if she's taking the blame for mishaps that aren't her fault. When she's only partially to blame, she looks entirely in the wrong.

I recently sat in on a meeting at an insurance company where the sole   7
woman, Helen, said "I'm sorry" or "I apologize" repeatedly. At one point she said, "I'm thinking out loud. I apologize." Yet the meeting was intended to be an informal brainstorming session, and *everyone* was thinking out loud.

The reason Helen's apologies stood out was that she was the only person   8
in the room making so many. And the reason I was concerned was that Helen felt the annual bonus she had received was unfair. When I interviewed her colleagues, they said that Helen was one of the best and most productive workers — yet she got one of the smallest bonuses. Although the problem

might have been outright sexism, I suspect her speech style, which differs from that of her male colleagues, masks her competence.

Unfortunately, not apologizing can have its price too. Since so many women use ritual apologies, those who don't may be seen as hard-edged. What's important is to be aware of how often you say you're sorry (and why), and to monitor your speech based on the reaction you get.

2. Criticism

A woman who cowrote a report with a male colleague was hurt when she read a rough draft to him and he leapt into a critical response — "Oh, that's too dry! You have to make it snappier!" She herself would have been more likely to say, "That's a really good start. Of course, you'll want to make it a little snappier when you revise."

Whether criticism is given straight or softened is often a matter of convention. In general, women use more softeners. I noticed this difference when talking to an editor about an essay I'd written. While going over changes she wanted to make, she said, "There's one more thing. I know you may not agree with me. The reason I noticed the problem is that your other points are so lucid and elegant." She went on hedging for several more sentences until I put her out of her misery: "Do you want to cut that part?" I asked — and of course she did. But I appreciated her tentativeness. In contrast, another editor (a man) I once called summarily rejected my idea for an article by barking, "Call me when you have something new to say."

Those who are used to ways of talking that soften the impact of criticism may find it hard to deal with the right-between-the-eyes style. It has its own logic, however, and neither style is intrinsically better. People who prefer criticism given straight are operating on an assumption that feelings aren't involved: "Here's the dope. I know you're good; you can take it."

3. Thank-Yous

A woman manager I know starts meetings by thanking everyone for coming, even though it's clearly their job to do so. Her "thank-you" is simply a ritual.

A novelist received a fax from an assistant in her publisher's office; it contained suggested catalog copy for her book. She immediately faxed him her suggested changes and said, "Thanks for running this by me," even though her contract gave her the right to approve all copy. When she thanked the assistant, she fully expected him to reciprocate: "Thanks for giving me such a quick response." Instead, he said, "You're welcome." Suddenly, rather than an equal exchange of pleasantries, she found herself positioned as the recipient of a favor. This made her feel like responding, "Thanks for nothing!"

Many women use "thanks" as an automatic conversation starter and closer; there's nothing literally to say thank you for. Like many rituals typical of women's conversation, it depends on the goodwill of the other to restore the balance. When the other speaker doesn't reciprocate, a woman may feel like someone on a seesaw whose partner abandoned his end. Instead of balancing in the air, she has plopped to the ground, wondering how she got there. 15

4. Fighting

Many men expect the discussion of ideas to be a ritual fight — explored through verbal opposition. They state their ideas in the strongest possible terms, thinking that if there are weaknesses someone will point them out, and by trying to argue against those objections, they will see how well their ideas hold up. 16

Those who expect their own ideas to be challenged will respond to another's ideas by trying to poke holes and find weak links — as a way *of helping*. The logic is that when you are challenged you will rise to the occasion: Adrenaline makes your mind sharper; you get ideas and insights you would not have thought of without the spur of battle. 17

But many women take this approach as a personal attack. Worse, they find it impossible to do their best work in such a contentious environment. If you're not used to ritual fighting, you begin to hear criticism of your ideas as soon as they are formed. Rather than making you think more clearly, it makes you doubt what you know. When you state your ideas, you hedge in order to fend off potential attacks. Ironically, this is more likely to *invite* attack because it makes you look weak. 18

Although you may never enjoy verbal sparring, some women find it helpful to learn how to do it. An engineer who was the only woman among four men in a small company found that as soon as she learned to argue she was accepted and taken seriously. A doctor attending a hospital staff meeting made a similar discovery. She was becoming more and more angry with a male colleague who'd loudly disagreed with a point she'd made. Her better judgment told her to hold her tongue, to avoid making an enemy of this powerful senior colleague. But finally she couldn't hold it in any longer, and she rose to her feet and delivered an impassioned attack on his position. She sat down in a panic, certain she had permanently damaged her relationship with him. To her amazement, he came up to her afterward and said, "That was a great rebuttal. I'm really impressed. Let's go out for a beer after work and hash out our approaches to this problem." 19

5. Praise

A manager I'll call Lester had been on his new job six months when he   20
heard that the women reporting to him were deeply dissatisfied. When he
talked to them about it, their feelings erupted; two said they were on the verge
of quitting because he didn't appreciate their work, and they didn't want to
wait to be fired. Lester was dumbfounded: He believed they were doing a fine
job. Surely, he thought, he had said nothing to give them the impression he
didn't like their work. And indeed he hadn't. That was the problem. He had
said *nothing* — and the women assumed he was following the adage "If you
can't say something nice, don't say anything." He thought he was showing
confidence in them by leaving them alone.

Men and women have different habits in regard to giving praise. For   21
example, Deirdre and her colleague William both gave presentations at a conference. Afterward, Deirdre told William, "That was a great talk!" He thanked
her. Then she asked, "What did you think of mine?" and he gave her a lengthy
and detailed critique. She found it uncomfortable to listen to his comments.
But she assured herself that he meant well, and that his honesty was a signal
that she, too, should be honest when he asked for a critique of his performance.
As a matter of fact, she had noticed quite a few ways in which he could have
improved his presentation. But she never got a chance to tell him because he
never asked — and she felt put down. The worst part was that it seemed she
had only herself to blame, since she *had* asked what he thought of her talk.

But had she really asked for his critique? The truth is, when she asked for   22
his opinion, she was expecting a compliment, which she felt was more or less
required following anyone's talk. When he responded with criticism, she figured, "Oh, he's playing 'Let's critique each other'" — not a game she'd initiated,
but one which she was willing to play. Had she realized he was going to criticize
her and not ask her to reciprocate, she would never have asked in the first place.

It would be easy to assume that Deirdre was insecure, whether she was   23
fishing for a compliment or soliciting a critique. But she was simply talking
automatically, performing one of the many conversational rituals that allow us
to get through the day. William may have sincerely misunderstood Deirdre's
intention — or may have been unable to pass up a chance to one-up her when
given the opportunity.

6. Complaints

"Troubles talk" can be a way to establish rapport with a colleague. You   24
complain about a problem (which shows that you are just folks) and the other
person responds with a similar problem (which puts you on equal footing).

But while such commiserating is common among women, men are likely to hear it as a request to *solve* the problem.

One woman told me she would frequently initiate what she thought would be pleasant complaint-airing sessions at work. She'd talk about situations that bothered her just to talk about them, maybe to understand them better. But her male office mate would quickly tell her how she could improve the situation. This left her feeling condescended to and frustrated. She was delighted to see this very impasse in a section in my book *You Just Don't Understand*, and showed it to him. "Oh," he said, "I see the problem. How can we solve it?" Then they both laughed, because it had happened again: He short-circuited the detailed discussion she'd hoped for and cut to the chase of finding a solution.

Sometimes the consequences of complaining are more serious: A man might take a woman's lighthearted griping literally, and she can get a reputation as a chronic malcontent. Furthermore, she may be seen as not up to solving the problems that arise on the job.

7. Jokes

I heard a man call in to a talk show and say, "I've worked for two women and neither one had a sense of humor. You know, when you work with men, there's a lot of joking and teasing." The show's host and the guest (both women) took his comment at face value and assumed the women this man worked for were humorless. The guest said, "Isn't it sad that women don't feel comfortable enough with authority to see the humor?" The host said, "Maybe when more women are in authority roles, they'll be more comfortable with power." But although the women this man worked for *may* have taken themselves too seriously, it's just as likely that they each had a terrific sense of humor, but maybe the humor wasn't the type he was used to. They may have been like the woman who wrote to me: "When I'm with men, my wit or cleverness seems inappropriate (or lost!) so I don't bother. When I'm with my women friends, however, there's no hold on puns or cracks and my humor is fully appreciated."

The types of humor women and men tend to prefer differ. Research has shown that the most common form of humor among men is razzing, teasing, and mock-hostile attacks, while among women it's self-mocking. Women often mistake men's teasing as genuinely hostile. Men often mistake women's mock self-deprecation as truly putting themselves down.

Women have told me they were taken more seriously when they learned to joke the way the guys did. For example, a teacher who went to a national conference with seven other teachers (mostly women) and a group of administrators (mostly men) was annoyed that the administrators always found reasons to leave boring seminars, while the teachers felt they had to stay and take notes. One evening, when the group met at a bar in the hotel, the principal asked her how one such seminar had turned out. She retorted, "As soon as you left, it got much better." He laughed out loud at her response. The playful insult appealed to the men — but there was a trade-off. The women seemed to back off from her after this. (Perhaps they were put off by her using joking to align herself with the bosses.)

There is no "right" way to talk. When problems arise, the culprit may be   30
style differences — and *all* styles will at times fail with others who don't share or understand them, just as English won't do you much good if you try to speak to someone who knows only French. If you want to get your message across, it's not a question of being "right"; it's a question of using language that's shared — or at least understood.

Journal Writing

Tannen's ANECDOTE about the newspaper columnist (par. 4) illustrates that much of what we say is purely automatic. Do you excuse yourself when you bump into inanimate objects? When someone says, "Have a good trip," do you answer, "You, too," even if the other person isn't going anywhere? Do you find yourself overusing certain words or phrases such as "like" or "you know"? Pay close attention to these kinds of verbal tics in your own and others' speech. Over the course of a few days, note as many of them as you can in your journal.

Questions on Meaning

1. What is Tannen's PURPOSE in writing this essay?
2. What does Tannen mean when she writes, "Conversation is a ritual" (par. 1)?
3. What does Tannen see as the fundamental difference between men's and women's conversational strategies?
4. Why is "You're welcome" not always an appropriate response to "Thank you"?

Questions on Writing Strategy

1. This essay has a large cast of characters: twenty-three to be exact. What function do these characters serve? How does Tannen introduce them to the reader? Does she describe them in sufficient detail?
2. Whom does Tannen see as her primary AUDIENCE? ANALYZE her use of the pronoun *you* in paragraphs 9 and 19. Whom does she seem to be addressing? Why?

3. Analyze how Tannen develops the category of apologies in paragraphs 4–9. Where does she use EXAMPLE, DEFINITION, and COMPARISON AND CONTRAST?

4. How does Tannen's characterization of a columnist as "well-known" (par. 4) contribute to the effectiveness of her example?

5. **OTHER METHODS**   For each of her seven areas of miscommunication, Tannen compares and contrasts male and female communication styles and strategies. SUMMARIZE the main source of misunderstanding in each area.

Questions on Language

1. What is the EFFECT of "I put her out of her misery" (par. 11)? What does this phrase usually mean?

2. What does Tannen mean by a "right-between-the-eyes style" (par. 12)? What is the FIGURE OF SPEECH involved here?

3. What is the effect of Tannen's use of figurative verbs, such as "barking" (par. 11) and "erupted" (20)? Find at least one other example of the use of a verb in a nonliteral sense.

4. Look up any of the following words whose meanings you are unsure of: synonymous, self-deprecating (par. 4); lucid, tentativeness (11); intrinsically (12); reciprocate (14); adrenaline, spur (17); contentious, hedge (18); sparring, rebuttal (19); adage (20); soliciting (23); commiserating (24); initiate, condescended, impasse (25); chronic, malcontent (26); razzing (28); retorted (29).

Suggestions for Writing

1. **FROM JOURNAL TO ESSAY**   Write an essay classifying the examples from your journal entry (p. 305) into categories of your own devising. You might sort out the examples by context ("phone blunders," "faulty farewells"), by purpose ("nervous tics," "space fillers"), or by some other principle of classification. Given your subject matter, you might want to adopt a humorous TONE.

2. How true do you find Tannen's assessment of miscommunication between the sexes? Consider the conflicts you have experienced yourself or observed — between your parents, among fellow students or coworkers, in fictional portrayals in books and movies. You could also go beyond your personal experiences and observations by researching the opinions of other experts (linguists, psychologists, sociologists, and so on). Write an essay confirming or questioning Tannen's GENERALIZATIONS, backing up your (and perhaps others') views with your own examples.

3. **CRITICAL WRITING**   Tannen insists that "neither [communication] style is intrinsically better" (par. 12), that "[t]here is no 'right' way to talk" (30). What do you make of this refusal to take sides in the battle of the sexes? Is Tannen always successful? Is absolute neutrality possible, or even desirable, when it comes to such divisive issues?

4. **CONNECTIONS**   Tannen offers some of her own experiences as examples of communication blunders, and she often uses the first-person *I* or *we* in explaining her
categories. In contrast, the author of the next essay, William Lutz, takes a more
distant approach in classifying types of misleading language called *doublespeak*.
Which of these approaches, personal or more distant, do you find more effective,
and why? When, in your view, is it appropriate to inject yourself into your writing, and when is it not?

Deborah Tannen on Writing

Though "But What Do You Mean?" is written for a general audience, Deborah Tannen is a linguistics scholar who does considerable academic writing.
One debate among scholarly writers is whether it is appropriate to incorporate personal experiences and biases into their papers, especially given the goal
of objectivity in conducting and reporting research. The October 1996 *PMLA
(Publications of the Modern Language Association)* printed a discussion of the
academic uses of the personal, with contributions from more than two dozen
scholars. Tannen's comments, excerpted here, focused on the first-person *I*.

When I write academic prose, I use the first person, and I instruct my
students to do the same. The principle that researchers should acknowledge
their participation in their work is an outgrowth of a humanistic approach to
linguistic analysis. . . . Understanding discourse is not a passive act of decod-
ing but a creative act of imagining a scene (composed of people engaged in
culturally recognizable activities) within which the ideas being talked about
have meaning. The listener's active participation in sense making both results
from and creates interpersonal involvement. For researchers to deny their
involvement in their interpreting of discourse would be a logical and ethical
violation of this framework. . . .

[O]bjectivity in the analysis of interactions is impossible anyway. Whether
they took part in the interaction or not, researchers identify with one or
another speaker, are put off or charmed by the styles of participants. This
one reminds you of a cousin you adore; that one sounds like a neighbor you
despise. Researchers are human beings, not atomic particles or chemical elements. . . .

Another danger of claiming objectivity rather than acknowledging and
correcting for subjectivity is that scholars who don't reveal their participation in interactions they analyze risk the appearance of hiding it. "Following

is an exchange that occurred between a professor and a student," I have read in articles in my field. The speakers are identified as "A" and "B." The reader is not told that the professor, A (of course the professor is A and the student B), is the author. Yet that knowledge is crucial to contextualizing the author's interpretation. Furthermore, the impersonal designations A and B are another means of constructing a false objectivity. They obscure the fact that human interaction is being analyzed, and they interfere with the reader's understanding. The letters replace what in the author's mind are names and voices and personas that are the basis for understanding the discourse. Readers, given only initials, are left to scramble for understanding by imagining people in place of letters.

Avoiding self-reference by using the third person also results in the depersonalization of knowledge. Knowledge and understanding do not occur in abstract isolation. They always and only occur among people. . . . Denying that scholarship is a personal endeavor entails a failure to understand and correct for the inevitable bias that human beings bring to all their enterprises.

The Brief Bedford Reader on Writing

In arguing for the use of the first-person *I* in scholarly prose, Tannen is speaking primarily about its use in her own field, linguistics. From your experience with ACADEMIC WRITING, is her argument applicable to other disciplines, such as history, biology, psychology, or government? What have your teachers in other courses advised you about writing in the first person? For our guidelines on choosing an appropriate POINT OF VIEW for your writing and using it consistently, check pages 48, 65–66, and 216.

WILLIAM LUTZ

William Lutz was born in 1940 in Racine, Wisconsin. He received a BA from Dominican College, an MA from Marquette University, a PhD from the University of Nevada at Reno, and a JD from Rutgers School of Law. For much of his career, Lutz's interest in words and composition has made him an active campaigner against misleading and irresponsible language. For fourteen years he edited the *Quarterly Review of Doublespeak*, and he has written three popular books on such language, the last being *Doublespeak Defined: Cut through the Bull**** and Get to the Point!* (1999). He has also written for many periodicals, including the *Los Angeles Times*, the *London Times*, and *USA Today*. In 1996 Lutz received the George Orwell Award for Distinguished Contribution to Honesty and Clarity in Public Language. He is professor emeritus at Rutgers University in Camden, New Jersey.

The World of Doublespeak

In the previous essay, Deborah Tannen examines the ways gender differences in speaking can cause innocent misunderstandings. But what if misunderstandings are the result of speech crafted to obscure meaning? Such intentional fudging, or *doublespeak*, is the sort of language Lutz specializes in, and here he uses classification to expose its many guises. "The World of Doublespeak" abridges the first chapter in Lutz's book *Doublespeak: From Revenue Enhancement to Terminal Living* (1989); the essay's title is the chapter's subtitle.

There are no potholes in the streets of Tucson, Arizona, just "pavement deficiencies." The Reagan Administration didn't propose any new taxes, just "revenue enhancement" through new "user's fees." Those aren't bums on the street, just "non–goal oriented members of society." There are no more poor people, just "fiscal underachievers." There was no robbery of an automatic teller machine, just an "unauthorized withdrawal." The patient didn't die because of medical malpractice, it was just a "diagnostic misadventure of a high magnitude." The US Army doesn't kill the enemy anymore, it just "services the target." And the doublespeak goes on.

Doublespeak is language that pretends to communicate but really doesn't. It is language that makes the bad seem good, the negative appear positive, the unpleasant appear attractive or at least tolerable. Doublespeak is language that avoids or shifts responsibility, language that is at variance with its real or purported meaning. It is language that conceals or prevents thought; rather than extending thought, doublespeak limits it.

Doublespeak is not a matter of subjects and verbs agreeing; it is a matter   3
of words and facts agreeing. Basic to doublespeak is incongruity, the incongruity between what is said or left unsaid, and what really is. It is the incongruity between the word and the referent, between seem and be, between the essential function of language — communication — and what doublespeak does — mislead, distort, deceive, inflate, circumvent, obfuscate.

How to Spot Doublespeak

How can you spot doublespeak? Most of the time you will recognize dou-   4
blespeak when you see or hear it. But, if you have any doubts, you can identify doublespeak just by answering these questions: Who is saying what to whom, under what conditions and circumstances, with what intent, and with what results? Answering these questions will usually help you identify as doublespeak language that appears to be legitimate or that at first glance doesn't even appear to be doublespeak.

First Kind of Doublespeak

There are at least four kinds of doublespeak. The first is the euphemism,   5
an inoffensive or positive word or phrase used to avoid a harsh, unpleasant, or distasteful reality. But a euphemism can also be a tactful word or phrase which avoids directly mentioning a painful reality, or it can be an expression used out of concern for the feelings of someone else, or to avoid directly discussing a topic subject to a social or cultural taboo.

When you use a euphemism because of your sensitivity for someone's   6
feelings or out of concern for a recognized social or cultural taboo, it is not doublespeak. For example, you express your condolences that someone has "passed away" because you do not want to say to a grieving person, "I'm sorry your father is dead." When you use the euphemism "passed away," no one is misled. Moreover, the euphemism functions here not just to protect the feelings of another person, but to communicate also your concern for that person's feelings during a period of mourning. When you excuse yourself to go to the "restroom," or you mention that someone is "sleeping with" or "involved with" someone else, you do not mislead anyone about your meaning, but you do respect the social taboos about discussing bodily functions and sex in direct terms. You also indicate your sensitivity to the feelings of your audience, which is usually considered a mark of courtesy and good manners.

However, when a euphemism is used to mislead or deceive, it becomes 7
doublespeak. For example, in 1984 the US State Department announced that
it would no longer use the word "killing" in its annual report on the status of
human rights in countries around the world. Instead, it would use the phrase
"unlawful or arbitrary deprivation of life," which the department claimed
was more accurate. Its real purpose for using this phrase was simply to avoid
discussing the embarrassing situation of government-sanctioned killings in
countries that are supported by the United States and have been certified by
the United States as respecting the human rights of their citizens. This use of
a euphemism constitutes doublespeak, since it is designed to mislead, to cover
up the unpleasant. Its real intent is at variance with its apparent intent. It is
language designed to alter our perception of reality.

The Pentagon, too, avoids discussing unpleasant realities when it refers 8
to bombs and artillery shells that fall on civilian targets as "incontinent ord-
nance." And in 1977 the Pentagon tried to slip funding for the neutron bomb
unnoticed into an appropriations bill by calling it a "radiation enhancement
device."

Second Kind of Doublespeak

A second kind of doublespeak is jargon, the specialized language of a 9
trade, profession, or similar group, such as that used by doctors, lawyers, engineers, educators, or car mechanics. Jargon can serve an important and useful
function. Within a group, jargon functions as a kind of verbal shorthand that
allows members of the group to communicate with each other clearly, efficiently, and quickly. Indeed, it is a mark of membership in the group to be able
to use and understand the group's jargon.

But jargon, like the euphemism, can also be doublespeak. It can be — and 10
often is — pretentious, obscure, and esoteric terminology used to give an
air of profundity, authority, and prestige to speakers and their subject matter. Jargon as doublespeak often makes the simple appear complex, the ordinary profound, the obvious insightful. In this sense it is used not to express
but impress. With such doublespeak, the act of smelling something becomes
"organoleptic analysis," glass becomes "fused silicate," a crack in a metal support beam becomes a "discontinuity," conservative economic policies become
"distributionally conservative notions."

Lawyers, for example, speak of an "involuntary conversion" of property 11
when discussing the loss or destruction of property through theft, accident,
or condemnation. If your house burns down or if your car is stolen, you have
suffered an involuntary conversion of your property. When used by lawyers in
a legal situation, such jargon is a legitimate use of language, since lawyers can
be expected to understand the term.

However, when a member of a specialized group uses its jargon to   12
communicate with a person outside the group, and uses it knowing that the
nonmember does not understand such language, then there is doublespeak.
For example, on May 9, 1978, a National Airlines 727 airplane crashed while
attempting to land at the Pensacola, Florida, airport. Three of the fifty-two
passengers aboard the airplane were killed. As a result of the crash, National
made an after-tax insurance benefit of $1.7 million, or an extra 18¢ a share
dividend for its stockholders. Now National Airlines had two problems: It did
not want to talk about one of its airplanes crashing, and it had to account for
the $1.7 million when it issued its annual report to its stockholders. National
solved the problem by inserting a footnote in its annual report which explained
that the $1.7 million income was due to "the involuntary conversion of a
727." National thus acknowledged the crash of its airplane and the subsequent profit it made from the crash, without once mentioning the accident or
the deaths. However, because airline officials knew that most stockholders in
the company, and indeed most of the general public, were not familiar with
legal jargon, the use of such jargon constituted doublespeak.

Third Kind of Doublespeak

A third kind of doublespeak is gobbledygook or bureaucratese. Basically,   13
such doublespeak is simply a matter of piling on words, of overwhelming the
audience with words, the bigger the words and the longer the sentences the
better. Alan Greenspan, then chair of President Nixon's Council of Economic
Advisors, was quoted in *The Philadelphia Inquirer* in 1974 as having testified
before a Senate committee that "It is a tricky problem to find the particular
calibration in timing that would be appropriate to stem the acceleration in
risk premiums created by falling incomes without prematurely aborting the
decline in the inflation-generated risk premiums."

Nor has Mr. Greenspan's language changed since then. Speaking to the   14
meeting of the Economic Club of New York in 1988, Mr. Greenspan, now
Federal Reserve chair, said, "I guess I should warn you, if I turn out to be
particularly clear, you've probably misunderstood what I've said." Mr. Greenspan's doublespeak doesn't seem to have held back his career.[1]

Sometimes gobbledygook may sound impressive, but when the quote is   15
later examined in print it doesn't even make sense. During the 1988 presidential campaign, vice-presidential candidate Senator Dan Quayle explained the
need for a strategic-defense initiative by saying, "Why wouldn't an enhanced
deterrent, a more stable peace, a better prospect to denying the ones who

---

[1] Greenspan retired from the Federal Reserve in 2006. He is now a private consultant. — EDS.

enter conflict in the first place to have a reduction of offensive systems and an introduction to defense capability? I believe this is the route the country will eventually go."

The investigation into the *Challenger* disaster in 1986 revealed the   16
doublespeak of gobbledygook and bureaucratese used by too many involved in the shuttle program. When Jesse Moore, NASA's associate administrator, was asked if the performance of the shuttle program had improved with each launch or if it had remained the same, he answered, "I think our performance in terms of the liftoff performance and in terms of the orbital performance, we knew more about the envelope we were operating under, and we have been pretty accurately staying in that. And so I would say the performance has not by design drastically improved. I think we have been able to characterize the performance more as a function of our launch experience as opposed to it improving as a function of time." While this language may appear to be jargon, a close look will reveal that it is really just gobbledygook laced with jargon. But you really have to wonder if Mr. Moore had any idea what he was saying.

Fourth Kind of Doublespeak

The fourth kind of doublespeak is inflated language that is designed to   17
make the ordinary seem extraordinary; to make everyday things seem impressive; to give an air of importance to people, situations, or things that would not normally be considered important; to make the simple seem complex. Often this kind of doublespeak isn't hard to spot, and it is usually pretty funny. While car mechanics may be called "automotive internists," elevator operators members of the "vertical transportation corps," used cars "preowned" or "experienced cars," and black-and-white television sets described as having "non-multicolor capability," you really aren't misled all that much by such language.

However, you may have trouble figuring out that, when Chrysler "initiates   18
a career alternative enhancement program," it is really laying off five thousand workers; or that "negative patient-care outcome" means the patient died; or that "rapid oxidation" means a fire in a nuclear power plant.

The doublespeak of inflated language can have serious consequences. In   19
Pentagon doublespeak, "pre-emptive counterattack" means that American forces attacked first; "engaged the enemy on all sides" means American troops were ambushed; "backloading of augmentation personnel" means a retreat by American troops. In the doublespeak of the military, the 1983 invasion of Grenada was conducted not by the US Army, Navy, Air Force, and Marines, but by the "Caribbean Peace Keeping Forces." But then, according to the Pentagon, it wasn't an invasion, it was a "predawn vertical insertion." . . .

The Dangers of Doublespeak

Doublespeak is not the product of carelessness or sloppy thinking. Indeed, most doublespeak is the product of clear thinking and is carefully designed and constructed to appear to communicate when in fact it doesn't. It is language designed not to lead but mislead. It is language designed to distort reality and corrupt thought. . . . In the world created by doublespeak, if it's not a tax increase, but rather "revenue enhancement" or "tax base broadening," how can you complain about higher taxes? If it's not acid rain, but rather "poorly buffered precipitation," how can you worry about all those dead trees? If that isn't the Mafia in Atlantic City, but just "members of a career-offender cartel," why worry about the influence of organized crime in the city? If Supreme Court Justice William Rehnquist wasn't addicted to the pain-killing drug his doctor prescribed, but instead it was just that the drug had "established an interrelationship with the body, such that if the drug is removed precipitously, there is a reaction," you needn't question that his decisions might have been influenced by his drug addiction. If it's not a Titan II nuclear-armed intercontinental ballistic missile with a warhead 630 times more powerful than the atomic bomb dropped on Hiroshima, but instead, according to air force colonel Frank Horton, it's just a "very large, potentially disruptive reentry system," why be concerned about the threat of nuclear destruction? Why worry about the neutron bomb escalating the arms race if it's just a "radiation enhancement weapon"? If it's not an invasion, but a "rescue mission" or a "predawn vertical insertion," you won't need to think about any violations of US or international law. [20]

Doublespeak has become so common in everyday living that many people fail to notice it. Even worse, when they do notice doublespeak being used on them, they don't react, they don't protest. Do you protest when you are asked to check your packages at the desk "for your convenience," when it's not for your convenience at all but for someone else's? You see advertisements for "genuine imitation leather," "virgin vinyl," or "real counterfeit diamonds," but do you question the language or the supposed quality of the product? Do you question politicians who don't speak of slums or ghettos but of the "inner city" or "substandard housing" where the "disadvantaged" live and thus avoid talking about the poor who have to live in filthy, poorly heated, ramshackle apartments or houses? Aren't you amazed that patients don't die in the hospital anymore, it's just "negative patient-care outcome"? [21]

Doublespeak such as that noted earlier that defines cab drivers as "urban transportation specialists," elevator operators as members of the "vertical transportation corps," and automobile mechanics as "automotive internists" can be considered humorous and relatively harmless. However, when a fire in a nuclear reactor building is called "rapid oxidation," an explosion in a nuclear power plant is called an "energetic disassembly," the illegal overthrow of a [22] legitimate government is termed "destabilizing a government," and lies are seen as "inoperative statements," we are hearing doublespeak that attempts to avoid responsibility and make the bad seem good, the negative appear positive, something unpleasant appear attractive; and which seems to communicate but doesn't. It is language designed to alter our perception of reality and corrupt our thinking. Such language does not provide us with the tools we need to develop, advance, and preserve our culture and our civilization. Such language breeds suspicion, cynicism, distrust, and, ultimately, hostility.

Doublespeak is insidious because it can infect and eventually destroy the 23 function of language, which is communication between people and social groups. This corruption of the function of language can have serious and far-reaching consequences. We live in a country that depends upon an informed electorate to make decisions in selecting candidates for office and deciding issues of public policy. The use of doublespeak can become so pervasive that it becomes the coin of the political realm, with speakers and listeners convinced that they really understand such language. After a while we may really believe that politicians don't lie but only "misspeak," that illegal acts are merely "inappropriate actions," that fraud and criminal conspiracy are just "miscertification." President Jimmy Carter in April of 1980 could call the aborted raid to free the American hostages in Teheran an "incomplete success" and really believe that he had made a statement that clearly communicated with the American public. So, too, could President Ronald Reagan say in 1985 that "ultimately our security and our hopes for success at the arms reduction talks hinge on the determination that we show here to continue our program to rebuild and refortify our defenses" and really believe that greatly increasing the amount of money spent building new weapons would lead to a reduction in the number of weapons in the world. If we really believe that we understand such language and that such language communicates and promotes clear thought, then the world of 1984,[2] with its control of reality through language, is upon us.

Journal Writing

Now that you know the name for it, when have you read or heard examples of doublespeak? Over the next few days, jot down examples of doublespeak that you recall or that you read and hear — from politicians or news commentators; in the lease for your

---

[2] In a section omitted from this abridgement of his chapter, Lutz discusses *Nineteen Eighty-Four*, the 1949 novel by George Orwell in which a frightening totalitarian state devises a language, called *newspeak*, to shape and control thought in politically acceptable forms. — EDS.

dwelling or your car; in advertising and catalogs; from bosses, teachers, or other figures of authority; in overheard conversations.

Questions on Meaning

1. What is Lutz's THESIS? Where does he state it?
2. According to Lutz, four questions can help us identify doublespeak. What are they? How can they help us distinguish between truthful and misleading language?
3. What, according to Lutz, are "the dangers of doublespeak"?
4. What ASSUMPTIONS does the author make about his readers' educational backgrounds and familiarity with his subject?

Questions on Writing Strategy

1. What principle does Lutz use for creating his four kinds of doublespeak — that is, what mainly distinguishes the groups?
2. How does Lutz develop the discussion of euphemism in paragraphs 5–8?
3. Lutz quotes Alan Greenspan twice in paragraphs 13–14. What is surprising about the comment in paragraph 14? Why does Lutz include this second quotation?
4. Lutz uses many quotations that were quite current when he first published this piece in 1989 but that now may seem dated — for instance, references to Presidents Carter and Reagan or to the nuclear arms race. Do these EXAMPLES undermine Lutz's essay in any way? Is his discussion of doublespeak still valid today? Explain your answers.
5. **OTHER METHODS**   Lutz's essay is not only a classification but also a DEFINITION of *doublespeak* and an examination of CAUSE AND EFFECT. Where are these other methods used most prominently? What do they contribute to the essay?

Questions on Language

1. How does Lutz's own language compare with the language he quotes as doublespeak? Do you find his language clear and easy to understand?
2. ANALYZE Lutz's language in paragraphs 22 and 23. How do the CONNOTATIONS of words such as "corrupt," "hostility," "insidious," and "control" strengthen the author's message?
3. The following list of possibly unfamiliar words includes only those found in Lutz's own sentences, not those in the doublespeak he quotes. Be sure you can define variance (par. 2); incongruity, referent (3); taboo (5); esoteric, profundity (10); condemnation (11); ramshackle (21); cynicism (22); insidious (23).

Suggestions for Writing

1. **FROM JOURNAL TO ESSAY** Choose at least one of the examples of doublespeak noted in your journal (p. 315), and write an essay explaining why it qualifies as doublespeak. Which of Lutz's categories does it fit under? How did you recognize it? Can you understand what it means?

2. Just about all of us have resorted to doublespeak at one time or another — when making an excuse, when trying to wing it on an exam, when trying to impress a potential employer. Write a NARRATIVE about a time you used deliberately unclear language, perhaps language that you yourself didn't understand. What were the circumstances? Did you consciously decide to use unclear language, or did it just leak out? How did others react to your use of this language?

3. **CRITICAL WRITING** Can you determine from his essay who Lutz believes is responsible for the proliferation of doublespeak? Whose responsibility is it to curtail the use of doublespeak: just those who use it? the schools? the government? the media? we who hear it? Write an essay that considers these questions, citing specific passages from the essay and incorporating your own ideas.

4. **CONNECTIONS** While Lutz looks at language "carefully designed and constructed to appear to communicate when in fact it doesn't," Deborah Tannen, in the previous essay, takes the position that "conversation is a ritual" — that we don't often think about what we're saying and miscommunicate as a result. How do you resolve the apparent contradictions in these two writers' underlying assumptions about language? Is most of our speech deliberate, or is it automatic? Why do you think so? In an essay that draws on examples and EVIDENCE from each of these two essays as well as from your own experience, explain what you see as the major causes of miscommunication.

William Lutz on Writing

In 1989 C-SPAN aired an interview between Brian Lamb and William Lutz. Lamb asked Lutz about his writing process. "I have a rule about writing," Lutz answered, "which I discovered when I wrote my dissertation: You never write a book, you write three pages, or you write five pages. I put off writing my dissertation for a year, because I could not think of writing this whole thing. . . . I had put off doing this book [*Doublespeak*] for quite a while, and my wife said, 'You've got to do the book.' And I said, 'Yes, I am going to, just as soon as I . . . ,' and, of course, I did every other thing I could possibly think of before that, and then I realized one day that she was right, I had to start writing. . . . So one day, I sit down and say, 'I am going to write five pages — that's all — and when I am done with five pages, I'll reward myself.'

So I do the five pages, or the next time I will do ten pages or whatever number of pages, but I set a number of pages."

Perhaps wondering just how high Lutz's daily page count might go, Lamb asked Lutz how much he wrote at one time. "It depends," Lutz admitted. "I always begin a writing session by sitting down and rewriting what I wrote the previous day — and that is the first thing, and it does two things. First of all, it makes your writing a little bit better, because rewriting is the essential part of writing. And the second thing is to get you flowing again, get back into the mainstream. Truman Capote[1] once gave the best piece of advice for writers ever given. He said, 'Never pump the well dry; always leave a bucket there.' So, I never stop writing when I run out of ideas. I always stop when I have something more to write about, and write a note to myself, 'This is what I am going to do next,' and then I stop. The worst feeling in the world is to have written yourself dry and have to come back the next day, knowing that you are dry and not knowing where you are going to pick up at this point."

The Brief Bedford Reader on Writing

You aren't writing whole books for your classes, of course, but Lutz's advice, scaled down, should remind you that you needn't write an essay all at once, only a few paragraphs at a time. Do you think Lutz's REVISION strategy — of rewriting before he starts writing about the idea he didn't develop on the previous day — is a good one? For other ways to approach the sometimes daunting tasks of drafting and revising, see Chapter 2 of this book, especially pages 34–42.

---

[1] Truman Capote (1924–84) was an American journalist and fiction writer. — EDS.

RUSSELL BAKER

Russell Baker is one of America's notable humorists and political satirists. Born in 1925 in Virginia, Baker was raised in New Jersey and Maryland by his widowed mother. After serving in the navy during World War II, he earned a BA from Johns Hopkins University in 1947. He became a reporter for the *Baltimore Sun* that year and then joined the *New York Times* in 1954, covering the State Department, the White House, and Congress. From 1962 until he left the *Times* in 1998, he wrote a popular syndicated column that ranged over the merely bothersome (unreadable menus) and the serious (the Cold War). Many of Baker's columns and essays have been collected in books, such as *There's a Country in My Cellar* (1990). Baker has twice received the Pulitzer Prize, once for distinguished commentary and again for the first volume of his autobiography, *Growing Up* (1982). He has also written fiction and children's books, edited *Russell Baker's Book of American Humor* (1993), and served as host of *Masterpiece Theatre* on public television. Now retired, Baker lives in Leesburg, Virginia.

The Plot against People

The critic R. Z. Sheppard has commented that Baker can "best be appreciated for doing what a good humorist has always done: writing to preserve his sanity for at least one more day." In this piece from the *New York Times* in 1968, Baker uses classification for that purpose, taking aim, as he has often done, at inanimate objects. In the decades since this piece was written, the proliferation of electronic devices has, if anything, intensified the plot Baker imagines.

Inanimate objects are classified into three major categories — those that 1 don't work, those that break down and those that get lost.

The goal of all inanimate objects is to resist man and ultimately to defeat 2 him, and the three major classifications are based on the method each object uses to achieve its purpose. As a general rule, any object capable of breaking down at the moment when it is most needed will do so. The automobile is typical of the category.

With the cunning typical of its breed, the automobile never breaks down 3 while entering a filling station with a large staff of idle mechanics. It waits until it reaches a downtown intersection in the middle of the rush hour, or until it is fully loaded with family and luggage on the Ohio Turnpike.

Thus it creates maximum misery, inconvenience, frustration and irritability among its human cargo, thereby reducing its owner's life span. 4

Washing machines, garbage disposals, lawn mowers, light bulbs, automatic laundry dryers, water pipes, furnaces, electrical fuses, television tubes, hose nozzles, tape recorders, slide projectors — all are in league with the automobile to take their turn at breaking down whenever life threatens to flow smoothly for their human enemies. 5

Many inanimate objects, of course, find it extremely difficult to break down. Pliers, for example, and gloves and keys are almost totally incapable of breaking down. Therefore, they have had to evolve a different technique for resisting man. 6

They get lost. Science has still not solved the mystery of how they do it, and no man has ever caught one of them in the act of getting lost. The most plausible theory is that they have developed a secret method of locomotion which they are able to conceal the instant a human eye falls upon them. 7

It is not uncommon for a pair of pliers to climb all the way from the cellar to the attic in its single-minded determination to raise its owner's blood pressure. Keys have been known to burrow three feet under mattresses. Women's purses, despite their great weight, frequently travel through six or seven rooms to find hiding space under a couch. 8

Scientists have been struck by the fact that things that break down virtually never get lost, while things that get lost hardly ever break down. 9

A furnace, for example, will invariably break down at the depth of the first winter cold wave, but it will never get lost. A woman's purse, which after all does have some inherent capacity for breaking down, hardly ever does; it almost invariably chooses to get lost. 10

Some persons believe this constitutes evidence that inanimate objects are not entirely hostile to man, and that a negotiated peace is possible. After all, they point out, a furnace could infuriate a man even more thoroughly by getting lost than by breaking down, just as a glove could upset him far more by breaking down than by getting lost. 11

Not everyone agrees, however, that this indicates a conciliatory attitude among inanimate objects. Many say it merely proves that furnaces, gloves and pliers are incredibly stupid. 12

The third class of objects — those that don't work — is the most curious of all. These include such objects as barometers, car clocks, cigarette lighters, flashlights and toy-train locomotives. It is inaccurate, of course, to say that they never work. They work once, usually for the first few hours after being brought home, and then quit. Thereafter, they never work again. 13

In fact, it is widely assumed that they are built for the purpose of not working. Some people have reached advanced ages without ever seeing some of these objects — barometers, for example — in working order. 14

Science is utterly baffled by the entire category. There are many theories   15
about it. The most interesting holds that the things that don't work have
attained the highest state possible for an inanimate object, the state to which
things that break down and things that get lost can still only aspire.

They have truly defeated man by conditioning him never to expect any-   16
thing of them, and in return they have given man the only peace he receives
from inanimate society. He does not expect his barometer to work, his electric
locomotive to run, his cigarette lighter to light or his flashlight to illuminate,
and when they don't it does not raise his blood pressure.

He cannot attain that peace with furnaces and keys and cars and women's   17
purses as long as he demands that they work for their keep.

Journal Writing

What other ways can you think of to classify inanimate objects? In your journal, try
expanding on Baker's categories, or create new categories of your own based on a
different principle — for example, objects no student can live without or objects no
student would want to be caught dead with.

Questions on Meaning

1. What is Baker's THESIS?

2. Why don't things that break down get lost, and vice versa?

3. Does Baker have any PURPOSE other than to make his readers smile?

4. How have inanimate objects "defeated man" (par. 16)?

Questions on Writing Strategy

1. What is the EFFECT of Baker's principle of classification? What categories are
   omitted here, and why?

2. In paragraphs 6–10, how does Baker develop the category of things that get lost?
   Itemize the strategies he uses to make the category clear.

3. Find three places where Baker uses hyperbole. (See FIGURES OF SPEECH in the
   Glossary if you need a definition.) What is the effect of the hyperbole?

4. How does the essay's INTRODUCTION help set its TONE? How does the CONCLUSION
   reinforce the tone?

5. **OTHER METHODS**   How does Baker use NARRATION to portray inanimate objects
   in the act of "resisting" people? Discuss how these mini-narratives make his
   classification more persuasive.

Questions on Language

1. Look up any of these words that are unfamiliar: plausible, locomotion (par. 7); invariably, inherent (10); conciliatory (12).

2. What are the CONNOTATIONS of the word "cunning" (par. 3)? What is its effect in this context?

3. Why does Baker use such expressions as "man," "some people," and "their human enemies" rather than *I* to describe those who come into conflict with inanimate objects? How might the essay have been different if Baker had relied on *I*?

Suggestions for Writing

1. **FROM JOURNAL TO ESSAY**   Write a brief, humorous essay based on one classification system from your journal entry (p. 321). It may be helpful to use narration or DESCRIPTION in your classification. Figures of speech, especially hyperbole and understatement, can help you establish a comic tone.

2. Think of a topic that would not generally be considered appropriate for a serious classification (some examples: game-show winners, body odors, stupid pet tricks, knock-knock jokes). Select a principle of classification, and write a brief essay sorting the subject into categories. You may want to use a humorous tone; then again, you may want to approach the topic "seriously," counting on the contrast between subject and treatment to make your IRONY clear.

3. **CRITICAL WRITING**   In a short essay, discuss the likely AUDIENCE for Baker's essay. (Recall that it first appeared in the *New York Times*.) What can you INFER from his EXAMPLES about Baker's own age and economic status? Does he ASSUME his audience is similar? How do the connections between author and audience help establish the essay's humor? Does this humor exclude some readers?

4. **CONNECTIONS**   Baker's essay bears comparison with "Remembering My Childhood on the Continent of Africa" by another humorist, David Sedaris (p. 180). Each man writes about himself with a self-deprecating, mock-serious tone. Read both works closely, and write an essay in which you COMPARE AND CONTRAST the words the authors use to present themselves and their situations.

JEAN-PIERRE DE BEER

Jean-Pierre (JP) De Beer was born in Pittsburgh, Pennsylvania, in 1999 and grew up in suburban Ohio and Illinois, rural South Carolina, and remote Queensland, Australia. He is currently a senior at Jefferson Township High School in northern New Jersey and hopes to embark to Paris, France, for college. A dual citizen of the United States and Belgium, De Beer has also had occasion to visit parts of Europe, New Zealand, and Japan. In addition to world travel he enjoys snowboarding, acting, massive multiplayer online games, and science fiction.

Stars of Life

De Beer wrote this essay especially for *The Brief Bedford Reader* in 2016. His original intention was to classify computer games, but, he tells us, he quickly realized that his categories were hopelessly overlapped. In a burst of inspiration, he composed a rough draft of "Stars of Life," a curious investigation of the possibilities for life on other planets, in a matter of a few hours. De Beer then devoted a week or so to revising it — refining his purpose, locating sources of information, fleshing out the details, and shaping the organization — and then another day to editing.

Notice that the finished essay is based on Web research. In accordance with MLA style (see pp. 499–513), De Beer names his sources in the text and lists them at the end. Most of his parenthetical citations do not include page numbers because most of his sources do not have them.

"I don't think the human race will survive the next thousand years, unless we spread into space."

— Stephen Hawking

Sooner than later humanity will need to abandon the small asteroid it lives on and find a place to live out among the stars. While most stars could potentially have Earth-like planets orbiting within their habitable zones, many are too short-lived, too unpredictable, or too uncommon to support human life in the long term. Moreover, in the years of the great move people will need to acquire and harness an abundant source of energy to power the space-age contraptions that will be required to reach and colonize a new home. If we wish to survive, humanity will need to find a long-term solution by identifying stars that can support our endeavors and last trillions of years.

Ranging from the runt OGLE-TR-122b to the enormous VY Canis Majoris, there are some 100 billion burning gas balls in our galaxy and 1 billion trillion of them in the observable universe (Howell). Astronomers generally classify these stars into seven major categories and fifty-six subcategories

("Star Types"). Of these, three types stand out as the most potentially beneficial to humankind and prolonging its existence: supergiants, yellow dwarfs, and red dwarfs. Each kind of star varies in different aspects such as temperature, life span, and number, and each offers distinct contributions should humanity succeed in spreading to space. The red dwarf, however, is or at least will be the most important star because of its incredibly long life span and relative abundance in our immense universe.

Supergiants earned their name because they are some of the largest and hottest stars known to science. With temperatures that can exceed 20,000 kelvin (about five times hotter than the sun), supergiants are among the stars with the greatest energy output. With this massive energy comes a cost, though: Where our sun will last about 10 billion years, supergiants tend to last only 10 to 50 million years. Because of their relatively short lifespan supergiants are extremely rare; they account for less then .0001% of all stars still alive, or about one in a million (Lang 140). Nonetheless, supergiant stars could be an immense source of energy for the future. Assuming that scientists could tap into that energy, an entire new world of possibility arises. 3

Intergalactic relocation will likely require an extraordinary amount of energy to power a range of demanding devices: space crafts, terraforming machines, life-support systems, and more. Harnessing the energy released by supergiant stars could theoretically accelerate development, power deep-space missions to other galaxies, and provide a basically infinite supply of fuel to sustain life on other planets. Studying and eventually applying the vast amount of heat and force a supergiant generates could lead to a range of new and stronger tools, materials, and matter that would be otherwise unobtainable. When humankind needs to acquire new forms of energy in any quantity and store it, the universe's greatest power source — the supergiant star — should be able to provide. 4

While supergiants promise to be of assistance in the future, yellow dwarfs deserve special appreciation because they have already been a massive help to humankind: Our current sun is a yellow dwarf. Yellow dwarf stars typically hit a surface temperature of around 5,600 kelvin (about 15 times hotter than boiling water), causing a relatively stable energy output. The low energy gives dwarf stars a longer life span than that of supergiants, commonly about 10 billion years (Cain). Should humanity need to find a new home quickly and nearby, a yellow dwarf would be our best bet. Approximately 20% of the stars in the known universe are yellow dwarfs, and it is likely that at least some host inhabitable planets for humankind to colonize on, at least for a little while. 5

Because of a yellow dwarf's mass and the amount of energy it releases, any rock planet that is in the habitable zone (like Earth) would be relatively safe from solar flares. The long life span of a yellow dwarf star ensures that once the 6 big move is finished, humanity will have plenty of time to colonize, develop, and adapt to the new landscape and solar system. In the event that we find a new home near a yellow dwarf star, we will have a workable base of operations — at least until a more long-term solution can be found.

Red dwarfs, the real stars of the show, are the most likely to help out 7 humankind in the long run. They are the smallest known stars in the universe (but still massive) and consistently hit a temperature of around 4,000 kelvin — a very low energy output in the spectrum of the stars. Because of their relative size and slow release of energy they will last for a cool ten trillion years, give or take a few billion ("Last Star"). Red dwarfs are also abundant, making up about 70% of all the stars in the universe. What's more, NASA's Kepler space telescope mission has found that at least half of the observable red dwarfs host a rock planet near the size of Earth, and many of them are in the "Goldilocks zone" of moderate temperature, atmospheric pressure, and the possibility of water. In the Milky Way alone about 5% of red dwarfs host roughly Earth-sized, inhabitable planets — that's more than four billion potential homes nearby!

The renowned cosmologist Stephen Hawking once said that humanity will 8 not survive unless we relocate. While all types of stars have the potential to host or at least help us, supergiants, yellow dwarfs, and red dwarfs especially will prove to be invaluable in the not-so-distant future. Supergiants and their unparalleled source of energy will power the devices needed to move and rebuild. Yellow dwarfs provide a viable alternative to Earth's sun should we need to evacuate quickly. Red dwarfs, however, give humanity a nearly infinite amount of space to grow, colonize, and hunker down for the long haul. Because of their immense life span, they will provide a place to live after all other stars have died out. And because of how common they are, they offer practically endless amounts of prime real estate just waiting to be claimed. If we look to them for our future, the entire universe will be at our fingertips for trillions of years to come.

Works Cited

Cain, Fraser. "What Kind of Star Is the Sun?" *Universe Today*, 1 Aug. 2008, www.universetoday.com/16350/what-kind-of-star-is-the-sun/.

Hawking, Stephen. "Colonies in Space May Be Only Hope." Interview by Roger Highfield. *The Telegraph*, 16 Oct. 2001, www.telegraph.co.uk/news/uknews/1359562/Colonies-in-space-may-be-only-hope-says-Hawking.html.

Howell, Elizabeth. "How Many Stars Are in the Milky Way?" *Space.com*, Purch, 21 May 2014, www.space.com/25959-how-many-stars-are-in-the-milky-way.html.

Lang, Kenneth R. *The Life and Death of Stars*. Cambridge UP, 2013. *Google Books*, books.google.com/books/about/The_Life_and_Death_of_Stars.html?id=MN-UCkUK9pcC.

"The Last Star in the Universe: Red Dwarfs Explained." *Kurzgesagt — In a Nutshell*, 31 Jan. 2016. *YouTube*, www.youtube.com/watch?v=LS-VPyLaJFM.

NASA. *Kepler: A Search for Habitable Planets*. Ames Research Center, 18 Jan. 2016, kepler.nasa.gov/.

"Star Types." *All about Astronomy*, Enchanted Learning, 2015, www.enchantedlearning.com/subjects/astronomy/stars/startypes.shtml.

Journal Writing

Do you think there could be life on other planets? If no, why not? If yes, what forms might such extraterrestrial life take: intelligent beings with social structures and civilizations akin to ours, or something more basic, like flora and fauna — or simple microbes? Or perhaps you imagine beings and societies far more evolved than our own? In your journal, ponder the possibilities.

Questions on Meaning

1. How seriously does De Beer take his subject? What seems to be his PURPOSE in classifying stars?

2. What is a planet's "Goldilocks zone" (par. 7)? Where does the term come from?

3. Where does De Beer state his THESIS? Is any part of his main idea left unsaid?

Questions on Writing Strategy

1. "Stars of Life" opens with a short quotation from Stephen Hawking. Why? What is the function of this epigraph? Where in the essay does De Beer return to it, and to what EFFECT?

2. For whom would you say De Beer is writing? What ASSUMPTIONS does he make about his AUDIENCE?

3. Identify the principle of classification De Beer uses to organize types of stars. What does each type have in common?

4. What consistent pattern does De Beer use to develop the paragraphs for each of his categories? How effective do you find this approach?

5. **OTHER METHODS**   What role does CAUSE-AND-EFFECT analysis play in De Beer's classification?

Questions on Language

1. How would you describe De Beer's general DICTION? Why is — or isn't — his language appropriate for his subject, his purpose, and his audience?

2. Locate some FIGURES OF SPEECH and COLLOQUIAL EXPRESSIONS in De Beer's writing and explain what they contribute to his essay.

3. Look up any of the following words whose meanings you are unsure of: asteroid, habitable, harness, contraptions, endeavors (par. 1); runt (2); kelvin (3); intergalactic, terraforming (4); spectrum (7); cosmologist (8).

Suggestions for Writing

1. **FROM JOURNAL TO ESSAY** Taking off from your speculations in your journal, respond to De Beer's proposal that humanity will need to move to another planet to survive. Is such a move really necessary, or possible? And if so, what are the ethical implications of colonizing habitable planets, especially if they already host some forms of life? Do we have the right to "spread into space"? What could happen if we did? Might there be wars and fights over resources, perhaps, the spread of disease, changes to human biology, interspecies development, some other consequences? Be as lighthearted or as serious as you wish, but be as imaginative as you can.

2. Look into the mission, history, and findings to date of the Kepler space telescope team (you might start with the home page De Beer identifies in his works-cited list). What are NASA's goals for the program? What has it achieved? How supportive of its budget has Congress been? Based on your findings, write an essay defending and justifying the use of government funding for the Kepler mission or another program such as the Hubble telescope or the New Horizons spacecraft. This essay will require some research because you will need to argue that the benefits of NASA's programs outweigh their costs, and you will need to support your claims with factual evidence. Or approach the issue from a skeptic's point of view and argue against using taxpayers' money for space exploration. Substantiate your argument with data, and be sure to propose alternative methods for exploring the cosmos and funding such investigations.

3. **CRITICAL WRITING** Most of the information De Beer provides comes from general-interest space and astronomy sites, and all of it comes from the Web. How convincing do you find this EVIDENCE? Does the nature of De Beer's sources weaken his essay in any way, or does his classification remain valid? Why do you think so? (You might, if time allows, look for more scholarly works on astronomy or the search for habitable planets, and consider how they apply to De Beer's conclusions.) Explain your evaluation in a brief essay.

4. **CONNECTIONS** Jean-Pierre De Beer's "Stars of Life" and Diane Ackerman's "Black Marble" (p. 127) both deal with space travel and the ultimate fate of the Earth. In an essay, COMPARE AND CONTRAST the two writers' treatment of their subjects. What strategies do De Beer and Ackerman have in common, and where do their perspectives diverge? How does the TONE of each essay contribute to its effect?

ADDITIONAL WRITING TOPICS

Classification

Write an essay by the method of classification, in which you sort one of the following subjects into categories of your own. Make clear your PURPOSE in classifying and the basis of your classification. Explain each class with DEFINITIONS and EXAMPLES (you may find it helpful to make up a name for each group). Check your classes to be sure they neither gap nor overlap.

People who use public transportation

Urban wildlife

Smartphone users or apps

Gym members

Late-night television shows

The drawbacks or benefits of small-town life

Your playlists

Families

Health-care providers

Politicians

Internships

College students

Movies for teenagers or men or women

Difficult coworkers

Graphic novels

Monsters

Sports announcers

Inconsiderate people

Social media platforms

Sources of energy

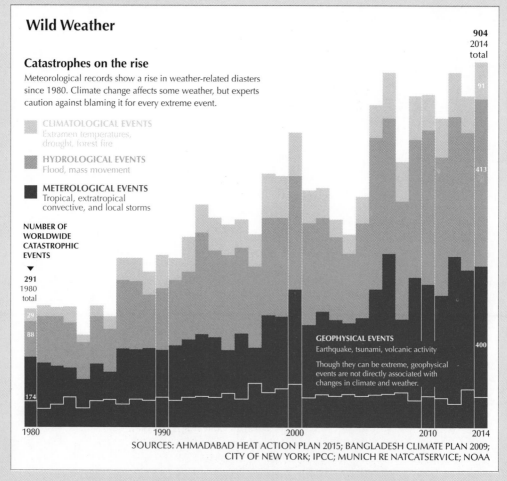

Wild Weather

904
2014
total

Catastrophes on the rise

Meteorological records show a rise in weather-related disasters since 1980. Climate change affects some weather, but experts caution against blaming it for every extreme event.

CLIMATOLOGICAL EVENTS
Extramen temperatures,
drought, forest fire

HYDROLOGICAL EVENTS
Flood, mass movement

METEROLOGICAL EVENTS
Tropical, extratropical
convective, and local storms

NUMBER OF
WORLDWIDE
CATASTROPHIC
EVENTS
▼
291
1980
total

29

88

174

91

413

400

GEOPHYSICAL EVENTS
Earthquake, tsunami, volcanic activity

Though they can be extreme, geophysical
events are not directly associated with
changes in climate and weather.

1980   1990   2000   2010   2014

SOURCES: AHMADABAD HEAT ACTION PLAN 2015; BANGLADESH CLIMATE PLAN 2009;
CITY OF NEW YORK; IPCC; MUNICH RE NATCATSERVICE; NOAA

Credit: Matt Twombly and Lawson Parker.

10

CAUSE AND EFFECT

Asking Why

◀ **Cause and effect in a bar graph**

With simple visuals and perhaps a few words, infographics often make striking comments on events and trends. This bar graph by *National Geographic*, published in a 2015 special issue devoted to climate change, proposes some disturbing effects of a well-known but sometimes disputed cause. What is the cause? What, according to the authors, have been three of the major effects, and how are they related? What other effects might result from the cause depicted here? Why do "experts caution against blaming it for every extreme event"? Do you agree or disagree with *National Geographic*'s claims? Why?

THE METHOD

Press the button of a doorbell and, inside the house or apartment, chimes sound. Why? Because the touch of your finger on the button closed an electrical circuit. But why did you ring the doorbell? Because you were sent by your dispatcher: You are a bill collector calling on a customer whose payments are three months overdue.

The touch of your finger on the button is the *immediate cause* of the chimes: the event that precipitates another. That you were ordered by your dispatcher to go ring the doorbell is a *remote cause:* an underlying, more basic reason for the event, not apparent to an observer. Probably, ringing the doorbell will lead to some results: The door will open, and you may be given a check — or have the door slammed in your face.

To figure out reasons and results is to use the method of CAUSE AND EFFECT. Either to explain events or to argue for one version of them, you try to answer the question "Why did something happen?" or "What were the consequences?" or "What might be the consequences?" Seeking causes, you can ask, for example, "Why do birds migrate?" "What led to America's involvement in the war in Vietnam?" Looking for effects, you can ask, "How has legalization of gay marriage changed the typical American family?" "What impact have handheld computers had on the nursing profession?" You can look to a possible future and ask, "Of what use might a course in psychology be to me if I become an office manager?" "Suppose an asteroid the size of a sofa were to strike Philadelphia — what would be the probable consequences?"

Don't confuse cause and effect with the method of PROCESS ANALYSIS (Chap. 7). Some process analysis essays, too, deal with happenings; but they focus more on repeatable events (rather than unique ones) and they explain *how* (rather than why) something happened. If you were explaining the process by which the doorbell rings, you might break the happening into stages — (1) the finger presses the button; (2) the circuit closes; (3) the current travels the wire; (4) the chimes make music — and you'd set forth the process in detail. But why did the finger press the button? What happened because the doorbell rang? To answer those questions, you need cause and effect.

In trying to explain why things happen, you can expect to find a whole array of causes — interconnected, perhaps, like the strands of a spiderweb. To produce a successful essay, you'll want to do an honest job of unraveling, and this may take time. Before you start to write, devote some extra thought to seeing which facts are the causes and which matter most. To answer the questions "Why?" and "What followed as a result?" may sometimes be hard, but it can be satisfying — even illuminating. Indeed, to seek causes and effects is one way for the mind to discover order in a reality that otherwise might seem random and pointless.

THE PROCESS

Subject and Purpose

The method of cause and effect tends to suggest itself: If you have a subject and soon start thinking "Why?" or "What results?" or "What if?" then you are on the way to analyzing causation. Your subject may be impersonal — like a change in voting patterns or the failure or success of a business — or it may be quite personal. Indeed, an excellent cause-and-effect paper may be written on a subject very near to you. You can ask yourself why you behaved in a certain way at a certain moment. You can examine the reasons for your current beliefs and attitudes. Writing such a paper, you might happen upon a truth you hadn't realized before.

Whether your subject is personal or impersonal, make sure it is manageable: You should be able to get to the bottom of it, given the time and information available. For a 500-word essay due Thursday, the causes of teenage rebellion would be a less feasible topic than why a certain thirteen-year-old you know ran away from home.

Before rushing to list causes or effects, stop a moment to consider what your PURPOSE might be in writing. Much of the time you'll seek simply to explain what did or might occur, discovering and laying out the connections as clearly and accurately as you can. But when reasonable people could disagree over causes or effects, you'll want to go further, arguing for one interpretation over others. You'll still need to be clear and accurate in presenting your interpretation, but you'll also need to treat the others fairly. (See Chap. 12 on argument and persuasion.)

Thesis

When you have a grip on your subject and your purpose, you can draft a tentative THESIS STATEMENT to express the main point of your analysis. The essays in this chapter provide good examples of thesis statements that put across, concisely, the author's central finding about causes and effects. Here are two examples:

> A bill like the one we've just passed [to ban imports from factories that use child labor] is of no use unless it goes hand in hand with programs that will offer a new life to these newly released children.
>
> — Chitra Divakaruni, "Live Free and Starve"

> To begin to solve the problem [of the illegal drug trade], we need to understand what's happening in drug-source countries, how the United States can and can't help there, and what, instead, can be done at home.
>
> — Marie Javdani, "*Plata o Plomo:* Silver or Lead"

Your own thesis statement may be hypothetical at the discovery stage, before you have gathered EVIDENCE and sorted out the complexity of causes and effects. Still, a statement framed early can help direct your later thinking and research.

Causal Relations

Your toughest job in writing a cause-and-effect essay may be figuring out what caused what. Sometimes one event will appear to trigger another, and it in turn will trigger yet another, and another still, in an order we call a *causal chain*. Investigators at the scene of a ten-car pileup, for instance, might determine that a deer ran across the highway, causing a driver to slam on the brakes suddenly, causing another driver to hit the first car, causing the next driver to swerve and hit the embankment, and so on.

In reality, causes are seldom so easy to find as that stray deer: They tend to be many and complicated. Even a simple accident may happen for more than one reason. Perhaps the deer was flushed out of the woods by a hunter. Perhaps the first driver was distracted by a crying child in the back seat. Perhaps winter had set in and the road was icy. Perhaps the low glare of the setting sun made it difficult for any of the drivers to see clearly. Still, one event precedes another in time, and in discerning causes you don't ignore chronological order; you pay attention to it.

When you can see a number of apparent causes, weigh them and assign each a relative importance. Which do you find matter most? Often, you will see that particular causes are more important or less so: major or minor. If you seek to explain why your small town has fallen on hard times, you might note that two businesses shut down: a factory employing three hundred and a drugstore employing six. The factory's closing is a *major cause*, leading to significant unemployment in the town, while the drugstore's closing is perhaps a *minor cause* — or not a cause at all but an effect. In writing about the causes, you would emphasize the factory and mention the drugstore only briefly if at all.

When seeking remote causes, look only as far back as necessary. Explaining your town's misfortunes, you might see the factory's closing as the immediate cause. You could show what caused the shutdown: a dispute between union and management. You might even go back to the cause of the dispute (announced layoffs) and the cause of the layoffs (loss of sales to a competitor). A paper showing effects might work in the other direction, moving from the factory closing to its impact on the town: unemployment, the closing of stores (including the drugstore), people packing up and moving away.

Two cautions about causal relations are in order here. One is to beware of confusing coincidence with cause. In the logical FALLACY called *post hoc* (short for the Latin *post hoc, ergo propter hoc,* "after this, therefore because of this"), one assumes, erroneously, that because A happened before B, A must have caused B. This is the error of the superstitious man who decides that he lost his job because a black cat walked in front of him. Another fallacy is to oversimplify causes by failing to recognize their full number and complexity — claiming, say, that violent crime is simply a result of "all those first-person shooter games." Avoid such wrong turns in reasoning by patiently looking for evidence before you write, and by giving it careful thought. (For a fuller list of logical fallacies, or errors in reasoning, see p. 412.)

Discovery of Causes

To help find causes of actions and events, you can ask yourself a few searching questions. These have been suggested by the work of the literary critic Kenneth Burke:

1. **What act am I trying to explain?**
2. **What is the character, personality, or mental state of whoever acted?**
3. **In what scene or location did the act take place, and in what circumstances?**
4. **What instruments or means did the person use?**
5. **For what purpose did the person act?**

Burke calls these elements a *pentad* (or set of five): the *act,* the *actor,* the *scene,* the *agency,* and the *purpose.* If you were a detective trying to explain why a liquor store burned down, you might ask these questions:

1. **Act:** Was the fire deliberately set by someone, or was there an accident?
2. **Actors:** If the fire was arson, who set it: the store's worried, debt-ridden owner? a mentally disturbed antialcohol crusader? a drunk who had been denied a purchase?
3. **Scene:** Was the store near a church? a mental hospital? a fireworks factory?
4. **Agency, or means of the act:** Was the fire caused by faulty electrical wiring? a carelessly tossed cigarette? a flaming torch? rags soaked in kerosene?
5. **Purpose:** If the fire wasn't accidental, was it set to collect insurance? to punish drinkers? to get revenge?

You can further deepen your inquiry by seeing relationships between the terms of the pentad. Ask, for instance, what does the actor have to do with this

Cause and Effect

scene? (Is he or she the neighbor across the street, who has been staring at the liquor shop resentfully for years?)

Don't worry if not all the questions apply or if not all the answers are immediately forthcoming. Burke's pentad isn't meant to be a grim rigmarole; it is a means of discovery, to generate a lot of possible material for you — insights, observations, hunches to pursue. It won't solve each and every human mystery, but sometimes it will helpfully deepen your thought.

Educated Guesses

In stating what you believe to be causes and effects, don't be afraid to voice a well-considered hunch. Your instructor doesn't expect you to write, in a short time, a definitive account of the causes of an event or a belief or a phenomenon — only to write a coherent and reasonable one. To discern all causes — including remote ones — and all effects is beyond the power of any one human mind. Still, admirable and well-informed writers on matters such as politics, economics, and world and national affairs are often canny guessers and brave drawers of inferences. At times, even the most cautious and responsible writer has to leap boldly over a void to strike firm ground on the far side. Consider your evidence. Focus your thinking. Look well before leaping. Then take off.

FOCUS ON CLARITY AND CONCISENESS

While drafting a cause-and-effect analysis, you may need to grope a bit to discover just what you think about the sequence and relative importance of reasons and consequences. Your sentences may grope a bit, too, reflecting some initial confusion or a need to circle around your ideas in order to find them. The following draft passage reveals such difficulties:

WORDY AND UNCLEAR Employees often worry about suggestive comments from others. The employee may not only worry but feel the need to discuss the situation with coworkers. One thing that is an effect of sexual harassment, even verbal harassment, in the workplace is that productivity is lost. Plans also need to be made to figure out how to deal with future comments. Engaging in these activities is sure to take time and concentration from work.

Drafting this passage, the writer seems to have built up to the idea about lost productivity (third sentence) after providing support for it in the first two sentences. The fourth sentence then adds more support. And sentences 2–4 all show a writer working out his ideas: Sentence subjects and verbs do not focus on the main actors and actions of the sentences, words repeat unnecessarily, and word groups run longer than needed for clarity.

These problems disappear from the edited version below, which moves the idea of the passage up front, uses subjects and verbs to state what the sentences are about (underlined), and cuts unneeded words.

> CONCISE AND CLEAR   Even verbal sexual <u>harassment</u> in the workplace <u>causes</u> a loss of productivity. Worrying about suggestive comments from others, discussing those comments with coworkers, planning how to deal with future comments — these <u>activities</u> <u>consume</u> time and concentration that a harassed employee could spend on work.

CHECKLIST FOR REVISING A CAUSE-AND-EFFECT ESSAY

✔ **Subject.** Have you been able to cover your subject adequately in the time and space available? Should you perhaps narrow the subject so that you can fairly address the important causes and/or effects?

✔ **Thesis.** For your readers' benefit, have you focused your analysis by stating your main idea succinctly in a thesis statement?

✔ **Completeness.** Have you included all relevant causes or effects? Does your analysis reach back to locate remote causes or forward to locate remote effects?

✔ **Causal relations.** Have you presented a clear pattern of causes or effects? Have you distinguished the remote from the immediate, the major from the minor?

✔ **Accuracy and fairness.** Have you avoided the *post hoc* fallacy, assuming that A caused B just because A preceded B? Have you also avoided oversimplifying and instead covered causes or effects in all their complexity?

✔ **Clarity and conciseness.** Have you edited your draft to foreground your main points and tighten your sentences?

CAUSE AND EFFECT IN ACADEMIC WRITING

A History Textbook

These paragraphs from Alan Brinkley's *American History: A Survey* explain the causes behind President Lyndon Johnson's decision in the 1960s to escalate the ongoing conflict in Vietnam into "a full-scale American war" — a decision that, as the author's text goes on to explain, had grave and far-reaching consequences for the United States.

Many factors played a role in Johnson's decision. But the most
obvious explanation is that the new president faced many pressures
to expand the American involvement and very few to limit it. As
the untested successor to a revered and martyred president, he felt
obliged to prove his worthiness for the office by continuing the policies of his predecessor. Aid to South Vietnam had been one of the
most prominent of those policies. Johnson also felt it necessary to
retain in his administration many of the important figures of the
Kennedy years. In doing so, he surrounded himself with a group of
foreign policy advisers — Secretary of State Dean Rusk, Secretary of
Defense Robert McNamara, National Security Adviser McGeorge
Bundy, and others — who firmly believed that the United States
had an important obligation to resist Communism in Vietnam.
A compliant Congress raised little protest to, and indeed at one
point openly endorsed, Johnson's use of executive powers to lead
the nation into war. And for several years at least, public opinion
remained firmly behind him — in part because Barry Goldwater's
bellicose remarks about the war during the 1964 campaign made
Johnson seem by comparison to be a moderate on the issue.

Above all, intervention in South Vietnam was fully consistent with nearly twenty years of American foreign policy. An anti-
Communist ally was appealing to the United States for assistance;
all the assumptions of the containment doctrine, as it had come
to be defined by the 1960s, seemed to require the nation to oblige.
Vietnam, Johnson believed, was a test of American willingness to
fight Communist aggression, a test he was determined not to fail.

Margin annotations:

Topic sentence: summary of causes to be discussed

Causes:
- Need to prove worthiness

- Advisers urging involvement

- Congressional cooperation

- Support of public opinion

- Consistency with American foreign policy against Communism

A Letter to the Editor

To encourage interaction between readers and writers, most newspapers,
magazines, and journals, as well as some Web sites, solicit and publish letters
to the editor. Unlike the anonymous comments readers may attach to news
and opinion articles online, letters to the editor are signed by their authors
and screened by editors. To be published, such letters generally must take a
calm tone and express ideas rationally. In most cases, the writer refers to the
original article or other piece that prompted the letter and responds by agreeing or disagreeing (or a little of both). The point is to add a new perspective
and move a conversation forward.

An ardent supporter of her school's track team, Kate Krueger was a sophomore during the team's first winning season in many years. At the end of the
season, the student newspaper published a sports column crediting the successes to a new coach. Krueger found this explanation inadequate and wrote
her own cause-and-effect analysis in the following letter to the newspaper's
editor. Notice that because Krueger actually agreed with the original writer

that the coach had helped the team, she acknowledged the coach's contributions while also detailing the other causes she saw at work.

May 2, 2016

To the Editor:

I take issue with Tom Boatz's column that was printed in the April 30 *Weekly*. Boatz attributes the success of this year's track team solely to the new coach, John Barak. I have several close friends who are athletes on the track team, so as an interested observer and fan I believe that Boatz oversimplified the causes of the team's recent success.

To be sure, Coach Barak did much to improve the training regimen and overall morale, and these have certainly contributed to the winning season. Both Coach Barak and the team members themselves can share credit for an impressive work ethic and a sense of camaraderie unequaled in previous years. However, several factors outside Coach Barak's control were also influential.

This year's team gained several phenomenal freshman athletes, such as Kristin Hall, who anchored the 4x400 and 4x800 relays and played an integral part in setting several school records, and Eric Montgomery-Asper, who was undefeated in the shot put.

Even more important, and also unmentioned by Tom Boatz, is the college's increased funding for the track program. Last year the school allotted fifty percent more for equipment, and the results have been dramatic. For example, the new vaulting poles are now the correct length and correspond to the weights of the individual athletes, giving them more power and height. Some vaulters have been able to vault as much as a foot higher than their previous records. Similarly, new starting blocks have allowed the team's sprinters to drop valuable seconds off their times.

I agree with Tom Boatz that Coach Barak deserves some credit for the track team's successes. But the athletes do, too, and so does the college for at last supporting its track program.

— Kate Krueger '18

Margin annotations:

Reason for writing: Original author oversimplified a cause-and-effect relationship

Point of agreement: The new coach was one cause of the team's success

Thesis statement: Other causes played a role

Other causes:
- Talented new team members

- Financial support from the college

Examples of positive effects:
- Improved vaulting performance

- Improved sprinting times

Conclusion summarizes Krueger's analysis

Cause and Effect

CHITRA DIVAKARUNI

Born in 1956 in Calcutta, India, Chitra Banerjee Divakaruni spent nineteen years in her homeland before immigrating to the United States. She holds a BA from the University of Calcutta, an MA from Wright State University, and a PhD from the University of California, Berkeley. Her books, often addressing the immigrant experience in America, include the novels *The Mistress of Spice* (1997), which was named one of the best books of the twentieth century by the *San Francisco Chronicle, One Amazing Thing* (2009), and *Oleander Girl* (2013); the story collections *Arranged Marriage* (1995) and *The Unknown Errors of Our Lives* (2001); and the poetry collections *Leaving Yuba City* (1997) and *Black Candle* (2000). Divakaruni has received a number of prizes for her work including the Before Columbus Foundation's 1996 American Book Award; in 2015, the *Economic Times* listed her among the twenty most globally influential Indian women. She teaches creative writing at the University of Houston and serves on the boards of several organizations that help women and children.

Live Free and Starve

Many of the consumer goods sold in the United States — shoes, clothing, toys, rugs — are made in countries whose labor practices do not meet US standards for safety and fairness. Americans have been horrified at tales of children put to work by force or under contracts (called *indentures*) with the children's parents. Some in the US government have tried to stop or at least discourage such practices: For instance, the bill Divakaruni cites in her first paragraph, which was signed into law, requires the Customs Service to issue a detention order on goods that are suspected of having been produced by forced or indentured child labor. In this essay from *Salon* in 1997, Divakaruni argues that such efforts, however well intentioned, can mean dreadful consequences for the very people they are designed to protect.

For a different perspective on the effects of globalization, see the next essay, Marie Javdani's *"Plata o Plomo:* Silver or Lead."

Some days back, the House passed a bill that stated that the United States   1
would no longer permit the import of goods from factories where forced or
indentured child labor was used. My liberal friends applauded the bill. It was
a triumphant advance in the field of human rights. Now children in Third
World countries wouldn't have to spend their days chained to their posts in

factories manufacturing goods for other people to enjoy while their childhoods slipped by them. They could be free and happy, like American children.

I am not so sure.   2

It is true that child labor is a terrible thing, especially for those children   3
who are sold to employers by their parents at the age of five or six and have
no way to protect themselves from abuse. In many cases it will be decades —
perhaps a lifetime, due to the fines heaped upon them whenever they make
mistakes — before they can buy back their freedom. Meanwhile these children,
mostly employed by rug-makers, spend their days in dark, ill-ventilated rooms
doing work that damages their eyes and lungs. They aren't even allowed to
stand up and stretch. Each time they go to the bathroom, they suffer a pay cut.

But is this bill, which, if it passes the Senate and is signed by President   4
Clinton, will lead to the unemployment of almost a million children, the
answer? If the children themselves were asked whether they would rather work
under such harsh conditions or enjoy a leisure that comes without the benefit
of food or clothing or shelter, I wonder what their response would be.

It is easy for us in America to make the error of evaluating situations in the   5
rest of the world as though they were happening in this country and propose
solutions that make excellent sense — in the context of our society. Even we
immigrants, who should know better, have wiped from our minds the memory
of what it is to live under the kind of desperate conditions that force a parent
to sell his or her child. Looking down from the heights of Maslow's pyramid,[1] it
seems inconceivable to us that someone could actually prefer bread to freedom.

When I was growing up in Calcutta, there was a boy who used to work in   6
our house. His name was Nimai, and when he came to us, he must have been
about ten or so, just a little older than my brother and I. He'd been brought
to our home by his uncle, who lived in our ancestral village and was a field
laborer for my grandfather. The uncle explained to my mother that Nimai's
parents were too poor to feed their several children, and while his older
brothers were already working in the fields and earning their keep, Nimai
was too frail to do so. My mother was reluctant to take on a sickly child who
might prove more of a burden than a help, but finally she agreed, and Nimai
lived and worked in our home for six or seven years. My mother was a good
employer — Nimai ate the same food that we children did and was given
new clothes during Indian New Year, just as we were. In the time between his
chores — dusting and sweeping and pumping water from the tube-well and
running to the market — my mother encouraged him to learn to read and

---

[1] The psychologist Abraham Maslow (1908–70) proposed a "hierarchy of needs" in the
shape of a five-level pyramid with survival needs at the bottom and "self-actualization" and
"self-transcendence" at the top. According to Maslow, one must satisfy the needs at each level
before moving up to the next. — EDS.

write. Still, I would not disagree with anyone who says that it was hardly a desirable existence for a child.

But what would life have been like for Nimai if an anti–child-labor law   7
had prohibited my mother from hiring him? Every year, when we went to visit our grandfather in the village, we were struck by the many children we saw by the mud roads, their ribs sticking out through the rags they wore. They trailed after us, begging for a few paise.[2] When the hunger was too much to bear, they stole into the neighbors' fields and ate whatever they could find — raw potatoes, cauliflower, green sugar cane and corn torn from the stalk — even though they knew they'd be beaten for it. Whenever Nimai passed these children, he always walked a little taller. And when he handed the bulk of his earnings over to his father, there was a certain pride in his eye. Exploitation, you might be thinking. But he thought he was a responsible member of his family.

A bill like the one we've just passed is of no use unless it goes hand in   8
hand with programs that will offer a new life to these newly released children. But where are the schools in which they are to be educated? Where is the money to buy them food and clothing and medication, so that they don't return home to become the extra weight that capsizes the already shaky raft of their family's finances? Their own governments, mired in countless other problems, seem incapable of bringing these services to them. Are we in America who, with one blithe stroke of our congressional pen, rendered these children jobless, willing to shoulder that burden? And when many of these children turn to the streets, to survival through thievery and violence and begging and prostitution — as surely in the absence of other options they must — are we willing to shoulder that responsibility?

Journal Writing

Write a journal response to Divakaruni's argument against legislation that bans goods produced by forced or indentured child laborers. Do you basically agree or disagree with the author? Why?

Questions on Meaning

1. What do you take to be Divakaruni's PURPOSE in this essay? When was it clear?

2. What is Divakaruni's THESIS? Where is it stated?

---

[2] *Paise* (pronounced "pie-say") are the smallest unit of Indian currency, worth a fraction of an American penny. — EDS.

3. What are "Third World countries" (par. 1)?

4. From the further information given in the footnote on page 341, what does it mean to be "[l]ooking down from the heights of Maslow's pyramid" (par. 5)? What point is Divakaruni making here?

5. In paragraph 8 Divakaruni suggests some of the reasons that children in other countries may be forced or sold into labor. What are they?

Questions on Writing Strategy

1. In her last paragraph, Divakaruni asks a series of RHETORICAL QUESTIONS. What is the EFFECT of this strategy?

2. How does the structure of paragraph 3 clarify causes and effects?

3. **OTHER METHODS**   What does the extended EXAMPLE of Nimai (pars. 6–7) contribute to Divakaruni's argument? What, if anything, does it add to Divakaruni's authority? What does it tell us about child labor abroad?

Questions on Language

1. Divakaruni says that laboring children could otherwise be "the extra weight that capsizes the already shaky raft of their family's finances" (par. 8). How does this metaphor capture the problem of children in poor families? (See FIGURES OF SPEECH in the Glossary for a definition of *metaphor*.)

2. What do the words in paragraph 7 tell you about Divakaruni's attitude toward the village children? Is it disdain? pity? compassion? horror?

3. Consult a dictionary if you need help in defining the following: indentured (par. 1); inconceivable (5); exploitation (7); mired, blithe (8).

Suggestions for Writing

1. **FROM JOURNAL TO ESSAY**   Starting from your journal entry, write a letter to your congressional representative or one of your senators who takes a position for or against laws such as that opposed by Divakaruni. You can use quotations from Divakaruni's essay if they serve your purpose, but the letter should center on your own views of the issue. When you've finished your letter, send it. (You can find your representative's and senators' names and addresses on the Web at *house.gov/ representatives/* and *senate.gov*.)

2. David Parker, a photographer and doctor, has documented child laborers in a series of powerful photographs (*childlaborphotographs.com*). He asks viewers, "Under what circumstances and conditions should children work?" Look at Parker's photographs, and answer his question in an essay. What kind of paid work, for how many hours a week, is appropriate for, say, a ten- or twelve-year-old child? Consider: What about children working in their family's business? Where do you draw the line between occasional babysitting or lawn mowing and

full-time factory work? You might want to research the history of child labor in the United States, including the development of child labor laws, to help support your answer.

3. **CRITICAL WRITING** Divakaruni's essay depends significantly on appeals to readers' emotions (see p. 409). Locate one emotional appeal that either helps to convince you of the author's point or, in your mind, weakens the argument. What does the appeal ASSUME about the reader's feelings or values? Why are the assumptions correct or incorrect in your case?

4. **CONNECTIONS** In the next essay, *"Plata o Plomo:* Silver or Lead," Marie Javdani examines another global relationship that can harm children: the international traffic in cocaine, heroin, and other drugs. To what extent do you think the people in one country are responsible for what happens in other countries as a result of their actions? Write a brief essay that answers this question, explaining clearly the beliefs and values that guide your answer.

Chitra Divakaruni on Writing

Chitra Divakaruni is also a community worker, reaching out through organizations such as Maitri, a refuge for abused women that she helped to found. In a 1998 interview in *Atlantic Unbound*, Katie Bolick asked Divakaruni how her activism and writing affected each other. Here is Divakaruni's response.

Being helpful where I can has always been an important value for me. I did community work in India, and I continue to do it in America, because being involved in my community is something I feel I need to do. Activism has given me enormous satisfaction — not just as a person, but also as a writer. The lives of people I would have only known from the outside, or had stereotyped notions of, have been opened up to me. My hotline work with Maitri has certainly influenced both my life and my writing immensely. Overall, I have a great deal of sensitivity that I did not have before, and a lot of my preconceptions have changed. I hope that translates into my writing and reaches my readers.

The Brief Bedford Reader on Writing

Do you have a project or an activity comparable to Divakaruni's activism that you believe positively affects your writing? What is it? How does it help you as you write? For additional help with having your "preconceptions" challenged, or CRITICAL THINKING, turn to pages 16–18.

MARIE JAVDANI

Marie Javdani was born in Albuquerque, New Mexico, and attended the University of Oregon, where she earned a BA and an MA in geography and was published in *Harvest*, the university's annual writing publication. As an undergraduate Javdani became interested in international development. She worked as a research assistant for Harvard's Center for International Development and traveled to Malawi to conduct research on the connection between fertilizer subsidies and food security. Currently involved with a nonprofit organization devoted to bringing clean water to communities in Kenya, Javdani is also a musician whose instrument of choice is the marimba, an African percussion device similar to the xylophone.

Plata o Plomo: Silver or Lead

Like Chitra Divakaruni in the previous selection, Javdani is concerned in this essay with how actions taken in the United States can affect people in other countries, often without our realizing it. To make her argument concrete, Javdani tells the stories of two boys, Eric, an American, and Miguel, a Colombian. (Colombia is a country in South America.) Reminding us that global problems start and end with people, the boys represent cause and effect at their most specific. Javdani wrote this paper for a freshman writing course and revised it for us in 2004. It is documented in MLA style, described on pages 499–513.

At 8:00 on a Friday night, Eric walks down the street in his American hometown whistling. Tonight, for the first time in almost a week, Eric does not have to do homework or chores. Tonight Eric is a free spirit. Best of all, tonight Eric has scored some drugs. He and his friends will trade their bland, controlled existence for some action and a little bit of fun.

At 8:00 on a Friday night, Miguel creeps down the road in his Colombian village praying. Tonight, for the last time in his life, Miguel will have to watch where he is going and listen anxiously for distant gunshots. Tonight Miguel will die. The guerillas who have been threatening him and his father will end his life for some coca and a lot of money.

Eric and Miguel represent opposite poles in what the United States government refers to as the "war on drugs." Miguel's home is where it starts. In his little village, drug production is the only possible way of life. Eric's home is where it ends. In his suburban paradise, the stress of homework and

345

ex-girlfriends requires weekend breaks for drugs. All but ignoring both youths, congresspeople, governors, and presidents talk about how their actions will combat the flow of drugs into our homeland. In an attempt to find the quickest route around a complicated problem, the United States sends billions in aid dollars every year to the governments of Latin American "drug-source" countries such as Colombia, Ecuador, Bolivia, and Peru (Carpenter 205). But the solution isn't working: Political turmoil and violence continue to plague the countries to which we are sending aid, and illegal drug use in the United States remains fairly constant (Vásquez 571–75). To begin to solve the problem, we need to understand what's happening in drug-source countries, how the United States can and can't help there, and what, instead, can be done at home.

Miguel's country, Colombia, is one of the top recipients of US money   4
and military weaponry and equipment. According to the US Department of State, Colombia produces nearly 80% of the world's cocaine as well as a significant amount of the US heroin supply. Drug production has become a way of life for Colombians. Some call it the *plata o plomo* mentality. As Gonzalo Sanchez explains it, *plata o plomo* is literally translated as "silver or lead" and means that one can either take the money — drug money, bribe money, and so on — or take a bullet (7). Since 1964, the country has been essentially run by drug lords and leftist extremists, mainly the FARC (the military wing of the Colombian Communist Party), whose guerilla presence is much stronger and more threatening than that of the actual government. In response, extreme right-wing paramilitary forces act in an equally deadly manner. Both of these groups raid villages continually, looking to root out "traitors" and executing whomever they please (Sanchez 12–15).

According to the humanitarian organization Human Rights Watch, US   5
aid money has helped fund, supply, and train Colombian military units that maintain close alliances with paramilitary groups (*World Report*). Although Colombia has recently taken a tougher stance toward the paramilitaries and peace negotiations are in progress, the US State Department, major human rights organizations, and the United Nations claim that the Colombian government is still linked to illicit paramilitary activities. For example, government forces have often invaded, emptied, and then left a guerilla-held area, clearing the way for paramilitary fighters to take control (Carpenter 162). Human rights groups also criticize what Adam Isacson calls a "forgive and forget" government policy toward paramilitary leaders accused of crimes, including promises of amnesty in return for gradual demobilization (251–52). Although the US has threatened to suspend aid if Colombia does not break such ties with paramilitary groups, the full amount of promised aid continues to be granted (*World Report*).

For the past forty years, the people of Colombia have found themselves   6
between a rock and a hard place over the production of coca, the plant used
for making cocaine and heroin. Under threats from the rebel drug lords, who
now control many areas, civilians must either allow their land to be cultivated
for the growth of coca or put themselves and their families at deadly risk. At
the same time, however, the consequence of "cooperation" with the rebels
is execution by paramilitary groups or even by the Colombian government.
Some coca farmers, fearful of the government, willingly form alliances with
rebels who offer to protect their farms for a fee (Vásquez 572).

Entire villages get caught in the crossfire between paramilitaries and reb-   7
els. In the past ten years, over 35,000 civilians have lost their lives in the
conflict and hundreds of thousands have been forced from their homes (Carpenter 215). A terrible incident in the town of Bellavista was reported in the
New York Times in 2002 (Forero, "Colombian War"). Paramilitary forces took
over the town in an attempt to gain control of jungle smuggling routes. When
leftist rebels arrived ready to fight a battle, the paramilitaries fled, leaving the
civilians trapped and defenseless. Most of the villagers huddled together in
their church, and 117 were killed when a stray rocket destroyed the church.

What is to be done to prevent such atrocities? The United States rushes   8
aid to Colombia, hoping to stop the violence and the drugs. Unfortunately,
the solutions attempted so far have had their own bad results. For instance,
eradicating coca fields has alienated peasants, who then turn to the rebels
for support, and it has also escalated violence over the reduced coca supply
(Vásquez 575). Money intended to help peasants establish alternative crops
has ended up buying weapons for branches of the military that support paramilitary operations (*World Report*). Not long ago $2 million intended for the
Colombian police just disappeared (Forero, "Two Million").

Obviously, the United States needs to monitor how its dollars are used   9
in Colombia. It can continue to discourage the Colombian government
from supporting the paramilitaries and encourage it to seek peace among the
warring factions. But ultimately the United States is limited in what it can
do by international law and by the tolerance of the US people for foreign
intervention.

Instead, the United States should be looking to its home front and should   10
focus on cutting the demand for drugs. Any economist will affirm that where
there is demand, there will be supply. A report by the United Nations Office
on Drugs and Crime connects this basic economic principle to illegal drugs:

> Production of illicit drugs is market driven. In the United States alone, illicit
> drugs are an $80 billion market. More than $70 billion of that amount goes
> to traffickers, those who bring the drugs to market. Stopping the demand
> would stop their business. (26)

The United States should reduce demand by dramatically increasing both treatment and education. The first will help people stop using drugs. The second will make users aware of the consequences of their choices.

The war on drugs is not fought just in the jungles of some distant country.   11
It takes place daily at our schools, in our homes, and on our streets. People my age who justify their use of illegal drugs by saying "It's my life, and I can do with it what I please" should be made aware that they are funding drug lords and contributing to the suffering of people across the globe, including in Colombia. Eric's "little bit of fun" is costing Miguel his life.

Works Cited

Carpenter, Ted Galen. *Peace and Freedom: Foreign Policy for a Constitutional Republic*. Cato Institute, 2002.

Forero, Juan. "Colombian War Brings Carnage to Village Altar." *The New York Times*, 9 May 2002, www.nytimes.com/2002/05/09/world/colombia-war-brings-carnage-to-village-altar.html.

– – –. "Two Million in US Aid to Colombia Missing from Colombian Police Fund." *The New York Times*, 11 May 2002, www.nytimes.com/2002/05/11/world/2-million-in-us-aid-is-missing-from-colombian-police-fund.html.

Isacson, Adam. "Optimism, Pessimism, and Terrorism: The United States and Colombia in 2003." *The Brown Journal of World Affairs*, vol. 10, no. 2, 2004, pp. 245–55.

Sanchez, Gonzalo. *Violence in Colombia*. Scholarly Resources, 1992.

United Nations. *Drug Consumption Stimulates Cultivation and Trade*. UN Office on Drugs and Crime, 2003.

United States, Department of State. *International Narcotics Control Strategy Report, 2003*. Government Printing Office, 2004.

Vásquez, Ian. "The International War on Drugs." *Cato Handbook for Congress: Policy Recommendations for the 108th Congress*, edited by Edward H. Crane and David Boaz, Cato Institute, 2003, pp. 567–76. *Cato Institute*, www.cato.org/cato-handbook-policymakers/cato-handbook-congress-policy-recommendations-108th-congress-2003.

World Report 2003. Human Rights Watch, 2004, www.hrw.org/legacy/wr2k3/.

Journal Writing

What do you think about Javdani's solution to the twin problems of violence in drug-producing countries and drug use in the United States (pars. 10–11)? Do you think her solution would work? Why, or why not?

Questions on Meaning

1. Where does Javdani state her THESIS? How does she develop the thesis?

2. Why do the Colombian peasants often support the Communist rebels rather than the government?

3. What, according to Javdani, are the problems caused by the US government's sending "billions in aid dollars every year to the governments of Latin American 'drug-source' countries" (par. 3)? What does Javdani offer as a solution?

Questions on Writing Strategy

1. Who seems to be Javdani's intended AUDIENCE for this essay? How does she appeal to this audience?

2. With whom do Javdani's sympathies lie? What EVIDENCE in the essay supports your answer?

3. Javdani cites a variety of outside sources throughout the essay. What is the EFFECT of her use of these sources?

4. **OTHER METHODS**   Why does Javdani use COMPARISON AND CONTRAST in her opening paragraphs? What is the effect of her returning to this comparison in her conclusion?

Questions on Language

1. In paragraph 6 Javdani describes the people of Colombia as "between a rock and a hard place over the production of coca." What does she mean?

2. How and why does Javdani use IRONY to describe Eric in paragraph 3?

3. Why does Javdani use quotation marks around *traitors* (par. 4) and *cooperation* (6)?

4. Consult a dictionary if you are unsure of the meanings of any of the following words: guerillas (par. 2); turmoil, plague (3); paramilitary (4); humanitarian, amnesty, demobilization (5); atrocities, eradicating, alienated (8).

Suggestions for Writing

1. **FROM JOURNAL TO ESSAY**   Working from your journal writing and, like Javdani, drawing on research, develop an essay that lays out your view of the most effective ways to curtail either the production or the consumption of illegal drugs. Which current US government efforts are successful, and which fall short? What more could be done?

2. Write a report on the use of illegal drugs by US adolescents, focusing on an aspect of the problem that interests you, such as how widespread it is, what groups it affects most and least, or what drugs are involved. An excellent starting place for your research is Monitoring the Future, a long-term study of "the behavior, attitudes, and values" of students and young adults. Its annual report, *Monitoring the Future Results,* is available at *drugabuse.gov/related-topics /trends-statistics/monitoring-future.*

3. **CRITICAL WRITING**   Is Javdani's essay an effective ARGUMENT? Consider the thesis development, the organization, the evidence, and the clarity of the presentation. What would you say are the strengths and weaknesses of this argument?

4. **CONNECTIONS**   Javdani's essay and Chitra Divakaruni's "Live Free and Starve" (p. 340) both look at effects of globalization, the increasing economic, cultural, and political connections among nations and their people. Write a brief essay discussing what you see as the main advantages and the main disadvantages of globalization. For instance, advantages might include the availability in this country of varied ethnic foods or of relatively inexpensive consumer goods that were produced elsewhere, while disadvantages might include the loss of American manufacturing jobs to foreign factories or the strong international drug trade.

Marie Javdani on Writing

In an interview for this book, we asked Marie Javdani to describe her writing process. She also offered suggestions for college writers based on her own experiences as a student.

Depending on my writing topic, it can often take a while to get a good start. If it's a topic I chose myself and am interested in or am at least somewhat knowledgeable about, the first steps are usually much easier. I usually start by brainstorming an outline by just writing things as I think of them. What questions do I want to answer? How does this topic actually affect people? Once I get a start, the writing process usually goes fairly quickly. I try to write in a way that I would speak if I were, for instance, teaching on the subject. That tends to make my work more readable. As for the introduction, I try to stay away from prescribed formats. I try to think of what would make me want to read more about a topic or to put a spin on it that makes it stand out. Also, I tend to write my introduction last. I've found that if I write it first it typically doesn't match what I write once I get "on a roll." If I plan ahead properly, I don't usually have to do more than two drafts unless I come upon new research that makes me need to rearrange my arguments. I try to write early enough to leave it alone for a few days before I go back and proofread it. . . .

From a student's perspective, the best thing you can do to improve your writing is to be interested in your topic. On the same note, however, don't soapbox. Just say what you want to say, support it, and move on. If you're writing for an assignment for which you weren't able to choose the topic, try to take an angle that you think no one else will take. . . . Do take the time to spell-check and edit your writing. The spelling checker on the computer is not sufficient. You're (not *your*) in college and you know (not *no*) better. Try reading your writing out loud to yourself. If it doesn't sound good when you say it, it doesn't sound good on paper either.

The Brief Bedford Reader on Writing

Do you share Javdani's experience that it's usually easier to write when you're interested in your topic? For tips on finding your interest in a subject, your own personal angle, before you start writing, refer to "Focusing on a Thesis" on pages 35–36 and "Developing Ideas" on pages 36–37. And for some of those "prescribed formats" Javdani avoids when she turns to her opening paragraphs (they can be quite helpful, really) see "Shaping the Introduction and Conclusion" (pp. 37–39).

RANDALL MUNROE

Randall Munroe (born 1984) is the creator of *xkcd*, a stick-figure "Web comic of romance, sarcasm, math, and language" that has gained a cult following since the author first started uploading his doodles on a whim in 2005. He graduated from Christopher Newport University in Newport News, Virginia, with a degree in physics and worked for a while as a roboticist at NASA's Langley Research Center. When his contract with NASA ended in 2006 he turned to writing the comic full time. Munroe now lives in Somerville, Massachusetts, and earns his living selling T-shirts and other *xkcd* merchandise online. When not drawing or writing, he likes to "climb things, open strange doors, and go to goth clubs dressed as a frat guy so [he] can stand around and look terribly uncomfortable."

Everybody Jump

In 2012, Munroe started a corollary to *xkcd* called "What If?" Once a week, he answers a fan's question about physics with his trademark mix of knowledge, wit, and graphing paper; a collection of his carefully researched posts was published in the book *What If? Serious Scientific Answers to Absurd Hypothetical Questions* in 2015. The illustrated entry we include here offers Munroe's take on what would happen if everybody on the planet got together and jumped at the same time. (He cites his sources in APA style, explained on pages 519–529.)

> **Q.** What would happen if everyone on Earth stood
> as close to each other as they could and jumped,
> everyone landing on the ground at the same instant?
> — Thomas Bennett (and many others)

A. This is one of the most popular questions submitted through my Web 1
site. It's been examined before, including by *ScienceBlogs* (2010) and *The Straight Dope* (1984). They cover the kinematics pretty well. However, they don't tell the whole story.

Let's take a closer look. 2

At the start of the scenario, the entire Earth's population has been magi- 3
cally transported together into one place.

352

This crowd takes up an area the size of Rhode Island. But there's no reason 4 to use the vague phrase "an area the size of Rhode Island." This is our scenario; we can be specific. They're *actually* in Rhode Island.

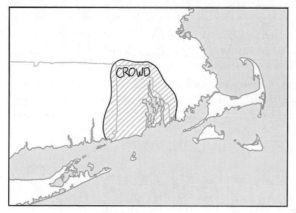

At the stroke of noon, everyone jumps.   5

As discussed elsewhere, it doesn't really affect the planet. Earth outweighs 6 us by a factor of over ten trillion. On average, we humans can vertically jump maybe half a meter on a good day. Even if the Earth were rigid and responded instantly, it would be pushed down by less than an atom's width.

Next, everyone falls back to the ground.   7

Technically, this delivers a lot of energy into the Earth, but it's spread out 8 over a large enough area that it doesn't do much more than leave footprints in a lot of gardens. A slight pulse of pressure spreads through the North American continental crust and dissipates with little effect. The sound of all those feet hitting the ground creates a loud, drawn-out roar lasting many seconds.

Eventually, the air grows quiet.   9

Seconds pass. Everyone looks around.   10
There are a lot of uncomfortable glances. Someone coughs.   11

A cell phone comes out of a pocket. Within seconds, the rest of the   12
world's five billion phones follow. All of them — even those compatible with
the region's towers — are displaying some version of "NO SIGNAL." The cell
networks have all collapsed under the unprecedented load. Outside Rhode
Island, abandoned machinery begins grinding to a halt.

    The T. F. Green Airport in Warwick, Rhode Island, handles a few thou-   13
sand passengers a day. Assuming they got things organized (including sending
out scouting missions to retrieve fuel), they could run at 500% capacity for
years without making a dent in the crowd.

    The addition of all the nearby airports doesn't change the equation much.   14
Nor does the region's light rail system. Crowds climb on board container ships

in the deep-water port of Providence, but stocking sufficient food and water for a long sea voyage proves a challenge.

Rhode Island's half-million cars are commandeered. Moments later, I-95,   15 I-195, and I-295 become the sites of the largest traffic jam in the history of the planet. Most of the cars are engulfed by the crowds, but a lucky few get out and begin wandering the abandoned road network.

Some make it past New York or Boston before running out of fuel. Since   16 the electricity is probably not on at this point, rather than find a working gas pump, it's easier to just abandon the car and steal a new one. Who can stop you? All the cops are in Rhode Island.

The edge of the crowd spreads outward into southern Massachusetts   17 and Connecticut. Any two people who meet are unlikely to have a language in common, and almost nobody knows the area. The state becomes a chaotic patchwork of coalescing and collapsing social hierarchies. Violence is common. Everybody is hungry and thirsty. Grocery stores are emptied. Fresh water is hard to come by and there's no efficient system for distributing it.

Within weeks, Rhode Island is a graveyard of billions.   18

The survivors spread out across the face of the world and struggle to   19 build a new civilization atop the pristine ruins of the old. Our species staggers on, but our population has been greatly reduced. Earth's orbit is completely unaffected — it spins along exactly as it did before our species-wide jump.

But at least now we know.   20

References

Science Blogs, Dot Physics. (26 August 2010). What if everyone jumped? Retrieved from http://scienceblogs.com/dotphysics/2010/08/26/what-if -everyone-jumped/

Straight Dope, The. (6 April 1984). If everyone in China jumped off chairs at once, would the Earth be thrown out of its orbit? Retrieved from http://www.straightdope.com/columns/read/142/if-all-chinese-jumped-at -once-would-cataclysm-result

Journal Writing

Have you recently been struck by curiosity, perhaps because of a question someone asked you, as happened to Munroe, or because of something you've read, or because of a phenomenon you've noticed? What question has been raised in your mind, and why does it interest you? Make note of the question, and your thoughts about it, in your journal.

Questions on Meaning

1. What does Munroe mean by "kinematics" (par. 1)? Why does he not focus on that aspect of the reader's question in his answer?
2. Does Munroe have a THESIS? What does he claim *would* happen if everybody on the planet got together and jumped at the same time?

Questions on Writing Strategy

1. For whom is Munroe writing? What clues in the text reveal how he imagines his AUDIENCE?
2. What is the point in paragraphs 12–18? How does the causal chain Munroe describes there relate to his thesis?
3. What EVIDENCE does Munroe offer to support his analysis of causes and effects? How seriously does he take his subject?
4. What do Munroe's drawings contribute to his essay?
5. **OTHER METHODS**   Why do you think Munroe chose Rhode Island to serve as the EXAMPLE for his scenario?

Questions on Language

1. How would you describe the overall TONE of this essay: academic? detached? amused? something else? Point to some words and phrases that support your answer.
2. Check a dictionary for definitions of the following words: scenario (par. 3); factor (6); dissipates (8); commandeered, engulfed (15); coalescing, hierarchies (17); pristine (19).
3. In speculating about future events, Munroe writes in the present tense. Why? What is the EFFECT of this choice?

Suggestions for Writing

1. **FROM JOURNAL TO ESSAY**   Follow Munroe's lead and look for answers to the question (or questions) you posed in your journal. Try searching the Internet for

information, as well as researching published scholarly works or interviewing an expert or two. Then write an essay that presents your findings, providing plenty of EVIDENCE to support your thesis.

2. Munroe observes that the "five billion" (par. 12) people who populate the Earth (as of 2016 the number is closer to seven billion) consume a lot of resources — "machinery" (12), "food and water" (14), "fuel" (16), and so forth — and his scenario concludes with a human "population [that] has been greatly reduced" (19). Is that a bad thing? In an essay, consider the problem of overpopulation and its effects on the environment. How many people can the planet reasonably hold? Do those in some regions (North America, for instance, or China) consume more than their fair share of resources? To what extent are human beings responsible for changes in the environment? What, if anything, can be done to make human life on Earth more sustainable? How do you envision the future of the planet, and of humanity?

3. **CRITICAL WRITING**   The "kinematics" explanations that Munroe cites at the start of his post and in his list of References are still available online. Read them both for yourself and in an essay, weigh Munroe's use of evidence: Does he represent the math and science accurately and fairly? How well does he adapt technical information for an audience of nonspecialists? What stylistic cues does he seem to take from his sources? Is his approach successful? Why, or why not?

4. **CONNECTIONS**   While Munroe jokes that the collapse of civilization would have no real effect on the Earth itself, Joan Didion, in "Earthquakes" (p. 465), writes about civilization's feelings of powerlessness in the face of natural disasters. What ASSUMPTIONS about human impacts on the Earth (and vice versa) do these writers seem to share, and where do they diverge? How might the apparent contradictions between their two perspectives be resolved?

CHRISTOPHER BEAM

Christopher Beam is a reporter for *Slate* who specializes in politics and crime. His writing has also been published in *New York* magazine, *Business Week*, the *New Republic, Gentlemen's Quarterly*, and other magazines. The son of a *Boston Globe* columnist, Beam grew up in Newton, Massachusetts, attended the Roxbury Latin school, and in 2006 completed a degree in American history at Columbia University. With his friend Nick Summers he cofounded *IvyGate*, a popular college news and gossip blog. Beam currently lives in Beijing, China, where he is studying as a Luce Scholar with the Asia Foundation and, by his own account, performing miserably at table tennis.

Blood Loss

Television crime dramas regularly feature plots in which a series of murders are committed by the same person. But how common are such characters in real life? In this 2011 article for *Slate*, Beam reports a surprising trend: Serial killings occur much less often than they did a generation ago. He suggests that shifting cultural anxieties, not just police work, can explain the decline.

When it came to serial killing, Stephen Griffiths did everything by the book. He targeted prostitutes in the slums of Bradford, a city in Northern England. He chose a unique murder weapon: a crossbow. He claimed to have eaten parts of his victims — two of them cooked, one of them raw. "I'm misanthropic," he told police investigators when he was finally caught in 2010. "I don't have much time for the human race." When he appeared in court, he gave his name as the "crossbow cannibal." It was as if he'd studied up on the art of serial murder. (In fact, he had: Griffiths was a part-time PhD student at Bradford University, where he was studying criminology.) And yet, for all his efforts, he got only one short blurb in the *New York Times* when he was sentenced last month.

Serial killers just aren't the sensation they used to be. They haven't disappeared, of course. Last month, Suffolk County, New York, police found the bodies of four women dumped near a beach in Long Island. Philadelphia police have attributed the murders of three women in the city's Kensington neighborhood to one "Kensington Strangler." On Tuesday, an accused serial stabber in Flint, Michigan, filed an insanity plea.

But the number of serial murders seems to be dwindling, as does the public's fascination with them. "It does seem the golden age of serial murderers is probably past," says Harold Schechter, a professor at Queens College of the City University of New York who studies crime.

Statistics on serial murder are hard to come by — the FBI doesn't keep   4
numbers, according to a spokeswoman — but the data we do have suggests
serial murders peaked in the 1980s and have been declining ever since. James
Alan Fox, a criminology professor at Northeastern University and coauthor
of *Extreme Killing: Understanding Serial and Mass Murder*, keeps a database of
confirmed serial murderers starting in 1900. According to his count, based on
newspaper clippings, books, and Web sources, there were only a dozen or so
serial killers before 1960 in the United States. Then serial killings took off:
There were 19 in the 1960s, 119 in the '70s, and 200 in the '80s. In the '90s,
the number of cases dropped to 141. And the 2000s saw only 61 serial murderers. (Definitions of *serial murder* vary, but Fox defines it as "a string of four or
more homicides committed by one or a few perpetrators that spans a period
of days, weeks, months, or even years." To avoid double-counting, he assigns
killers to the decade in which they reached the midpoint of their careers.)

There are plenty of structural explanations for the rise of reported serial   5
murders through the 1980s. Data collection and record-keeping improved,
making it easier to find cases of serial murder. Law enforcement developed
more sophisticated methods of investigation, enabling police to identify link-
ages between cases — especially across states — that they would have otherwise ignored. The media's growing obsession with serial killers in the 1970s and
'80s may have created a minor snowball effect, offering a short path to celebrity.

But those factors don't explain away the decline in serial murders since   6
1990. If anything, they make it more significant. Then why the downtrend?

Trends in Serial Killing

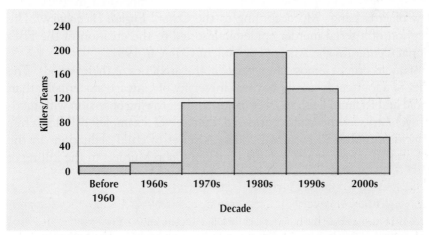

Source: James Alan Fox and Jack Levin. *Extreme Killing: Understanding Serial and Mass Murder*. Sage Publications, 2011.

It's hard to say. Better law enforcement could have played a role, as police catch would-be serial killers after their first crime. So could the increased incarceration rate, says Fox: "Maybe they're still behind bars." Whatever the reason, the decline in serial murders tracks with a dramatic drop in overall violent crime since the '80s. (One caveat: The numbers for the 2000s may skew low, since some serial killers haven't been caught yet.)

As the raw numbers have declined, the media have paid less attention,   7
too. Sure, you've still got the occasional Beltway sniper or Grim Sleeper who terrorizes a community. But nothing in the last decade has captured the popular imagination like the sex-addled psychopaths of the '70s and '80s, such as Ted Bundy (feigned injuries to win sympathy before killing women; about thirty victims), John Wayne Gacy (stored bodies in his ceiling crawl-space; thirty-three victims), or Jeffrey Dahmer (kept body parts in his closet and freezer; seventeen victims). These crimes caused media frenzies in part because of the way they tapped into the obsessions and fears of the time: Bundy, a golden boy who worked on Nelson Rockefeller's presidential cam-paign in Seattle, seemed to represent the evil lurking beneath America's cheery exterior. Gacy, who dressed up as a clown and preyed on teenage boys, was every parent's nightmare. "Son of Sam" David Berkowitz milked — and, in so doing, mocked — the media's obsession with serial killers by sending a letter to *New York Daily News* reporter Jimmy Breslin.

The media returned the favor, inflating the perception that serial kill-   8
ers were everywhere and repeating the erroneous statistic that there were five thousand serial murder victims every year. These horror stories were not exactly discouraged by the FBI, one of whose agents coined the term "serial killer" in 1981. (The phrase "serial murderer" first appeared in 1961, in a review of Fritz Lang's M,[1] according to the *Oxford English Dictionary*.) The perception of a serial murder epidemic also led to the creation of the FBI's National Center for the Analysis of Violent Crime in 1981.

Infamous crimes almost always needle the anxieties of their periods. The   9
murder of a fourteen-year-old boy by University of Chicago students Nathan Leopold and Richard Loeb in 1924 captured the growing obsession with mod-ern psychiatry, as the pair considered themselves examples of Nietzsche's *Übermensch*,[2] unbound by moral codes. A series of child abductions in the 1920s and '30s, from the Wineville Chicken Coop Murders to the killing of

---

[1] A 1931 movie about the hunt for a child killer in Germany. — Eds.
[2] Friedrich Nietzsche (1844–1900) was a German philosopher. The concept of *Über-mensch*, loosely translated as "superhuman," embodies his idea that human beings should strive for God-like perfection. — Eds.

Charles Lindbergh's son, became a symbol of societal decay during the Depression. Charles Manson, who presided over the Tate murders in 1969, embodied a sexual revolution gone mad. The Columbine massacre preyed on parental fears of the effects of violent movies and video games.

Conversely, sensational crimes that *don't* play into a larger societal narrative fade away. In 1927, Andrew Kehoe detonated three bombs at a school in Bath Township, Michigan, killing thirty-eight children and seven adults, including Kehoe — one of the largest cases of domestic terrorism before the Oklahoma City bombing in 1995. The disaster made headlines, but was soon eclipsed by Charles Lindbergh's trans-Atlantic flight. "It was a crime that was ahead of its time," says Schechter.   10

Indeed, if something like the Bath School massacre happened today, it would probably resonate more deeply than it did in the 1920s. What child abductors were to the '20s and serial killers were to the '70s and '80s, terrorists are to the early twenty-first century. After 9/11, fear of social unraveling has been replaced by anxiety over airplanes, bombs, and instant mass annihilation. Stephen Griffiths isn't the new Jeffrey Dahmer. The Times Square bomber is.   11

Journal Writing

Since Beam wrote this essay, "something like the Bath School massacre" (par. 11) *did* occur. On December 14, 2012, a shooter forced his way into Sandy Hook Elementary School in Newtown, Connecticut, murdering twenty children and six adults before turning the gun on himself. And as Beam predicted, the slaughter of innocents touched a nerve in the national consciousness. How did you react to the news? In your journal, write down what you recall most vividly about your emotions in the wake of the shooting.

Questions on Meaning

1. What seems to be Beam's primary PURPOSE in this piece? Does he want to inform his readers about a trend? express relief that serial killings are on the decline? expose a new threat to public safety? propose a theory? How can you tell?

2. Although Beam gives details about some of the killers he discusses, he mentions others — such as the Beltway sniper, the Grim Sleeper, David Berkowitz, the Times Square bomber — without explaining who they are or what they did. Why? What ASSUMPTIONS does he make about his readers' interests and knowledge? Must one be familiar with the particulars of the crimes Beam cites to understand his point?

3. According to Beam, what role do the media play in the rise and fall of certain types of crime? Does he really mean to suggest that journalists are at least partly to blame for the spike in serial murders in the 1980s?

4. How would you summarize Beam's THESIS? Where in the essay does he state it most directly?

Questions on Writing Strategy

1. Why do you think Beam opens his essay as he does? What is the EFFECT of this opening?

2. What does Beam mean by "structural explanations" (par. 5)? What point is he making here?

3. How does Beam explain the drop in serial killings over the past two decades? What possible causes does he dismiss?

4. In paragraph 4 and the bar graph on page 421, Beam cites a number of statistics, or facts expressed numerically. How reliable are these statistics? What do they accomplish?

5. **OTHER METHODS**   Where in the essay does Beam use DEFINITION to clarify the meaning of *serial murder*?

Questions on Language

1. Find some examples of formal and informal DICTION in the essay. What is the effect of Beam's word choice?

2. What does Beam mean by "golden boy" in paragraph 7? What are the CONNOTA-TIONS of this term, especially as applied to Ted Bundy?

3. If any of the following words are new to you, look them up in a dictionary: cross-bow, misanthropic, criminology (par. 1); incarceration, caveat (6); feigned (7); erroneous, epidemic (8); needle (9); conversely, eclipsed (10); annihilation (11).

Suggestions for Writing

1. **FROM JOURNAL TO ESSAY**   The horror at Newtown, and several mass shootings since then, has sparked a movement to stop publicizing the names of shooters, as the media attention is thought to encourage others to seek a similar limelight. Research the major ARGUMENTS that have taken shape on both sides of the issue since December 2012. Then build on the emotions you described in your journal entry (p. 361) to argue your position on some aspect of the debate. Do mass murderers kill for the attention, or do other motives come into play? Can their actions be considered a form of terrorism? How has the continued threat of such attacks affected your life and the lives of others you know? How has the threat affected the country more generally? Do journalists have an obligation to identify

mass shooters by name, or should they focus solely on the victims? Why do you think so? Make appropriate emotional APPEALS as you draft your essay, but be sure to keep your argument grounded in reason.

2. Choose a subject that has seen significant change in the past twenty years or so — for example, gender roles, communication technology, fashion, manners, a particular sport, ideals of beauty, or attitudes toward a particular group such as gays and lesbians, African Americans, Muslims, or immigrants. Do some research on the topic, and then write an essay that examines the causes and effects of the change. Support your essay with specific EVIDENCE from your experience, observation, and research.

3. **CRITICAL WRITING** Take a close look at Beam's use of SUMMARY, PARAPHRASE, and direct QUOTATION. In an essay, analyze the way he SYNTHESIZES information and ideas from SOURCES. Why does he quote directly where he does? How effective are his summaries and paraphrases? How does he combine source materials to develop a thesis of his own?

4. **CONNECTIONS** Like Christopher Beam, Guillermo del Toro and Chuck Hogan, in "Vampires Never Die" (p. 282), and Alain de Botton, in "Tragedy" (p. 199), also examine mass media. What do news outlets have in common with popular culture productions such as movies and TV dramas? How are they different? Drawing on the ideas presented in all three essays as well as your own experience and observations, write an essay of your own that considers the ways in which the media both reflect and shape cultural anxieties, whether for good or bad.

ADDITIONAL WRITING TOPICS

Cause and Effect

1. In *Blue Highways* (1982), an account of his rambles around the United States, William Least Heat-Moon explains why Americans, and not the British, settled the vast tract of northern land that lies between the Mississippi and the Rockies. He traces what he believes to be the major cause in this paragraph:

> Were it not for a web-footed rodent and a haberdashery fad in eighteenth-century Europe, Minnesota might be a Canadian province today. The beaver, almost as much as the horse, helped shape the course of early American history. Some *Mayflower* colonists paid their passage with beaver pelts; and a good fur could bring an Indian three steel knives or a five-foot stack could bring a musket. But even more influential were the trappers and fur traders penetrating the great Northern wilderness between the Mississippi River and the Rocky Mountains, since it was their presence that helped hold the Near West against British expansion from the north; and it was their explorations that opened the heart of the nation to white settlement. These men, by making pelts the currency of the wilds, laid the base for a new economy that quickly overwhelmed the old. And all because European men of mode simply had to wear a beaver hat.

In a Heat-Moon–like paragraph of your own, explain how a small cause produced a large effect. You might generate ideas by browsing in a history book—where you might find, for instance, that a cow belonging to Mrs. Patrick O'Leary is believed to have started the Great Chicago Fire of 1871 by kicking over a lighted lantern—or a collection of *Ripley's Believe It or Not*. If some small event in your life has had large consequences, you might care to write instead from personal experience.

2. In an essay, explain *either* the causes *or* the effects of a situation that concerns you. Narrow your topic enough to treat it in some detail, and provide more than a mere list of causes or effects. If you focus on causes, you will have to decide carefully how far back to go in your search for remote causes. If stating effects, fill your essay with examples. Here are some topics to consider:

Labor strikes in professional sports

Rising hostility in partisan politics

State laws mandating the use of seat belts in cars or the wearing of helmets when riding motorcycles

Efforts to make police forces more ethnically diverse

The fact that women increasingly take jobs formerly regarded as being for men only, and vice versa

Some quirk in your personality, or a friend's

Income inequality

The invention of 3D printing

The popularity of a particular TV program, comic strip, or performer

The steady increase in college costs

The absence of a military draft

The fact that many couples are choosing to have only one child, or none at all

Being "born again"

The emphasis on competitive sports in high school and college

The pressure on students to get a good grade

The scarcity of people training for employment as skilled workers: plumbers, tool and die makers, electricians, masons, and carpenters, to name a few

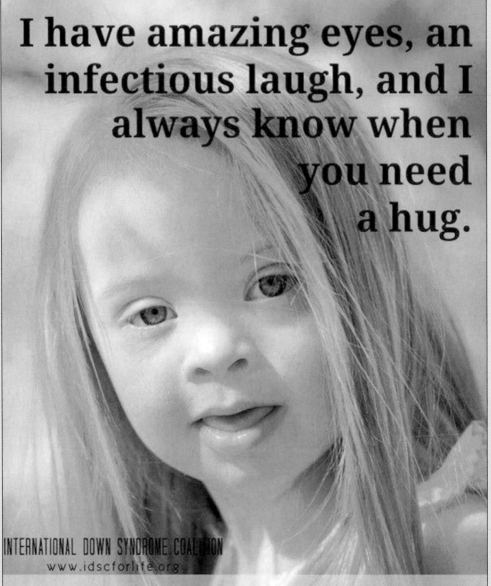

I also have Down syndrome.
It's a part of me, not a
definition of who I am.

International Down Syndrome Coalition

11

DEFINITION

Tracing Boundaries

◀ **Definition in a poster**

This social media poster doesn't define *Down syndrome*. Instead, it invites viewers to rethink their assumptions about people who have the condition. The poster is part of a "photo campaign" launched by the International Down Syndrome Coalition, a volunteer support and advocacy group. Family members submit pictures of their loved ones and work with the IDSC to create captions that highlight the dignity and achievements of people with Down syndrome; the group then distributes the posters on *Twitter, Facebook*, and *Pinterest*. Who seem to be the intended viewers of such photos? What goals of the advocacy group does the campaign seem meant to address? What needs and concerns in viewers might the poster appeal to? What does the photograph of the girl contribute to the appeal? What does the text contribute, and why are some words printed in color? At the same time, what concerns in viewers does the poster ignore or even reject?

THE METHOD

As a rule, when we hear the word DEFINITION, we immediately think of a dictionary. In that helpful storehouse — a writer's best friend — we find the literal and specific meaning (or meanings) of a word. The dictionary supplies this information concisely: in a sentence, in a phrase, or even in a *synonym* — a single word that means the same thing ("**narrative** [năr-e-tĭv] *n.* **1:** story . . .").

Stating such a definition is often a good way to begin an essay when basic terms may be in doubt. A short definition can clarify your subject to your reader, and perhaps help you limit what you have to say. If, for instance, you are writing a psychology paper about schizophrenia, you might offer a short definition at the outset, clarifying your subject and your key term.

In constructing a short definition, the usual procedure is to state the general class to which the subject belongs and then add any particular features that distinguish it. You could say: "Schizophrenia is a brain disease" — the general class — "whose symptoms include hallucinations, disorganized behavior, incoherence, and, often, withdrawal." Short definitions are useful whenever you introduce a technical term that readers may not know.

When a term is central to your essay or likely to be misunderstood, a *stipulative definition* may be more helpful. This fuller explanation stipulates, or specifies, the particular way you are using a term. The following paragraph, defining *TV addiction*, could serve as a stipulative definition in an essay about the causes and cures of the addiction.

> Who is addicted to television? According to Marie Winn, author of *The Plug-in Drug: Television, Children, and Family Life*, TV addicts are similar to drug or alcohol addicts: They seek a more pleasurable experience than they can get from normal life; they depend on the source of this pleasure; and their lives are damaged by their dependency. TV addicts, says Winn, use television to screen out the real world of feelings, worries, demands. They watch compulsively — four, five, even six hours on a work day. And they reject (usually passively, sometimes actively) interaction with family or friends, work at hobbies or chores, and chances for change and growth.

In this chapter we are mainly concerned with *extended definition*, a kind of expository writing that relies on a variety of other methods. Suppose you wanted to write an essay to make clear what *poetry* means. You would specify its elements — rhythm, IMAGES, and so on — by using DIVISION or ANALYSIS. You'd probably provide EXAMPLES of each element. You might COMPARE AND CONTRAST poetry with prose. You might discuss the EFFECT of poetry on the reader. In fact, extended definition is perhaps less a method in itself than the application of a variety of methods to achieve a purpose. Like DESCRIPTION, extended definition tries to *show* a reader its subject. It does so by establishing boundaries, as its writer tries to differentiate a subject from anything that might be confused with it.

An extended definition can define a word (like *poetry*), a thing (a laser beam), a condition (schizophrenia), a concept (TV addiction), or a general phenomenon (the popularity of *SnapChat*). Unlike a sentence definition or any you would find in a dictionary, an extended definition takes room: at least a paragraph, often an entire essay. Also unlike a dictionary definition, which sets forth meaning in an unimpassioned manner, an extended definition often reflects or champions the author's bias. When Tal Fortgang, in his essay in this chapter, seeks to define the word *privilege*, he examines his experiences as a white male, specifying the meaning of his subject in a particular political context.

THE PROCESS

Discovery of Meanings

The purpose of almost any extended definition is to explore a topic in its full complexity, to explain its meaning or sometimes to argue for (or against) a particular meaning. To discover this complexity, you may find it useful to ask yourself the following questions. To illustrate how the questions might work, at least in one instance, let's say you plan to write a paper defining *sexism*.[1]

- **Is this subject unique, or are there others of its kind? If it resembles others, in what ways? How is it different?** These questions invite you to compare and contrast. Applied to the concept of sexism, they might prompt you to compare sexism with one or two other -isms, such as racism or ageism. Or the questions might remind you that sexists can be both women and men, leading you to note the differences.

- **In what different forms does it occur, while keeping its own identity?** Specific examples might occur to you: a story you read about a woman's experiences in the army and a girlfriend who is nastily suspicious of all men. Each form — the soldier and the girlfriend — might rate a description.

- **When and where do we find it? Under what circumstances and in what situations?** Well, where have you been lately? at any parties where sexism reared its ugly head? in any classroom discussions? Consider other areas of your experience: Did you encounter any sexists while holding a job?

---

[1] The six questions that follow are freely adapted from those first stated by Richard E. Young, Alton L. Becker, and Kenneth L. Pike in *Rhetoric: Discovery and Change* (1970).

Definition

- **What is it at the present moment?** Perhaps you might make the point that sexism was once considered an exclusively male preserve but is now an attribute of women as well. Or you could observe that many men have gone underground with their sexism, refraining from expressing it blatantly while still harboring negative attitudes about women. In either case you might care to draw examples from life.

- **What does it do? What are its functions and activities?** Sexists stereotype and sometimes act to exclude or oppress people of the opposite sex. These questions might also invite you to reply with a PROCESS ANALYSIS: You might show, for instance, how a personnel director who determines pay scales systematically eliminates women from better-paying jobs.

- **How is it put together? What parts make it up? What holds these parts together?** You could apply analysis to the various beliefs and assumptions that, all together, make up sexism. This question might work well in writing about an organization: the personnel director's company, for instance, with its unfair hiring and promotion policies.

Not all these questions will fit every subject under the sun, and some may lead nowhere, but you will usually find them well worth asking. They can make you aware of points to notice, remind you of facts you already know. They can also suggest interesting aspects you need to find out more about.

Methods of Development

The preceding questions will give you a good start in using whatever method or methods of writing can best answer the overall question "What is the nature of this subject?" You will probably find yourself making use of much that you have learned earlier in this book. A short definition like the one for *schizophrenia* on page 368 may be a good start for an essay, especially if readers need a quick grounding in the subject. (But feel no duty to place a dictionaryish definition in the INTRODUCTION of every essay you write: The device is overused.) In explaining schizophrenia, if your readers already have at least a vague idea of the meaning of the term and need no short, formal definition of it, you could open your extended definition with a description of the experiences of a person who has the disease:

> On his twenty-fifth birthday, Michael sensed danger everywhere. The voices in his head argued loudly about whether he should step outside. He could see people walking by who he knew meant him harm — the trick would be to wait for a break in the traffic and make a run for it. But the arguing and another noise — a clanging like a streetcar bell — made it difficult to concentrate, and Michael paced restlessly most of the day.

You could proceed from this opening to explain how Michael's experiences illustrate some symptoms of schizophrenia. You could provide other examples of symptoms. You could, through process analysis, explain how the disease generally starts and progresses. You could use CAUSE AND EFFECT to explore some theories of why schizophrenia develops.

Thesis

Opening up your subject with questions and developing it with various methods are good ways to see what it has to offer, but you might be left with a welter of ideas and a blurred focus. As in description, when all your details build to a DOMINANT IMPRESSION, so in definition you want to center all your ideas and evidence about the subject on a single controlling idea, a THESIS. It's not essential to state this idea in a THESIS STATEMENT, but it is essential that the idea govern.

Here, from the essays in this chapter, are two thesis statements. Notice how each makes an assertion about the subject, and how we can detect the author's bias toward the subject.

> I have checked my privilege. And I apologize for nothing.
> — Tal Fortgang, "Checking My Privilege"

> If you are reading this essay, you have some kind of privilege. It may be hard to hear that, I know, but if you cannot recognize your privilege, you have a lot of work to do; get started.
> — Roxane Gay, "Peculiar Benefits"

Evidence

Writing an extended definition, you are like a mapmaker charting a territory, taking in what lies within the boundaries and ignoring what's outside. The boundaries, of course, may be wide; and for this reason, drafting an extended definition sometimes tempts a writer to sweep across a continent and to soar off into abstract clouds. Like any other method of expository writing, though, definition will work only for the writer who remembers the world of the senses and supports every GENERALIZATION with concrete evidence.

Never lose sight of the reality you are attempting to enclose, even if its frontiers are as inclusive as those of *psychological burnout* or *human economic rights*. Give examples, narrate an illustrative story, bring in specific description — whatever method you use, keep coming back inside. Without your eyes on the world, you will define no reality. You might define *animal husbandry* till the cows come home and never make clear what it means.

Definition

FOCUS ON UNITY

When drafting a definition, you may find yourself being pulled away from your subject by the narratives, descriptions, examples, comparisons, and other methods you use to specify meaning. Let yourself explore the byways of your subject — doing so will help you discover what you think. But in revising you'll need to make sure that all paragraphs focus on your thesis and, within paragraphs, that all sentences focus on the paragraph topic, generally expressed in a TOPIC SENTENCE. In other words, you'll need to ensure the UNITY of your essay and its paragraphs.

Meghan Daum's "Narcissist — Give It a Rest" (p. 390), for instance, opens with a complaint that "a whole lot of people" (par. 1) are misusing the word *narcissist* as a general insult, then proceeds methodically to specify the word's meaning as Daum understands it. As shown in the following outline, the paragraphs begin with topic sentences that state parts of the definition, which Daum then illustrates with examples and analyses.

PARAGRAPH 2	The concept of narcissism as a broad cultural condition, and the word's use as an everyday term, goes back several decades. . . .
PARAGRAPH 3	But lately the word seems to be enjoying a resurgence, often among people who give the impression that they just discovered it. . . .
PARAGRAPH 5	Here's the problem with the charge of narcissism. . . .
PARAGRAPH 7	So perhaps it's time to declare a moratorium on the indiscriminate use of this particular n-word. . . .

CHECKLIST FOR REVISING A DEFINITION

✔ **Meanings.** Have you explored your subject fully, turning up both its obvious and its not-so-obvious meanings?

✔ **Methods of development.** Have you used an appropriate range of other methods to develop your subject?

✔ **Thesis.** Have you focused your definition and kept within that focus, drawing clear boundaries around your subject?

✔ **Evidence.** Is your definition specific? Do examples, anecdotes, and concrete details both pin the subject down and make it vivid for readers?

✔ **Unity.** Do all paragraphs focus on your thesis, and do individual paragraphs or groups of paragraphs focus on parts of your definition?

DEFINITION IN ACADEMIC WRITING

A Biology Textbook

This paragraph from *Life: The Science of Biology*, by William K. Purves and Gordon H. Orians, defines a term, *homology*, that is useful in explaining the evolution of different species from a common ancestor (the topic at this point in the textbook). The paragraph provides a brief definition, a more extensive one, and finally examples of the concept.

When the character traits found in any two species owe their resemblance to a common ancestry, taxonomists say the states are *homologous*, or are *homologues* of each other. *Homology* is defined as correspondence between two structures due to inheritance from a common ancestor. Homologous structures can be identical in appearance and can even be based on identical genes. However, such structures can diverge until they become very different in both appearance and function. Nevertheless, homologous structures usually retain certain basic features that betray a common ancestry. Consider the forelimbs of vertebrates. It is easy to make a detailed, bone-by-bone, muscle-by-muscle comparison of the forearm of a person and a monkey and to conclude that the forearms, as well as the various parts of the forearm, are homologous. The forelimb of a dog, however, shows marked differences from those of primates in both appearance and function. The forelimb is used for locomotion by dogs but for grasping and manipulation by people and monkeys. Even so, all of the bones can still be matched. The wing of a bird and the flipper of a seal are even more different from each other or from the human forearm, yet they too are constructed around bones that can be matched on a nearly perfect one-to-one basis.

Definition of homology *and related words*

Short definition

Refined definition

Examples:
- *Similar appearance, function, and structure*
- *Dissimilar appearance and function, but similar structure*

An Essay Exam

You might worry about essay exams — many students do — but take heart: Instructors who assign timed essays don't expect prize-winning compositions. They expect students to demonstrate their knowledge and critical thinking about important concepts covered in lectures and assignments.

Often you'll need to interpret the wording of an exam question to figure out what kind of response is appropriate. Questions that ask *why*, for example, might call for CAUSE-AND-EFFECT analysis, while those that ask *how* might lead to a PROCESS ANALYSIS. Keep in mind that an essay you write for an in-class exam will be less polished than one you write at home.

Definition

That's fine — as long as you draft an accurate, detailed, and coherent answer to the question asked.

The midterm exam for Martin Ward's introductory government class included multiple-choice questions, a short-answer section, and one essay question: "Explain the meaning of *civil liberties*, including an explanation of how civil liberties differ from civil rights." Ward quickly recognized that "explain the meaning of" called for a definition and that "differ" called for an element of COMPARISON AND CONTRAST. Following the advice of the teaching assistant in the exam review session, Ward quickly outlined the points he needed to cover before he started writing. Then he composed the following response.

Civil liberties are the freedoms that individuals have against state intrusion. Laws protecting civil liberties limit or prohibit government action. The Constitution's Bill of Rights guarantees many of these liberties, including freedom of expression, freedom of religion, and freedom from unreasonable searches and seizures. Historically, the protection of civil liberties was established before the US Constitution in documents such as the English Magna Carta (1215). Since that time, free countries have defined themselves against authoritarian countries by their respect for — and legal protections of — these freedoms.

Short definition of *civil liberties*

Examples

Brief history of the concept

While most people agree that civil liberties are essential to a free state, there is some controversy surrounding their meaning. People don't always agree which rights are civil liberties. For example, the debate over abortion reflects a dispute over whether the Constitution protects privacy rights that include the right to have an abortion. There is also disagreement about what constitutes a violation of civil liberties. As the federal government has taken measures to protect the country from terrorism, many have questioned whether practices such as warrantless wiretapping violate privacy rights, speech rights, or the prohibition of unreasonable searches and seizures.

Extended definition considers issues that complicate meaning:

• Which rights are civil liberties?

• What violates civil liberties?

People often confuse civil liberties with civil rights. Civil liberties are freedoms from government intrusion protected primarily by the Bill of Rights. Civil rights, however, concern the equal treatment of individuals in society and are established mainly by the Equal Protection Clause of the Fourteenth

Point-by-point contrast with civil rights

Amendment. An example is the right of citizens to attend public schools regardless of their color or gender. Civil liberties and civil rights differ in another important way as well: While protections of civil liberties prohibit government action, the government must often act to protect civil rights, as in the creation of antidiscrimination laws.

TAL FORTGANG

Tal Fortgang is a student at Princeton University, majoring in politics. Born in 1994, he grew up in New Rochelle, New York, graduated from SAR High School (an Orthodox Jewish academy) in the Bronx, and then studied the Talmud for a year in Israel. After college he plans to attend law school and pursue a career that combines his two major passions: American political thought and hockey.

Checking My Privilege

Fortgang wrote this essay as a freshman and published it in *The Princeton Tory*, a conservative campus journal, in 2014. Shortly thereafter, *Time* magazine reprinted it for a national audience, generating a flurry of discussion online. As you'll see, Fortgang was inspired by a criticism leveled at him in class to examine his own experiences and to question the intent of an accusation that he believes is heard on campus all too often.

The essay following this one, Roxane Gay's "Peculiar Benefits," responds indirectly to Fortgang and counters his point about context and meaning.

There is a phrase that floats around college campuses, Princeton being no exception, that threatens to strike down opinions without regard for their merits, but rather solely on the basis of the person that voiced them. "Check your privilege," the saying goes, and I have been reprimanded by it several times this year. The phrase, handed down by my moral superiors, descends recklessly, like an Obama-sanctioned drone, and aims laser-like at my pinkish-peach complexion, my maleness, and the nerve I displayed in offering an opinion rooted in a personal Weltanschauung.[1] "Check your privilege," they tell me in a command that teeters between an imposition to actually explore how I got where I am, and a reminder that I ought to feel personally apologetic because white males seem to pull most of the strings in the world.

I do not accuse those who "check" me and my perspective of overt racism, although the phrase, which assumes that simply because I belong to a certain ethnic group I should be judged collectively with it, toes that line. But I do condemn them for diminishing everything I have personally accomplished, all the hard work I have done in my life, and for ascribing all the fruit I reap

---

[1] German word meaning, roughly, worldview or philosophy. — EDS.

not to the seeds I sow but to some invisible patron saint of white maleness who places it out for me before I even arrive. Furthermore, I condemn them for casting the equal protection clause, indeed the very idea of a meritocracy, as a myth, and for declaring that we are all governed by invisible forces (some would call them "stigmas" or "societal norms"), that our nation runs on racist and sexist conspiracies. Forget "you didn't build that";[2] check your privilege and realize that nothing you have accomplished is real.

But they can't be telling me that everything I've done with my life can   3
be credited to the racist patriarchy holding my hand throughout my years of education and eventually guiding me into Princeton. Even that is too extreme. So to find out what they are saying, I decided to take their advice. I actually went and checked the origins of my privileged existence, to empathize with those whose underdog stories I can't possibly comprehend. I have unearthed some examples of the privilege with which my family was blessed, and now I think I better understand those who assure me that skin color allowed my family and me to flourish today.

Perhaps it's the privilege my grandfather and his brother had to flee their   4
home as teenagers when the Nazis invaded Poland, leaving their mother and five younger siblings behind, running and running until they reached a Displaced Persons camp in Siberia, where they would do years of hard labor in the bitter cold until World War II ended. Maybe it was the privilege my grandfather had of taking on the local Rabbi's work in that DP camp, telling him that the spiritual leader shouldn't do hard work, but should save his energy to pass Jewish tradition along to those who might survive. Perhaps it was the privilege my great-grandmother and those five great-aunts and uncles I never knew had of being shot into an open grave outside their hometown. Maybe that's my privilege.

Or maybe it's the privilege my grandmother had of spending weeks upon   5
weeks on a death march through Polish forests in subzero temperatures, one of just a handful to survive, only to be put in Bergen-Belsen concentration camp where she would have died but for the Allied forces who liberated her and helped her regain her health when her weight dwindled to barely eighty pounds.

Perhaps my privilege is that those two resilient individuals came to America   6
with no money and no English, obtained citizenship, learned the language and met each other; that my grandfather started a humble wicker basket business with nothing but long hours, an idea, and an iron will — to paraphrase the man I never met: "I escaped Hitler. Some business troubles are going to ruin me?"

---

[2] Phrase from a 2012 campaign speech in which President Barack Obama argued that individual successes arise from the support of others. — Eds.

Maybe my privilege is that they worked hard enough to raise four children, and to send them to Jewish day school and eventually City College.

Perhaps it was my privilege that my own father worked hard enough in 7 City College to earn a spot at a top graduate school, got a good job, and for twenty-five years got up well before the crack of dawn, sacrificing precious time he wanted to spend with those he valued most — his wife and kids — to earn that living. I can say with certainty there was no legacy involved in any of his accomplishments. The wicker business just isn't that influential. Now would you say that we've been really privileged? That our success has been gift-wrapped?

That's the problem with calling someone out for the "privilege" which 8 you assume has defined their narrative. You don't know what their struggles have been, what they may have gone through to be where they are. Assuming they've benefitted from "power systems" or other conspiratorial imaginary institutions denies them credit for all they've done, things of which you may not even conceive. You don't know whose father died defending your freedom. You don't know whose mother escaped oppression. You don't know who conquered their demons, or may still be conquering them now.

The truth is, though, that I have been exceptionally privileged in my life, 9 albeit not in the way any detractors would have it.

It has been my distinct privilege that my grandparents came to America. 10 First, that there was a place at all that would take them from the ruins of Europe. And second, that such a place was one where they could legally enter, learn the language, and acclimate to a society that ultimately allowed them to flourish.

It was their privilege to come to a country that grants equal protection 11 under the law to its citizens, that cares not about religion or race, but the content of your character.

It was my privilege that my grandfather was blessed with resolve and an 12 entrepreneurial spirit, and that he was lucky enough to come to the place where he could realize the dream of giving his children a better life than he had.

But far more important for me than his attributes was the legacy he sought 13 to pass along, which forms the basis of what detractors call my "privilege," but which actually should be praised as one of altruism and self-sacrifice. Those who came before us suffered for the sake of giving us a better life. When we similarly sacrifice for our descendents by caring for the planet, it's called "environmentalism," and is applauded. But when we do it by passing along property and a set of values, it's called "privilege." (And when we do it by raising questions about our crippling national debt, we're called Tea Party radicals.) Such sacrifice of any form shouldn't be scorned, but admired.

My exploration did yield some results. I recognize that it was my parents' 14
privilege and now my own that there is such a thing as an American dream
which is attainable even for a penniless Jewish immigrant.

I am privileged that values like faith and education were passed along 15
to me. My grandparents played an active role in my parents' education, and
some of my earliest memories included learning the Hebrew alphabet with
my Dad. It's been made clear to me that education begins in the home, and
the importance of parents' involvement with their kids' education — from
mathematics to morality — cannot be overstated. It's not a matter of white or
black, male or female or any other division which we seek, but a matter of the
values we pass along, the legacy we leave, that perpetuates "privilege." And
there's nothing wrong with that.

Behind every success, large or small, there is a story, and it isn't always 16
told by sex or skin color. My appearance certainly doesn't tell the whole story,
and to assume that it does and that I should apologize for it is insulting. While
I haven't done everything for myself up to this point in my life, someone
sacrificed themselves so that I can lead a better life. But that is a legacy I am
proud of.

I have checked my privilege. And I apologize for nothing. 17

Journal Writing

As a college student, have you ever been told, or heard someone else be told, "Check
your privilege"? What was your reaction? In your journal, reflect on the advantages
and disadvantages you believe may have helped or hindered you in establishing your
current position in life. How do you think others perceive your background?

Questions on Meaning

1. How does Fortgang define the customary use of "Check your privilege" (par. 1)?
   What does he interpret the phrase to mean?

2. Fortgang acknowledges that he has "been exceptionally privileged in [his] life,
   albeit not in the way any detractors would have it" (par. 9). In what way (or ways)
   does he consider himself privileged? Why does he resent implications that his
   color and gender have given him any advantages?

3. To what is Fortgang referring when he mentions the "equal protection clause"
   (par. 2) and "equal protection under the law" (11)? Why does he invoke this
   concept?

4. What would you say is Fortgang's primary PURPOSE in this essay? How well does
   he succeed?

Questions on Writing Strategy

1. Who was Fortgang's intended AUDIENCE? How do you suppose he expected readers to respond? What do you think he hoped they would take away from their reading? What in the essay supports your answer?

2. In his first three paragraphs Fortgang discusses privilege in the ABSTRACT. How are these paragraphs connected to his stories about his family's history? Why do you think he begins the essay this way? Is this INTRODUCTION effective or not? Why?

3. Identify the TRANSITIONS Fortgang repeats in paragraphs 4–7 and 9–12. How do they create UNITY and COHERENCE in his definition?

4. Look back at the last two sentences of Fortgang's essay. What is the EFFECT of ending on this idea?

5. **OTHER METHODS**   Fortgang's definition is based largely on EXAMPLES and CAUSE-AND-EFFECT. Does his analysis seem sound to you? Do you think he overemphasizes any causes or effects or overlooks others? Explain.

Questions on Language

1. Give some examples of FIGURES OF SPEECH in Fortgang's essay. Do any *metaphors* or *similes* strike you as particularly fresh and inventive?

2. Why does Fortgang put quotation marks around "privilege" at some points in his essay? What other words and phrases does he single out this way?

3. The phrase "content of your character" (par. 11) comes from the famous civil rights speech "I Have a Dream" by Martin Luther King, Jr.: "I have a dream," he said, "that my four little children will one day live in a nation where they will not be judged by the color of their skin but by the content of their character." How does this ALLUSION serve Fortgang?

4. If you don't know the meanings of the following words, look them up in a dictionary: reprimanded, imposition (par. 1); overt, condemn, ascribing, meritocracy, stigmas, conspiracies (2); patriarchy, empathize (3); resilient (6); legacy (7); conspiratorial, conceive, oppression (8); detractors (9); acclimate (10); resolve, entrepreneurial (12); attributes, altruism, descendents (13); perpetuates (15).

Suggestions for Writing

1. **FROM JOURNAL TO ESSAY**   Based on your journal writing (p. 379), compose an essay in which you define your own privilege (or lack thereof). What advantages and disadvantages do you share with other people like you, and which are particular to yourself or your family? Be sure your essay has a clear THESIS and plenty of examples to make your definition precise.

2. Think about the values Fortgang cites in paragraphs 13 and 15: "altruism," "self-sacrifice," "faith," "education," "morality." Choose one of these words, or another

of the values Fortgang mentions in the essay, and write an essay that explains its meanings for you. Use examples from your own experience, observations, and reading to make the definition complete.

3. Research the history of Jewish immigration to the United States. When and why did the initial wave of immigration occur? What forces have led to other patterns of immigration over the years? Have Jewish Americans faced different kinds of discrimination or enjoyed different opportunities than other immigrants have? In an essay, answer these or other questions that occur to you.

4. **CRITICAL WRITING**   Evaluate Fortgang's TONE in this essay. What contributes to this tone, and to what extent does it serve his purpose in writing? How might a different tone have changed your response to the essay?

5. **CONNECTIONS**   The next essay, Roxane Gay's "Peculiar Benefits," examines privilege from the perspective of a woman born to Haitian immigrants. Write an essay that COMPARES AND CONTRASTS Fortgang's understanding of the concept with Gay's. How does context and personal background help to shape each writer's definition? Whose ARGUMENT do you find more persuasive, and why?

Tal Fortgang on Writing

Tal Fortgang garnered a lot of media attention — both positive and negative — with "Checking My Privilege," but he stands by his argument. In comments he wrote for this book, he reflects on his writing process and considers how being passionate about a belief can lead to a strong thesis.

I distinctly remember how the idea for this piece came to me. I was in the shower (all good ideas start in the shower; the best piece of advice I can give you is if you're stuck or out of good ideas, take a hot shower and let your mind wander) and thinking about how certain things, like money or values, are passed from generation to generation. So I started thinking about possible arguments against estate taxes, wherein I might contend that governments were taking too much money from parents who saved up in hopes of passing down to their children. This tax, to me, was antithetical to the "American dream." That got me thinking about "privilege" and how it was being framed on my campus: Is there something wrong with my parents' and grandparents' hard work being passed along? Not that my family is fabulously wealthy by any stretch, but should I be embarrassed that someone before me wanted to give me a better life, and was successful in allowing me to be born into comfort? And that's how I got to talking about privilege, which is way more interesting than estate taxes, in my opinion.

My method of writing is pretty unusual. I can focus on one thing really well for about forty-five minutes at a time, so I'll usually sit down and pour out everything in my head for that long (again, usually while wearing only a towel and sopping wet because if I took the time to get dressed I'd forget all my deep shower thoughts). Then I'll step away and do something else for a while before coming back an hour or few later. I still do this. I'm writing this piece the same way. I don't know if I recommend it for everyone, but if whatever you've been doing isn't working, don't be afraid to try it out.

More important than how you go about getting your writing done is the content. (I don't think anyone would disagree with that, but it seemed like a nicely authoritative topic sentence.) Central to your content is your thesis, or the thing you know you always need to have but aren't quite sure if you do or don't yet have. I think there's a way of thinking about thesis development that really simplifies the process. Here goes: Making arguments is tough, but the good news is that you probably think things. You may even believe things you think! So you're well on your way to arguing for something you think and/or believe. When you're presented with a prompt or a question or a topic, try to capture your gut-reaction answer. Now channel your inner five-year-old and ask "why?" Then ask "why?" again. And again. As many "whys" as you need to whittle your gut reaction down to its fundamental parts. When you've reached something fundamental — the "nuclear argument" is what I like to call it — you can argue that you think it is true, and is the basis of what you believe.

I'll add that it helps to argue something you deeply, truly, believe from the bottom of your heart and the entirety of your soul. Just ask yourself why you believe it. Your writing will be stronger and you might even learn something about yourself in the process.

The Brief Bedford Reader on Writing

Aside from the "sopping wet" part, Tal Fortgang's DRAFTING process isn't unusual at all. We certainly recommend you try writing freely in concentrated spurts, as time and focus allow (but you might want to put on some clothes). For additional thoughts on how you can narrow a subject until you reach your point of interest, try turning to pages 32–36 of this book. And for help developing your own "nuclear argument" with specifics — the "whys" — see "Supporting the Thesis" (pp. 36–37).

ROXANE GAY

Roxane Gay describes herself as just a "bad feminist . . . trying to make sense of this world we live in," but she is a rising star admired for crafting sharp critiques that bridge academia and popular culture with a solid sense of humor. She was born in 1974 to Haitian immigrants and grew up "a loner, shy and awkward." Shuttled around the suburbs of Nebraska, New Jersey, Colorado, Illinois, and Virginia, she read voraciously for company and wrote to entertain herself. Raped by classmates at the age of twelve, she retreated into herself and deliberately turned to overeating as a way of shielding her body and surviving the trauma. Gay graduated from Phillips Exeter Academy in New Hampshire in 1992, earned an MA in English from the University of Nebraska, Lincoln, and completed a PhD in rhetoric and technical communication at Michigan Technological University in 2010. While teaching at Eastern Illinois University and blogging innumerable essays for sites ranging from *Jezebel* to the *New York Times*, she put together her first book, *Ayiti* (2011), a mixture of poetry, fiction, and prose focused on the experiences of Haitian emigrants. In 2014 she published both *An Untamed State*, a novel, and *Bad Feminist*, a collection of essays. *Hunger*, a critical memoir of obesity, followed in 2016. Currently an associate professor at Purdue University, Gay is also an aggressive Scrabble player who regularly competes in tournaments and the founder of Tiny Hardcore Press, an experimental publishing house.

Peculiar Benefits

As a Haitian American woman "who has been queer identified at varying points in her life," Gay nonetheless considers herself extraordinarily fortunate in the opportunities that have been afforded her. In "Peculiar Benefits," she thoughtfully examines her own privilege, mildly chastising those who cannot or will not acknowledge theirs. The essay first appeared on the online forum *The Rumpus* in 2012 and was revised for inclusion in *Bad Feminist* in 2014, just as the Internet was buzzing with debate over Tal Fortgang's "Checking My Privilege" (p. 376).

When I was young, my parents took our family to Haiti during the summers. For them, it was a homecoming. For my brothers and me it was an adventure, sometimes a chore, and always a necessary education on privilege and the grace of an American passport. Until visiting Haiti, I had no idea what poverty really was or the difference between relative and absolute poverty. To see poverty so plainly and pervasively left a profound mark on me.

To this day, I remember my first visit, and how at every intersection, men   2
and women, shiny with sweat, would mob our car, their skinny arms stretched
out, hoping for a few gourdes[1] or American dollars. I saw the sprawling slums,
the shanties housing entire families, the trash piled in the streets, and also the
gorgeous beach and the young men in uniforms who brought us Coca-Cola
in glass bottles and made us hats and boats out of palm fronds. It was hard for
a child to begin to grasp the contrast of such inescapable poverty alongside
almost repulsive luxury, and then the United States, a mere eight hundred
miles away, with its gleaming cities rising out of the landscape and the well-
maintained interstates stretching across the country, the running water and
the electricity. It wasn't until many, many years later that I realized my education on privilege began long before I could appreciate it in any meaningful way.

Privilege is a right or immunity granted as a peculiar benefit, advantage, or   3
favor. There is racial privilege, gender (and identity) privilege, heterosexual
privilege, economic privilege, able-bodied privilege, educational privilege,
religious privilege, and the list goes on and on. At some point, you have to
surrender to the kinds of privilege you hold. Nearly everyone, particularly in
the developed world, has something someone else doesn't, something someone else yearns for.

The problem is, cultural critics talk about privilege with such alarming fre-   4
quency and in such empty ways, we have diluted the word's meaning. When
people wield the word "privilege," it tends to fall on deaf ears because we hear
that word so damn much it has become white noise.

One of the hardest things I've ever had to do is accept and acknowledge   5
my privilege. It's an ongoing project. I'm a woman, a person of color, and the
child of immigrants, but I also grew up middle class and then upper middle
class. My parents raised my siblings and me in a strict but loving environment.
They were and are happily married, so I didn't have to deal with divorce or
crappy intramarital dynamics. I attended elite schools. My master's and doc-
toral degrees were funded. I got a tenure-track position my first time out. My
bills are paid. I have the time and resources for frivolity. I am reasonably well
published. I have an agent and books to my name. My life has been far from
perfect, but it's somewhat embarrassing for me to accept just how much privilege I have.

It's also really difficult for me to consider the ways in which I lack privi-   6
lege or the ways in which my privilege hasn't magically rescued me from a
world of hurt. On my more difficult days, I'm not sure what's more of a pain in
my ass — being black or being a woman. I'm happy to be both of these things,

[1] Official paper currency of Haiti. One Haitian gourde is worth approximately two American
cents. — EDS.

but the world keeps intervening. There are all kinds of infuriating reminders of my place in the world — random people questioning me in the parking lot at work as if it is unfathomable that I'm a faculty member, the persistence of lawmakers trying to legislate the female body, street harassment, strangers wanting to touch my hair.

We tend to believe that accusations of privilege imply we have it easy,   7 which we resent because life is hard for nearly everyone. Of course we resent these accusations. Look at white men when they are accused of having privilege. They tend to be immediately defensive (and, at times, understandably so). They say, "It's not my fault I am a white man," or "I'm [insert other condition that discounts their privilege]," instead of simply accepting that, in this regard, yes, they benefit from certain privileges others do not. To have privilege in one or more areas does not mean you are wholly privileged. Surrendering to the acceptance of privilege is difficult, but it is really all that is expected. What I remind myself, regularly, is this: The acknowledgment of my privilege is not a denial of the ways I have been and am marginalized, the ways I have suffered.

You don't necessarily *have* to do anything once you acknowledge your   8 privilege. You don't have to apologize for it. You need to understand the extent of your privilege, the consequences of your privilege, and remain aware that people who are different from you move through and experience the world in ways you might never know anything about. They might endure situations you can never know anything about. You could, however, use that privilege for the greater good — to try to level the playing field for everyone, to work for social justice, to bring attention to how those without certain privileges are disenfranchised. We've seen what the hoarding of privilege has done, and the results are shameful.

When we talk about privilege, some people start to play a very pointless   9 and dangerous game where they try to mix and match various demographic characteristics to determine who wins at the Game of Privilege. Who would win in a privilege battle between a wealthy black woman and a wealthy white man? Who would win a privilege battle between a queer white man and a queer Asian woman? Who would win in a privilege battle between a working-class white man and a wealthy, differently abled Mexican woman? We could play this game all day and never find a winner. . . .

Too many people have become self-appointed privilege police, patrolling   10 the halls of discourse, ready to remind people of their privilege whether those people have denied that privilege or not. In online discourse, in particular, the specter of privilege is always looming darkly. When someone writes from experience, there is often someone else, at the ready, pointing a trembling finger, accusing that writer of having various kinds of privilege. How dare someone speak to a personal experience without accounting for every possible configuration of privilege or the lack thereof? We would live in a world of silence if the only people who were allowed to write or speak from experience or about difference were those absolutely without privilege.

When people wield accusations of privilege, more often than not, they 11 want to be heard and seen. Their need is acute, if not desperate, and that need rises out of the many historical and ongoing attempts to silence and render invisible marginalized groups. Must we satisfy our need to be heard and seen by preventing anyone else from being heard and seen? Does privilege automatically negate any merits of what a privilege holder has to say? Do we ignore everything, for example, that white men have to say?

We need to get to a place where we discuss privilege by way of obser- 12 vation and acknowledgment rather than accusation. We need to be able to argue beyond the threat of privilege. We need to stop playing Privilege or Oppression Olympics because we'll never get anywhere until we find more effective ways of talking through difference. We should be able to say, "This is my truth," and have that truth stand without a hundred clamoring voices shouting, giving the impression that multiple truths cannot coexist. Because at some point, doesn't privilege become beside the point?

Privilege is relative and contextual. Few people in the developed world, and 13 particularly in the United States, have no privilege at all. Among those of us who participate in intellectual communities, privilege runs rampant. We have disposable time and the ability to access the Internet regularly. We have the freedom to express our opinions without the threat of retaliation. We have smartphones and iProducts and desktops and laptops. If you are reading this essay, you have some kind of privilege. It may be hard to hear that, I know, but if you cannot recognize your privilege, you have a lot of work to do; get started.

Journal Writing

Gay's "bills are paid," she notes, and she has a good job and is "reasonably well published" (par. 5). In your journal, consider the meaning of *success*, focusing on these questions: Whom do you consider to be successful, and why? Where do your ideas of success come from — your parents? your friends? your schooling? the media?

Questions on Meaning

1. In your own words, SUMMARIZE Gay's definition of *privilege*.

2. What does Gay mean by "the difference between relative and absolute poverty" (par. 1)? How does that difference apply to her understanding of privilege?

3. What does Gay believe to be the most basic reason people object when they're "accused of having privilege" (par. 7)?

4. In paragraph 7, Gay says that acknowledging her privilege "is not a denial of the ways [she has] been and [is] marginalized." What does she mean? How do you explain this contradiction?

5. What seems to be Gay's PURPOSE in this essay? What solution to the problem of privilege does she propose? Is she optimistic or pessimistic that people can be encouraged to be more empathetic to others?

Questions on Writing Strategy

1. Why does Gay open by detailing her first family trip to Haiti? How does this INTRODUCTION lead into her subject?

2. What does Gay assume about her AUDIENCE? To what extent do you fit her assumptions?

3. Why is Gay so careful to enumerate her own privileges in paragraph 5? What is the EFFECT of her admissions?

4. **OTHER METHODS**   How does Gay use CLASSIFICATION to sort out the types of privilege she sees in the contemporary world? What categories does she identify? What, if any, forms of privilege might you add to her lists?

Questions on Language

1. Find some examples of both formal and informal DICTION in the essay. What is the effect of Gay's word choices?

2. Why does Gay capitalize the phrases "Game of Privilege" and "Oppression Olympics" in paragraphs 9 and 12? What does she mean by these terms?

3. What is "white noise" (par. 4)? Why is this metaphor particularly apt, given Gay's subject and purpose? (For a definition of *metaphor*, see FIGURES OF SPEECH in the Glossary.)

4. Notice that Gay shifts POINT OF VIEW in paragraph 8 and again in her conclusion, addressing readers directly as *you*. What is the effect of the last two sentences of the essay in particular?

5. Be sure you know the meanings of the following words, checking a dictionary if necessary: pervasively (par. 1); shanties (2); immunity, peculiar (3); intramarital, frivolity (5); intervening, unfathomable, legislate (6); marginalized (7); disenfranchised (8); demographic (9); discourse, specter, configuration (10); acute (11); clamoring (12).

Suggestions for Writing

1. **FROM JOURNAL TO ESSAY**   Compose an extended definition of *success* that includes an examination of the sources of your definition, as you explored them in your

journal writing. The sources could be negative as well as positive — that is, your ideas of success may have formed in reaction *against* others' ideas and privileges as well as in agreement with or appreciation of them.

2. Propose some course of action in a situation you consider an injustice. Racial privilege is one possible area, or unfairness to any disenfranchised group, such as women, children, the elderly, ex-convicts, the disabled, the poor. If possible, narrow your subject to a particular incident or a local situation on which you can write knowledgeably.

3. As Gay suggests in the introduction to her essay, Haiti is the poorest country in the Americas. Do some research to learn about the natural disasters and decades of social and political upheaval — including violent conflicts between the government and rebels — that have plagued the country, prompted intervention by the United Nations, and encouraged many Haitians to seek asylum in the United States. In an essay, report your findings, considering in particular the CAUSES and EFFECTS of poverty in the Caribbean islands.

4. **CRITICAL WRITING**   Write an essay examining the organization of Gay's essay. What does the author accomplish in each paragraph? How effectively does she use TRANSITIONS to move from paragraph to paragraph?

5. **CONNECTIONS**   In some ways Gay's essay is an admonition to readers to "check your privilege," the phrase that Tal Fortgang, in the previous essay (p. 376), finds so maddening. Read or reread Fortgang's essay and consider the extent to which he fits Gay's understanding of why white men in particular react badly "when they are accused of having privilege" (par. 7). How well do Gay's characterizations describe Fortgang? How might he respond to her definition?

Roxane Gay on Writing

Gay is known for writing regularly in multiple genres on any number of subjects — personal essays on her *Tumblr* blog, scholarly analyses of culture for her *New York Times* column, pithy Tweets on current events, poetry and fiction for a general audience. In a 2014 interview with Tina Essmaker for *The Great Discontent*, she explained why she writes as much as she does.

Writing is not a tortured act for me. I don't have any angst about it, and I don't find it to be a painful misery. Writing is the one endeavor that makes me purely happy, and it comes fairly easily to me. I don't know why I'm that lucky, but it's true.

There are definitely times when I have writer's block, and it's infuriating, but writers love to dramatize the suffering of the writer. I don't judge them on that, because it's their truth, but I'm suffering when I'm *not* writing: It's what

I do for fun. When people say I'm prolific, I think, "Well, it's kind of my self-medication, and it doesn't feel like work."

I'm a happy writer, and although that hasn't always been the case, I count my blessings. I'm finally in the place I've always dreamed of. Maybe my dreams weren't that big, but I just wanted to write and have people read what I had to say one way or another. I have that.

The Brief Bedford Reader on Writing

It seems that Roxane Gay's unassuming PURPOSE for writing — simply expressing herself and reaching an AUDIENCE — makes the task easy for her. How can knowing your readers and having something to say to them work for you? Turn to pages 30–32 to find out.

MEGHAN DAUM

Born in 1970 in Palo Alto, California, Meghan Daum is a writer known for provocative, witty essays on American life. Daum graduated from Vassar College with a BA in English in 1992 and earned an MA in writing from Columbia University in 1996. A former contributing editor for *Harper's Bazaar* and since 2005 a syndicated columnist for the *Los Angeles Times*, Daum has published her work in a variety of newspapers and magazines, including *The New Yorker*, *Gentlemen's Quarterly*, *Vogue*, and the *New York Times Book Review*. She is the author of a number of books, including *The Quality of Life Report* (2003), a novel; *Life Would Be Perfect If I Lived in That House* (2011), a humorous memoir; and *My Misspent Youth* (2001) and *The Unspeakable* (2014), essay collections. Winner of the 2015 PEN Center USA award for creative nonfiction, Daum is also an occasional guest on National Public Radio and has contributed to *Marketplace*, *Morning Edition*, and *This American Life*. She lives in Los Angeles.

Narcissist — Give It a Rest

In this column first published in the *Los Angeles Times* in 2011, Daum takes issue with the current usage of one particular word. We might be a nation of narcissists, she concedes, except we're not. As far as Daum is concerned, Americans are something else entirely.

1 At any given moment a whole lot of people are accusing a whole lot of other people of being narcissists. In recent years, the term for a self-destructive "personality disorder" has become the insult of choice for almost anyone doing almost anything.

2 The concept of narcissism as a broad cultural condition, and the word's use as an everyday term, goes back several decades. Christopher Lasch published *The Culture of Narcissism* in 1979, three years after Tom Wolfe[1] declared the era the "me decade." The 1980s turned out to be even more "me" than the '70s had been, and by the 1990s, the rise of identity politics, the birth of reality television and the proliferation of the language of self-help (remember Wendy Kaminer's *I'm Dysfunctional, You're Dysfunctional?*) effectively elevated self-absorption from a passing (if protracted) trend to, well, pretty much just the way things were. To accuse someone of being a narcissist was kind of like accusing them of breathing. In other words, what was the point?

[1] American journalist (born 1931) best known for *The Electric Kool-Aid Acid Test* (1968) and *The Right Stuff* (1979). — Eds.

But lately the word seems to be enjoying a resurgence, often among people   3
who give the impression that they just discovered it. Professional pundits love
it, as do bloggers, politicians, religious leaders, celebrity shrinks, cultural critics, Internet commenters and blowhards at parties. And why shouldn't we?
(Yes, I include myself in this mix; I am, after all, a you-know-what.) It's the
handiest weapon in our arsenal: a derogatory *apercu*[3] that's one-size-fits-all.

Democrats, Republicans, red state folks, blue state folks, baby boomers,   4
Gen Xers, millennials: all narcissists! Parents, nonparents, vegans, meat eat-
ers, city dwellers, rural dwellers, people who travel a lot, people who refuse to
travel, writers who use the first person: all vectors in the national scourge of
self-involvement. In practice, any behavior you don't like can be dismissed
as abrasively, idiotically, dangerously self-centered, with a $10, three-syllable
word that has a way of making even a nincompoop feel like he's saying something intellectual. . . .

Here's the problem with the charge of narcissism. The term has been mis-   5
used and overused so flagrantly that it's now all but meaningless when it comes
to labeling truly destructive tendencies. These days, you can be called a narcissist
merely by having self-esteem and showing a little ambition — in other words,
for trying to survive in the world. In fact, so fluid has the definition become that
narcissism's true home for the last forty-four years, the *Diagnostic and Statistical
Manual of Mental Disorders*, has dropped the diagnosis from its roster.

As for anyone still itching to attribute our collective addiction to *Face-*   6
book and e-mail and other self-referential forms of communication to a
narcissism epidemic, I beg to differ. That stuff hasn't made us into egomaniacs;
it's made us into boring, semi-verbal zombies who bang into each other when
we exit movie theaters because we're buried in our iPhones.

So perhaps it's time to declare a moratorium on the indiscriminate use   7
of this particular n-word. After all, we're not a nation of narcissists. We're a
nation of jerks. Which also happens to be a lot easier to spell.

Journal Writing

Daum writes that "baby boomers, Gen Xers, [and] millennials" (par. 4) have all been
characterized as narcissists. To what generation do you belong? How do you and your
peers tend to be described in the media? Do you agree that people in your age group
are "dangerously self-centered" (4) or otherwise unpleasant to others? In your journal,
write down your own characterization of members of your generation.

[3] French, "perception" or "insight." Daum uses the word in its colloquial sense of linguistic
shorthand. — Eds.

Questions on Meaning

1. When, according to Daum, did people start misusing the word *narcissist*? Why is the timing significant to her?

2. What would you say is Daum's PURPOSE in this essay?

3. Does Daum have a THESIS? In which sentence or sentences does she state her main idea most directly?

Questions on Writing Strategy

1. What AUDIENCE probably would not like this essay? Why would they not like it?

2. Daum defines mostly by negation. In your own words, SUMMARIZE her implied definition of *narcissist*. How does it differ from the meanings commonly attached to the word?

3. Analyze the organization of this essay. What does Daum discuss in each of her paragraphs? How does she create UNITY among them?

4. **OTHER METHODS**   Where in the essay does Daum list some of the people and attitudes that have been called narcissistic? What seems to be the intended EFFECT of these EXAMPLES?

Questions on Language

1. How would you describe the TONE of this essay?

2. Be sure you know the meanings of the following words, checking a dictionary if necessary: proliferation, protracted (par. 2); resurgence (3); vegans, vectors, scourge (4); flagrantly, roster (5); moratorium, indiscriminate (7).

3. What is the effect of "you-know-what" in paragraph 3 and "this particular n-word" in paragraph 7? Why doesn't Daum just say "narcissist" in these instances?

Suggestions for Writing

1. **FROM JOURNAL TO ESSAY**   Write an essay giving an extended definition of the age group of which you consider yourself a member, drawing on your journal entry (p. 391), Daum's essay, and any other sources that offer ideas. You might use one of the labels Daum cites (baby boomers, Gen Xers, millennials) or come up with a name of your own. Keep in mind that characterizing such a large and diverse group requires GENERALIZATION. How does your definition compare with other definitions you have heard in the media? Does any attempt to characterize an age group necessarily oversimplify? Do you find value or interest in the exercise?

2. Think of another word or phrase that is commonly misused or overused (or both). Examples might include *literally, amazing, hero, like, LOL, I could care less,* or *beg the question.* Following Daum's essay as a model, write an essay of your own explaining your objections and imploring people to stop using the word or phrase.

3. Daum suggests that, thanks to "self-referential forms of communication" (par. 6) such as social media and smartphones, Americans have become increasingly self-absorbed and rude. Write an essay in which you offer your own viewpoint on this idea. Are we, in fact, "a nation of jerks" (7)? If you generally agree, offer specific examples and speculate about the causes of this change. If you generally disagree, challenge Daum's assumptions with examples that counter her claim.

4. **CRITICAL WRITING**   The decision to remove narcissistic personality disorder from the *Diagnostic and Statistical Manual of Mental Disorders* raised some controversy when it was announced in late 2010 — just a few weeks before Daum wrote her essay. Research the controversy so that you understand the views for and against retaining narcissism as a psychiatric diagnosis. In an essay, briefly summarize the controversy, and then analyze Daum's essay as a contribution to the conversation. On which side of the debate does her position seem to fall? Does she agree with the decision to drop the disorder from the psychiatrists' manual? Or does she seem to think it should have stayed? Use PARAPHRASES and QUOTATIONS from the essay to support your conclusions.

5. **CONNECTIONS**   In her essay "An Obligation to Prevent Trauma on Campus" (p. 426), Brianne Richson examines another type of psychiatric diagnosis that seems often misunderstood. How does Richson define *post-traumatic stress disorder*? Does she portray it as a personality trait on a par with Daum's *narcissism*, or as more of a medical problem? Write an essay that COMPARES AND CONTRASTS post-traumatic stress disorder and narcissism as Richson and Daum define them. Why might some people argue that trauma victims deserve special treatment, for instance? Is it possible that people accused of narcissism suffer from mental illness? Should either condition be formally classified as a disorder? Why, or why not?

Meghan Daum on Writing

At least once a week, Daum claims, she hears from a "student who's been assigned a paper about my writing and wants me to tell her what to say." In this excerpt from a 2011 *Los Angeles Times* column, she explains why those students should not expect a response.

I know, I know. I should be flattered. I should be heartened that the youth of America are reading newspapers (albeit under duress) and, for that matter, that anyone's reading my column at all. . . . Still, I find myself consistently irked over this whole phenomenon, and not just because I feel guilty when I don't answer these e-mails and resentful when I do. It's because in a world of hyper-accessibility, writers are expected not only to write things but then engage with readers via e-mail or comment boards or book festival Q&As about why they wrote it and what they meant. Nothing is ever considered enough. Readers don't want to simply read stuff and mull it over on their own; they want a personal dialog with the writer about what they were supposed to get out of it.

Students, especially, should be figuring out the how and why of a piece of writing based not on what the author explains to them in an Internet chat room but by tapping into the pure recesses of their own minds. That kind of approach is the highest compliment a reader can give a writer. It's also, by definition, the one we just can't offer any help on.

The Brief Bedford Reader on Writing

What does Daum mean when she says that students should be "tapping into the pure recesses of their own minds" instead of asking writers what they meant? To learn how to "simply read stuff and mull it over on [your] own," also known as CRITICAL THINKING, read (or reread) Chapter 1 of this book, especially "Developing an Understanding" and "Analyzing Essays," pages 15–22.

AUGUSTEN BURROUGHS

Augusten Burroughs was born Christopher Robison in Pittsburgh, Pennsylvania, in 1965 and raised in western Massachusetts. He dropped out of school in the sixth grade, earned a GED, and legally changed his name when he turned eighteen. By his own account Burroughs has been repeatedly victimized by circumstances, many of them recounted in a series of best-selling memoirs. In *Running with Scissors* (2002) he tells of being raised by his mother's psychiatrist and becoming trapped in a relationship with a pedophile. In *Dry* (2003) he examines a period of alcoholism worsened after losing a boyfriend to AIDS. And in *A Wolf at the Table* (2008) he recalls childhood abuse at the hands of his father. Critics sometimes question the details of Burroughs's tales, yet most admire the emotional honesty and gothic humor that pervade his work. In addition to memoirs, Burroughs has also written a novel, *Sellevision* (2000); two collections of essays, *Magical Thinking* (2004) and *Possible Side Effects* (2006); a compilation of Christmas stories, *You'd Better Not Cry* (2009); and, most recently, a self-help book, *This Is How: Proven Aid in Overcoming Shyness, Molestation, Fatness, Spinsterhood, Grief, Disease, Lushery, Decrepitude and More* (2012). He lives in rural Connecticut.

How to Identify Love
by Knowing What It's Not

In *This Is How,* the book Burroughs says he "was born to write," the author draws on his life experiences to offer straightforward if unconventional advice on topics ranging from riding elevators to changing the world. "How to Identify Love by Knowing What It's Not," a chapter from the book, explores the delusions that can lead people to mistake cruelty for caring.

Love doesn't use a fist. 1

Love never calls you fat or lazy or ugly. 2

Love doesn't laugh at you in front of friends. 3

It is not in Love's interest for your self-esteem to be low. 4

Love is a helium-based emotion; Love always takes the high road. 5

Love does not make you beg. 6

Love does not make you deposit your paycheck into its bank account. 7

Love certainly never, never, never brings the children into it. 8

Love does not ask or even want you to change. But if you change, Love is 9
as excited about this change as you are, if not more so. And if you go back to the way you were before you changed, Love will go back with you.

Love does not maintain a list of your flaws and weaknesses. 10

Love believes you. 11

Love is patient; Love does not make a point of showing you how patient 12
it is. It is critical to understand the distinction.

Patience is like donating a large sum of money to a charity anonymously. 13
What matters to you as the donor is that the charity receives the funding, not
who wrote the check, even if knowing who donated such a huge check would
wildly impress the world.

So, patience is exhibited only by a lack of pressure. This is how you know 14
it's there.

But when you see on the face of your partner or spouse an expression that 15
reads, "I'm being very patient with you," this could be the single detail that
alerts you to the fact that you are in an abusive relationship.

You can be in such a relationship and not even know it. You can receive 16
so many black eyes, you forget it's abnormal to have even one.

Physical violence is one kind of abuse. Emotional violence is another 17
kind of abuse. These assaults are delivered with concepts. People usually say,
emotional abuse is about words: fat, ugly, stupid, lazy. But it's not about words
because an emotionally abusive person doesn't always resort to using the verbal club, but rather the verbal untraceable poison.

They may, in fact, speak very kind words to you. And appear nothing but 18
supportive to those around you: Their covert abuse is administered in small, cunning ways. Over time. So the impact is gradual, not fist-to-the-eye immediate.

An abusive partner is controlling. They are manipulative. They might 19
make a special point of coyly sharing information that they actually know will
upset you. They might supply reasonable arguments as to why they and not
you should make important decisions.

If you possess talent or a natural ease and comfort with a particular ability 20
and your abusive partner is resentful, abuse might arrive in the form of sub-
traction: no remark at all, not a compliment or a gesture of support. Perhaps
one small, internally flawless diamond of a criticism will be presented.

Silence when there should be discussion to resolve an issue is another 21
method of abuse if the silence is used as a tool to frustrate or sadden or otherwise intentionally manipulate the emotions of another.

I knew of somebody . . . who was many years into an abusive relationship 22
but did not know it. She knew only that she had been so happy when they
met and that it seemed to her this feeling was bled out of her year after year,
and she found that she now resembled her partner, whom she had once seen
as strong and silent and loving but had come to understand was emotionally
disturbed and was not silent in his mind, but roiling.

When she finally left him she did so still loving him. She had been more 23
financially stable so she had given him their home. He had admitted to her

that for the last couple of years, he had been occupied with planning his suicide. He told her he'd worked out all the details and would do it in a quaint
West Coast town right on the Pacific that they had frequently spoken of visiting but never seen.

When she left him she left their beloved dog with him because she wor-   24
ried a totally empty house would be dangerous.

Their plan had been to share the dog but he wanted nothing more to do   25
with her. And the regular updates and photographs he had sent when they
first parted stopped now completely.

Months passed and she heard nothing until he sent a brief email inform-   26
ing her that the dog now had a potential serious health problem and that he
would take care of it.

She could not help but feel that he had taken a small measure of satisfac-   27
tion knowing how brutal the news would be to her ears and how helpless she
would feel being able to do nothing, not even see this dog she had loved for
so long.

Emotional abuse is the process of breaking the spirit or shattering the   28
confidence of another for one's own purpose.

Abusive people never change. There is no point of pursuing couples' ther-   29
apy when one member of the relationship is abusive. A therapist may tell you
otherwise. But I'm telling you the not-for-profit truth. Abusers do not change.

It will only get worse.   30

The difference between physical violence like a slap on the face or a shove   31
and homicide can be as small as a few centimeters or the angle of approach.

Also, abusers are always very, very sorry. Men who abuse women probably   32
shed more tears in one year than the combined tears of all the girls in the
audience of a Renée Zellweger movie opening weekend at the Paris Theatre
in Manhattan.

That's how sorry he is.   33

Or so he says, with his tears.   34

Of course, he's not sorry. She is.   35

Unless the roles are reversed. And the abuser is a woman, not a man.   36

Women can and do physically and emotionally abuse their partners. The   37
perception that the abuser is always a man is false. . . .

People remain in abusive relationships for the same reasons they remain   38
in loving ones: they've built a life together, they have children, financial
interests, habit, nothing better. Lots of reasons.

But probably the number-one reason is simply not knowing they're in one.   39

You think of domestic violence and you think of a character and a weak   40
victim: macho, powerful bully and a passive, frail woman and you don't recognize that. So it can't be you.

It might help, then, for me to show you in clinical terms what domestic   41
violence actually looks like on the printed page. This checklist is from the
National Domestic Violence Hotline. Ask yourself, does your partner:

- Embarrass you with put-downs
- Look at you or act in ways that scare you
- Control what you do, who you see or talk to, or where you go
- Stop you from seeing your friends or family members
- Take your money or Social Security check, make you ask for money, or
  refuse to give you money
- Make all of the decisions
- Tell you that you're a bad parent or threaten to take away or hurt your
  children
- Prevent you from working or attending school
- Act like the abuse is no big deal, it's your fault, or even deny doing it
- Destroy your property or threaten to kill your pets
- Intimidate you with guns, knives, or other weapons
- Shove you, slap you, choke you, or hit you
- Force you to try and drop charges
- Threaten to commit suicide
- Threaten to kill you

Think about the answers before you answer. Does he prevent you from   42
working? No, he encourages you, that's terrific.

Or does he?   43

Does he *maybe* prevent you a little by getting drunk and then, say, being   44
unable to find a certain pair of shoes so he turns the house upside down, creating such a scene, a ME, ME, ME moment that you can't possibly work?

Might he always, over and over, bring it all back to himself? Leaving no   45
room or time for you to work on your crafts, aka possible future home business
aka threat to him?

Domestic violence is extremely difficult to detect when it is happening to   46
you because domestic violence always only happens to other people, and you
are too smart and sophisticated to ever, for one moment, be with somebody
abusive. The thought is absurd. Domestic violence is a lower-class problem,
something that afflicts only those whose homes are clad in aluminum siding.

Besides, you would know if you were being abused.   47

Except the truth is, some things are too terrible to know; too impossible   48
to see; too painful to realize; too heartbreaking to face.

You could be in an abusive relationship and be unaware that you are, unable to see the abuse for what it is. 49

Sometimes the truth must unspool slowly. It's simply impossible to grasp it all at once. Perhaps, one day, you will be able to see a glimpse of abuse in your relationship. 50

In time, you'll be able to see more. 51

Because if you allow yourself to have one small serving of reality, the hard part, the opaque part, is over. And eventually, you'll be able to see the rest. 52

Also, the more unlikely it is that you would ever be in an abusive relationship, the closer you need to look at your relationship. Not because you want to try to see something sinister that simply isn't there, but because you're more likely to be blind to abuse if it is there. 53

Just, you know, pay attention. To all those familiar, everyday things they say to you or do to you. Ask, "If he said that to my friend, would I think it was mean?" 54

Try to actually hear what the person says to you. Try to hear it fresh. Try to see if what they say to you might, in a way, also be a kind of steering wheel. 55

It's a spectrum, too. Maybe your partner isn't exactly "abusive" so much as a little controlling. This is fairly easy to see. 56

What's difficult to see is when you're with somebody who is a full-strength abuser. And maybe one reason it's so difficult to see something that to the rest of the world — at least on paper — is so obvious is because there's no contrast. They are controlling and abusive and this is what they are. 57

If you realize you are in an abusive relationship, you may want to call this phone number — it's toll-free so it won't cost you anything and it won't show up on your phone bill. If possible, take the number with you and call from somewhere else: 58

National Domestic Violence Hotline 1-800-799-SAFE (7233) 59

Seventy-nine-nine, seventy-two, thirty-three. 60

If you have children and your spouse is abusing them physically, mentally, or sexually, leave now. 61

It never takes courage to leave. 62

It takes love. 63

Journal Writing

Anybody could be in an abusive relationship, Burroughs insists, although recognizing the abuse can be difficult or even impossible. Do you agree? Have you witnessed any of the behaviors he describes, whether in one of your relationships or in someone else's?

In your journal, describe the troubling aspects of that relationship. Did you recognize the behavior as abusive? Who was the victim, and who the abuser? Has the relationship ended, or is it still in place?

Questions on Meaning

1. What exactly does Burroughs define in this essay? Is his subject love, as the title suggests it will be, or something else entirely?

2. Where does Burroughs first state his THESIS? At what points does he restate his main idea? Why do you suppose he repeats himself as he does?

3. What do you make of the essay's final sentence? What, to the author, is the true measure of love? How and where does he define it?

4. How do you suppose Burroughs hoped readers would respond to this essay? What is his PURPOSE? What is your response, and why?

Questions on Writing Strategy

1. Many of Burroughs's paragraphs consist of a single sentence. Do you recognize the ALLUSION in paragraphs 1–12? What is the EFFECT of this allusion and of the other very short paragraphs in the essay?

2. This essay is a model of an *extended* definition, yet it also includes several *stipulative* definitions (see p. 368). Locate at least two of these. What do they contribute to Burroughs's meaning?

3. Examine the organization of the essay. What major sections does it fall into? Why do you think Burroughs chose to order the essay as he did?

4. Why does Burroughs provide a checklist from the National Domestic Violence Hotline in paragraph 41 and give the organization's phone number in paragraphs 60 and 61?

5. **OTHER METHODS**   How does Burroughs use a single extended EXAMPLE to clarify his point about emotional abuse?

Questions on Language

1. In much of the essay, Burroughs addresses readers directly, using the second-PERSON *you*. What does this language choice reveal about how he imagines his AUDIENCE?

2. Burroughs often uses the plural pronoun *they* to refer back to a singular *he*, *partner*, or *person*, as in "An abusive partner is controlling. They are manipulative" (par. 19). Where else does he do this? Does Burroughs seem to break the rules of pronoun-antecedent agreement for a reason, or is he guilty of using bad grammar? Why do you think so? (If necessary, refer to p. 52 for an explanation of pronoun-antecedent agreement.)

3. Consult a dictionary if you don't know the meaning of any of the following words: helium (par. 5); covert, cunning (18); coyly (19); roiling (22); clinical (41); unspool (50); opaque (52); sinister (53); spectrum (56).

4. How would you characterize the TONE of this essay: serious? detached? earnest? angry? compassionate? something else? Point to some words and phrases that support your answer.

Suggestions for Writing

1. **FROM JOURNAL TO ESSAY**   Expand your journal writing (pp. 399–400) into an essay explaining why and how a specific someone should leave an abusive relationship. You might write about somebody you know, about yourself, about a public figure, or about a fictional abuse victim, but take care to protect the person's anonymity. In your essay, draw on Burroughs's definitions and advice as appropriate to support your points, but be sure to develop a unique thesis of your own and to offer plenty of specifics to support your claims.

2. Write an essay that defines *love* or another strong feeling, such as *hate, compassion, happiness,* or *fear.* You might, like Burroughs, choose to focus on what the feeling is *not,* or you might prefer to define it by explaining what it *is.* In either case, be sure to provide a wide range of examples to suggest the various aspects of your subject.

3. **CRITICAL WRITING**   ANALYZE Burroughs's use of FIGURES OF SPEECH in this essay. How does the author combine *personification, metaphor, simile, paradox,* and similar devices to add meaning and a sense of empathy to his definition of abuse? In your analysis, pay particular attention to those figures of speech you find especially fresh or compelling.

4. **CONNECTIONS**   Compare Burroughs's "How to Identify Love by Knowing What It's Not" with Junot Díaz's "The Dreamer" (p. 84). Of these two highly subjective essays dealing with abuse, which is more personal? Write a brief essay answering this question, and support your answer with quotations and PARAPHRASES from Burroughs and Díaz.

ADDITIONAL WRITING TOPICS

Definition

1. Write an essay in which you define an institution, trend, phenomenon, or abstraction as specifically and concretely as possible. Following are some suggestions designed to stimulate ideas. Before you begin, limit your subject.

Responsibility	Fairness
Fun	Leadership
Empathy	Leisure
Plagiarism	Originality
Community	Integrity
Education	Imagination
Progress	Socialism
Advertising	A smile
Happiness	A classic (of music, literature, art, or film)
Fads	Success
Feminism	Meditation
Marriage	Friendship

2. In a brief essay, define one of the following. In each instance, you have a choice of something good or something bad to talk about.

    A good or bad boss
    A good or bad parent
    A good or bad host
    A good or bad athlete
    A good or bad physician
    A good or bad nurse
    A good or bad minister, priest, rabbi, or imam
    A good or bad roommate
    A good or bad driver
    A good or bad business

3. In a paragraph, define a slang expression or specialized term for someone who has never heard it. Possible expressions include *cisgender, sick, hook up, vaping, clickbait, wicked, poser, vine, swag, chill, hot mess.*

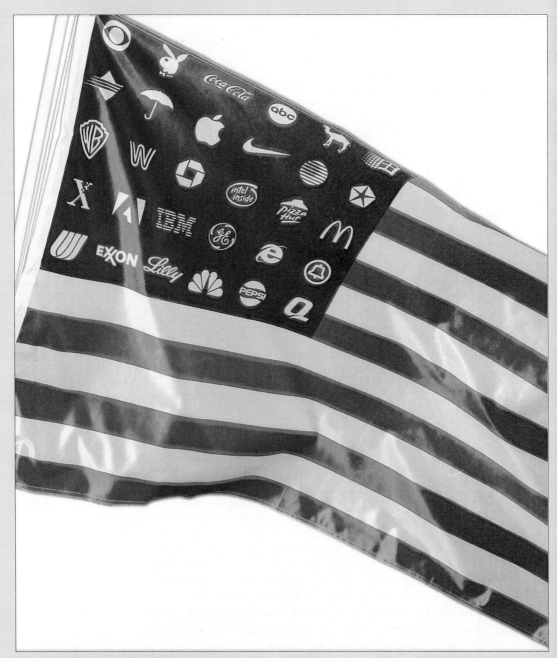

Courtesy of Adbusters Media Foundation

12

ARGUMENT AND PERSUASION

Stating Opinions and Proposals

◀ **Argument and persuasion in an image**

Adbusters Media Foundation, an activist group "concerned about the erosion of our physical and cultural environments by commercial forces," launched its Corporate America flag in 1999. This version appeared in a full-page advertisement in the *New York Times*. Showing the American flag's stars replaced by well-known corporate logos, the image adapts a symbol that many Americans revere to make a strong argument about the United States. What is the argument? How do you respond to the image: Are you offended? persuaded? amused? Why? Whatever your view, do you understand why others might think differently?

THE METHOD

Practically every day, we try to persuade ourselves or someone else. We usually attempt such persuasion without being aware that we follow any special method at all. Often, we'll state an *opinion*: We'll tell someone our way of viewing things. We say to a friend, "I'm starting to like Senator Clark. Look at all she's done to help people with disabilities. Look at her voting record on the minimum wage." And, having stated these opinions, we might go on to make a *proposal*, to recommend that some action be taken. Addressing our friend, we might suggest, "Hey, Senator Clark is speaking on campus at four-thirty. Want to come with me and listen to her?"

Sometimes you try to convince yourself that a certain way of interpreting things is right. You even set forth your opinion in writing — as in a post to a social media site complaining about unreasonable return policies at a certain retailer. You might write an e-mail of protest to a landlord who wants to raise your rent, pointing out that the bathroom hot water faucet doesn't work. As a concerned citizen, you may wish to speak your mind in an occasional letter to an editor or to an elected representative.

Many professions involve persuading people in writing as well. Before arguing a case in court, lawyers prepare briefs setting forth all the points in favor of their sides. Businesspeople regularly put in writing their ideas for new products and ventures, for improvements in cost control and job efficiency. Researchers write proposals for grants to obtain money to support their work. Scientists write and publish papers to persuade the scientific community that their findings are valid, often stating hypotheses, or tentative opinions.

Even if you never produce a single persuasive work (which is very unlikely), you will certainly encounter such works directed at you. We live our lives under a steady rain of opinions and proposals. Organizations that work for causes campaign with broadcast media and direct mail, all hoping that we will see things their way. Moreover, we are bombarded with proposals from people who wish us to act. Religious leaders urge us to lead more virtuous lives. Advertisers urge us to rush right out and buy the large economy size.

Small wonder, then, that argument and persuasion — and CRITICAL THINK-ING about argument and persuasion — may be among the most useful skills a college student can acquire. Time and again, your instructors will ask you to criticize or to state opinions, either in class or in writing. You may be asked to state your view of anything from the Electoral College to animal rights. You may be asked to judge the desirability or undesirability of compulsory testing for drugs or revision of the existing immigration laws. Critically reading other people's arguments and composing your own, you will find, helps you discover what you think, refine it, and share what you believe.

Be aware that the terms *argument* and *persuasion* have somewhat different meanings: PERSUASION aims to influence readers' actions, or their support for an action, by engaging their beliefs and feelings, while ARGUMENT aims to win readers' agreement with an assertion or claim by engaging their powers of reasoning. However, most effective argument or persuasion contains elements of both methods. In this book we tend to use the terms interchangeably.

One other point: We tend to talk here about *writing* arguments, but most of what we say has to do with *reading* them as well. When we discuss your need, as a writer, to support your claims, we are also discussing your need, as a reader, to question the support other authors provide for their claims. In reading arguments critically, you apply the critical-thinking skills we discussed in Chapter 1 — ANALYSIS, INFERENCE, SYNTHESIS, and EVALUATION — to a particular kind of writing.

Audience and Common Ground

Unlike some advertisers, responsible writers of argument do not try to storm people's minds. In writing a paper for a course, you persuade by gentler means: by sharing your view with an AUDIENCE willing to consider it. You'll want to learn how to express your view clearly and vigorously. But to be fair and persuasive, it is important to understand your readers' views as well.

In stating your opinion, you present the truth as you see it: "The immigration laws discourage employers from hiring nonnative workers," perhaps, or "The immigration laws protect legal aliens." To persuade your readers that your view makes sense, you need not begin by proclaiming that your view is absolutely right and should prevail. Instead, you might begin by trying to state what your readers probably think, as best you can infer it. You don't consider views that differ from your own merely to flatter your readers. You do so to balance your own view and make it more accurate. Writer and reader become two sensible people trying to find COMMON GROUND, or points on which both can agree. This approach will relieve you, whenever you have to state your opinions in writing, of the terrible obligation to be one hundred percent right at all times.

Elements of Argument

The British philosopher Stephen Toulmin has proposed a useful division of argument into distinct elements. Adapted to the terminology of this book, they are *claims*, *evidence*, *appeals*, and *assumptions*.

Claims and Thesis Statements

A CLAIM is an assertion that requires support. It is what an argument tries to convince readers to accept. The central claim — the main point — is almost always stated explicitly in a THESIS STATEMENT like one of the following:

Argument and Persuasion

A CLAIM ABOUT REALITY   The war on drugs is not winnable because laws cannot eradicate demand or the supply to meet it.

A CLAIM OF VALUE   Drug abuse is a personal matter that should not be subject to government interference.

A CLAIM FOR A COURSE OF ACTION   The United States must intensify its efforts to reduce production of heroin in Afghanistan.

Usually, but not always, you'll state your thesis at the beginning of your essay, making a play for readers' attention and clueing them in to your purpose. But if you think readers may have difficulty accepting your thesis until they've heard some or all of your argument, then you might save the thesis statement for the middle or end.

The essays in this chapter provide a variety of thesis statements as models. Here are four examples:

> The fact that so many illegal immigrants are intertwined with American citizens or legal residents, either as spouses or parents, should give pause to those who'd like to see all illegal immigrants rounded up and deported or their lives made so miserable they leave on their own.
>
> — Linda Chavez, "Supporting Family Values"

> Such measures [calling for "trigger warnings" on college syllabi] certainly have a potential to be taken too far, but our obligation to prevent a trauma survivor's class time becoming a living hell outweighs concerns about a stunted learning environment.
>
> — Brianne Richson, "An Obligation to Prevent Trauma on Campus"

> My main gripe with trigger warnings . . . is that while they aim to be sensitive to people suffering from afflictions like post-traumatic stress disorder, they threaten to stifle some of the most important conversations and lessons in college.
>
> — Jon Overton, "Beware the Trigger Warning"

> Ads that pop up on your screen might seem useful, or at worst, a nuisance. But they are much more than that. The bits and bytes about your life can easily be used against you. . . . We need a do-not-track law, similar to the do-not-call one.
>
> — Lori Andrews, "*Facebook* Is Using You"

Evidence

Claims are nothing without the EVIDENCE to make them believable and convincing. Toulmin calls evidence *data* or *grounds*, using terms that convey how specific and fundamental it is. Depending on your subject, your evidence may include facts, statistics (facts expressed in numbers), expert opinions, examples, and reported experiences. These kinds of evidence should meet certain criteria.

- **Accuracy:** Facts, examples, and opinions should be taken from reliable sources and presented without error or distortion.

- **Representation:** The evidence should reflect reality, neither slanting nor exaggerating it.

- **Relevance:** All evidence should apply directly to the claims, reflecting current thinking by recognized experts.

- **Adequacy:** The evidence should be sufficient to support the claims entirely, not just in part.

Appeals

To strengthen the support for your claims, you can also make APPEALS to readers either directly or indirectly, in the way you present your evidence. In classical argument these appeals are often referred to as *logos*, *ethos*, and *pathos*; we refer to them as RATIONAL APPEALS, ETHICAL APPEALS, and EMOTIONAL APPEALS, respectively.

- **Rational appeals** rely on sound reasoning (*logos*) and marshal evidence that meets the criteria above. See pages 410–413 for more on reasoning.

- **Ethical appeals** show readers that you are a well-informed person of goodwill, good sense, and good moral character — and, therefore, to be believed (*ethos*). Strengthen your ethical appeal by collecting ample evidence, reasoning carefully, demonstrating respect for opposing views, using an appropriate emotional appeal (see below), and minding your TONE (see p. 416).

- **Emotional appeals** acknowledge what you know of readers' sympathies and beliefs and show how your argument relates to them (*pathos*). An example in this chapter appears in Linda Chavez's "Supporting Family Values": The author argues for immigration reform by appealing to readers' respect for intact families and fear of cultural disintegration. Carefully used, an emotional appeal can stir readers to constructive belief and action by engaging their feelings as well as their minds, as long as the appeal is appropriate for the audience and the argument.

Argument and Persuasion

Assumptions

Another element of argument, the ASSUMPTION, is in Toulmin's conception the connective tissue between grounds, or evidence, and claims: An assumption explains why the evidence leads to and justifies a claim. Called a *warrant* by Toulmin, an assumption is usually a belief, a principle, or an inference whose truth the writer takes for granted. Here is how an assumption might figure in an argument for one of the claims given earlier:

CLAIM   The United States must intensify its efforts to reduce the production of heroin in Afghanistan.

EVIDENCE   Afghanistan is the world's largest heroin producer and a major supplier to the United States.

ASSUMPTION   The United States can and should reduce the production of heroin in other countries when its own citizens are affected.

As important as they are, the assumptions underlying an argument are not always stated. As we will see in the discussion of deductive reasoning, which begins on the next page, unstated assumptions can sometimes pitch an argument into trouble.

Reasoning

When we argue rationally, we reason — that is, we make statements that lead to a conclusion. Two reliable methods of rational argument date back to the classical Greek philosopher Aristotle, who identified the complementary processes of inductive and deductive reasoning.

Inductive Reasoning

In INDUCTIVE REASONING, the method of the sciences, we collect bits of evidence on which to base a GENERALIZATION, the claim of the argument. The assumption linking evidence and claim is that what is true for some circumstances is true for others as well. For instance, you might interview a hundred representative students about their attitudes toward changing your school's honor code. You find that 65% of the interviewees believe that the code should remain as it is, 15% believe that the code should be toughened, 10% believe that it should be loosened, and 10% have no opinion. You then assume that these statistics can be applied to the student body as a whole and make a claim against changing the code because 65% of students don't want change.

The more evidence you have, the more trustworthy your claim will be, but it would never be airtight unless you interviewed every student on campus. Since such thoroughness is almost always impractical if not impossible, you assume in an *inductive leap* that the results can be generalized. The smaller the leap — the more evidence you have — the better.

Deductive Reasoning

DEDUCTIVE REASONING works the opposite way of inductive reasoning: It moves from a general statement to particular cases. The basis of deduction is the SYLLOGISM, a three-step form of reasoning practiced by Aristotle:

> All men are mortal.
>
> Socrates is a man.
>
> Therefore, Socrates is mortal.

The first statement, called a *major premise*, is an assumption: a fact, principle, or inference that you believe to be true. The second statement, or *minor premise*, is the evidence — the new information about a particular member of the larger group named in the major premise. The third statement, or *conclusion*, is the claim that follows inevitably from the premises. If the premises are true, then the conclusion must be true. Following is another example of a syllogism. You may recognize it from the discussion of assumptions on page 410, only here the statements are simplified and arranged differently:

> MAJOR PREMISE (ASSUMPTION)   The United States can and should reduce heroin production when its own citizens are affected.
>
> MINOR PREMISE (EVIDENCE)   A major producer of heroin for the US market is Afghanistan.
>
> CONCLUSION (THESIS)   The United States can and should reduce heroin production in Afghanistan.

Problems with deductive reasoning start in the premises. Consider this untrustworthy syllogism: "To do well in school, students must cheat a little. Jolene wants to do well in school. Therefore, she must cheat." This is bad deductive reasoning, and its flaw is in its major premise, which is demonstrably untrue: Plenty of students do well without cheating. Because the premise is false, the conclusion is necessarily false as well.

When they're spelled out neatly, bad syllogisms are pretty easy to spot. But many deductive arguments are not spelled out. Instead, one of the premises goes unstated, as in this statement: "Mayor Perkins was humiliated in his recent bid for reelection, winning only 2,000 out of 5,000 votes." The unstated assumption here, the major premise, is "Winning only two-fifths of the votes humiliates a candidate." (The rest of the syllogism: "Mayor Perkins received only two-fifths of the votes. Thus, Mayor Perkins was humiliated.")

The unstated premise isn't necessarily a problem in argument — in fact, it's quite common. But it *is* a problem when it's wrong or unfounded. For instance, in the statement "She shouldn't be elected mayor because her husband has bad ideas on how to run the city," the unstated assumption is that the candidate cannot form ideas independently of her husband. This is a possibility, perhaps, but it requires its own discussion and proof, not concealment behind other assertions.

Logical Fallacies

In arguments we read and hear, we often meet logical FALLACIES: errors in reasoning that lead to wrong conclusions. From the time you start thinking about your thesis and claims and begin planning your paper, you'll need to watch out for them. To help you recognize logical fallacies when you see them or hear them, and so guard against them when you write, here is a list of the most common.

- **Non sequitur** (from the Latin, "it does not follow"): stating a conclusion that doesn't follow from one or both premises.

  I've lived in this town a long time — why, my great-grandfather was one of the first settlers — so I'm against putting fluoride in the drinking water.

- **Oversimplification:** supplying neat and easy explanations for large and complicated phenomena.

  No wonder drug abuse is out of control. Look at how the courts have hobbled police officers.

  Oversimplified solutions are also popular:

  All these teenage kids that get in trouble with the law — why, they ought to put them in work camps. That would straighten them out!

- **Post hoc, ergo propter hoc** (from the Latin, "after this, therefore because of this"), or *post hoc* for short: a form of oversimplification assuming that because B follows A, B was caused by A.

  Ever since the city suspended height restrictions on skyscrapers, the city budget has been balanced.

  (For more on *post hoc* and oversimplification, see the discussion in Chapter 10 on cause-and-effect analysis, pp. 334–335.)

- **Either/or reasoning:** assuming that a reality may be divided into only two parts or extremes or assuming that a given problem has only one of two possible solutions.

  What's to be done about the trade imbalance with Asia? Either we ban all Asian imports, or American industry will collapse.

  Obviously, either/or reasoning is a kind of extreme oversimplification.

- **Hasty generalization:** leaping to a generalization from inadequate or faulty evidence. The most familiar hasty generalization is the stereotype.

  Men aren't sensitive enough to be day-care providers.

  Women are too emotional to fight in combat.

- **Argument from doubtful or unidentified authority:** citing an unreliable source.

  Uncle Oswald says that we ought to imprison all sex offenders for life.

  According to an anonymous informant, my opponent is lying.

- **Argument ad hominem** (from the Latin, "to the man"): attacking a person's views by attacking his or her character.

  Mayor Burns is divorced and estranged from his family. How can we listen to his pleas for a city nursing home?

- **Begging the question:** taking for granted from the start what you set out to demonstrate. When you reason in a *logical* way, you state that because something is true, then, as a result, some other truth follows. When you beg the question, however, you repeat that what is true is true.

  Dogs are a menace to people because they are dangerous.

  This statement proves nothing, because the idea that dogs are dangerous is already assumed in the statement that they are a menace. Beggars of questions often just repeat what they already believe, only in different words. This fallacy sometimes takes the form of arguing in a circle, or demonstrating a premise by a conclusion and a conclusion by a premise.

  I am in college because that is the right thing to do. Going to college is the right thing to do because it is expected of me.

- **False analogy:** the claim of persuasive likeness when no significant likeness exists. An ANALOGY asserts that because two things are comparable in some respects, they are comparable in other respects as well. Analogies cannot serve as evidence in rational arguments because the differences always outweigh the similarities; but analogies can reinforce such arguments *if* the subjects are indeed similar in some ways. If they aren't, the analogy is false. Many observers see the "war on drugs" as a false and damaging analogy because warfare aims for clear victory over a specific, organized enemy, whereas the complete eradication of illegal drugs is probably unrealistic and, in any event, the "enemy" isn't well defined: the drugs themselves? users? sellers? producers? the producing nations? (These critics urge approaching drugs as a social problem to be skillfully managed and reduced.)

THE PROCESS

Finding a Subject

Your way into a subject will probably vary depending on whether you're writing an argument that supports an opinion or one that proposes a change. In stating an opinion, you set forth and support a claim — a truth you believe. You may find such a truth by thinking and feeling, by reading, by talking to your instructors or fellow students, by listening to a discussion of some problem or controversy. Before you run with a subject, take a minute to weigh it: Is this something about which reasonable people disagree? Arguments go nowhere when they start with ideas that are generally accepted (pets should not have to endure physical abuse from their owners) or are beyond the pale (pet owners should be able to hurt their animals if they want).

In stating a proposal, you already have an opinion in mind, and from there, you go on to urge an action or a solution to a problem. Usually, these two statements will take place within the same piece of writing: You will first set forth a view ("The campus honor code is unfair to first offenders"), provide the evidence to support it, and then present your proposal as a remedy ("The campus honor code should be revised to give more latitude to first offenders").

Whatever your subject, resist the temptation to make it big. If you have two weeks to prepare, an argument about the litter problem in your town is probably manageable: In that time you could conduct your own visual research and talk to town officials. But an argument about the litter problem in your town compared with that in similar-sized towns across the state would surely demand more time than you have.

Organizing

There's no one right way to organize an argument because so much depends on how your readers will greet your claim and your evidence. Below we give some ideas for different situations.

Introduction

In your opening paragraph or two, draw readers in by connecting them to your subject if possible, showing its significance, and providing any needed background. End the INTRODUCTION with your thesis statement if you think readers will entertain it before they've seen the evidence. Put the thesis statement later, in the middle or even at the end of the essay, if you think readers need to see some or all of the evidence in order to be open to the idea.

Body

The BODY of the essay develops and defends the points that support your thesis. Generally, start with your least important point and build in a crescendo to your strongest point. However, if you think readers may resist your ideas, consider starting strong and then offering the more minor points as reinforcement.

For every point you make, give the evidence that supports it. The methods of development can help here, providing many options for injecting evidence. Say you were arguing for or against further reductions in welfare funding. You might give EXAMPLES of wasteful spending, or of neighborhoods where welfare funds are still needed. You might spell out the CAUSES of social problems that call for welfare funds, or foresee the likely EFFECTS of cutting welfare programs or of keeping them. You could use NARRATION to tell a pointed story; you could use DESCRIPTION to portray certain welfare recipients and their neighborhoods.

Response to Objections

Part of the body of the essay, but separated here for emphasis, a response to probable objections is crucial to effective argument. If you are arguing fairly, you should be able to face potential criticisms fairly and give your critics due credit, reasoning with them, not dismissing them. This is the strategy Linda Chavez uses later in this chapter in "Supporting Family Values" (p. 421) by conceding, more than once, that arguments against immigration have some merit ("But the greater concern for some opponents," "It is true that," and so on) before she points out what she sees as their logical flaws. As Chavez does, you can tackle possible objections throughout your essay, as they pertain to your points. You can also field objections near the end of the essay, an approach that allows you to draw on all of your evidence. But if you think that readers' own opposing views may stiffen their resistance to your argument, you may want to address those views very early, before developing your own points.

Conclusion

The CONCLUSION gives you a chance to gather your points, restate your thesis in a fresh way, and leave readers with a compelling final idea. In an essay with a strong emotional component, you may want to end with an appeal to readers' feelings. But even in a mostly rational argument, try to involve readers in some way, showing why they should care or what they can do.

FOCUS ON TONE

Readers are most likely to be persuaded by an argument when they sense that the writer is reasonable, trustworthy, and sincere. Sound reasoning, strong evidence, and acknowledgment of opposing views do much to convey these attributes, but so does tone, the attitude implied by choice of words and sentence structures.

Generally, you should try for a tone of moderation in your view of your subject and a tone of respectfulness and goodwill toward readers and opponents.

- **State opinions and facts calmly:**

OVEREXCITED   One clueless administrator was quoted in the newspaper as saying she thought many students who claim learning disabilities are "faking" their difficulties to obtain special treatment! Has she never heard of dyslexia, attention deficit disorders, and other well-established disabilities?

CALM   Particularly worrisome was one administrator's statement, quoted in the newspaper, that many students who claim learning disabilities may be "faking" their difficulties to obtain special treatment.

- **Replace arrogance with deference:**

ARROGANT   I happen to know that many students would rather party or just bury their heads in the sand than get involved in a serious, worthy campaign against the school's unjust learning-disabled policies.

DEFERENTIAL   Time pressures and lack of information about the issues may be what prevent students from joining the campaign against the school's unjust learning-disabled policies.

- **Replace sarcasm with plain speaking:**

SARCASTIC   Of course, the administration knows even without meeting students what is best for every one of them.

PLAIN   The administration should agree to meet with each learning-disabled student to learn about his or her needs.

- **Choose words whose CONNOTATIONS convey reasonableness** rather than anger, hostility, or another negative emotion:

HOSTILE   The administration <u>coerced</u> some students into dropping their lawsuits. [*Coerced* implies the use of threats or even violence.]

REASONABLE   The administration <u>convinced</u> some students to drop their lawsuits. [*Convinced* implies the use of reason.]

(For more on connotations and tone in general, refer to the Glossary and to pages 48–49 in Chapter 2.)

> ### CHECKLIST FOR REVISING ARGUMENT AND PERSUASION
>
> ✔ **Audience.** Have you taken account of your readers' probable views? Have you reasoned with readers, not attacked them? Are your emotional appeals appropriate to readers' likely feelings? Do you acknowledge opposing views?
>
> ✔ **Thesis.** Does your argument have a thesis, a claim about how your subject is or should be? Is the thesis narrow enough to argue convincingly in the space and time available? Is it stated clearly? Is it reasonable?
>
> ✔ **Evidence.** Is your thesis well supported with facts, statistics, expert opinions, and examples? Is your evidence accurate, representative, relevant, and adequate?
>
> ✔ **Assumptions.** Have you made sound connections between your evidence and your thesis and other claims?
>
> ✔ **Logical fallacies.** Have you avoided common errors in reasoning, such as oversimplifying or begging the question? (See pp. 412–413 for a list of fallacies.)
>
> ✔ **Structure.** Does your organization lead readers through your argument step by step, building to your strongest ideas and frequently connecting your evidence to your central claim?
>
> ✔ **Tone.** Is the tone of your argument reasonable and respectful?

ARGUMENT AND PERSUASION IN ACADEMIC WRITING

A Public Relations Textbook

Taken from *Public Relations: Strategies and Tactics*, by Dennis L. Wilcox, Phillip H. Ault, and Warren K. Agee, the following paragraph argues that lobbyists (who work to persuade public officials on behalf of a cause) are not slick manipulators but something else. The paragraph falls in the textbook's section on lobbying as a form of public relations, and its purpose is to correct a mistaken definition.

Although the public stereotypes a lobbyist as a fast-talking person twisting an elected official's arm to get special concessions, the reality is quite different. Today's lobbyist, who may be fully employed by one industry or represent a variety of clients, is often a quiet-spoken, well-educated man or woman armed with statistics and research reports. Robert Gray, former head of Hill and Knowlton's Washington office and a public affairs expert for thirty years, adds, "Lobbying is no longer a booze and buddies business. It's presenting

Topic sentence: the claim

Evidence:
* Expert opinion

Argument and Persuasion

honest facts and convincing Congress that your side has more merit
than the other." He rejects lobbying as being simply "influence ped-
dling and button-holing" top administration officials. Although the
public has the perception that lobbying is done only by big business,
Gray correctly points out that a variety of special interests also do it.
These may include such groups as the Sierra Club, Mothers Against   • Facts and examples
Drunk Driving, the National Association of Social Workers, the
American Civil Liberties Union, and the American Federation of
Labor. Even the American Society of Plastic and Reconstructive
Surgeons hired a Washington public relations firm in their battle
against restrictions on breast implants. Lobbying, quite literally, is
an activity in which widely diverse groups and organizations engage
as an exercise of free speech and representation in the marketplace
of ideas. Lobbyists often balance each other and work toward legislative compromises that benefit not only their self-interests but
society as a whole.

A Proposal

In many courses and occupations, you'll be expected to write proposals
that identify specific problems or related sets of problems and argue for reasonable solutions. A proposal usually addresses clearly defined readers who are
in a position to take action or approve an action. It addresses those readers'
unique needs and concerns, anticipating objections and offering evidence to
demonstrate the benefits of the solution.

As a nursing student in California as well as a mother, Adrianne Silver
knew that school districts across the nation had been struggling with an
escalating problem of bullying and that many states had recently insti-
tuted new laws to address the issue. Eager to see her own state government
improve its response, she researched possible changes and also attitudes
toward change on the part of schoolteachers and administrators. The following paragraphs come from her longer proposal for a law mandating pros-
ecution and counseling for bullies. Before this section, Silver opened with
an overview of the problem and of recent laws that had been passed in
response to bullied students' suicides. After this section, Silver explained
her solution in greater detail, suggested steps for implementing it, and
addressed objections more fully.

Yet with all the anti-bullying policies, procedures, and   Transition from
training being implemented nationwide, not much is being done   discussion of problem
to address the behavior before it reaches the level of violence.
Unfortunately, many teachers have the opinion that teasing

and taunting is just "kids being kids" and that nothing needs to be done. But these kids grow up to become teenagers with destructive behaviors. If we are to reduce aggression, we must understand the cause and deal with the offender while the behavior can still be corrected.

In order to reduce the problem of school bullying, I propose to establish a new law . . . to make bullying or discrimination and harassment a summary offense, which does not require a jury trial. Unlike existing laws that provide only guidelines to protect students from acts of bullying, this new law will take the course of action one step further: If a student is accused of bullying, it will be mandatory for the incident to be reported to the police. The student will be charged and must appear in juvenile court for disciplinary action.

The penalty for this offense will include court-mandated counseling to determine the severity of the student's behavior. In accordance with the California Education Code, suspension from school may be recommended, and family counseling may also be imposed. The student's parents or guardians will be responsible for adhering to all treatment(s) as recommended by the court counselor. . . . If the student commits a second offense, he or she will receive a one-week suspension and family counseling will be required as a condition of returning to school. A third offense will result in mandatory expulsion. Each incident and court ruling will be noted in the student's permanent school records and police record.

Enforcement of this new anti-bullying law will be the key to its success. It will be the responsibility of the teachers, school counselors, school administrators, and parents or guardians of each student to ensure that all claims of discrimination and harassment are reported and investigated. Failure of a school administrator to investigate any complaint can be reported to the school board, and the school board will be obligated to compel an immediate investigation.

Once a student is found guilty of discrimination and harassment, the police and juvenile court will enforce the penalty. The court will monitor the individual's progress through

family counseling, and the school administrator will be advised
of the student's status.

    Each day another bully becomes empowered when his or   Response to objections
her actions are dismissed and the victim's cries are ignored.
We must be more proactive in dealing with these offenders
before more young lives are needlessly lost.

LINDA CHAVEZ

An outspoken commentator on issues of civil rights and affirmative action, Linda Chavez was born in 1947 in Albuquerque, New Mexico, to a Spanish American family long established in the Southwest. She graduated from the University of Colorado (BA, 1970) and did graduate work at the University of California at Los Angeles and at the University of Maryland. She has held a number of government positions, including director of the White House Office of Public Liaison under President Ronald Reagan and chair of the National Commission on Migrant Education under President George H. W. Bush. She has published three books: *Out of the Barrio: Toward a New Politics of Hispanic Assimilation* (1991), which argues against affirmative action and bilingual education; *An Unlikely Conservative: The Transformation of an Ex-Liberal (Or How I Became the Most Hated Hispanic in America)* (2002); and *Betrayal: How Union Bosses Shake Down Their Members and Corrupt American Politics* (with Daniel Gray, 2004). Chavez currently directs the Becoming American Institute, a nonprofit public policy organization. She also writes a syndicated newspaper column and is a political analyst for Fox News. She lives in Purcellville, Virginia.

Supporting Family Values

In this piece written in 2009 for *townhall.com*, a conservative news and information site, Chavez makes an unusual case in favor of immigration, legal or not. Presenting evidence that challenges the stereotype of immigrants as unstable and unable to adapt to life in the United States, she argues that established American citizens should be taking life lessons from their newest neighbors.

1   A new report out this week from the Pew Hispanic Center confirms what many observers already suspected about the illegal immigrant population in the United States: It is made up increasingly of intact families and their American-born children. Nearly half of illegal immigrant households consist of two-parent families with children, and 73% of these children were born here and are therefore US citizens.

2   The hard-line immigration restrictionists will, no doubt, find more cause for alarm in these numbers. But they should represent hope to the rest of us. One of the chief social problems afflicting this country is the breakdown in the traditional family. But among immigrants, the two-parent household is alive and well.

"Supporting Family Values" from *townhall.com*, Friday, April 17, 2009. Reprinted by permission of Linda Chavez and Creators Syndicate, Inc.

Only 21% of native households are made up of two parents living with   3
their own children. Among legal immigrants, the percentage of such households jumps to 35%. But among the illegal population, 47% of households
consist of a mother, a father and their children.

Age accounts for the major difference in household composition between   4
the native and foreign-born populations: Immigrants, especially illegal
immigrants, tend to be younger, while the native population includes large
numbers of older Americans whose children have already left home. But out-
of-wedlock births and divorce, which are more common among the native
born — especially blacks, but also Hispanics and whites — also mean that
even young native households with children are more likely to be headed by
single women than immigrant households are.

But the greater concern for some opponents of immigration — legal and   5
illegal — is the fear that these newcomers will never fully adapt, won't learn
English, will remain poor and uneducated, and transform the United States
into a replica of Mexico or some other Latin American country. The same
fears led Americans of the mid-nineteenth century to fear German and Irish
immigrants, and in the early twentieth century to fear Italians, Jews, Poles and
others from Eastern and Southern Europe.

Such worries are no more rational today — or born out of actual   6
evidence — than they were a hundred years ago. It is true that Hispanic
immigrants today take a while to catch up with the native born just as their
European predecessors did, and illegal immigrants never fully do so in terms
of education or earnings. But there is still some room for optimism in the
Pew Hispanic report. Nearly half of illegal immigrants between the ages of
18 and 24 who have graduated from high school attend college. A surprising
25% of illegal immigrant adults have at least some college, with 15% having
completed college.

And although earnings among illegal immigrants are lower than among   7
either the native population or legal immigrants, they are far from destitute.
The median household income for illegal immigrants was $36,000 in 2007
compared with $50,000 for native-born households. And illegal immigrant
males have much higher labor force participation rates than the native born,
94% compared with 83% for US-born males.

The inflow of illegal immigrants has slowed substantially since the peak,   8
which occurred during the economic boom of the late 1990s, not in recent
years, contrary to popular but uninformed opinion. The Pew Hispanic Center
estimates there are nearly 12 million illegal immigrants living in the United
States now, a number that has stabilized over the last few years as a result both
of better border enforcement and the declining job market. As a result, there

might never be a better time to grapple with what to do about this population than right now.

The fact that so many illegal immigrants are intertwined with American 9 citizens or legal residents, either as spouses or parents, should give pause to those who'd like to see all illegal immigrants rounded up and deported or their lives made so miserable they leave on their own. A better approach would allow those who have made their lives here, established families, bought homes, worked continuously and paid taxes to remain after paying fines, demonstrating English fluency and proving they have no criminal record. Such an approach is as much about supporting family values as it is granting amnesty.

Journal Writing

How do you feel about illegal immigrants? Are they criminals who should be punished? victims of circumstance who should be helped? something in between? In your journal, explore your thoughts on illegal immigration. Why do you feel as you do?

Questions on Meaning

1. What seems to have prompted Chavez's essay? How can you tell?
2. What distinctions, if any, does Chavez make between legal and illegal immigrants? Are such distinctions important to her?
3. What is Chavez's point in paragraphs 5 and 6, and how does this point fit into her larger argument?
4. At what point does Chavez reveal her PURPOSE in writing? Why do you suppose she chose not to state her THESIS in the introduction?

Questions on Writing Strategy

1. How does Chavez characterize those who hold opposing views? What does this characterization suggest about how she imagines her AUDIENCE?
2. On what underlying ASSUMPTION does Chavez base her argument? Is that assumption reasonable?
3. As a whole, is Chavez's essay an appeal to emotion or a reasoned argument, or both? Give EVIDENCE to support your answer.
4. **OTHER METHODS** Where and how does Chavez use CLASSIFICATION to support her argument?

Questions on Language

1. Consult a dictionary if you are unsure of the meaning of any of the following: restrictionists (par. 2); wedlock (4); replica (5); predecessors (6); destitute, median (7); stabilized, grapple (8); intertwined, amnesty (9).

2. What does Chavez mean by "native" households and populations? Do you detect any IRONY in her use of the word?

3. How would you describe Chavez's TONE in this essay?

Suggestions for Writing

1. **FROM JOURNAL TO ESSAY**   Based on your journal entry (p. 423), draft an essay in which you respond directly to Chavez, explaining why you agree or disagree with her position. If you wish, write your essay as a letter to the editor of *townhall. com*, the online journal in which Chavez's essay was published. (See p. 338 for an example of a letter to the editor.)

2. Write an essay in which you present your view on an aspect of US immigration policy or practice that you have strong opinions about — for example, amnesty for illegal immigrants, treatment of asylum seekers, border control, or restrictions on immigration. Before beginning your draft, do some research to support your position and also to explore opposing views so that you answer them squarely and fairly.

3. Identify a current controversy over national policy — raising taxes for the wealthy, the right to carry a concealed weapon, government funding for private schools, and so on. Read newspaper and weekly magazine editorials, letters to the editor, and other statements on the subject of the controversy. You could also discuss the issue with your friends and family. Based on your research, write a classification essay in which you group people according to their stand on the issue. Try to be as objective as possible.

4. **CRITICAL WRITING**   Write an essay in which you ANALYZE the main CLAIMS of Chavez's argument. What evidence does she provide to back up these claims? Do you find the evidence adequate? (You may wish to track down and examine the source Chavez cites in her introduction: Published by the Pew Hispanic Center on April 14, 2009, its title is *A Portrait of Unauthorized Immigrants in the United States*.)

5. **CONNECTIONS**   While defending the status of some illegal immigrants, Chavez stresses the need for all immigrants to "fully adapt," or assimilate, to American culture. Read Tal Fortgang's "Checking My Privilege" (p. 376), which touches on the author's grandparents' experiences as Polish refugees during World War II. What does it mean to be "American" in a country as diverse as the United States? In an essay, define, defend, or dispute the concept of assimilation. To what extent should recent immigrants be expected to trade ethnic or national identity for a new American identity? What might such an identity encompass, and how could it be obtained? What is gained, or lost, when immigrants become "Americanized"?

Linda Chavez on Writing

To Linda Chavez, telling writers they don't need to know the rules of grammar is like "telling aerospace engineers they don't need to learn the laws of physics." In a 2002 article for *The Enterprise*, Chavez writes about her affection for the lost art of diagramming sentences — using a branching structure to identify sentence parts and map their relationships. She fondly recalls her years in elementary school, then called "grammar school," when learning "where to place a modifier and whether to use an adverb or adjective" was an essential part of the curriculum. Abandoning grammar instruction, she writes, is leaving students scrambled.

Chavez criticizes recent classroom practices of emphasizing creativity over accuracy in composition: "For years now, schools have been teaching students to 'express' themselves, without worrying about transmitting the finer points of grammar and syntax. . . . But effective communication always entails understanding the rules. There are no short-cuts to good writing." According to Chavez, self-expression and grammar are not at odds with each other at all. As she sees it, a solid grasp of grammar is what allows a writer to clearly communicate meaning. In her own writing, Chavez follows the adage of her childhood teacher: "If you can't diagram it, don't write it."

The Brief Bedford Reader **on Writing**

Like many of the educators Chavez criticizes, we, too, suggest setting sentence-level concerns aside when you begin to write, because doing so is an important tool in getting that first draft done (see p. 34). A finished essay needs a different set of tools, however, and we have to agree with Chavez that grammar is a useful one. For a rundown of ways to bring polish to your writing, and to correct common grammatical errors in particular, check out "Editing" in Chapter 2 (pp. 47–53).

BRIANNE RICHSON

Brianne Richson was born in 1992 in Wisconsin and as a teenager moved to New Jersey and attended Summit High School. Richson returned to the Midwest to study English, journalism, and psychology at the University of Iowa, where she also competed on the swim team and wrote a regular opinion column for the *Daily Iowan*. She graduated in 2015 and plans to pursue a PhD in clinical psychology.

An Obligation to Prevent Trauma on Campus

"An Obligation to Prevent Trauma on Campus" (editors' title) first appeared, in slightly different form, in Richson's column for the *Daily Iowan*, the student newspaper of the University of Iowa. Showing empathy toward classmates who may be suffering from post-traumatic stress disorder (PTSD), Richson urges her readers to support the inclusion of "trigger warnings," or advance notices of potentially upsetting material, in all class syllabi.

In the essay following this one, "Beware the Trigger Warning," fellow University of Iowa student Jon Overton shares Richson's concerns for trauma victims but argues against adopting trigger warnings on campus.

We all have that one memory that we'd prefer people not bring up because we want to block it from our consciousness forever. Hopefully, such memories become more vague as we grow further removed from them with time, but what about a memory that has legitimately traumatized a person? A memory that has even made its holder a victim of post-traumatic stress disorder (PTSD)? 1

Students at colleges across the country are taking a term originating from the world of blogs, "trigger warning," and calling for its direct use on class syllabi, to alert them to potential adverse reactions to sensitive academic material. This might include anything from sexual assault — a prominent issue on college campuses — to eating disorders, violent graphic content, or topics of race. The list goes on. 2

One might consider such measures as dramatic and symptomatic of what I have often heard my father refer to as the "every kid gets a trophy" generation: a generation full of coddling and cushioning when things go wrong. It isn't fair, however, to compare modern parents' affinity for sheltering their children from failure with the generation's demand to be protected from reliving that which was traumatic. 3

Is it too much to ask that a rape survivor be forewarned when a profes-   4
sor is about to cover material on the topic or to ask that a person who was
confronted with a racial slur and beaten up be allowed to leave the lecture
hall before course material sends her or him into a tizzy of hypervigilance, a
hallmark characteristic of PTSD?

A great difficulty that goes along with PTSD is that it can surface at any   5
given time following a traumatic event — in weeks or years. It is one thing to
be aware of what sensory elements could trigger an episode for you, but it is
another to have the ability to actively avoid these potentially toxic situations.

University of California–Santa Barbara has passed a resolution that profes-   6
sors should indicate in syllabi when emotionally or physically stressful material
would be presented in class, prompting a *Los Angeles Times* editorial to stamp
the measure as "antithetical to college life." The same editorial suggests that
trigger warnings are a cop-out for students not wishing to engage with a diverse
set of subject material or to face traditionally uncomfortable issues head-on.

Victims of PTSD do not have more to learn about the academic subject   7
matter that is traumatic for them; they have lived it. Not everyone has the
luxury of dealing with issues upfront and immediately after a trauma. And no
one has the right to force you to do so. In Ohio, Oberlin College has gone so
far as to suggest that trigger material should not even be included in a course
if it is not clear how the students might learn from the material.

Such measures certainly have a potential to be taken too far, but our   8
obligation to prevent a trauma survivor's class time becoming a living hell
outweighs concerns about a stunted learning environment.

Journal Writing

As a student yourself, you've probably had at least one experience with the sort of
uncomfortable course materials Richson describes, whether as the person upset or as a
witness to someone else's negative reaction. Do you agree with Richson that students
should be "forewarned" of such materials so they can avoid them, or do you think it's
more beneficial to confront disturbing materials directly? Or are your feelings mixed?
In your journal, explore your thoughts on the inclusion of "traumatizing" subject matters in a college education.

Questions on Meaning

1. What is Richson's PURPOSE for writing? What problem does she identify, and
   what solution does she propose?
2. What is a "trigger warning," as Richson explains it? Where did the practice originate?

3. What is the THESIS of Richson's argument? Where is this thesis stated most clearly?

4. Richson mentions, in paragraph 7, that "Oberlin College has gone so far as to suggest that trigger material should not even be included in a course if it is not clear how the students might learn from the material." How does she seem to feel about this suggestion?

Questions on Writing Strategy

1. "An Obligation to Prevent Trauma on Campus" was directed at a very specific AUDIENCE. Who were Richson's intended readers? What ASSUMPTIONS does she make about them?

2. Where and how does Richson address opposing points of view? Do her concessions seem adequate to you? Why, or why not?

3. Clearly Richson's argument relies on EMOTIONAL APPEAL, but it is nonetheless based on an implied SYLLOGISM. Tease out her major claim, minor claim, and conclusion, and express them in your own words. (For help, refer to pp. 410–412 on deductive reasoning.)

4. **OTHER METHODS**   Discuss how Richson uses EXAMPLES to explain the experiences of people suffering from post-traumatic stress disorder, or PTSD. Why do you suppose she highlights just a few potential reactions?

Questions on Language

1. Find some COLLOQUIAL EXPRESSIONS in Richson's essay. What is the effect of such language? Does it strike you as appropriate for an academic argument?

2. Be sure you are familiar with the following words, checking a dictionary if necessary: traumatized (par. 1); adverse (2); coddling (3); forewarned, hypervigilance, hallmark (4); sensory, toxic (5); resolution (6).

3. Examine the language Richson uses to describe people who suffer from PTSD. Is it OBJECTIVE? sympathetic? negative?

Suggestions for Writing

1. **FROM JOURNAL TO ESSAY**   Working from your journal entry, write an essay that responds to Richson's argument, putting forth your own position on calls for trigger warnings in college syllabi. Under what circumstances (if any) is it acceptable, or even necessary, to study potentially traumatic subjects? Are some subjects more likely to trigger negative responses than others? Do the benefits of preventing discomfort indeed outweigh the drawbacks? Why do you think so? Like Richson, you may arrange your thoughts into an argument for or against using trigger warnings, or you may prefer to structure your essay as a personal NARRATIVE focused on your own experiences.

2. Do some research on another issue related to free speech on campus. For example: Should schools adopt codes banning speech that might offend any group based on race, gender, ethnicity, religion, or sexual orientation? Should administrators have control over what students publish in school newspapers? What is the proposed Academic Bill of Rights, and how would its enactment affect the exchange of ideas on campus? Write an essay in which you give background information on the issue and support your own view in a well-reasoned argument.

3. **CRITICAL WRITING**   Find the original version of Richson's *Daily Iowan* column online and compare it to the version we present here (titled "Colleges Should Adopt Trigger Warnings," it was first published on May 6, 2014). What REVISION and EDITING strategies did Richson use to improve her essay? What additional changes might you suggest?

4. **CONNECTIONS**   In the next essay Jon Overton writes about what he sees as the problem with trigger warnings. Write an essay in which you COMPARE AND CONTRAST the ways Richson and Overton present their cases. Which argument do you find more effective? Why?

Brianne Richson on Writing

As a recent graduate, Brianne Richson tells us that she enjoyed having "the privilege of studying creative nonfiction, the punchy world of journalism, and the research-driven writing of clinical psychology" while in school. In this reflection on her own writing process, written especially for *The Brief Bedford Reader*, Richson stresses the importance of having something to say and then saying it clearly, whatever the subject.

I find that my writing is most successful when I have a thorough handle on what it is exactly that I'm trying to get across. One thing most disciplines have in common is that no matter what, it is very important that each sentence drives home your point. This is not to say that I don't include contradictions or sentences in which I play the devil's advocate. However, if I am struggling with a particular piece, I will often write my thesis last, after reading what I have managed to flesh out. It is easy when drafting a thesis to write something that misses the mark of what you're trying to say, and it's a tricky position to write an entire piece feeling obligated to what you thought was your original stance. Saving the thesis sentence for later ensures that it encompasses your true, unencumbered thoughts.

When I write, I try to think about my thesis (or what it might ultimately be) and also about my audience, but I have spent a lot of time caught up in trying to impress readers with fancy words or experimental prose.

With experience, I have realized that the most authentic pieces say what they really mean and do not need the excess dressings to do so. I think that oftentimes writers like to fluff up their writing with strange words or unconventional style because saying what they are really trying to say can be scary, particularly in the context of nonfiction or opinion pieces. Nevertheless, it is your duty to your stance and to your readers to say what you mean.

The Brief Bedford Reader on Writing

Richson's practice of putting off writing a THESIS STATEMENT until she has worked out her ideas is one that many writers find helpful, as we discuss on pages 35–36. For suggestions on how to "say what you mean" as directly as possible, refer to "Clear and Engaging Sentences" (pp. 49–50) and "Focus on Clarity and Conciseness" (p. 336–337).

JON OVERTON

Born in Marshalltown, Iowa, in 1993, Jon Overton first got involved with journalism in high school, reporting for his school paper. As a student at the University of Iowa, he served as media editor for the Iowa Peace Network and wrote
editorials and opinion columns for *The Daily Iowan*. Overton earned degrees
in sociology and in ethics and public policy (BA, 2015) and is now a graduate
student at Kent State University. His interests include social psychology, politics,
inequality, and science.

Beware the Trigger Warning

Overton first published "Beware the Trigger Warning" in his *Daily Iowan* column, one day after Brianne Richson's argument (p. 426) appeared. Responding
directly to her claims, Overton counters that adopting trigger warnings in course
syllabi threatens to undermine the very purpose of a college education.

Brianne Richson suggests that US colleges and universities should adopt   1
trigger warnings on syllabi, on the grounds that people who've suffered traumatic experiences may be exposed to course material that would trigger memories of those events.

I agree that we should be considerate toward people who suffer from psy-   2
chological illnesses. My main gripe with trigger warnings more broadly, however, is that while they aim to be sensitive to people suffering from afflictions
like post-traumatic stress disorder, they threaten to stifle some of the most
important conversations and lessons in college.

Trigger warnings run into the same problem as proposed hate-speech laws: 3
Where do they stop? Anything can be a trigger, from hot dogs to Nazis to
Mike Tyson[1] to the color yellow. The right smell, sound, word, or image can
initiate a painful flashback for a particular person, who can't always anticipate
them. The triggers don't have to be traditionally traumatic words, phrases, or
concepts, so you can't easily predict what will set someone off.

And yet in Ohio, Oberlin College recently issued a policy that advised   4
instructors to "remove triggering material when it does not contribute directly

---

[1] Tyson (born 1966) is an American boxer with a history of violent behavior both in and
out of the ring, including a rape conviction in 1992. — EDS.

to the course learning goals." This implies that professors ought to go through their syllabi line by line to consider what might trigger a traumatic memory for some students.

Students at the University of California–Santa Barbara also passed a res- 　5
olution encouraging faculty to include a list of potential triggers on course syllabi and not punish students for leaving early if triggering content arises. Some of the most extreme trigger warning advocates have even attacked classical literature like *Things Fall Apart* and *The Great Gatsby*.[2]

Thanks to some highly vocal faculty at Oberlin, the attack on academic 　6
freedom there was shot down, but these examples illustrate perfectly what is so dangerous about trigger warnings. They threaten to transform higher education into a horrific nightmare in which political correctness on steroids allows students to avoid any information with which they disagree. One of the great things about colleges and universities is that they challenge your worldview. They force you to confront information that makes you rethink cherished beliefs. This can be distressing, but that's the point: to expose yourself to new ideas and points of view.

The motivations behind trigger warnings are undoubtedly admirable. 　7
They reflect the pinnacle of empathy and compassion. However, it's up to the students who suffer from PTSD to tell their instructors in advance if they're concerned about a potential trigger from specific course material. As much as we'd like to help trauma victims, we can't know what's going to initiate a panic attack, and trying to prevent any and all of them endangers academic discourse.

Journal Writing

Think of a proposal or development that some people view positively but that you view differently because of its risks, unintended effects, or ethical implications: space travel? stem-cell research? wind farms? an everyday convenience such as Bitcoin or location tracking? In your journal, explore your thoughts about this proposal or development.

Questions on Meaning

1. What do you take to be Overton's main PURPOSE in writing? What is his THESIS, and where does he state it?

2. Why, according to Overton, are trigger warnings a bad idea? What exactly are "triggers," as he explains them? What's wrong with listing them in syllabi?

[2] Chinua Achebe's *Things Fall Apart* (1958) has been singled out for themes of racial conflict and colonialism; F. Scott Fitzgerald's *The Great Gatsby* (1925) includes violence against women. — EDS.

3. What does Overton believe to be the purpose of a college education? Where does he spell out the primary ASSUMPTION behind his argument? .

4. What alternative solution to the problem identified by Richson does Overton propose?

Questions on Writing Strategy

1. Why does Overton open and close his essay by saying he agrees with Richson and admires her motivations (pars. 2, 7)? Do you think he fully understands the issue she addresses?

2. Does Overton seem to expect his AUDIENCE to agree or disagree with his position? In answering this question, consider his TONE and his use of pronouns (*we* and *you* especially). What audience reaction does he seem to be seeking?

3. To what extent does Overton use rational, emotional, and ethical APPEALS in his argument? Identify examples of each kind of appeal in your answer.

4. **OTHER METHODS**   Examine the way Overton uses EXAMPLE to develop his response to Richson. From where does he draw his examples? How persuasive are they as EVIDENCE for his claim about trigger warnings' potential to "stifle some of the most important conversations and lessons in college" (par. 2)?

Questions on Language

1. Check a dictionary if you are unfamiliar with the meanings of any of the following words: traumatic (par. 1); afflictions, stifle (2); initiate, flashback (3); resolution (5); distressing (6); pinnacle, empathy, discourse (7).

2. What does Overton mean by "political correctness on steroids" (par. 6)? Do you notice any other FIGURES OF SPEECH that underscore his attitude toward trigger warnings?

3. How do the ALLUSIONS to *Things Fall Apart* and *The Great Gatsby* in paragraph 5 support (or undermine) Overton's point?

Suggestions for Writing

1. **FROM JOURNAL TO ESSAY**   Compose an essay in which you explain why you believe that the proposal or development you wrote about in your journal has or may have negative consequences ignored by others. Be sure to acknowledge what others see as the benefits. Also keep in mind that some readers may not immediately agree with you, so you will need to defend your views carefully and fully.

2. In paragraph 6 Overton asserts that the purpose of higher education is to "challenge your worldview [and] force you to . . . rethink cherished beliefs." When has your mind been expanded by exposure to a view that was different from your own? Perhaps you attended a religious service with a friend, visited another country, took a course with an instructor whose political views you disagreed with, or

learned something interesting from a book you thought you would hate. What did you gain from the experience? Write an essay about the importance of challenging your worldview, using concrete examples (or a single extended example) to support your point.

3. Expand your knowledge about post-traumatic stress disorder (PTSD) by researching the condition. You might start with its definition in the *Diagnostic and Statistical Manual of Mental Disorders*, Fifth Edition, published by the American Psychiatric Association and available in most college libraries. Look also for scholarly articles in a periodical database, and perhaps some personal accounts by people who have the condition. What causes PTSD, and what are some of its symptoms? How is it treated? How do "triggers" come into play? In an essay SYNTHESIZE what you discover.

4. **CRITICAL WRITING**   In an essay, EVALUATE Overton's argument. How truly does it resonate with your own experience? How persuasive do you find his evidence? How well does he convince you of the threats posed by trigger warnings? How well do you think he develops his proposed solutions?

5. **CONNECTIONS**   On what points does Overton seem to agree with *Daily Iowan* columnist Brianne Richson (p. 426)? On what points does he disagree? To what extent do the two writers' perspectives explain their difference of opinion? What are *your* thoughts on the issue they debate, and how does your own perspective influence your opinion? Answer these questions in an essay.

Jon Overton on Writing

Asked to tell us about his experience writing arguments, Jon Overton took it upon himself to do some research to learn more about the method and how to be effective at persuading readers. Here he shares his findings.

Effective persuasion requires empathy.

It's hard to build an argument that actually changes someone's opinion, especially when your stance contradicts audience members' firmly held beliefs. Social psychologists have long known that once people form an opinion, and especially if that opinion is important to their identity, it's incredibly hard to change.

To a degree, you can still reason with people. But you have to understand why they think the way they do. It helps if you can establish common ground with opponents from the beginning. This makes them more likely to listen to you once you lay out your case.

From there, your argument should appeal not only to your moral intuitions, but to the moral intuitions of those who disagree with you. Recent research by Feinberg and Willer (2015) illustrated that arguments that appeal to ideological opponents' values are far more persuasive than arguments that simply rely on your sides' values.

The more you consider the opposing side's position, the more persuasive your argument will be.

Reference

Feinberg, M., & Willer, R. (2015). From gulf to bridge: When do moral arguments facilitate political influence? *Personality and Social Psychology Bulletin, 41*(12), 1665–1681. doi:10.1177/0146167215607842

The Brief Bedford Reader on Writing

Overton's quick research follows APA style, outlined on pages 519–529 of the Appendix. You can find additional suggestions for building COMMON GROUND with readers on page 407 of this chapter.

NICHOLAS CARR

Nicholas Carr was born in 1959 and educated at Dartmouth College and Harvard University. He worked as a management consultant for a private firm and as executive editor for *Harvard Business Review* and is currently an editorial advisor for *Encyclopaedia Britannica*. Carr is best known, however, for his worrisome insights into computers and culture. He has stirred controversy with his books, all skeptical of the benefits of technology: *Does IT Matter? Information Technology and the Corrosion of Competitive Advantage* (2004), *The Big Switch: Rewiring the World, from Edison to Google* (2008), *The Shallows: What the Internet Is Doing to Our Brains* (2011), and *The Glass Cage: How Our Computers Are Changing Us* (2014). Carr's writing has also appeared in several newspapers and magazines, including *The Atlantic Monthly*, *Financial Times*, *Wired*, the *New York Times*, and *Advertising Age*. He is a sought-after speaker on the business lecture circuit and a regular commentator on television and radio.

Tracking Is an Assault on Liberty

Carr is a leading critic of the Internet and often writes about the dangers of spending time online. In this 2010 essay for the *Wall Street Journal*, he cites examples of how corporations collect and use our personal information, warns of potential abuses of such data mining, and advocates new rules protecting consumer privacy. The essays following this one — Jim Harper's "Web Users Get as Much as They Give" (p. 443) and Lori Andrews's "*Facebook* Is Using You" (p. 449) — address the same issue.

In a 1963 Supreme Court opinion, Chief Justice Earl Warren observed 1
that "the fantastic advances in the field of electronic communication constitute a great danger to the privacy of the individual." The advances have only accelerated since then, along with the dangers. Today, as companies strive to personalize the services and advertisements they provide over the Internet, the surreptitious collection of personal information is rampant. The very idea of privacy is under threat.

Most of us view personalization and privacy as desirable things, and we 2
understand that enjoying more of one means giving up some of the other. To have goods, services and promotions tailored to our personal circumstances and desires, we need to divulge information about ourselves to corporations, governments or other outsiders.

This tradeoff has always been part of our lives as consumers and citizens.   3
But now, thanks to the Net, we're losing our ability to understand and control
those tradeoffs — to choose, consciously and with awareness of the consequences, what information about ourselves we disclose and what we don't.
Incredibly detailed data about our lives are being harvested from online databases without our awareness, much less our approval.

Even though the Internet is a very social place, we tend to access it in   4
seclusion. We often assume that we're anonymous as we go about our business
online. As a result, we treat the Net not just as a shopping mall and a library
but as a personal diary and, sometimes, a confessional. Through the sites we
visit and the searches we make, we disclose details not only about our jobs,
hobbies, families, politics and health, but also about our secrets, fantasies,
even our peccadilloes.

But our sense of anonymity is largely an illusion. Pretty much everything   5
we do online, down to individual keystrokes and clicks, is recorded, stored
in cookies and corporate databases, and connected to our identities, either
explicitly through our user names, credit-card numbers and the IP addresses
assigned to our computers, or implicitly through our searching, surfing and
purchasing histories.

A few years ago, the computer consultant Tom Owad published the results of   6
an experiment that provided a chilling lesson in just how easy it is to extract sensitive personal data from the Net. Mr. Owad wrote a simple piece of software that
allowed him to download public wish lists that *Amazon.com* customers post to
catalog products that they plan to purchase or would like to receive as gifts. These
lists usually include the name of the list's owner and his or her city and state.

Using a couple of standard-issue PCs, Mr. Owad was able to download   7
over 250,000 wish lists over the course of a day. He then searched the data for
controversial or politically sensitive books and authors, from Kurt Vonnegut's
Slaughterhouse-Five[1] to the Koran. He then used *Yahoo!* People Search to identify addresses and phone numbers for many of the list owners.

Mr. Owad ended up with maps of the United States showing the locations   8
of people interested in particular books and ideas, including George Orwell's
Nineteen Eighty-Four.[2] He could just as easily have published a map showing the residences of people interested in books about treating depression or
adopting a child. "It used to be," Mr. Owad concluded, "you had to get a
warrant to monitor a person or a group of people. Today, it is increasingly easy
to monitor ideas. And then track them back to people."

---

[1] A 1969 novel about alien abduction, time travel, and the bombing of Dresden, Germany,
in World War II. — Eds.

[2] A 1949 novel critical of communism and mind control. — Eds.

What Mr. Owad did by hand can increasingly be performed automatically, 9
with data-mining software that draws from many sites and databases. One of
the essential characteristics of the Net is the interconnection of diverse stores
of information. The "openness" of databases is what gives the system much of
its power and usefulness. But it also makes it easy to discover hidden relationships among far-flung bits of data.

In 2006, a team of scholars from the University of Minnesota described 10
how easy it is for data-mining software to create detailed personal profiles of
individuals — even when they post information anonymously. The software
is based on a simple principle: People tend to leave lots of little pieces of
information about themselves and their opinions in many different places on
the Web. By identifying correspondences among the data, sophisticated algorithms can identify individuals with extraordinary precision. And it's not a big
leap from there to discovering the people's names. The researchers noted that
most Americans can be identified by name and address using only their ZIP
code, birthday and gender — three pieces of information that people often
divulge when they register at a website.

The more deeply the Net is woven into our work lives and leisure activities, 11
the more exposed we become. Over the last few years, as social-networking services have grown in popularity, people have come to entrust ever more intimate
details about their lives to sites like *Facebook* and *Twitter*. The incorporation of
GPS transmitters into cellphones and the rise of location-tracking services like
Foursquare provide powerful tools for assembling moment-by-moment records of
people's movements. As reading shifts from printed pages onto networked devices
like the Kindle and the Nook, it becomes possible for companies to more closely
monitor people's reading habits — even when they're not surfing the Web.

"You have zero privacy," Scott McNealy remarked back in 1999, when 12
he was chief executive of Sun Microsystems. "Get over it." Other Silicon
Valley CEOs have expressed similar sentiments in just the last few months.
While Internet companies may be complacent about the erosion of personal
privacy — they, after all, profit from the trend — the rest of us should be wary.
There are real dangers.

First and most obvious is the possibility that our personal data will fall into 13
the wrong hands. Powerful data-mining tools are available not only to legitimate corporations and researchers, but also to crooks, con men and creeps. As
more data about us is collected and shared online, the threats from unsanc-
tioned interceptions of the data grow. Criminal syndicates can use purloined
information about our identities to commit financial fraud, and stalkers can
use locational data to track our whereabouts.

The first line of defense is, of course, common sense. We need to take personal 14
responsibility for the information we share whenever we log on. But no amount
of caution will protect us from the dispersal of information collected without our

knowledge. If we're not aware of what data about us are available online, and how they're being used and exchanged, it can be difficult to guard against abuses.

A second danger is the possibility that personal information may be used   15
to influence our behavior and even our thoughts in ways that are invisible to us. Personalization's evil twin is manipulation. As mathematicians and marketers refine data-mining algorithms, they gain more precise ways to predict people's behavior as well as how they'll react when they're presented with online ads and other digital stimuli. Just this past week, Google CEO Eric Schmidt acknowledged that by tracking a person's messages and movements, an algorithm can accurately predict where that person will go next.

As marketing pitches and product offerings become more tightly tied to our   16
past patterns of behavior, they become more powerful as triggers of future behavior. Already, advertisers are able to infer extremely personal details about people by monitoring their Web-browsing habits. They can then use that knowledge to create ad campaigns customized to particular individuals. A man who visits a site about obesity, for instance, may soon see a lot of promotional messages related to weight-loss treatments. A woman who does research about anxiety may be bombarded with pharmaceutical ads. The line between personalization and manipulation is a fuzzy one, but one thing is certain: We can never know if the line has been crossed if we're unaware of what companies know about us.

Safeguarding privacy online isn't particularly hard. It requires that soft-   17
ware makers and site operators assume that people want to keep their information private. Privacy settings should be on by default and easy to modify. And when companies track our behavior or use personal details to tailor messages, they should provide an easy way for us to see what they're doing.

The greatest danger posed by the continuing erosion of personal privacy   18
is that it may lead us as a society to devalue the concept of privacy, to see it as outdated and unimportant. We may begin to see privacy merely as a barrier to efficient shopping and socializing. That would be a tragedy. As the computer security expert Bruce Schneier has observed, privacy is not just a screen we hide behind when we do something naughty or embarrassing; privacy is "intrinsic to the concept of liberty." When we feel that we're always being watched, we begin to lose our sense of self-reliance and free will and, along with it, our individuality. "We become children," writes Mr. Schneier, "fettered under watchful eyes."

Privacy is not only essential to life and liberty; it's essential to the pursuit   19
of happiness, in the broadest and deepest sense. We human beings are not just social creatures; we're also private creatures. What we don't share is as important as what we do share. The way that we choose to define the boundary between our public self and our private self will vary greatly from person to person, which is exactly why it's so important to be ever vigilant in defending everyone's right to set that boundary as he or she sees fit.

Journal Writing

"The more deeply the Net is woven into our work lives and leisure activities, the more exposed we become," Carr writes (par. 11). Do you agree? Draft a narrative account of an experience you have had of feeling exposed while using a medium such as *Google*, *Facebook*, or *Instagram*. If you've never felt exposed, explain why not.

Questions on Meaning

1. What problem does Carr identify? What solution, if any, does he propose?
2. How, according to Carr, do "corporations, governments or other outsiders" (par. 2) obtain personal information about individual Internet users?
3. "There are real dangers" to losing privacy online, says Carr (par. 12). What are those dangers, as he sees them?
4. What seems to be Carr's PURPOSE? Is he writing to express a concern, offer a solution, influence government regulations, change attitudes, or do something else? What details from the essay support your answer?

Questions on Writing Strategy

1. What does the author accomplish by opening with a discussion of the "tradeoff" (par. 3) between privacy and personalization?
2. Is this essay an appeal to emotion or a reasoned argument, or both? Give evidence for your answer.
3. Why is Carr so concerned about "manipulation" (pars. 15–16)? What exactly does he think could happen if advertisers customize their messages to individual Internet users' interests and behaviors? Do you think his concerns are valid? What does he seem to ASSUME about his readers' CRITICAL-THINKING abilities?
4. **OTHER METHODS** How does Carr use DEFINITION to clarify the meaning of *privacy*? By what means does he bring his argument around to the subject of liberty?

Questions on Language

1. How would you describe Carr's attitude toward his subject? What is the overall TONE of his argument?
2. Who are Earl Warren (par. 1), Tom Owad (6), Scott McNealy (12), Eric Schmidt (15), and Bruce Schneier (18)? What does Carr achieve by quoting and paraphrasing them?
3. Be sure you are familiar with the following words, checking a dictionary if necessary: surreptitious (par. 1); peccadilloes (4); algorithms (10); complacent (12); syndicates, purloined (13); dispersal (14); stimuli (15); intrinsic, fettered (18).

Suggestions for Writing

1. **FROM JOURNAL TO ESSAY** Expand on the narrative account you drafted in your journal to write an essay that assesses the CAUSE-AND-EFFECT relationship between the Internet and loss of privacy, being sure to define what you mean by *privacy*. Do you believe that online tools encourage people to share "ever more intimate details about their lives" (par. 11)? Do you think such exposure is a problem? Why, or why not?

2. Both of the novels Carr mentions — *Slaughterhouse-Five* and *Nineteen Eighty-Four* — present pessimistic visions of imagined societies in which governments control individual citizens' minds and behaviors. Choose one novel and read it (or a reputable synopsis of it), keeping Carr's argument in mind. Why do searches for these novels represent especially apt examples of the issues surrounding data tracking? What might a government agency in particular infer about a person who reads one of these works?

3. **CRITICAL WRITING** Write an essay in which you analyze and evaluate any one of Carr's ideas. Some possibilities: Do "[m]ost of us view personalization and privacy as desirable things" (par. 2)? Are the dangers of online exposure as "real" (12) as he claims? Are we becoming resigned to a lack of privacy as he says (18)? Do we really need privacy in the first place (19)? Support your view with evidence from your experience, observation, or reading.

4. **CONNECTIONS** While Carr expresses deep concern about the theoretical implications of data mining, and Lori Andrews (p. 449) argues that tracking poses serious practical risks for Internet users, Jim Harper, the author of the next essay, sees little reason to worry. On what major point do these authors agree and disagree? How do the tones of the three essays compare? Does any one writer seem more convinced of being in the right than the others do? Which essay do you find most convincing, and why?

Nicholas Carr on Writing

Carr is well known for his concern that constant exposure to electronic stimuli shortens one's attention span. In a 2010 blog post for both the *Futurist* and *Encyclopaedia Britannica,* he offers a dour prediction of how new technologies will continue to affect not only reading but also writing.

I have little doubt that in 2050 — or 2100, for that matter — we'll still be happily reading and writing. Even if we come to be outfitted with nifty Web-enabled brain implants, most of the stuff that's beamed into our skulls will likely take the form of text. Even our robots will probably be adept at reading.

What will change — what already is changing, in fact — is *the way we read and write*. In the past, changes in writing technologies, such as the shift from scroll to book, had dramatic effects on the kind of ideas that people put down on paper and, more generally, on people's intellectual lives. Now that we're leaving behind the page and adopting the screen as our main medium for reading, we'll see similarly far-reaching changes in the way we write, read, and even think.

Our eager embrace of a brand new verb — *to text* — speaks volumes. We're rapidly moving away from our old linear form of writing and reading, in which ideas and narratives wended their way across many pages, to a much more compressed, nonlinear form. What we've learned about digital media is that, even as they promote the transmission of writing, they shatter writing into little, utilitarian fragments. They turn stories into snippets. They transform prose and poetry into quick, scattered bursts of text.

Writing will survive, but it will survive in a debased form. It will lose its richness. We will no longer read and write words. We will merely process them, the way our computers do.

The Brief Bedford Reader on Writing

Do you share Carr's concern that new technologies will diminish our talent for CRITICAL THINKING? To hone your own analytic skills, read Chapter 1, especially pages 16–18. And for tips on developing "quick, scattered bursts of text" into writing that has UNITY and COHERENCE, see pages 41–42 of Chapter 2.

JIM HARPER

Jim Harper is the Web master of *WashingtonWatch*, a site that tracks federal spending; the editor of *Privacilla*, a Web-based think tank; and the director of information policy studies at the Cato Institute in Washington, DC. He is also a founding member of the Data Privacy and Integrity Advisory Committee for the Department of Homeland Security. Harper studied political science at the University of California at Santa Barbara and in 1994 received a law degree from Hastings College of the University of California. His articles about privacy and security have appeared in *Administrative Law Review*, the *Minnesota Law Review*, the *Hastings Constitutional Law Quarterly*, the *Blaze*, and the *Technology Liberation Front*. He has also published two books: *Identity Crisis: How Identification Is Overused and Misunderstood* (2006) and *Terrorizing Ourselves: Why US Counterterrorism Policy Is Failing and How to Fix It* (2010), coedited with Benjamin H. Friedman and Christopher A. Preble. As an expert in the legal complications surrounding new technologies, Harper has testified at several congressional hearings and lectured widely.

Web Users Get as Much as They Give

With so much useful (and not so useful) material available free of charge, some might say that privacy is a fair price for Web users to pay. In this essay published in the *Wall Street Journal* alongside the previous selection, Nicholas Carr's "Tracking Is an Assault on Liberty" (p. 436), Harper argues that contemporary business models and opportunities to customize advertising justify the use of data mining. The next essay, "*Facebook* Is Using You," by Lori Andrews (p. 449), offers a third perspective on the subject.

If you surf the Web, congratulations! You are part of the information economy. Data gleaned from your communications and transactions grease the gears of modern commerce. Not everyone is celebrating, of course. Many people are concerned and dismayed — even shocked — when they learn that "their" data are fuel for the World Wide Web.

Who is gathering the information? What are they doing with it? How might this harm me? How do I stop it?

These are all good questions. But rather than indulging the natural reaction to say "stop," people should get smart and learn how to control personal information. There are plenty of options and tools people can use to protect privacy — and a certain obligation to use them. Data about you are not "yours" if you don't do anything to control them. Meanwhile, learning about the information economy can make clear its many benefits.

It's natural to be concerned about online privacy. The Internet is an inter-   4
active medium, not a static one like television. Every visit to a Web site sends information out before it pulls information in. And the information Web surfers send out can be revealing.

Most Web sites track users, particularly through the use of cookies, little   5
text files placed on Web surfers' computers. Sites use cookies to customize a visitor's experience. And advertising networks use cookies to gather information about users. A network that has ads on a lot of sites will recognize a browser (and by inference the person using it) when it goes to different Web sites, enabling the ad network to get a sense of that person's interests. Been on a site dealing with SUVs? You just might see an SUV ad as you continue to surf. Most Web sites and ad networks do not "sell" information about their users. In targeted online advertising, the business model is to sell space to advertisers — giving them access to people ("eyeballs") based on their demographics and interests. If an ad network sold personal and contact info, it would undercut its advertising business and its own profitability.

Some people don't like this tracking, for a variety of reasons. For some, it   6
feels like a violation to be treated as a mere object of commerce. Some worry that data about their interests will be used to discriminate wrongly against them, or to exclude them from information and opportunities they should enjoy. Excess customization of the Web experience may stratify society, some believe. If you are poor or from a minority group, for example, the news, entertainment and commentary you see on the Web might differ from others', preventing your participation in the "national" conversation and culture that traditional media may produce. And tied to real identities, Web-surfing data could fall into the hands of government and be used wrongly. These are all legitimate concerns that people with different worldviews prioritize to differing degrees.

"Surreptitious" use of cookies is one of the weaker complaints. Cookies   7
have been integral to Web browsing since the beginning, and their privacy consequences have been a subject of public discussion for over a decade. Cookies are a surreptitious threat to privacy the way smoking is a surreptitious threat to health. If you don't know about it, you haven't been paying attention. But before going into your browser settings and canceling cookies, Web users should ask another question about information sharing in the online world. What am I getting in return?

The reason why a company like *Google* can spend millions and millions   8
of dollars on free services like its search engine, Gmail, mapping tools, *Google*

Groups and more is because of online advertising that trades in personal information. And it's not just *Google*. *Facebook*, *Yahoo!*, *MSN* and thousands of blogs, news sites, and comment boards use advertising to support what they do. And personalized advertising is more valuable than advertising aimed at just anyone. Marketers will pay more to reach you if you are likely to use their products or services. (Perhaps online tracking makes everyone special!)

If Web users supply less information to the Web, the Web will supply 9 less information to them. Free content won't go away if consumers decline to allow personalization, but there will be less of it. Bloggers and operators of small Web sites will have a little less reason to produce the stuff that makes our Internet an endlessly fascinating place to visit. As an operator of a small government-transparency Web site, *WashingtonWatch*, I add new features for my visitors when there is enough money to do it. More money spent on advertising means more tools for American citizens to use across the Web.

Ten years ago — during an earlier round of cookie concern — the Federal 10 Trade Commission asked Congress for power to regulate the Internet for privacy's sake. If the FTC had gotten authority to impose regulations requiring "notice, choice, access, and security" from Web sites — all good practices, in varying measure — it is doubtful that *Google* would have had the same success it has had over the past decade. It might be a decent, struggling search engine today. But, unable to generate the kind of income it does, the quality of search it produces might be lower, and it may not have had the assets to produce and support all its fascinating and useful products. The rise of *Google* and all the access it provides was not fated from the beginning. It depended on a particular set of circumstances in which it had access to consumer information and the freedom to use it in ways that some find privacy-dubious.

Some legislators, privacy advocates and technologists want very badly to 11 protect consumers, but much "consumer protection" actually invites consumers to abandon personal responsibility. The *caveat emptor*[1] rule requires people to stay on their toes, learn about the products they use, and hold businesses' feet to the fire. People rise or fall to meet expectations, and consumer advocates who assume incompetence on the part of the public may have a hand in producing it, making consumers worse off. If a central authority such as Congress or the FTC were to decide for consumers how to deal with cookies, it would generalize wrongly about many, if not most, individuals' interests, giving them the wrong mix of privacy and interactivity. If the FTC ruled that third-party cookies required consumers to opt in, for example, most would not, and the wealth of "free" content and services most people take for granted would quietly fade from view. And it would leave consumers unprotected

---

[1] Latin, "buyer beware." — Eds.

from threats beyond their jurisdiction (as in Web tracking by sites outside the United States). Education is the hard way, and it is the only way, to get consumers' privacy interests balanced with their other interests.

But perhaps this is a government vs. corporate passion play, with government as the privacy defender. The *Wall Street Journal* reported last week that engineers working on a new version of Microsoft's Internet Explorer browser thought they might set certain defaults to protect privacy better, but they were overruled when the business segments at Microsoft learned of the plan. Privacy "sabotage," the Electronic Frontier Foundation called it. And a *Wired* news story says Microsoft "crippled" online privacy protections. But if the engineers' plan had won the day, an equal, opposite reaction would have resulted when Microsoft "sabotaged" Web interactivity and the advertising business model, "crippling" consumer access to free content. The new version of Microsoft's browser maintained the status quo in cookie functionality, as does *Google*'s Chrome browser and *Firefox*, a product of the nonprofit Mozilla Foundation. The "business attacks privacy" story doesn't wash.   12

This is not to say that businesses don't want personal information — they do, so they can provide maximal service to their customers. But they are struggling to figure out how to serve all dimensions of consumer interest, including the internally inconsistent consumer demand for privacy along with free content, custom Web experiences, convenience and so on.   13

Only one thing is certain here: Nobody knows how this is supposed to come out. Cookies and other tracking technologies will create legitimate concerns that weigh against the benefits they provide. Browser defaults may converge on something more privacy-protective. (Apple's *Safari* browser rejects third-party cookies unless users tell it to do otherwise.) Browser plug-ins will augment consumers' power to control cookies and other tracking technologies. Consumers will get better accustomed to the information economy, and they will choose more articulately how they fit into it. What matters is that the conversation should continue.   14

Journal Writing

Harper acknowledges, in paragraph 6, that some people are concerned that by narrowing the kinds of information certain segments of the population are exposed to, customized news outlets limit "participation in the 'national' conversation and culture that traditional media may produce." What kind of news do you follow, and how do you gain access to it? Why do you choose to follow the stories you do on the outlets you do?

Questions on Meaning

1. What connection does Harper make between personal data and the "information economy" (par. 1)? Express his THESIS in a sentence or two of your own.

2. What are cookies, and how are they used? Why is Harper not bothered by them?

3. Where does Harper ultimately place the blame for the average American's loss of privacy online? What solution does he suggest?

4. What seems to be the author's primary PURPOSE in this essay: to discredit critics of Internet tracking? to reassure Web users that their personal information is safe? to advance an economic theory? Do you think Harper accomplishes his purpose? Why, or why not?

Questions on Writing Strategy

1. To understand Harper's strategy, make an outline of the main points in his argument. Which of these points directly counter points made by Nicholas Carr in the previous essay (pp. 436–439)? Which of Carr's points does Harper not address directly? In what ways is his emphasis different from Carr's?

2. What ASSUMPTIONS does Harper seem to make about the readers of this essay? (Recall that it was first published in the *Wall Street Journal*.) Are the assumptions correct in your case?

3. In paragraph 9 Harper discusses his role as "an operator of a small government-transparency Web site." What persuasive tactic is he employing here? Does it work, in your opinion?

4. What examples of past efforts to protect consumer privacy does Harper present? What do these examples contribute to his point?

5. **OTHER METHODS**   Much of Harper's argument is developed by CAUSE-AND-EFFECT analysis. What does he claim would be the result of new regulations protecting privacy online?

Questions on Language

1. Harper uses FIGURES OF SPEECH throughout his essay, such as the metaphor "grease the gears of modern commerce" (par. 1), and the personification "advertising that trades in personal information" (8). Locate a few more figures of speech and comment on their effectiveness. What do they contribute to Harper's TONE?

2. Check a dictionary if you are unfamiliar with the meanings of any of the following words: gleaned (par. 1), demographics (5), stratify (6), surreptitious (7), jurisdiction (11), status quo (12), augment (14).

3. A "passion play" (par. 12) is a traditional Christian pageant that celebrates the death and resurrection of Jesus. What does Harper accomplish by making an ALLUSION to this particular dramatic GENRE? Does it strengthen his argument, or weaken it? Why?

Suggestions for Writing

1. **JOURNAL TO ESSAY**   Beginning with an analysis of your own preferences in news reporting and sources, write an essay in which you consider how important you think it is for people to stay informed about what's happening in the world around them. In your essay, also consider the kinds of news you believe people should follow and what you see as the best sources for gaining access to such news.

2. Write an essay in which you compare and contrast two related types of communication or entertainment media: for example, print books and e-readers, television and *YouTube*, radio and streaming music services, laptops and tablets. Your approach may be either lighthearted or serious, but make sure you come to some conclusion about your subjects. Which technology do you favor? Why?

3. **CRITICAL WRITING**   Harper writes that "[s]ome people don't like . . . tracking, for a variety of reasons" (par. 6). He then lists several of these reasons and acknowledges that such concerns are legitimate, but doesn't go into them in any detail. Pick one of the issues he raises and explore it in an essay. Does it, for instance, "feel like a violation to be treated as a mere object of commerce" (6)? Could data mining lead to discrimination or stratification in society? What might happen if information falls into the wrong hands? You may wish to think broadly about this issue, but bring your essay down to earth by focusing on one specific concern — perhaps one that you've experienced or witnessed yourself.

4. **CONNECTIONS**   Jim Harper and Nicholas Carr (p. 436) both assume that Internet tracking is used to collect data so that advertisers can customize their messages to a targeted audience. But Lori Andrews, in the next essay ("*Facebook* Is Using You"), asserts that data mining is conducted for a much different — and more disturbing — purpose. What is that purpose, and why do you suppose neither Harper nor Carr dwell on it? How does Andrews's perspective affect your understanding of the issue? Should the uses to which data may be put affect people's willingness (or refusal) to sacrifice privacy online? Why, or why not? Answer these questions in an essay.

LORI ANDREWS

Lori Andrews was born in Chicago, Illinois, in 1952 and earned her under-graduate and law degrees from Yale University. She has published ten books on the legal issues associated with subjects ranging from infertility and cloning to genetic screening. Her most recent book, *I Know Who You Are and I Saw What You Did* (2012), looks at the cultural and political consequences of online social networking. Considered a leading expert on bioethics and emerging tech-nologies, Andrews is a frequent contributor to newspapers and magazines and a popular guest on TV news programs, including *Good Morning America*, *Night-line*, and *60 Minutes*. She is also the author of three mystery novels. Andrews teaches at the Illinois Institute of Technology's Chicago–Kent College of Law, where she is director of the Institute of Science, Law, and Technology.

Facebook Is Using You

In this 2012 essay for the *New York Times*, Andrews extends the debate between Nicholas Carr and Jim Harper in the previous two essays. Despite the many opportunities and advantages offered by the Internet, Andrews warns, data-collection technologies also pose practical threats to Web users. As she sees it, individual privacy settings are insufficient. What we need, she insists, are new laws to protect us from harm.

Last week, *Facebook* filed documents with the government that will allow it to sell shares of stock to the public. It is estimated to be worth at least $75 billion. But unlike other big-ticket corporations, it doesn't have an inven-tory of widgets or gadgets, cars or phones. *Facebook*'s inventory consists of personal data — yours and mine.

Facebook makes money by selling ad space to companies that want to reach us. Advertisers choose key words or details — like relationship status, loca-tion, activities, favorite books and employment — and then *Facebook* runs the ads for the targeted subset of its 845 million users. If you indicate that you like cupcakes, live in a certain neighborhood and have invited friends over, expect an ad from a nearby bakery to appear on your page. The magnitude of online information *Facebook* has available about each of us for targeted mar-keting is stunning. In Europe, laws give people the right to know what data companies have about them, but that is not the case in the United States.

Facebook made \$3.2 billion in advertising revenue last year, 85% of its   3
total revenue. Yet *Facebook*'s inventory of data and its revenue from advertising are small potatoes compared to some others. *Google* took in more than
ten times as much, with an estimated \$36.5 billion in advertising revenue
in 2011, by analyzing what people sent over Gmail and what they searched
on the Web, and then using that data to sell ads. Hundreds of other companies have also staked claims on people's online data by depositing software
called cookies or other tracking mechanisms on people's computers and in
their browsers. If you've mentioned anxiety in an e-mail, done a *Google* search
for "stress" or started using an online medical diary that lets you monitor your
mood, expect ads for medications and services to treat your anxiety.

Ads that pop up on your screen might seem useful, or at worst, a nuisance.   4
But they are much more than that. The bits and bytes about your life can easily be used against you. Whether you can obtain a job, credit or insurance can
be based on your digital doppelgänger — and you may never know why you've
been turned down.

Material mined online has been used against people battling for child   5
custody or defending themselves in criminal cases. LexisNexis has a product
called Accurint for Law Enforcement, which gives government agents
information about what people do on social networks. The Internal Revenue
Service searches *Facebook* and *MySpace* for evidence of tax evaders' income
and whereabouts, and United States Citizenship and Immigration Services
has been known to scrutinize photos and posts to confirm family relationships or weed out sham marriages. Employers sometimes decide whether to
hire people based on their online profiles, with one study indicating that 70%
of recruiters and human resource professionals in the United States have
rejected candidates based on data found online. A company called Spokeo
gathers online data for employers, the public and anyone else who wants it.
The company even posts ads urging "HR Recruiters — Click Here Now!" and
asking women to submit their boyfriends' e-mail addresses for an analysis of
their online photos and activities to learn "Is He Cheating on You?"

Stereotyping is alive and well in data aggregation. Your application for   6
credit could be declined not on the basis of your own finances or credit history,
but on the basis of aggregate data — what other people whose likes and dislikes
are similar to yours have done. If guitar players or divorcing couples are more
likely to renege on their credit-card bills, then the fact that you've looked at
guitar ads or sent an e-mail to a divorce lawyer might cause a data aggregator
to classify you as less credit-worthy. When an Atlanta man returned from his
honeymoon, he found that his credit limit had been lowered to \$3,800 from
\$10,800. The switch was not based on anything he had done but on aggregate
data. A letter from the company told him, "Other customers who have used

their card at establishments where you recently shopped have a poor repayment history with American Express."

Even though laws allow people to challenge false information in credit reports, there are no laws that require data aggregators to reveal what they know about you. If I've Googled "diabetes" for a friend or "date rape drugs" for a mystery I'm writing, data aggregators assume those searches reflect my own health and proclivities. Because no laws regulate what types of data these aggregators can collect, they make their own rules.

In 2007 and 2008, the online advertising company NebuAd contracted with six Internet service providers to install hardware on their networks that monitored users' Internet activities and transmitted that data to NebuAd's servers for analysis and use in marketing. For an average of six months, NebuAd copied every e-mail, Web search or purchase that some 400,000 people sent over the Internet. Other companies, like Healthline Networks Inc., have in-house limits on which private information they will collect. Healthline does not use information about people's searches related to HIV, impotence or eating disorders to target ads to people, but it will use information about bipolar disorder, overactive bladder and anxiety, which can be as stigmatizing as the topics on its privacy-protected list.

In the 1970s, a professor of communication studies at Northwestern University named John McKnight popularized the term *redlining* to describe the failure of banks, insurers and other institutions to offer their services to inner city neighborhoods. The term came from the practice of bank officials who drew a red line on a map to indicate where they wouldn't invest. But use of the term expanded to cover a wide array of racially discriminatory practices, such as not offering home loans to African-Americans, even those who were wealthy or middle class.

Now the map used in redlining is not a geographic map, but the map of your travels across the Web. The term *Weblining* describes the practice of denying people opportunities based on their digital selves. You might be refused health insurance based on a *Google* search you did about a medical condition. You might be shown a credit card with a lower credit limit, not because of your credit history, but because of your race, sex or ZIP code or the types of Web sites you visit.

Data aggregation has social implications as well. When young people in poor neighborhoods are bombarded with advertisements for trade schools, will they be more likely than others their age to forgo college? And when women are shown articles about celebrities rather than stock market trends, will they be less likely to develop financial savvy? Advertisers are drawing new redlines, limiting people to the roles society expects them to play.

Data aggregators' practices conflict with what people say they want. A 2008 *Consumer Reports* poll of two thousand people found that 93% thought

Internet companies should always ask for permission before using personal information, and 72% wanted the right to opt out of online tracking. A study by Princeton Survey Research Associates in 2009 using a random sample of one thousand people found that 69% thought that the United States should adopt a law giving people the right to learn everything a Web site knows about them. We need a do-not-track law, similar to the do-not-call one. Now it's not just about whether my dinner will be interrupted by a telemarketer. It's about whether my dreams will be dashed by the collection of bits and bytes over which I have no control and for which companies are currently unaccountable.

Journal Writing

What does your online self look like? Consider not just any profiles you have created but also records of searches you have conducted, transactions you have completed, and information others may have posted about you. (You may wish to search the Web for your name to see what comes up.) In your journal, create two lists of adjectives: one for how you think you appear to others online and one for how you think you really are.

Questions on Meaning

1. In which sentence or sentences does Andrews state her THESIS most directly?

2. What is a "data aggregator" (par. 6)? How are data aggregators different from advertisers? Why is the distinction important?

3. How, according to Andrews, do data aggregators stereotype Web users? Why does the practice concern her?

4. What would you say is the PURPOSE of this essay? What, specifically, does Andrews propose, and why?

Questions on Writing Strategy

1. Despite the title and the INTRODUCTION, this essay is not concerned exclusively with *Facebook*. What does Andrews accomplish by opening with a discussion of the company's initial stock offering and business earnings?

2. As a whole, is this essay an APPEAL to emotion or a reasoned argument, or both? What ASSUMPTIONS does Andrews seem to make about her readers? Give evidence for your answer.

3. In her final paragraph, Andrews cites the results of two surveys. How convincing do you find this EVIDENCE? Why?

4. Where in the essay does Andrews write about herself? What is the point of her doing so?

5. **OTHER METHODS**   How does Andrews use EXAMPLES to support her argument?

Questions on Language

1. How would you characterize Andrews's prevailing DICTION? Why does she also use COLLOQUIAL EXPRESSIONS? Find at least three examples of everyday speech and explain their EFFECT.

2. Andrews writes, "Whether you can obtain a job, credit or insurance can be based on your digital doppelgänger" (par. 4). What does she mean? What is a *doppelgänger*?

3. What is *Weblining* (par. 10)? What is the source of this term?

4. Use a dictionary if necessary to help you define any of the following words: magnitude (par. 2); revenue, mechanisms (3); scrutinize (5); renege (6); proclivities (7); stigmatizing (8); bombarded, forgo (11).

Suggestions for Writing

1. **FROM JOURNAL TO ESSAY**   Based on the list you created in your journal, write an essay in which you COMPARE AND CONTRAST how you view yourself with how you think the digital world views you. You might focus on a single aspect of your identity (for example, you may see yourself as fun-loving, while you're careful to appear serious online) or on a number of characteristics that make up your persona as a whole.

2. Andrews bases much of her argument on objections to stereotyping. Have you ever witnessed or been the object of unfair treatment based on race, ethnicity, marital status, medical history, shopping habits, or something else? What happened, and what was your reaction? Write an essay discussing stereotypes and how they can harm people. Use vivid details to re-create the incident and your reaction to it, but also reflect on its larger significance. Do you view the incident as fairly unusual, or do you think it is symptomatic of widespread stereotyping? What are the causes of this stereotyping, and how does it affect the people it is directed against?

3. **CRITICAL WRITING**   In an essay, examine the organization of Andrews's argument. What does Andrews accomplish in each paragraph? How effectively does she use TRANSITIONS to move from one idea to the next?

4. **CONNECTIONS**   Write an essay in which you establish your own position on the debate over Internet privacy. Are new laws necessary, or unwise? Do you agree with Andrews that loss of privacy causes real damage to people's lives? Do you take Nicholas Carr's (p. 436) view that privacy is a fundamental right not to be given up lightly? Or do you accept Jim Harper's (p. 443) position that privacy is

a reasonable price to pay for the content available online? Perhaps your opinion falls somewhere in between? As much as possible, use examples from your own experience (or from the experiences of those close to you) to support your argument.

Lori Andrews on Writing

"I love to write," says Lori Andrews in a faculty interview for the Chicago–Kent College of Law, "and in fact, I put myself through college and law school writing magazine articles and other things that I published in legal literature." As a lawyer and bioethicist, she has since written hundreds of articles and legal briefs and more than a dozen books of nonfiction. But when she started work on her first mystery novel, a project inspired by the human dramas she witnessed as an ethics advisor for the Human Genome Project, Andrews discovered her writing had room for improvement.

"I found," she explains, that "since I had written things that were almost always conceptual and oriented on the mind . . . I had to learn the way to describe things in a totally different context that had to do with people's bodies, not just with their ideas." In another faculty interview, for *Illinois Institute of Technology Magazine*, she continues: "I realized that I had no sense of physicality. For example, someone can't get shot and talk normally five seconds later. That was the biggest issue — leading an academic life of the mind, and then writing about very physical, tangible things."

The Brief Bedford Reader on Writing

Andrews reflects here on the impact that GENRE can have on readers' expectations. Writing for a scientific or legal AUDIENCE, she discovered, requires an approach that doesn't work with fiction. You may make a similar discovery when writing for classes in different disciplines. Refer back to "Assessing the Writing Situation" (pp. 30–32) for advice on adapting your style to your SUBJECT and PURPOSE.

ADDITIONAL WRITING TOPICS

Argument and Persuasion

1. Write a persuasive essay in which you express a deeply felt opinion. In it, address a particular person or audience. For instance, you might direct your essay to any of the following readers:

    A friend unwilling to attend a ballet performance (or a car race) with you on the grounds that such an event is a waste of time

    A teacher who asserts that the prevalence of texting has led to a decline in students' writing skills

    A developer who plans to tear down a historic building

    Someone who sees no purpose in studying a foreign language

    A high-school class whose members don't want to commit to public service

    An older generation insistent on the value of home ownership

    A skeptic who asserts that religion is a leading cause of violence

    The members of a community organization who want to ban pit bulls or another breed of dog

2. Write a letter to your campus newspaper or a city newspaper in which you argue for or against a certain cause or view. You may wish to object to a particular feature or editorial in the paper. Send your letter and see if it is published.

3. Write a short letter to your congressional or state representative, arguing in favor of (or against) the passage of some pending legislation. Look in a news magazine or a newspaper for a worthwhile bill to write about. Or else write in favor of some continuing cause: for instance, requiring (or not requiring) cities to provide shelter for homeless people, reducing (or increasing) military spending, providing (or refusing) aid to the arts, solving (or ignoring) income inequality.

4. Write an essay arguing that something you feel strongly about should be changed, removed, abolished, enforced, repealed, revised, reinstated, or reconsidered. Be sure to propose some plan for carrying out whatever suggestions you make. Possible topics, listed to start you thinking, are these:

    Drug laws
    Unpaid internships
    Women in combat
    Police brutality
    Graffiti
    Fraternities and sororities
    Genetically modified organisms (GMOs) in food
    Public transportation

PART THREE

MIXING THE METHODS

Everywhere in this book, we have tried to prove how flexible the methods of development are. All the preceding essays offer superb examples of DEFINITION or CLASSIFICATION or ARGUMENT, but every one illustrates other methods, too — DESCRIPTION in PROCESS ANALYSIS, NARRATION in COMPARISON, ANALYSIS and EXAMPLES in CAUSE AND EFFECT.

In this part of the book, we take this point even further by presenting a collection of essays that share a significant feature: All the authors draw on whatever methods of development, at whatever length, will help them achieve their PURPOSES. To show how the writers combine methods, we highlight the most significant ones in the notes preceding each essay.

You have already begun to command the methods by focusing on them individually, making each a part of your kit of writing tools. Now, when you face a writing assignment, you can consider whether and how each method may help you sharpen your focus, develop your ideas, and achieve your aim. Indeed, one way to approach a subject is to apply each method to it, one by one. The following list offers a set of questions that you can ask about any subject.

- **Narration:** Can you tell a story about the subject?
- **Description:** Can you use your senses to illuminate the subject?
- **Example:** Can you point to instances that will make the subject concrete and specific?
- **Comparison and contrast:** Will setting the subject alongside another one generate useful information?
- **Process analysis:** Will a step-by-step explanation of how the subject works add to readers' understanding?
- **Division or analysis:** Can slicing the subject into parts produce a clearer vision of it?
- **Classification:** Is it worthwhile to sort the subject into kinds or groups?
- **Cause and effect:** Does it help to ask why something happened or what its results are?
- **Definition:** Can you trace boundaries that will clarify the meaning of the subject?
- **Argument and persuasion:** Can you back up an opinion or make a proposal about the subject?

Rarely will every one of these questions produce fruit for a given essay, but inevitably some will. Try the whole list when you're stuck at the beginning of an assignment or when you're snagged in the middle of a draft. You'll find the questions are as good at removing obstacles as they are at generating ideas.

JUDY BRADY

Judy Brady was born in 1937 in San Francisco, where she now lives, and earned a BFA in painting from the University of Iowa in 1962. Drawn into political action by her work in the feminist movement, she went to Cuba in 1973, where she studied class relationships as a way of understanding change in a society. When she was diagnosed with cancer in 1980, Brady became an activist against what she calls "the cancer establishment." ("Cancer is, after all, a multibillion-dollar business," she says.) In 1991 she published *One in Three: Women with Cancer Confront an Epidemic*, an anthology of writings by women. She is a board member of Greenaction, an environmental justice organization, and a founding member of the Toxic Links Coalition, which seeks to educate people about the links between environmental toxins and public health. She provided a chapter for the book *Sweeping the Earth: Women Taking Action for a Healthy Planet* (1999), and she writes articles for Breast Cancer Action in San Francisco. Brady is also featured in the 2011 movie *Pink Ribbons, Inc.*, a documentary critiquing corporate breast cancer philanthropy.

I Want a Wife

After reading "I Want a Wife" aloud at a 1970 women's meeting in San Francisco, Brady submitted the essay for the Spring 1972 issue of *Ms.* magazine, which had started the year before as a vehicle for the modern feminist movement, then in its first decade. "I Want a Wife" became one of the best-known manifestos in popular feminist writing. In the essay Brady trenchantly examines the multiple duties and functions expected of a wife, leading to an inescapable conclusion.

On the whole a definition (Chap. 11) of *wife* that relies on division or analysis (Chap. 8) to identify the parts of the role, "I Want a Wife" uses several other methods of development to show both how Brady sees her expected duties in marriage and why she resents them:

Example (Chap. 5): paragraphs 2–4
Comparison and contrast (Chap. 6): paragraphs 5, 7
Process analysis (Chap. 7): paragraphs 4, 6
Classification (Chap. 9): paragraphs 3–7
Cause and effect (Chap. 10): paragraph 3

I belong to that classification of people known as wives. I am A Wife. And, not altogether incidentally, I am a mother.

Not too long ago a male friend of mine appeared on the scene fresh from a recent divorce. He had one child, who is, of course, with his ex-wife. He is looking for another wife. As I thought about him while I was ironing one evening, it suddenly occurred to me that I, too, would like to have a wife. Why do I want a wife?

I would like to go back to school so that I can become economically independent, support myself, and, if need be, support those dependent upon me. I want a wife who will work and send me to school. And while I am going to school I want a wife to take care of my children. I want a wife to keep track of the children's doctor and dentist appointments. And to keep track of mine, too. I want a wife to make sure my children eat properly and are kept clean. I want a wife who will wash the children's clothes and keep them mended. I want a wife who is a good nurturant attendant to my children, who arranges for their schooling, makes sure that they have an adequate social life with their peers, takes them to the park, the zoo, etc. I want a wife who takes care of the children when they are sick, a wife who arranges to be around when the children need special care, because, of course, I cannot miss classes at school. My wife must arrange to lose time at work and not lose the job. It may mean a small cut in my wife's income from time to time, but I guess I can tolerate that. Needless to say, my wife will arrange and pay for the care of the children while my wife is working.

I want a wife who will take care of my physical needs. I want a wife who will keep my house clean. A wife who will pick up after my children, a wife who will pick up after me. I want a wife who will keep my clothes clean, ironed, mended, replaced when need be, and who will see to it that my personal things are kept in their proper place so that I can find what I need the minute I need it. I want a wife who cooks the meals, a wife who is a *good* cook. I want a wife who will plan the menus, do the necessary grocery shopping, prepare the meals, serve them pleasantly, and then do the cleaning up while I do my studying. I want a wife who will care for me when I am sick and sympathize with my pain and loss of time from school. I want a wife to go along when our family takes vacation so that someone can continue to care for me and my children when I need a rest and change of scene.

I want a wife who will not bother me with rambling complaints about a wife's duties. But I want a wife who will listen to me when I feel the need to explain a rather difficult point I have come across in my course of studies. And I want a wife who will type my papers for me when I have written them.

I want a wife who will take care of the details of my social life. When my wife and I are invited out by my friends, I want a wife who will take care of the babysitting arrangements. When I meet people at school that I like and want to entertain, I want a wife who will have the house clean, will prepare a special meal, serve it to me and my friends, and not interrupt when I talk about things that interest me and my friends. I want a wife who will have arranged that the children are fed and ready for bed before my guests arrive so that the children do not bother us. I want a wife who takes care of the needs of my guests so that they feel comfortable, who makes sure that they have an ashtray, that they are passed the hors d'oeuvres, that they are offered a second helping of the food, that their wine glasses are replenished when necessary, that their coffee is served to them as they like it. And I want a wife who knows that sometimes I need a night out by myself.

I want a wife who is sensitive to my sexual needs, a wife who makes love 7 passionately and eagerly when I feel like it, a wife who makes sure that I am satisfied. And, of course, I want a wife who will not demand sexual attention when I am not in the mood for it. I want a wife who assumes the complete responsibility for birth control, because I do not want more children. I want a wife who will remain sexually faithful to me so that I do not have to clutter up my intellectual life with jealousies. And I want a wife who understands that *my* sexual needs may entail more than strict adherence to monogamy. I must, after all, be able to relate to people as fully as possible.

If, by chance, I find another person more suitable as a wife than the wife I 8 already have, I want the liberty to replace my present wife with another one. Naturally, I will expect a fresh, new life; my wife will take the children and be solely responsible for them so that I am left free.

When I am through with school and have a job, I want my wife to quit 9 working and remain at home so that my wife can more fully and completely take care of a wife's duties.

My God, who *wouldn't* want a wife? 10

Journal Writing

Brady addresses the traditional obligations of a wife and mother. In your journal, jot down what you perceive to be the parallel obligations of a husband and father.

Questions on Meaning

1. Sum up the duties of a wife as Brady sees them.
2. To what inequities in the roles traditionally assigned to men and to women does "I Want a Wife" call attention?
3. What is the THESIS of this essay? Is it stated or implied?
4. Is Brady unfair to men?

Questions on Writing Strategy

1. What EFFECT does Brady obtain with the title "I Want a Wife"?

2. What do the first two paragraphs accomplish?

3. What is the TONE of this essay?

4. How do you explain the fact that Brady never uses the pronoun *she* to refer to a wife? Does this make her prose unnecessarily awkward?

5. Knowing that this essay was first published in Ms. magazine in 1972, what can you guess about its intended readers? Does "I Want a Wife" strike a college AUDIENCE today as revolutionary?

6. **OTHER METHODS**   What principle of ANALYSIS does Brady use to analyze the role of wife? Can you think of some other principle for analyzing the role?

7. **OTHER METHODS**   Although she mainly divides or analyzes the role of wife, Brady also creates a DEFINITION by using CLASSIFICATION to sort the many duties and responsibilities into manageable groups. What are the groups?

Questions on Language

1. What is achieved by the author's frequent repetition of the phrase "I want a wife"?

2. Be sure you know how to define the following words as Brady uses them: nurturant (par. 3); replenished (6); adherence, monogamy (7).

3. In general, how would you describe the DICTION of this essay? How well does it suit the essay's intended audience?

Suggestions for Writing

1. **FROM JOURNAL TO ESSAY**   Working from your journal entry (p. 461), write an essay titled "I Want a Husband" in which, using examples as Brady does, you enumerate the roles traditionally assigned to men in our society.

2. Imagining that you want to employ someone to do a specific job, divide the task into its duties and functions. Then, guided by your analysis, write an accurate job description in essay form.

3. **CRITICAL WRITING**   As indicated in the note introducing it, Brady's essay was first published in 1972 in Ms., a feminist magazine. Do some research about the women's movement of the 1960s and '70s. Where did women stand in higher education (studying and teaching), in medicine and other professions, in the workforce, as wives and mothers, as homemakers, and so on? What kinds of change did feminists seek, and how did they go about demanding those changes? How did society as a whole seem to respond? Based on your research, write an essay in which you SUMMARIZE Brady's view as you understand it and then EVALUATE her essay. Consider: Is Brady fair? If not, is unfairness justified? Provide specific EVIDENCE from your experience, observation, and research.

4. **CONNECTIONS**   Both "I Want a Wife" and Augusten Burroughs's "How to Identify Love by Knowing What It's Not" (p. 395) address domestic partnerships and traditional expectations of spouses. However, Brady's STYLE is fast paced and her tone is sarcastic, while Burroughs's is more methodical and earnest. Which method of addressing relationship issues do you find more effective? Why? Write an essay that COMPARES AND CONTRASTS the essays' tones, styles, POINTS OF VIEW, and language. What conclusions can you draw about the connection between the writers' strategies and their messages?

5. **CONNECTIONS**   In "But What Do You Mean?" (p. 299), Deborah Tannen looks at some of the ways in which women and men communicate. In a brief essay, consider how Tannen's discussion of gender differences, particularly in instances of "Troubles Talk," might add another layer of meaning to Brady's complaints about traditional roles for husbands and wives.

Judy Brady on Writing

Before Judy Brady penned "I Want a Wife" in 1970, she had never considered being a writer. In a 2007 interview with Dick Gordon on American Public Media, Brady recalled that the idea of writing the essay was planted at a women's movement gathering at Glide Memorial Church in San Francisco: "Well, I was complaining at one of the consciousness-raising group meetings and somebody just said, 'Why don't you write it?' Which hadn't occurred to me. And I went home and did."

Brady says that although writing the essay took her only a couple of hours, its inspiration had been brewing for the decade of marriage and motherhood that preceded it. Brady remembers feeling spitefully awakened when she began to speak with other women about their position in the home and in society: "There was tremendous anger when I began to understand how I had been . . . how can I say this? . . . how I had been *molded* by forces about which I was totally unconscious."

At a rally celebrating the fiftieth anniversary of American women's right to vote, Brady read "I Want a Wife" aloud (and "totally terrified") to a gathering of both supporters and hecklers. Her now ex-husband bought her flowers after the event, a gesture that Brady describes as "bizarre." "He meant it well, but he sort of didn't get it," she says.

Inspired by the response to her essay, Brady became an active supporter of social and political causes, volunteering in Cuba, advocating for cancer patients, and getting involved in the environmental movement while continuing to work for women's rights. Reflecting on the impact of "I Want a

Wife" forty years later, Brady is still frustrated by what she sees as a lack of meaningful change for women and for underprivileged people in general. Writing the piece did, however, affect her personally: "I've had a much more interesting life than I would have had had I not found the women's movement and not . . . done this essay."

The Brief Bedford Reader on Writing

Judy Brady discovered her subject matter long before she ever considered writing about it, and her hastily written speech became a component of her activism — a public ARGUMENT against expectations for women. For tips on finding a subject for an argument of your own, see page 414. Then, consider the revision checklist on page 417. In your estimation, does "I Want a Wife" meet all of the criteria for an effective argument? If Brady were to revise her essay to make a case for modern women, what changes would you suggest?

JOAN DIDION

A writer whose fame is fourfold — as novelist, essayist, journalist, and screen-writer — Joan Didion was born in 1934 in California, where her family had lived for five generations. After graduation from the University of California at Berkeley, she spent a few years in New York, working as a feature editor for the fashion magazine *Vogue*. She gained wide notice in the 1960s and 1970s with the publication of the essay collections *Slouching towards Bethlehem* (1968) and *The White Album* (1979) and the novels *River Run* (1963), *Play It as It Lays* (1971), and *A Book of Common Prayer* (1977). *Salvador* (1983), her book-length essay based on a visit to war-torn El Salvador, and *Miami* (1987), a study of Cuban exiles in Florida, also received close attention. With her late husband, John Gregory Dunne, Didion coauthored a number of screenplays, notably for *A Star Is Born* (1976), *True Confessions* (1981), and *Up Close and Personal* (1996). Her latest books are *The Year of Magical Thinking* (2005), an examination of her reactions to Dunne's sudden death, and *Blue Nights* (2011), an emotional memoir of losing their adult daughter after an extended illness.

Earthquakes

Long a resident of California, Didion knows firsthand the experience of earth-quakes and the peculiar blend of dread and denial with which most Californians view seismic catastrophe. This piece is a self-contained excerpt from a longer essay, "Los Angeles Days," that appeared first in 1988 in *The New Yorker* and then in Didion's collection *After Henry* (1992).

"Earthquakes" relies on a range of methods to depict the attitudes of Didion herself and of her fellow Californians toward "the Big One":

Narration (Chap. 3): paragraphs 1, 2–7, 8, 9
Description (Chap. 4): paragraphs 1, 2, 9
Example (Chap. 5): paragraphs 1, 2, 8, 9
Process analysis (Chap. 7): paragraph 2
Cause and effect (Chap. 10): paragraphs 1, 7–9
Definition (Chap. 11): paragraphs 1, 8, 9

During one of the summer weeks I spent in Los Angeles in 1988 there was a 1 cluster of small earthquakes, the most noticeable of which, on the Garlock Fault, a major lateral-slip fracture that intersects the San Andreas in the Tehachapi range north of Los Angeles, occurred at six minutes after four on a Friday after-noon when I happened to be driving in Wilshire Boulevard from the beach. People brought up to believe that the phrase *terra firma*[1] has real meaning often

[1] Latin, "solid earth." — Eds.

find it hard to understand the apparent equanimity with which earthquakes are accommodated in California, and tend to write it off as regional spaciness. In fact it is less equanimity than protective detachment, the useful adjustment commonly made in circumstances so unthinkable that psychic survival precludes preparation. I know very few people in California who actually set aside, as instructed, a week's supply of water and food. I know fewer still who could actually lay hands on the wrench required to turn off, as instructed, the main gas valve; the scenario in which this wrench will be needed is a catastrophe, and something in the human spirit rejects planning on a daily basis for catastrophe. I once interviewed, in the late sixties, someone who did prepare: a Pentecostal minister who had received a kind of heavenly earthquake advisory, and on its quite specific instructions was moving his congregation from Port Hueneme, north of Los Angeles, to Murfreesboro, Tennessee. A few months later, when a small earthquake was felt not in Port Hueneme but in Murfreesboro, an event so novel that it was reported nationally, I was, I recall, mildly gratified.

A certain fatalism comes into play. When the ground starts moving all   2
bets are off. Quantification, which in this case takes the form of guessing where the movement at hand will rank on the Richter scale, remains a favored way of regaining the illusion of personal control, and people still crouched in the nearest doorjamb will reach for a telephone and try to call Caltech, in Pasadena, for a Richter reading. "Rock and roll," the DJ said on my car radio that Friday afternoon at six minutes past four. "This console is definitely shaking . . . no word from Pasadena yet, is there?"

"I would say this is a three," the DJ's colleague said.   3

"Definitely a three, maybe I would say a little higher than a three."   4

"Say an eight . . . just joking."   5

"It felt like a six where I was."   6

What it turned out to be was a five-two, followed by a dozen smaller   7
after-shocks, and it had knocked out four of the six circuit breakers at the A. D. Edmonston pumping plant on the California Aqueduct, temporarily shutting down the flow of Northern California water over the Tehachapi range and cutting off half of Southern California's water supply for the weekend. This was all within the range not only of the predictable but of the normal. No one had been killed or seriously injured. There was plenty of water for the weekend in the system's four southern reservoirs, Pyramid, Castaic, Silverwood, and Perris lakes. A five-two earthquake is not, in California, where the movements people remember tend to have Richter numbers well over six, a major event, and the probability of earthquakes like this one had in fact been built into the aqueduct: The decision to pump the water nineteen hundred feet over the Tehachapi was made precisely because the aqueduct's engineers rejected the idea of tunneling through an area so geologically

complex, periodically wrenched by opposing displacements along the San Andreas and the Garlock, that it has been called California's structural knot.

Still, this particular five-two, coming as it did when what Californians call "the Big One" was pretty much overdue (the Big One is the eight, the Big One is the seven in the wrong place or at the wrong time, the Big One could even be the six-five centered near downtown Los Angeles at nine on a weekday morning), made people a little uneasy. There was some concern through the weekend that this was not merely an ordinary five-two but a "foreshock," an earthquake prefiguring a larger event (the chances of this, according to Caltech seismologists, run about one in twenty), and by Sunday there was what seemed to many people a sinister amount of activity on other faults: a three-four just east of Ontario at twenty-two minutes past two in the afternoon, a three-six twenty-two minutes later at Lake Berryessa, and, four hours and one minute later, northeast of San Jose, a five-five on the Calaveras Fault. On Monday, there was a two-three in Playa del Rey and a three in Santa Barbara.

Had it not been for the five-two on Friday, very few people would have registered these little quakes (the Caltech seismological monitors in Southern California normally record from twenty to thirty earthquakes a day with magnitudes below three), and in the end nothing came of them, but this time people did register them, and they lent a certain moral gravity to the way the city happened to look that weekend, a temporal dimension to the hard white edges and empty golden light. At odd moments during the next few days people would suddenly clutch at tables, or walls. "Is it going," they would say, or "I think it's moving." They almost always said *it*, and what they meant by *it* was not just the ground but the world as they knew it. I have lived all my life with the promise of the Big One, but when it starts going now even I get the jitters.

Journal Writing

What potential threat or threats in your life most give you "the jitters"? Write a journal entry exploring your specific worries.

Questions on Meaning

1. What does Didion mean by "protective detachment" in referring to Californians' attitude toward earthquakes (par. 1)?

2. How, according to Didion, do Californians maintain the illusion of personal control during earthquakes?

3. Why was the earthquake Didion writes about a cause of special concern, even though it was not a major disturbance?

4. What is the ultimate threat of "the Big One"? Why does its possibility give Didion "the jitters" (par. 9)?

Questions on Writing Strategy

1. Why in paragraphs 1 and 8 is Didion so specific about the times of the earthquakes?

2. How does Didion use IRONY in paragraph 1?

3. Why do you suppose Didion quotes the on-air conversation between the radio DJ and his associate in paragraphs 2–6?

4. **MIXED METHODS**   What other method does Didion use in paragraph 8 to DEFINE "the Big One"?

5. **MIXED METHODS**   What CAUSE-AND-EFFECT relationship does Didion explore in paragraph 9?

Questions on Language

1. What is the effect of Didion's use of "as instructed" twice in the middle of paragraph 1?

2. Throughout the essay Didion refers to specific Richter-scale numbers when describing earthquakes. Why does she do so?

3. What does Didion mean by the phrase "temporal dimension" in paragraph 9? What does *temporal* mean?

4. Check a dictionary if any of the following are unfamiliar to you: equanimity, precludes, scenario (par. 1); fatalism (2); displacements (7); seismologists (8); magnitudes (9).

Suggestions for Writing

1. **FROM JOURNAL TO ESSAY**   Expand your journal entry (p. 467) into an essay in which you explore your concerns about a potential threat in your life. What has led you to feel the way you do? Do you think many other people share your concern? How do you cope with your feelings? What might you do if the threat became real?

2. Do some research about the incidence and probability of earthquakes in the United States. (A good starting point would be the Geologic Hazards Team of the US Geological Survey: *geohazards.usgs.gov.*) Is California the only state vulnerable to earthquakes? (The answer may surprise you.) What kinds of damage and loss of life have been caused by earthquakes in this country? Write a report about earthquakes in which you answer these questions and others that interest you.

3. **CRITICAL WRITING**   Didion is noted for a distinctive STYLE of writing. In an essay, ANALYZE her style in "Earthquakes." What seems notable about the words Didion chooses and the ways she structures her sentences? What is her TONE? What does her style say about her? How do you respond to it?

4. **CONNECTIONS**   In "Stars of Life" (p. 323), student writer Jean-Pierre De Beer also speculates about the end of the world as we know it. Write an essay that COMPARES AND CONTRASTS Didion's and De Beer's essays. How are the authors' assumptions, conclusions, self-presentations, and attitudes toward catastrophe similar and different?

5. **CONNECTIONS**   Like that in "Earthquakes," Didion's reporting often involves herself as part of the story. In "Live Free and Starve" (p. 340) Chitra Divakaruni is also involved in the situation she reports. Write an essay that considers how the presence of the writer affects each essay. How would the essays be different if they had been written from a completely OBJECTIVE perspective?

Joan Didion on Writing

In "Why I Write," an essay published by the *New York Times Book Review*, adapted from her Regents' Lecture at the University of California at Berkeley, Joan Didion writes, "I stole the title for this talk, from George Orwell. One reason I stole it was that I like the sound of the words: Why I Write. There you have three short unambiguous words that share a sound, and the sound they share is this:

I

I

I

In many ways writing is the act of saying *I*, of imposing oneself upon other people, of saying *listen to me, see it my way, change your mind. . . .*"

Didion's "way," though, comes not from notions of how the world works or should work but from its observable details. She writes, "I am not in the least an intellectual, which is not to say that when I hear the word 'intellectual' I reach for my gun, but only to say that I do not think in abstracts. During the years when I was an undergraduate at Berkeley I tried, with a kind of hopeless late-adolescent energy, to buy some temporary visa into the world of ideas, to forge for myself a mind that could deal with the abstract. . . . In short, I tried to think. I failed. My attention veered inexorably back to the specific, to the tangible, to what was generally considered, by everyone I knew then and for that matter have known since, the peripheral. I would try to contemplate the Hegelian dialectic and would find myself concentrating instead on the flowering pear tree outside my window and the particular way the petals fell on my floor."

Later in the essay, Didion writes, "During those years I was traveling on what I knew to be a very shaky passport, forged papers: I knew that I was no legitimate resident in any world of ideas. I knew I couldn't think. All I knew then was what I wasn't, and it took me some years to discover what I was.

"Which was a writer.

"By which I mean not a 'good' writer or a 'bad' writer but simply a writer, a person whose most absorbed and passionate hours are spent arranging words on pieces of paper. Had my credentials been in order I would never have become a writer. Had I been blessed with even limited access to my own mind there would have been no reason to write. I write entirely to find out what I'm thinking, what I'm looking at, what I see, and what it means. What I want and what I fear. . . . *What is going on in these pictures in my mind?*"

In the essay, Didion emphasizes that these mental pictures have a grammar. "Grammar is a piano I play by ear, since I seem to have been out of school the year the rules were mentioned. All I know about grammar is its infinite power. To shift the structure of a sentence alters the meaning of that sentence, as definitely and inflexibly as the position of a camera alters the meaning of the object photographed. Many people know about camera angles now, but not so many know about sentences. The arrangement of the words matters, and the arrangement you want can be found in the picture in your mind. The picture dictates the arrangement. The picture dictates whether this will be a sentence with or without clauses, a sentence that ends hard or a dying-fall sentence, long or short, active or passive. The picture tells you how to arrange the words and the arrangement of the words tells you, or tells me, what's going on in the picture."

The Brief Bedford Reader on Writing

Didion writes, she says, to make sense of her observations and to learn what she thinks. That is, she doesn't start with a THESIS but works her way into it, as we suggest you try when you draft your own essays (see pp. 34–36). For quick guidelines on how to harness the "infinite power" of grammar and sentences for yourself, turn to "Editing" in Chapter 2 (pp. 47–53).

E. B. WHITE

For half a century Elwyn Brooks White (1899–1985) was a regular contributor to *The New Yorker*, and his essays, editorials, anonymous features for "The Talk of the Town," and fillers helped build the magazine a reputation for wit and good writing. If as a child you read *Charlotte's Web* (1952), you have met E. B. White before. The book reflects some of his own life on a farm in North Brooklin, Maine. White wrote other children's books, including *Stuart Little* (1945), and in 1970 he received the Laura Ingalls Wilder Award for his "substantial and lasting contribution to literature for children." He is also widely known for revising and expanding *The Elements of Style* (50th anniversary edition, 2008), a writer's guide by his college professor William Strunk, Jr. White's *Letters* were collected in 1976, his *Essays* in 1977, and his *Poems and Sketches* in 1981. On July 4, 1963, President Kennedy named White in the first group of Americans to receive the Presidential Medal of Freedom, with a citation that called him "an essayist whose concise comment . . . has revealed to yet another age the vigor of the English sentence."

Once More to the Lake

"Once More to the Lake" first appeared in *Harper's* magazine in 1941. Perhaps if a duller writer had written the essay, or an essay with the same title, we wouldn't much care about it, for at first its subject seems as personal and ordinary as a letter home. White's loving and exact portrayal, however, brings this lakeside camp to life for us. In the end, the writer arrives at an awareness that shocks him — shocks us, too, with a familiar sensory detail.

"Once More to the Lake" is a stunning mixture of description and narration, but it is also more. To make his observations and emotions clear and immediate, White relies extensively on several methods of development.

Narration (Chap. 3): throughout
Description (Chap. 4): throughout
Example (Chap. 5): paragraphs 2, 7–8, 11, 12
Comparison and contrast (Chap. 6): paragraphs 4–7, 9–10, 11–12
Process analysis (Chap. 7): paragraphs 9, 10, 12

August 1941

One summer, along about 1904, my father rented a camp on a lake in Maine and took us all there for the month of August. We all got ringworm from some kittens and had to rub Pond's Extract on our arms and legs night and morning, and my father rolled over in a canoe with all his clothes on; but outside of that the vacation was a success and from then on none of us ever thought there was any place in the world like that lake in Maine. We returned summer after summer — always on August 1 for one month. I have since become a salt-water man, but sometimes in summer there are days when the restlessness of the tides and the fearful cold of the sea water and the incessant wind that blows across the afternoon and into the evening make me wish for the placidity of a lake in the woods. A few weeks ago this feeling got so strong I bought myself a couple of bass hooks and a spinner and returned to the lake where we used to go, for a week's fishing and to revisit old haunts.

I took along my son, who had never had any fresh water up his nose and   2
who had seen lily pads only from train windows. On the journey over to the lake I began to wonder what it would be like. I wondered how time would have marred this unique, this holy spot — the coves and streams, the hills that the sun set behind, the camps and the paths behind the camps. I was sure that the tarred road would have found it out, and I wondered in what other ways it would be desolated. It is strange how much you can remember about places like that once you allow your mind to return into the grooves that lead back. You remember one thing, and that suddenly reminds you of another thing. I guess I remembered clearest of all the early mornings, when the lake was cool and motionless, remembered how the bedroom smelled of the lumber it was made of and of the wet woods whose scent entered through the screen. The partitions in the camp were thin and did not extend clear to the top of the rooms, and as I was always the first up I would dress softly so as not to wake the others, and sneak out into the sweet outdoors and start out in the canoe, keeping close along the shore in the long shadows of the pines. I remembered being very careful never to rub my paddle against the gunwale for fear of disturbing the stillness of the cathedral.

The lake had never been what you would call a wild lake. There were   3
cottages sprinkled around the shores, and it was in farming country although the shores of the lake were quite heavily wooded. Some of the cottages were owned by nearby farmers, and you would live at the shore and eat your meals at the farmhouse. That's what our family did. But although it wasn't wild, it was a fairly large and undisturbed lake and there were places in it that, to a child at least, seemed infinitely remote and primeval.

I was right about the tar: It led to within half a mile of the shore. But when   4
I got back there, with my boy, and we settled into a camp near a farmhouse and into the kind of summertime I had known, I could tell that it was going to be pretty much the same as it had been before — I knew it, lying in bed the first morning smelling the bedroom and hearing the boy sneak quietly out and go off along the shore in a boat. I began to sustain the illusion that he was I, and therefore, by simple transposition, that I was my father. This sensation persisted, kept cropping up all the time we were there. It was not an entirely new feeling, but in this setting it grew much stronger. I seemed to be living a

dual existence. I would be in the middle of some simple act, I would be picking up a bait box or laying down a table fork, or I would be saying something and suddenly it would be not I but my father who was saying the words or making the gesture. It gave me a creepy sensation.

We went fishing the first morning. I felt the same damp moss covering the worms in the bait can, and saw the dragonfly alight on the tip of my rod as it hovered a few inches from the surface of the water. It was the arrival of this fly that convinced me beyond any doubt that everything was as it always had been, that the years were a mirage and that there had been no years. The small waves were the same, chucking the rowboat under the chin as we fished at anchor, and the boat was the same boat, the same color green and the ribs broken in the same places, and under the floorboards the same fresh water leavings and debris — the dead hellgrammite, the wisps of moss, the rusty discarded fishhook, the dried blood from yesterday's catch. We stared silently at the tips of our rods, at the dragonflies that came and went. I lowered the tip of mine into the water, tentatively, pensively dislodging the fly, which darted two feet away, poised, darted two feet back, and came to rest again a little farther up the rod. There had been no years between the ducking of this dragon-fly and the other one — the one that was part of memory. I looked at the boy, who was silently watching his fly, and it was my hands that held his rod, my eyes watching. I felt dizzy and didn't know which rod I was at the end of.

We caught two bass, hauling them in briskly as though they were mackerel, pulling them over the side of the boat in a businesslike manner without any landing net, and stunning them with a blow on the back of the head. When we got back for a swim before lunch, the lake was exactly where we had left it, the same number of inches from the dock, and there was only the merest suggestion of a breeze. This seemed an utterly enchanted sea, this lake you could leave to its own devices for a few hours and come back to, and find that it had not stirred, this constant and trustworthy body of water. In the shallows, the dark, water-soaked sticks and twigs, smooth and old, were undulating in clusters on the bottom against the clean ribbed sand, and the track of the mussel was plain. A school of minnows swam by, each minnow with its small individual shadow, doubling the attendance, so clear and sharp in the sunlight. Some of the other campers were in swimming, along the shore, one of them with a cake of soap, and the water felt thin and clear and unsubstantial. Over the years there had been this person with the cake of soap, this cultist, and here he was. There had been no years.

Up to the farmhouse to dinner through the teeming dusty field, the road under our sneakers was only a two-track road. The middle track was missing, the one with the marks of the hooves and the splotches of dried, flaky manure. There had always been three tracks to choose from in choosing which track to walk in; now the choice was narrowed down to two. For a moment I missed terribly the middle alternative. But the way led past the tennis court, and something about the way it lay there in the sun reassured me; the tape had loosened along the backline, the alleys were green with plantains and other weeds, and the net (installed in June and removed in September) sagged in the dry noon, and the whole place steamed with midday heat and hunger and emptiness. There was a choice of pie for dessert, and one was blueberry and one was apple, and the waitresses were the same country girls, there having been no passage of time, only the illusion of it as in a dropped curtain — the waitresses were still fifteen; their hair had been washed, that was the only difference — they had been to the movies and seen the pretty girls with the clean hair.

Summertime, oh, summertime, pattern of life indelible, the fade-proof   8
lake, the woods unshatterable, the pasture with the sweetfern and the juniper forever and ever, summer without end; this was the background, and the life along the shore was the design, the cottages with their innocent and tranquil design, their tiny docks with the flagpole and the American flag floating against the white clouds in the blue sky, the little paths over the roots of the trees leading from camp to camp and the paths leading back to the outhouses and the can of lime for sprinkling, and at the souvenir counters at the store the miniature birchbark canoes and the postcards that showed things looking a little better than they looked. This was the American family at play, escaping the city heat, wondering whether the newcomers in the camp at the head of the cove were "common" or "nice," wondering whether it was true that the people who drove up for Sunday dinner at the farmhouse were turned away because there wasn't enough chicken.

It seemed to me, as I kept remembering all this, that those times and those   9
summers had been infinitely precious and worth saving. There had been jollity and peace and goodness. The arriving (at the beginning of August) had been so big a business in itself, at the railway station the farm wagon drawn up, the first smell of the pine-laden air, the first glimpse of the smiling farmer, and the great importance of the trunks and your father's enormous authority in such matters, and the feel of the wagon under you for the long ten-mile haul, and at the top of the last long hill catching the first view of the lake after eleven months of not seeing this cherished body of water. The shouts and cries of the other campers when they saw you, and the trunks to be unpacked, to give up their rich burden. (Arriving was less exciting nowadays, when you sneaked up in your car and parked it under a tree near the camp and took out the bags and in five minutes it was all over, no fuss, no loud wonderful fuss about trunks.)

Peace and goodness and jollity. The only thing that was wrong now, really,   10
was the sound of the place, an unfamiliar nervous sound of the outboard motors. This was the note that jarred, the one thing that would sometimes

break the illusion and set the years moving. In those other summertimes all
motors were inboard; and when they were at a little distance, the noise they
made was a sedative, an ingredient of summer sleep. They were one-cylinder
and two-cylinder engines, and some were make-and-break and some were
jump-spark, but they all made a sleepy sound across the lake. The one-lungers
throbbed and fluttered, and the twin-cylinder ones purred and purred, and
that was a quiet sound, too. But now the campers all had outboards. In the
daytime, in the hot mornings, these motors made a petulant irritable sound;
at night in the still evening when the afterglow lit the water, they whined
about one's ears like mosquitoes. My boy loved our rented outboard, and his
great desire was to achieve single-handed mastery over it, and authority, and
he soon learned the trick of choking it a little (but not too much), and the
adjustment of the needle valve. Watching him I would remember the things
you could do with the old one-cylinder engine with the heavy flywheel, how
you could have it eating out of your hand if you got really close to it spiritually.
Motorboats in those days didn't have clutches, and you would make a landing
by shutting off the motor at the proper time and coasting in with a dead rud-
der. But there was a way of reversing them, if you learned the trick, by cutting
the switch and putting it on again exactly on the final dying revolution of the
flywheel, so that it would kick back against compression and begin reversing.
Approaching a dock in a strong following breeze, it was difficult to slow up
sufficiently by the ordinary coasting method, and if a boy felt he had complete
mastery over his motor, he was tempted to keep it running beyond its time and
then reverse it a few feet from the dock. It took a cool nerve, because if you
threw the switch a twentieth of a second too soon you would catch the flywheel when it still had speed enough to go up past center, and the boat would
leap ahead, charging bull-fashion at the dock.

We had a good week at the camp. The bass were biting well and the sun   11
shone endlessly, day after day. We would be tired at night and lie down in the
accumulated heat of the little bedrooms after the long hot day and the breeze
would stir almost imperceptibly outside and the smell of the swamp drift in
through the rusty screens. Sleep would come easily and in the morning the
red squirrel would be on the roof, tapping out his gay routine. I kept remembering everything, lying in bed in the mornings — the small steamboat that
had a long rounded stern like the lip of a Ubangi, and how quietly she ran on
the moonlight sails, when the older boys played their mandolins and the girls
sang and we ate doughnuts dipped in sugar, and how sweet the music was on
the water in the shining night, and what it had felt like to think about girls
then. After breakfast we would go up to the store and the things were in the
same place — the minnows in a bottle, the plugs and spinners disarranged
and pawed over by the youngsters from the boys' camp, the Fig Newtons and

the Beeman's gum. Outside, the road was tarred and cars stood in front of the store. Inside, all was just as it had always been, except there was more Coca-Cola and not so much Moxie and root beer and birch beer and sarsaparilla. We would walk out with a bottle of pop apiece and sometimes the pop would backfire up our noses and hurt. We explored the streams, quietly, where the turtles slid off the sunny logs and dug their way into the soft bottom; and we lay on the town wharf and fed worms to the tame bass. Everywhere we went I had trouble making out which was I, the one walking at my side, the one walking in my pants.

One afternoon while we were at the lake a thunderstorm came up. It was   12
like the revival of an old melodrama that I had seen long ago with childish awe. The second-act climax of the drama of the electrical disturbance over a lake in America had not changed in any important respect. This was the big scene, still the big scene. The whole thing was so familiar, the first feeling of oppression and heat and a general air around camp of not wanting to go very far away. In midafternoon (it was all the same) a curious darkening of the sky, and a lull in everything that had made life tick; and then the way the boats suddenly swung the other way at their moorings with the coming of a breeze out of the new quarter, and the premonitory rumble. Then the kettle drum, then the snare, then the bass drum and cymbals, then crackling light against the dark, and the gods grinning and licking their chops in the hills. Afterward the calm, the rain steadily rustling in the calm lake, the return of light and hope and spirits, and the campers running out in joy and relief to go swimming in the rain, their bright cries perpetuating the deathless joke about how they were getting simply drenched, and the children screaming with delight at the new sensation of bathing in the rain, and the joke about getting drenched linking the generations in a strong indestructible chain. And the comedian who waded in carrying an umbrella.

When the others went swimming my son said he was going in, too. He   13
pulled his dripping trunks from the line where they had hung all through the shower and wrung them out. Languidly, and with no thought of going in, I watched him, his hard little body, skinny and bare, saw him wince slightly as he pulled up around his vitals the small, soggy, icy garment. As he buckled the swollen belt, suddenly my groin felt the chill of death.

Journal Writing

White strongly evokes the lake camp as a place that was important to him as a child. What place or places were most important to you as a child? In your journal, jot down some memories.

Questions on Meaning

1. How do you account for the distortions that creep into the author's sense of time?

2. What does the discussion of inboard and outboard motors (par. 10) have to do with the author's divided sense of time?

3. To what degree does White make us aware of his son's impression of this trip to the lake?

4. What do you take to be White's main PURPOSE in the essay? At what point do you become aware of it?

Questions on Writing Strategy

1. In paragraph 4 the author first introduces his confused feeling that he has gone back in time to his own childhood, an idea that he repeats and expands throughout his account. What is the function of these repetitions?

2. Try to describe the impact of the essay's final paragraph. By what means is it achieved?

3. To what extent is this essay written to appeal to any but middle-aged readers? Is it comprehensible to anyone whose vacations were never spent at a Maine summer cottage?

4. What is the TONE of White's essay?

5. **MIXED METHODS**   White's DESCRIPTION depends on many IMAGES that are not FIGURES OF SPEECH but literal translations of sensory impressions. Locate four such images.

6. **MIXED METHODS**   Within White's description and NARRATION of his visit to the lake, what purpose is served by the COMPARISON AND CONTRAST between the lake now and when he was a boy?

Questions on Language

1. Be sure you know the meanings of the following words: incessant, placidity (par. 1); gunwale (2); primeval (3); transposition (4); hellgrammite (5); undulating, cultist (6); indelible, tranquil (8); petulant (10); imperceptibly (11); premonitory (12); languidly (13).

2. Comment on White's DICTION in his reference to the lake as "this unique, this holy spot" (par. 2).

3. Explain what White is describing in the sentence that begins, "Then the kettle drum . . ." (par. 12). Where else does the author use figures of speech?

Suggestions for Writing

1. **FROM JOURNAL TO ESSAY**   Choose one of the places suggested by your journal entry (p. 476), and write an essay describing the place now, revisiting it as an adult. (If you haven't visited the place since childhood, you can imagine what

seeing it now would be like.) Your description should draw on your childhood memories, making them as vivid as possible for the reader, but you should also consider how your POINT OF VIEW toward the place differs now.

2. In a descriptive paragraph about a real or imagined place, try to appeal to each of your reader's five senses.

3. **CRITICAL WRITING**   While on the vacation he describes, White wrote to his wife, "This place is as American as a drink of Coca-Cola. The white collar family having its annual liberty." Obviously, not everyone has a chance at the lakeside summers White enjoyed. To what extent, if at all, does White's privileged point of view deprive his essay of universal meaning and significance? Write an essay answering this question. Back up your ideas with EVIDENCE from White's essay.

4. **CONNECTIONS**   In White's "Once More to the Lake" and Brad Manning's "Arm Wrestling with My Father" (p. 111), the writers reveal a changing sense of what it means to be a father. Write an essay that examines the similarities and differences in their definitions of fatherhood. How does a changing idea of what it means to be a son connect with this redefinition of fatherhood?

5. **CONNECTIONS**   White's essay is full of images that place readers in an important setting of his childhood. David Sedaris, in "Remembering My Childhood on the Continent of Africa" (p. 180), also uses vivid images to evoke childhood, both his own and that of his partner. After reading these two essays, write an essay of your own ANALYZING four or five images from each that strike you as especially evocative. What sense impression does each image draw on? What does each one tell you about the author's feelings?

COLSON WHITEHEAD

Hailed by *Contemporary Black Biography* as "one of the most promising — and certainly one of the hippest — young writers on the literary scene today," Colson Whitehead is a popular author of fiction, essays, and offbeat journalism. Born in 1969 and raised in Manhattan, he (just barely) graduated from Harvard University with a degree in English in 1991 and took an entry-level job with the *Village Voice* in New York City. While sorting the mail and learning to write book reviews and television criticism on deadline, Whitehead began working in his spare time on the experimental and conceptual novels that have earned him a Pulitzer nomination, a MacArthur "genius" grant, and a devoted following: *The Intuitionist* (1999), *John Henry Days* (2001), *Apex Hides the Hurt* (2006), *Sag Harbor* (2009), *Zone One* (2011), and, most recently, *The Underground Railroad* (2016). His nonfiction works include *The Colossus of New York* (2003), a collection of essays, and *The Noble Hustle: Poker, Beef Jerky, and Death* (2014), a chronicle of the author's effort, on a magazine assignment, to compete in the 2011 World Series of Poker in Las Vegas and see how far an amateur player could rise. Currently residing in Brooklyn, Whitehead has never learned to drive.

Loving Las Vegas

"Loving Las Vegas" is extracted from *The Noble Hustle* and was first published in *Harper*'s magazine as a self-contained essay in 2013. In this piece, Whitehead relates with precision and nostalgia his first impressions, formed on a postgraduation road trip with aimless college friends, of "what the prudes get wrong about Sin City."

Primarily a blend of narration and description, Whitehead's essay mixes in several other methods of development to reveal the hopes and anxieties of a recent college graduate with an uncertain future.

Narration (Chap. 3): throughout
Description (Chap. 4): throughout
Example (Chap. 5): paragraphs 1, 2, 5, 14, 15–20
Comparison and contrast (Chap. 6): paragraphs 15–20
Process analysis (Chap. 7): paragraphs 3–4, 19
Division or analysis (Chap. 8): paragraphs 10, 15–20
Cause and effect (Chap. 10): paragraphs 2, 8–12, 23
Definition (Chap. 11): paragraph 2

I pity people who've never been to Vegas. Who dismiss the city without 1
setting foot on its carpeted sidewalks. I recognized myself in the town the first time I laid eyes on it, during a cross-country trip the summer after college.

My friend Darren had a gig writing for *Let's Go*, the student-produced series of travel guides. *Let's Go: USA*, *Let's Go: Europe*, *Let's Go: North Korea* (they always lost a few freshmen updating that one). The previous year his beat had been New York City. We'd spent the summer eating 50¢ hot dogs at Gray's Papaya for breakfast, lunch, and dinner and "researching" dive bars like Downtown Beirut and King Tut's Wah Wah Hut, which were beacons of pure, filthy truth in a city still years away from its Big Cleanup. This summer he was assigned the Southwest. The subways didn't run that far out, but his roommate Dan had a car, a brown '83 Toyota Tercel, and the idea was we'd hit the open road and split the writing duties and the money three ways.

It was 1991. We'd just been diagnosed as Generation X, and certainly we had all the symptoms, our designs and life plans as scrawny and undeveloped as our bodies. Sure, we had dreams. Dan had escaped college with a degree in visual arts, was a cartoonist en route to becoming an animator. Darren was an anthro major who'd turned to film, fancying himself a Lynchian[1] auteur in those early days of the indie art-house wave. I considered myself a writer but hadn't got much further than wearing black and smoking cigarettes. I wrote two five-page short stories, two five-page epics, to audition for my college's creative-writing workshops and was turned down both times. I was crushed, but in retrospect it was perfect training for being a writer. You can keep "write what you know" — for a true apprenticeship, internalize the world's indifference and accept rejection and failure into your very soul. 2

First thing, Dan hooked up our ride with new speakers. We didn't have money or prospects, but we had our priorities straight. I couldn't drive. That spring I'd sworn I'd get my license so I could contribute my fair share, but no. 3

I promised to make it up to Dan and Darren by being a Faithful Navigator, wrestling with the Rand McNally[2] and feeding the cassette deck with dub.[3] Dub, Lee "Scratch" Perry, deep deep cuts off side six of *Sandinista!* — let these be indicators of the stoner underpinnings of our trip out west. As if our eccentric route were not enough. From New York down to Lancaster, Pennsylvania, to visit a college pal. He took me to my first mall. Even then, I had a weakness for those prefab palaces. "I asked Andy why there were no security guards around," I wrote in my notebook. "He told me I had a New Yorker's mentality." 4

Then hundreds of miles to Chicago for a disappointing pilgrimage too complicated and inane to detail here. We bought two tiny replicas of the Sears Tower as consolation. Veered south, taking in the territory, cooking up plots. 5

---

[1] David Lynch (1946–) is an American director known for gritty, surrealist films. — Eds.
[2] Rand McNally publishes printed foldout roadmaps and atlases. — Eds.
[3] A subgenre of electronic dancehall music, emerged from reggae. — Eds.

Inspiration: "discussing the plot of the movie Darren wants to write, about 7-Elevens that land in cornfields." Down to New Orleans, where we slept in a frat house, on mattresses still moldy and damp from the spring floods. One of Darren's childhood friends belonged to the frat. His brothers wanted to know why he was "bringing niggers and Jews" into their chill-space. We sure were seeing a lot of America on this trip.

Then west to tackle our Let's Go assignment proper. We wrote up the   6
Grand Canyon and Lake Mead. Decided to keep driving so we could spend the night in Las Vegas, the camping thing not really taking. ("Hours of agony. Impossible to sleep. Bugs. A consistent feeling of itchiness.") Miles and miles of black hills and winding roads, and then at one crest it manifested, this smart white jellyfish flopping on the desert floor. We suited up in a cheap motel downtown. Anticipating all the sweaty, laundryless days and nights we'd spend in the Tercel, we'd hit Domsey's, the famous Brooklyn thrift store, before we left New York City. We required proper gear for our Vegas debut. Dead men's spats, ill-fitting acrylic slacks and blazers with stiff fibers sticking out of the joints and seams. Roll up the sleeves of the sports jacket to find the brown stains corresponding to the previous owner's track marks. We looked great.

The whole trip out I'd maintained that I wasn't going to gamble. Gam-   7
bling was a weakness of the ignorant masses, the suckers inhabiting the Great American Middle we'd just driven through. I was an intellectual, see, could quote Beckett[4] on the topic of the abyss, had a college degree and everything. I can't remember the name of our hotel — the place was long ago demolished to make way for the Fremont Street Experience.[5] It wasn't a proper casino, just a grim box with rooms upstairs, but the first floor had rows of low-stakes gambling apparatuses to keep the reception desk company. On our way to check-in, we passed the geriatric zombies in tracksuits installed at the slots, empty coin buckets overturned on their oxygen tanks. These gray-skinned doomed tugged on the levers, blinked, tugged again. Blink. Tug. Blink.

Grisly. We were about to get our first glimpse of the hurly-burly of down-   8
town Vegas. Before we pushed open the glass doors, what the heck, I dropped a nickel into a one-armed bandit and won two dollars.

In a dank utility room deep in the sub-basements of my personality, a little   9
man wiped his hands on his overalls and pulled the switch: *More*. Remembering it now, I hear a sizzling sound, like meat being thrown into a hot skillet. I didn't do risk, generally. So I thought. But I see now I'd been testing the House Rules the previous few years. I'd always been a goody-goody. Study

[4] Samuel Beckett (1906–89), Irish author and playwright. — Eds.
[5] A pedestrian mall and "entertainment district" covered by a five-block long LED video canopy. — Eds.

hard, obey your parents, hut-hut-hut through the training exercises of decent society. Then, in college, now that no one was around, I started to push the boundaries, a little more each semester. I was an empty seat in lecture halls, slept late in a depressive funk, handed in term papers later and later to see how much I could get away with before the House swatted me down.

Push it some more. We go to casinos to tell the everyday world that we   10
will not submit. There are rules and codes and institutions, yes, but for a few hours in this temple of pure chaos, of random cards and inscrutable dice, we are in control of our fates. My little gambles were a way of pretending that no one was the boss of me. I hadn't had time for driving lessons before our trip because I'd been too busy cramming a semester of work into exam period. It had been touch and go whether I'd graduate, as I'd barely shown up for my final semester's religion course. The last thing I'd wanted to hear about was some sucker notion of the Divine. There's a man in the sky who watches over everything you do, as all-seeing as the thousands of security cameras embedded in casino ceilings. So what? Nothing escapes his attention, and nothing will move him to intervene.

After a few phone calls, the administration released me into the world   11
with a D minus. What was it to them? My passive-aggressive rebellion against the system was meaningless. The House doesn't care if you piss away your chances, are draining the college fund, letting the plumber's bill slide until next month. Ruin yourself. The cameras above record it all, but you're just another sap passing in the night.

The nickels poured into the basin, sweet music. If it worked once, it will   12
work again.

We hit the street.   13

Before we left town, we bought dozens of tiny plastic slot machines from a   14
trinket shop. Pink, red, lime green. They joined the Museum of Where We'd Been. Everybody's a walking Museum of Where They've Been, but we decided to make it literal. We had serious epoxy. Each place we stopped, we picked up souvenirs and glued them to the Tercel. Two Sears Towers sticking up over the engine, a row of small turquoise stones just above the windshield, toy buffalo stampeding across the great brown plain of the hood. Bull's horns from Arizona, in case we needed to gore someone at ramming speed, you never know, and four refrigerator magnets with Elvis's face on the front grille, to repel ghosts. We dotted the hood with glue and stuck the slot machines on, the polyethylene totems marking us as goofball heathens.

Weeks later, we were in Berkeley,[6] sleeping on a friend's floor. The friend   15
was catsitting for a drug dealer, weed mostly. I didn't approve of the drug dealer's lifestyle choices — for vacation, he went camping. We wrote up our time in the

---

[6] City in northern California. — Eds.

land of Circus Circus and the El Cortez, the cheap steaks and watered-down drinks. Let's Go's previous correspondent had been a prissy little [thing], filling his/her copy with snobby asides. ("But what do you *do* there?") He/she wrote:

> Forget Hollywood images of Las Vegas glamor, the city at base is nothing but a desert Disneyland. As a small, small world of mild, middle-aged debauchery, Vegas simply replaces Mickey and Minnie with overbright neon marquees, monolithic hotel/casinos, besequinned Ziegfieldesque [*sic*] entertainers, quickly marrying them in rococo wedding chapels.

Percy, where are my smelling salts?

And what's wrong with Disneyland? It brings joy to millions of people   16
and tutors children about the corporate, overbranded world they've been born into. "It's a Small World" is a delightful ditty, an ode to that quality of everyday existence by which the soul is crushed, diminished, *made entirely small*. No need to denigrate it. Better to worry about the lack of a clear antecedent for "them" in that last sentence. I would protect Vegas. How about:

> The magic formula of this oasis of mild, middle-aged debauchery — offer everything but the gambling cheaply, and if you gild it, they will come — was hit upon by Bugsy Siegel in the 1940s. Das Kapital is worshipped here, and sacrifices from all major credit cards are happily accepted.

Much more upbeat, although I apologize if some readers were tricked into thinking the city is devoted to Karl Marx's book.[7] I think we were just trying to get fancy with "capital."

Some of the classic joints we wrote about are gone now, and we captured   17
a time before Las Vegas made a science of demography, but most of the basic observations in our Let's Go entry remain solid. In between games of Risk (board-game version), we cut up the previous year's text, discarded what we disliked, and glued (more glue) what remained onto white paper alongside our revisions and additions. "But remember that casinos function on the basis of most tourists leaving considerably closer to the poverty line than when they arrived; don't bring more than you're prepared to lose cheerfully" became "But always remember: *In the long run, chances are you're going to lose money. Don't bring more than you're prepared to lose cheerfully.*" No, casinos are not out to destroy you. The destroyed do not return to redeem reward-card perks and lose more money. No one forces doom upon you, folks. You need to seek it out.

---

[7] German philosopher Karl Marx (1818–83) was a revolutionary socialist and the author (with Friedrich Engels, 1820–95) of *The Communist Manifesto* (1848) and *Das Kapital* (1894), a three-volume critique of capitalist society. — Eds.

We kept "Drinks in most casinos cost 75¢–$1, free to those who look like   18
they're playing" but added "Look like you're gambling; acting skills will stretch
your wallet, but don't forget to tip that cocktail waitress in the interesting get-
up." Out with the general tsk-tsking and upper-middle-class disdain, in with
"For best results, put on your favorite loud outfit, bust out the cigar and pinky
rings, and begin." You have been granted a few days' reprieve from who you
are. Celebrate the gift of a place that allows you to be someone else for a time.

Then Darren wigged out and caught a plane home. He still had his child-   19
hood room. Dan was going to drive back east in August, maybe get a Eurail
pass that autumn and check out some . . . castles or whatever. I was out of
money when Dan set off, and I asked whether he had any room in the car, as
the guy we'd been crashing with, the catsitter, was bailing out of California,
too, and bringing all his stuff. After all, I was a good navigator. As luck would
have it, they intended to stop off in Vegas on the way back.

No one laid a hand on the Museum when we were on the road. Odd,   20
moonfaced kids — a motel owner's brood — gawked at it when we stopped at
night but dared not touch. A cop pulled us over for speeding in Massachusetts
the last day of our return trip. "What's all this?" We shrugged. What to say? He
wrote us a ticket. The Museum lasted a few days in Cambridge before teenagers or disaffected housewives or whoever stripped everything. We'd made it
home, and the spell had worn off.

We grew up. Our generational symptoms faded bit by bit. I got a job work-   21
ing for the books section of a newspaper. We ran fiction sometimes, mixed in
with reviews. When the writing teacher who had rejected my work in college submitted a story, I passed on it. Not out of revenge; it just wasn't up to
snuff. As in cards, it was business, not personal. I badgered one editor for an
assignment, that assignment led to another, and soon enough I was paying
my bills freelancing. Played poker at Dan's house every Sunday for a couple
years, and one day we picked up Hold'em. Dan got into computer animation
and founded a visual-effects company, rendering animation for movies such as
Requiem for a Dream and *Black Swan*, which Darren directed. We'd waited for
cards, and then we played them.

Journal Writing

Do you find the Las Vegas gambling industry and its visitors, as described by Whitehead, to be ridiculous, depressing, amusing, criminal, harmless, something else? Why?
Compose a one- or two-paragraph answer in your journal.

Questions on Meaning

1. Against what did the author rebel as a college student? What forms did his rebellion take, and what was the result?

2. Why does Whitehead "pity people who've never been to Vegas" (par. 1)? What does the place represent to him?

3. How does Whitehead explain the SYMBOLISM of the trinkets he and his friends glued to their car? What, to him, do the souvenirs signify?

4. What do you take to be Whitehead's PURPOSE in writing this piece? How well does he accomplish it?

5. What would you say is Whitehead's implied THESIS?

Questions on Writing Strategy

1. Closely examine how Whitehead appeals to each of the five senses in his descriptions of his trip to Las Vegas. Choose two or three particularly effective sensory IMAGES, and explain their purpose and their effect.

2. Identify some of the TRANSITIONS throughout the essay. How do they create COHERENCE among the different episodes that Whitehead recounts?

3. Where, and why, does Whitehead quote passages from the JOURNAL he kept in 1991?

4. **MIXED METHODS**   How does Whitehead use CAUSE AND EFFECT to explain the appeal of gambling?

5. **MIXED METHODS**   What role does DIVISION or ANALYSIS play in paragraphs 15–18? How do the revisions to the *Let's Go* guidebook made by Whitehead and his friends COMPARE with the original text?

Questions on Language

1. Find examples of both formal and informal DICTION in the essay and consider their intent. What do Whitehead's word choices reveal about the way he imagines his AUDIENCE?

2. Identify some FIGURES OF SPEECH in Whitehead's essay, especially metaphors and understatements, and explain their effect. Why do some of the stories of failure, in particular, come off as slightly funny?

3. What are the implications of Whitehead's ALLUSIONS to the works of Samuel Beckett (par. 7) and Karl Marx (16)?

4. In quoting the *Let's Go* passage in paragraph 15, what does Whitehead intend by the use of *sic* in brackets?

5. Why do you suppose Whitehead chose to capitalize "Faithful Navigator" (par. 4), "Great American Middle" (7), and "Museum of Where We'd Been" (14)?

6. Define en route, auteur, retrospect, apprenticeship (par. 2); prospects (3); pilgrim-age, inane (5); manifested (6); abyss, apparatuses, geriatric (7); hurly-burly (8); inscrutable (10); passive-aggressive (11); literal, polyethylene, totems, heathens (14); denigrate, antecedent (16); demography (17); brood, disaffected (20); ren-dering (21).

Suggestions for Writing

1. **FROM JOURNAL TO ESSAY**   Write an essay, drawn from your journal entry (p. 484), in which you spell out and explain your response to Whitehead's essay. If you find it depressing, for instance, what depresses you — the elderly gamblers? the casino workers? the aimless college students? Why do they depress you? What do you think these people say about American culture? If you find the essay reassuring, on the other hand, explain what exactly in Whitehead's observations cheers you, and why.

2. Like Los Angeles, New York, and some other American cities, Las Vegas is a place with a reputation. What does Las Vegas mean to you? Base your answer on firsthand experience if you can, but also on information in the media (TV, movies, books, magazines). In an essay giving specific examples, describe the city as you understand it.

3. Whitehead writes of experiencing a "depressive funk" (par. 9) in his last year of college in 1991. Has the problem of depression (or anxiety) among college stu-dents improved or worsened since then? Research the problem in several studies published since 1991 — the more recent the better. Then write an essay in which you explain current trends in mental illness in college, what you think causes it, and how it might be addressed.

4. **CRITICAL WRITING**   How serious is Whitehead when he counsels young readers and aspiring writers to "internalize the world's indifference and accept rejection and failure into your very soul" (par. 2)? Where else does he return to this notion or something like it? In an essay, analyze Whitehead's TONE. How does the writer present himself and his apparent attitude toward life, risk, and writing? How appropriate do you find this tone, given Whitehead's subject and purpose? How do you respond to it?

5. **CONNECTIONS**   Both Whitehead and Naomi Shihab Nye, in "Museum" (p. 78), write many years later about the emotions they felt while visiting a new place. Write an essay in which you COMPARE AND CONTRAST how the two writers describe their travels and how each writer uses the arts to make a larger point about desire.

6. **CONNECTIONS**   Like "Loving Las Vegas," E. B. White's "Once More to the Lake" (p. 471) also blends narration and description. Examine the two essays together, not so much on their purposes, which are somewhat different, but on this blending. What senses do the authors rely on? How do they keep their nar-ratives moving? How much of themselves do they inject into their essays?

Colson Whitehead on Writing

As a successful and popular novelist, Colson Whitehead often gives creative writing workshops. He has been the writer in residence at the University of Richmond, the University of Wyoming, and Vassar College; and he has also taught aspiring writers at Brooklyn College, the University of Houston, Princeton, Columbia, and Wesleyan, to name just a few appointments. In 2012 Whitehead published "How to Write," a breakdown of the "rules" he stresses with his students, in *The New York Times*. A condensed version of the essay appears below.

The art of writing can be reduced to a few simple rules. I share them with you now.

Rule No. 1: Show and Tell. Most people say, "Show, don't tell," but I stand by Show and Tell, because when writers put their work out into the world, they're like kids bringing their broken unicorns and chewed-up teddy bears into class in the sad hope that someone else will love them as much as they do. . . . Show and Tell, followed by a good nap.

Rule No. 2: Don't go searching for a subject, let your subject find you. You can't rush inspiration. . . . Once your subject finds you, it's like falling in love. It will be your constant companion. Shadowing you, peeping in your windows, calling you at all hours to leave messages like, "Only you understand me." Your ideal subject should be like a stalker with limitless resources, living off the inheritance he received after the suspiciously sudden death of his father. He's in your apartment pawing your stuff when you're not around, using your toothbrush and cutting out all the really good synonyms from the thesaurus. Don't be afraid. . . .

Rule No. 3: Write what you know. . . . How do you make that which is your everyday into the stuff of literature? Listen to your heart. Ask your heart, Is it true? And if it is, let it be. Once the lawyers sign off, you're good to go.

Rule No. 4: Never use three words when one will do. Be concise. Don't fall in love with the gentle trilling of your mellifluous sentences. Learn how to "kill your darlings," as they say. . . . and don't be shy about softening them up in the hostage pit for a few days before you do.

Rule No. 5: Keep a dream diary.

Rule No. 6: What isn't said is as important as what is said. . . . Try to keep all the good stuff off the page. Some "real world" practice might help. The next time your partner comes home, ignore his or her existence for thirty minutes, and then blurt out "That's it!" and drive the car onto the neighbor's lawn. When your children approach at bedtime, squeeze their shoulders meaningfully and, if you're a woman, smear your lipstick across your face with the back of your wrist, or, if you're a man, weep violently until they say, "It's okay, Dad." Drink out of a chipped mug, a souvenir from a family vacation or weekend getaway in better times, one that can trigger a two-paragraph compare/contrast description later on. It's a bit like Method acting. Simply let this thought guide your every word and gesture: "Something is wrong — can you guess what it is?" If you're going for something a little more postmodern, repeat the above, but with fish.

Rule No. 7: Writer's block is a tool — use it. When asked why you haven't produced anything lately, just say, "I'm blocked." . . . Being blocked is the perfect cover for when you just don't feel like working. The gods of creativity bless you, they forsake you, it's out of your hands and whatnot. Writer's block is like "We couldn't get a baby sitter" or "I ate some bad shrimp," an excuse that always gets you a pass. . . . But don't overdo it. In the same way the baby-sitter bit loses credibility when your kids are in grad school, there's an expiration date. . . .

Rule No.   8: Is secret.

Rule No.   9: Have adventures. . . . Get out and see the world. It's not going to kill you to butch it up a tad. Book passage on a tramp steamer. Rustle up some dysentery; it's worth it for the fever dreams alone. Lose a kidney in a knife fight. You'll be glad you did.

Rule No. 10: Revise, revise, revise. I cannot stress this enough. Revision is when you do what you should have done the first time, but didn't. It's like washing the dishes two days later instead of right after you finish eating. Get that draft counter going. Remove a comma and then print out another copy — that's another draft right there. Do this enough times and you can really get those numbers up, which will come in handy if someone challenges you to a draft-off. When the ref blows the whistle and your opponent goes, "26 drafts!," you'll bust out with "216!" and send 'em to the mat.

Rule No. 11: There are no rules. If everyone jumped off a bridge, would you do it, too? No. There are no rules except the ones you learned during your Show and Tell days. Have fun. If they don't want to be friends with you, they're not worth being friends with. Most of all, just be yourself.

The Brief Bedford Reader on Writing

Whitehead offers a lot of advice on writing, most of it tongue in cheek yet useful nonetheless. Two of our favorites are "let your subject find you" (Rule No. 2) and "Revise, revise, revise" (Rule No. 10). If you find yourself stuck for something to write about, revisit the suggestions under "Discovering Ideas" (p. 32). And for details on how revision is the key to successful writing, check out "Revising" on pages 32–34. Whitehead may lean otherwise, but we keep no secrets.

APPENDIX

FINDING AND DOCUMENTING SOURCES

Responding to the readings in this book — thinking critically about them and synthesizing the writers' ideas with your own — prepares you for the researched writing that will occupy you for much of your college career. The academic disciplines — history, psychology, chemistry, and the like — examine different subjects and take different approaches, but they share the common goal of using reading and writing to build and exchange knowledge.

Reading critically and writing effectively are both key skills for this kind of ACADEMIC WRITING, which calls on your ability to think critically about what you read. Part One of this book shows you how to read and write in response to a single SOURCE, such as any of the selections in Part Two. This appendix covers the essentials of using multiple sources in your writing: finding and evaluating them (below), synthesizing source material without plagiarizing (p. 496), and documenting sources using the styles of the Modern Language Association (MLA) for papers in English and most humanities (p. 499) or the

American Psychological Association (APA) for papers in the social sciences and business (p. 519).

CONDUCTING RESEARCH

Research is a process of inquiry, driven by curiosity. Whatever discipline you are working in, the process is most productive when you start with a specific question that interests you enough to spend some time investigating. Often such questions will be provided for you, as is the case with many of the writing suggestions that accompany the essays in this book. Other times, you will need to come up with intriguing questions for yourself. In either case, try to focus on a question you care about, because you will put a good deal of effort into finding and examining sources that can help you answer it.

Using the Library

You have two paths to sources for a research project: your school's library and a public search engine such as *Google* or *Bing*. Although it may seem easier to turn to the open Internet first, always start with the library: Its Web portal will lead you to books, scholarly journals, reputable newspapers, and other quality sources that information professionals have deemed worthwhile. Furthermore, some of the most useful source material is not freely available or online at all. Your library can link you to online resources that are accessible only to paid subscribers, and it can provide periodicals and specialized reference works that exist only in print.

The Internet is home to many valuable sources as well, but finding them requires ingenuity and an extra degree of caution. Tapping a question into a search engine will not lead you to the best materials as if by magic. A quick keyword search can give you an overview of your subject and generate ideas, but it can just as easily direct you to the rantings of extremists, advertisements posing as science, and dubious claims in anonymous posts. It will also generally bring up an unwieldy number of hits, with little indication of which ones are worthy of your attention. Most of the quality material you can find on the Web is indexed on your library's home page; searching from there will save you time and trouble in the long run.

Evaluating Sources

When examining multiple works for possible use in your paper, you of course want each one to be relevant to your subject and to your question. But you also want it to be reliable — that is, based on good evidence and carefully reasoned. To evaluate relevance and reliability, you'll depend on your critical-reading skills of analysis, inference, and synthesis (see pp. 16–18). Use the questions for evaluating sources in the box below and the following discussion of the criteria. Take extra care when evaluating Internet sources you have reached directly, for those materials have not been filtered and are therefore inherently less reliable.

QUESTIONS FOR EVALUATING SOURCES

ALL SOURCES

✔ What is the PURPOSE of the source?

✔ Who is the intended AUDIENCE?

✔ Is the material a primary or a secondary source?

✔ Is the author an expert? What are his or her credentials?

✔ Does the author's bias affect his or her argument?

✔ Is the argument supported with EVIDENCE that is complete and up to date?

INTERNET SOURCES

✔ What is the origin of the source? Can you identify the author?

✔ Who created the Web site? Does the sponsor have any biases or agendas?

✔ Does the site contain links to sources used as evidence? Is the evidence credible?

✔ How current is the source?

Purpose and Audience

The potential sources you find may have been written for a variety of reasons — for instance, to inform the public, to publish new research, to promote a product or service, to influence readers' opinions about a particular issue. The first two of these purposes might lead to a balanced approach to the subject, one that treats all sides fairly. The second two are likely to be biased toward one view, and you'll need to weigh what they say accordingly.

A source's intended audience can suggest relevance. Was the work written for general readers? Then it may provide a helpful overview but not much detail. Was the work written for specialists? Then it will probably cover the topic in depth, but understanding it may require careful reading or consulting additional sources for clarification.

Primary versus Secondary Sources

Primary sources are works by people who conducted or saw events firsthand. They include research reports, eyewitness accounts, diaries, and personal essays as well as novels, poems, and other works of literature. *Secondary sources*, in contrast, present and analyze the information in primary sources and include histories, reviews, and surveys of a field. Both types of sources can be useful in research writing. For example, if you were writing about the debate over the assassination of President John F. Kennedy, you might seek an overview in books that discuss the evidence and propose theories about what happened — secondary sources. But you would be remiss if you did not also consult eyewitness accounts and law-enforcement documents — the primary sources.

Author's Credentials and Bias

Before you use a source to support your ideas, investigate the author's background to be sure that he or she is trustworthy. Look for biographical information in the introduction or preface of a book or in a note at the beginning or end of an article. Is the author an expert on the topic? Do other writers cite the author of your source in their work?

Often you won't be able to tell easily, or at all, who put a potential source on the Internet and thus whether that author is credible and reliable. Specific background may require digging. On Web sites, look for pages that have information about the author or sponsor or links to such information on other sites. On blogs and social media, ask anonymous writers for information about themselves. If you can't identify an author or a sponsor at all, you probably should not use the source.

Investigating an author's background and credentials will likely also uncover any bias — that is, the author's preference for a particular view of an issue. Bias itself is not a problem: Everyone has a unique outlook created by experience, training, and even research techniques. What does matter is whether the author deals frankly with his or her bias and argues reasonably despite it. (See Chap. 12 for a discussion of reasoning.)

Evidence

Look for strong and convincing evidence to support the ideas in a source: facts, examples, reported experience, expert opinions. A source that doesn't muster convincing evidence, or much evidence at all, is not a reliable source. For very current topics, such as in medicine or technology, the source's ideas and evidence should be as up to date as possible.

The most reliable sources acknowledge borrowed evidence and ideas and tell you where they came from, whether with general mentions in the case of journalism, with formal references in scholarly works, or (sometimes online) with links to the borrowed material. Check out references or links to be sure they represent a range of views. Be suspicious of any work that doesn't acknowledge sources at all.

Currency

If you are writing about a current topic, you want your sources to be up to date. Online sources tend to be more current than print sources, but they also have some potential disadvantages. Very current information may not have been tested by others and therefore may not be reliable. And because Web sites change constantly, information you locate one day could be missing or altered the next. Finally, sites that seem current may actually be dated because their authors or sponsors have not tended them. Look for a date of copyright, publication, or last revision to gauge currency. If you don't find a date (and you may not), compare the source with others you know to be recent before using its information.

Preparing an Annotated Bibliography

Whether for your own use or as part of an assignment, preparing an annotated bibliography during research can help you keep track of your sources and your evaluation of them, ensuring that you use them effectively.

A common form of annotated bibliography contains a two-part entry for every potential source: (1) full publication information for the source, so that you can find it again and cite it accurately in your paper; and (2) your own comments on the source, including an overview and a brief ANALYSIS that identifies its contents, addresses its value in its field, and considers its usefulness to you. One student, for instance, researched and wrote a literary analysis about revenge in the works of Edgar Allan Poe, focusing on the parallels in Poe's life and fiction. She read and reread several of Poe's short stories and then searched her school's library and the Internet for critical analyses of the author's work. At her instructor's request, she compiled an annotated bibliography that listed and commented on the sources she thought would be most helpful in writing her paper, using MLA style (p. 499) to format the publication information. Here are two of her entries:

Allen, Brooke. "The Tell-Tale Artist: Edgar Allan Poe Turns 200." *The Weekly Standard*, 28 Sept. 2009, pp. 28–31.
Source: magazine article

A literary critic's view of Poe's place in literary history and popular culture on the 200th anniversary of his birth. Allen claims that Poe essentially invented horror fiction, science
Contents of article

1. Poe's influence

fiction, and the detective story. She also sees parallels between
Poe himself and the characters in his fiction. Allen's focus
on Poe's mental instability and its effects on his creativity is
helpful in understanding some themes in his work, particularly
revenge. Poe's sensitivity to insults, for example, connects to
Montressor in "The Cask of Amontillado," who kills to avenge
an unnamed slight.

> 2. Parallels between
> Poe's life and work
>
> Potential use of source

The Edgar Allan Poe Society of Baltimore. 1997–2016, www
    .eapoe.org/. Accessed 26 Feb. 2016.
A comprehensive online collection of all of Poe's works, including letters and other documents, as well as links to critical articles from the journal *Poe Studies/Dark Romanticism.* The site's
most useful features are essays by scholars that address common misconceptions about Poe, particularly that his poems
and stories about anger, loss, fear, and vengeance mirror events
and relationships in his own life. This perspective is valuable to
balance Allen and other writers who make a great deal of the
connections between Poe's life and work. At the same time,
the site seems somewhat defensive about Poe and protective of
him, so information about Poe and his life needs to be verified
in other sources.

> Source: Web site
>
> Contents of Web site
> 1. Collection of Poe's
>   works
>
> 2. Scholarly criticism
>
> 3. Balancing
>   perspectives
>
> Potential use of source

You may or may not be required to include an annotated bibliography
with the final draft of a research paper. But if you do, the annotations along
with the publication information can help readers locate and assess your
sources for themselves.

WRITING WITH SOURCES

In researched writing, you test and support a THESIS by exploring and
orchestrating a range of opinions and evidence found in multiple sources. The
writing is source *based* but not source *dominated*: As when responding to a
single work, your critical reading and your views set the direction and govern
the final presentation.

Integrating Source Material

Writing with sources, you have an opportunity and an obligation to
think critically — to analyze, infer, evaluate, and synthesize as described on
pages 16–18. Key to SYNTHESIS is first deciding how to present evidence from
your research and then working the evidence into your paper smoothly and
informatively so it flows with your own ideas.

Depending on what the source material contributes to your thesis, you might use summary, paraphrase, or quotation to integrate it with your text. When you SUMMARIZE or PARAPHRASE a source, you express its ideas in your own words; when you QUOTE, you use the source's exact words, in quotation marks. See pages 42–47 in Chapter 2 for guidelines and examples. And remember that *all summaries, paraphrases, and quotations must be acknowledged with source citations*, as modeled in the sections on MLA and APA documentation later in this appendix (pp. 499–529).

Synthesizing Multiple Sources

In research writing as in response writing, your views should predominate over those of others. You decide which sources to use, how to treat them, and what conclusions to draw from them in order to test and support your thesis. In your writing, this thinking about sources' merits and relevance should be evident to readers. Here, for example, is a paragraph from a student writer's research paper about the problem of mental illness in college. Notice how the writer states her idea at the outset, guides us through the presentation of evidence from three sources, and finally concludes by tying the evidence back to her idea.

> Despite the prevalence of depression and related disorders on campus, however, most students avoid seeking help when they need it. The American Psychiatric Association maintains that most mental-health issues can be managed or overcome with treatment by therapy and/or medication. But among students with a history of depression, according to the American College Health Association, a mere 10% currently receive any kind of treatment (35). One reason for such low numbers can be found in a study published in *Journal of Mental Health Counseling:* Four in five American students are unwilling to ask for help even when they are certain they need it, because they perceive mental illness as embarrassing or shameful (Aegisdóttir et al. 327–28). Thus students who need help suffer additional pain — and no treatment — because they fear the stigma of mental illness.

(Margin annotations:) Writer's idea · Evidence from a Web site · Evidence from a survey · Evidence from a scholarly journal · Writer's interpretation of the evidence

This paragraph illustrates the techniques of synthesis detailed in pages 42–47 of Chapter 2:

- **Summarize and paraphrase data and ideas from sources,** stressing your own voice and your mastery of the source material.

- **Integrate each summary or paraphrase into your sentences.** Use SIGNAL PHRASES that name the source authors, and tell readers how the borrowed material relates to your idea.
- **Clearly indicate what material is borrowed and where it is borrowed from.** Such source citation is crucial to avoid plagiarism, discussed in the next section.

Avoiding Plagiarism

Academic knowledge building depends on the integrity and trust of its participants. PLAGIARISM — the theft of someone's ideas or written work — violates that trust. Most students know that passing off another writer's work as their own, or copying long passages from published texts, are unacceptable practices that can bring severe punishments. Such intentional plagiarism is obviously cheating and is easily detected.

But plagiarism is often more subtle, the result of carelessness or misunderstanding. Writers of researched papers must be cautious in their use of sources to avoid instances of unintentional plagiarism, such as poorly handled paraphrases or missing quotation marks. As you synthesize the information and ideas gathered through research in your writing, it is essential that you make clear to readers what ideas are your own and what ones are borrowed, *always citing the sources of borrowed material.* Avoid plagiarism by following these guidelines:

- **Identify the sources of all borrowed information and ideas.** Introduce every summary, paraphrase, or quotation and name the author in a signal phrase or a parenthetical citation. See pages 42–47 on integrating source material.
- **Indicate where the material can be found.** Follow any information or idea taken from a source with a parenthetical citation that provides the name of the author (if not mentioned in a signal phrase) and the page number(s), if available. (If you are using APA style, give the year of publication as well.) See pages 500–03 on MLA parenthetical citations and pages 520–22 on APA parenthetical text citations.
- **Mark direct quotations.** Whether sentences, phrases, or distinctive words, another writer's language must be clearly distinguished from your own. (See p. 45.) Enclose brief quotations in quotation marks. Set off longer quotations with an indentation. See page 515 for an example in MLA style.

- **Take care to express all paraphrases and summaries in your own words.** Check your sentences against the original sources, making sure that you haven't picked up any of the writers' phrasings or sentence structures. For examples of acceptable and unacceptable summary and paraphrase, see pages 43–44.
- **Include a list of sources.** On a separate page (or pages) at the end, provide a complete list of the sources cited within your paper, with full publication information for each. See pages 499–519 for guidelines on creating an MLA list of works cited and see pages 519–535 for guidelines on creating an APA and a references list.
- **Recognize common knowledge.** Not all information from sources must be cited. Some falls under the category of common knowledge — facts so widely known or agreed upon that they are not attributable to a specific source. You may not know that President Dwight Eisenhower coined the term *military-industrial complex* during his 1961 farewell address, for example, but because anyone can easily find that fact in encyclopedias, in books, and in articles about Eisenhower, it requires no citation (as long as you express it in your own words). In contrast, a scholar's argument that Eisenhower waited too long to criticize the defense industry, or the president's own comments, would need to be credited because each remains the property of its author.

Be especially cautious about plagiarism when you are working online. Whether accidentally or deliberately, you can download source material directly into your own document with a few clicks. And you might be tempted to buy complete papers from term-paper sites. Don't. *It is plagiarism to use downloaded material without credit, even accidentally, and it is plagiarism to submit someone else's work as your own, even if you paid for it.* Getting caught is more than likely, too, because anything from the Internet is easy to trace.

SOURCE CITATION USING MLA STYLE

In this section we explain the documentation style of the Modern Language Association, as described in the *MLA Handbook*, 8th edition (2016). This style — used in English, foreign languages, and some other humanities — involves providing a citation in your text that names the author of borrowed material and gives the page number(s) in the source where the material appears. Readers can use the name to locate the full source information in a list of works cited at the end of your text, and they can find the location of the borrowed material in the source itself.

In your text, the author's name may appear in a SIGNAL PHRASE, or it may appear in parentheses. In either case, put any page numbers in parentheses:

TEXT CITATION, AUTHOR NAMED IN SIGNAL PHRASE

As Quindlen suggests, people's dwellings seem to have lost their emotional hold and to have become just investments (185).

TEXT CITATION, AUTHOR NAMED IN PARENTHESES

People's dwellings seem to have lost their emotional hold and to have become just investments (Quindlen 185).

ENTRY IN LIST OF WORKS CITED

Quindlen, Anna. "Homeless." *The Brief Bedford Reader*, edited by
    X. J. Kennedy et al., 13th ed., Bedford/St. Martin's, 2017, pp. 184-86.

MLA Parenthetical Citations

The following examples of MLA text citations show the author named in a signal phrase or named in parentheses.

MLA Parenthetical Citations

A work with two authors 500	An entire work or a work with no reference numbers 502
A work with three or more authors 500	A work in more than one volume 502
A work with a group author 501	An indirect source 502
A work with no identified author 501	A literary work 502
Two or more works by the same author(s) 501	More than one work in the same citation 503
A source without page numbers 502	

A work with two authors

By shortening the time to product-in-hand, 3D printing enables designers and engineers to create prototypes quickly and cheaply (Lipson and Kurman 30).

A work with three or more authors

With three or more authors, name only the first author followed by et al. (*et alii,* "and others").

Gilman herself created the misconception that doctors tried to ban her story "The Yellow Wallpaper" when it appeared in 1892 (Dock et al. 61).

A work with a group author

For a work that lists an organization as author — for instance, a government agency or a corporation — treat the group's name as the author name.

> In a tongue-in-cheek graphic novel, the Centers for Disease Control and Prevention invokes the threat of a zombie apocalypse to encourage Americans to gather materials for an all-purpose emergency kit and keep them readily at hand (United States 5).

If the group author is also the publisher of the work, however, you will need to alphabetize it by title in your works-cited list (see p. 503), so provide the title in a parenthetical citation.

> According to the National Coalition for the Homeless, several city governments have passed legislation meant to discourage individuals and charitable organizations from providing food to homeless people (*Share No More* 4).

A work with no identified author

Cite an unsigned work by its title. In a signal phrase, use the full title. In a parenthetical citation, shorten a long title to the first one, two, or three main words.

> A growing number of national chain hotels allow guests to bring dogs and cats with them — a welcome relief for travelers whose pets require specialized care ("Rooming" 10).

Two or more works by the same author(s)

If you cite more than one work by the same author or authors, include a short version of each work's title. The full titles for the citations below are "The Case for Reparations" and "The Black Family in the Age of Mass Incarceration."

> Ta-Nehisi Coates argues that a long history of systemic oppression, discrimination, and racial injustice has inflicted "practical damage" that can only be repaired with government payments of cash to African Americans ("Case" 55).

> One example of such oppression can be found in contemporary imprisonment rates: At least 25% of black men living in America today have been jailed, affecting not only those incarcerated but also their families and their larger communities (Coates, "Black Family" 66).

A source without page numbers

Cite an unpaginated source, such as an HTML document, a sound recording, or a DVD, as you would any printed source: by author's name or, if there is no author specified, by title. If a source numbers paragraphs instead of pages, give the reference number after par. (one paragraph) or pars. (more than one paragraph). If a source's numbering system is unstable, as is often the case with e-books, refer to section or chapter numbers (sec., secs.; ch., chs.) instead of page numbers. For a source with no reference numbers at all, use the model for an entire work below.

> One nurse questions whether doctors are adequately trained in tending
> patients' feelings (Van Eijk, pars. 6-7).

> Kozol believes that most people do not understand the effect that tax and
> revenue policies have on the quality of urban public schools (ch. 2).

An entire work or a work with no reference numbers

Omit page numbers when you cite an entire work or cite a work that does not number pages, paragraphs, or other parts.

> Vogel recommends that new entrants into the job market strive to create their
> own professional roles, rather than search for existing positions.

A work in more than one volume

If you cite two or more volumes of a multivolume work, identify the volume number before the page number. Separate volume number and page number with a colon and a space.

> According to Gibbon, during the reign of Gallienus "every province of the
> Roman world was afflicted by barbarous invaders and military tyrants" (1: 133).

An indirect source

Use qtd. in ("quoted in") to indicate that you found the source you quote within another source.

> Despite his tendency to view human existence as an unfulfilling struggle,
> Schopenhauer disparaged suicide as "a vain and foolish act" (qtd. in Durant 248).

A literary work

Because novels, poems, and plays may be published in various editions, the page number may not be enough to lead readers to the quoted line or passage. For a novel, specify the chapter number after the page number and a semicolon.

> Among South Pacific islanders, the hero of Conrad's *Lord Jim* found "a totally new set of conditions for his imaginative faculty to work upon" (160; ch. 21).

For a verse play or a poem, omit the page number in favor of line numbers.

> In "Dulce et Decorum Est," Wilfred Owen undercuts the heroic image of warfare by comparing suffering soldiers to "beggars" and "hags" (lines 1-2) and describing a man dying in a poison-gas attack as "guttering, choking, drowning" (17).

If the work has parts, acts, or scenes, cite those as well (below: act 1, scene 5, lines 16–17).

> Lady Macbeth worries about her husband's ambition: "Yet I do fear thy nature; / It is too full o' the milk of human kindness" (1.5.16-17).

More than one work in the same citation

> In the post-Watergate era, journalists have often employed aggressive reporting techniques not for the good of the public but simply to advance their careers (Fallows 64; Gopnik 92).

MLA List of Works Cited

Your list of works cited is a complete record of your sources. Follow these guidelines for the list:

- **Title the list** Works Cited.
- **Double-space the entire list.**
- **Arrange the sources alphabetically** by the last name of the first author or by the first main word of the title if the source has no named author.
- **Begin the first line of each entry at the left margin,** and indent subsequent lines one-half inch.

Following are the essentials of a works-cited entry:

- **Reverse the names of the author,** last name first, with a comma between. (If there are two authors, give the second name in normal order.) Conclude the author name(s) with a period.
- **Give the full title of the work,** capitalizing the first, last, and all important words. Italicize the titles of books, periodicals, and Web sites; use quotation marks for the titles of parts of books, articles in periodicals, and pages on Web sites. Place a period after the title.

- **Give publication information.** For this information, MLA style operates on a principle of nested "containers." For a scholarly article, for instance, the journal that published it is the primary container; if you accessed the article through a periodicals database, the database is a second container. In each container, list as many of the following elements that apply to the source, in the order listed: Title of the container, names and functions of additional contributors, version of the material (a revised edition of a book, for example), sequence numbers (such as volumes and issues for journals), publisher or sponsor, date of publication, and location details (typically page numbers or a URL). Separate the elements within a container with commas, and separate each container with a period.

- **Include any additional information that might help clarify the nature of the source.** Optional elements include descriptive labels such as Review, Letter, or Address; access dates for some online sources; and original publication information for republished works.

In the pages that follow, we demonstrate how the MLA system works when applied to several common types of sources. You may need to combine the following models for a given source — for instance, combine "Three or more authors," "An article in a scholarly journal," and "A short work on a Web site," for an online journal article with five authors.

Authors

One author

Olson, W. Scott. "Nine Variations on the Idea of Street Music." *Utne Reader*,
    Winter 2015, pp. 80-83.

Two authors

Ansari, Aziz, and Eric Klinenberg. *Modern Romance*. Penguin Press, 2016.

Three or more authors

List only the first author followed by et al. (*et alii*, "and others").

DiGiovanni, Janine, et al. "The New Exodus." *Newsweek*, 3 Apr. 2015, pp. 24-33.

A group author

For a publication by an organization, corporation, or government agency, use the group name as the author name. If the group is also the publisher, omit the author name and start with the title of the work.

Associated Press. "Civil Rights Leaders Press NBA on Diversity." *Sports Illustrated*, 4 June 2014, www.si.com/nba/2014/06/04/ap-bkn-clippers-sharpton.

Share No More: The Criminalization of Efforts to Feed People in Need. National Coalition for the Homeless, 2014, nationalhomeless.org/wp-content/uploads/2014/10/Food-Sharing2014.pdf. Accessed 5 Apr. 2016.

MLA List of Works Cited

No identified author

"Sit Down and Shut Up." *Outside*, Mar. 2016, p. 51.

More than one work by the same author(s)

Coates, Ta-Nehisi. "The Black Family in the Age of Mass Incarceration." *The Atlantic*, Oct. 2015, pp. 60-84.

---. "The Case for Reparations." *The Atlantic*, June 2014, www.theatlantic .com/magazine/archive/2014/06/the-case-for-reparations/361631/.

Periodicals: Journals, Magazines, and Newspapers

An article in a scholarly journal

After the journal title, give the volume and issue numbers, the date of publication, and the page numbers of the article. If the journal numbers issues but not annual volumes, give just the issue number after the title.

Hansen, Luke O., et al. "'You Get Caught Up': Youth Decision-Making and Violence." *The Journal of Primary Prevention*, vol. 35, no. 1, Feb. 2014, pp. 21-31.

Rogoss, Jay. "The Paris Diet." *Able Muse*, no. 19, 2015, pp. 24-25.

For journals published online, provide a location where the article can be accessed. If the article has been assigned a DOI (digital object identifier), use that as its locator; if there is no DOI, provide the URL.

Resane, Thomas. "The Theological Responses to the Socio-Economic Activities that Undermine Water as a Resource." *HTS Teologiese Studies / Theological Studies*, vol. 66, no. 1, June 2010, doi:10.4102/hts.v66i1.328.

Zhou, Coco. "Magical Girl as a Shōjo: Genre and the Male Gaze." *Flow*, vol. 22, no. 4, Feb. 2016, www.flowjournal.org/2016/02/magical-girl-as-a-shojo-genre/.

An article in a magazine

Acocella, Joan. "The Lure of the Fairytale." *The New Yorker*, 23 July 2012, pp. 73-78.

McWilliams, James. "Vegan Feud." *Slate*, 7 Sept. 2012, www.slate.com/ articles/life/food/2012/09/hsus_vs_abolitionists_vs_the_meat_ industry_why_the_infighting_should_stop_.html.

Nolan, Rachel. "Displaced in the Dominican Republic: A Country Strips 210,000 of Citizenship." *Harper's Magazine*, May 2015, pp. 38-47.

An article in a newspaper

Boylan, Jennifer Finney. "The Year of the Angry Voter." *The New York Times*,
10 Feb. 2016, www.nytimes.com/2016/02/11/opinion/the-year-of-the-
angry-voter.html?_r=0.

Gasper, Christopher L. "Hopefully, Optimism Pays Off." *The Boston Globe*,
greater Boston ed., 4 Mar. 2016, pp. D1+.

The page number D1+ in the second example means that the article begins
on page 1 of section D and continues on a later page. If the newspaper has an
edition, such as greater Boston ed. in the example, it will be labeled at the top
of the first page.

A review

Tóibín, Colm. "She Played Hard with Happiness." Review of *The Complete
Stories*, by Clarice Lispector. *The New York Review of Books*, 17 Dec. 2015,
pp. 61-63.

A periodical article from a database

For an article that you obtain from a library or online database, provide
publication information using the models above. Add the database title and
the DOI (if available) or URL.

Conway, Daniel W. "Reading Henry James as a Critic of Modern Moral Life."
Inquiry, vol. 45, no. 3, Aug. 2002, pp. 319-30. *Academic Search Elite*,
doi:10.1080/002017402760258169.

Wortham, Stanton, et al. "Scattered Challenges, Singular Solutions: The
New Latino Diaspora." *The Phi Delta Kappan*, vol. 94, no. 6, Mar. 2013,
pp. 14-19. *JSTOR*, www.jstor.org/stable/23611744.

Books

A book with an author

Oldstone-Moore, Christopher. *Of Beards and Men*. U of Chicago P, 2015.

A book with an editor or editors

Clarke, Jaime, editor. *Don't You Forget about Me: Contemporary Writers on the
Films of John Hughes*. Simon & Schuster, 2007.

Gessen, Keith, and Stephen Squibb, editors. *City by City: Dispatches from the
American Metropolis*. N+1 / Farrar, Straus and Giroux, 2015.

A book with an author and an editor

Austen, Jane. *Northanger Abbey: An Annotated Edition*. Edited by Susan J.
Wolfson, Harvard UP, 2014.

A later edition

Friedan, Betty. *The Feminine Mystique*. 50th anniversary ed., W. W. Norton,
2015.

A work in a series

Macleod, Jenny. *Gallipoli*. Oxford UP, 2015. Great Battles.

An anthology or collection

Kennedy, X. J., et al., editors. *The Brief Bedford Reader*. 13th ed., Bedford/St.
Martin's, 2017.

Cite an entire anthology only when you are citing the work of the
editor(s) or you are cross-referencing it, as in the Doyle and Lipsyte models
below.

A selection from an anthology or collection

The numbers at the end of the following entry identify the pages on which
the entire cited selection appears.

Doyle, Brian. "A Note on Mascots." *The Brief Bedford Reader*, edited by
X. J. Kennedy et al., 13th ed., Bedford/St. Martin's, 2017, pp. 160-62.

If you cite more than one selection from the same anthology, you may
give the anthology as a separate entry and cross-reference it by the editor's or
editors' last name(s) in the entries for the selections. Place each entry in its
proper alphabetical place in the list of works cited.

Doyle, Brian. "A Note on Mascots." Kennedy et al., pp. 160-62.
Kennedy, X. J., et al., editors. *The Brief Bedford Reader*. 13th ed., Bedford/St.
Martin's, 2017.
Lipsyte, Robert. "Jock Culture." Kennedy et al., pp. 276-79.

A reference work

Cheney, Ralph Holt. "Coffee." *Collier's Encyclopedia*, 2007 ed.
"Seagrass Beds." *Ocean: A Visual Encyclopedia*, Dorling Kindersley, 2015.

A book on the Web

Addington, H. Bruce. *Historic Ghosts and Ghost Hunters*. Moffat, Yard, 1908.
   Project Gutenberg, www.gutenberg.org/files/28699/28699-h/28699-h
   .htm. Accessed 6 Apr. 2016.

Visual, Audio, and Multimedia Sources

A photograph, painting, sculpture, or other work of art

For a work of art that you see in the original, follow this format:

van Gogh, Vincent. *The Starry Night*. 1889, Museum of Modern Art,
   New York.

For a work of art that you see online or in a reproduction, provide the
publication information for the source you used:

Doble, Rick. *Spring Rain Abstraction*. 2009. *Digital Art Photography*, 2010,
   www.rickdoble.net/. Accessed 18 Dec. 2015.

Hockney, David. *Nichols Canyon*. 1980. *David Hockney: A Retrospective*, edited
   by Maurice Tuchman and Stephanie Barron, Los Angeles County Museum
   of Art, 1988, p. 205.

If the image originally or simultaneously appeared in another medium, you
may provide the information for the other medium before the publication
information:

Matisse, Henri. *La Musique*. 1939, Albright-Knox Gallery, Buffalo. *WebMuseum*,
   www.ibiblio.org/wm/paint/auth/matisse/matisse.musique.jpg. Accessed
   3 Mar. 2016.

A map, graph, or chart

If the title doesn't make the type of visual clear, provide a label describing
it at the end of the entry.

Fisk, Charles. "Las Vegas Annual Precipitation, 1949-2015." *Climate Stations*,
   www.climatestations.com/wp-content/uploads/2016/01/lvannp.gif.
   Graph.

An advertisement

Maxwell House. Advertisement. *Rolling Stone*, 18 Jun. 2015, p. 35.

A television or radio broadcast

What information you provide, and in what order, depends on your focus in using the source. If your emphasis is on a particular contributor, start with that person's name and function:

> Chase, Zoe, performer. "That's One Way to Do It." *This American Life*, hosted
> by Ira Glass, episode 580, Chicago Public Media, 19 Feb. 2016.

If your focus is on an episode or the series as a whole, start with the relevant title and list any significant contributors:

> "That's One Way to Do It." *This American Life*, hosted by Ira Glass, perfor-
> mances by Zoe Chase and Sigrid Frye-Revere, episode 580, Chicago
> Public Media, 19 Feb. 2016.
>
> *This American Life*. Hosted by Ira Glass, Chicago Public Media, 1995-2016.

A television program on the Web

Cite the program using one of the models above, followed with information about the Web source.

> "Breath Play." *Criminal Minds*, season 10, episode 17, CBS, 11 Mar. 2015.
> *Netflix*, www.netflix.com/search/criminalminds. Accessed 19 July 2015.
>
> Joubert, Beverly, and Dereck Joubert, narrators. "Soul of the Elephant."
> *Nature*, season 34, episode 4, WNET, 14 Oct. 2015. *PBS*, www.pbs.org/
> wnet/nature/soul-elephant-full-episode/12956/.

A podcast or sound recording

> "The Alibi." *Serial*, narrated by Sarah Koenig, season 1, episode 1, WBEZ
> Chicago, 3 Oct. 2014. *iTunes*, itunes.apple.com/us/podcast/serial/
> id917918570?mt=2.
>
> Mendelssohn, Felix. *A Midsummer Night's Dream*. Conducted by Erich Leinsdorf,
> Boston Symphony Orchestra. RCA, 1982.
>
> Roosevelt, Franklin D. Inaugural address. 20 Jan. 1941. *Vincent Voice Library*,
> Michigan State University, 2015, www.lib.msu.edu/cs/branches/vvl/
> presidents/fdr.html.

A film or video

For untitled works, provide a generic description of the content. If a video recording originally or simultaneously appeared in another medium, you may provide the information for the other medium before the publication information:

> Edison, Thomas A. Gordon sisters boxing. Edison Manufacturing, 1901.
> *American Memory*, Library of Congress, NCN046321, memory.loc.gov/
> mbrs/varsmp/1628.mpg.

Manufacturing Consent: Noam Chomsky and the Media. Directed by Mark
    Achbar and Peter Wintonick, Humanist Broadcasting Foundation, 1992.
    Zeitgeist Video, 2002.

vlogbrothers. *Is the Gender Pay Gap Real? YouTube*, 2 Feb. 2016, www
    .youtube.com/watch?v=it0EYBBl5LI.

Other Online Sources

Online sources vary greatly, and they may be and often are updated. Your
aim in citing such a source should be to tell what version you used and how
readers can find it for themselves. If you don't see a model for the type of
source you used, follow a model that comes close. If you can't find all the
information shown in a model, give what you can find.

A short work on a Web site

The following example shows the basic elements to include when citing
a source from the Web: (1) author's name, (2) title of the work, (3) title of
the site, (4) sponsor or publisher of the site, (5) date of the online publication
or last update, (6) URL (omitting "http://"), and (7) date you consulted the
source (optional).

Speer, Cindy Lynn. "Neil Gaiman's Film Work." *Neil Gaiman*, Harper Collins
Publishers, Aug. 2007, www.neilgaiman.com/Cool_Stuff/Essays/Essays
_About_Neil/Neil_Gaiman's_Film_Work. Accessed 28 Apr. 2016.

An entire Web site

Civic Engagement. University of Chicago, civicengagement.uchicago.edu/.
    Accessed 10 Feb. 2016.

A government publication on the Web

United States, Department of Education. "Teaching Academic Content and
    Literacy to English Learners in Elementary and Middle School." *What
    Works Clearinghouse*, Institute of Education Sciences, Feb. 2010, ies
    .ed.gov/ncee/wwc/pdf/practice_guides/english_learners_pg_040114
    .pdf. Accessed 2 Mar. 2016.

A wiki

"Carnival." *Wikipedia*, 10 Feb. 2016, en.wikipedia.org/wiki/Carnival. Accessed
    26 Feb. 2016.

A blog post or comment

Allan, Patrick. "The Power of Going It Alone." *Life Hacker*, Gawker Media,
    16 May 2016, lifehacker.com/the-power-of-going-it-alone-1776843438.
EasyBakeGirl. Comment on "The Power of Going It Alone," by Patrick Allen.
    Life Hacker, Gawker Media, 17 May 2016, lifehacker.com/the-power-of-
    going-it-alone-1776843438.
Sullivan, Andrew. "The Years of Writing Dangerously." *The Dish*, 6 Feb. 2015,
    dish.andrewsullivan.com/2015/02/06/the-years-of-writing-dangerously/.

A posting to a discussion group

Olney, Alexandra. "First-Person Pronouns." *Teaching and Learning Forum*, National
    Council of Teachers of English, 4 Nov. 2015, ncte.connectedcommunity
    .org/communities/community-home/digestviewer/viewthread
    ?GroupId=757&MID=24714&CommunityKey=6e95458a-28cf-448e-b907-
    7974ab61b95c&tab=digestviewer#bm0.
Peckham, Irvin. "RE: First-Person Pronouns." *Teaching and Learning
    Forum*, National Council of Teachers of English, 5 Nov. 2015, ncte
    .connectedcommunity.org/communities/community-home/digestviewer/
    viewthread?GroupId=757&MID=24714&CommunityKey=6e95458a-28cf-
    448e-b907-7974ab61b95c&tab=digestviewer#bm6.

If the posting has no title, use the label Online posting in the place of a
title.

Twitter and social media

Provide the user name or pseudonym as the author name; you may follow
it with the writer's real name (if known) in parentheses. If a posting has a title,
use it. Otherwise, quote the entire content of a tweet or a short message, citing the date and time of the post. End with the URL.

@NASA (United States, National Aeronautics and Space Administration).
    "Newly discovered Kepler-452b is first near-Earth-size planet in
    'habitable zone' around a sun-like star." *Twitter*, 23 Jul. 2015, 7:32
    p.m., twitter.com/NASA/status/624406765707268097?lang=en.
Reich, Robert. "An Open Letter to the Republican Establishment." *Facebook*,
    29 Feb. 2016, 12:22 p.m., www.facebook.com/RBReich/.
Sedaris, David. "I Am 'America's Most Beloved Author' David Sedaris. AMA."
    Reddit, 8 Oct. 2014, www.reddit.com/r/IAmA/comments/2iokd7/i_am_
    americas_most_beloved_author_david_sedaris/.

Personal Communications

E-mail

Dove, Chris. "Re: Bishop's Poems." Received by Rhonda Blake, 7 May 2016.

A letter

For a letter that you receive, list the source under the writer's name, use the label Letter to the author, and provide the date of the correspondence.

Dove, Chris. Letter to the author. 14 May 2016.

List a published letter under the author's name, and provide full publication information.

Stetson, James A. Letter to Dolly W. Stetson. 8 Feb. 1845. *Letters from an American Utopia: The Stetson Family and the Northampton Association, 1843-1847*, edited by Christopher Clark and Kerry W. Buckley, U of Massachusetts P, 2004, pp. 133-34.

An interview

Arnaldo, Donald. Personal interview. 13 May 2016.

Brownstein, Carrie. Interview by Rachel Brodsky. *Spin*, 27 Oct. 2015, www.spin.com/2015/10/carrie-brownstein-hunger-makes-me-a-modern-girl-memoir-interview/.

A SAMPLE RESEARCH PAPER IN MLA STYLE

Margaret Lundberg wrote the following research paper for a first-year writing course at Tacoma Community College in Washington State and revised and updated it for *The Brief Bedford Reader*. We present Lundberg's paper for three reasons: It illustrates many techniques of using and documenting sources, which are highlighted in the marginal comments; it demonstrates elements of effective ARGUMENT, also noted in the margins; and it shows a writer working with a topic that interests her in a way that arouses the readers' interest as well.

Lundberg's advice to other writers is straightforward: "Keep a notebook handy at all times," she says. "You never know when that 'perfect' idea will show up."

Margaret Lundberg

Professor Fox

English 101

12 April 2016

Eating Green

When I was a child, our family's diet was important to
my mother. We had two vegetables with every meal, ate plain
yogurt for breakfast, and exercised with Jack LaLanne. Later, as
a young mom myself, I learned to cook meals from scratch, froze
and canned fresh produce, and did aerobics with Jane Fonda.
I was concerned with my sons' nutrition, having learned early
that good health didn't just happen — you had to work for it.
Now that my family circle has widened to include grandchildren,
I find that my concerns go beyond just the health of my own
family, to the health of the planet we live on. I believe that our
personal and global health is tightly interconnected, and what
benefits one will benefit the other.

I became a vegetarian about three years ago, and "went
vegan" last spring. I could tout all sorts of reasons, but suffice
it to say that I look and feel better at fifty-two than I did five
years ago. For *my* health and well-being, becoming a vegetarian
was the best thing I could have done. Which got me thinking —
what if we could establish that a vegetarian diet would benefit
not only our personal health, but the health of the planet as
well? Between pollution, greenhouse gases, and dependence on
a dwindling supply of fossil fuels, our little blue planet isn't feeling too well. If all of us adopting a vegetarian diet could slow
or stop all of these ills, shouldn't we consider it? The idea is not
as far-fetched as it might sound: A vegetarian diet could be just
what the doctor ordered for our global health.

Eating meat is such a big part of the American way of life
that it almost feels unpatriotic to spurn it. Would it still be
Thanksgiving without the turkey, the Fourth of July without the
hamburgers, a baseball game without the hotdogs? All of these
things seem to be permanently interwoven into our culture.
But the great American love affair with burgers and fries also
has a dark side. Just as the standard American diet is killing us
individually — with skyrocketing rates of obesity, diabetes, heart

Title arouses readers'
curiosity.

Introduction provides
context and establishes
Lundberg's purpose.

Evidence from
personal experience.
No source citation
needed for Lundberg's
generalizations.

Thesis statement.

Acknowledgment of
opposing viewpoint
(see p. 415).

Refutation of opposing
viewpoint.

disease, and a host of other ills — it is also having devastating effects on our planet. Pollution, global warming, and an alarming dependence on fossil fuels can all be traced back, in large part, to the agricultural practices that are required to feed our ever-growing craving for meat. Dietician Kate Geagan compares the environmental impact of the American diet with that of "our love affair with SUVs," warning that the energy use involved in the "production, transport, processing, packaging, storing, and preparation [of food] is now the single largest contributor to global warming" (x).

> *Quotation integrated into Lundberg's text. Brackets indicate change to original wording (see p. 45).*
>
> *Citation includes page number only because author (Geagan) is named in the text.*

Livestock production in this country and throughout the Western world has come a long way from the era of the American cowboy. The days of cattle grazing serenely on huge expanses of prairie pasture land are pretty much over. As journalist Michael Pollan points out in his book *The Omnivore's Dilemma*, raising cattle and other livestock is a multi-billion dollar operation that is now more manufacturing plant than traditional ranching. Cows no longer spend their lives grazing the hillsides until they are ready for slaughter. They are warehoused and fed a diet that is contrary to their very physiology — intended to eat grass, they are now fattened on corn, in as short a time as possible. In the early 1900s it took four to five years to ready a steer for slaughter; it now takes fourteen to sixteen months (ch. 4).

> *Citation for summary uses a chapter number because the source, an e-book, does not have stable page numbers.*

The corn-based diet they are fed leads to a variety of health issues for the cattle. In his article "The Ecology of Eating: The Power of the Fork," Mark Hyman offers an example:

> Of the 24 million pounds of antibiotics produced each year in this country, 19 million are put in the factory-farmed animals' feed to prevent infection, which results from overcrowding, and to prevent the cow's stomach from exploding with gas from the fermentation of the corn. (15)

> *Quotation of more than four lines is indented one-half inch.*
>
> *Parenthetical citation for set-off quotation falls outside final period.*

As a result of what is basically indigestion, Hyman explains, cattle belch vast amounts of methane, which is twenty-three times more potent at trapping heat than carbon dioxide. Livestock manure is the source of two-thirds of the man-made nitrous oxide now circulating in our atmosphere — a greenhouse gas that is three hundred times more potent than carbon dioxide (14).

> *Citation of a paraphrase. Citation includes only page number because author (Hyman) is named in the text.*

Lundberg 3

Other statistics are equally grim. Kate Geagan reports that livestock raised for meat production are responsible for 18% of greenhouse gas emissions — more than the cars we drive. The food sector is responsible for 20% of the total energy use in the United States every year, and most of that comes from the raising and packaging of livestock animals (30). The average household could make a bigger impact on greenhouse gas emissions by cutting their meat consumption in half than by cutting their driving in half!

A nonvegetarian diet requires 2.9 times more water, 2.5 times more energy, 13 times more fertilizer (also made from petroleum products), and 1.4 times more pesticides than does a vegetarian diet — and the greatest difference comes from beef consumption (Marlow et al. 1699). Less than half of the harvested acreage in the United States is used to grow food for people, and it takes sixteen pounds of grain and soybeans fed to cattle to get one pound of meat ready for us to eat. Ten times as much land is required for meat-protein production than is required for plant-protein production, and producing one pound of animal protein uses almost a hundred times more water than it takes to produce one pound of plant protein ("Land").

As a population's income rises, its people have traditionally eaten more meat and dairy foods, replacing wheat and rice in their diets — exactly what we have been experiencing over the last fifty years (Bittman). Nevertheless, between global warming and decreased natural resources such as farmable land and water, the earth simply can't support any greater increase in meat production. In my lifetime, the world population has doubled, and it is still growing exponentially. Yet, with finite resources, how will we continue to feed us all? Factory farming is simply unsustainable. Even Dennis Avery, director of the Centre for Global Food Issues (a very pro-livestock organization), has commented that "[t]he world must create 5 billion vegans in the next several decades, or triple its total farm output without using more land" (qtd. in "Land"). If *he* thinks so, it *must* be time to rethink our diet!

But what about our burgers? For far too many of us, giving up meat seems like an unreasonable thing to ask.

Statistics provided as evidence.

Author's name above and parenthetical page number clearly indicate the beginning and end of paraphrased material.

Lundberg's interpretation of the evidence.

Paragraph synthesizes information from two sources to support Lundberg's argument (see pp. 497–98).

Citation includes author's name and page number; "et al." ("and others") indicates more than two authors.

Citation includes title of source published by a group author. Online source has no page or reference numbers.

Paragraph synthesizes information from two sources to support Lundberg's argument.

Lundberg's interpretation of the evidence.

Expert opinion offered as evidence. Brackets indicate change to original passage (see p. 45).

Source quoted in another source.

Acknowledgment of opposing viewpoint.

Meat is good for us, isn't it? Maybe. But the average American consumes nearly 200 pounds of meat a year — 33% more than five decades ago. We eat about 110 grams of protein a day (more than three-quarters of which is animal protein), while the USDA's Food Pyramid recommends less than half that — an amount still nearly twice the 30 grams most other experts say we actually *need* (Bittman). Since the advent of products like McDonald's Quarter Pounder with Cheese (30 grams of protein all by itself!), it has become entirely too easy to eat much more meat than any of us could ever need ("USA Nutrition"). Our expanding waistlines and rising levels of diabetes and heart disease prove that any benefit we might gain from a modest amount of meat in our diet is being overcome by the sheer amount we are eating on a daily basis.

With growing evidence that human activities in general — and livestock production in particular — are causing large-scale environmental effects, many major corporations are attempting to make changes and "do their part" for the environment. A group of dairy farmers in New York State, for example, is teaming with General Electric to produce renewable energy from cow manure. Apparently manure from 2,500 cows can generate enough electricity for 200 homes. In a state with over 600,000 dairy cows, that's a lot of potential kilowatts. "We've estimated that this could generate $38 million in new revenue for dairy farmers around the country and offset 2 million tons of carbon dioxide equivalents annually by 2020," says Rick Naczi, executive vice president at Dairy Management Inc., in a press release ("GE"). Naczi reports that the dairy industry has committed to reducing greenhouse gas emissions by 25% by 2020 — the equivalent of getting "1.25 million passenger cars off the road every year." That's a lot of gas.

But even if we *can* make electricity from "cow pies," does that make up for the fact that we in the Western world are using far more than our fair share of the earth's limited resources? We use substantial amounts of fossil fuels and other nonrenewable resources to grow a "crop" that many in our global population cannot access; one that pollutes and sickens the planet — and its inhabitants — in ways we are only beginning to comprehend.

Marginal notes:

Refutation of opposing viewpoint.

Citation uses shortened version of title for work with corporate author and no page numbers.

Lundberg's interpretation of the evidence.

Acknowledgment of opposing viewpoint.

Citation uses shortened version of title for work with no named author. Online source has no page numbers.

Lundberg's comment on the evidence.

Refutation of opposing viewpoint.

No source citation for common knowledge.

Lundberg 5

In the face of a looming worldwide crisis where food prices are rising and nearly 3 billion people earn less than two dollars a day, two of every three people in the world already subsist on a vegetarian diet (Clemmit 1). Yet in the industrialized world over 50% of the grain that we grow is used to fatten livestock (Hyman 14). Peter Timmer, a fellow at the Washington-based Center for Global Development, states, "There's still plenty of food for everyone, but only if everyone eats a grain and legume-based diet. If the diet includes large . . . amounts of animal protein . . . , food demand is running ahead of global production" (qtd. in Clemmit 3).

Citation of a quotation from an indirect source. Ellipses indicate omission from quotation (see p. 45).

With finite resources already being stretched thin by a growing global population, is it rational for us to continue on as we are? Our food systems are not sustainable, and today's livestock production methods make potential food crises more likely every day. If greenhouse gases continue to build as they have over the last fifty years, the effects on today's farmlands may be irreversible. As global temperatures continue to rise, Alaska may become the new "Corn Belt" and the Midwest could become a desert. How much of the land we now depend on to feed us could be lost to agriculture? A vegetarian diet would enable us to healthfully feed many more people, and make much better use of the resources we have. Do we really want to wait until it's too late to change our way of eating?

Conclusion summarizes Lundberg's main points and restates her thesis.

Paper ends with a provocative question.

Works Cited

Bittman, Mark. "Rethinking the Meat-Guzzler." *The New York Times*, 27 Jan. 2008, www.nytimes.com/2008/01/27/weekinreview/27bittman.html?_r=0. Accessed 2 Apr. 2016.

Clemmit, Marcia. "Global Food Crisis: What's Causing the Rising Prices?" *Social Problems: Selections from* CQ Researcher, Sage, 2010, pp. 1-24.

Geagan, Kate. *Go Green Get Lean: Trim Your Waistline with the Ultimate Low-Carbon Footprint Diet*. Rodale, 2009.

"GE, US Dairy Industry Shine Light on Potential of 'Cow Power' in New York." *Business Wire*, 29 Oct. 2009, www.businesswire.com/news/home/20091029006166/en/GE-U.S.-Dairy-Industry-Shine-Light-Potential. Accessed 4 Apr. 2016.

List of works cited provided at end of paper.

An article in the Web version of a newspaper.

A selection in an anthology.

A print book.

A newspaper article posted on the Web.

Lundberg 6

Hyman, Mark. "The Ecology of Eating: The Power of the Fork."
    Alternative Therapies in Health and Medicine, vol. 15, no.
    4, July/Aug. 2009, pp. 14-15.

"Land." *Information Resources*, The Vegan Society, www.vegansociety
    .com/resources. Accessed 18 Mar. 2016.

Marlow, Harold J., et al. "Diet and the Environment: Does What
    You Eat Matter?" *American Journal of Clinical Nutrition*,
    vol. 89, no. 5, May 2009, pp. 1699-1703. *General One File*,
    doi:10.3945/.

Pollan, Michael. *The Omnivore's Dilemma: A Natural History of
    Four Meals*. Penguin Books, 2006.

"USA Nutrition Facts for Popular Menu Items." *Nutrition Choices*,
    McDonald's, nutrition.mcdonalds.com/getnutrition/
    nutritionfacts.pdf. Accessed 25 Mar. 2016.

Annotations (right margin):

An article from a print journal.

A short work from a Web site published by a group author.

Journal article from a database. "Et al." ("and others") indicates more than two authors.

An e-book.

A short work from a Web site published by a corporate author.

SOURCE CITATION USING APA STYLE

In this section we explain the documentation style of the American Psychological Association, as described in the *Publication Manual of the American Psychological Association*, 6th edition (2010). This style — used in psychology, sociology, business, education, economics, and other social sciences — involves a citation within the text that identifies the author and date of a source, as well as the page number(s) for a quotation or paraphrase (page numbers are not required for a summary).

In your text, the author's name may appear in a SIGNAL PHRASE, or it may appear in parentheses along with the date and any page numbers. Either way, the citation information directs readers to the source's full publication information in a list of references at the end of the text:

TEXT CITATION, AUTHOR NAMED IN SIGNAL PHRASE

As Quindlen (2017) has suggested, people's dwellings seem to have lost their emotional hold and to have become just investments (p. 165).

TEXT CITATION, AUTHOR NAMED IN PARENTHESES

One observer has suggested that people's dwellings seem to have lost their emotional hold and to have become just investments (Quindlen, 2017, p. 165).

ENTRY IN REFERENCE LIST

Quindlen, A. (2017). Homeless. In X. J. Kennedy, D. M. Kennedy, J. E. Aaron, &
    E. K. Repetto (Eds.), *The Brief Bedford Reader* (13th ed., pp. 164-166).
    Boston: Bedford.

APA Parenthetical Citations

The following examples of APA text citations show the author named in a signal phrase or named in parentheses.

APA Parenthetical Citations

A work with two authors

Comer and White (2016) reported that a mere 1.5% of writing students enrolled in their Massive Open Online Course earned a certificate of accomplishment, presumably because only a small number of enrollees intended to complete the work in the first place (p. 320).

A work with three to five authors

With more than two but fewer than six authors, list all of the authors in the first parenthetical citation. Separate the names with commas, and precede the final name with &.

Emergency room visitors over 65 years old are twice as likely as younger patients to be admitted for a hospital stay (Murdoch, Turpin, Johnston, MacLullich, & Losman, 2015, p. 1).

In later references to the same source, shorten the citation to the first author's name followed by et al. (*et alii,* "and others").

Murdoch et al. (2015) have suggested that all medical personnel need to be better trained in recognizing and addressing the unique needs of a growing elderly population (p. 6).

A work with six or more authors

Name only the first author followed by et al. (*et alii,* "and others").

In the midst of a global economic downturn in the early twenty-first century, household spending in the United States actually increased (Thiel et al., 2010, p. 26).

A work with a group author

For a work published under the name of an organization, such as a government agency or a corporation, use the name of the group as the author.

> The United States Conference of Mayors (2015) reported that most cities do not have enough emergency shelter beds to accommodate the needs of homeless residents (p. 2).

A work with no identified author

Cite an unsigned work by using the first one or two main words of the title (excluding any initial "A," "An," or "The").

> A full decade after Hurricane Katrina devastated New Orleans, some six thousand families remain unable to rebuild their homes ("Long Way," 2015, p. 39).

Two or more works by exactly the same author(s)

If you cite more than one work by the same author or authors, in most cases the year of publication will indicate which work you're referring to. If two or more works were published in the same year, assign lowercase letters to the years in your list of references (see p. 525) and include the same letters in your parenthetical citations.

> Gladwell (2011a) has argued that although popular wisdom held that Apple founder "[Steve] Jobs stole the personal computer from Xerox," the reality was that he refined ideas that Xerox showed little interest in pursuing (p. 48).

> According to Gladwell (2011b), Jobs's most significant personality trait—more so than his perfectionism, his aggressiveness, or his resilience—was his preference to "tweak" other people's inventions instead of innovate from scratch.

A source without page numbers

Cite an unpaginated source, such as an HTML document, a sound recording, or a DVD, as you would any print source: by author's name or, if there is no author indicated, by title. If a source numbers paragraphs instead of pages, give the appropriate number(s) as in the following model, after para. (one paragraph) or paras. (more than one paragraph).

> For six years in the 1970s, folk singer Joni Mitchell occasionally appeared on stage disguised as a black man, a deviant practice that Grier (2012) has claimed gave her "legitimacy and authority" among rock musicians (para. 1).

For a source with no page or paragraph numbers, provide a heading for the section in which the cited material appears (abbreviated if it is long), followed by the paragraph number within the section, as determined by your own count.

> One patient developed a painful, swollen rash that dermatologists attributed to an exclusive diet of fast food; in the months he abstained from such meals, his condition improved (Sundhar et al., 2012, Case section, para. 1).

An indirect source

Use as cited in to indicate that you found the source you quote within another source.

> Of the many difficulties of living in space, astronaut Norm Thagard felt that "boredom was the most common problem" (as cited in Roach, 2010, p. 28).

More than one work in the same citation

List the names in alphabetical order and separate the entries with a semicolon.

> Moving welfare recipients out of blighted neighborhoods has been shown to increase their happiness, if not their earning potential (Edsall, 2014; Rothwell, 2015).

Personal communications

Interviews you conduct and letters, e-mails, and messages you receive should be cited in your text with the correspondent's initials and last name, the words personal communication, and the full date. Because readers cannot retrieve such materials, they are not included in the list of references.

> A county health inspector explained that meat must be shelved at the bottom of refrigeration units to reduce the risk of contaminating vegetables and dairy products with bacteria (M. K. Edwards, personal communication, May 30, 2016).

APA Reference List

Your reference list is a complete record of your sources. Follow these guidelines for the list:

- **Title the list** References.

- **Double-space the entire list.**

- **Arrange the sources alphabetically** by the last name of the first author or by the first main word of the title if the source has no named author.

- **Begin the first line of each entry at the left margin.** Indent the subsequent lines of the entry one-half inch or five spaces.

Following are the essentials of a reference-list entry:

- **Reverse the names of the authors,** last name first, followed by a comma and initials for first and middle names (even if the names are given in full on the source), with another comma after the initials.

- **Provide a publication date** in parentheses after the name or names.

- **Give the full title of the work.** For titles of books, use italics and capitalize only the first word of the title and subtitle and any proper nouns. Use the same capitalization style for titles of articles, but don't italicize them or enclose them in quotation marks. For titles of periodicals, capitalize all major words and italicize the title.

- **Give publication information.** For books, include the city and state of publication and the publisher's name. For periodicals, include the volume number and sometimes the issue number along with the page numbers for the article you cite. For print periodical articles, also include a digital object identifier (DOI) if one is available. Always include the DOI or a URL for online periodical articles. (See pp. 525–26 for more on DOIs and URLs.)

- **Use periods between parts of each entry,** but do not include a period at the end of a DOI or URL.

You may need to combine some of the following models to document a particular source — for instance, combine "Eight or more authors" and "A periodical article from a database" for an online database article with twelve listed authors.

Authors

One author

Jordan, J. A. (2015). *Edible memory: The lure of heirloom tomatoes and other forgotten foods*. Chicago, IL: University of Chicago Press.

Two to seven authors

McFadden, J., & Al-Khalili, J. (2014). *Life on the edge: The coming of age of quantum biology*. New York, NY: Crown.

Murdoch, I., Turpin, S., Johnston, B., Maclullich, A., & Losman, E. (2015). *Geriatric emergencies*. Malden, MA: Wiley-Blackwell.

APA Reference List

Eight or more authors

Name the first six authors, insert ellipses, and end with the name of the last listed author.

Adams, J. D., Kavouras, S. A., Robillard, J. I., Bardis, C. N., Johnson, E. C.,
    Ganio, M. S., . . . White, M. A. (2016). Fluid balance of adolescent
    swimmers during training. *Journal of Strength and Conditioning Research,
    30,* 621-25.

A group author

U.S. Department of Justice, Cybersecurity Unit. (2015). *Best practices for
    victim response and reporting of cyber incidents.* Retrieved from http://
    www.justice.gov/sites/default/files/criminal-ccips/legacy/2015/04/30
    /04272015reporting-cyber-incidents-final.pdf

No identified author

Start the entry with the title of the work, followed by the date and publication information.

If you can't stand the heat. (2015, November 28). *The Economist, 417*(8966),
    10-13.

More than one work by exactly the same author(s)

When you cite two or more works by the same author that were published in *different* years, include the author's name in each entry and list the entries in chronological order by publication date.

> Turkle, S. (2011). *Alone together: Why we expect more from technology and less from each other.* New York, NY: Basic Books.
>
> Turkle, S. (2015). *Reclaiming conversation: The power of talk in a digital age.* New York, NY: Penguin Press.

When you cite two or more works by the same author that were published in the *same* year, list the works in alphabetical order by title and add lowercase letters (a, b, c, etc.) to the date. Use the same letters with the date in the corresponding parenthetical citations (see p. 521).

> Gladwell, M. (2011a, May 16). Creation myth: Xerox PARC, Apple, and the truth about innovation. *The New Yorker, 87*(13), 44-53.
>
> Gladwell, M. (2011b, November 14). The tweaker: The real genius of Steve Jobs. *The New Yorker, 87*(36), 32-35.

Periodicals: Journals, Magazines, and Newspapers

An article in a journal

Most journals number issues consecutively throughout the year, so that the first page of issue 3, for instance, might begin on page 409. In such cases, follow the journal title with the volume number (italicized), a comma, the inclusive page numbers of the article, and a period. If a journal starts each issue with page 1, include the issue number in parentheses (not italicized) after the volume number. APA strongly recommends listing the digital object identifier (DOI) for any article that has one assigned to it.

> Conti, R. (2015). Compassionate parenting as a key to satisfaction, efficacy and meaning among mothers of children with autism. *Journal of Autism and Developmental Disorders, 45,* 2008-2018. doi:10.1007/s10803-015-2360-6
>
> Ryan, C. (2014). Empowering teachers and students through formative assessment. *Council Chronicle, 23*(3), 6-9.

Base an entry for an online journal article on one of the above models for print journals. Include the DOI if one is provided.

> Yu, Z., Day, D. A., Connal-Nicolaou, A., & Enders, F. T. (2011). Early food allergen exposure may be protective against food allergies: An extension of the hygiene hypothesis. *Internet Journal of Epidemiology, 10*(1). doi:10.5580/243a

If no DOI is provided, give the URL of the journal's home page after **Retrieved from**.

> Peel, M. (2015). Assessing fitness to detain in police custody. *Nursing Standard, 30*(11), 43-49. Retrieved from http://nursingstandard .rcnpublishing.co.uk

(If you must break a DOI or URL, do it after the two slashes following http:// or before a single slash, a period, or another punctuation mark. Do not add a hyphen.)

An article in a magazine

Include the complete date in parentheses and provide volume and issue numbers.

> Fallows, J. (2015, November). The (planet-saving, capitalism-subverting, surprisingly lucrative) investment secrets of Al Gore. *The Atlantic, 316*(4). Retrieved from http://www.theatlantic.com
>
> Helgoe, L. (2010, October). Revenge of the introvert. *Psychology Today, 43*(5), 54-61.
>
> Von Drehle, D. (2015, April 20). Line of fire. *Time, 185*(14), 24-28.

An article in a newspaper

Include the year, month, and day in the date. List all page numbers, preceded by p. (for one page) or pp. (for multiple pages).

> Kaplan, S. (2016, March 3). Whose advice is it? Doctors promoting treatments on social media routinely fail to disclose ties to drug makers. *The Boston Globe*, pp. C1, C7.

For an article from the Web version of a newspaper, replace page numbers with the URL for the full site.

> Ferdman, R. A. (2016, March 4). The magical thing eating chocolate does to your brain. *The Washington Post*. Retrieved from https://www .washingtonpost.com/

A periodical article from a database

For an article that you obtain from a library or online database, provide print publication information using the models for journals, magazines, and newspapers above. Add the DOI or, if there is none, the URL of the periodical's home page. Do not include the name of the database.

Reed, M. G., & George, C. (2011). Where in the world is environmental
    justice? *Progress in Human Geography, 35,* 835-842. doi:10.1177
    /0309132510388384
Scudellari, M. (2015, July 31). The kids aren't all right. *Newsweek, 165*(5),
    44-47. Retrieved from http://www.newsweek.com

Books

A book with an author

Sacks, O. (2012). *Hallucinations.* New York, NY: Knopf.

A book with an editor or editors

Masih, T. L. (Ed.). (2012). *The chalk circle: Intercultural prizewinning essays.*
    Deadwood, OR: Wyatt-MacKenzie.
Zeigler-Hill, V., & Marcus, D. K. (Eds.). (2016). *The dark side of personality:
    Science and practice in social, personality, and clinical psychology.* Wash-
    ington, DC: American Psychological Association.

A later edition

Patterson, K., Grenny, J., McMillan, R., & Switzler, A. (2012). *Crucial conver-
    sations: Tools for talking when stakes are high* (2nd ed.). New York, NY:
    McGraw-Hill.

A selection from an anthology

Use the anthology's publication year after the author's name, even if the
selection was originally published earlier. In the page numbers in parentheses,
give the location of the cited selection within the anthology.

Barnet, R. (2010). Why didn't the boat sink? How a kindertransportee kept
    afloat. In S. Kriger (Ed.), *Marking humanity: Stories, poems, and essays by
    Holocaust survivors* (pp. 64-67). Toronto, Canada: Soul Inscriptions Press.

A book on the Web

Instead of print publication information, provide the URL you used to
retrieve the book. In this example, the final parenthesis provides the date of
the book's original publication:

Barker, C. H. (2004). *Wanted, a young woman to do housework: Business prin-
    ciples applied to housework.* Retrieved from http://www.gutenberg.org
    /files/14117/14117-h/14117-h.htm (Original work published 1915)

A book on an e-reader

For an electronic book on an e-reader such as a Kindle, Nook, or iPad, add the type of file in brackets after the title, followed by the URL where you retrieved the book.

> Cohen, A. (2016). *Imbeciles: The Supreme Court, American eugenics, and the sterilization of Carrie Buck* [iBooks version]. Retrieved from http://www .itunes.apple.com
>
> Urrea, L. A. (1996). *By the lake of sleeping children: The secret life of the Mexican border* [Kindle version]. Retrieved from http://www.amazon.com

Other Online and Multimedia Sources

Online sources vary greatly, and they may be and often are updated. Your aim in citing such a source should be to tell what version you used and how readers can find it for themselves. Include the date on which you accessed the source only if the source is likely to change or if it lacks a publication date or version number (see the first model below for an example). Substitute n.d. (for "no date") in parentheses if a source is undated. If you don't see a model for the type of source you used, follow a model that comes close. If you can't find all the information shown in a model, give what you can find.

A document from a Web site

Include as much of the following information as you can find: author's name, date of publication or last update, title, and URL.

> Rigoglioso, M. (2012, April 17). *The psychology around voter turnout.* Retrieved from http://csi.gsb.stanford.edu/getting-out-vote

If no author is listed, begin the entry with the title followed by the date in parentheses. The following example also includes the date of retrieval because the source has no publication date and is likely to change.

> *Lyme disease.* (n.d.). Retrieved September 18, 2015, from http://www.webmd .com/rheumatoid-arthritis/arthritis-lyme-disease

A video or audio recording

Include a description of the medium or file type in brackets after the title of the work.

> Campbell, M. (Director). (2011). *Green lantern* [DVD]. Burbank, CA: Warner Bros.

Fraser, S. (2012, May). Why eyewitnesses get it wrong [Video file]. Retrieved
    from http://www.ted.com/talks/scott_fraser_the_problem_with
    _eyewitness_testimony.html

Montgomery, S. (2014, November/December). Predators in the barnyard
    [Audio file]. Retrieved from https://orionmagazine.org/article
    /sy-montgomery-reads-predators-in-the-barnyard/

Waits, T. (1976). The piano has been drinking (not me). On *Small change*
    [CD]. New York, NY: Elektra/Asylum Records.

A podcast

Crespi, S., & Grimm, D. (Hosts). (2016, January 8). Dancing dinosaurs, naked
    black holes, and more [Audio podcast]. *Science podcasts*. Retrieved from
    http://www.sciencemag.org/podcasts

A posting to a blog or discussion group

HypnoToad72. (16 July 2012). Re: Go mobile or go home: From augmented
    reality to language learning to virtual classrooms, the word is mobile
    [Blog comment]. Retrieved from http://www.zdnet/article/go-mobile
    -or-go-home

Northrup, L. (2016, February 16). Our growing e-commerce addiction means
    mountains of cardboard [Blog post]. Retrieved from http://consumerist.com

SAMPLE PAPER IN APA STYLE

As a bioengineering major and pre-med student at the University of
Pennsylvania in Philadelphia, Eric Kim enrolled in the sophomore-level composition seminar "The Novelist and the Neuroscientist" to fulfill a critical
writing requirement. "Writing has always been difficult" for him, Kim says, but
he enjoyed the course because "it was nice to write on a topic he is interested
in." The paper we present on the following pages explores Kim's interest in
one recently discovered aspect of the human brain; it also demonstrates the
uses of APA documentation style in a brief yet thoroughly developed sample
of researched writing. Kim revised and updated the essay for *The Brief Bedford
Reader*.

Notice that in accordance with APA style, the writer provides a title page
with an (optional) author note and a running head that continues through
the paper; he also follows the American Psychological Association's convention of using past tense or past perfect tense in signal phrases that introduce
the findings of other researchers.

Running head: BRAIN   1   Title page provides a
                                                                 shortened version of
                                                                 title used as a running
                                                                 head throughout paper.

                        The Brain That Changes   Title, author name, and
                              Eric Kim   school are centered on
                                                                 page.
                      University of Pennsylvania

                                                                 Optional author note
                                                                 provides additional
                                                                 information about
Author Note: This paper was prepared for *Critical Writing Seminar in Psychology:*   course and lists any
The Novelist and the Neuroscientist, taught by Professor Charbonnier.   acknowledgements.

Until recently, neuroscientists held the notion that the structure of the brain was fixed after infancy; neurons could never regenerate or form new networks. Less than two decades ago, however, researchers documented neural cell division in adult primates (Gould, Tanapat, McEwen, Flügge, & Fuchs, 1998). A flurry of subsequent experiments illustrated that the brain continuously changes throughout life. This property has been termed *neuroplasticity* and it involves modifying neural connections, building new neural networks, destroying old neurons, and generating new neurons. Through neuroplasticity, everything from experiences, injuries, and even thoughts can change the fabric of the brain (Carr, 2011, p. 27). In fact, if this concept is new to you, your brain is undergoing reorganization as you read. For some, this might be a startling notion: Are these structural changes in the brain taking place for better or worse? After all, in a system as complex as the brain, any changes might disrupt a natural balance. On the other hand, neuroplasticity implies an opportunity to improve the brain. Human experience shows both results can occur. For the most part, however, neuroplasticity is beneficial.

It would be wrong to ignore that, in some cases, neuroplasticity can lead to harmful conditions. For example, neuroplasticity may malfunction in response to injury. Normal injuries rearrange nerve cells to help enforce a feeling of pain. These neural changes eventually revert, and the pain subsides. With severe injuries, however, the neural changes may become irreversible, leading to many cases of chronic pain. Amputees often develop this problem in their severed limbs, a disorder known as "phantom limb" pain (Carr, 2011, p. 30). Many other harmful results of neuroplasticity have been documented. For example, writers who used hand muscles frequently strengthened corresponding networks in the motor cortex. In some cases, this development led to a hyperactive motor cortex that caused painful, involuntary contractions of hand muscles (Johnston, 2009, p. 99). Likewise, drug use can overstimulate and change neural pathways, ultimately leading to addiction (Rácz, 2014). While

Citation of a source with five authors not named in the text. No page number required for a summary.

Citation of a source with one author not named in the text. Page number provided for paraphrase.

Introduction engages readers' interest and identifies Kim's research question.

Thesis statement answers research question.

Acknowledgment of opposing viewpoint (see p. 415).

Paragraph synthesizes information from four sources (see pp. 497–98).

Page numbers provided for quotations (Carr) and paraphrases (Johnston), but not for summaries (Rácz and Wilson & Hunt [on next page]).

neuroplasticity can have harmful results, virtually all biological functions have some negative effects. Errors in nuclear division, for example, can lead to Down syndrome; likewise, faulty protein synthesis can result in diabetes, cystic fibrosis, cancer—the list goes on (Wilson & Hunt, 2015). However, normal functioning of nuclear division and protein synthesis are both critical for human life. Similarly, while neuroplasticity can have some problems, it still plays an overall positive role in our biology.

> Refutation of opposing viewpoint.

For one, neuroplasticity allows the brain to improve useful mental functions. When the brain engages in a challenging mental task, it structures a network of neurons to perform the task. With repetition, the neurons thicken, and new connections are added to the network to make it more advanced. To study this role of neuroplasticity, a research team at the University of Dokuz Eylül in Turkey examined the parietal lobes of mathematicians; this part of the brain helps process the abstract creativity used in advanced mathematics. The results showed that the density of neurons and neural connections in the parietal lobes "were strongly correlated with the time spent [training] as an academician" (Aydin et al., 2007, p. 1859). Other studies found similar correlations between violinists and the motor and auditory cortexes, as well as taxi cab drivers and brain regions that store spacial information (Wilson, Conyers, & Rose, 2015, Redefining section, para. 2). In other words, practicing a skill, such as mathematicians do when repeatedly solving difficult problems, leads to lasting changes in the brain that make a person better at that skill. Just like physical exercises that can strengthen specific body parts, mental exercises can literally reshape the brain to suit different functions as needed. Without neuroplasticity, the brain would be a fixed structure and any improvements would be impossible.

> Paragraph synthesizes information from two sources.

> Quotation integrated into Kim's text. Brackets indicate word added for clarity (see p. 45).

> Citation of a source with eight authors not named in the text; page number required for quotation.

> Citation of source with three authors not named in the text; abbreviated section heading and paragraph number for paraphrase from an unpaged document.

> Kim's interpretation of the evidence.

Beyond improving the usual roles of brain regions, neuroplasticity allows brain regions to adopt radically new functions. This mechanism plays a critical role in compensating for the disruption or loss of a function. The first experiment to illustrate this notion was conducted by MIT neuroscientists von Melchner,

Pallas, and Sur (2000), who disturbed retinal connections in newborn ferrets by redirecting them to the auditory cortex. Because the structure of the auditory cortex cannot process light, the ferrets should have been completely blind. Remarkably, the ferrets still responded to light stimuli. Brain imaging showed that neurons in the auditory cortex had reorganized to resemble networks normally present in the visual cortex (pp. 874-875). Thus, neuroplasticity can adapt brain regions to suit new needs. Later studies have found numerous parallels in humans. Deaf subjects, for instance, can use the auditory cortex to interpret sign language, while blind people can use the visual cortex to read Braille; if a finger is lost, its brain area can be taken over by the remaining fingers to make them more efficient (Carr, 2011, p. 29; Johnston, 2009, pp. 96-97). These studies have shown that when regions of the brain can no longer be used for their normal functions, they are adapted for other purposes. In this context, neuroplasticity operates to constantly make the most of the brain's neural real estate. This efficiency cushions the impact when normal processes are compromised.

Moreover, neuroplasticity helps patients recover from physical brain injuries. Because the brain is such an integral part of normal functioning, brain injuries often have devastating consequences. Strokes, for example, can destroy an entire hemisphere of the brain, leading to paralysis in half of the body. Other brain injuries can occur from surgeries, tumors, and blood vessel disorders; these commonly result in severe speech impairments, disrupted vision, and memory problems. Luckily, neuroplasticity acts as a built-in healing mechanism. When the brain senses injury, it forms new neurons and synapses to repair the damaged networks, often leading to dramatic improvements. Stroke patients, for example, can recover almost full speech and motor function (Johnston, 2009). In this way, neuroplasticity prevents brain damage from leading to permanent disability.

In a related manner, neuroplasticity assists in recovery from psychological disorders. Insight into this process was first gained by studying the brains of Buddhist monks after

Names and date here and page number later in the paragraph frame evidence paraphrased from a source.

Two sources cited in a single citation.

Kim's interpretation of the evidence.

No citation needed for common knowledge, or generally accepted information that cannot be traced to any single source.

No page numbers for a summary.

meditation (Kaufman, 2005). The results indicated that brain
regions associated with positive attitudes and happiness under-
went lasting changes during meditation that made them more
active. In other words, conscious thoughts (such as the positive ones common during meditation) can fundamentally alter
the brain, and these thoughts can be controlled. Thus, it is
not surprising that in many cases of depression and anxiety, patients reported marked improvements by simply thinking positive
thoughts (Marx, 2013). In this context, neuroplasticity allows
us to actively improve our mental health. When something goes
wrong, we have the power to fix it.

Neuroplasticity has shattered the concept of a static brain.
Within less than twenty years of its discovery, numerous benefits
of neuroplasticity have been identified. Such broad implications
are beginning to change old notions. In education, for example,
neuroplasticity has strongly swung the nature-nurture debate
in favor of the nurturists; educators are helping children overcome learning difficulties and actually improve their intelligence
through training programs that restructure the brain (Wilson,
Conyers, & Rose, 2015). Neuroplasticity is impacting the adult
population as well. As news of a malleable brain spreads, people
are engaging in mental exercises to proactively improve themselves (Marx, 2013). Meditation, anyone?

Paragraph synthesizes information from two sources.

Kim's interpretation of the evidence.

Conclusion considers implications of the research.

Citation for a source with three authors not named in the text; no page numbers for a summary.

References

Aydin, K., Ucar, A., Oguz, K. K., Okur, O. O., Agayev, A., Unal, Z., . . . Ozturk, C. (2007). Increased gray matter density in the parietal cortex of mathematicians: A voxel-based morphometry study. *Neuroradiology, 28*, 1859-64. Retrieved from http://link.springer.com/journal/234

Carr, N. (2011). *The shallows: What the Internet is doing to our brains.* New York, NY: Norton.

Gould, E., Tanapat, P., McEwen, B. S., Flügge, G., & Fuchs, E. (1998). Proliferation of granule cell precursors in the dentate gyrus of adult monkeys is diminished by stress. *Proceedings of the National Academy of Sciences of the United States of America, 95*, 3168-71.

Johnston, M. V. (2009). Plasticity in the developing brain: Implications for rehabilitation. *Developmental Disabilities Research Reviews, 15*(2), 94-101. doi:10.1002/ddrr.64

Kaufman, M. (2005, January 3). Meditation gives brain a charge, study finds. *The Washington Post.* Retrieved from http://www.washingtonpost.com

Marx, P. (2013, July 29.) Mentally fit: Workouts at the brain gym. *The New Yorker, 89*(22), 24-28.

Rácz, I. (2014). Neuroplastic changes in addiction. *Frontiers in Molecular Neuroscience, 6*(56). doi:10.3389/fnmol2013.00056

von Melchner, L., Pallas, S. L., & Sur, M. (2000). Visual behavior mediated by retinal projections directed to the auditory pathway. *Nature, 404*, 871-75.

Wilson, D., Conyers, M., & Rose, K. (2015). Rethinking learning potential. *Independent School, 75*(1). Retrieved from https://www.nais.org

Wilson, J. H., & Hunt, T. (2015). *Molecular biology of the cell* (6th ed.). New York, NY: Garland Science.

Reference list begins on a new page.

An article with eight authors and no DOI from a database.

A print book with one author.

An article with five authors from a print journal.

A journal article with a DOI from a database.

A newspaper article on the Web.

A print article from a weekly magazine.

An online scholarly journal without page numbers.

An article with three authors from a print journal.

A journal article without page numbers or a DOI from a database.

A print book with two authors in a later edition.

GLOSSARY OF USEFUL TERMS

Abstract and concrete   Two kinds of language. *Abstract* words refer to ideas, conditions, and qualities we cannot directly perceive: *truth, love, happiness, courage, evil, poverty, progressive*. *Concrete* words indicate things we can know with our senses: *tree, chair, bird, pen, courthouse, motorcycle, perfume, thunderclap*. Concrete words lend vigor and clarity to writing, for they help a reader to picture things. See IMAGE.

    Writers of expository and argumentative essays tend to shift back and forth from one kind of language to the other. They often begin a paragraph with a general statement full of abstract words ("There is *hope* for the *future* of *driving*"). Then they usually go on to give examples and present evidence in sentences full of concrete words ("Inventor *Jones* claims his *car* will go from *Fresno* to *Los Angeles* on a *gallon* of *peanut oil*"). Inexperienced writers often use too many abstract words and not enough concrete ones. See also pages 48 and 108.

Academic writing   The kind of writing generally undertaken by scholars and students, in which a writer responds to another's work or uses multiple SOURCES to develop and support an original idea. Typically based on one or more TEXTS, all academic writing calls on a writer's CRITICAL THINKING, READING, AND WRITING abilities and shares the common goal of using reading and writing to build and exchange knowledge. See Chapter 2, pp. 42–47, and the Appendix, pp. 496–99.

Active voice   The form of the verb when the sentence subject is the actor: *Trees* [subject] *shed* [active verb] *their leaves in autumn.* Contrast PASSIVE VOICE.

Allude, allusion   To refer to a person, place, or thing believed to be common knowledge (*allude*), or the act or result of doing so (*allusion*). An allusion may point to a famous event, a familiar saying, a noted personality, or a well-known story or song. Usually brief, an allusion is a space-saving way to convey much meaning. For example, the statement "The game was Coach Johnson's Waterloo" informs the reader that, like Napoleon meeting defeat in a celebrated battle, the coach led a confrontation resulting in his downfall and that of his team. If the writer is also showing Johnson's character, the allusion might further tell us that the coach is a man of Napoleonic ambition and pride. To make an effective allusion, you have to ensure that it will be clear to your audience. Not every reader, for example, would understand an allusion to a neighbor, to a seventeenth-century Russian harpsichordist, or to a little-known stock-car driver.

Analogy   An extended comparison based on the like features of two unlike things: one familiar or easily understood, the other unfamiliar, abstract, or complicated. For instance, most people know at least vaguely how the human eye works: The pupil adjusts to admit light, which registers as an image on the retina at the back of the eye. You might use this familiar information to explain something less familiar to many people, such as how a camera works: The aperture (like the pupil) adjusts to admit light, which registers as an image on the film (like the retina) at the back of the camera. Analogies are especially helpful for explaining technical information in a way that is nontechnical, more easily grasped. For example, the spacecraft *Voyager 2* transmitted spectacular pictures of Saturn to Earth. To explain the difficulty of their achievement, NASA scientists compared their feat to a golfer sinking a putt from five hundred miles away. Because it can make abstract ideas vivid and memorable, analogy is also a favorite device of philosophers, politicians, and preachers.

Analogy is similar to the method of COMPARISON AND CONTRAST. Both identify the distinctive features of two things and then set the features side by side. But a comparison explains two obviously similar things — two Civil War generals, two responses to a mess — and considers both their differences and their similarities. An analogy yokes two apparently unlike things (eye and camera, spaceflight and golf) and focuses only on their major similarities. Analogy is thus an extended *metaphor*, the FIGURE OF SPEECH that declares one thing to be another — even though it isn't, in a strictly literal sense — for the purpose of making us aware of similarity: "Hope," writes the poet Emily Dickinson, "is the thing with feathers / That perches in the soul."

In an ARGUMENT, analogy can make readers more receptive to a point or inspire them, but it can't prove anything because in the end the subjects are dissimilar. A false analogy is a logical FALLACY that claims a fundamental likeness when none exists. See page 413.

Analyze, analysis   To separate a subject into its parts (*analyze*), or the act or result of doing so (*analysis*, also called *division*). Analysis is a key skill in CRITICAL THINKING, READING, AND WRITING; see pages 16, 18–22, and 24–25. It is also considered a method of development; see Chapter 8.

Anecdote   A brief NARRATIVE, or retelling of a story or event. Anecdotes have many uses: as essay openers or closers, as examples, as sheer entertainment. See Chapter 3.

Appeals   Resources writers draw on to connect with and persuade readers:

- A **rational appeal** *(logos)* asks readers to use their intellects and their powers of reasoning. It relies on established conventions of logic and evidence.
- An **emotional appeal** *(pathos)* asks readers to respond out of their beliefs, values, or feelings. It inspires, affirms, frightens, angers.
- An **ethical appeal** *(ethos)* asks readers to look favorably on the writer. It stresses the writer's intelligence, competence, fairness, morality, and other qualities desirable in a trustworthy debater or teacher.

See also page 409.

Argument   A mode of writing intended to win readers' agreement with an assertion by engaging their powers of reasoning. Argument often overlaps PERSUASION. See Chapter 12.

Assume, assumption   To take something for granted (*assume*), or a belief or opinion taken for granted (*assumption*). Whether stated or unstated, assumptions influence a writer's choices of subject, viewpoint, EVIDENCE, and even language. See also pages 17 and 410.

Audience   A writer's readers. Having in mind a particular audience helps the writer in choosing strategies, such as which method(s) to use, what details to include, and how to shape an ARGUMENT. You can increase your awareness of your audience by asking yourself a few questions before you begin to write. Who are to be your readers? What is their age level? background? education? Where do they live? What are their beliefs and attitudes? What interests them? What, if anything, sets them apart from most people? How familiar are they with your subject? Knowing your audience can help you write so that your readers will not only understand you better but care more deeply about what you say. See also pages 20, 30, and 407.

Body   The part of an essay, usually several PARAGRAPHS, that develops the writer's main idea. See pages 36–37.

Cause and effect   A method of development in which a writer ANALYZES reasons for an action, event, or decision, or analyzes its consequences. See Chapter 10. See also EFFECT.

Chronological order   The arrangement of events as they occurred or occur in time, first to last. Most NARRATIVES and PROCESS ANALYSES use chronological order.

Claim   The proposition that an ARGUMENT demonstrates, generally expressed in a THESIS STATEMENT. See pages 407–08.

Classification   A method of development in which a writer sorts out multiple things (contact sports, college students, kinds of music) into categories. See Chapter 9.

Cliché   A worn-out, trite expression that a writer employs thoughtlessly. Although at one time the expression may have been colorful, from heavy use it has lost its luster. It is now "old as the hills." In conversation, most of us sometimes use clichés, but in writing they "stick out like sore thumbs." Alert writers, when they revise, replace a cliché with a fresh, CONCRETE expression. Writers who have trouble recognizing clichés should be suspicious of any phrase they've heard before and should try to read more widely. Their problem is that, because so many expressions are new to them, they do not know which ones are full of moths.

Climactic order   The arrangement of points from least to most important, weakest to strongest. Essays organized by EXAMPLE and CAUSE AND EFFECT often use climactic order, as do many ARGUMENTS.

Coherence   The clear connection of the parts in effective writing so that the reader can easily follow the flow of ideas between sentences, paragraphs, and larger divisions, and can see how they relate successively to one another.

   In making your essay coherent, you may find certain devices useful. TRANSITIONS, for instance, can bridge ideas. Reminders of points you have stated earlier are helpful to a reader who may have forgotten them — as readers tend to do sometimes, particularly if an essay is long. However, a coherent essay is not one merely pasted together with transitions and reminders. It derives its coherence from the clear relationship between its THESIS (or central idea) and all its parts. See also pages 41–42 and 257–58.

Colloquial expressions   Words and phrases occurring primarily in speech and in informal writing that seeks a relaxed, conversational tone. "I need a burger and a shake" or "This mess is making me twitchy" may be acceptable in talking to a roommate, in corresponding with a friend, or in writing a humorous essay for general readers. Such choices of words, however, would be out of place in formal writing — in, say, a laboratory report or a letter to your senator. Contractions (*let's*, *don't*, *we'll*) and abbreviated words (*pic*, *sales rep*, *ad*) are the shorthand of spoken language. Good writers use such expressions with an awareness that they produce an effect of casualness.

Common ground   One or more aspects of an ARGUMENT on which both writer and reader can agree. A writer arguing in favor of raising highway speed limits might, for example, start by acknowledging the importance of safe driving before citing evidence showing that higher average speeds would have little effect on accident rates. By conceding the validity of opposing points or identifying ASSUMPTIONS shared by people on both sides of an issue, the writer establishes the fairness of his or her position and helps to win over readers who may otherwise be inclined to reject the argument outright. See page 407.

Comparison and contrast   Two methods of development usually found together. Using them, a writer examines the similarities and differences between two things to reveal their natures. See Chapter 6.

Conclusion   The sentences or paragraphs that bring an essay to a satisfying and logical end. See pages 38–39.

Concrete   See ABSTRACT AND CONCRETE.

Connotation and denotation   Two types of meanings most words have. *Denotation* is the explicit, literal, dictionary definition of a word. *Connotation* refers to a word's implied meaning, resonant with associations. The denotation of *blood* is "the fluid that circulates in the vascular system." The connotations of *blood* range from *life force* to *gore* to *family bond*. A doctor might use the word *blood* for its denotation, and a mystery writer might rely on the word's connotations to heighten a scene.

   Because people have different experiences, they bring to the same word different associations. A conservative's emotional response to the word *welfare* is not likely to be the same as a liberal's. And referring to your senator as a *diplomat* evokes a different response, from the senator and from others, than would *baby-kisser*, *political hack*, or even *politician*. The effective use of words involves knowing both what they mean literally and what they are likely to suggest.

Critical thinking, reading, and writing   A group of interlocking skills that are
essential for college work and beyond. Each seeks the meaning beneath the
surface of a statement, poem, editorial, picture, advertisement, Web site, or
other TEXT. Using ANALYSIS, INFERENCE, SYNTHESIS, and often EVALUATION, the
critical thinker, reader, and writer separates a text into its elements in order to see
and judge meanings, relations, and ASSUMPTIONS that might otherwise remain
buried. See also pages 12, 25–26, 255, and 406–07.

Data   A name for EVIDENCE favored by philosopher Stephen Toulmin in his conception of ARGUMENT. See pages 408–09.

Deductive reasoning, deduction   The method of reasoning from the general to the
particular: From information about what we already know, we deduce what we
need or want to know. See Chapter 12, pages 411–12.

Definition   A statement of the literal and specific meaning or meanings of a word
or a method of developing an essay. In the latter, the writer usually explains the
nature of a word, a thing, a concept, or a phenomenon. Such a definition may
employ NARRATION, DESCRIPTION, or any other method. See Chapter 11.

Denotation   See CONNOTATION AND DENOTATION.

Description   A mode of writing that conveys the evidence of the senses: sight,
hearing, touch, taste, smell. See Chapter 4.

Dialog   The quoted speech of participants in a story. Dialog is commonly included
in a NARRATIVE, especially fiction, but it can also be useful in bringing any form
of reported writing to life. See pages 68.

Diction   The choice of words. Every written or spoken statement uses diction of some
kind. To describe certain aspects of diction, the following terms may be useful:

- **Standard English:** the common American language, words, and grammatical
  forms that are used and expected in schools, businesses, and other formal sites.
- **Nonstandard English:** words and grammatical forms such as *theirselves* and
  ain't that are used mainly by people who speak a dialect other than standard
  English.
- **Dialect:** a variety of English based on differences in geography, education,
  or social background. Dialect is usually spoken but may be written. Shirley
  Jackson's story in Chapter 3 transcribes the words of dialect speakers ("'I looked
  out the window and the kids was gone, and then I remembered it was the
  twenty-seventh and came a-running'").
- **Slang:** certain words in highly informal speech or writing, or in the speech of
  a particular group — for example, *blow off, dweeb, wack*.
- **Colloquial expressions:** words and phrases from conversation. See COLLOQUIAL
  EXPRESSIONS for examples.
- **Regional terms:** words heard in a certain locality, such as *spritzing* for "raining"
  in Pennsylvania Dutch country.
- **Technical terms:** words and phrases that form the vocabulary of a particular discipline (*monocotyledon* from botany), occupation (*drawplate* from die-
  making), or avocation (*interval training* from running). See also JARGON.
- **Archaisms:** old-fashioned expressions, once common but now used to suggest
  an earlier style, such as *ere* and *forsooth*.
- **Obsolete diction:** words that have passed out of use (such as the verb *werien*,
  "to protect or defend," and the noun *isetnesses*, "agreements"). *Obsolete* may

also refer to certain meanings of words no longer current (*fond* for foolish, *clipping* for hugging or embracing).

- **Pretentious diction:** use of words more numerous and elaborate than necessary, such as *institution of higher learning* for "college," and *partake of solid nourishment* for "eat."

Archaic, obsolete, and pretentious diction usually have no place in good writing unless for ironic or humorous effect: The journalist and critic H. L. Mencken delighted in the hifalutin use of *tonsorial studio* instead of barber shop. Still, any diction may be the right diction for a certain occasion: The choice of words depends on a writer's PURPOSE and AUDIENCE.

Discovery   The stage of the writing process before the first draft. It may include deciding on a topic, narrowing the topic, creating or finding ideas, doing reading and other research, defining PURPOSE and AUDIENCE, or planning and arranging material. Discovery may follow from daydreaming or meditation, reading, or perhaps carefully ransacking memory. In practice, though, it usually involves considerable writing and is aided by the act of writing. The operations of discovery — reading, research, further idea creation, and refinement of subject, purpose, and audience — may all continue well into drafting as well. See also pages 32–34.

Division   See ANALYZE, ANALYSIS.

Dominant impression   The main idea a writer conveys about a subject through DESCRIPTION — that an elephant is gigantic, for example, or an experience scary. See Chapter 4.

Drafting   The stage of the writing process during which a writer expresses ideas in complete sentences, links them, and arranges them in a sequence. See also pages 34–39 and 53–54.

Editing   The final stage of the writing process, during which a writer corrects errors and improves stylistic matters by, for example, using the ACTIVE VOICE and reworking sentences to achieve PARALLEL STRUCTURE. Contrast with REVISION. And see pages 47–53 and 58.

Effect   The result of an event or action, usually considered together with CAUSE as a method of development. See the discussion of cause and effect in Chapter 10. In discussing writing, the term *effect* also refers to the impression a word, a sentence, a paragraph, or an entire work makes on the reader: how convincing it is, whether it elicits an emotional response, what associations it conjures up, and so on.

Emotional appeal (*pathos*)   See APPEALS.

Emphasis   The stress or special importance given to a certain point or element to make it stand out. A skillful writer draws attention to what is most important in a sentence, a paragraph, or an essay by controlling emphasis in any of the following ways:

- **Proportion:** Important ideas are given greater coverage than minor points.
- **Position:** The beginnings and ends of sentences, paragraphs, and larger divisions are the strongest positions. Placing key ideas in these spots helps draw attention to their importance. The end is the stronger position, for what stands last stands out. A sentence in which less important details precede the main point is called a **periodic sentence**: "Having disguised himself as a guard and walked through the courtyard to the side gate, the prisoner made his escape."

A sentence in which the main point precedes less important details is a **loose sentence**: "Autumn is orange: gourds in baskets at roadside stands, the harvest moon hanging like a pumpkin, and oak leaves flashing like goldfish."

- **Repetition:** Careful repetition of key words or phrases can give them greater importance. (Careless repetition, however, can cause boredom.)
- **Mechanical devices:** Italics (underlining), capital letters, and exclamation points can make words or sentences stand out. Writers sometimes fall back on these devices, however, after failing to show significance by other means. Italics and exclamation points can be useful in reporting speech, but excessive use makes writing sound exaggerated or bombastic.

For additional ways to emphasize ideas at the sentence level, see pages 49–50.

Essay   A short nonfiction composition on one central theme or subject in which the writer may offer personal views. Essays are sometimes classified as either formal or informal. In general, a **formal essay** is one whose DICTION is that of the written language (not colloquial speech), whose TONE is serious, and whose focus is on a subject the writer believes is important. (For example, see Alain de Botton's "Tragedy.") An **informal essay**, in contrast, is more likely to admit COLLOQUIAL EXPRESSIONS; the writer's tone tends to be lighter, perhaps humorous, and the subject is likely to be personal, sometimes even trivial. (See Naomi Shihab Nye's "Museum.") These distinctions, however, are rough ones: An essay such as Judy Brady's "I Want a Wife" uses colloquial language and speaks of personal experience, but its tone is serious and its subject important. See also EXPOSITION.

Ethical appeal (*ethos*)   See APPEALS.

Euphemism   The use of inoffensive language in place of language that readers or listeners may find hurtful, distasteful, frightening, or otherwise objectionable — for instance, a police officer's announcing that someone *passed on* rather than *died*, or a politician's calling for *revenue enhancement* rather than *taxation*. Writers sometimes use euphemism out of consideration for readers' feelings, but just as often they use it to deceive readers or shirk responsibility. (For more on euphemism, see William Lutz's "The World of Doublespeak" in Chap. 9.)

Evaluate, evaluation   To judge the merits of something (*evaluate*) or the act or result of doing so (*evaluation*). Evaluation is often part of CRITICAL THINKING, READING, AND WRITING. In evaluating a work of writing, you base your judgment on your ANALYSIS of it and your sense of its quality or value. See also pages 17–18, 23, 26, and 492–95.

Evidence   The details that support an argument or an explanation, including facts, examples, and expert opinions. A writer's opinions and GENERALIZATIONS must rest upon evidence. See pages 408–09.

Example   Also called **exemplification** or **illustration**, a method of development in which the writer provides instances of a general idea. See Chapter 5. An *example* is a verbal illustration.

Exposition   The mode of prose writing that explains (or exposes) its subject. Its function is to inform, to instruct, or to set forth ideas: the major trade routes in the Middle East, how to make a dulcimer, why the United States consumes more energy than it needs. Exposition may call various methods to its service: EXAMPLE, COMPARISON AND CONTRAST, PROCESS ANALYSIS, and so on. Most college writing is at least partly exposition, and so are most of the ESSAYS in this book.

Fallacies   Errors in reasoning. See pages 412–13 for a list and examples.

Figures of speech   Expressions that depart from the literal meanings of words for the sake of emphasis or vividness. To say "She's a jewel" doesn't mean that the subject of praise is literally a kind of shining stone; the statement makes sense because the CONNOTATIONS of *jewel* come to mind: rare, priceless, worth cherishing. Some figures of speech involve comparisons of two objects apparently unlike:

- A **simile** (from the Latin, "likeness") states the comparison directly, usually connecting the two things using *like*, *as*, or *than*: "The moon is like a snowball"; "He's as lazy as a cat full of cream"; "My feet are flatter than flyswatters."
- A **metaphor** (from the Greek, "transfer") declares one thing to *be* another: "A mighty fortress is our God"; "The sheep were bolls of cotton on the hill." (A **dead metaphor** is a word or phrase that, originally a figure of speech, has come to be literal through common usage: "the *hands* of a clock.")
- **Personification** is a simile or metaphor that assigns human traits to inanimate objects or abstractions: "A stoop-shouldered refrigerator hummed quietly to itself"; "The solution to the math problem sat there winking at me."

Other figures of speech consist of deliberate misrepresentations:

- **Hyperbole** (from the Greek, "throwing beyond") is a conscious exaggeration: "I'm so hungry I could eat a saddle"; "I'd wait for you a thousand years."
- The opposite of hyperbole, **understatement**, creates an ironic or humorous effect: "I accepted the ride. At the moment, I didn't feel like walking across the Mojave Desert."
- A **paradox** (from the Greek, "conflicting with expectation") is a seemingly self-contradictory statement that, on reflection, makes sense: "Children are the poor person's wealth" (wealth can be monetary, or it can be spiritual). *Paradox* may also refer to a situation that is inexplicable or contradictory, such as the restriction of one group's rights in order to secure the rights of another group.

Flashback   A technique of NARRATION in which the sequence of events is interrupted to recall an earlier period.

Focus   The narrowing of a SUBJECT to make it manageable. Beginning with a general subject, you concentrate on a certain aspect of it. For instance, you may select crafts as a general subject, then decide your main interest lies in weaving. You could focus your essay still further by narrowing it to operating a hand loom. You also focus your writing according to who will read it (AUDIENCE) or what you want it to achieve (PURPOSE).

General and specific   Terms that describe the relative number of instances or objects included in the group signified by a word. *General* words name a group or class (*flowers*); *specific* words limit the class by naming its individual members (*rose, violet, dahlia, marigold*). Words may be arranged in a series from more general to more specific: *clothes, pants, jeans, Levis*. The word *cat* is more specific than *animal*, but less specific than *tiger*, or *Garfield*. See also ABSTRACT AND CONCRETE and pages 48 and 108.

Generalization   A statement about a class based on an examination of some of its members: "Lions are fierce." The more members examined and the more representative they are of the class, the sturdier the generalization. The statement

"Solar energy saves home owners money" would be challenged by home owners who have yet to recover their installation costs. "Solar energy can save home owners money in the long run" would be a sounder generalization. Insufficient or nonrepresentative EVIDENCE often leads to a hasty generalization, such as "All freshmen hate their roommates" or "Men never express their feelings." Words such as *all*, *every*, *only*, *never*, and *always* have to be used with care: "Some men don't express their feelings" is more credible. Making a trustworthy generalization involves the use of INDUCTIVE REASONING (discussed on pp. 410–411).

Genre   The category into which a piece of writing fits. Shaped by PURPOSE, AUDIENCE, and context, genres range from broad types (such as fiction and nonfiction) to general groups (novel, essay) to narrower groups (science fiction novel, personal narrative) to specific document formats (steampunk graphic novel, post on a retail workers' forum) — and they tend to overlap. The genres of college writing vary widely. Examples appear on pages 71 (police log), 109 (field observation), 146 (job-application letter), 178 (review), 218 (lab report), 259 (critical analysis), 297 (résumé), 338 (letter to the editor), 373 (essay exam), and 418 (proposal).

Most readers are instinctively aware of individual genres and the characteristics that distinguish them, and they expect writers to follow the genre's conventions for POINT OF VIEW, structure and organization, types of EVIDENCE, language, TONE, length, appearance, and so forth. Consider, for instance, a daily newspaper: Readers expect the news articles to be objective statements of fact, with none of the reporters' personal thoughts and little rhetorical flourish; but when they turn to the op-ed page or their favorite columnists, such opinions and clever turns of phrase are precisely what they're looking for. Similar expectations exist for every kind of writing, and good writers make a point of knowing what they are. See also pages 10, 32, and 40 and the individual chapter introductions in Part Two.

Grounds   A name for EVIDENCE favored by philosopher Stephen Toulmin in his conception of ARGUMENT. See page 408–09.

Hyperbole   See FIGURES OF SPEECH.

Illustration   Another name for EXAMPLE. See Chapter 5.

Image   A word or word sequence that evokes a sensory experience. Whether literal ("We picked two red apples") or figurative ("His cheeks looked like two red apples, buffed and shining"), an image appeals to the reader's memory of seeing, hearing, smelling, touching, or tasting. Images add concreteness to fiction — "The farm looked as tiny and still as a seashell, with the little knob of a house surrounded by its curved furrows of tomato plants" (Eudora Welty in a short story, "The Whistle") — and are an important element in poetry. But writers of essays, too, use images to bring ideas down to earth. See also FIGURES OF SPEECH.

Inductive reasoning, induction   The process of reasoning to a conclusion about an entire class by examining some of its members. See pages 410–11.

Infer, inference   To draw a conclusion (*infer*), or the act or result of doing so (*inference*). In CRITICAL THINKING, READING, AND WRITING, inference is the means to understanding a writer's meaning, ASSUMPTIONS, PURPOSE, fairness, and other attributes. See also pages 16–17, 23, and 25.

Introduction   The opening of a written work. Often it states the writer's subject, narrows it, and communicates the writer's main idea (THESIS). See page 38.

Irony   A manner of speaking or writing that does not directly state a discrepancy, but implies one. **Verbal irony** is the intentional use of words to suggest a meaning other than literal: "What a mansion!" (said of a shack); "There's nothing like sunshine" (said on a foggy morning). (For more examples, see the essays by Jessica Mitford and Judy Brady.) If irony is delivered contemptuously with an intent to hurt, we call it **sarcasm**: "Oh, you're a real friend!" (said to someone who refuses to lend the speaker the coins to operate a clothes dryer). With **situational irony**, the circumstances themselves are incongruous, run contrary to expectations, or twist fate: Juliet regains consciousness only to find that Romeo, believing her dead, has stabbed himself. See also SATIRE.

Jargon   Strictly speaking, the special vocabulary of a trade or profession. The term has also come to mean inflated, vague, meaningless language of any kind. It is characterized by wordiness, ABSTRACT terms galore, pretentious DICTION, and needlessly complicated word order. Whenever you meet a sentence that obviously could express its idea in fewer words and shorter ones, chances are that it is jargon. For instance: "The motivating force compelling her to opt continually for the most labor-intensive mode of operation in performing her functions was consistently observed to be the single constant and regular factor in her behavior patterns." Translation: "She did everything the hard way." (For more on such jargon, see William Lutz's "The World of Doublespeak" in Chap. 9.)

Journal   A record of one's thoughts, kept daily or at least regularly. Keeping a journal faithfully can help a writer gain confidence and develop ideas. See also page 33.

Logos   See APPEALS.

Metaphor   See FIGURES OF SPEECH.

Narration, narrative   The mode of writing (*narration*) that tells a story (*narrative*). See Chapter 3.

Narrator   The teller of a story, usually either in the first PERSON (*I*) or in the third (*he, she, it, they*). See pages 65–66.

Nonstandard English   See DICTION.

Objective and subjective   Kinds of writing that differ in emphasis. In *objective* writing the emphasis falls on the topic; in *subjective* writing it falls on the writer's view of the topic. Objective writing occurs in factual journalism, science reports, certain PROCESS ANALYSES (such as recipes, directions, and instructions), and logical arguments in which the writer attempts to downplay personal feelings and opinions. Subjective writing sets forth the writer's feelings, opinions, and interpretations. It occurs in friendly letters, journals, bylined feature stories and columns in periodicals, personal essays, and ARGUMENTS that appeal to emotion. Few essays, however, contain one kind of writing exclusive of the other.

Organization   The way ideas and supporting evidence are structured in the BODY of an essay. The methods of development typically lend themselves to different approaches, discussed in the introductions to Chapters 3–12. Independent of the methods, a successful writer orders subpoints and details in whatever way will best get the main idea across. While a NARRATIVE or a PROCESS ANALYSIS typically follows a CHRONOLOGICAL ORDER, for instance, the writer may need to step back to relate previous or concurrent events. DESCRIPTION often uses a SPATIAL ORDER, arranging details the way one's eyes might take them in. And the writer of an essay that presents EXAMPLES or an ARGUMENT may choose to move from most compelling points to least, or vice versa with a CLIMACTIC ORDER, depending on the desired EFFECT. See pages 20–21, 27, 68–69 (narration), 106–07 (description), 174–76 (COMPARISON AND CONTRAST), 214 (process analysis), 257 (DIVISION OR ANALYSIS), 294–95 (CLASSIFICATION), and 414–15 (argument or persuasion).

Paradox   See FIGURES OF SPEECH.

Paragraph   A group of closely related sentences that develop a central idea. In an essay, a paragraph is the most important unit of thought because it is both self-contained and part of the larger whole. Paragraphs separate long and involved ideas into smaller parts that are more manageable for the writer and easier for the reader to take in. Good paragraphs, like good essays, possess UNITY and COHERENCE. The central idea is usually stated in a TOPIC SENTENCE, often found at the beginning of the paragraph and related directly to the essay's THESIS. All other sentences in the paragraph relate to this topic sentence, defining it, explaining it, illustrating it, providing it with evidence and support. If you come across a unified and coherent paragraph that has no topic sentence, it will contain a central idea that no sentence in it explicitly states, but that every sentence in it clearly implies. See also pages 41–42, 257–58 (paragraph coherence); 41, 295–96 (paragraph development); and 41, 372 (paragraph unity).

Parallelism, parallel structure   A habit of good writers: keeping related ideas of equal importance in similar grammatical form. A writer may place nouns side by side ("*Trees* and *streams* are my weekend tonic") or in a series ("Give me *wind*, *sea*, and *stars*"). Phrases, too, may be arranged in parallel structure (*"Out of my bed, into my shoes, up to my classroom* — that's my life"), as may clauses ("Ask not what your country can do for you; ask what you can do for your country").

Parallelism may be found not only in single sentences but in larger units as well. A paragraph might read: "Rhythm is everywhere. It throbs in the rain forests of Brazil. It vibrates ballroom floors in Vienna. It snaps its fingers on street corners in Chicago." In a whole essay, parallelism may be the principle used to arrange ideas in a balanced or harmonious structure. See the famous speech given by Judy Brady (p. 459), in which paragraphs 4–7 all begin with the words "I want a wife who will" and describe an imagined partner. Not only does such a parallel structure organize ideas, but it also lends them force. See also pages 50 and 176–77.

Paraphrase   Putting another writer's thoughts into your own words. In writing a research paper or an essay containing EVIDENCE gathered from your reading, you will find it necessary to paraphrase — unless you are using another writer's very words with quotation marks around them — and to acknowledge your sources. Contrast SUMMARY. And see page 44.

Passive voice   The form of the verb when the sentence subject is acted upon: *The report* [subject] *was published* [passive verb] *anonymously*. Contrast ACTIVE VOICE.

Pathos   See APPEALS.

Person   A grammatical distinction made between the speaker, the one spoken to, and the one spoken about. In the first person (*I*, *we*), the subject is speaking. In the second person (*you*), the subject is being spoken to. In the third person (*he*, *she*, *it*), the subject is being spoken about. The point of view of an essay or work of fiction is often specified according to person: "This short story is told from a first-person point of view." See also POINT OF VIEW.

Personification   See FIGURES OF SPEECH.

Persuasion   A mode of writing intended to influence people's actions by engaging their beliefs and feelings. Persuasion often overlaps ARGUMENT. See Chapter 12.

Plagiarism   The use of someone else's ideas or words as if they were your own, without acknowledging the original author. See pages 42–45 and 498–99.

Point of view   In an essay, the physical position or the mental angle from which a writer beholds a SUBJECT. On the subject of starlings, the following three writers would likely have different points of view: An ornithologist might write OBJECTIVELY about the introduction of these birds into North America, a farmer might advise other farmers how to prevent the birds from eating seed, and a bird watcher might SUBJECTIVELY describe a first glad sighting of the species. Whether objective or subjective, point of view also encompasses a writer's biases and ASSUMPTIONS. For instance, the scientist, farmer, and bird watcher would likely all have different perspectives on starlings' reputation as nuisances: Although such perspectives may or may not be expressed directly, they would likely influence each writer's approach to the subject. See also PERSON.

Premise   A proposition or ASSUMPTION that leads to a conclusion. See pages 411–12 for examples.

Process analysis   A method of development that most often explains step by step how something is done or how to do something. See Chapter 7.

Purpose   A writer's reason for trying to convey a particular idea (THESIS) about a particular subject to a particular AUDIENCE of readers. Though it may emerge gradually during the writing process, in the end, purpose should govern every element of a piece of writing.

   In trying to define the purpose of an essay you read, ask yourself, "Why did the writer write this?" or "What was this writer trying to achieve?" Even though you cannot know the writer's intentions with absolute certainty, an effective essay will make some purpose clear. See also pages 19, 31–32, and 40.

Rational appeal   See APPEALS.

Revision   The stage of the writing process during which a writer "re-sees" a draft from the viewpoint of a reader. Revision usually involves rethinking fundamental matters such as PURPOSE and organization as well as rewriting to ensure COHERENCE and UNITY. See pages 39–42 and 55–57. See also EDITING.

Rhetoric   The study (and the art) of using language effectively. *Rhetoric* also has a negative CONNOTATION of empty or pretentious language meant to waffle, stall, or even deceive. This is the meaning in "The president had nothing substantial to say about taxes, just the usual rhetoric."

Rhetorical question   A question posed for effect, one that requires no answer. Instead, it often provokes thought, lends emphasis to a point, asserts or denies something without making a direct statement, launches further discussion, introduces an opinion, or leads the reader where the writer intends. Sometimes a writer throws one in to introduce variety in a paragraph full of declarative sentences. The following questions are rhetorical: "When will the United States learn that sending people into space does not feed them on the earth?" "Shall I compare thee to a summer's day?" "What is the point of making money if you've no one but yourself to spend it on?" Both reader and writer know what the answers are supposed to be: (1) Someday, if the United States ever wises up. (2) Yes. (3) None.

Sarcasm   See IRONY.

Satire   A form of writing that employs wit to attack folly. Unlike most comedy, the purpose of satire is not merely to entertain, but to bring about enlightenment — even reform. Usually, satire employs irony — as in Koji Frahm's "How to Write an A Paper." See also IRONY.

Scene   In a NARRATION, an event retold in detail to re-create an experience. See Chapter 3.

Sentimentality   A quality sometimes found in writing that fails to communicate. Such writing calls for an extreme emotional response on the part of an AUDIENCE, although its writer fails to supply adequate reason for any such reaction. A sentimental writer delights in waxing teary over certain objects: great-grandmother's portrait, a lock of hair from baby's first trip to the barber, an empty popcorn box saved from the World Series of 1996. Sentimental writing usually results when writers shut their eyes to the actual world, preferring to snuffle the sweet scents of remembrance.

Signal phrase   Words used to introduce a quotation, PARAPHRASE, or SUMMARY, often including the source author's name and generally telling readers how the source material should be interpreted: "Nelson argues that the legislation will backfire." See also page 47.

Simile   See FIGURES OF SPEECH.

Slang   See DICTION.

Source   Any outside TEXT or material that a writer uses to develop and support ideas. Often found through the process of researching a subject, a single source might be the focus of an essay (as when you write about a selection in this book), or a writer might SYNTHESIZE multiple sources as EVIDENCE for one or more points. Any source referred to in an essay must be documented with an in-text citation and an entry in a works-cited or references list. See Chapter 2 on academic writing, especially pages 42–47, and the Appendix on research and documentation.

Spatial order   An organizational technique in which a writer DESCRIBES an object or scene by presenting details parallel to the way people normally view them — for instance, near to far, top to bottom, left to right. See also pages 106–07.

Specific   See GENERAL AND SPECIFIC.

Standard English   See DICTION.

Strategy   Whatever means a writer employs to write effectively. The methods set forth in this book are strategies; but so are narrowing a SUBJECT, organizing ideas clearly, using TRANSITIONS, writing with an awareness of your AUDIENCE, and other effective writing practices.

Style   The distinctive manner in which a writer writes. Style may be seen especially in the writer's choice of words and sentence structures. Two writers may write on the same subject, even express similar ideas, but it is style that gives each writer's work a personality.

Subject   What a piece of a writing is about. The subject of an essay starts with a general topic, but because writers narrow their FOCUS on a subject until they have a specific point to make about it, multiple works on the same topic will typically be very different from one another. See also page 30, PURPOSE, and THESIS.

Subjective   See OBJECTIVE AND SUBJECTIVE.

Summarize, summary   To condense a work (essay, movie, news story) to its essence (*summarize*), or the act or result of doing so (*summary*). Summarizing a piece of writing in one's own words is an effective way to come to understand it. (See pp. 15–16.) Summarizing (and acknowledging) others' writing in your own text is a good way to support your ideas. (See pp. 43, 44, and 46.) Contrast PARAPHRASE.

Suspense   Often an element in NARRATION: the pleasurable expectation or anxiety we feel that keeps us reading a story. In an exciting mystery story, suspense is constant: How will it all turn out? Will the detective get to the scene in time to prevent another murder? But there can be suspense in less melodramatic accounts as well.

Syllogism   A three-step form of reasoning that employs DEDUCTION. See page 411 for an illustration.

Symbol   A visible object or action that suggests further meaning. The flag suggests country; the crown suggests royalty — these are conventional symbols familiar to us. Life abounds in such clear-cut symbols. Football teams use dolphins and rams for easy identification; married couples symbolize their union with a ring.

In writing, symbols usually do not have such a one-to-one correspondence, but evoke a whole constellation of associations. In Herman Melville's *Moby-Dick*, the whale suggests more than the large mammal it is. It hints at evil, obsession, and the untamable forces of nature. Such a symbol carries meanings too complex or elusive to be neatly defined.

Although more common in fiction and poetry, symbols can be used to good purpose in nonfiction because they often communicate an idea in a compact and concrete way.

Synthesize, synthesis   To link elements into a whole (*synthesize*), or the act or result of doing so (*synthesis*). In CRITICAL THINKING, READING, AND WRITING, synthesis is the key step during which you use your own perspective to reassemble a work you have ANALYZED or to connect the work with others. (See pp. 17 and 25.) Synthesis is a hallmark of ACADEMIC WRITING in which you respond to others' work or use multiple sources to support your ideas. (See pp. 46–47 and 496–98.)

Text   Any creation — written, visual, auditory, physical, or experiential — that can be interpreted or used as a SOURCE for writing. The starting point for most ACADEMIC WRITING, texts include written documents such as essays, articles, and books, of course, but also photographs, paintings, advertisements, Web sites, performances, musical scores, experiments, conversations, lectures, field observations, interviews, dreams, jokes — anything that invites a response, sparks an idea, or lends itself to CRITICAL THINKING, READING, AND WRITING. See pages 26–28.

Thesis, thesis statement   The central idea in a work of writing (*thesis*), to which everything else in the work refers; one or more sentences that express that central idea (*thesis statement*). In some way, each sentence and PARAGRAPH in an effective essay serves to support the thesis and to make it clear and explicit to readers. Good writers, while writing, often set down a thesis statement to help them define their purpose. They also often include this statement in their essay as a promise and a guide to readers. See pages 19, 35–36, 40–41, and the introductions to Chapters 3–12.

Tone   The way a writer expresses his or her regard for subject, AUDIENCE, or self. Through word choice, sentence structures, and what is actually said, the writer conveys an attitude and sets a prevailing spirit. Tone in writing varies as greatly as tone of voice varies in conversation. It can be serious, distant, flippant, angry, enthusiastic, sincere, sympathetic. Whatever tone a writer chooses, usually it informs an entire essay and helps a reader decide how to respond. For examples of strong tone, see the essays by Diane Ackerman, Brian Doyle, Jessica Mitford, David Sedaris, Russell Baker, Chitra Divakaruni, Tal Fortgang, and Judy Brady. See also page 416.

Topic sentence   The statement of the central idea in a PARAGRAPH, usually asserting one aspect of an essay's THESIS. Often the topic sentence will appear at (or near) the beginning of the paragraph, announcing the idea and beginning its development. Because all other sentences in the paragraph explain and support this central idea, the topic sentence is a way to create UNITY.

Transitions   Words, phrases, sentences, or even paragraphs that relate ideas. In moving from one topic to the next, a writer has to bring the reader along by showing how the ideas are developing, what bearing a new thought or detail has on an earlier discussion, or why a new topic is being introduced. A clear purpose, strong ideas, and logical development certainly aid COHERENCE, but to ensure that the reader is following along, good writers provide signals, or transitions.

To bridge sentences or paragraphs and to point out relationships within them, you can use some of the following devices of transition:

- Repeat or restate words or phrases to produce an echo in the reader's mind.
- Use PARALLEL STRUCTURES to produce a rhythm that moves the reader forward.
- Use pronouns to refer back to nouns in earlier passages.
- Use transitional words and phrases. These may indicate a relationship of time (*right away, later, soon, meanwhile, in a few minutes, that night*), proximity (*beside, close to, distant from, nearby, facing*), effect (*therefore, for this reason, as a result, consequently*), comparison (*similarly, in the same way, likewise*), or contrast (*yet, but, nevertheless, however, despite*). Some words and phrases of transition simply add on: *besides, too, also, moreover, in addition to, second, last, in the end.*

Understatement   See FIGURES OF SPEECH.

Unity   The quality of good writing in which all parts relate to the THESIS. In a unified essay, all words, sentences, and PARAGRAPHS support the single central idea. Your first step in achieving unity is to state your thesis; your next step is to organize your thoughts so that they make your thesis clear. See also pages 41 and 372.

Voice   In writing, the sense of the author's character, personality, and attitude that comes through the words. See TONE.

Warrant   The name for ASSUMPTION favored by philosopher Stephen Toulmin in his conception of ARGUMENT. See page 410.

DIRECTORY TO THE WRITERS ON WRITING

COLLABORATION

COMPUTERS

CRITICAL THINKING

DESCRIPTION

DETAILS

DISCOVERING IDEAS

DRAFTING

EDITING

ESSAYS

EVIDENCE

EXAMPLES

FEEDBACK

GENRE

GRAMMAR

HUMOR

INTRODUCTIONS

JOURNALISM

LANGUAGE

MEANING

NARRATION

OBSERVATION

ORGANIZATION

PLANNING

POETRY

POINT OF VIEW

VOICE

Acknowledgments

Ackerman, Diane. "Black Marble," from *The Human Age: The World Shaped by Us.* © 2014 by Diane Ackerman. Used by permission of W. W. Norton Company, Inc. and HarperCollins Publishers Ltd. All rights reserved.

Andrews, Lori. "*Facebook* is Using You" from *The New York Times*, Feb. 5, 2012. Copyright © 2012 by The New York Times. All rights reserved. Used by permission and protected by the Copyright Laws of the United States. The printing, copying, redistribution, or retransmission of this Content without express written permission is prohibited.

Baker, Russell. "The Plot against People" from The New York Times, June 18, 1968. Copyright © 1968 by The New York Times. All rights reserved. Used by permission and protected by the Copyright Laws of the United States. The printing, copying, redistribution, or retransmission of the Material without express written permission is prohibited.

Beam, Christopher. "Blood Loss" from *Slate*, Jan. 5, 2011. Copyright © 2011 by The Slate Group. All rights reserved. Used by permission and protected by the Copyright Laws of the United States. The printing, copying, redistribution, or retransmission of the Material without express written permission is prohibited.

Birkerts, Sven. "Ladder" from *The Other Walk: Essays.* Copyright © 2011 by Sven Birkerts. Reprinted with the permission of The Permissions Company, Inc. on behalf of Graywolf Press, Minneapolis, Minnesota, *www.graywolfpress.org.*

Brady, Judy. "I Want a Wife." Copyright © 1970 by Judy Brady. Reprinted with the permission of the author.

Burroughs, Augusten. "How to Identify Love by Knowing What It's Not" from *This Is How: Surviving What You Think You Can't* (St. Martin's Press). Copyright © 2012 by Augusten Inc., published by permission of Augusten Burroughs c/o Selectric Artists LLC.

Carr, Nicholas. "The Great Privacy Debate: Tracking Is an Assault on Liberty, With Real Dangers" from *The Wall Street Journal*, Aug. 6, 2010. Reprinted with permission of The Wall Street Journal. Copyright © 2010 Dow Jones & Company, Inc. All Rights Reserved Worldwide. Used under license.

Carr, Nicholas. "The Rapid Evolution of Text" was originally published in *The Futurist*, vol. 43, no. 6, Nov.–Dec. 2009. Used with permission from the author.

Catton, Bruce. "Grant and Lee: A Study in Contrasts," copyright © 1956 by United States Capitol Historical Society. All rights reserved. Reprinted with permission.

Chavez, Linda. "Supporting Family Values," *townhall.com*, Friday, April 17, 2009. By permission of Linda Chavez and Creators Syndicate, Inc.

Cofer, Judith Ortiz. "The Cruel Country," first published in *Brevity* magazine, Issue 40, Fall 2012. Reprinted by permission of University of Georgia Press.

Daum, Meghan. "Narcissist — Give It a Rest" from *The Los Angeles Times*, Jan. 6, 2011. Reprinted by permission of the author.

Daum, Meghan. "On Writing" from "Kids, Do Your Own Homework," *The Los Angeles Times*, April 21, 2011. Reprinted by permission of the author.

de Botton, Alain. "Tragedy" from *The News: A User's Manual.* Copyright © 2014 by Alain de Botton. Used by permission of Pantheon Books, an imprint of the Knopf Doubleday Publishing Group, a division of Penguin Random House LLC. All rights reserved.

del Toro, Guillermo, and Chuck Hogan. "Why Vampires Never Die" from *The New York Times*, July 13, 2009. Copyright © 2009 by The New York Times. All rights reserved. Used by permission and protected by the Copyright Laws of the United States. The printing, copying, redistribution, or retransmission of the Material without express written permission is prohibited.

Díaz, Junot. "The Dreamer," first published in *More Magazine*, copyright © 2011 by Junot Díaz. Reprinted by permission of Junot Díaz and Aragi, Inc.

Díaz, Junot. Excerpts from "Becoming a Writer," first published in O, *The Oprah Magazine*, copyright © 2009 by Junot Díaz. Reprinted by permission of Junot Díaz and Aragi, Inc.

Quindlen, Anna. Excerpt from "In the Beginning," from *Living Out Loud*. Copyright © 1988 by Anna Quindlen. Used by permission of Random House, Inc. Any third party use of this material, outside of this publication, is prohibited. Interested parties must apply directly to Random House, Inc. for permission.

Rae, Issa. "The Struggle." Reprinted with the permission of 37 Ink/Atria Books, a Division of Simon & Schuster, Inc., from *The Misadventures of Awkward Black Girl* by Issa Rae. Copyright © 2015 Issa Rae Productions, Inc.

Richson, Brianne. "Colleges Should Adopt Trigger Warnings." *The Daily Iowan*, May 6, 2014. Reprinted by permission.

Sedaris, David. "Remembering My Childhood on the Continent of Africa" from *Me Talk Pretty One Day*. Copyright © 2000 by David Sedaris. By permission of Little, Brown and Company. Electronic use by permission of Don Congdon Associates, Inc.

Staples, Brent. "Black Men and Public Space," *Harper's*, December 1986. Used by permission of the author.

Tan, Amy. "Fish Cheeks." Copyright © 1987 by Amy Tan. First appeared in *Seventeen Magazine*. Reprinted by permission of the author and the Sandra Dijkstra Literary Agency.

Tannen, Deborah. "But What Do You Mean?" text (as adapted in the October 1994 issue of *Redbook* magazine) from *Talking from 9 to 5* by Deborah Tannen. Copyright © 1994 by Deborah Tannen. Reprinted by permission of HarperCollins.

Tannen, Deborah. From "Forum: The Inevitability of the Personal," *PMLA*, (1996): 1151–52. Reprinted by permission of the Modern Language Association of America.

White, E. B. "Once More to the Lake" from *One Man's Meat*, text copyright © 1941 by E. B. White. Copyright renewed. Reprinted by permission of International Creative Management. All rights reserved.

Whitehead, Colson. Excerpt(s) from *The Noble Hustle: Poker, Beef Jerky, and Death*. Copyright © 2014 by Colson Whitehead. Used by permission of Doubleday, an imprint of the Knopf Doubleday Publishing Group, a division of Penguin Random House LLC. All rights reserved.

INDEX

Page numbers in boldface refer to definitions in the Glossary of Useful Terms.